A HISTORY OF THE AMERICAN THEATRE

FROM ITS ORIGINS TO 1832

A History of the
American Theatre
from Its Origins
to 1832

WILLIAM DUNLAP

Introduction by
Tice L. Miller

UNIVERSITY OF ILLINOIS PRESS
Urbana and Chicago

Introduction © 2005 by the Board of Trustees
of the University of Illinois

Manufactured in the United States of America

∞ This book is printed on acid-free paper.

1 2 3 4 5 C P 5 4 3 2 1

Typeset from the 1832 edition by J. & J. Harper, New York
Cataloging-in-Publication data is available
from the Library of Congress.
ISBN 0-252-03030-3 (cloth : alk. paper)
ISBN 0-252-07285-5 (paper : alk. paper)

DEDICATED TO

JAMES FENNIMORE COOPER, ESQ.

BY HIS FRIEND,

THE AUTHOR

Where's that palace whereinto sometimes
Foul things intrude not?

The corruption of the Theatre is no disproof
of its innate and primitive utility.

⇥ CONTENTS ⇤

➤➤ INTRODUCTION ◄◄

Tice L. Miller

In his diary entry for October 26, 1832, William Dunlap wrote: "The Harpers advertise to publish my book this day."[1] This was a little more than four months after he had left his manuscript for *A History of the American Theatre* with publishers J. & J. Harper at 82 Cliff Street in lower Manhattan, and two weeks after he had deposited the title page in the District Clerk's Office to copyright the work. Although no extant contract exists, diary entries indicate that J. & J. Harper had planned an edition of 1,500 copies. Eugene Exman in *The Brothers Harper* suggests that the book might have been "published on a half-profits arrangement or purchased outright (which seems likely)," and calculates that Dunlap bought copies from the publishers at $1.33 and sold them at $1.93 for a profit of 60 cents a copy.[2] It is clear from Dunlap's diary that Dunlap was expected to collect subscribers and perhaps had worked out some arrangement with the Harpers to get his friends to subscribe. Many did, including Gouverneur Kemble, who ordered a hundred copies. Critical reaction was favorable: the *Albion* of October 27 praised the author for greatly adding "to our stock of knowledge on the early history of the American stage" and recommended "this entertaining book to our readers."[3] A brief notice in the November 3 *New York Mirror* praised Dunlap for being "[i]ntimately acquainted with the subject from experience and personally acquainted with all the great actors, authors and critics of his day. . . . [H]is book ought to meet prompt and efficient support. Everybody should purchase it without delay."[4] And in December, the *American Quarterly Review* weighed in with a lengthy review that quoted extensively from the book, examining it chapter by chapter. Of importance to this critic was the book's moral tone: "Our author endeavors, throughout his work, to elevate the stage and render it subservient to the great interests of society and morality, by stimulating those who write for it, as well as those who represent what is written, to a just estimate of the duties they have assumed." The critic concluded that Dunlap "appears to be a man of sound principles and excellent feelings. He is a veteran in service as well as in years, and we hope his book will meet with a reception to gratify his self-love, and replenish his purse."[5] Noted in Dunlap's diary are letters lavish in their praise from friends such as Washington Irving and Matthew Carey. And while Dunlap was awaiting the publication of his book at home, he was sending advance sheets to Paris to his friend James Fenimore Cooper, who was arranging for a London edition with publisher Richard Bentley in early 1833. A pioneering effort, Dunlap's *History of the American Theatre* was the first attempt at chronicling our native theatre, and the reference point for all subsequent stage histories of the United States. With the interest today in early American history and culture, the reissuing of the book by University of Illinois Press seems timely.

Born in 1766, in Perth Amboy, New Jersey, William Dunlap enjoyed a privileged upbringing as the only child of a prosperous Tory shopkeeper. In his *History,* he recalls a childhood spend reading books and plays, owing first to an aged neighbor who served as an unofficial tutor, and later to a Quaker tutor who encouraged the young man to read Shakespeare and Homer. Almost sixty years later, he could still recall British soldiers marching through his village and "the heavy rumbling of the wagons over the frozen earth, and the groans of those who were borne to the hospitals."[6] The family spent much of the Revolutionary War in occupied New York, where young William attended his first play, George Farquhar's *The Beaux' Stratagem,* presented by a company of English soldiers at the John Street Theatre, renamed the Theatre Royal. It was during this time, in 1778, that through a playground accident, Dunlap lost the sight of his right eye. After the war he took up painting and had occasion to paint a portrait of George Washington in 1783. Evidently convinced that his son had talent, Dunlap's father, Samuel, sent him to London the following year to study painting with expatriate American painter Benjamin West. In the three years he was abroad, Dunlap spent more time at the theatre and in entertaining than he did developing his skills as an artist. Called home in 1787, he returned to New York with no specific career in mind, setting himself up as a portrait painter but with little success.

Again the theatre came to occupy much of his time, and he was encouraged by the success of Royal Tyler's *The Contrast* in 1786. The play had introduced an American character, Jonathan, played in Yankee dialect by comedian Thomas Wignell. This inspired Dunlap to write a five-act comedy, *The Modest Soldier; or, Love in New York,* with a Yankee character for Wignell. The play had a reading before managers of the American Company, Lewis Hallam Jr. and John Henry. In spite of being accepted for production, the piece was never performed because, as Dunlap learned, there were no suitable parts for either Henry or his wife. He would not make this mistake in his second play, *The Father; or, American Shandyism* (later *The Father of an Only Child*). Borrowing part of the title and some of the characters and plot from Lawrence Sterne's *Tristram Shandy* (1760), he crafted stock characters to fit the talents of the company, including the Henrys and Wignell. He tailored the comic role of Doctor Quiescent (later revised as Dr. Tattle) for Wignell. First produced at the John Street Theatre in September 1789, *The Father* received four performances in New York, two in Philadelphia, and one in Baltimore, a successful premiere for the day.[7] The same year, Dunlap wrote an interlude, *Darby's Return,* again for Wignell, who performed it at his benefit in November with President Washington in the audience. Darby was a low comic character that Wignell had made famous in John O'Keeffe's *The Poor Soldier* (1786), one of the most popular plays of the time. In this short interlude, Darby returns to Ireland after adventures in Europe and America to tell his countrymen about the chaos of the French Revolution and orderly process in the United States of adopting a constitution and inaugurating a president. For performance, Dunlap deleted references to Darby's visit to France, perhaps because he feared they would incite a riot from Republicans who were pro-French.[8] It is clear that at this time the playwright held Federalist views of the French Revolution, and these are expressed in the play.

Although Dunlap showed some talent as a playwright, his efforts were not financially rewarding enough to support a family. In February 1789, he married Elizabeth Woolsey, a descendent of an old New York merchant family. In December of that year, their first child, a son, was born. Shortly after this, probably in early 1790, his father took him into his business as a partner in Samuel Dunlap and Son, an importer of lamps, glasses, and china. In 1791 he inherited the business when his father died, but life as a merchant held little interest for him. He freed the family slaves and worked for organizations supporting the abolition of slavery. Within two years, he had turned the running of the import shop to one of his wife's relatives, although he retained a share of the profits. It was at this time that he pursued playwriting seriously, turning out *The Miser's Wedding,* a comedy, in 1793; *Leicester,* a blank verse tragedy, in 1793 (first performed under the title *The Fatal Deception; or, The Progress of Guilt*); *Fontainville Abbey,* a mystery, with incidents borrowed from the Gothic novels of Ann Radcliffe, in 1795; and *The Archers,* an opera based on the William Tell legend, in 1796. Dunlap was influenced by the novels of Radcliffe and Matthew Gregory Lewis; a vogue for Gothic drama had swept New York at the end of the eighteenth century, and *Fontainville Abbey* included the machinery typical of the genre: "travellers in gloomy landscapes, fostered in a ruinous abbey, and beset by villains of the deepest die."[9]

The young playwright could have continued writing plays and profiting from the family business had he not succumbed to an offer in 1796 to become a partner in the American Company at John Street Theatre with Lewis Hallam Jr. and

John Hodgkinson. Founded as the Comedians from London in 1752 by Lewis Hallam Sr. and his brother William, the company with a name change had survived the Revolutionary War in Jamaica and reestablished itself afterward in New York. In 1792 the managers, Lewis Hallam Jr. and John Henry, reorganized the company and recruited actors from England, including the talented Hodgkinson. Quickly establishing himself as the best actor in the company, Hodgkinson displaced Henry in his major roles and in 1794 bought out his shares. But by 1796 Hodgkinson and Hallam had become bitter rivals for principal roles and needed someone to act as a buffer between them, manage the theatre, and supply needed finances. Hodgkinson offered to sell Dunlap half of his shares with the agreement that he would serve as manager and have "sole control of the pieces to be brought before the public."[10] Idealism and practical concerns prompted Dunlap's decision. He persuaded himself that "it was his duty to take the direction of so powerful an engine as the stage," concluding that he "should have the power to do much good." And he was persuaded that he could make money and get his own plays before an audience. George Odell notes that "Dunlap entered into the agreement, tempted . . . by the prospect of being able to produce his own plays without let or hindrance."[11] From the perspective of 1832, Dunlap admitted that he should have doubted "his powers" to direct the company.

There were difficulties from the beginning. At first, Hallam refused to sign the agreement, with Hallam accusing Hodgkinson of stealing his major roles, preventing his plays from being performed, and forcing his wife off the stage, thus depriving her of her livelihood. Mrs. Hallam allegedly had been drunk during performances, and Hodgkinson would not allow her back on the stage. There was much bad blood between the two, and Dunlap quickly found himself in the middle. Finally, the two managers and Dunlap signed articles of agreement in May 1796 that gave Dunlap the authority to determine the weekly schedule including new plays.[12] On September 26, 1796, Dunlap began as head of what Odell called the "ill-assorted Cerberus of Hallam, Hodgkinson and Dunlap."

It was a decision Dunlap soon came to regret. Although the agreement seemed to clarify how the company would be managed, the reality of working with Hodgkinson and Hallam taxed all of his patience and business acumen. His first year of management was filled with strife, not only from his two principal actors but also from the necessity of borrowing money to meet the payroll. Dunlap was forced to use his own property as collateral to meet basic expenses. But if his main objective in managing the American Company was to produce his own work, he found some measure of success. In October 1796, he produced his third tragedy, *The Mysterious Monk,* drawing on the vogue for Gothic subjects. In January 1797, he added a farce, *Tell Truth and Shame the Devil,* adapted from a French one-act play, *Jérôme Pointu,* by A. L. B. Robineau. In June a comedy that owed its origins to both Dunlap and Hodgkinson, *The Man of Fortitude*, closed the first season. Hodgkinson took the company to Hartford and Boston over the summer to help shore up finances; but the box office did not even cover expenses, and Dunlap had to borrow money to make up the difference. The burden of keeping the American Company solvent would soon exhaust all of his resources.

Part of the problem was that the John Street Theatre had become dilapidated and in need of major renovation. An effort had begun in 1794 to build a new theatre in New York. The *Daily Advertiser* of July 8, 1794, contained a notice that a committee formed to erect the new theatre desired investors or subscribers.[13] The committee apparently discussed terms for a lease with Hallam and Hodgkinson; prominent New Yorkers signed on as shareholders; and by the time Dunlap became involved, the building of the New Theatre in Park Row (later called the Park Theatre) was well underway. In June 1797, Dunlap and Hodgkinson reached some kind of understanding about a four-year lease with the proprietors. Hallam retired from management, selling his property to the two comanagers with the agreement that he would receive one-fourth of the profits and that he and his wife would be retained as actors. In anticipation that the 1796–97 season would be their last in John Street, Dunlap and Hodgkinson hired a larger company and planned their debut at the Park Theatre for October 1797. Unfortunately, the theatre was not finished and the Company stayed in John Street until late January 1798, losing money with the expanded company. A more serious problem developed: in negotiating the four-year lease, the managers had failed to get the proprietors' signatures, and consequently, the terms negotiated in May 1797 were changed. According to Odell, the building had cost more than originally planned: "It is one thing to plan a building at a cost of $42,375 and quite another to erect it at an outlay of over $130,000."[14] Dunlap notes that the committee in charge of raising money and erecting the theatre "had contracted debts for the building on their own responsibility, and now were about to call upon the proprietors to assume them."[15] The rent agreed upon had been based on a percentage of box office receipts, but the committee now added the stipulation that managers were to provide free tickets to each performance for all the stockholders (Dunlap mentions both 130 and 113 stockholders). A final compromise reduced the rent but kept the free tickets. Since these were the persons most likely to attend the theatre, the loss of revenue was a major blow for the enterprise. Other changes in the original terms also served to cast a shadow over the theatre's opening.

Still unfinished, the Park Theatre opened on January 29, 1798, with Shakespeare's *As You Like It*. The production brought out a large house, but because of confusion, "great numbers entered without paying at the door or delivering tickets." Despite this, the night earned receipts of $1,232.[16] It seemed for a time that the managers' gamble might pay off, but after some early successes, the theatre began to lose money. The appearance of Thomas Abthorpe Cooper on February 28 as Hamlet again brought strong houses for a time. Cooper had been recruited from England in 1796 by Wignell, now manager of the Chestnut Street Theatre in Philadelphia, and Cooper established himself as the leading actor on the American stage. But he had a disagreement with the management in Philadelphia and was enticed to play in New York.

An important premiere occurred on March 30, 1798, with Dunlap's blank-verse tragedy *André*. Arguably his best play, *André* is based on the 1780 capture, trial, and execution of British officer Major John André, who conspired with the Continental general Benedict Arnold to surrender West Point to the British. Dunlap's sympathetic treatment of André drew criticism, as did Cooper's performance of Bland, a young American officer who had been befriended by André when he was a prisoner of the British. When his petition for mercy before Washington had been denied, Bland tore the black cockade from his hat and threw it on the stage. The audience thought this act unpatriotic and hissed the actor. Although Dunlap revised the play, adding a speech in the last act where Bland apologizes for his hasty actions, the play received only three performances and was not revived.[17] Clearly, the public was not receptive to a tragedy about recent history, especially one in which a sympathetic British officer is hanged for being a spy, a sentence considered necessary by Washington. And current political events may have overwhelmed the play. In March 1798, war with France seemed likely over the XYZ Affair: the nation was badly divided, with the Republicans defending the French and the Federalists urging war.[18] As a measure of the times, during the summer of 1798, the Federalists who controlled Congress passed the infamous Alien and Sedition Acts in response to the perceived threat from French émigrés, clearly a violation of the First Amendment to the Constitution. Nationalistic sentiments were always present in the early American theatre and threatened any new play. Here, both sides used *André* to advance their agenda. Dunlap diluted the politics and reworked the material in 1803 for a Fourth of July celebration, and this version was revived regularly.

Finances continued to plague Dunlap in his tenure as manager of the Park Theatre. The original lease had based the rent on a percentage of the box office. Having made no money the first year, the proprietors for the second season dropped the percentage and demanded a flat fee of $5,000. The popular Hodgkinson left in spring of 1798 to manage the Federal Street Theatre in Boston, and Dunlap found himself the sole manager of the company. His financial condition was rapidly becoming desperate, and to add to his woes, yellow fever closed all public places for the 1798 fall season. It was not until December 3 that he was able to open the theatre with Sheridan's *The School for Scandal*. He scheduled three plays a week and needed about $400 a night to break even. Attendance was sparse the first week, and receipts of $997 did not cover expenses of $1161.[19] For his second week, Dunlap turned to his adaptation of Augustus Von Kotzebue's *Menschenhass und Reue* (1794), which had been playing in London in various adaptations under the title *The Stranger*. The German playwright had been wildly popular in Europe, and his appeal extended to New York. His plays offered a mixture of sentimental and sensational plot devices that thrilled audiences tired of the same old round of Shakespeare and eighteenth-century English dramas. Joseph Addison's neoclassical tragedy *Cato* might have been Washington's favorite play, but contemporary audiences were drawn to Kotzebue's romantic tales of incestuous marriages, self-immolations, murders, and violence of all kinds.

The Stranger explores a theme similar to Nicholas Rowe's *The Tragedy of Jane Shore* (1714) of whether adultery by a wife and mother can ever be forgiven. In the play, a mysterious woman has been working as a housekeeper on the country estate of Countess de Wintersen for the past three years. A mysterious stranger known only as a misanthrope has been living in a cottage at the edge of the estate. Both characters keep to themselves, and their paths never cross. As the plot thickens, we learn that the woman had abandoned her husband and children for a lover but has since repented and taken refuge with the Countess. Both the woman and the misanthrope reveal themselves to be generous and charitable toward the poor. When they finally meet in a powerfully emotional scene at the end of the fourth act, they recognize each other as husband and wife. In the last tearful act, the stranger forgives his wife, but she does not feel worthy of him and they agree to separate forever. The arrival of their two children whom neither has seen for three years brings more tears, a happy reunion of the family, and a fast curtain. The *New York Commercial Advertiser* reported that "the effect of the pathetic scenes was beyond any former example within our remembrance."[20] In her study of Kotzebue, Jenny Broekman de Vries praises the play for its "originality and even courage in presenting an adulterous wife as the heroine of a sentimental comedy."[21] Kotzebue seems to suggest that an arranged marriage, a too-youthful bride, and a villainous seducer must share responsibility for the woman's actions. It is love, not parental arrangements, that should govern marriages in Kotzebue's world, a theme that will come to dominant nineteenth-century melodrama.

American critics were not kind to Kotzebue and his moral universe, but his plays refitted for an American audience did well at the box office and proved a lifesaver for the American Company. Dunlap's version of *The Stranger* was performed at the Park Theatre twelve times during the season. Odell writes, "There was something about the tone of *The Stranger* that exactly fitted into the mood of the last years of the Eighteenth Century. The melancholy and misanthropy of the mysterious stranger . . . typified, no doubt, to many sentimental souls the very essence of what we have since learned to call the romantic revival."[22] Local audiences favored anything written by this "German Shakespeare." Dunlap's translation of his *The Natural Son* as *Lovers' Vows* played in March and dealt with an unwed mother and her son. While unwed mothers in the theatre usually faced a slow and painful death in the last act, Kotzebue challenged that convention. The play ends much like *The Stranger* in that the son brings father and mother back together for a three-handkerchief ending.

Sentimental and melodramatic, Kotzebue's plays created such a demand at the box office that it was easy in April 1799 for Dunlap to pass off his own *The Italian Father* as written by the German. He did not identify the author in the program, and the final scene resembled Kotzebue's style. In reality, Dunlap had borrowed the second half of Thomas Dekker and Thomas Middleton's *The Honest Whore* (1604) and added parts of other English plays to piece together a comedy. He believed that if audiences knew that he was the author, the play would not be as successful. His version of Kotzebue's *Indians in England* closed the season. The romantic drama had arrived in New York, displacing the traditional English repertoire. Critics denounced Kotzebue and all German drama for challenging the social conventions of the age. But for a time, emotion was everything, and the Teutonic taste in literature was in vogue.

Hodgkinson and his wife returned to the Park Theatre for the 1799 fall season as salaried actors, because Hodgkinson's management of the Federal Street Theatre in Boston had proved to be financially unrewarding. Just as things were returning to normal, in December Thomas Cooper withdrew from the company. He had gone to Philadelphia on business, missing two performances, and did not like the way his absences were announced from the stage.[23] Without his star actor, Dunlap turned again to Kotzebue. Two of the theatre's most popular attractions of the 1799–1800 season were Kotzebue's *The Virgin of the Sun* and its sequel, *Pizarro in Peru; or, The Death of Rolla,* both adapted by Dunlap from other adaptations, the latter by Richard Brinsley Sheridan. Both plays dealt with the Spanish conquest of Peru and Inca resistance, subjects of special interest to Western audiences at the end of the eighteenth century. The importance of Kotzebue to Dunlap can be seen in that thirty of the one hundred playing nights in 1799 were dedicated to the "German Shakespeare."[24] The death of Washington on December 14 added to Dunlap's financial woes. When the news became known in New York on December 20, the theatres were closed until December 30, and they remained draped in black until February 22, Washington's birthday.

The next two seasons were disrupted by the yellow fever epidemic. The 1800–1801 season did not open until October 20, when Dunlap again turned to *Lovers' Vows* and his own *Fraternal Discord,* adapted from Kotzebue's *Bruder's Twist.*

Although the play was given six performances, the *Monthly Magazine* questioned if Kotzebue's fame had about run its course. Finding the right combination of plays and actors to keep the Park Theatre open continued as Dunlap's main occupation. He returned to English drama with a revival of Thomas Morton's *Speed the Plow* (1800) and its favorite character, Mrs. Grundy. He offered Matthew Gregory Lewis's new comedy, *The East Indian*. On Evacuation Day, November 25, he staged John Burk's *Bunker Hill*, a play he considered worthless, but patriotism would draw and Dunlap needed a paying audience.

With yellow fever delaying the 1801–2 opening until November 16, Dunlap revived *Lovers' Vows* in an attempt to rescue the season. His most successful production, *Blue Beard*, by George Colman the younger, opened in March and received twelve performances. Odell credited the piece with satisfying "a craving for Gothic thrills, and for a spectacle of oriental magnificence."[25] Dunlap imported the talented Mrs. Anne Merry from the Chestnut Street Theatre in Philadelphia for a two-week engagement in April. It was artistically satisfying, but the theatre continued to lose money and he continued to borrow to keep it afloat.

Odell rates the 1802–3 season as Dunlap's most brilliant at the Park Theatre. He had hired a strong company including Mrs. Merry, Thomas A. Cooper, and Hodgkinson. The continuing popularity for Gothic subjects prompted the revival of *The Mysterious Monk*, now renamed *Ribbemont; or, the Feudal Baron*. Cooper announced that he was returning to London to perform at the Drury Lane Theatre, and he gave several farewell performances in his favorite roles: Hamlet, Richard III, Shylock, and Macbeth. In February Dunlap's *The Voice of Nature* introduced many of the elements of mélodrame to the New York stage. Invented five years earlier by Guilbert de Pixerécourt in Paris, mélodrame differed little from the Gothic drama except for the use of music to heighten the dramatic effect. Its popularity received a boost in the United States when Thomas Holcroft's *A Tale of Mystery*, an adaptation of Pixerécourt's *Coelina*, opened at the Park Theatre in March. On July 4, Dunlap brought out his *The Glory of Columbia–Her Yeomanry!* adapted from the failed *André*. Whereas the first play had made a hero out of a British officer, the revised version made heroes out of the common soldiers who had captured André. Dunlap had switched the appeal away from federalism to republicanism, from the classes to the masses. The play was cobbled together with songs and dances to satisfy Fourth of July audiences and was revived for years. As a theatre manager trying to survive, he did what he could to adapt to rapidly changing social and political conditions in America. That Dunlap realized he had lowered his personal standards to gain an audience is seen in his comparing *The Glory of Columbia* to John Burk's *Bunker Hill*, a play he considered worthless.

The 1803–4 season was not successful and moved Dunlap a step closer to bankruptcy. The American Company had lost its most popular actors: Cooper was in London; Hodgkinson had left to join Alexander Placide in Charleston. New performers such as comedian John E. Harwood from Philadelphia were hired as replacements, but they did not have the following of either Cooper or Hodgkinson. Novelties followed in quick succession, including spectacular pantomimes, operas with gorgeous scenery, and Gothic subjects with Gothic treatment. Nothing seemed to draw an audience. On one occasion "a mill with a running stream and a burning house lent interest to the evening's program."[26] The popular light comedian Mrs. Johnson played Young Norval in *Douglas* for her husband's benefit in June, one of the earliest attempts in America of an actress playing a breeches role. The heavily mortgaged theatre was put up for auction and sold for a fraction of its investment.

The end came rather suddenly during Dunlap's final season at the Park, which began on October 22, 1804. Times were hard, New York faced a terrible winter, and benefits were given for the poor all over the city. Cooper returned from London in November for a twelve-night engagement, at first drawing good houses for his round of plays including *Macbeth, Jane Shore, Hamlet, Richard III, Lovers' Vows,* and *Pizzaro.* Then Cooper ceased to draw, and on February 18 Dunlap placed a notice in the newspaper: "The public are respectfully informed on account of the want of patronage, the manager is under the necessity of closing the theatre, and this evening is positively the last night of the present season."[27] He lost everything in bankruptcy except his mother's house in Perth Amboy. The loss affected him deeply and tempered the idealism with which he had begun the enterprise. He had attempted to uplift the American stage by offering the classics and the best of contemporary drama. Now sick and in debt, he contemplated how he would survive and make a living.

Dunlap had begun his career as a painter, and after 1805 he turned to his brushes once again to support his family. He traveled the eastern seaboard seeking commissions as a miniature portraitist and even journeyed to Canada to seek work. Later he added large-scale historical paintings and oil portraits, exhibiting them commercially and giving lectures to make money. At the same time, he undertook to publish his plays, coming out in 1806 with the first volume that included four of his early works: *The Father of an Only Child, Leicester, Fontainville Abbey,* and *Darby's Return.* He intended ten volumes, but the first did not sell, so he abandoned the project. Ten years later, his publisher assembled volumes two and three. Also in 1806 he began working as an assistant to Thomas A. Cooper, who had leased the Park Theatre. Dunlap had picked up odd jobs to support his family; one of his most interesting was as traveling companion for English actor George Frederick Cooke during the 1810–11 season. Taking advantage of this situation, he published his *Memoirs of Cooke* in 1813. Other jobs included serving as assistant paymaster-general of the New York militia and as keeper and librarian for the American Academy of Fine Arts. He served as director of the American Academy of Design in 1817 and as a founder of the National Academy of Design in 1826. He also taught historical painting at the National Academy from 1830–39.

Dunlap continued to paint on large canvasses, exhibiting his 18 x 12 foot *Christ Rejected* in 1822 and adding several other religious paintings in 1824 and 1825, all in imitation of Benjamin West. In 1828 he exhibited his *Calvary,* a large canvas that took three years to paint, which he considered his masterpiece. The same year, he wrote his last play, *A Trip to Niagara; or, Travellers in America,* which opened at the Bowery Theatre on November 28 with an eye to skewering English travelers such as Mrs. Trollope and offering twenty-five thousand feet of moving panorama scenery of the Hudson River. *A Trip to Niagara* included Irish, French, and Yankee characters, as well as a new type, Leatherstocking, borrowed from his friend James Fenimore Cooper.[28]

In 1832 Dunlap prepared an exhibition of his major biblical paintings and lectured on them, hoping they would draw a paying audience. In this he was only partially successful. Even though he had some talent as a painter, he lacked imagination, and his work seemed to his contemporaries (and to us today) as derivative. He was not an artist of the first rank but a good craftsman, borrowing inspiration from better artists as he had borrowed dramatic plots from better dramatists. Yet in 1834, he wrote the first book on the arts in this country: *History of the Rise and Progress of the Arts of Design in the United States.* His contemporaries considered it an important book, and we continue to value it today. It remains a major source of information about the fine arts in the young republic.

Poverty and ill health continued to plague Dunlap during the last decade of his life. A theatrical benefit held at the Park Theatre on February 28, 1833, brought him about $2,500 and the thanks of some of the most distinguished persons in New York. In 1838 fellow artists arranged a picture exhibit at the Stuyvesant Institute that netted him about $1,000. He continued to write and paint. His last publication in 1839 was the two-volume *History of the New Netherlands, Province of New York, and State of New York, to the Adoption of the Federal Constitution.* In ill health and struggling to make ends meet, he died in New York on September 28, 1839.

William Dunlap was the first American to attempt a history of the professional theatre in this country. He begins his chronicle with the arrival of the Hallams from London in 1752, and he ends with the engagement of the English star George Frederick Cooke in 1810–12. He describes a culture being challenged by the new spirit of romanticism, a theatre facing an invasion from the Continent, and a society undergoing the cultural leveling of republicanism. He recounted the legal challenges to the theatre from the Puritans, the establishment of theatrical criticism led by Washington Irving, and attempts to make the theatre a respectable institution. Although Dunlap was a failure as a manager, he was America's first professional playwright creating original scripts as well as adapting European successes. He sought a drama of ideas like that of ancient Greece, but to attract an audience and keep his theatre open, he was forced to write for the pit and galleries, rather than the boxes. He adjusted his political views to the realities of running a theatre, the most public of the arts, and nothing demonstrates this more than his rewriting *André* into *The Glory of Columbia* to appeal to republican tastes. His views were not always consistent: he wanted a theatre "controlled by the enlightened portion of the public that the accumulation of money shall not be the object of their directors."[29] He was so impressed with the Théâtre Français that he included its regulations in an appendix. On the other hand, he decried European aristocratic privilege and looked to a natural aristocracy—"nature's noblemen"—to uphold the highest standards of politics, art, and literature. Yet, as Joseph Ellis notes, he failed to grasp that "unprecedented individual freedom" did not prevent the nation's new natural aristocrats from cherishing "money more than moral or aesthetic truth."[30]

Posterity has treated Dunlap's *History of the American Theatre* with critical respect for the most part. His most vocal critic, George O. Seilhamer (*History of the American Theatre, 1888–91*), found a number of inaccuracies, especially in the first section on colonial theatres. Writing in *Theatre Magazine* in November 1916, Monrose J. Moses pointed out that Dunlap was not always careful in his dates or in his statements.[31] Oral S. Coad's biography in 1917 recognized that through oversight and inaccessibility of materials, Dunlap had made errors but defended his pioneering work because it remains the authority in so many areas. A more recent biographer, Robert H. Canary (1970), finds Dunlap's study more of a personal memoir than a history, providing Dunlap's personal reactions to actors and events. Perhaps this is the correct way we should read it.

Other scholars have drawn heavily on Dunlap. Arthur Hobson Quinn included a chapter on Dunlap in volume 1 of his *History of the American Drama* (1923), as did Joseph J. Ellis in *After the Revolution* (1979). George C. D. Odell drew extensively on Dunlap's history in writing volume 2 of his *Annals of the New York Stage* (1927). Richard Moody and Barnard Hewitt quote extensively from Dunlap in their histories: *America Takes the Stage* (1955) and *Theatre U.S.A.* (1959). David Grimsted begins his *Melodrama Unveiled* with Dunlap and Kotzebue (1968). And at least thirty references to Dunlap are included in volume 1 of Wilmeth and Bigsby's *Cambridge History of the American Theatre* (1998). Because he wrote from memory and incomplete records, Dunlap was not always accurate, but these errors do not lessen the value of his personal observations of actors, plays, theatres, and events of his time. His *History of the American Theatre* remains a treasured resource because it is an original source with its incumbent strengths and weaknesses.

NOTES

1. Dunlap, *Diary,* 627.
2. Exman, *The Brothers Harper,* 27.
3. *Albion,* October 27, 1832, 167.
4. *New York Mirror,* November 3, 1832, 143.
5. *American Quarterly Review,* December 1832, 509–31.
6. Dunlap, *History of the American Theatre* (hereafter cited as *HAT*), 237.
7. Coad, *William Dunlap,* 20.
8. Rinehart, "Manly Exercises," 271–72.
9. Odell, *Annals,* 1: 382.
10. Dunlap, *HAT,* 9–148.
11. Odell, *Annals,* 1: 414.
12. Hodgkinson, "A Narrative," 16–18.
13. Odell, *Annals,* 1: 361.
14. Odell, *Annals,* 2: 2.
15. Dunlap, *HAT,* 216.
16. Ibid., 218.
17. Rinehart, "Manly Exercises," 278–79.
18. Wilmer, *Theatre, Society, and the Nation,* 74–76.
19. Dunlap, *HAT,* 248, 253.
20. Odell, *Annals,* 2: 44–45.
21. Broekman de Vries, "Kotzebue on the American Stage," 78.
22. Odell, *Annals,* 2: 44.
23. Odell, *Annals,* 2: 88.
24. Coad, *William Dunlap,* 234.
25. Odell, *Annals,* 2: 133.
26. Coad, *William Dunlap,* 79.
27. Odell, *Annals,* 2: 219.
28. Canary, *William Dunlap,* 73–74.
29. Dunlap, *HAT,* 86.
30. Ellis, *After the Revolution,* 117.
31. Moses, "Early American Dramatists," 276.

SELECTED BIBLIOGRAPHY

Albion or, *British Colonial, and Foreign Weekly Gazette* 2 no. 21 (October 27, 1832): 167. American Periodical Series, 1800–1850, Rl. 707. Ann Arbor: University Microfilms, 1954.

American Quarterly Review (December 1832): 509–31. American Periodical Series, 1800–1850, Rl. 299. Ann Arbor: University Microfilms, 1954.

Bordman, Gerald. *Oxford Companion to American Theatre.* 2d ed. New York: Oxford University Press, 1992.

Broekman de Vries, Jenny. "*Kotzebue* on the American Stage, 1798–1840." Ph.D. diss., University of Virginia, 1972.

Brown, Jared. *The Theatre in America during the Revolution.* New York: Cambridge University Press, 1995.

Brown, T. Allston. *A History of the New York Stage.* 3 vols. New York: Dick and Fitzgerald, 1870.

Canary, Robert H. *William Dunlap.* New York: Twayne, 1970.

Clark, Barrett H., gen. ed. *America's Lost Plays.* 20 vols. Princeton University Press, 1940–41.

Coad, Oral S. *William Dunlap.* New York: The Dunlap Society, 1917.

Dunlap, William. *Adaptations of European Plays.* Delmar, N.Y.: Scholars' Facsimiles and Reprints, 1988.

———. *André.* In *Early American Drama,* ed. Jeffrey H. Richards, 58–108. New York: Penguin, 1997.

———. *Darby's Return.* In *Washington and the Theatre,* ed. Paul L. Ford, appendix pp. 1–14. New York: The Dunlap Society, 1899.

———. *Diary of William Dunlap, 1766–1839.* 1930. Reprint, New York: Benjamin Blom, 1969.

———. *Five Plays of William Dunlap.* Delmar, N.Y.: Scholars' Facsimiles and Reprints, 1991.

———. *History of the American Theatre.* New York: J. and J. Harper, 1832.

———. *History of the Rise and Progress of the Art of Design in the United States.* 2 vols. New York: George P. Scott, 1834.

Durham, Weldon B., ed. *American Theatre Companies, 1749–1887.* Westport, Conn.: Greenwood Press, 1986.

Ellis, Joseph J. *After the Revolution: Profiles of Early American Culture.* New York: W. W. Norton, 1979.

Engle, Ron, and Tice L. Miller, eds. *The American Stage: Social and Economic Issues from the Colonial Period to the Present.* New York: Cambridge University Press, 1993.

Exman, Eugene. *The Brothers Harper.* New York: Harper and Row, 1965.

Gates, Robert Allan. "William Dunlap's Managership of the Park Theatre, New York, 1798–1805." Ph.D. diss., New York University, 1978.

Getchell, Charles Munro. "The Mind and Art of William Dunlap, 1766–1839." Ph.D. diss., University of Wisconsin, 1946.

Grimsted, David. *Melodrama Unveiled: American Theater and Culture, 1800–1850.* Chicago: University of Chicago Press, 1968.

Hewitt, Barnard. *Theatre U.S.A., 1665–1957.* New York: McGraw Hill, 1959.

Hodgkinson, John. "A Narrative of His Connection with the Old American Company." New York: J. Oram, 1797. Reprint with William Dunlap, *History of the American Theatre.* vol. 3. New York: Burt Franklin, 1963.

Hornblow, Arthur. *A History of the Theatre in America.* 2 vols. Philadelphia: J. B. Lippincott, 1919.

Hughes, Glenn. *A History of the American Theatre, 1700–1950.* New York: Samuel French, 1951.

Ireland, Joseph. *Records of the New York Stage, from 1750 to 1860.* 2 vols. New York: T. H. Morrell, 1866–67.

Kotzebue, August. *The Stranger.* 6th ed., Trans. A. S[chin]k, London: C. Dilly, 1799.

McConachie, Bruce A. *Melodramatic Formations: American Theatre and Society, 1820–1870.* Iowa City: University of Iowa Press, 1992.

McNamara, Brooks. *The American Playhouse in the Eighteenth Century.* Cambridge, Mass.: Harvard University Press, 1969.

Meserve, Walter J. *An Emerging Entertainment: The Drama of the American People to 1828.* Bloomington: Indiana University Press, 1977.

Moody, Richard. *America Takes the Stage: Romanticism in American Drama and Theatre, 1750–1900.* Bloomington: Indiana University Press, 1955.

———, ed. *Dramas from the American Theatres 1762–1909.* Cleveland: World Publishing, 1966.

Moses, Montrose J. *The American Dramatist.* Boston: Little, Brown, 1925.

———. "Early American Dramatists." *The Theatre Magazine.* November 1916, 276, 323.

———, ed. *Representative Plays by American Dramatists.* New York: E. P. Dutton, 1918–21.

Moses, Montrose J., and John Mason Brown, eds. *The American Theatre as Seen by Its Critics, 1752–1934.* New York: Norton, 1934.

New York Mirror. November 3, 1832, 143.

Odell, George C. D. *Annals of the New York Stage.* 15 vols. New York: Columbia University Press, 1927–49.

Quinn, Arthur Hobson. *A History of the American Drama from the Beginning to the Civil War,* 2d ed. New York: F. S. Crofts and Co. 1944.

Richardson, Gary A. *American Drama from the Colonial Period through World War I: A Critical History.* New York: Twayne, 1993.

Rinehart, Lucy Elizabeth. "'Manly Exercises': Post-Revolutionary Performances of Authority in the Theater Career of William Dunlap." *Early American Literature* 36, no. 2 (2001): 263–93.

———. "'A Most Conspicuous Theatre': The Rise of American Theater and Drama, 1787–1829." Ph.D. diss., Columbia University, 1994.

Seilhamer, George O. *History of the American Theatre.* 3 vols. 1888–91. Reprint, New York: Haskell House, 1969.

Wilmer, S. E. *Theatre, Society, and the Nation,* Cambridge: Cambridge University Press, 2002.

Wilmeth, Don B., and Christopher Bigsby, eds. *The Cambridge History of American Theatre.* 3 vols. Cambridge: Cambridge University Press, 1998–2000.

Wilmeth, Don B., and Tice L. Miller, eds. *Cambridge Guide to American Theatre.* New York: Cambridge University Press, 1993.

Wilson, Garff B. *Three Hundred Years of American Drama and Theatre.* Englewood Cliffs, N.J.: Prentice-Hall, 1973.

A HISTORY OF THE AMERICAN THEATRE
FROM ITS ORIGINS TO 1832

⇥ PREFACE ⇤

Colley Cibber, in his Apology, the best book ever written on the subject of the theatre, thus speaks of the increase of play-houses in London, and the effect on the actors and the public. "Their extraordinary number of course reduced them to live upon the gratification of such hearers as they knew would be best pleased with public offence: and public offence, of what kind soever, will always be a good reason for making laws to restrain it."

We have seen acted over and over again in America, that which Cibber describes and laments as occurring in his time—"they were reduced to have recourse to foreign novelties: L'Abbe, Balon, and Mademoiselle Subligny, three of the then most famous dancers of the French opera, were at several times brought over at extraordinary rates, to revive that sickly appetite which plain sense and nature had satiated. But alas! there was no recovering to a sound constitution by those merely costly cordials; the novelty of a dance was but of a short duration, and perhaps hurtful in its consequence; for it made a play without a dance less endured than it had been before, when such dancing was not to be had," and the same may be said of every deviation from "plain sense and nature."

Colley Cibber's is one of those books in which a man finds all that he wants to know or say on the subject he is considering.

Would we not think that instead of Cibber, some writer of the present day, who had seen what he thought better days, some old fellow of seventy, in the year 1832, wrote the following?—"Polite hearers," in former days, "would be content with polite entertainments; and I remember the time when plays, without the aid of farce or pantomime, were as decently attended as operas or private assemblies; where a noisy sloven would have passed his time as uneasily in a front box as in a drawing-room; when a hat upon a man's head there would have been looked upon as a sure mark of a brute or a booby: but of all this I have seen, too, the reverse—where, in the presence of ladies at a play, common civility has been set at defiance, and the privilege of being a rude clown, even to a nuisance, has in a manner been demanded as one of the rights of English lib-

1

erty." "Yet, methinks, the liberty of seeing a play in quiet has as laudable a claim to protection as the privilege of not suffering you to do it has to impunity."

Here the question is fairly stated as to the right which the decent or "polite hearer" has to protection from all indecency or annoyance; and that right appears so evident as to need no argument. The director of the theatre is obligated to afford this protection to the persons whom he has invited to see and hear the pieces advertised. The director is bound to exclude any improper person, known to be such—to prohibit the entrance of persons known as coming for improper or immoral purposes, and of any person intoxicated or evincing improper character by behaviour—and if any such gain admittance, to employ force to expel them.

Another question is treated of by Cibber,—that of licensing the performances which shall be brought on the stage. He decides in favour of a licenser, and compares the liberty of throwing abroad improper maxims or indecent jokes to another species of liberty, "I mean that," says he, "of throwing squibs and crackers at all spectators without distinction."—If he had not added "on a lord mayor's day" we should have supposed that the passage was written in New-York, after a fourth of July. The laws for the government of the *Theatre Françoise* remedy this, and the other evils attendant on the English and American theatre.

In ages of barbarism, the professors of the fine arts were under the necessity of becoming the servants of the lords of the earth, the Nimrods, the mighty hunters and exterminators of men, for protection and bread. They were patronised. The poet, the musician, the painter, and the player looked to one ignorant prince or baron for protection from the injuries threatened by another. Thus the companies of players were "the king's servants"—"the duke's"—"the lord admiral's"—or the lord's of the castle, or other stronghold.

Brute force lorded it over intellect and the arts, and their professors were considered servile. Where intellect predominates, the arts are honoured, and their professors hold the highest place in public esteem. On the contrary, the brute of the good old times, and the fool of the improved modern day, have thought, and would have it thought, that artists are their inferiors.

As the arts, in the course of progressive civilization, emancipated themselves, like other slaves, at the moment of acquiring liberty, they were inclined to become licentious; thus the poet and the player required legal restraint.

The first licenser we read of for the English drama was Sir James Hawes, the lord mayor of London. The office was subsequently, in England, filled by the lord chamberlain.

The first paid attention particularly to morals, the subsequent were occupied principally by politics or the protection of royalty.

From what has been said of the state of the histrionic art in the dark ages, and its abasement when it was the slave of ignorance clothed with power, and when, being partly emancipated, it became mischievous as the encourager of licentiousness; it will be seen that it has been progressively improving to the present time; and although occasionally in some respects retrograding, yet the drama in its moral character is now purer than in any former time since the glories of Grecian republicanism and literature.

To secure and further this improvement, the laws and regulations above recommended would be found sufficient in our republic.

I will here make my acknowledgments to the friends who have aided me in my work. The valuable library of the Historical society has been open to me, through the politeness of John Delafield, Esq. I have been encouraged and assisted by James K. Paulding, and John Inman, Esqrs. The researches of Elias Hicks, Esq. into the early history of the theatre of our country, have been liberally communicated, and have been of great use to me. Doctors Hosack and Francis will be seen to have furnished me with valuable materials. And to William B. Wood, Esq., I owe a particular expression of gratitude, for indefatigable attention to my inquiries, and such prompt answers to my letters as have enabled me to record much valuable matter that must otherwise have escaped me.

I have made use of the authority of Colley Cibber, in this preface, and cannot better conclude it than in his words. "I would fain flatter myself, that those who are not too wise to frequent the theatre (or have wit enough to distinguish what sort of sights there either do honour or disgrace to it,) may think their national diversion no contemptible subject for a more able historian than I pretend to be. If I have any particular qualification for the task more than another, it is that I am perhaps the only person living (however unworthy) from whom the same materials can be collected."

→ CHAPTER 1 ←

1752 — Use and Abuse of the Theatre — State of the English Stage from the year 1741 to 1752 — The Hallams — Plan of the Voyage of Discovery and Adventure by the first Company of Players that crossed the Atlantic — The Company — Occupation at Sea — Arrival at Yorktown — First regular Theatrical Performance in America — First Play — Prologue for the Occasion — Singleton's Poems.

If the fine arts, as we believe, are effective instruments for promoting the best interests of man—if the pleasure of the virtuous, as Plato tells us, is their aim and the test of their success—if their great sphere and scope is that *beau ideal* which lifts us above the groveling, the vile, and the sensual—it is the duty of every good citizen to encourage their cultivation in the country of his birth or residence, and to cherish the memories of those, whatever their motives, who introduced them.

The histrionic art is so inseparably connected with the drama in our minds, that in contemplating tragedy and comedy, we see Roscius and Garrick, Talma and Clarion, Kemble and Siddons, Cooper and Merry, Lewis and Farren, Hodgkinson, Moreton, Wood, Wignell, Jefferson, Harwood, and the long list of artists who imbodied in themselves the spirits of Eschylus and Sophocles, Shakespeare and Jonson, Racine and Molière, and the hundreds who have delighted and will continue to delight millions by exciting terror and pity, or contempt for baseness, and admiration of magnanimity.

The professors of the histrionic art become commentators on the works of the poet, and living illustrations of his ideas. By the magic of this art, the immortal works of the dramatist are endowed with a more vivid immortality, and Hamlet, Macbeth, and Richard, Desdemona, Viola, and Juliet, have doubly "a local habitation and a name." The pictures of folly, ignorance, or humorous absurdity, alive in the closet, have a double life on the stage.

Dramatic poetry is one of the first of the fine arts. The histrionic art, not complete in itself, because dependent on the poet, is still so important as the handmaid of poetry, that its history, as a part of the history of any country, is positively necessary to the understanding of its literature and its manners. The rise, progress, and cultivation of the drama mark the progress of refinement and the state of manners at any given period in any country.

Without the aid of the actor, there are thousands who would never have heard

5

the name of Shakespeare; but who, by his aid, are familiar with the most sublime, moral, and beautiful sentiments that ever adorned a language. That there are evils, and perversions, and abuses attendant upon theatrical exhibitions, as on all sublunary things, no one is more ready to admit than the writer, and it shall be his aim to point them out as it is his wish to remedy them; but he firmly believes that the theatre is in itself a powerful engine well adapted to the improvement of man, and that it only wants the directing hand of an enlightened society to make it the pure source of civilization and virtue.

Entertaining these views, it appears to us that a history of the American theatre is a subject of importance as connected with the history of our literature and manners. Such a history will tend to mark the growth and improvement of our country, and may be eminently subservient to the cause of morals, whether the theatre as it exists is so or not. With this object in view, we shall endeavour to rescue from oblivion such facts relative to the drama in this country as can now be collected, and to combine them with the knowledge personally belonging to us, gained by a diversified experience of many years. The whole would soon, if not thus recorded, be swept from the memory of man; for few now live who can assist to throw light on the early dramatic history of the New World.

Before we embark with the adventurers who introduced the drama in its living shape among the English colonists of America, we will look at the state of the stage in the mother country at that period.

Garrick had reached the summit of fame and perfection in his arduous profession about the year 1745. He had been rejected by Fleetwood and Rich, the managers of Drury Lane and Covent Garden in 1741; and after a probation at Ipswich, he was received and fostered at the theatre in Goodman's Fields by his friend Giffard; the predecessor, as proprietor and manager of that place of entertainment, of William Hallam; deservedly called the father of the American stage.

On the boards of Goodman's Fields theatre, from which ten years after issued the leaders of that company which planted the drama in America, the English Roscius first displayed his unrivalled talents to a London audience, and perfected himself in that art which has immortalized him; embalming his name with that of the far greater artist and man, who "exhausted worlds and then imagined new." Let every artist hold in mind that Garrick rose to this height by hard study, and established his reputation as a *man* and a *gentleman,* as well as his fame for unrivalled skill in his profession as an actor.

In consequence of the success of Garrick, Goodman's Fields theatre became the centre of attraction. Drury Lane and Covent Garden were deserted. At the end of the season of 1742, Fleetwood was glad to engage both manager and actor. Giffard, now befriended by Garrick, was invited to Drury Lane, and Roscius entered upon the scene of his future triumphs in the brilliant career of fame and fortune.

Mr. William Hallam succeeded Giffard at Goodman's Fields, becoming the proprietor of Garrick's cradle, rendered famous, but unprofitable, from the circumstance of having had such a nursling. Drury Lane flourished, and the successor of Giffard and Garrick became bankrupt in 1750. This event led to the voyage of discovery planned by the manager and executed by his brother Lewis, the father of that Lewis Hallam who is remembered still as old Mr. Hallam.

It is well known that the state of the drama was in 1750 much more brilliant than it has been for the last half century, or is now in Great Britain. The best and greatest men of the country wrote plays and attended their performance. The pit of the theatre was the resort of wit and learning; while fashion, beauty, taste, and refinement, the proud and exclusive aristocracy of the land, took their stations in the boxes, surrounding the assemblage of poets and critics below. In the course of our history we may find the causes which have degraded the drama, while every other species of literature and art have been rising in estimation, and every science progressing to its destined perfection.

The William and Lewis Hallam mentioned above were brothers of Admiral Hallam. There was a fourth brother, an actor, who was killed accidentally in the green-room by the celebrated Charles Macklin, the original of all the Shylocks from that time to this, and author of The Man of the World. Lewis was a member of his brother William's company at Goodman's Fields, and sustained the line of first low comedian. His wife, who was related to Mr. Rich, the manager of Covent Garden, played the first line of tragedy and comedy. To have been the first low comedian, and the first tragic and comic actress in a company which had to strive against Covent Garden, and to vie with Drury Lane, having Garrick as its leader, gives us reason to believe that Mr. and Mrs. Hallam were far above mediocrity in their profession; and tradition fully supports the belief.

As we have said, in the year 1750, William Hallam, the manager of Goodman's Fields, failed. On winding up his business, his debt proved five thousand pounds, a trifling sum as the amount of loss in such a complicated and hazardous speculation. The accounts and conduct of Mr. Hallam were so fair and satisfactory to his creditors that they presented him with the wardrobe and other theatrical property of the establishment; thus discharging him from debt, and leaving him in possession of a capital to commence business anew. Under these circumstances he turned his thoughts to the New World, and conceived the plan of sending a company of players to the colonies. The thought proves that William Hallam was no common man, and his confiding such a scheme to Lewis is equally in favour of the character of the latter.

Lewis and his wife having consented to cross the Atlantic and seek their fortunes in what might then not improperly be called the western wilderness, the ex-manager's next step was to find suitable persons to fill up the *corps drama-*

tique, and to induce them to join his brother and sister in this theatrical forlorn hope. He succeeded in enlisting a good and efficient company, willing to leave their country (and perhaps their creditors), and fitted to ensure success to the perilous adventure. The emigrants were next assembled at the house of William Hallam; a list of *stock plays* produced by him, with attendant farces, and the *cast* of the whole agreed upon in full assembly of the body politic: which appears to have been a well organized republic, every member of which had his part assigned to him, both private and public, behind and before the curtain. Lewis Hallam was appointed manager, chief magistrate, or king, and William, who staid at home, was to be "viceroy over him," according to Trinculo's division of offices. The brothers were to divide profits equally after deducting the expenses and *shares.* Thus William was entitled to half of such profits as projector and proprietor, and Lewis to the other half as manager and conductor.

The names of the persons who under the direction of the Hallams introduced the drama into our country, having been communicated to the writer by one of the number, he takes pleasure in recording them, and feels that although under other circumstances they would be, perhaps, suffered to float down the tide of time consigned to oblivion, their adventure and its consequences render them worthy subjects for the pen of the dramatic historian, and interesting to all who take an interest in the literature of our country. Mr. and Mrs. Hallam were first in consequence and in talents. Mr. Rigby played the first line in tragedy and comedy, and was only inferior to the leaders. Mrs. Rigby does not appear to have had high pretensions. Mr. and Mrs. Clarkson were of the class called useful. Miss Palmer, Mr. Singleton, Mr. Herbert, Mr. Winnell, or Wynel, Mr. Adcock, and Mr. Malone completed the company, and filled the *dramatis personæ* of the plays that were cast at the proprietor's house.

Of the twenty-four plays and their attendant farces, *cast* and *put in study* before leaving England, we have the names of the following:—The Merchant of Venice, The Fair Penitent, The Beaux' Stratagem, Jane shore, The Recruiting Officer, King Richard the Third, The Careless Husband, The Constant Couple, Hamlet, Othello, Theodosius (a great favourite everywhere, added our informant), Provoked Husband, Tamerlane, The Inconstant, Woman's a Riddle, The Suspicious Husband, The Conscious Lovers, George Barnwell, The Committee, and The Twin Rivals. We cannot record the names of these twenty plays without interest. They were doubtless the favourites of the metropolis of Great Britain at that time, and stood paramount wherever the stage spoke the English tongue. How many of them now hold possession of the scene? At most, six. And of the six, four are Shakespeare's, the only four from his pen in the twenty. All Farquhar's comedies, whose dialogue for wit was unrivalled but by Shakespeare's, are laid on the shelf, or occasionally revived at a benefit, *cut down* to afterpieces.

Colley Cibber's The Careless Husband, pronounced by Pope the best comedy in the language, cannot be tolerated; and even Bishop Hoadley's The Suspicious Husband exhibits licentiousness that we turn from as unfit for representation. The farces cast and studied for the common stock were, Lethe, The Lying Valet, Miss in her Teens, The Mock Doctor, The Devil to Pay, Hob in the Well, Damon and Phillida, and The Anatomist. In the last it is recorded that Rigby was so excellent in the French doctor, that the farce stood first on the list for popularity and profit. From this we gather that Mr. Rigby had talents of Hodgkinsonian order, as he was the first in tragedy and genteel comedy, and excellent in farce.

Of pantomimes, the company had but one for many years, which was called Harlequin Collector, or the Miller Deceived.

We will remark of these eight farces, that three were Garrick's, and two of the three are still played.

Lewis Hallam, jun., known by those who remember him by the familiar appellation of old Hallam (the son of the Lewis Hallam who led these adventurers as manager and first low comedian), from whom this account of the adventure and its origin is derived, was at the time a boy of twelve years of age, and at a grammar school at Cambridge. The choice was given him of remaining at his school, or going with his parents, and he had no hesitation in preferring the latter. A younger son, Adam, and a daughter, soon introduced on the stage as Miss Hallam, made a part of the company of emigrants, and eventually of the company of players.

A daughter, still younger, being then six years of age, was left with her uncle William, and became afterward famous in dramatic history as Mrs. Mattocks.

We have said that the profits of the adventure were to be equally divided between the original proprietor and projector, and his brother the conductor and manager. These profits were to be the ersidue and remainder, after deducting the shares, for this was what is known among players as a sharing company or scheme, and so continued until some time after our revolution. In such *schemes* the manager has one or more shares as reward for the trouble of governing; one or more shares pay him for the use, wear, and tear of the property; one or more shares according to his abilities or reputation as an actor; and he generally avails himself of the power which rests with him of casting plays so as to keep up his reputation by appropriating the best or most popular parts to himself. The remaining shares, after the manager is satisfied, are divided among the members of the commonwealth according to ability, reputation in the profession, or the influence obtained by becoming favourites with the public.

Hallam's company, under the appellation of the *American* Company, in process of time underwent a change. The principal performers became partners in the property; the number of sharers were diminished; actors were engaged on weekly salaries; and by degrees the present system was established, in which one man, or a company forming a copartnership are lessees or proprietors, and the stage-manager and performers are hired.

It is proper in the early history of the stage in this country to state many particulars which would be out of place in a record of the affairs of a more recent date. As we have the power to lay before the reader the original proportions in which the receipts of this first company were divided, with the shares assigned to each individual, we shall proceed so to do.

The number of shares was fixed at eighteen. The number of adult performers was twelve, including the manager, each being entitled to one share. Mr. Hallam had another share as manager. Four shares were assigned to the property, and one share was allowed for the manager's three children. It is to be presumed that the four shares assigned for the property were to be divided between the brothers, as the profits of the partnership, otherwise it is hard to say from whence profit was to accrue.

Having despatched these preliminaries, we will attend this band of adventurers on their voyage of experiment. Early in the month of May they embarked in the "Charming Sally," Captain Lee, and after a voyage of six weeks, a short passage in those days, arrived safely at Yorktown, Virginia.

How many reflections does the name of this place suggest? What recollections to the American of the present day! Yorktown, the scene of that great drama of real life, or rather the catastrophe of the military drama, which secured never-dying laurels on the brow of that man in 1780, who, sent by Governor Dinwiddie in 1753, the year after the arrival of our adventurers, to summon the French posts on the Ohio to surrender to the arms of England, is called by the writers of the Universal History *one Major Washington.* This Major Washington very probably witnessed the first representation of plays in Virginia; and one at least of the same company of players (the second Lewis Hallam, then a boy) performed repeatedly before him, when he was the first magistrate of the greatest republic the world had ever seen, and the theme of eulogium to every enlightened or philanthropic statesman the world possessed.

In 1610, the first effectual colonization of English America took place. In 1751, Franklin calculated the English population of the colonies at one million. Such was the increase in one hundred and forty years, and the arts, following in the train of civilization, already prepared to rear the standard of taste.

As the first settlers of Virginia were of the established English Church, and that form of religion was supported by law to the exclusion of all others, it is probable that William Hallam was induced to send his company thither in preference to the other colonies, from the knowledge that Episcopalians were then more liberal in regard to the drama than most other sects, although equally intolerant in respect to religious creeds or worship as their Presbyterian breth-ren, and more so than most other denominations of Christians.

The foresight exercised by the Hallams in preparing their company for im-mediate action on their arrival in America, merits applause. The pieces had been selected, cast, and put in study before embarkation; and during the passage they were regularly rehearsed. The quarter-deck of the Charming Sally was the stage, and whenever the winds and weather permitted, the heroes and heroines of the sock and buskin performed their allotted parts, rehearsing all the plays that had been selected, particularly those fixed upon to form the first theatrical exhibi-tion which was to enliven the wilds of America.

It is easy to imagine the *fun* which these rehearsals, with the drilling of the corps, must have created among the tars. We know the salutary effect of the admirable plan of that skilful navigator Parry, who by introducing the amuse-ments of the theatre when his ship was locked up amid the gloom of a half-year's polar night, preserved the health of his crew by preserving their cheerfulness. Sailors are peculiarly alive to dramatic representations,—in that, as in some other points, they resemble children; and the novelty of having such a set of passengers, with the humour of many of the pieces rehearsed, must have de-lighted Jack; while the nautical drollery of the audience must have been occa-sionally a source of equal amusement to the players.

The circumstance of a complete company of comedians crossing the Atlan-tic together and regularly drilling during the voyage, each one in his respective line, must have given a degree of precision to the first dramatic performances in the New World, which is found wanting in many theatres, even metropoli-tan, at this time.

Williamsburg was then the capital of Virginia; and thither the players pro-ceeded from Yorktown, the place of their landing. Upon application made to Governor Dinwiddie, permission was granted to erect or fit up a building for a theatre.* Hallam found a building which he judged to be sufficient for his pur-pose, and proceeded to metamorphose it into pit, box, gallery, and stage. It was a long house in the suburbs of the town, probably erected as a store-house by the early emigrants; it was unoccupied, and the manager purchased it. This was the first theatre opened in America by a company of regular comedians, and although within the boundaries of the metropolis of the Ancient Dominion, the seat of William and Mary College, and residence of all the officers of his majes-ty's government, was so near the woods that the manager could stand in the door

* Burke, in his History of Virginia, says (ch. ii.), That under the presidency of Thomas Lee, the New-York company of comedians obtained permission to erect a theatre in Williamsburg, i.e. in the year 1750, when no New-York company existed, or any other on the continent. Governor Dinwiddie arrived in 1752.

and shoot pigeons for his dinner, which he more than once actually did. This theatre was situated on the spot occupied now by the house of the late Judge Tucker. After its destruction by fire, another was erected below the old capitol. The reader will observe that the proprietors of this enterprise had not included an orchestra in the plan of their establishment; but fortunately a professor of music had been before them as a pioneer of the fine arts, and Mr. Pellham, who taught the harpsichord in the town, was engaged with his instrument to represent that splendid assemblage of wind and stringed instruments which we now look for in an orchestra.

On the fifth of September, 1752, at Williamsburg, the capital of Virginia, the first play performed in America by a regular company of comedians was represented to a delighted audience. The piece was the Merchant of Venice, and it was followed by the farce of Lethe. Thus Shakespeare had the first place in time as in merit as the dramatist of the western world, and Garrick the honour of attending upon his master. Lethe was at that time new even in London, and a popular afterpiece. The cast of the first play and farce represented in America is worth recording, and shows the strength of the company and the various *lines* of the performers, who are all included in the following bill, except Mrs. Clarkson, Mrs. Rigby, and Adam Hallam, a child.

THE MERCHANT OF VENICE.

Bassanio,	Mr. Rigby.
Antonio,	Clarkson.
Gratiano,	Singleton.
Salanio and Duke,	Herbert.
Salarino and Gobbo,	Winnell.
Launcelot and Tubal,	Hallam.
Shylock,	Malone.
Servant to Portia,	Master Lewis Hallam
(being his first appearance on any stage),	
Nerissa,	Miss Palmer.
Jessica (her first appearance on any stage)	Hallam.
Portia,	Mrs. Hallam.

LETHE.

Esop,	Mr. Clarkson.
Old Man,	Malone.
Fine Gentleman,	Singleton.
Frenchman,	Rigby.
Charon,	Herbert.
Mercury,	Adcock.
Drunken Man and Tattoo,	Hallam.
John,	Winnell.

| Mrs. Tattoo, | Miss Palmer. |
| Fine Lady, | Mrs. Hallam. |

The Tailor was *cut out*, and Lord Chalkstone was not in being when the company left home. He was an after-thought of the authors.

It will be observed by the above bill that the first night of performing in America was the first night of appearance on any stage of Lewis Hallam the second. He had one line to speak, apparently an easy task, but when he found himself in presence of the audience he was panic-struck. He stood motionless and speechless, until bursting into tears he walked off the stage making a most inglorious exit. We need not say that he was the hero and favourite in tragedy and comedy for nearly half a century.

This night's performance is rendered the more memorable as it gave occasion for the first composition connected with the drama which was written for, or addressed particularly to an American audience. A prologue especially composed for the purpose, probably on ship-board, by Mr. Singleton. It was spoken by Mr. Rigby. These lines were written down as recited at the request of the author by Lewis Hallam the second, forty years after their *debut*. Mr. Hallam seemed to remember every transaction of that period, every circumstance attending these first histrionic adventures, as though they were of yesterday.

We think lines brought forward under such auspices are worthy of record, and accordingly give them.

> To this New World, from fam'd Britannia's shore,
> Through boist'rous seas where foaming billows roar,
> The Muse, who Britons charm'd for many an age,
> Now sends her servants forth to tread your stage;
> Britain's own race, though far removed, to show
> Patterns of every virtue they should know.
> Though gloomy minds through ignorance may rail,
> Yet bold examples strike where languid precepts fail.
> The world's a stage where mankind act their parts;
> The stage a world to show their various arts;
> While the soul touch'd by Nature's tenderest laws,
> Has all her passions rous'd in virtue's cause.
> Reason we hear, and coolly may approve,
> But all's inactive till the passions move.
> Such is the human mind, so weak, so frail,
> "Reason's her chart, but passion is her gale."
> Then raise the gale to waft fair virtue o'er
> The sea of life where reason points the shore.
> But ah! let reason guide the course along,
> Lest passion listening to some siren's song

Rush on the rocks of vice, where all is lost,
And shipwreck'd virtue renders up the ghost.
　　Too oft, we own, the stage with dangerous art,
In wanton scenes has play'd the siren's part.
Yet if the muse, unfaithful to her trust,
Has sometimes stray'd from what is pure and just,
Has she not oft with awful, virtuous rage,
Struck home at vice, and nobly trod the stage?
Made tyrants weep, the conscious murderer stand
And drop the dagger from his trembling hand?
Then, as you treat a favourite fair's mistake,
Pray spare her foibles for her virtue's sake.
And while her chastest scenes are made appear
(For none but such will find admittance here)
The muse's friends, we hope, will join our cause,
And crown our best endeavours with applause.

Mr. Singleton afterwards published a volume of poems, the principal or longest was descriptive, or intended so to be, of the West India islands.

➤➤ CHAPTER 2 ◀◀

Departure of Company from Virginia — Annapolis — First Theatre in New-York — First Theatre in Philadelphia — Death of Hallam, the first Manager in America — Succeeded by Douglass — Old American Company in New-York under Douglass — Second Theatre in New-York — Second and third Theatres in Philadelphia — Third Theatre in New-York — Newport — Theatrical Expenses and Profits — Customs of the Theatre — Benefit Bill — Destruction of the third New-York Theatre.

The precise date at which the comedians left Williamsburg is not mentioned in the memoranda taken from the dictation of Lewis Hallam the second. At their departure Governor Dinwiddie gave the manager a certificate signed in council, recommending the company as comedians, and testifying to the propriety of their behaviour as men.

There would be no useful end obtained by following the Thespians in their manifold wanderings, but a notice of the time and manner of introducing the theatre into our principal cities, and some of the changes which occurred in the company shall be recorded as far as information can be now obtained.

A writer in the Maryland Gazette, under date of June 19th, 1828, claims for Annapolis the first theatre, in point of time, erected in the United States. He says,

"In the year 1752, it appears from the files of the Maryland Gazette, that plays were performed in what is there called the new theatre. So called I presume in contradistinction to the temporary theatres previously used, which I am told were such commercial warehouses as could be gotten, and substituted for the purpose."* This writer gives the following advertisement.

"By permission of his Honour the President. At the new theatre in Annapolis, by the company of comedians, on Monday next, being the 13th of this instant, July, 1752, will be performed a comedy called The Beaux' Stratagem. Likewise a farce called The Virgin Unmasked. To begin precisely at 7 o'clock. Tickets to be had at the printing-office. Box 10 shillings, pit 7 and 6 pence, gallery 5 shillings. No person to be admitted behind the scenes." This writer says, "the names of the company, as no dramatic personæ are given, I am unable to ascertain. In the advertisement of Richard the III, which was acted twice, the character of Richard was performed by a Mr. Wynell, and that of Richmond by a Mr. Herbert. In another play the name of Mr. Eyarson is mentioned."

In the first chapter, the account given by Lewis Hallam, the son of the manager is followed. He was then twelve years of age. It appears that the company arrived at Yorktown in June, as the passage was six weeks, and they sailed early in May. From his account they did not play at Williamsburg until the 5th of September, which leaves ample time for Winnell (Wynell) and Herbert to have gone to Annapolis, and to have performed with a Mr. Eyarson, who as we have seen was not one of William Hallam's company, and others who had associated for the purpose of performing plays. Winnell and Herbert were inferiors in Hallam's company, and their performing the parts of Richard and Richmond accords with this supposition.

The writer in the Maryland Gazette goes on to say, that "The theatre (in Annapolis) which in 1752 is called the new theatre, was a neat brick building, tastefully arranged, and competent to contain between five and six hundred persons. It was built upon ground which had been leased from the Protestant Episcopal church in this city. When the lease, about ten or twelve years ago, had expired, the church took possession of the theatre. It was sold. It was pulled down merely to procure the materials of which it was built. Scarcely a fragment of it now remains. It was the oldest theatre in the United States. It was the earliest temple reared in our country to the dramatic muse. Perhaps it was the first spot upon which the characters of Shakespeare were exhibited to the people of the western world. It would hereafter have become an object at which the citizens of this ancient metropolis would have pointed with pride; which the curious would

* Probably used by boys or young men to enact plays after their fashion, as was the case, and will be the case, everywhere.

have sought, and which the admirers of genius and the drama would have revered."

Such is the claim put in by the citizens of Annapolis. That the whole of Hallam's company were not there is proved by the silence of his son Lewis, and by the circumstance of two inferior performers playing the first parts. Winnell and Herbert we find at Williamsburg in September, playing in their subordinate stations.

The claim for Annapolis of having erected the first theatre, the first temple to the dramatic muse, appears fully made out; notwithstanding the second Lewis Hallam's statement as given above; and yet that this circumstance should have escaped him, who played in Annapolis again and again, in his father's company probably, in Douglass's certainly, in 1772, and after, when the company was under the firm of Hallam and Henry, appears very unaccountable.

The third stage on which the productions of the dramatic muse were exhibited to the inhabitants of the New World was in Nassau-street, New-York. A theatre was erected on the spot long since occupied by the old Dutch Church. This was the second building expressly erected for the purpose of dramatic exhibitions in America. We have seen that the first appearance of the histrionic artists was at Williamsburg, Virginia, in a house which had been previously occupied for other purposes, probably a store-house. Annapolis has the honour of having raised the first temple to the Muses, and thither the company led by Lewis Hallam proceeded from Williamsburg, and after performing their stock plays and farces, visited and performed at Upper Marlborough, Piscataway, and Port Tobacco, then places of wealth and consequence in Maryland. Hallam opened his theatre in Nassau-street, New-York, on the 17th of September, 1753, one year after the first dramatic representations at Williamsburg.

It has been remarked that the south, from the universally admitted character of its population, was best fitted for the reception of the drama. The Presbyterians of the New-England provinces were opposed to any innovations upon their ascetic habits, and particularly to the introduction of those "profane stage-plays" which had been the delight of the Jacobite cavaliers, the enemies of their forefathers. New-York, originally a Dutch province, retained much of the language and manners of that people, and could only be considered as a resort after the southern provinces. The Quakers of Philadelphia were of all people the most opposed to scenic representations; and that population which, by its influx and increase, has changed the city of Penn from its drab-coloured austerity to the bland and polished amenity of the many-coloured receptacle of literature and the fine arts, was then in its incipient state. It was therefore wisely, as we have seen, that William Hallam, the manager of the London theatre in which Garrick attained to fame, directed his brother Lewis to the genial south, and Virginia and Maryland received the adventurers with a joyous welcome.

After the south, New-York presented the fairest field for the efforts of the comedians, and they opened their theatre with the following bill, which is given as a historic document. Particularity of this kind would be unnecessary in regard to events of more recent date, and out of place in a history of the theatre; but in this early stage of the work before us we think a play-bill a valuable source of information, and gladly insert it.

"By his Excellency's authority.
By a Company of Comedians from London, at the New Theatre in Nassau-street, the present evening being the 17th of September (1753), will be presented a comedy called

THE CONSCIOUS LOVERS.

The part of Young Bevil to be performed by Mr. Rigby.
The part of Mr. Sealand to be performed by Mr. Malone.

Sir John Bevil	by Mr. Bell.
Myrtle	by Mr. Clarkson.
Cimberton	by Mr. Miller.
Humphrey	by Mr. Adcock.
Daniel	by Master L. Hallam.

The part of Tom to be performed by Mr. Singleton.
The part of Phillis to be performed by Mrs. Becceley.

Mrs. Sealand	by Mrs. Clarkson.
Lucinda	by Miss Hallam.
Isabella	by Mrs. Rigby.

And the part of Indiana to be performed by Mrs. Hallam.
To which will be added the Ballad Farce called

DAMON AND PHILLIDA.

Arcas	by Mr. Bell.
Ogon	by Mr. Rigby.
Korydon	by Mr. Clarkson.
Cymon	by Mr. Miller.
Damon	by Mr. Adcock.
Phillida	by Mrs. Becceley.

A new occasional prologue to be spoken by Mr. Rigby. An epilogue (addressed to the ladies) by Mrs. Hallam. Prices, box 8s. pit 6s. gallery 3s. No person whatever to be admitted behind the scenes. N.B. Gentlemen and ladies that choose tickets may have them at the new printing-office in Beaver-street.* To begin at 6 o'clock."

* This was the office of the Gazette, printed by Parker and Weyman.

The days of performance were Mondays, Wednesdays, and Fridays; and so continued for half a century. On the second night of performing the prices were announced as box 6s. pit 5s. gallery 3s.; and towards the middle of October, the pit and gallery were reduced to 4s. and 2s.

It will be seen by the above bill that Sir Richard Steele was the first dramatist presented to the inhabitants of New-York. "The Conscious Lovers" is worthy of one of the authors of the Spectator, the coadjutor of Addison.

It appears that an accession had been made to the company. The names of Mr. Bell, Mr. Miller, and Mrs. Becceley are not in the list of adventurers who embarked in the Charming Sally, Captain Lee. Besides these three performers, Mr. and Mrs. Love now made part of the company, and Mr. Hulett.

The latter was an apprentice to William Hallam of Goodman's Fields, and was sent out to the company as a dancer and violin player. He was for many years the only dancing master in New-York, and some of us *old fellows* remember the lessons and the steps taught by this worthy man; whose sons were the teachers of succeeding generations, and live in the memories of the middle-aged of New-York.

On the 20th November the following curious note appeared on the play-bills. "N.B. Gentlemen and ladies that intend to favour us with their company are desired to come by six o'clock, (we) being determined to keep to our hour; as it would be a great inconvenience to them to be kept out late, *and a means to prevent disappointment.*" And on the 20th of December the bills gave notice that "nothing under the full price would be taken during the whole performance." It might be inferred from this notice that half price had been received heretofore; or it may have been intended to prevent the disappointment of those who had been accustomed to admittance in London at half price after the third act.

The early history of our drama brings us in contact with the antiquities of our country, particularly of our cities, and we shall take occasion to describe their boundaries and point out their progressive extent and improvements as far as we may do so, without abandoning that branch of history assigned to us, or as lawyers say, "travelling out of the record."

The theatre in Nassau-street was closed on the 18th of March, 1754, with The Beggar's Opera and The Devil to Pay. The company had given one night's performance to the poor. The play was "Love for Love," played to a full house with applause. The benefits commenced the latter part of January, 1754, and ended the 18th of March. After which appeared the following notice. Lewis Hallam, comedian, intending for Philadelphia, begs the favour of those that have any demands upon him to bring in their accounts and receive their money."

Taking it for granted that we can hardly be too particular in this part of our work, and that every thing connected with the introduction of the drama into

our country, has become interesting in proportion as the traces of this commencement and early progress becomes dim and would soon be lost, we will
give Mr. Hallam's account of the negotiation of his father with the authorities
and citizens of Philadelphia for permission to enact plays in their city.

Already had the religious toleration wisely and benevolently established by
William Penn, peopled his city with inhabitants of every sect and denomination. While Presbyterianism was intolerant and exclusive in the east, and Epis-
copacy in the south, Penn and Baltimore, the Quaker and the Roman Catholic,
had opened Pennsylvania and Maryland as lands of refuge for liberty of conscience. The consequence was that the plain Quaker-colour made only a part
of the garb of the citizens of Philadelphia even at this early period; but still *drab*
was the livery of the majority. A large portion of the inhabitants, however, saw
no offence to morality or religion in any of the colours which diversify and
beautify the works of creation; or any of those innocent amusements which
bring men together to sympathize in joys or sorrows, uniting them in the same
feelings and expressions with a brotherly consciousness of the same nature and
origin. Many, also, had been accustomed to the representations of the dramatists in their native land, and longed to renew the associations of their youth.
Others who had only read the works of Shakespeare were anxious to experience
the influence of the living personification of those thoughts and characters
which had delighted them in the closet, and looked towards the sister and then
secondary city of New-York with a strong desire to participate in her pleasures
and advantages. These causes produced an application to the manager while the
company were playing at New-York. Several gentlemen from Philadelphia urged
Mr. Hallam to apply to Governor Hamilton for permission to open a theatre in
that city, and pledged themselves for the success notwithstanding any opposition from the followers of Penn. They suggested that it would be best to make
application for liberty to play for a few nights.

Hallam received these overtures with pleasure, and looked around upon his
companions for a man fitted for the task of opening the way to so desirable an
acquisition as this hitherto hostile city would be to the cause of the Muse. Such
a pioneer and negotiator needed address and talents, and we must suppose that
Mr. Malone had evinced powers of persuasion, and possessed engaging manners or accomplishments superior to most of his fellows, as he was selected by
the manager for the important and difficult mission.

The nature of the reward offered to induce Malone to undertake this *long
journey,* and trust himself, face to face, with these broad-brimmed, brown-
wigged Quakers in their own stronghold, lets us into some of the secrets of the
green-room. "He undertook the business," says our informant, "on condition,
that if successful, he should have for his reward the parts of *Falstaff* in "Henry

the Fourth" and "The Merry Wives," and of *Don Lewis* in "Love makes a Man, or the Fop's Fortune."

At that period, and long since, the parts in which an actor was cast, if the manager's decree was confirmed by the public, became his inalienable property while in the company, and ofttimes the proprietor continued to figure as a youthful hero or lover long after all nature's qualifications for the parts had become the prey of time the despoiler, and the wrinkles of age, and the cracked voice changed to "childish treble" should have consigned him to the representation of the lean and slippered pantaloon.

The tenacity of players is sometimes the subject of ridicule, and sometimes of surprise or wonder; but this will cease when we consider that the consequence or standing of the individual is estimated by the parts he plays, and that the good part marks and sometimes makes the good actor. We must also remember, that the salary, the share, and the benefit, may be measured by the cast of parts.

Malone willingly undertook the embassy with the hope of attaining this brilliant accession to his theatrical property, but he experienced such a strenuous opposition, and found the strife with these disciples of peace so perilous, that he wrote for the manager to come to his assistance. The cry was "Hallam to the rescue." The manager flew, as fast as mortals could then fly, to the assistance of his emissary. The relief was effectual, for "the king's name is a tower of strength," or was in those good old times. The manager found the city of brotherly love and passive peace divided into two hostile factions, as violent as the green and red of Constantinople when charioteers shook the empire of the Cesars to its foundation. Here it was not one colour against its opposite, but colours against colourless: the rainbow struggling through a cloud.

The Quakers and their adherents carried a petition to the governor for the prohibition of profane stage-plays. Counter petitions were signed and presented, and finally the friends of action and passion prevailed, and the manager was favoured by Governor Hamilton with a permission to open a theatre and cause twenty-four plays with their attendant afterpieces to be performed, on condition that they "offered nothing indecent and immoral," and performed one night for the benefit of the poor of the city,—and further, that the manager gave security for all debts contracted, and all contracts entered into by the company. How characteristic is all this of the time.

Such was the treaty by which the first histrionic adventurers gained a narrow and precarious footing in a new region which seemed forbidden ground. Once within the walls they extended the boundaries of their conquest, not without opposition, until the whole city submitted to the invaders, who by degrees, like the Tartar invaders of the Celestial empire, have become one and the same with the people they had conquered—not that the players became Quakers, but peaceable and good citizens, no longer living on sufferance or obliged to give bonds for their good behaviour.

All this had taken place previous to the 18th of March, 1754, and a place secured for the representation of plays in Philadelphia. Accordingly the players proceeded thither, and commenced theatrical exhibitions. This was the first theatre opened in the capital of Pennsylvania by artists or actors by profession. As early as 1749, it is on record that the magistracy of the city had been disturbed by some idle young men perpetrating the murder of sundry plays in the skirts of the town, but the culprits had been arrested and bound over to their good behaviour, after confessing their crime and promising to spare the poor poets for the future.

The first regular company of comedians opened their theatre, the store-house of Mr. William Plumstead, on the corner of the first alley above Pine-street, and commenced playing in April, 1754, with the tragedy of the Fair Penitent. The place has since been occupied as a sail-loft, and the remains or traces of scenic decoration were to be seen within forty years. This was called the new theatre. The word "new" seems to have applied to all the places or buildings used by this company, although there had been no previous establishment of the kind. The prices of admittance were, box 6 shillings, pit 4 shillings, gallery 2 shillings and 6 pence. The company gained money and reputation, notwithstanding a continued and vigorous opposition. Pamphlets were published and distributed gratis during the whole theatrical campaign, and every effort made to show the evils attendant upon plays and players, and play-houses; but Shakespeare and his followers prevailed. The tree was planted and could not be rooted out. The effort of the wise should be to improve its fruit by cultivation, trimming, and grafting.

The Fair Penitent and Miss in her Teens were the first dramatic pieces presented to the inhabitants of Philadelphia; Nicholas Rowe and David Garrick, the first dramatists who spoke from the stage in the city of Penn. The tragedy was thus cast:

Sciotto,	Mr. Malone.
Horatio,	Rigby.
Lothario,	Singleton.
Altamont,	Clarkson.
Calista,	Mrs. Hallam.
Lavinia,	Adcock.
Lucetta,	Miss Hallam.

The house was, as might be expected from the excitement, full to overflowing. In the course of the evening a great tumult was occasioned by the discovery of one of the unfriendly petitioners in the pit. He was considered as a spy, and peace was not restored until he was hustled out.

The governor added six nights to the twenty-four first granted to the players. Thus they held possession of the town until July, as their thirty nights, three in each week, occupied ten weeks.

In addition to the pleasure of success, the Thespians were gladdened by a visit from William Hallam, the father of the American stage, the original projector of this prosperous scheme. He landed in June, 1754. There is reason to believe that Lewis purchased all the property, interest, and good-will, from his brother William the original owner, as he returned to England immediately after a settlement of their accounts, and we hear no more of him.

Lewis, now not only manager but sole proprietor, transported his company to the West Indies, and dying in Jamaica, his widow married David Douglass, and placed him on the theatrical throne of the western hemisphere.

During the absence of the company in the West Indies, the theatre in Nassau-street, New-York, was taken down, and Douglass procured a building more according to his views to be erected for the reception of his company when they should return to that city. This building, the third theatre erected in the United States, was on Cruger's wharf, between what are now called Old-slip and Coffee-house-slip. At that time the south-east side of Water-street was unbuilt, and the place of the earth on which it stands was occupied by the tide-water. "Cruger's wharf" was the name given to a projecting block of buildings to the east of "Little Dock-street," bounded by the water, and having the water on each side, in what were called docks.

Douglass had built his theatre without obtaining permission from the magistracy to enact plays. This was a sad mistake, and no doubt offended dignity had determined before his arrival to punish him for neglecting those "boos" which the patron exacts from the patronized. The manager was made sensible of his neglect immediately upon his arrival in the autumn of 1758 (for until this time it would appear that the Thespians were roving among the West India islands). Upon application for permission to perform plays, the "gentlemen in power" refused it.

Douglass made an appeal to the public in Gaine's Mercury of November 6th, stating that he had "to his great mortification, met with a positive and absolute denial" when he "applied to the gentlemen in power for permission to play." He goes on to say that "he has in vain represented that such are his circumstances and those of the other members of the company, that it is impossible for them to move to another place; and although in the humblest manner he begged the magistrates would indulge him in acting as many plays as would barely defray the expenses he and the company have been at in coming to this city, and enable them to proceed to another, he has been unfortunate enough to be peremptorily refused it. As he has given over all thoughts of acting, he begs leave to inform the public, that in a few days he will open a HISTRIONIC ACADEMY, of which notice will be given in this paper."

This was considered as an attempt to evade, or resist, the prohibition of the magistrates, and on the 8th of December, Douglass found it necessary to deny all such intention, and concludes his apology thus: "The expense of our coming here, our living since our arrival, the charge of building, &c. amount to a sum that would swallow up the profits of a great many nights' acting, had we permission. I shall conclude with humbly hoping that those gentlemen who have entertained an ill opinion of me from my supposed presumption will do me the favour to believe that I have truly explained the advertisement, and that I am to them and the public a very humble and devoted servant." His explanation of his Histrionic Academy, was that he "proposed to deliver dissertations on subjects *moral, instructive,* and *entertaining,* and to endeavour to qualify such as would favour him with attendance *to speak in public with propriety.*"

This man appears to have been by descent and education a gentleman. He afterward filled the office of one of his majesty's judges. He had failed to bow the knee to power even before he had approached within its bounds, and he was thus made to lick the dust before a gracious permission was granted, to enlighten his judges, their satellites, and the people entrusted to their care, by the recitation of the pride of English poetry and wit.

Permission was at length obtained to perform thirteen nights, and the second theatre in New-York was opened with Jane Shore. Singleton's prologue was spoken by the second Lewis Hallam, now eighteen years of age; and an epilogue, written probably by Mr. Singleton, was delivered by Mrs. Douglass, Hallam's mother.

The epilogue, as marking the opposition which the theatre now had to sustain, and the degree of ability with which that opposition was met, and likewise the improvement of poet Singleton by his transplantation, shall be inserted here.

> Much has been said at this censorious time,
> To prove the treading of the stage a crime.
> Mistaken zeal, in terms not quite so civil,
> Consigns both plays and players to the devil.
> Yet wise men own, a play well chose may teach
> Such useful moral truths as churchmen preach.
> May teach the heart another's grief to know,
> And melt the soul to salutary wo.
>   So when the unhappy virtuous fair complains
> In Shakespeare's, Lee's, or Otway's moving strains,
> The narrowest hearts expanded wide appear,
> And soft compassion drops the pitying tear.

Or would you warn the thoughtless youth to shun
Such dangerous arts as numbers have undone,
A Barnwell's fate can never fail to move,
And strike with shame and terror, lawless love.
See, plunged in ruin, with a virtuous wife,
The Gamester weeps, despairs, and ends his life.
When Cato bleeds he spends his latest breath,
To teach the love of country, strong in death.
With these examples and a thousand more,
Of godlike men who lived in times of yore,
The tragic Muse recalls this long-past age,
And brings heroic virtue, living, on the stage.
    But when to social gayety inclined
The comic Muse shall feast the cheerful mind,
Fools of all sorts, and fops a brainless crew,
To raise your mirth, we'll summon to your view;
Make e'en the coxcomb laugh to see his brother,
And one knave blush with shame to see another,
'Tis magic ground we tread, and at our call
Those sprites appear that represent you all.
    Yet hold—methinks I hear some snarler cry,
"Pray madam, why so partial—rat me—why
Don't you do justice on your own sweet sex?
Are there no prudes, coquettes, or jilts to vex?"
Granted—there are. For folly's not confined
To sex, it sways despotic all of human kind.
We frankly own—indeed we may as well—
For every fluttering beau, we find a simpering belle.
    But oft, above the pert, the dull, the vain,
The comic Muse exalts her moral strain;
To laugh at folly will not be confined,
But tries to mend as well as please mankind.
So when vile custom by false honour's breath,
For one rash word would doom two friends to death,
Steele's moral Muse the impressive lesson shows,
Teaching the unhallow'd tyrant's will t' oppose.
Showing a Bevil, generous as brave,
Too wise to be insensate custom's slave,
Above the fear of death, but not above
The law of God, prescribing peace and love.
    Thus human life's our theme—a fruitful field
Of moral themes a plenteous store to yield—
Sages upheld our art in ancient time,

And to paint nature was not thought a crime;
For if the soul in virtue's cause we move,
The friends of virtue cannot disapprove—
We trust they do not, by the splendid sight
Of sparkling eyes that grace our scenes to-night;
Then bravely dare to assert the taste you've shown,
Nor be ashamed so just a cause to own;
And tell our foes, what Shakespeare said of old
(Our former motto spoke it, I am told),
That here the world in miniature you see,
And all mankind are players as well as we.

The "former motto" alluded to was "Totus Mundus aget Histrionem." Some one has paraphrased Shakespeare thus—

"Yes, all the world's a stage, and full of cares,
And all mankind poor strutting, fretting players."

In the year 1759, David Douglass opened the second theatre in Philadelphia. It was situated at the south-west corner of Vernon and South-streets, at a place formerly called "Society Hill."

Strictly speaking, this was the first theatre opened in Philadelphia or its suburbs, unless we call every place a theatre which is fitted up for the temporary exhibition of plays. This was, however, the first building erected as a theatre. The manager had cautiously taken his stand without the precincts of the city authorities, in what is called the Southern Liberties, but this did not prevent the revival of the civil strife of 1754. The Quakers and others arrayed themselves in opposition, and applied to Judge Allen (probably because the place was within the peculiar limits assigned to his rule), with denunciations of the players, and petitions that his power might be exerted for the putting down of these intruders, these disturbers of the sleepy quiet of the formal city. The judge gave them an answer which must have been very unpalatable. Watson says he rejected the petition, and among other matter told the petitioners that "he had learned more moral virtue from plays than from sermons." What was the consequence? The play-house was opened, and the wife of the judge fell sick and died. Such is the warning which tradition has handed down to us that wives may hereafter prevent their husbands giving countenance to theatres.

It is probable that Douglass, profiting by experience, had applied to Allen and obtained his permission before he ventured to erect a theatre, thus avoiding the prohibition which had troubled him at New-York.

This temple of the dramatic muse was, as may be supposed, an ordinary wooden building, and was afterward converted into three dwelling-houses, which are still standing at the corner of Vernon and South-streets. The inhab-itants of Philadelphia remember Mr. and Mrs. Douglass, Miss Cheer, and Miss Morris as the most prominent performers of that day.

The easternmost boundary of the theatrical empire at this time was Newport, Rhode Island, where the next theatre was built. From Williamsburg to Newport the company ranged, occasionally playing besides at the cities of Annapolis, Philadelphia, and New-York, and in smaller places, where a court-house could be transformed to a play-house, and scenes of imaginary heroic guilt be allowed to take the place of vulgar plebeian crime.

Perth Amboy, then the capital of the province of New-Jersey, and the residence of his majesty's governors, judges, treasurers, attorney-generals, and collectors, with a garrison usually of a regiment of foot, occasionally received the visits of the Thespians, and the writer has heard old ladies speak, almost in raptures, of the beauty and grace of Mrs. Douglass, and the pathos of her personation of Jane Shore.

In 1759 and long after, Newport, Williamsburg, Annapolis, and Perth Amboy, were places of comparative importance, now sunk into little more than villages, while neighbouring towns have sprung up, towering above them and overshad-owing them, producing a sickly existence or absolute decay. A description of the first has been elegantly and truly given by the American novelist, James Fenni-more Cooper, in his Red Rover. The health inspiring garden of the north, where the southern planters, from the West Indies and the Carolinas, met in the great slave market of the English provinces.

The Thespians did not visit New-York from 1759 to 1761, but in the year 1760, Douglass built a larger theatre in Philadelphia, and after giving a benefit at So-ciety Hill for the college of the city "for improving youth in the divine art of psalmody and church music," he opened the theatre in Southwark, which re-mained the only theatre of the metropolis of Pennsylvania until the building of the beautiful house in Chestnut-street, erected for Wignell and Reinagle in 1791, of which hereafter.

The house erected in 1760 was of sufficient size for the population at that time and long after, and was well adapted for theatrical representations. It was of wood principally and painted red, without outward ornament, and in its ap-pearance no ornament to the city. It was partly burnt some years ago, and is now used as a distillery. Once pouring out a mingled strain of good and evil, it now dispenses purely evil. Yet distillers are not stigmatised in society.

This place was used for the exhibition of players, though not the performance of plays, as late as August, 1800, when Messrs. Hodgkinson and Barrett opened it with portions of plays, recitations, and music, for two nights.

In the beginning of August, 1761, "his honour the lieutenant-governor was pleased to give Mr. Douglass permission to build a theatre to perform in," in the city of New-York, "the ensuing winter." We lost sight of the theatre on Cruger's wharf, and a new house in Beekman-street was erected, and ready for opening on the 18th of November, on which night Rowe's *The Fair Penitent* and Garrick's *Lethe* were performed. This, the third theatre erected in New-York, was situated a little below the junction of Nassau and Beekman-street, on the south or southwest side of the latter street.

At this time the company came from Newport, Rhode Island, where they left a favourable impression, as appears by the following extract from Gaine's Mercury of November 9th, 1761.

> Newport, November 3d. On Friday evening last, the company of comedians finished their performances in this town by enacting the tragedy of Douglass for the benefit of the poor. This *second* charity is undoubtedly meant as an expression of gratitude for the countenance and favour the town has shown them; and it cannot without an uncommon degree of malevolence be ascribed to an interested or selfish view, because it is given at a time when the company are just leaving the place, and consequently can have neither fear nor hope from the public. In return for this generosity it ought in justice to be told, that the behaviour of the company here has been irreproachable: and with regard to their skill as players, the universal pleasure and satisfaction they have given is their best and most honourable testimony. The character they brought from the governor and gentlemen of Virginia has been fully verified, and therefore we shall run no risk in pronouncing "that they are capable of entertaining a sensible and polite audience."

It appears from this, that the Thespians found foes among the slave dealers of Newport, who probably thought a stage-player a greater abomination than the kidnapper, or receiver and abetter of the kidnapper, of the miserable negro. It likewise appears that the actors carried and exhibited *a character* from place to place, vouching for their capability, and took care at this time to smooth their way in New-York by this commendation, republished from the Gazette of Newport. Notwithstanding this policy, a strenuous opposition was still made to the players, and permission was only given to them at this time to perform two months. They played twice a week. The house held 180 pounds or 450 dollars. They calculated their average receipts at three hundred dollars, which for the sixteen nights allowed them, gave four thousand eight hundred dollars. They stated the current expenses of the sixteen nights to amount to two hundred and fifty pounds, or six hundred and twenty-five dollars (at 39 dollars 7 cents per night). The cost of the theatre was estimated at sixteen hundred and twenty-five dollars. By this we may judge of the size and elegance of the building, and compare it with the theatres of the present day. The cost of scenery and wardrobe was set down at four hundred pounds, or one thousand dollars. Making the money expended amount to thirteen hundred pounds, or three thousand one hundred and fifty dollars, leaving a balance of six hundred and twenty pounds, or fifteen hundred and fifty dollars, to pay their individual expenses while in New-York and their travelling charges. This curious statement and calculation was published by Douglass as an answer to an enemy who had asserted in the journals of the day that the company would cost the city six thousand pounds.

Play tickets were advertised to be sold by Hugh Gaine at the Bible and Crown. Box 8 shillings, pit 5 shillings, gallery 3 shillings. "The doors to be opened at four, and the play to begin precisely at six o'clock. No person to be admitted behind the scenes."

Many of our older citizens will remember Mr. Gaine with respect. He was Irish by birth, and rose to fortune like Franklin, by industrious application to the type and the press. Industry does not always imply economy, but with this worthy man they went hand in hand, until that wealth, their inevitable result, justified the assumption of a more swelling port. He was never ostentious or prodigal, but ever liberal both of time and property for the service of the public, or of meritorious individuals. His business was attended to with the same punctuality, the same brown wig—such as we should look for in vain in these degenerate days—the same long-skirted brown coat, the same shrewdness and good-humour which had characterized him from early life. He printed and edited the newspaper called the Mercury, which had afterward the additional title of the Weekly Gazette for many years, conducting it through the war of the revolution under the auspices of the Bible and Crown. It is needless to say that in 1783 the crown fell, but the Bible continued as the sign of his printing-office and bookstore, in Hanover-square, now Pearl-street, near Wall-street, for many years after it had lost its companion. This separation betokened that of church from state, which is one of the safeguards of our liberty.

Pearl-street then extended only from the Battery to Whitehall; the present street bore the additional names of Dock-street, Hanover-square, and Queen-street, and ended where Pearl crosses Chatham.

The old American Company at this period, 1761, consisted of Messrs. Douglass, Hallam (the second, his son-in-law), Allyn, Morris, Quelch, Tomlinson, Sturt, Reed, Tremaine, and Master A. Hallam. Mesdames Douglass, Morris, Crane, Allyn, and Miss Hallam.

The oppositionists continued their attacks through the medium of the public prints, and the players defended themselves by repeating their prologue and epilogue, revised by the author, and by acting a play for the benefit of "such poor families as are not provided for by the public."

The profits arising from the representation of Othello, after deducting the charges of the night (exclusive of remuneration to actors, who all gave their services to appease opposition and feed the poor), was one hundred and fourteen pounds ten shillings, or two hundred and eighty-six dollars and a quarter. This sum was paid by Mr. Douglass to George Harrison, Esq., and Mr. John Vanderspiegle, who undertook the distribution of the charity.

The amount of the receipts on this occasion was one hundred and thirty-three pounds and six pence, or three hundred and thirty-two dollars and fifty-six cents. The account rendered by the manager of receipts and expenses is inserted as a curiosity.

	s.	£	s.	d.
"Box tickets sold at the door,	116 a 8 -	46	8	
Pit " " "	146 5 -	36	10	
Gallery " "	90 3 -	13	10	
Cash received at the doors		36	12	6
		£133	00	6

Charges.

"To candles, 26 lb. of spermaceti at	3s.	6d. ⎫	
" 14 lb. tallow	1s.	⎬ £5 5	
To music, Messrs. Harrison & Van Dienval at	36s.	3 12	
To the front door-keeper, 16s., stage door-keeper,	8s.	1 4	
To the assistants, 13s., bill sticker,	4s.	17	
To the men's dresser, 4s., stage-keeper, 32s., drummer, 4s.		2	
To wine in the second act,	2s.	6d.	2 6
To Hugh Gaine, for two sets of bills, advertisements, and commissions		5 10	
		£18 10 6	

Balance, £114 10s.

Notwithstanding the notification of "no person admitted behind the scenes," the disorderly and improper practice of permitting gentlemen to mingle with the actors and actresses behind the scenes, and even to show themselves on the stage, was common at this time, as is proved by the following public notice of Dec. 31st, 1761. "Complaints having been several times made that a number of gentlemen crowd the stage and very much interrupt the performance, and as it is impossible the actors, when thus obstructed, should do that justice to their parts they otherwise would; it will be taken as a particular favour if no gentleman will be offended that he is absolutely refused admittance at the stage-door, unless he has previously secured himself a place in either the stage or upper boxes." This is a picture of the state of things behind the scenes, which it is now scarcely possible to conceive. We know from the history of the English stage that such was the practice in London for many years.* On benefit nights, the stage would be nearly filled, the auditory seated so as to allow a small portion of the boards for the actors. The practice was abolished long before our first knowledge of theatres.

We cannot resist the temptation of inserting the benefit bill of the first actress in the country, and wife to the manager. Besides other customs of the time, the last paragraph shows the existence in Feb., 1762, the date of the bill, of a custom probably common in England at the time.

> For the benefit of Mrs. Douglass, the tragical history of KING RICHARD THE THIRD, containing the distress and death of King Henry the Sixth in the Tower; the usurpation of the crown by Richard; the inhuman murder of the young King Edward the Fifth, and his brother the Duke of York; the fall of the Duke of Buckingham; the landing of the Earl of Richmond (afterwards Henry the Seventh) at Milford; the battle of Bosworth Field, and death of Richard, which put an end to the contention between the houses of York and Lancaster; with many other historical passages.
>
> King Richard,   by Mr. Douglass;
> Richmond,   by Mr. Hallam;
>
> King Henry, by Mr. Allyn; King Edward the Fifth, by Master A. Hallam; Duke of York, by a young Master for his diversion; Duke of Buckingham, by Mr. Tomlinson; Lord Stanly, by Mr. Morris; Lieutenant of the Tower, by Mr. Sturt; Catesby, by Mr. Reed; Tressel, by Mr. Hallam; Dutchess of York, by Mrs. Crane; Lady Anne, by Mrs. Morris, and Queen Elizabeth, by Mrs. Douglass.
>
> To which will be added, a dramatic satire called LETHE, with the additional character of Lord Chalkstone. Lord Chalkstone, by Mr. Allyn; Æsop, by Mr. Douglass; Fine Gentleman, Mr. Hallam; Mercury, Mr. Sturt; Frenchman, Mr. Allyn; Charon, Mr. Tomlinson; Old Man, Mr. Morris; Mr. Tattoo, Mr. Reed; Bowman, Mr. Tomlinson; Drunken Man, Mr. Hallam; Mrs. Riot, by Mrs. Douglass.
>
> Tickets to be had of Mr. Gaine, printer, at the sign of the bible and Crown, in Hanover-square, and of Mrs. Douglass, at her lodgings near the theatre, where places in the boxes may be taken. Box 8s., pit 5s., gallery 3s.
>
> The ceremony of waiting on ladies and gentlemen at their houses with bills has been for some time left off in this company; the frequent solicitations on these occasions having been found rather an inconvenience to the person so waited on, than a compliment.

---

* In 1721, a riot was occasioned at Rich's theatre, by the insolence of the people *of quality* behind the curtain, which ended in a fight between the nobles and the players, and the final capture of the *men of condition,* and triumph of the actors.

It is not alone on the state of theatrical manners and customs that these notices from bills and advertisements throw light; we gain a peep at our long-buried
ancestors of the colonies, which, aided by an active imagination, conjures up
scenes of real life that otherwise would have slept in oblivion. We see the beaux
of 1761, with their powdered wigs, long stiff-skirted coats and waistcoats, with
flaps reaching nearly to the knees of their inexpressibles; their silk stockings,
short-quartered shoes, and silver or paste buckles, crowding and ogling the actresses on the stage, having secured the box ticket for the purpose of gaining
admission behind the scenes. The ladies in the boxes looking now on the actor,
and now on a friend or brother by his side. And we see the actor or actress going from house to house, presenting benefit bills, and soliciting patronage—
"rather an inconvenience to the person so waited upon."

The company finished their labours in New-York on the 26th of April, 1762,
with a play for the benefit of the Charity School, and "a handsome sum was
raised and delivered by Mr. Douglass to the church wardens."

From this time until 1767, we have no documents of any special value relative to the state of the company, or the feelings of the people towards them. They
went their rounds on the continent, and in the English West Indies.

The "troubles," however, which agitated the colonies in consequence of the
stamp act, occasioned the destruction of the third New-York theatre. The arts
can only be cherished in seasons of peace and prosperity. During the civil wars
in England, the theatres were shut, and the players entered the king's army, in
opposition to the republic. The republicans of New-York, in 1764, whether remembering the predilection of the actors for monarchy, or from other causes,
determined to overthrow the play-house in Beekman-street, and a gentleman
late residing on Long Island, then a boy, told us that he was engaged in the work
of destruction. He said that a number of persons assembled in a yard, or open
space opposite the theatre, in the evening, and set on the boys to commence the
work, which once begun, found hands enough to aid in it. Thus it appears that
the first cloud portending civil war, discharged its thunders on the temple of
the Muses: the cloud passed off, and left the political horizon in a state of flattering calm and brightness—flattering because deceitful.

During this calm, Thos. Godfrey, of Philadelphia, the son of the inventor of
the quadrant, in 1765, published a play called "The Prince of Parthia," a tragedy, founded on, but deviating from history; whether intended for the stage, or
only for the closet, is unknown. That it was not performed by the players is certain. This is the first American drama on record.

In 1767 we find further records of the dramatic muse, which require a new
chapter.

➤➤ CHAPTER 3 ◀◀

Theatre in John-street, New-York — John Henry — Theatre in Albany — New-York Hospital — Doctor Cooper — First Theatre in Charleston, S.C. — The four Misses Storer — Miss Cheer — Congress recommends the closing of Theatres, or rather resolves to discourage extravagance and dissipation, and names Theatres as among the sources — The resolution communicated by Peyton Randolph — Wignell arrives — Antiquities.

In the summer of 1767, the theatre in John-street, New-York, was built very much upon the plan of that in the Southern Liberties at Philadelphia, already mentioned. It was principally of wood; an unsightly object, painted red. The situation of this house was on the north side of the street, nearly opposite the present Arcade (1832). It was about 60 feet back from the street, having a covered way of rough wooden material from the pavement to the doors. There is reason to believe that at this time the dressing-rooms and green-room were under the stage, for after the revolution, Hallam and Henry added on the west side of the building a range of rooms for dressing, and a commodious room for assembling previous to being called to "*go on.*" Two rows of boxes, with a pit and gallery, could accommodate all the play-going people of that time, and yield to the sharers eight hundred dollars when full, at the usual prices. The stage was of good dimensions, as far as memory serves, equal to that of Colman's theatre in the Haymarket, London, originally Foote's.

The John-street theatre was opened on the 7th of December, 1767, with Farquhar's lively and licentious comedy of The Beaux' Stratagem, which now cannot be tolerated, and Garrick's Lethe.

On this occasion, Mr. John Henry, long known as one of the firm of Hallam and Henry, and one of the best performers in the colonies, made his first appearance in America, in the character of Aimwell, and judging from his appearance twenty years after, he must have been as handsome an Aimwell as ever trod the stage.* Henry, an Irishman by birth, had been liberally educated, and made his *debut* in London, under the patronage of the elder Sheridan, author of the once fashionable pronouncing dictionary, well known as an actor, and better known as the father of the author of The School for Scandal. The success of

---

* Carpenter, an English or Irish historian of the stage, with an accuracy similar to that of Burk, the Irish historian of Virginia, says that Hallam, the son-in-law and successor of Douglass, found Henry an actor at Drury Lane after our revolution, and entering into partnership with him, he made his first appearance in consequence (see The Mirror of Taste) of this arrangement, and of course after 1783.

Henry on the London stage had not been sufficient to gain him a place among the successors of Garrick; but to fail of success in London was the lot of Garrick on his first appearance, and afterwards Siddons experienced the same neglect.

The company was still Douglass's, but many changes had occurred. Many of the original adventurers, and even of their successors, had disappeared, and in their places on the play-bills we find the names of Messrs. Henry, Wall, Roberts, Greville, Wools, and Raworth, with Mesdames Harman, Wall, Cheer, Wainwright, Storer, F. Storer, and M. Storer. The last and first Miss Storer were afterward in turn Mrs. Henry, the youngest died first of the three, as Mrs. Henry; and after Henry's death, the two elder sisters were known as Mrs. Mechler and Mrs. Hogg. Mrs. Storer and *four* daughters had joined the company in Jamaica; the daughters were designated as Miss Storer, Miss Ann Storer, Miss Fanny Storer, and Miss Maria Storer. Henry married the eldest, but during a voyage from Jamaica, the vessel in which she was a passenger, whether he was with her or not, we know not, was burnt, and she with it. This accident took place on our eastern coast. The second sister, Ann or Nancy, was the mother of a son, born to Henry, and afterward a captain of a ship. The third sister, Fanny, was afterward Mrs. Mechler. Maria, the fourth sister, died Mrs. Henry. The second sister, Ann or Nancy, was afterward Mrs. Hogg.

This gives us a glimpse at the state of manners and morals among these teachers of virtue and morality, and such instances, even if rare, accounts for that repelling principle which keeps the cautious and the pure in private society aloof from those who delight them in public. Those who attract public attention should be able to bear the scrutiny of the public. It is not players alone that are found wanting when weighed in the balance, and it is unjust to fix a stigma on a profession which appertains to an unworthy individual.

The name of Miss Cheer appears for the first time on occasion of opening the house in John-street. She played the part of Mrs. Sullen, and from this time shared the first rank of characters with Mrs. Douglass.*

The youngest Miss Storer possessed beauty and talent. She was, until the year 1792, the best public singer America had known. She played tragedy and comedy with spirit and propriety, although her figure was rather petite for the first, or for the elegant females of Congreve and Cibber.

Wools was for many years the first singer of the company, continuing to figure as such long after all voice had left him, and snuff and snuffle characterized his attempts.

We must be permitted to insert the bill for the opening of the theatre in John-

---

* We have before us a Philadelphia play-bill, in which Hallam is announced for Macbeth, and Miss Cheer as Lady Macbeth.

street, a place which yet lives in the memories of some hundreds of the citizens of New-York.

"By permission of his Excellency the Governor. By the American Company. At the theatre in John-street, this present evening, being the 7th instant, December, will be presented a comedy called the Stratagem.

Archer, Mr. Hallam; Aimwell, Mr. Henry; Sullen, Mr. Tomlinson; Freeman, Malone; Foigard, Allyn; Gibbet, Wools; Scrub, Wall; Boniface, Douglass; Dorinda, Miss Hallam; Lady Bountiful, Mrs. Harman; Cherry, Miss Wainwright; Gipsey, Mrs. Wall; Mrs. Sullen, Miss Cheer. An occasional epilogue by Mrs. Douglass."

The afterpiece of Lethe gave Mr. Wools an opportunity of singing as Mercury, and a song in character was sung by Miss Wainwright. The bill concludes "*Vivant Rex et Regina.*"

On the 14th of December, nine chiefs of the Cherokee nation attended the theatre. Richard the Third was played for their edification, and the journal remarks that "they regarded the play with attention, but seemed to express nothing but surprise; the *Oracle* and *Harlequin's Vagaries* drew forth some proofs of their being diverted." Soon after the bills announce that "the Cherokee chiefs and warriors being desirous of making some return for the friendly reception and civilities they have received in this city, have offered to entertain the public with a war-dance;" and "it is humbly presumed that no part of the audience will forget the proper decorum so essential to all public assemblies, particularly on this occasion, as the persons who have *condescended* to contribute to their entertainment are of rank and consequence in their own country." How many reflections does this precious *morceau* give rise to—but the reader shall not be anticipated.

In December, the papers of the day announce that Mrs. Morris, of the theatre (together with her maid servant), was drowned in crossing the ferry at *Kill Vankeel.* The husband of the person here mentioned appears to have joined the company in 1761; he is remembered as a part of it until 1800. He was a low comedian, and played the old men of farce and comedy when the shuffling gait, and whistling treble, which time had forced upon him, were applauded as most exquisite imitations of old age, whose imperfections are ever the jest of the thoughtless vulgar. Those who can look back to 1788, will remember him a little shrivelled old man, with a voice palsied by years, having for his second wife a tall elegant woman, the favourite comedy lady, and the admiration of the public.

The first notice of a custom which prevailed within the remembrance of the writer, is thus mentioned on a play-bill dated January 16, 1768. "Ladies will please to send their servants to keep their places, at four o'clock." From four until six and after, the front seats of the boxes were occupied by blacks of every age, waiting until their masters and mistresses made their appearance.

On the 16th of January, 1769, the theatre in John-street was opened under the direction of Douglass, with "King John, and The Old Maid." The only new names in the bills are Byerley, Parker, and Darby.

The 17th of March, "The Busy Body and Brave Irishman" were announced to be performed by particular desire of the GRAND KNOT of the *friendly brothers* of St. Patrick. The charter song by Mr. Wools.

March 28. The Tender Husband and Upholsterer were advertised for "the entertainment of the R. W. Grand Master, the M. W. and brethren of the ancient and honourable Society of Free and Accepted Masons." To the bill was annexed the following invitation: "The company of *all the brethren* in town is earnestly requested to meet at Burn's at 5 o'clock on the day of performance, and walk from thence in *procession* to the theatre, where the pit will be reserved for their accommodation."

In the New-York Journal of April 10th, we find Othello and Hob in the Well advertised. "The part of Othello to be attempted by a gentleman, assisted by other gentlemen in the characters of the Duke and Senate of Venice, from a benevolent and generous design of encouraging the theatre, and relieving the performers from some embarrassments in which they are involved."

Miss Wainwright, who appears to have been a principal comic actress, retired from the stage about this time, and Mrs. Douglass, who had, as Mrs. Hallam, been the heroine of Goodman's Fields theatre in the time of Garrick's first success and after; and who, as we have seen, had been the favourite of the West Indian and North American colonists from 1752, was now declining in health, and approaching the final exit.

On the 19th of June, the theatre closed with the play of Love for Love, and for the sixth time, The Padlock. Mr. Hallam, the son of Mrs. Douglass, who, as we have seen, came from England with his parents at the age of twelve, was not the principal comedian and tragedian of the company. He ascribed his success to the instructions of Rigby, who was the first male player of the original band. In The Padlock, Mr. Hallam was unrivalled to his death, giving the Mungo with a truth derived from study of the negro slave character, which Dibdin the writer could not have conceived.

Albany was visited by the servants of the Muses for the first time in July of this year; having gained permission "for one month only," from "his Excellency the Governor." On the 3d of July, 1769, the first play was performed in the city, now the seat of government of the great state of New-York. The entertainments were the tragedy of Venice Preserved, with a farce, and the price of admission, boxes 6 shillings, pit 4 shillings, gallery 2 shillings. The days of playing, as everywhere else, were Mondays, Wednesdays, and Fridays. The company performed in the Hospital.

The last visit of Douglass and his company to New-York seems to have been unfortunate, and the "embarrassments" above alluded to probably deterred them from a visit to John-street for some months to come. They had other homes, and Philadelphia was one of the best, though the island of Jamaica was the warmest. We find them in Annapolis in 1772, where the reader will recollect that the first theatre was built, and *that,* a brick building, whereas no other was erected of more permanent materials than wood, until the Chestnut-street Philadelphia theatre was built forty years after it.

In the Maryland Gazette of 1772, we see, "By authority. By the American Company. On Tuesday, Sept. 1st. The theatre will be opened with a comedy written by Hugh Kelley, author of False Delicacy, &c., called *A Word to the Wise.*" On this occasion we find, for the first time, the names of Messrs. Goodman and Johnson, and Mrs. Morris, the actress mentioned above, as Mr. Morris's second wife.

Scenery is for the first time particularly announced. We have reason to believe that the department of the drama which depended upon the painter had not hitherto created much of illusion, or even sensation. On this occasion the bills say, "with a new set of SCENES, painted by Mr. Richards of London." It is reasonable to conclude, that as Annapolis saw the first theatre in America, she likewise saw displayed the first well-painted set of scenery. There appears to have been no gallery in the Annapolis theatre, as the prices given are "Boxes 7 shillings and 6 pence, pit 5 shillings." We notice another circumstance, which is the first mention made of a box book. It is in these words: "places in the boxes to be had at the theatre, where a book is kept for that purpose."

The usual routine of playing and travelling, from the North American colonies to the West Indies and back again, occupied the Thespians without leaving any memorable trace until the year 1773, when on the 14th of April, Douglass opened the theatre in New-York, giving notice that it would be impossible to keep it open "longer than the end of May." It will be seen that the time was extended to August, from which we may conclude that the company was more successful than at their last visit.

On the 3d of May, the manager threatened the gallery gods that if they did not behave better, he would expel them from Olympus. "The repeated insults," he says, "which some mischievous persons in the gallery have given, not only to the stage and orchestra, but to the other parts of the house, call loudly for reprehension:" he then goes on to say, that unless this is amended, "the gallery for the future will be shut up." In this same month appeared Dryden's alteration of Shakespeare's Tempest, to which no other term will apply than that of a profanation—and yet it still is played, and still applauded.

About this time died Mrs. Catharine Maria Harman, of the American Company, a granddaughter of Colley Cibber, the poet laureate, the hero of Pope's Dunciad, the author of the Careless Husband, and of the most amusing work on his profession ever written, for he was likewise a player, and a very good one. His autobiography is unrivalled.

Mrs. Harman is recorded as a just actress and an exemplary woman—"sensible, humane, and benevolent."

This summer, several appearances of "gentlemen" in various characters diversify the bills, and on the 26th of July the tragedy of George Barnwell and the farce of The Padlock were performed, "as a support to the Hospital *about to be erected*. The following N.B. was added to the bill. "It is hoped that all who are charitably disposed, or wish well to so laudable and useful an undertaking, will countenance this play with their presence, or otherwise contribute their might towards so GOOD A WORK as providing a receptacle for the sick and needy. It is hoped by the friends of the Hospital, that the moral of the play to be acted will have some influence with those who are otherwise no friends to the theatre."

The Reverend Dr. Cooper, provost of King's (now Columbia) College, wrote the following prologue for the occasion, which was spoken by Mr. Hallam. The doctor, it will be seen, makes the players pledge themselves to support a moral stage. I fear that this was not always remembered, and managers and actors are too apt to lay the "flattering unction to their souls" which David Garrick provided for himself and them, that "they who live to please must please to live." The stage, however, became more and more cleansed from "the artful hint" and the "thoughts that modesty need blush to hear," which the writer of the verses makes the speaker, for his companions, disclaim. And inasmuch as the wise and the good countenance the drama, wisdom and morality must take the place of the "ribald page" of former times.

> Prologue, written by the Rev. Dr. Cooper on the occasion of a play
> being performed to assist in building the New-York Hospital.
>
> With melting breast the wretch's pangs to feel,
> His cares to soften or his anguish heal;
> Wo into peace by pity to beguile,
> And make disease, and want, and sorrow smile;
> Are deeds that nobly mark the generous mind
> Which swells with liberal love to human kind,
> and triumphs in each joy to others known
> As blissful portions added to his own.
> Small though our powers, we pant with honest heart
> In pity's cause to bear a humble part;
> We gladly give *this night* to aid a plan
> Whose object's charity and good to man.
> Patrons of charity! While time endures
> Be every bliss of conscious virtue your's!
> The hoary father snatch'd from want and pain,

Oft to his consort and his youthful train
Shall praise the hand that rais'd his drooping head,
When every hope, when every friend had fled,
That rais'd him, cold and naked, from the ground,
And pour'd the healing balsam in his wound.
With kindly art detain'd his parting breath,
And back repell'd the threat'ning dart of death.
The plaintive widow, shedding tears of joy,
As fondly watching o'er her darling boy,
Her anxious eyes with keen discernment trace
The dawn of health, relumining his face,
Shall clasp him to her breast with raptures new,
And pour the prayer of gratitude for you.
In you, the long lost characters shall blend,
Of guardian, brother, father, husband, friend!
And sure if bliss in mortal breast can shine,
That purest bliss, humanity! is thine.
　　Let not mistaken avarice deplore
Each mite diminish'd from his useless store,—
But tell the wretch—that liberal acts bestow
Delights which hearts like his can never know.
Tell—for you feel—that generous love receives
A double portion of the joy it gives,
Beams o'er the soul a radiance pure and even,
And antidates on earth the bliss of Heaven.
　　This night, to youth, our moral scene displays
How false, how fatal, are the wanton's ways;
Paints her alluring looks, fallacious wiles,
And the black ruin lurking in her smiles;—
Bids us the first approach of vice to shun,—
And claims a tear for innocence undone.
　　While scenes like this employ our humble stage,
We fondly hope your favours to engage;
No ribald page shall here admittance claim,
Which decency or virtue brands with shame:
No artful hint that wounds the virgin's ear,
No thought that modesty would blush to hear;—
We ask no patronage—disclaim applause—
But while we act and speak in virtue's cause.
This is our aim—and while we this pursue,
We ne'er can fail of patronage from you.

Hallam had now succeeded Rigby both as first player and as speaker of pro-
logues, and added besides the best parts in farce and the holiday magician,

Harlequin. The only new name added to the dramatis personæ this season is that of Blackler.

In August the theatre closed in New-York, with Goldsmith's new comedy of She Stoops to Conquer, and the company went to Annapolis, and thence to Philadelphia, where Mrs. Douglass (the mother of Mr. Hallam and Mrs. Mattocks) died.

This summer, the first theatre was built in Charleston, South Carolina, Douglass having gained permission from the magistrates and being invited by the inhabitants. In September he went thither, and the company followed him. They played fifty-one nights in that city, closing the campaign in June, 1774.

Hallam, Miss Hallam, and Wools proceeded from Charleston to London, and the remainder of the company arrived in New-York, intending to open the theatre in the fall; but the Provincial Congress had met in Philadelphia, and not seeing in a company of English players from the Theatre Royal fit instruments to second the cause of American liberty, or wishing to turn the attention of mankind to something more immediately necessary in their opinion to the welfare of the colonies than any branch of the fine arts, they recommended a suspension of all public amusements. Their recommendation was a law to those who looked up to them as the assertors of their rights—and theatres were closed—and the Thespians embarked for the more loyal colonies of the English West Indies.

It was on the 24th of October, 1774, that the first Congress passed the above resolution or recommendation. They agreed to discountenance and discourage every species of extravagance and dissipation; and among others named "gaming, cockfighting, exhibitions of shows, plays, and other expensive diversions and entertainments." A strange medley, plays ranked with cockfighting and gambling, and these last only censured because expensive. This resolution of Congress was conveyed to Douglass in a letter from the president, Peyton Randolph. And the committed of New-York gave him likewise notice of the same.

Wignell, so well known afterward throughout the continent, had been sent out by his cousin Hallam, on his arrival in London, and reached New-York the day before the news of the recommendation of Congress found its way to that city. He was sitting under his hair-dresser's hands when it was made known that all the theatres on the continent were virtually closed by this recommendation. Of course, he only joined the company to aid in their West India campaign, and remained unknown to North America until after she had become an independent nation.

Before commencing a new chapter, let us take a view of the boundaries, and note some of the antiquities, if any thing in this new world of European colonization can deserve the name, of two or three of our principal cities.

It is very difficult for one who remembers our cities, or, indeed our country generally as it was before the revolution, to conceive that the time which has since elapsed could have produced the immense changes which every where appear. Our cities are so dissimilar that we look for causes adequate to such effects. We find them in our republican institutions, and in the federal union which has given them stability. Before the revolution, Boston was in the eyes of Europe, America. Greatly as Boston has increased and improved, and deservedly ranking for intelligence with the most favoured places in either hemisphere, she now holds but a third place in the scale of political importance among the cities of the United republic. When she placed herself in the battle's front, and received as she had provoked the first blow in defence of the rights of Americans, the splendid bridges and magnificent causeways which connect the city with the surrounding main land had no existence. Beacon hill towered above the town, which meandered in crooked streets around its base, from *the neck* to *north end,* and looked over it on the beautiful bay to the east; Charlestown to the north; and upon the *common,* some straggling houses and rough fields or waste lands; to the south-west and west, with the town and hills of Roxbury—the hill has vanished; the fields are thickly covered with houses like palaces; the *common* remains a beautiful lawn, on two sides bordered by the Mall, the finest public walk in some respects which we know in America, and which was commenced by the troops of Great Britain when Gage defied the assembling bands of militia who took post on the surrounding heights of Roxbury and Cambridge. The English general thought he was forming a pleasure-walk for the future subjects of his, and his master's government. But a few years since, perhaps now, the excavation from which the gravel was taken to raise and level the Mall was seen, and the faint traces of the wheels on which it was borne from the west side of the common. The noble trees under whose shade we have seen the *ancient* and *honourable,* and Sargeant's light infantry, and other corps of militia, the best disciplined in the world, perform their military evolutions, were planted by the mercenaries who were expected by the parliament of England to march triumphantly over the fields and corpses of Americans from one end of the continent to the other. The paltry buildings which then served for Adams and Hancock to display their eloquence in, have given place to edifices such as did not then exist, even in the imaginations of the sober townsfolk. But Boston as it then existed does not perhaps fall within the province of the historian of the American theatre, for it was not until some years after the revolution that an institution of that nature was permitted to occupy a place within its limits, except when occupied by a hostile army.

Newport, as it existed before the year 1775, before Providence became the metropolis of the state of Rhode Island, is described by James Fennimore Cooper in his charming romance of the Red Rover. The slave market of the West Indies and the southern colonies, and the summer resort of the planters who sought health and pleasure in the breezes of the north, and profit in the forced labour of the African. One of its antiquities has occupied some attention, and is made by the novelist the scene of several incidents belonging to his plot. The conjectures respecting this object of antiquarian research, reminds the writer of a discovery of this nature made by him on his first visit to the city of Hudson. According to his custom, he had gone straightforward from the landing place to the highest ground he could perceive within his reach; a hill behind the town. There, after admiring the Catskill mountains, the magnificent river, and all the varied landscape below and around, his attention was arrested by a number of large blocks of stone, placed circularly on the summit of the hill. Conjecture and imagination were hard at work instantly. No other stones were near. These must have been brought thither from a distance and with much labour. Probably by the aborigines. Probability was very soon certainty. It must have been a rustic altar. No doubt they here offered to the great spirit the first fruit of their maize fields, or of their hunting. Imagination pictured their figures as they danced round this hallowed circle. The ceremonies; the sacrifices; perhaps of human victims taken in war. Filled with these images, the traveller returned to the town, and from the heights real and imaginary descended to the inn and mixed with every-day beings. But the Indians, and the important, if not magic circle, was uppermost in his thoughts, and an opportunity was sought and found to speak of it to an elderly gentleman of the town, who had been occupied by the newspaper. He listened—inquired the spot—was told—"Oh, on the hill; ah, where the old windmill used to stand." Never was imagination more quickly put to flight by reality. All was plain without further inquiry. The altar or temple, the scene of so many sacred rites and solemn sacrifices, was the foundation of an old windmill. The reader will remember Oldbuck and Eddy Ochiltree. We have travelled out of the record, but return to Newport. The theatre of this very pleasantly situated town was an apartment over the market-house, and as all that is metropolitan tends to the seat of commerce up the river, no other temple has been dedicated to the muse in Newport.

Baltimore must be left for consideration at a period subsequent to the war of independence, for the same reason that Boston is reserved. And we must refer the reader to Watson's Annals of Philadelphia for the antiquities of that city. This gentleman has been indefatigable in his research, and has preserved from oblivion very many valuable facts, and descriptions of buildings as they existed in former times, which but for him would have been lost. In a manuscript diary of a citizen of New-York, written when on a visit to Philadelphia in the winter of 1793–4, I find this memorandum.

> "This day visited Bush hill. During the late dreadful fever, this place was occupied as a hospital for the infected. It is now inhabited by French fugitives from St. Domingo. The house and grounds are all in ruins, though evidently once

a very delightful country residence. Many of the bedsteads used for the unhappy citizens who were conveyed hither from their homes, were standing by
the door. The committed took forcible possession of this house as a proper
place for the purpose or use intended. Two of the committee of health distinguished themselves in a remarkable manner. At a time when no attendants
or nurses could be procured, and the miserable subjects of this pestilence were
dying hourly in the hospital, Peter Helmes and Stephen Girard went thither
and officiated night and day in the lowest and most disgusting offices both
to dead and dying. These men are now alive."

Let us add, that Stephen Girard lived until 1832, the richest man in the United
States, and with the same benevolence which guided him in 1793, left his immense property for the promotion of human happiness.

Another extract from the above diary may be acceptable. "Visited the stranger's burying-ground, called Potters Field, and saw the manner of burying the
dead during the fever. The graves were dug in rows, very deep and large, and
four bodies deposited in each. Some of these pits are open, being a surplus, which
gave me an opportunity of judging of their size. They were scarcely a foot asun-
der, and I computed that in that field alone upwards of 1800 persons were interred. It was a melancholy scene. I looked with peculiar emotion on one of the
carts then employed in conveying the dead bodies." The traces of this cemetery
have long disappeared. In the midst of the beautiful city, a square full of life gives
no indication of the mansions of the dead by pestilence. Washington-square in
New-York is another instance of the abode of death being changed to a source
of life and pleasure.

In Watson's work above mentioned are notices of New-York, but as the writer
who now wishes to occupy the reader's attention has been familiar with the latter
city from childhood, he detects errors in what Mr. Watson has gleaned from the
memories of others, and thinks he shall do more service to the searcher into such
reminiscences of the past by giving his own recollections, than by adopting those
of any other if in contradiction to them. Besides, we are now to consider New-
York as it existed from 1767 to 1774.

It will be recollected that the second theatre built in New-York was situated
on Cruger's wharf. It was built in 1758. The place called Cruger's wharf appears
by a map of the city published in 1767, to have been a block projecting into the
harbour, having the water of the bay on each side, and being based upon "Little Dock-street," now that part of Water-street between Coenties-slip and Old-
slip. We will proceed along what is called the East river, and go northward and
eastward. The portion of Water-street between "Old-slip" and "Coffee-house-
slip," was unbuilt on its east side, the water occupying the space. From the
"Coffee-house-slip" to Fly or Vly Market-slip, or Long Island ferry, that which

is Water-street now was called "Burnet-street." It was built on both sides, and had a block somewhat similar to Cruger's wharf projecting into the harbour. Having crossed "Fly Market-slip" we find a similar projection serving as the foundation and continuation of Water-street to "Burling-slip," from whence, as we go north-east, the water occupied the east side of Water-street, except as piers or wharves projected into it. That part of Water-street which was then so called, commenced at "Peck's-slip," extending eastward till intersecting Cherry-street, which last terminates at what was afterward "New-slip," but then was the commencement of "the ship-yards."

Having travelled by the edge of the harbour on the east side of the town as far as it extended, we will return to our starting place on Cruger's wharf, and proceed south-west, on which side we find the tide-water flowing up to what is now Pearl-street and a long pier projecting into it. South-west of this pier were two basins called east and west dock. Further on was a small block, which was separated from the battery by "Whitehall-slip."

The battery, occupying the low point of the island, was founded on rocks, whose black faces appeared between the ramparts and the water, except at very high tide. This rocky margin was continued round the point unto the commencement of Broadway at the same spot it now commences. Number one Broadway was long known as Kennedy's house. Opposite to this well-known house, still standing but much enlarged, was an open space, which was afterward enclosed with iron railing, and called the Bowling-Green. In this enclosure until 1776 stood an equestrian statue of lead gilt, of the king of Great Britain, France, and Ireland, erected on occasion of the repeal of the stamp act. South of this place stood on a commanding eminence Fort George, which overlooked the Battery and the beautiful bay, and overhung the little narrow street called Pearl-street, which has given its name to what was once Dock-street, Hanover-square, Queen-street, and Magazine-street; like Aaron's rod, swallowing up all the serpent rods of the Egyptian Magi, all as crookedly serpentine as itself. The governor's house and garden were within the precincts of the fort, where were quarters or barracks for soldiers. Pearl-street in 1767 extended only from the Battery to Whitehall, following that line now so called, first came Dock-street to Old-slip, then Hanover-square to Coffee-house-slip, and then Queen-street ending in Chatham-road or row. This was a row on the east side of what is now Chatham-street, the west or north-west side was open from where Pearl-street now crosses Chatham, to the old jail lately metamorphosed into a Grecian temple. This open space was occupied by a rough bank and a hill called Windmill-hill.

Nearly opposite the place where Queen-street ended in Chatham-road, was the celebrated tea-water pump, from which the inhabitants were supplied by carts carrying casks, and attended by men and women, who distributed fresh water as regularly as now milk is dealt out. The inhabitants then kept their cows in the town, and cowherds received them in the morning and drove them to pasture, returning them in due time in the evening. The cow-pastures were, on the east upon a line with the present Grand-street, on the west as low down as the Hospital. Behind the tea-waterpump was situated the fresh water, or Kolk, or Collect, extending to the vicinity of Bayard's mount, afterward called Bunkerhill. This was a high and commanding sugar-loaf-shaped hill, situated on the north side of the present Grand-street, and west of Mott-street. To the east of Chatham-row the town was partially built on low swampy ground, intermingled with water to the ship-yards.

The Bowery, or Boston road, the only avenue to the city, began as now, but there were only a few houses beyond the tea-waterpump on that side. Farmhouses and gardens here commenced. To the east, and near the ship-yards, on the brink of a steep bank, a cemetery for the Jews was walled in. Their synagogue was in Mill-street, near Broad-street.

We will return, if the reader is not tired, to the commencement of Broadway at Kennedy's house. Behind this and several of the adjacent houses as we proceed up the street, were gardens whose walls rested on the beach, and were washed by the tide-water of the harbour, here called the North or Hudson river. Where Trinity Church now stands, a temple more purely Gothic in its architecture, and decorated with sculptured angels within its walls, reared its tall spire. On the site of Grace Church stood the Lutheran Church. Proceeding up Broadway the buildings were mean until we came to St. Paul's Chapel, and beyond that were two two-story brick houses, beyond which were public houses, gardens, fields, orchards, and swamps.

To the west of Broadway were streets bearing the names of Rector, Thames, Crown, Courtlandt, Partition, Vesey, Barclay, and Reed, the two last partly built; these streets ran to Greenwich-street, or rather to the wharves and water, which then occupied its place. Warren and Reed-streets were very narrow and ill-built, with here and there a house. The Hospital was built between the years 1773 and 1775. Since enlarged. King's College was a part of what is now Columbia College. The place now the Park was an open ground, called the Common. The Jail and Bridewell fronted on it.

We will now go south again to the commencement of Broad-street at the water. Here were the east and west dock, the Albany pier and basin. Here stood the Merchant's Exchange, a brick building, open below. A bridge or planked walk extended from this place where merchants congregated, up the street, covering a sewer, where formerly the dock let in the tide, which had once flowed up to above Garden-street, where stood the ferry-house immortalized in Cooper's Water-Witch, by the pen of genius, patriotism, and benevolence.

This street had many of the true Dutch houses, with the gable-ends for fronts, and at its head stood the City Hall, part court-house, part jail. This stood where afterward Federal Hall stood, and projected beyond the present Custom house.

The old Federal Hall is memorable as the seat of the first Congress under our constitution, and the place where Washington, in presence of the people assembled in Wall and Broad-streets, and the Senate and members of the House of Representatives surrounding him, standing in the balcony in all the simplicity of republicanism, took the oath as first president of the United States of America.

The front of this building projected into Wall-street, which commencing as now at Broadway, ended at the Coffee-house slip. The Coffee-house was at the corner of the slip and Burnet-street.

From the Old-slip ran Smith-street to Wall-street, where Pitt's statue stood, erected by the gratitude of the colony after the repeal of the stamp act. The street continued thence under the name it now bears, of William-street, terminating in Queen-street, and forming the string of an irregular bow.

From the Fly or Vly Market, Maiden-lane commenced, exceedingly narrow, and having like all the other streets at that time the gutter or kennel in the middle. Maiden-lane widened as it went west to Broadway, and sent off a branch called Crown-street, now Liberty, at the corner of which and Nassau stood the old Dutch Church, on the spot occupied in 1753 by the first theatre.

Nassau-street began obscurely at the back of the City Hall, with a narrow passage into Wall-street, and continued northward until it came to Chatham-row.

John-street began, as now, in Broadway, and was lost in a narrow lane called Goldenhill, which descended precipitously to Queen-street, opposite Burling-slip.

The Fly Market we have seen stood at the east end of Maiden-lane; at its west end, touching on Broadway, stood the Oswego Market; at its south side were some hovels and dram-shops. The Bear Market stood on what is now Greenwich-street, in front of the present Washington Market.

We have seen that the Jail and Bridewell fronted on the Common. Behind these buildings to the north were barracks for soldiers, and then the ground descended in rough unseemly sort to water and swamp; and on a kind of islet stood the Powder Magazine, which, when the place was filled up and a street built, gave it the name of Magazine-street, now a part of Pearl-street.

North of the Bridewell and Jail was the place of execution. As late as 1782–3, the effigies of two German officers were there suspended on a gallows, the originals of the portraits having deserted to the rebels.

Here close we our notes of New-York before the revolution. If any reader has accompanied the author, let him look abroad on what it now is—and think.

⇥ CHAPTER 4 ⇤

1776 — Description of New-York during the war of the Revolution — Military Thespians at Boston — Burgoyne's second Drama — A Cure for the Spleen — Theatre Royal, New-York — Captain Stanley's Prologue — Tragedy of Douglas — Names of the performers of the British Army — Theatre in Philadelphia — Advertisement for Ladies — Theatre Closed.

New-York, during the revolutionary war, is fully within the recollection of the writer. It will be remembered that when Washington withdrew his undisciplined army from the city after their defeat at Brooklyn, having with consummate skill crossed the sound called the East river, he led the yet unmanageable mass of citizen-soldiers beyond the reach of the enemy, and they saw the city they had left enveloped in flames, as they turned their eyes to the homes many looked back upon for the final adieu.

The conflagration which raged unchecked on the night the English troops first took their quarters in New-York as an enemy's city, destroyed all the buildings, with very few exceptions, from the lower part of Broadway on the west side, to Trinity Church, that beautiful Gothic edifice included; and then leaving the street, continued its ravages between it and the river until nearly in the rear of St. Paul's Chapel.

On the eastern side of Broadway, the same devastation spread from nearly opposite the site of Grace Church, southward, then occupied by the Lutheran Church, which had escaped the flames, to serve the royalists for a store-house. The fire only stopped after destroying all between Broadway and the water to the south-east, and on the east to Broad-street, including a part of the west side of that street in its ruinous march. Thus a great portion of what was then New-York was left for years a mass of black unsightly rubbish.

During the war, another fire added all the east side of what was then called Great Dock-street (now Pearl), and a great part of Little Dock-street (now Water-street), to the ruins. The walls and chimneys left by the first mentioned fire served the lowest followers of the army for shelter, by the aid of refuse boards, half-burned beams, poles, and pieces of sail-cloth, and the filthy congregation of vile materials went by the name of Canvass-town. This place of refuge for drunkenness, prostitution, and violence, was the resort of the sailors from the ships-of-war in the harbour, of negroes who fled from the neighbouring provinces, and others brought from the south by the troops in their southern expeditions. Canvass-town was the Wapping, the St. Giles's, and the Five Points of the desolated garrisoned city.

To the south of this scene of ruin and abomination, Pearl-street, consisting of some of the two-story houses yet remaining, escaped the conflagration. Pearl-street extended originally, and at that time, only from the Battery to Whitehall-street. Fort George, on the north, overlooked the houses of Pearl-street. A few houses remained at the south extremity of the west side of Broadway, the last and largest, then called Kennedy's house, was the residence of the British commanders-in-chief. Between these houses and the North river there were no buildings, and the waves washed the walls of their gardens.

On the eastern side, the city extended from the ruins caused by the fire to the New-slip; then commenced the ship-yards. Front-street and South-street were then water or wharves.

On the west side of the city, we have seen that the first great fire stopped its destructive progress on the side of Broadway nearest the river, after devouring Trinity Church; and the portion of the street between that church and St. Paul's was spared, most of the houses were however small and poor. There existed no brick houses beyond St. Paul's Chapel, except two two-story buildings, since enlarged to three stories—beyond, to the north, were wooden houses, inhabited by those who were allied in theory and practice to the inmates of Canvass-town, excepting two public houses, one having a billiard table in its front apartments, and behind it the five-alley made notorious, not to say famous, as the daily resort of Sir Henry Clinton and his *cortége*. The commander-in-chief, we presume, after the hour of morning business, was seen galloping from head-quarters, near the fort, up Broadway to this five-alley, and after exercising there, he again mounted and galloped like a sportsman at a fox-chase, out of town and in again, followed at full speed by his aids and favourites. There was another five-alley in John-street, near Broadway, on the same side with the theatre.

Beyond the town and elevated above it, stood, where it still stands, with many additions and improvements, that Hospital to which the Thespians of the American Company contributed their labours; and in the outskirts of the city, the college, since enlarged, where the writer of the prologue spoken on that occasion, Dr. Cooper, presided as provost. Mr. Hugh Gaine, who as usual sold the tickets for the play, was for many years one of the worthy governors of the charitable institution for which the comedians and the provost laboured.

That triangular space now called the Park, and so ornamental to the southern division of the city, was then beyond its northern limits, except that the Bridewell frowned on the base of the triangle to the west, and the Jail, then called the provo, where American prisoners suffered for asserting the rights of their country, scowled on the east. This place held in confinement but a small portion of the miserable prisoners of war. The prison-ships, those charnel houses of the living, had a greater share in the human victims, and the sugar-house in

Crown-street (now Liberty), might be seen, every window filled with heads, thrust one above another to the top of the scanty aperture, to catch a portion of the blessed air of Heaven, which could not find place to circulate within the massive walls and among the throng of miserable victims. The old Dutch Church adjoining this abode of wretchedness, was occupied as a riding-school for the dragoons, and had been used as a prison. This little portion of the globe (the site of the church), had been used and abused as a play-house, a church, a riding-school, and a prison, all within the space of one-fourth of a century. The Brick Church was the only building in Chatham-row, except such as we have described as the nuisances of the other side of the open space, called the Fields, and of Canvass-town.

The above mentioned space was a shapeless void, its surface undulating with hillocks of filth.

Where that building known as the Alms-house, Museum, Academy of Arts, and finally converted by legislative magic into part and parcel of the City Hall, now stands, then stood a range of soldier's barracks, looking down upon an open and desolate space descending to the Collect. The mass of mud and water which was known by that name extended from that part of Pearl-street, not long since called Magazine-street (from a powder magazine which stood there in former days), to that part of Canal-street which intersects Broadway, *then* and *there* called the new road. The waters of the Collect communicated with those of the low grounds on the other side of the road, called Lispenard's meadows, under a bridge, and the skaters of that day passed at will from one collection of waters when frozen to the other, i.e. from Pearl-street (as now called), to the sand beach of the North river, between Lispenard's mansion and the public gardens and house of Brennon; long known afterward as a place of entertainment kept by Tyler, for years an important member of the dramatic corps, and more recently by Hogg, another well-known Thespian. Those are now living here, and the writer among the number, who remember the present King of England, then a midshipman, essaying very awkwardly to skate, supported by generals, admirals, and their supporters, on the broad expanse of water which then in winter covered that ground, now covered by houses and churches and a population of thousands then unborn.

To the north of the waters of the Collect rose a pyramidal hill which overlooked the city and its beautiful bay, and which, if now standing, would be the finest spot from which to sketch a panorama that exists, short of Edinburgh or Naples. Its earth has since served in part to fill the cavities near it and transform the waters to dry land, and its site and miles beyond it is now loaded with brick and stone, and filled with the busy hum of men.

The Bowery, that noble street, was then the Bowery-road, and the only avenue from the city to the country. On each side were meadows and orchards.

The new road, now Broadway, stopped at the gardens which surrounded what has since been called the Sailor's Snug Harbour, then the country-seat of Andrew Elliot, Esq. At another spot, now the corner of Leonard-street and Broadway, stood a house and gardens, the rural retreat of our citizens, called from a retreat of the kind near London, the White conduit House, it has been since called Mount Vernon Gardens, and had, as will be seen, a theatre attached to it, the remains of which were visible within seventeen years. Nearly opposite, on the other side of the new road, were the remains of aqueducts and reservoirs begun some time before 1775, for the purpose of raising water from the Collect, the pond below and to the east, before mentioned, to supply the city with wholesome water, from the stagnant receptacle of filth which slaughter-houses and other nuisances poured into it.

On the eastern side, the city terminated as has been said by the ship-yards on the line of the water, and at a small distance from the shore by a steep bank, on which was walled-in a cemetery called the Jew's burying-ground. Near this bank stood a house, now a tavern, and called from its central situation "Centre House." Beyond the cemetery were orchards, gardens, and meadows, suffering decay from the effects of war.

To return to the extreme or south point of the island and town. Below the towering hill on which Fort George bristled with cannon, lay the battery, a fortification covering a portion of that health-giving space still bearing the name. Part of the ramparts advanced to the water's edge, and on the north between them and Broadway, the rocky foundation protruded, until the earth of the hill on which the towering fort stood was brought down, since the war of independence, to cover them.

Such were some of the features and boundaries of New-York during and after the revolution. The places of amusement were the ball-room of the City Tavern, on the spot where now a part of the City Hotel stands, the theatre in John-street, and *the Mall,* the walk in front of the ruins of Trinity Church, the resort of beaux and belles during the summer evenings, walking in thoughtless gayety or with measured steps to the music of the military bands placed by the officers amid the graves of the church-yard.

The military parade was each morning likewise in front of the ruins of Trinity Church, the divisions of soldier's assigned to each post of guard throughout the city were marched from thence to their several guard-houses; the main-guard being at the City Hall in Wall-street. Here might be seen the Hessian with his towering brass-fronted cap, mustachios coloured with the same material that coloured his shoes, his hair plastered with tallow and flour, and tightly drawn into a long appendage reaching from the back of the head to his waist, his blue uniform almost covered by the broad belts sustaining his cartouch-box, his brass-hilted sword, and his bayonet; a yellow waistcoat with flaps, and yellow breeches were met at the knee by black gaiters, and thus heavily equipped, he stood an automaton, and received the command or cane of the officer who inspected him. A contrast to the German was the Highlander, who though loaded with weapons and accoutrements, appeared free and flowing in the contour of his figure. His low checkered bonnet, his tartan or plaid, his short red coat, his kilt leaving his knees exposed to the view and the winds, and his legs partly covered by the many-coloured hose of his country. His musket, bayonet, broadsword, dirk, and pistols, showed a formidable array for the strife of blood, and the ornamental portion of his dress was completed by a pouch hanging in front of his kilt decorated with tassels. This costume was changed after the first or second campaign in a country whose temperature and warfare were both unsuited to it. These were the most striking and most contrasted costumes of the army of the king at this time, though we could describe perhaps graphically the gallant grenadiers of Anspach, with their towering black caps and sombre but military array—the gaudy *Waldeckers,* their cocked hats edged with yellow scallops, the German *Yagers,* and the various corps of English in glittering and gallant pomp, such as then was seen day by day, in that walk, now passed by our gay and peaceful citizens as they seek the breezes of the Battery, or obey the call of the church bell, or hurry to the banks, and broker's and insurance offices of Wall-street.

The main-guard of the city was at the City Hall, a clumsy building projecting into Wall-street at the head of Broad-street. For a short time General Lee was closely confined in this place.

The theatre in John-street was kept in preservation by the loyal adherents of the crown and the Episcopal Church, while the places of worship of the dissenters were most of them used as barracks, store-houses, and riding-schools.

The players were succeeded by the officers of his Britannic majesty's army and navy, and as a link in the chain of the theatrical history of the country, however imperfect and rusty the link may be thought, we will preserve what is now known of the drama of that time.

The military Thespians began their transatlantic histrionic career in Boston, as well as their less brilliant career of arms. As no theatre had been built in the town of Boston, some place admitting of the change must have been fitted up as such. The accomplished Burgoyne, who commenced dramatic author in 1775, by the "Maid of the Oaks," now produced his second drama in that stronghold of Puritanism and unconquerable liberty; and the Heiress was preceded by a farce called The Blockade of Boston, doubtless intended to ridicule the Yankees who then held the soldiers of Britain cooped up on that narrow neck of land, protected by their ships; soon after expelled them with disgrace; and subsequently received the surrendered sword of the unfortunate poet on the meadow of Saratoga; as dear to us, as the *Runnimede* to our English forefathers.

It is remembered that while the officers were performing Burgoyne's farce, an alarm was given that the rebels had assaulted the lines, and when a sergeant entered and announced the fact, the audience supposing his words, "The rebels have attacked the lines on the Neck," belonged to the farce, applauded the very natural acting of the man, and were not disturbed until successive *encores* convinced them that it was not to the play that the words, however apropos, belonged, and that the prompter of the speaker was not behind the scenes, but behind the trenches. This was, as far as is known, the second drama written in America, and the first, so written, that was performed, although not by professors of the art histrionic, but amateurs. Another piece in a dramatic form was published about this time, and perhaps ought to take chronological precedence. It bears no date, but as it was printed by James Rivington, in New-York, evidently previous to the occupation of that city by the British, and purports to have been originally printed in "New-England," it must have been published as soon, if not before, "the Blockade of Boston" was played by the British officers. That it was written before hostilities commenced, its politics and whole scope and tendency evince. Though its form is dramatic, it was not intended for representation, but by its humour and satire to attract readers and gain proselytes to the cause of royalty or toryism. It is entitled "The Americans Roused, in a Cure for the Spleen," and the dramatis personæ are Sharp, a country Parson; Bumper, a country Justice; Fillpot, an Innkeeper; Graveairs, a Deacon; Trim, a Barber; Brim, a Quaker; and Puff, a late Representative.

Trim, a political barber, conceited and talkative, a piece of a Quotem and a Lingo, and more of a Razor, is the advocate of the people in his shop, but merely because it serves his interest. The real advocates of freedom are Mr. Puff, who, to suit the author's views, is a stupid, ignorant, pretending blockhead, and Deacon Graveairs as stupid and ignorant as himself. The shrewd Quaker, the honest Justice, and the orthodox well-informed and perfect parson, are all friends to old England's paternal dominion and rights of rule over the colonists. The result is, that all become converts to the Parson's doctrine. The Barber says he is "determined to drop" his "shop preachments, or else to take the right side of the question," whatever becomes of his custom. The Deacon fears that he and his patriotic friends have been wrong. The Representative begins "to see things in a different light." The Landlord is glad he had "nothing to do with these matters." And the Quaker sums up, or as the players say, *tags* the piece, with, "Treason is an odious crime in the sight of God and men; may we none of us listen to the suggestions of Satan; but may the candle of the Lord within lighten our paths; and may the Spirit lead us in the way of truth, and preserve us from all sedition, privy conspiracy, and rebellion."

So much for the politics of the piece; as specimens of the character and dramatic humour, take the following.

Trim protesting against the banishment of politics from his shop because they are a part of his trade, Brim says, "Why I have often heard thee holding forth to thy customers with such apparent zeal against British tyranny and oppression, that I was verily persuaded thou wert infected with the epidemical phrensy of the times."

> *Trim.*—Aye, friend Brim, all trades have their mysteries, and one-half the world live by the *follies* of the other half.
> *Puff.*—But pray, Mr. Trim, are you such a tory as to turn all our grievances into scorn and derision, and only pretend to be a friend to your country for the sake of a living!
> *Trim.*—Why, between you and me and the post, Mr. Puff, I believe you, when you would be a representative, and Trim the barber when he would get and keep good custom, act upon the same principles," &c. Trim elsewhere says—"If I was denied the privilege of my shop to canvass politics, as a body may say, that is Lord North, East Indian company, constitution, charter-rights and privileges, duties, taxes, and the like o' that, body o' me sir, strip me of this darling privilege, and you may take my razors, soap, combs, and all."

The Parson compares the Americans to the Jews, who, though placed in the chosen land by their king who had "driven out the Canaanites, the Indians, before them, now vauntingly say, who shall be Lord over us?"

Brim wishes the clergyman to teach the truth to the republicans, for he "seems to be moved to become a light to their feet, and a lamp to their path."

> *Trim.*—*Face* is the latin for candle—I am dumb—"*Perge domine reverende.*"

The Parson thunders against the ministers who had used the pulpit to stir up rebellion.

Trim joins in with "As Dryden says,

> 'These lead the path tho' not of surest scent,
> Yet deepest mouth'd against the government.'

And Lilly's grammar ranks them with beasts and robbers—'*Bos, fur, sus atque sacerdos.*'—No offence to you, sir."

The author of "A Cure for the Spleen" was a dramatist. And although his work may not strictly belong to the History of the American Theatre, it may class with American dramatic literature, and therefore not be thought out of place here. Although the best plays are those originally intended for representation, many very excellent dramas have been written altogether for the closet, some to inculcate religious doctrines, some devoted to the delineation of passion, and others merely the sport of poetic imagination. This American drama was intended to instruct in government and politics, and however mistaken the author was, and has been proved, he possessed talents for the species of writing which comes under our consideration of no ordinary magnitude.

In the centre of the Bowling-Green stood the pedestal from which his leaden majesty George the Third had been hurled by his rebellious subjects, and his ponderous effigy and his still more ponderous horse, metamorphosed into bullets to repel the blessings his benevolent government would have forced upon them at the bayonet's point.

Another statue, though not equestrian, ornamented Wall-street, where it is crossed by William-street (or rather as then named, where Smith-street and William-street met in Wall-street). This was a marble representation of Lord Chatham, the hand which had been outstretched to enforce his eloquence, and the head from whence it flowed, had been stricken off, whether by the vulgar partisans of Whigism or Toryism, tradition sayeth not.

The Coffee-house of the city was on the south-east corner of Wall and Water-streets. A platform of wood occupied the centre of the street running from Queen-street to Water-street, and was called the Coffee-house-bridge. This was the place for auctioneers, then called vendue-masters, to cry and sell their wares. Rivington's celebrated printing-office was at the north-east corner of Wall and Queen-streets (now Pearl), and his bookstore occupied the lower story of the house, from which the criers of the newspapers (for then they depended on sale by these hawkers), issued with yells in every pitch of the human voice, from the "childish treble" to the bassoon sounds of a tall fellow, who roared in tones of thunder, "Bloody news—bloody news—bloody news—where are the rebels *now?*" And he was confident that Rivington had justified his triumphant shout, for every paper defeated some portion of the rebel army, and added glory to his majesty's arms.

Having been driven from Boston, the warriors of England triumphantly took possession of the city and theatre of New-York, such as both have been described above.

A corps dramatique was formed, and the theatre in John-street opened, on the 25th of January, 1777. The manager for several years and principal low comedian, was Doctor Beaumont, surgeon-general of his majesty's army in America. We remember his Scrub and Mock Doctor, characters which, seen a few years after in London as performed by Quick and Edwin, appeared, such is the force of first impressions in early life, very inferior to the representations of the manager-doctor of John-street. Col. French played Scrub likewise with great success.

Women's characters, as in the time of Shakespeare, were frequently performed by the younger subalterns of the army, and we have before us the name of Lieutenant Pennefeather as Estifania, in the well-known Rule a Wife of Beaumont and Fletcher. It is to be hoped that the allies of the English arms, the Mohawks, Senecas, Onondagos, and other supporters of his majesty's honour, and asserters of the cause of justice, mercy, and humanity, were ignorant that the warriors of their great father George submitted to the degradation of the petticoat.

Major Williams, of the Artillery, was the hero of tragedy, the Richard and Macbeth of the company, and the heroine bore his name, though not received as the legal possessor. Her comedy had great merit. Mrs. Sullen and Clarinda are particularly remembered. There were other females associated with the company, such as had "followed the drum," and these were paid for their services at the rate of two, three, and four guineas each performance. The names of Captain Oliver Delancy, 17th Dragoons; Captain Michael Seix, 22d Foot; Captain Wm. Loftus, Guards; Captain Edward Bradden, 15th Foot; Lieut. Pennefeather, Captain Phipps, Captain Stanley, Wm. Hewlet, and Wm. C. Hewlet, are recorded with that of Major Andre as performing at this time. We remember, besides these, many others, afterwards known in London, when peace and half-pay had deprived them of much of the heroic splendour which surrounded them in the streets and on the stage of New-York.

The house in John-street was now called the "Theatre Royal." The play-bills were headed "Charity," and sometimes "For the benefit of the orphans and widows of soldiers."

This company of comedians opened their Theatre Royal with a prologue, written for the occasion, and spoken by the author, Captain Stanley, and limited their efforts the first night to the performance of *Tom Thumb.*

Their loyal friends applauded the performers both at the theatre and in the Royal Gazette. They had opened the theatre shut up by the Congress. They possessed humour and spirit, and proved that "good education and knowledge of polite life are essentially necessary to form a good actor"—this was said when the performers had proved these qualifications only by playing *Tom Thumb.* The prologue was pronounced honourable to the "infant muse" of Captain Stanley,— and "the scenes painted by Captain Delancy," who by-the-by was a manager at this time, "would not disgrace a theatre under the management of a Garrick. The house was crowded with company, and the ladies made a brilliant appearance." Tickets were advertised to be had of "David Matthews, Esq. Mayor, Wm. Waddle, Esq. Alderman, and of the printer, Hugh Gaine, at the Bible and Crown." Captain Delancy was a performer, a manager, and scene painter, and Major Andre likewise played and painted scenery. Mr. Wm. Hewlet, at this time a teacher of dancing, occasionally performed—the reader will recollect that he joined the real comedians soon after their emigration to this country, having been sent out by Wm. Hallam, of Goodman's Fields theatre, in 1753. His son, Wm. C. Hewlet, a remarkably beautiful youth, occasionally played and danced. He entered the army as an officer, and soon after died in the West Indies.

It is not to be forgotten, that the profits arising from the amusements of

these lovers of the drama were applied to the relief of sufferers in that inclem-
ent season which prevented the operations of war, and gave leisure from military duty to these gentlemen of the army. Neither is this occupation of a
portion of their time, when the idleness of a garrison might have induced more
pernicious employment of leisure hours than studying the poets or reciting
them, to be severely, if at all, censured. It is not to be compared with the folly
of those young men who neglect their education or the sober pursuits destined for them by their parents, to associate clandestinely for the purpose of
acting plays, and enter into expenses which may lead to crime for their support, and in consequence of the applauses bestowed upon their performances
from their ignorant auditors, are led to abandon the pursuits intended to lead
them to honour, and to embrace a profession as full of hazards as of difficulty; a profession stigmatized, whether justly or not, is not now the question,
as one not congenial to the habits of ordinary life. These military men were
engaged in a profession which the world has chosen to honour, and their as-
sociating together and imitating players was not considered derogatory, neither did it lead to an abandonment of the road they had chosen for their path
to fortune or fame. They had, as observed, the further inducement for preferring this amusement to others, that the result relieved the miseries which
war and winter inflicted on the poor.

The following notice appeared upon the play-bill of Feb. 10th, 1777. "The
gentlemen concerned in the above charity, give notice, that they have lodged one
hundred pounds with Doctor Morris, treasurer to the charity; for the purpose
of giving such immediate relief to widows and orphans of soldiers who by certificates from commanding officers of corps, appear to be proper objects." It is
recorded that the expenses of a night's performance was £80, or $200. And fur-
ther, that Captain Madden was *famous* as Papillon and the Copper Captain.—
Captain Loftus as Young Wilding and Archer.—Captain Delancy as Boniface,
and Lieutenant Pennefeather as Estifania, in Rule a Wife and have a Wife.

On the 6th of January, 1778, the Theatre Royal was opened with Douglas and
the Apprentice. Gaine's Mercury of the 12th says, the audience was a crowded
one, and the play received with universal applause. The following prologue was
written for the opening, and spoken on the occasion:

> "Now that hoar winter o'er the frozen plain,
> Has spread the terrors of his dreary reign,
> Has bade awhile the din of battle cease,
> And mock these regions with the mask of peace.
> Once more the Scenic Muse exerts her power,
> And claims her portion of the leisure hour,
> To prompt the laugh, the brow of care to smooth,

(And this sad land has cares enough to sooth)
To wake to pity, and with soft control
Melt into tender sympathy the soul;
Vice to discourage, or with bolder aim,
Rouse to high deed and point the way to fame;
These are the ends which from the earliest age
Have been the boast and object of the stage.
We have a nobler purpose still in view,
A tribute to our falling comrades' due;
From us their helpless infants shall be fed,
And fainting misery receive its bread.

    O Britons! (and your generous thirst of fame
Has fully prov'd you worthy of the name),
Tho' scowling faction's interested band
At home asperse us, and with envious hand
Our well earn'd laurels tear, the public weal
Bids us not murmur whatsoe'er we feel;
But, to those honour'd names, whose free applause
Rewards the champions of their country's cause,
Whose generous breasts feel for each soldier slain,
Nor suffer blood so shed to flow in vain;
Whose liberal hand allays the widow's grief,
And to her starving babes affords relief;
To those whose bounty thus our toil repays,
O friends! withhold not the full meed of praise!
Their fair example bade our stage arise,
Blest be th' amusement which relief supplies
To infant wretchedness, to widow'd age,
And the maim'd victim of the battle's rage.
With you for judges, and such views as these,
(Although with anxious care and wish to please)
No fears distress us. To secure applause,
We'll plead no other merit than our cause."

This prologue is not unworthy of preceding the first appearance of Home's excellent tragedy in America. The author is unknown.

We insert the following curious account of the first rehearsal of the tragedy of Douglas, taken from the Edinburgh Evening Post.

> It may not be generally known that the first rehearsal of this tragedy took place in the lodgings in the Canongate occupied by Mrs. Sarah Ward, one of Digg's company; and that it was rehearsed by, and in the presence of, the most distinguished characters Scotland could ever boast of. The following was the cast of the piece on that occasion.

Lord Randolph,	Doctor Robertson, Principal, Edinburgh.
Glenalvon,	David Hume, Historian.
Old Norval,	Doctor Carlyle, Minister of Musselburg.
Douglas,	John Home, the Author.
Lady Randolph,	Doctor Ferguson, Professor.
Anna (maid),	Doctor Blair, Minister, high church.

The audience that day, besides Mrs. Diggs and Mrs. Sarah Ward, were the Right Honourable Lord Wilbank, Lord Milton, Lord Kaimes, Lord Monbodo (the two last were then only lawyers), the Rev. John Steel, and William Home, ministers. The company (all but Mrs. Ward) dined afterwards at the Griskin Club, in the Abbey.

The above is a signal proof of the strong passion for the drama which then obtained among the literati of this capital; since then, unfortunately, much abated. The rehearsal must have been conducted with very great secrecy; for what would the Kirk, which took such deep offence at the composition of the piece by one of its ministers, have said to the fact, of no less than four of these being engaged in rehearsing it, and two others attending the exhibition? The circumstance of the gentle Anna having been personated by Doctor Blair, minister of the high church, is a very droll one.

Cumberland's West Indian was first played in America, on the 15th of January, 1778. The house was so thronged as to exclude numbers who had purchased tickets. The receipts amounted to £310, or $776. Both the new plays, Douglas and the West Indian, were seen by the writer as represented by these performers. The Lady Randolph of Mrs. Siddons is the only image of that character remaining on the tablets of his memory, but the military Major O'Flaherty shares with the original Moody, and with John Henry, in making the picture of the best Irish gentleman belonging to the stage.

On the 27th of March, the tragedy of Othello was announced for performance. Major Moncrieff, of the Engineers, was the Othello, and from the following extract we may gather that the major had performed for his amusement, before the war, with the company of Douglass in New-York. "The gentleman who it is said is to appear in Othello (Major Moncrieff, of the Engineers), is eminent in tragedy, and has *figured much to his reputation in that distinguished part some years ago in this city,* to a crowded audience, and therefore much may be expected from his talents for the charitable purpose which occasions his intended appearance."

The theatre was announced to be closed on the 11th of May, but, says a bill of a later date, "The managers and gentlemen of the theatre, from a sense of the distress of those poor persons who did not fall within their original design, propose to give a play for *that purpose,* and accordingly, on Wednesday evening (May 20th), will be presented, the Recruiting Officer, with a farce called the Miller of Mansfield."

To some it may be interesting to have the names of the managers and perform-
ers for charity's sake, at the Theatre Royal, New-York, in 1778. Col. Guy Johnson,
and Doctor Hammond Beaumont, managers—the latter a performer as Iago—
Hecate—Lovegold—Scrub—Mock Doctor. Major Edward Williams (Artillery)
Richard—Macbeth. Captain Stephen Payne Adye (Artillery and Judge Advocate),
King Henry the Sixth. Major John Andre (Guards and Adjutant General). Cap-
tain Wm. Fawcet (Guards). Captain McDonell (71st Foot). Major O'Flaherty,
Ranger—Douglas. Captain Hardenbrook (Provincials), Belcour. Lieutenant Le
Grange (Provincials). Captain Thomas Shreve (Provincials), Duke of Venice—
Lord Mayor—Freeman. Major Lowther Pennington (Guards), Othello. Lieuten-
ant Butler (8th Foot), Stockwell. Major Moncrieff (Engineers), Othello. Lieuten-
ant Spencer of the Queen's Rangers. This gentleman played Richard the Third at
Bath in 1785, and the next day he was thus noticed in one of the papers. "The
debutant of last night has long been known as an excellent player—*at billiards.*"

As the officers had musicians at hand in their regimental bands, the orchestra was better filled than in the times of the real players. They had fourteen
performers at a dollar the night. Their scenery is said to have been wretched.
Their dresses elegant.

Notwithstanding this general censure of the scenery, we remember the usual
variety—streets—woods and wilds—chambers and palaces. It has likewise been
confidently asserted that Major Andre was expert at the brush. The scene department was likewise assisted by Mr. Thomas Barrow, originally a coach painter,
and for many years the only dealer in engravings known in New-York. Mr. Barrow had taste and knowledge in the art of design.

When the British army took possession of Philadelphia, the theatre in Southwark was opened and supported as that in John-street continued to be. Major
Andre and Captain Delancy were the scene painters here also, and it is recorded that a drop-curtain, painted by the first, continued to be used as long as the
house stood.

In addition to their amusements at the theatre, the military gentlemen of this
gay and chivalrous army *got up* with great splendour an entertainment which
they called a Maschienza, a mixture of Ball Masquerade and Tournament, which
does not fall within our limits, and for an account of which we refer the reader
to Watson's Antiquarian Researches.

In Gaine's Mercury of Nov. 15th, 1779, appeared this advertisement. "Theatre
Royal. Such ladies as are duly qualified, and inclined to perform on the stage
during the course of the ensuing winter, will please to send in their proposals,
sealed and directed, to the managers, to be left at Mr. Rivington's."

The office of prompter, so essential in a theatre, was filled by Mr. Hemsworth,
who occasionally played; he was not an officer, and for his benefit a play was

occasionally performed, otherwise, benefits could not be a part of the dramatic arrangement, where all was for the benefit of the poor.

From Nov. 13th, 1780, to June 11th, 1781, the theatre was kept open, and as the efforts of the managers of the great military drama became languid, so the ardour for the stage declined; and the theatre was abandoned by the military occupants before the town was surrendered to the man who had been their constant attendant, and sometimes rather an interruption to their sports, from the period of the blockade of Boston to the final sinking of the English flag, on the 25th of November, 1783.

⤞ CHAPTER 5 ⤝

The American Company received coldly on its Return — Hallam commences playing first in Philadelphia, then in New-York — Henry, Wignell, and others join Hallam — Hamlet first played — Celebrated Players of the Character — School for Scandal — Poor Soldier — Certificates first Issued — First Theatre in Baltimore — Richmond — Hallam and Henry open the Philadelphia Theatre — Debate in Pennsylvania Legislature — Second Theatre in Charleston.

The players by profession returned with peace, but not the whole company. Hallam arrived first, with a weak detachment, as if to gain a footing in the New Republic. Philadelphia was the place chosen at which to effect a landing, but the people received the runaways with frowns.

When our enlightened and beneficent ancestors, Hampden, Pym, Vane, Milton, and their glorious companions, raised the standard of humanity against that of ignorance and oppression, and put to flight the dramatic muse by the clang of the trumpet and thunder of the war-horse, her retainers being the king's servants, exchanged the mock truncheon and the foil of the green-room and the stage for real command and pointed weapons, in the ranks of their royal master; but it does not appear that any of the stage heroes of the American Company became leaders or followers in the regiments of George the Third. They seem to have gained a safe distance from the scene of strife when our more recent patriots defied and put to flight the standard and adherents of monarchy, and having seen the stage on which the contending parties had been playing a tragedy of ten acts cleared by the retreat of the royalists, they crept from their hiding-places and approached warily to the land in which they felt that they had no part or portion as partakers in its dangers, its sufferings, or its glories. The republicans received them at first with coldness, and many would have willingly continued the prohibition of stage plays which the caution of the first Continental Congress had so effectually recommended.

The theatre in Southwark was opened by Hallam, assisted by Mr. Allen, on the 11th of March, 1785. The Pennsylvania Mercury praises their entertainments, and expresses the hope "that Shakespeare, Addison, and Young, may be permitted once more to enforce on our citizens the love of virtue, liberty, and morality." It is added, that these gentlemen, the players, had presented to the poor of the city one hundred pounds, from the profits of their exhibitions.

The Legislature of Pennsylvania was in session at this time, and after the players had retired to New-York, a debate took place on the subject of prohibiting a theatre, which, as it may stand for a fair specimen of the opinions for and against the drama at this period, shall be laid before the reader in a brief abstract, ere we accompany the Thespians to John-street.

A motion was made to add a clause to a bill before the house for suppressing vice and immorality. This clause prohibited the erecting of any "play-house, stage, or scaffold" for the purpose of acting any kind of dramatic work, enumerating them from the tragedy to the pantomime, and fined all persons concerned in or abetting in any manner such immoral practices.

In the debate that followed, Gen. Wayne, the hero of Stoneypoint, was the first speaker. He hoped that the theatre would not be mentioned in a bill for suppressing vice and immorality. He asserted that a well-regulated theatre was universally acknowledged to be an efficient engine for the improvement of morals.

Doctor Logan thought that theatres were only fit for monarchies. He said the government of Geneva prohibited a theatre in that republic as inimical to their liberties. That the kings of France and Sardinia had endeavoured to establish a theatre in Geneva to subvert the republic. He however added, "if we had a theatre under proper regulations, where no plays should be exhibited but those calculated to expose vice or recommend virtue, I should have no objection."

Mr. Robert Morris, one of the greatest of our statesmen, and the ablest of financiers, boldly declared himself a friend to the theatre, as affording a rational, instructive, and innocent amusement. "As to the effect of the theatre on morals and manners, I hold it," said he, "to be favourable to both."

Mr. Clymer, in favour of the drama, argued that, say or do what we would, a theatre would be forced upon us; "it is a concomitant of an independent state. No civilized state is without it." He contended that it served to refine and purify manners. "Are we for ever," said he, "to be indebted to other nations for genius, wit, and refinement?"

Mr. Fitzsimmons wished the question of the utility of a theatre fully discussed.

Mr. Whitehill, the mover of the clause, avowed his opinion that no regulation could prevent the vice and immorality of a theatre; and said he would oppose the establishment of one in the state of Pennsylvania.

Mr. Smiley thought that by drawing the minds of the people to amusements, they were led to forget their political duties. "Cardinal Mazarine," he said, "established the academy of Arts and Sciences in France with this view. He avowed himself "no friend of the fine arts," and asserted that "they only flourished when states were on the decline."

The last mentioned speaker has at least the merit of consistency. He had sagacity enough to perceive that the fine arts were all connected, and must stand or fall together, and he knew that the drama was one of the number. He placed the theatre where it should be; for if the drama is injurious to a state, so are literature and the arts. His last assertion was the fruit of ignorance in the history of nations. He honestly confounded the abuse of things with the things themselves—what has been so abused to the purposes of evil as the press? What is so precious to man?

Mr. Finley saw in a theatre regulated by government "a dangerous tool" in its hands. Forgetting that the people who created the ministers of government were the judges of the representations brought on the stage, and that such an engine in the hands of government would be jealously watched by the people. A theatre directed by government would be attended by the best citizens; they would guaranty the purity of this source of instruction and delight, and the political impulse given must always accord with the opinion of the public; so must the laws of a state, or they become nugatory. Mr. Finley concluded that the state vitiated taste by representing unreal characters.

Mr. Clymer in reply, said, that "if the pieces represented are not immoral, the stage cannot be immoral." He asserted that as the people of Europe had progressed in civilization and refinement, their plays had improved in purity.

Mr. Robert Morris asserted that all celebrated nations had "permitted the establishment of theatres, and that they had improved the manners of the people. The writers for the theatre have generally been men of extensive genius." He thought the lessons given to vice and folly salutary. He hoped to see American poets suiting plays to our times, characters, and circumstances. "The taste and manners of a people," he said, "regulate the theatre; and the theatre has a reciprocal effect on the public taste and manners."

Gen. Wayne said he thought the prohibition of plays during the war, by Congress, was an ill-judged measure, as plays might have been represented that would have stimulated to heroic actions. "A theatre," he said, "in the hands of a republican government, regulated and directed by such, would be, instead of a dangerous instrument, a happy and efficient one."

Mr. Whitehill in reply, repeated his opinion that the establishment of a theatre tended "directly to the encouragement of licentiousness."

Mr. Robert Morris, after some further remarks in favour of the stage, concluded by saying, "in such large societies as are common in cities like this, people will find out amusements for themselves unless government do it." He expressed his belief as before, that a regulated theatre improved morals.

Mr. Robinson argued against the theatre from the bad tendency of many plays.

Mr. Smiley thought that the plays now in existence were in general unfit for our state of society.

Mr. Finley opposed fiction, and brought examples of plays inculcating immorality.

Gen. Wayne proposed that all plays previous to performance should be submitted to the executive council, who would be responsible to the people.

Mr. Clymer exposed that ignorance which asserted that the fine arts only flourished under despotism, or in the decline of liberty. He said Virgil and Horace were men before the republic was overthrown, and in Greece there was not a single author of eminence after the fall of republicanism. The clause which prohibited the drama as being one of the sources of vice and immorality was rejected.

After his attempt upon Philadelphia, Hallam, with his feeble band, effected a lodgement in the theatre of New-York, of which he was now the principal, if not the sole proprietor, and advertised a course of lectures, to begin with a prologue and terminate with a pantomime. The music selected and composed by Mr. Bentley. This was August 24, 1785.

They continued this skirmishing with farces and pantomimes until the 24th of October, when they came out boldly with a play and afterpiece.

The first play performed in the United States under the protection of the flag, called proudly by Americans *The Star Spangled Banner,* and in derision by England *the piece of striped bunting,* was "the Countess of Salisbury"; the afterpiece "The Ghost." The names in this feeble company were Hallam, Moore, Bentley, Lake, Allen, Durang, Mrs. Allen, and Miss Durang. The first alone possessing the skill of an artist in his profession. He was in this short campaign the hero of tragedy and comedy, the low comedian of farce, and the harlequin of pantomime. They closed the house on the 24th of October.

But The Star Spangled Banner could not protect a man from the censure of the magistrates in the enlightened city of New-York, for daring to invite the people of a free republic to hear recitations or lectures, or the works of the poet who had devoted himself to the tragic or the comic muse, as the following document proves.

"At a meeting of the Common Council, held in the city of New-York, at the City-Hall, on Friday, the 14th of October, 1785, present James Duane, mayor,

Richard Varick, recorder, &c. &c. 'Whereas, it has been represented to this board in behalf of Mr. Lawrence Embree, one of the commissioners of the alms-house, that the company of comedians in this city, some time since, presented him with forty pounds for the use of the poor; that as he disapproved of a donation so circumstanced, he thought it his duty to suffer it to be deposited with him until the sense of the magistrates respecting the same could be obtained.' Whereupon the board came to the following resolutions:

> "That it appears that the play-house was opened by said comedians without license or permission of the civil authority; which in the opinion of this board is a thing unprecedented and offensive. That while so great a part of this city still lies in ruins, and many of the citizens continue to be pressed with the distresses brought on them in consequence of the late war, there is a loud call for industry and economy; and it would in a particular manner be unjustifiable in this corporation to countenance enticing and expensive amusements; that among these a play-house, however regulated, must be numbered, when under no restraint it may prove a fruitful source of dissipation, immorality, and vice. That the acceptance of the said donation by the order of this board might authorise a conclusion that they approved of the opening of said theatre, and that therefore it be and it hereby is recommended to Mr. Embree to return the same to the person from whom he received it."

We personally knew and highly respect the memories of the persons here named. Mr. Embree, doubtless, acted by the guidance of the sect he belonged to, or the direction of the quarterly meeting of *Friends*. The names of Duane and Varick are unsullied. But the errors or prejudices of the best have no claim to respect.

A few days after, a writer in Oswald's Journal ironically praises the wisdom of the city magistrates for discountenancing the theatre, and preferring the licensing tippling-shops, they being harmless and yielding a revenue unpolluted by its source. This writer in the Journal takes it for granted that the Common Council sent from their own pockets the hundred dollars to the poor, which they so wisely prevented them from receiving as a donation from a play-house.

We have seen that Douglass, under the government of the king's officers, had committed the same oversight that Hallam now suffered for. He opened a theatre without having "boo'd to the gowden calves" in office. He suffered for it, and had to kneel to the delegates of majesty. Hallam perhaps thought that times, and things, and opinions, and therefore magistrates, had changed. He forgot that man only changes as he becomes individually enlightened. The ignorant are the same at all times, and the office-holder ever prone to the assumption of airs of superiority. The successors of King George's minions could not think themselves of less importance than their predecessors. Official dignity was offended. These players "without license or permission" had opened a play-house, "a thing in the opinion of this board unprecedented." Where did they look for precedents that made it necessary to obtain such license? To the government their wiser countrymen had overthrown, because it shackled the mind of man and bowed him to assumed superiority.

On the 21st of November, 1785, the New-York theatre was opened in form, under the management of Hallam and Henry. Mrs. Douglass, Hallam's mother, had been some time dead; Douglass remained in the island of Jamaica, where he played the part in real life of one of his Britannic majesty's judges. He relinquished the sceptre of the American Company to Hallam, who received for the partner of his throne Mr. John Henry. Did the monarchs obtain permission to "strut their hour?"

The company consisted of the managers, who were at the head both by their dignified office and their merit as actors, and of Messrs. Wignell, Harper, Morris, Biddle, Wools, Lake, and Durang. Mesdames Morris, Harper, Miss Tuke, Miss Durang, and occasionally Miss Storer (soon afterwards Mrs. Henry). Hallam, Henry, Wignell, Morris, and Wools, were sharers* or proprietors, the remainder were salaried. The motto over the stage was "*Qicquid agunt homines.*"

The Royal Gazette, conducted during the war of the revolution with great spirit and unbounded devotion to the cause of Britain, had now passed from the hands of James Rivington into those of Archibald McLean, under the title of the Independent Journal. In this journal we find it stated that on Monday evening, January 16th, 1786, Mr. Hallam made his first appearance in Hamlet.

This glorious emanation from the genius of the greatest poet and the most consummate searcher into the human heart which the world has known, although mentioned in the list of plays cast by Hallam's uncle before the company left London in 1752, may not, and probably was not, until this date, attempted on the stage in America. The play is difficult in the performance in proportion to the subtle, metaphysical, and philosophical character of its plot and dialogue. The part of Hamlet is the bow of Ulysses to the actor. We do not find the play mentioned in the records of the American Company previous to this time, and although the officers of the English army figured as Richards, Macbeths, and Othellos, all far above their reach, none attempted the philosophic, university-bred Prince of Denmark.

There is reason to believe that Betterton was the first true personator of Hamlet; and even Betterton, though instructed by Davenant, who had seen the original representative as taught by Shakespeare, though replete with talent and judgment, must have been in that part of the picture which depends on costume miserably deficient. We have Cibber's testimony in favour of the Hamlet of

---

* See Chap. i. p. 10.

Betterton, and on such subjects the poet laureate is good authority. "You have seen," he says, "a Hamlet perhaps, who on the first appearance of his father's spirit, has thrown himself into all the straining vociferation requisite to express rage and fury, and the house has thundered with applause, though the misguided actor was all the while, as Shakespeare terms it, "tearing a passion into rags." I am the more bold to offer you this particular instance, because the late Mr. Addison, while I sat by him to see the scene acted, made the same observation, asking me with some surprise if I thought Hamlet "should be in so violent a passion with the ghost, which though it might have astonished, had not provoked him, for you may have observed that in his beautiful speech the passion never rises beyond an almost breathless astonishment, or an impatience limited by filial reverence to inquire into the suspected wrongs that may have raised him from his peaceful tomb, and a desire to know what a spirit so seemingly distressed might wish to enjoin a sorrowful son to execute towards his future quiet in the grave." This was the light in which Betterton threw this scene, which he opened with a pause of mute amazement; then rising slowly to a solemn trembling of the voice, he made the ghost equally terrible to the spectator as to himself. Another author has said of this actor "that his countenance, naturally ruddy and sanguine, in the scene of the third act where his father's ghost appears, through the violent and sudden emotion of amazement and horror, turned instantly on the sight of his father's spirit as pale as his neckcloth, when his whole body seemed to be affected with a tremour inexpressible, so that had his father's ghost actually risen before him he could not have been seized with more real agonies; and this was felt so strongly by the audience, that the blood seemed to shudder in their veins likewise, and they in some measure partook of the astonishment and horror with which they saw this excellent actor affected."

Those who are familiar with the costume of Hamlet, as first introduced among us by Cooper, and that represented by Lawrence in his picture of Kemble, will see in the "neckcloth" of Betterton, and the wig, and other most unpoetical and most inappropriate parts of dress which we know he wore, that he had not those accessories to help the illusion of the scene which actors since have enjoyed who do not produce the "astonishment and horror" in the audience which Betterton effected. Betterton flourished from 1665 to 1700.

Wilks, a contemporary with Betterton, gained credit in other portions of the varied character of Hamlet, particularly his reproaches to his mother, and the pathos of his exclamation, "Mother, for the love of grace."

When Garrick has left Goodman's Fields theatre, the nursery from which afterwards the Hallams issued, he became the representative of Hamlet, and the same receding of colour from the face, and other symptoms of real horror and astonishment recorded of Betterton, are described as having the same effect upon his auditors. All will recollect Fielding's compliment put into the mouth of *Partridge* in Tom Jones. It is said that the line "I have that within which passeth show," was made so impressive by his manner as never to be forgotten by the hearers.

Lewis Hallam the second, whose representation of Hamlet has occasioned the above remarks, might have seen Garrick's Hamlet, as it will be remembered that he went from Annapolis to London in the summer of 1774, and Garrick, although declining and diseased, continued playing until the 10th of June, 1776. Certainly Hallam attempted the part at Covent Garden, and made no impression on the audience of that theatre of strength sufficient to induce an engagement.

We now, at the period to which our History of the American Theatre has been brought down, find the Independent Journal thus speaking of the first representation of Hamlet. "Mr. Hallam was received with that kindness and eclat which has been shown to him for these last thirty years." In the course of the performance the managers restored the scene of the grave-diggers, which, says the same paper, "had been discontinued of late years, from whim, by the late Mr. Garrick." Mr. Henry, who played the ghost, appeared in royal robes in the closet scene, taking the idea from the exclamation of young Hamlet,

> "My father in his habit as he lived."

"This alteration," says the critic, "was much approved, and more especially as this was the first time it had been noticed on the stage."

The scene of the grave-diggers had been restored to the London stage long before, and it will be remembered that it is in *that* scene Lawrence has represented Kemble moralizing on the scull of Yorick.

On the 14th of March, Miss Storer made her first appearance as Nysa in the burletta of Midas; and in June, Oswald's Journal speaks with enthusiasm of the delight received from her performance in the Maid of the Mill.

May 10th, The Busy Body and Rosina were performed for the benefit of the "distressed prisoners confined in the jail for debt. The sum of one hundred dollars was raised and paid to the sheriff.

The company was strengthened by the arrival from London of Mr. and Mrs. Kenna, Mr. J. Kenna, and Miss Kenna. Mrs. Kenna made her debut in Isabella, and her husband in Lissardo. Soon after the benefits commenced, and Miss M. Storer, who had not before appeared, played on the 29th of May for Henry's benefit, being announced as "a gentlewoman." She chose *Patty* in *The Maid of the Mill,* and *Daphne* in *Daphne and Amintor* for her opening characters, and afterwards for the benefit of Wools, she played *Rosetta* in *Love in a Village,* and *the Lady* in *Comus,* probably the first time Milton spoke from the stage in the New World.

Sheridan and O'Keefe came before the American public for the first time this theatrical season. The School for Scandal, The Duenna, and The Poor Soldier took their stand on the boards never to be removed. Wignell's Joseph Surface and Darby, Henry's Sir Peter Teazle and Patrick, are still remembered with pleasure after the lapse of nearly half a century. The first issuing of certificates for places in the boxes may be traced to the following notice. "Theatre. The public are respectfully informed, that on account of a number of complaints relative to *unfair preference in boxes,* many of which have been lately taken without being occupied, the managers, ever ready to show their attention to the accommodation of their friends and patrons, have adopted a mode to prevent any similar infringement in future by having tickets for the night, which will be delivered by the box-keeper, on payment, to the gentlemen taking boxes, with the number of places particularized; a measure which they flatter themselves will meet with general approbation. Hallam & Henry."

The friends and enemies of the drama continued their paper warfare during the whole time of the company's now performing in New-York. A *whig* attacks theatrical exhibitions in Loudon's New-York packet of September 29th. *Moralitas* answers him. Some months after a memorial was presented to the legislature of New-York praying the suppression of the theatre, and this was met by a counter memorial.

It appears from a publication in Loudon's New-York packet, that the clergy of the city went so far as to attack the stage from the pulpit, and so far inflamed a portion of their hearers, who doubtless thought themselves pious people, that they threatened to pull down the theatre. Some of these "well-meaning people," fortunately for themselves, consulted their spiritual agitators, and they prudently advised to petition the legislature then sitting to put down the theatre before they took upon themselves to pull it down. The clergy of the city are praised for having kindled this flame, and praised for setting bounds to it. Their forbearing to sanction the destruction of other people's property and jeopardizing the lives of their fellow-citizens shows a memorable degree of meekness and self-command. The writer (Impartialis) praises the clergy for opposing an institution which had been denounced by "the pious and learned in every age of the church." Besides, the clergy of the city "were whigs," and did not, as the players had done, run away to Jamaica, and leave others to fight the battles of the country. They battled from the pulpit, "drum ecclesiastic." This argument would have shut up or pulled down the Episcopal churches, whose orators had not indeed run away to Jamaica, but had prayed and preached most loyally for King George and for the overthrow of those in arms against him. The Rev. Doctor Beach and Doctor Provost were exceptions.

The memorial advised as above was presented to the legislature in April. This prayed for a law or amendment in existing laws to put down taverns, infamous houses, sabbath-breakers, profane-swearers, and the theatre. The memorialists assert that the stage has been opposed "by the wisest and best men, both heathens and Christians." They assert its enmity to the interests of religion, and its influence in causing "a scarcity of cash," and finally pray for an amendment of the laws against profaneness and immorality, and the suppression of the theatre. Signed by seven hundred names.

The counter memorialists were brief and moderate. They only petitioned that the legislature may not be misled by the first petition, and suppose that the citizens wished to suppress the theatre. They say "that they consider the institution in question as a source of innocent and rational entertainment, not more exceptionable in moral or political respects than any other species of public amusement, and affording advantages to which no other can pretend." They further observe, that if the exhibitions are contrary to good morals as alleged, they are amenable to the ordinary course of law; if they are not immoral, the interference of the legislature would deprive the citizens of that which they wished, and which had been approved of by great and enlightened minds. Signed by fourteen hundred names.

The opponents of the theatre published an extract from Josiah Quincey's Journal, dated May 11th, 1773, with which we will dismiss the subject for the present. "Went to the play-house in the evening, saw The Gamester and The Padlock performed. The players made an indifferent figure in tragedy. They make a much better in comedy. Hallam has merit in every character he acts. Mr. Wools in the character of Don Diego, and Mrs. Morris (the first Mrs. Morris) in that of Ursula, I thought, acted superlatively. I was however much gratified upon the whole, and I believe if I had staid in town (New-York) a month, I should go to the theatre every acting night. But as a citizen and friend to the morals and happiness of society, I should strive hard against the admission, and much more the establishment of a play-house in any state of which I was a member." This gentleman afterwards, on seeing the Beggar's Opera in London, says, "The stage is the nursery of vice, and disseminates the seeds far and wide with an amazing and baneful effect."

It would have been well if this distinguished patriot had given us facts, or any mode of devising how he draws such conclusions from such premises. The Gamester or The Padlock, particularly the first, one would suppose could not warrant the estimate he forms of the stage. He was delighted, and surely could not have been made worse. The Beggar's Opera has been censured, but the mind that could be injured by such a piece of satire must be weak indeed. Even if the pieces were in fault, it is no argument against a theatre any more than a vile book is against the press.

In the Independent Journal of August 5th, 1786, is found this notice of the second theatre in Charleston, South Carolina. "We hear from Charleston, S.C. that a principal merchant of that city and a Mr. Goodwin, comedian, have leased a lot of land for five years, and have erected a building called Harmony Hall, for the purpose of music meetings, dancing, and theatrical amusements. It is situated in a spacious garden in the suburbs of the city. The boxes are 22 in number, with a key to each box. The pit is very large, and the *theatrum* and orchestra elegant and commodious. It was opened with a grand concert of music *gratis* for the satisfaction of the principal inhabitants, who wished to see it previous to the first night's exhibition. The above building has cost £500 sterling. Salaries from 2 to 5 guineas per week, and a benefit night every nine months is offered to good performers."

While the company were in New-York, the managers caused a theatre to be erected in Baltimore, now rising to overshadow Annapolis, and on the 16th of August, 1786, the first play-house was opened in that city. This was a new soil for the players to cultivate, and their harvest was proportionably great. Their southern friends received them with smiles, and they continued their efforts in the new theatre of Maryland until the beginning of October, when they proceeded to Richmond, which had now become the rising sun of Virginia, and our histrionics appear to shun the sinking towns as naturally as rats fly foundering ships.

From Richmond, after playing a short time, the company in full force removed to Philadelphia, and again took their old stand in the theatre of Southwark, where the unfortunate Andre had left as a memorial of his taste a drop-curtain, which was used for several years after the melancholy termination of the last tragedy he performed in.

→➤ CHAPTER 6 ◄←

Reflections on the Drama — Plan for its Improvement and that of the Professors of the Histrionic Art — "The Contrast," a Comedy — "The Prince of Parthia" and "Mercenary Match," Tragedies — "May Day," Farce — Mrs. Henry and her Sisters — Harper — Doctor's Mob.

We have now arrived at an era from which we may date our literature as more distinct, more national, more diverging in character from that of our ancestors or brethren of England, and it may be chosen as a point in our theatrical history, convenient and proper for some reflections on the past and present character of the drama; its influence on society, and its capabilities of improvement.

There are no people on earth who have advanced the least step towards civilization, who have not had their public amusements. These may be purely for relaxation from weightier employment, or for instruction conveyed through such means as tend to delight at the moment they exalt and improve. Mankind, when congregated for the purposes of innocent pleasure, or the higher purposes of receiving lessons in life, morals, or religion, are by the sympathy of such association, more firmly bound and knit together in the kindlier feelings of our common nature. The merely meeting together for the same purpose, if that purpose is not evil, tends to good.

If we look back upon the history of nations, we shall find that their amusements mark the progress or degree of civilization they had attained at any one period, and their advancement in all that enobles our nature, or the retrograde movement, the falling off towards darkness and barbarism.

When Greece was at the pinnacle of her refinement, we see her citizens congregated at her public games, attracted by, and united in manly exercises, listening to the recitations of poets, witnessing the exhibitions of sculpture and painting, or the representations of the dramatic works of Eschylus, Aristophanes, or Sophocles. Rome, civilized by those she had conquered, never attained so high a point on the scale of mental elevation; she turned from the theatre to the circus, became enamoured of blood while viewing spectacles of triumph, captives in chains devoted to massacre, brutes striving with brutes or men, and men trained to the slaughter of each other for the amusement of a population devoted by such amusements to slavery and every debasing vice, until a new source of light should arise and dispel the moral darkness. Thus the knowledge and refinement of Greece is marked by her drama, the decline of both in Rome by her gladiatorial shows.

The ages of chivalry are marked by the amusement of the tournament, a step forward again in civilization; and the song of the minstrel, and the rude drama of the mystery, mark another step in the upward progress. As civilization, learning, and the arts increased; as morality and religion struggled through the darkness of barbarism and superstition, men congregated again for ameliorating amusement, and theatres and plays again appear. We see Calderon withdraw the Spaniard's eyes at times from the auto-da-fé and the bull-fight; the poets and musicians and painters of Italy, raising the stage where false religion and bad government counteracted its influence; the drama of France advancing as refinement advanced, but trammelled by false taste, and struggling against the maxims of despotic monarchy; and in England the dawning of "learning's triumph o'er her barbarous foes" is marked by the rearing of the stage, and mighty bursting forth of those dramatic luminaries whose light has only been obscured by the greater splendour of Shakespeare. Through the barbarism still clinging to our ancestors in his time, through the filth which he, *even he,* could not throw from him, he did more for the enlightenment of his country than any other individual, uninspired, before or since. Civil war and its evils followed. Our ancestors felt the influence of reason, advanced rapidly towards the goal of human excellence, but had to shake off the incubus of the damnable doctrine of divine right in kingship, and then men thought only of the struggle for and against oppression; of course, the theatre, with all literature, declined. The commonwealth and the protectorate were continued struggles of reason against intolerant bigotry; republicanism against profligate monarchy and daring apostacy and usurpation. The arts and the drama were silent. We are left to imagine what would have been the amusements of our ancestors, what would have been their drama, if the nation had been far enough advanced to have formed a true republican representative government—and a Milton, instead of being a Latin secretary to Cromwell, had written for and directed a theatre; the dramas he *did* write are worthy of the best ages of Greece. But our English ancestors were not yet a nation of republicans. Monarchy was restored—licentiousness prevailed, and the stage became a sink of profligacy. From this degraded state, the dramatic literature of England, which is ours, has been rising in purity, though declining in force.

When the drama was introduced into this country, the favourites of England were of course the favourites of the colonies. It is a subject for the historian of America. It is the duty of the historian of our literature to mark the changes from the plays then popular, plays full of wit, but fraught with indelicacies, not to say obscenities, their very plots so entwined with the loose manners and intrigues of the time as to be incapable of pruning so as to leave the wit, the better part, separated from the filth; it is his duty to point out these favourites of former times, and to show that as our society has improved, that these plays have fallen into desuetude, both here and in England. The indecency and immorality of the plays of Charles the Second's time, and after, belonged to the state of society, and not to the stage or the writers for it, otherwise than as a part of society. If the wise and the good frequent the theatre, its exhibitions must become schools of wisdom. The lessons taught must be those of patriotism, virtue, morality, religion. These lessons would not be thought misplaced as coming from the stage, if the stage had not been polluted by the licentiousness of its supporters; and when as may be, its supporters shall be the moral and the wise, the purest teachings will flow, mingled in the same stream with the delightful waters of Helicon, undefiled by the conduits from which they are received.

If the theatre is abandoned to the uneducated, the idle, and the profligate, mercenary managers will please their visiters by such ribaldry or folly, or worse, as is attractive to such patrons, and productive of profit to themselves.

As Puritanism or bigotry cannot shut the theatre, or even as in former times in England, fine the actors for repeating the words of the dramatists,* or banish the fine arts from society as being too worldly, or stigmatize their professors as ungodly worldlings, or frivolous, or vicious men,—let those who seek rational amusement and elevating pleasure, and know the value of such amusements in a political point of view upon the mass of the people—those who know that music, painting, poetry, and the art of the player may be made salutary instruments for refining the mass of the population, unite in supporting, and by their presence purifying and directing the theatre. Let the lovers of rational enjoyment, the enjoyment set before man by his benevolent Creator, join in the support and purification of every elegant art. What engine is more powerful than the theatre. No arts can be made more effectual for the promotion of good than the dramatic and histrionic. They unite music, poetry, painting, and eloquence. The engine is powerful for good or ill—it is for society to choose.

But the question arises—"How are the evils flowing from theatrical representations to be banished from them, and the good preserved and secured?" The answer is, make the theatre an object of governmental patronage; take the mighty engine into the hands of the people as represented by their delegates and magistrates. The stream of pure instruction flowing into a city, is of more worth than even the purity of the water which is to cleanse it, and afford an aliment to banish the poison of the licensed murderers at every corner and every avenue of our towns. If a state or city government directed a theatre, nothing could be represented that was not conformable to patriotism, morality, and religion. The petty princes of Germany, actuated by good taste, have done this, and the result has been, moral plays and moral players. Witness the life and plays of Iffland and others.

If an association of men of taste, literature, and moral standing in the community, should build and open a theatre upon a similar plan, select a man of acquirements fitted for the management, and pay him liberally, not allowing him any interest in the profits or losses, and supervising the whole by a committee or otherwise, the same result would follow. Gain would not be the object of such an association, and yet gain might accrue. Actors, in either case, of a theatre protected by the government or by an association of private individuals, should be well paid, and selected for their morals as well as talents; they would be then instruments of good at all times; and sheltered from the temptations which now beset the profession, they would be honoured in private as applauded in public.

In Greece, where the arts attained a perfection yet unrivalled, plays were the organs of the public and the stimulants to heroism and patriotic self-devotion. There artists of every description were the cherished instruments of taste and

---

* See Life of Betterton.

refinement. To make use of the language of a historian and philosopher, "shall we cast into the gulf of oblivion all the taste, and art, and invention, all the monuments of free thought, and sublime and glorious outgoings forth of the soul, which the republics of Rome and Greece have bequeathed us," in the form of drama, and all the knowledge contained in modern dramatic authors? Long ought we to strive to untwist the mingled web, and throw away the stained thread, before we consent to such destruction.

If the wise and the good desert the theatre, the directors, on the present plan, having only emolument in view, will attract the idle and vicious by such entertainments as suits their ignorance or depravity, and the school and the scholars depreciate together, each acting as cause, each suffering the effect. But is it visionary to suppose a free government, a government of the people, regulating and making more perfect, and even more attractive, an amusement which the people love, and will have, making it a school that shall invite to virtue and teach the truths of history, philosophy, patriotism, and morals? Or that an association of wealthy enlightened individuals should effect the same salutary object?

The establishment of a theatre and its support is costly. But the expense need be no objection. The price of admission might be very low, and still the expense paid. And a low price of admission would, with the superior excellence of performers and entertainments, put down competitors. Histrionic artists would then be honoured, and not as under other systems, shunned, and thereby degraded in their own eyes, and made a source of ill to themselves and others.

A history of the theatre of any country ought to show faithfully any ill that may flow from it or attend it, either to the people or to those engaged in supporting, directing, or treading the stage. Many players have been licentious, many have been the victims of intemperance; but what profession can say "we are free" from such members? It may be a part of our task to show that the temptations are strong which beset the player, and that they are such as the plan proposed above would remove. But we must not for a moment confound the actor—the histrionic artist—with the pretenders and low hangers-on of the theatre. The message deliverer is to the personater of Hamlet what the hod-carrier is to the architect. But even the lowest retainers of the play-house, if employed, sanctioned, protected by government, or an association such as above mentioned, must with such support, and under such control, be decent, if not virtuous members of society.

Let the legislators or the philosophers of a republic, governed by law, imitate the princes of Germany in good, and our players will be like Iffland, our dramatists like Schiller.

This plan may appear chimerical, and perhaps may be opposed, at first view, by players and managers, as well as by all the enemies of the theatre, who are such from the various motives of blind prejudice, or honest belief that it is a promoter of evil. But let not the latter determine rashly to oppose an engine which is so powerful; let them rather with me devise means to secure it as the auxiliary of all that is precious to man. Let them likewise consider that these remarks do not come from youth and inexperience, but from one long familiar with the subject, long wishing to remedy the evils connected with it, and fully acquainted with them.

With this experience, and this knowledge, his conclusion is, that the theatre ought to be supported, but that its direction should be wrested from the hands of any person, whose sole aim is profit (either by making money or increasing his professional celebrity), and guided by the enlightened portion of society.

A player's first motive is to increase his fame as an actor, and his popularity; and if he is the manager of a theatre, money, though an attendant on such popularity, is a secondary object. In his choice of pieces to bring before the public, he reads the work of the dramatist with the primary object of finding a character in it that will suit his powers, and gain him applause. If there is no such part he is tempted to pronounce it worthless. His office of manager may then come to his recollection, and he thinks of the probability of its bringing full houses. He has no thought of the quality of the auditors, and if the crowded house of boys, vulgar brawlers, drunkards, rioters, thoughtless or vicious persons of both sexes, fill his treasury as manager, or gratify his desire for applause as actor, he is content.

The manager, not a player, if merely looking to retrieve fortune, or make it, has but one object in view, and is as careless of the tendency of the plays he adopts for his stage as the player. Money is not his object. Both say, "we must please the public." But their public becomes that public which is pleased only with glitter, parade, false sentiments, and all that lulls conscience or excites to evil. The wise, the good, even the mere worldlings, who fear for their reputation, desert the place where the first are disgusted, and the last tremble for the character on which their prosperity depends.

Now all this would be, *must be* changed, if this powerful engine is in the hands of those whose only aim is to use it for moral purposes, to instruct, to inspire love of country, virtue, religion and morality, teaching and improving the public, who are attracted by the hope of amusement, and held by the delights of truth, conveyed by poetry, assisted by music, painting, and eloquence.

The historians of the celestial empire, if we remember aright, are prohibited the indulgence of reflections. As we are at liberty to reflect and remark upon the facts we record, and the personages appertaining to our history, we shall take other opportunities to pursue the subject touched upon above, and now return to the thread of our story, chronologically.

On the 12th of February, 1786, Hallam and Henry opened the theatre in John-street, New-York, with The Provoked Husband, and Miss in her Teens. The company had undergone no material change.

A Mrs. Giffard made a first appearance in Lady Rusport, in the West Indian, on the 16th. Hallam's Belcour, and Henry's O'Flaherty, made this a play as popular in America as in England. Cato was played about this time, *Sempronius* by a gentleman, soon after taking his place in the ranks as Mr. Smallwood.

On the 16th of April, 1786, was performed the first American play which had ever been got up on a regular stage, by a regular company of comedians. It was a comedy in five acts, called "The Contrast," written by Royall Tyler, Esq., of Boston, who was encouraged by the favour with which this first effort was received, to produce in the May following, a farce, for the benefit of Wignell, called, "May Day, or New-York in an uproar." We thus arrive at the commencement of the American drama as united with the American theatre.

As has been noticed, Godfrey's "The Prince of Parthia," was published in 1765, appearing in print at the place of the author's residence, Philadelphia.* And we have read the very pleasant and laugh-provoking tragedy of "The Mercenary Match," written by Barnaby Bidwell, Esq., and played by the students of Yale College, under the auspices of the late Rev. Ezra Styles, D. D., president, the author of a very interesting book on the fugitive judges of Charles the First, by the monarchists called regicides. This tragedy was, perhaps still is, in blank verse. The shouts of laughter produced by the reading of it in a company of young men some forty years ago, are vividly recollected, but only two passages are remembered. The first,

"Night follows day, and day succeeds to night,"

has never been contradicted. The second,

"Sure never was the like heard of before in Boston,"

though not so measured and harmonious, was equally applauded.

"The Contrast" ranks first in point of time of all American plays, which had been performed by players. It is extremely deficient in plot, dialogue, or incident, but has some marking in the characters, and in that of *Jonathan,* played by Wignell, a degree of humour, and knowledge of what is termed Yankee dialect, which, in the hands of a favourite performer, was relished by an audience gratified by the appearance of home manufacture—a feeling which was soon exchanged for a most discouraging predilection for foreign articles, and con-

---

* This author, Thomas Godfrey, was the son of the inventor of the quadrant; and wrote his poem, The Prince of Parthia, at the age of twenty-two.

tempt for every literary home-made effort. This comedy was given by the author to Wignell, who published it in 1790 by subscription. It was coldly received in the closet: yet Jonathan the First has, perhaps, not been surpassed by any of his successors. He was the principal character, perhaps, strictly speaking, the only character. We will give a specimen of Jonathan; and select his description of a play-house in New-York, and the performance of The School for Scandal, and The Poor Soldier.

> *Jenny.*—So, Mr. Jonathan, I hear you were at the play last night.
> *Jon.*—At the play! Why do you think I went to the devil's drawing-room?
> *Jenny.*—The devil's drawing-room?
> *Jon.*—Yes: why aint cards and dice the devil's device? And the play-house the shop where the devil hangs out the vanities of the world upon the tenter hooks of temptation? I believe you have not heard how they were acting the old boy one night, and the wicked one came among them, sure enough; and went right off in a storm, and carried one-quarter of the play-house with him. Oh, no, no, no! You won't catch me at a play-house, I warrant you.

To the question, "where were you about six o'clock?" He answers, "why I went to see one Mr. Morrison, the *hocus pocus* man; they said as how he could eat a case-knife. As I was going about here and there to find it," the place, "I saw a great crowd of folks going into a long entry, that had lanterns over the door" (see the commencement of the third chapter for a description of the theatre in John-street, New-York); "so I asked a man if that was the place where they played *hocus pocus?* He was a very civil kind of a man, though he did speak like the Hessians; he lifted up his eyes and said, 'They play *hocus pocus* tricks enough there, got knows, mine friend.' So I went right in, and they showed me away clean up to the garret, just like a meeting-house gallery. And so I saw a power of topping folks, all sitting round in little cabins just like father's corn-crib, and then there was such a squeaking of the fiddles, and such a tarnal blaze with the lights, my head was near turned. At length people that sat near me set up such a hissing— hiss—like so many mad cats, and then they went thump, thump, thump, just like our Peleg thrashing wheat, and stampt away just like the nation, and called out for one Mr. Langolee—I suppose he helps act the tricks."

> *Jenny.*—Well, and what did you do all this time?
> *Jon.*—Gor, I—I liked the fun, and so I thumpt away, and hissed as lustily as the best of them. One sailor-looking man that sat by me, seeing me stamp, and knowing I was a cute fellow, because I could make a roaring noise, clapped me on the shoulder and said, "You are a d—d hearty cock, smite my timbers." I told him so I was, but he needent swear so and make use of such wicked words.

Jenny.—Did you see the man with his tricks?

Jon.—Why, I vow, as I was looking out for him, they lifted up a great green cloth, and let us look right into the next neighbour's house. Have you a good many houses in New-York made in that 'ere way?

Jenny.—Not many. But did you see the family?

Jon.—Yes, swamp it, I seed the family.

Jenny.—Well, and how did you like them?

Jon.—Why, I vow, they were pretty much like other families;—there was a poor good-natured curse of a husband, and a sad rantipole of a wife.

Jenny.—But did you see no other folks?

Jon.—Yes. There was one youngster, they called him Mr. Joseph; he talked as sober and as pious as a minister; but like some ministers that I know, he was a sly tike in his heart, for all that; he was going to ask a young woman to spark it with him, and—the Lord have mercy on my soul—she was another man's wife.

Jenny.—And did you see any more folks?

Jon.—Why they came on as thick as mustard. For my part I thought the house was haunted. There was a soldier fellow that talked about his row-de-dow-dow, and courted a young woman; but of all the cute folk I saw, I liked one little fellow—he had red hair, and a little round plump face like mine, only not altogether so handsome. His name was Darby—that was his baptizing name—his other name I forget. Oh! it was Wig—Wag—Wag-all—Darby Wagall—pray, do you know him? I should like to take a sling with him, or a drop of cider with a pepper-pod in it, to make it warm and comfortable.

Jenny.—I can't say I have that pleasure.

Jon.—I wish you did, he's a cute fellow. But there was one thing I didn't like in that Mr. Darby, and that was, he was afraid of some of them 'ere shooting irons, such as your troopers wear on training days. Not I'm a true-born Yankee American son of liberty, and I never was afraid of a gun yet in all my life." Jenny tells him he "was certainly at the play-house," and he cries, "Marcy on my soul! Did I see the wicked players? Mayhap that 'ere Darby that I liked so, was the old serpent himself, and had his cloven foot in his picket. Why I vow, now I come to think on't, the candles seemed to burn blue, and I'm sure, where I sat, it smelt tarnally of brimstone.

He proceeds to tell of his demanding his money, because he had not seen the show; "the dogs a bit of a sight have I seen unless you call listening to people's private business a sight."

Royall Tyler, Esq., was a native of Massachusetts, received a liberal education, studied law, and served as an officer in quelling Shea's insurrection. After this, he wrote "The Contrast" and "May Day." Returning to Massachusetts, he became involved in pecuniary difficulties, and retired to Vermont, then a *new country*. He settled at Brattleborough, and grew with the state. He became a judge, and finally chief-justice. Besides the above comedy and farce, he wrote and published a novel, called the Algerine Captives, and several poems. He died in the year 1824.

Such is the beginning of the American theatre, as connected with our literature, and it is as connected with literature, manners, and morals, that its history is valuable. We prefer the dialogue of "A Cure for the Spleen," mentioned in chapter the fourth, to that of "The Contrast." It is more dramatic, though not intended for the stage.

In McLean's Journal of March 21st, will be found the following note from the managers, which marks public feeling at the time on the subjects of France and England. "It is with real concern the subscribers learn that a character in "*The Poor Soldier*" has given umbrage to any frequenters of the theatre: it is both their duty and invariable study to please, not to offend, as a proof of which, they respectfully inform the public, they have made such alterations in the part alluded to, as they trust will do away every shadow of offence." The part alluded to was *Bagatelle.*

It is well known that the *Frenchman* has, in English farce and comedy, been ever the butt of John Bull's ridicule and contempt. One legitimate proof of his inferiority and source of merriment at his expense, is the fact that he does not speak good English; this, with various other equally good reasons, may be given as proofs that he was, and is, a character only to be laughed at, and such was a portion of English education. Now Jonathan began to feel, some time before, that all the maxims of John Bull were not as true as holy writ, and having received aid from France and Frenchmen in the late struggle with England, and moreover, having had ocular demonstration that one Englishman cannot *always* whip three Frenchmen, took it into his head that he ought not to suffer Monsieur *Bag-and-tail* to be made a laughing-stock on the American stage; and the managers were obliged, as we see, to apologize, and make such alterations as appeased their Yankee audience.

On the 5th of May, The Contrast, for the fourth time, and Widow's Vows, were performed for the "benefit of the unfortunate sufferers by the fire in Boston."

The theatre closed the 9th of June. The benefits had proved very unsuccessful. Hallam tried three nights before he *made* a benefit or gave up the attempting to make one.

From New-York, Hallam and Henry, with their company, went to Baltimore, where they opened a new theatre, on the 16th of August, 1786.

Philadelphia appears to have been shunned at this time: probably the hostility against the drama was too strong to admit of a visit, for on the 21st of December, the company were again in New-York, and opened the theatre in John-street.

On this occasion the managers announced that "in compliance with the wish of many respectable patrons of the theatre, there would be only two night's performance in a week." *Since* then we have had four large theatres, and a circus in which farces were performed, all open six nights in the week.

The company now consisted of Messrs. Hallam, Henry, Biddle, Harper, Morris, Wignell, Wools, Heard, Macpherson, and Ryan the prompter. Mesdames Henry, Morris, Harper, Sewell, and Miss Tuke.

In April, the performers were again taking benefits, and the 7th of the month, Henry brought out for his wife's benefit a pageant entitled "The Convention, or the Columbian Father," which had little other effect than to remind the public that two years before (March, 1785), she had played under the denomination of "a gentlewoman" for Henry's benefit, and to draw forth a bitter remark in Greenleaf's Journal, that she had so done to serve a *brother* and *lover*. This person was the youngest of the four Miss Storers, and the second who enjoyed the name of Mrs. Henry. The older sisters, who had been on the stage in New-York, had disappeared from before the American public. Two of them afterwards reappeared as Mrs. Mechler and Mrs. Hogg. The three sisters came to America in the year 1767, having previously joined the company in Jamaica, with an elder sister, who was lost in the voyage to America (with the ship), as before mentioned. They were passengers in a vessel from Jamaica, which took fire at sea, the crew and passengers, with the one exception, were saved by the boats, and landed at Newport, Rhode Island.

Mr. Harper was a very useful man in the American Company at this time, and personated characters of every description from Charles Surface to Falstaff. In the latter part he gave great satisfaction. He was unrivalled, for there was no other, and had been no other Falstaff seen on this side of the Atlantic. About this time, April 14th, 1787, he had advertised the first part of Henry IV. for his benefit, but it was postponed from day to day in consequence of what has been called the "Doctor's Mob." Some students of anatomy and young surgeons had incautiously left the windows of a dissecting-room at the Hospital in such a situation, that boys at play about the building, at that time out of town, saw the subjects in a mutilated state. They communicated their horror to others, and a mob of men and boys assembled, broke into the house, and were so inflamed by the objects they discovered and the inferences they drew from them, that they threatened destruction to all surgeons. The most obnoxious of the profession were sheltered from their fury by being placed in the jail, and even then could only be protected by the armed militia. It was several days before the tumult was appeased sufficiently to allow Falstaff and Hotspur to meet at Shrewsbury.

The theatre was closed on the 28th of May, and the company proceeded to Philadelphia. The benefits had been unsuccessful. Even Wignell, the great favourite, was obliged to call upon a writer to plead for him, as one who was an object of commiseration from long-continued sickness. One of the company, Macpherson, either could not raise the wind for a voyage to Philadelphia, or had created some of those ties which are too strong to admit of change of place. He advertised lectures on heads, and endeavoured to excite the sympathy of the public as a father, who was unable to discharge the debts he had unavoidably contracted. Wignell appeared next year, restored to health and in the full tide of popular favour; of Macpherson, we never hear more.

⤙ CHAPTER 7 ⤚

Strollers — Authorship for the Stage — Managers — Dubellamy — Henry — Hallam — First Comedy accepted and delayed — Second brought out — The Father of an Only Child — Dramatis Personæ — Darby's Return — Washington.

When Kemble, or his sister Siddons, or his rival Cooke, went the round of the provincial theatres, were they not strollers? But they played in the theatres royal of Bath, or Liverpool, or Manchester. And the Douglasses and Hallams played in his majesty's theatres of the colonies by royal authority, delegated to the royal governors. If to be his majesty's servants gave dignity to the first, the same equivocal dignity belongs to the second. In the time of feudal barbarism, the musician, the poet, and the player could only be protected from the violence of the robber-baron by becoming the servant of the baron-robber, or of his liege lord the king. This is the origin of the honourable distinction enjoyed by the players of the London and other licensed English theatres. The barons no longer entertaining minstrels, or trouvers, or histrions, or jongleurs (jugglers), or players, and the law considering the unpatronised artist as a vagabond, the king became sole master of the players, and all established theatres were theatres royal.

Happily, the time is approaching when the painter, the musician, the poet, and the player may instruct or amuse the public without being called to account by the constable. It has not yet arrived in every part of the United States. The poems of Milton or Shakespeare, or the picture on which, as on the page of history, the painter has written lessons of eternal truth, teaching love to God and man, are all subjects of fine or tax, and are stigmatized as shows, and their exhibiters or reciters as showmen or strollers in some portions of our country. If merely moving from place to place for the purpose of exercising a calling makes that calling disreputable, and remaining in one spot for its exercise is dignified, it would seem to follow that the judge who goes the circuit—the lawyer who travels from court-house to court-house, from county to county—the preacher who obeys the call of those who want a teacher—the missionary who carries instruction to the ignorant who do not call for it, or the bishop who moves through his diocese to confirm and consecrate, are all in this respect as undignified as the player; and the cobbler, who sits from the first of January to the last of December in his stall, is the most dignified personage that can well be imagined. Let us return to players, plays, and the authors of plays.

About the end of summer, in the year 1787, the writer returned home, after a residence of more than three years in London. These years were those which occur between the ages of eighteen and twenty-two, a portion of life fraught with danger to all. The theatre had been his delight, and he had seen all the great performers on the English stage at that period, and as many plays as his finances permitted. The theatres of Drury Lane, Covent Garden, and the Haymarket had been visited for the sake of the performances exhibited, and not as scenes of dissipation. All Shakespeare's acting plays, and many others, especially the new pieces of the day, had been before him, represented by the immediate successors, and some of the contemporaries of Garrick.

Young, and filled with these recollections, he first saw the American Company on his return, performing upon the stage where, as a boy, he had witnessed the representations of Shakespeare, Home, and Cumberland by the officers of his Britannic majesty during the cessations of their military exertions for suppressing the rebellion. He heard of the success of "The Contrast," and although it was already put on the shelf of the prompter, or buried in his travelling chest, the praises bestowed upon it lit up the inflammable material brought from abroad, and a comedy in five acts was written in a few weeks.

A Yankee servant, a travelled American, an officer in the late revolutionary army, a fop, such as fops then were in New-York, an old gentleman and his two daughters, one of course lively and the other serious, formed the dramatis personæ. The play was read to critics as young and ignorant as the author, and praised to his heart's content. It has long slept in the tomb of the Capulets, and fortunately no traces remain of its merits or demerits.

Having written a play, how was the author to approach those awful personages, the managers. He had never been behind the scenes of a theatre. His ideas of managers were those formed from books, and Garrick, and Colman, and Sheridan, the arbiters of the fate of authors, and famed themselves for wit and learning, invested all managers with a splendour little short of regal dignity. He had not read that letter of Garrick to Colman, which says, "I know that fools may be, and that many fools have been managers." Little did the young author know how much these redoubted American kings wished for alliance with the citizens, and how gladly they would meet any overtures from the son of a merchant. In fact, he knew nothing of the theatre, its managers or its actors, but the mere outside.

As a medium of communication between the play writer and the managers, a man was pointed out who had for a time been of some consequence on the London boards, and now resided under another name in New-York. This was the Dubellamy of the English stage; a first singer and *walking-gentleman.* He was now past his meridian, but still a handsome man, and was found sufficiently easy of access and full of the courtesy of the old school. A meeting was arranged at the City Tavern, and a bottle of Madeira discussed with the merits of this first-born of a would-be author. The wine was praised, and the play was praised,—the first, perhaps, made the second tolerable,—that must be good which can repay a man of the world for listening to an author who reads his own play. Unless the work has uncommon merit, the listener's task is a hard one. The play was read with "good emphasis and discretion," in the reader's opinion, and apparently in that of the veteran Dubellamy. It was "excellent, wanted a little pruning, but far less the 'She Stoops to Conquer,' when Goldsmith read it to us in the green-room." Delightful draughts of flattery, from a man who had heard and seen the author of the Vicar of Wakefield, and She Stoops to Conquer! The comedy was called by the mawkish title of "The Modest Soldier, or Love in New-York."

An introduction to the managers was the next step; and a reading by appointment at Henry's house, to Messrs. Hallam and Henry and Mrs. Henry. The lady was polite, Henry complimented, Hallam was shy and silent.

Henry being the acting manager, several interviews with him succeeded. On one occasion the author of the comedy calling on him was ushered into his chamber by Mrs. Henry, and found him extended on a field-bed and apparently unable to rise. His gigantic figure appeared larger than ever, his face was flushed with fever, and the lower part covered by beard. His disease was gout, and he occasionally expressed his suffering, but spoke cheerfully, and even jocosely. The same evening he played the Youthful Lover in The Clandestine Marriage, and his morning visiter saw him in apparent health and elegantly apparelled, while his brother-manager Hallam, a Harlequin in activity, represented Lord Ogilby, a character he had seen performed by King at Drury Lane, and mimicked those twitches and excruciating pains which Henry, feeling in reality, covered with the mask of apparent ease and enjoyment. Such is one picture of theatrical life, and by no means the most extraordinary.

Henry was the only actor in America who kept a carriage. It was in the form of a coach, but very small, just sufficient to carry himself and wife to the theatre; it was drawn by one horse and driven by a black boy. Aware of the jealousy towards players, and that it would be said he *kept a coach,* he had caused to be painted on the doors, in the manner of those coats of arms which the aristocracy of Europe display, *two crutches* in heraldic fashion, with the motto, "*This or these.*"

It is remembered that Henry said, "I put this marked motto and device on my carriage to prevent any impertinent remarks on an actor keeping his coach. The wits would have taken care to forget that the actor could not walk."

The ride was not a long one for the actor and actress from their house to the theatre in John-street, as he lived in Fair-street (now Fulton), between Nassau-street and Broadway, in the same two-story brick house painted yellow in which Hodgkinson resided for some years. Mrs. Henry used to go ready dressed for the character she was to play, and shut up in the little boxlike vehicle. This residence in Fair-street was still more convenient for Hodgkinson's theatrical business, as a gate opened (and still opens) from the back of the house, directly opposite Theatre Alley.

The comedy of the young author was *accepted* and *cast*, but after some delays its appearance was by agreement deferred until the next winter, as the benefits were soon to commence previous to the company's leaving the city. While on this subject it is best to despatch it. The next season alterations were proposed and made to suit Mrs. Henry. The bringing out was still put off, and it was only time and experience that explained to the candidate for fame the mystery of his disappointment. There was no part suited to Henry, and he was the acting and efficient manager. There was no part suited to his wife, and she was another efficient manager. The best man's part was intended for Wignell. The best woman's part was cast by the author for Mrs. Morris, as the representative of the lively comedy lady. The acting manager and his manager were jealous of, and at variance with Hallam and Wignell, and Mrs. Morris was patronized by Wignell.

These were mysteries unthought of by the young author, who, buoyed up by hope and expectation, anticipating the success of this much-praised comedy, proceeded to write a second, in which, without design, one part was suited to Henry, another did not displease his wife, and the lively lady was evidently inferior to the character assigned to the manager's lady. This second comedy was seized with avidity by Henry. The author was easily persuaded to let the second come out first; and the first was ultimately consigned to oblivion. No doubt a merited oblivion, the flattery of Dubellamy, Hallam, Henry, and the rest notwithstanding.

About this time Mr. Samuel Low, then in the Bank of New-York, then the only bank of the city or state, wrote a comedy, which was rejected by the managers, and published for their justification by the author.

On the 13th of June, 1788, Mr. Kenna, who with his wife had made a part of the old American company, opened a theatre at Newbern, North Carolina, with the tragedy of Isabella, Mrs. Kenna playing the heroine; and in July, the same corps opened a theatre in Wilmington.

On the 7th of September, 1789, the second comedy above mentioned was brought out. It was called "The Father." It had been studied carefully, was played correctly, and received with great applause by the citizens. It was printed, and was the first play which had come from the American press, as performed by regular comedians. It was immediately reprinted in Halifax, and some years after, another edition was published, with an addition to the title of the words "of an Only Child."

This play was well performed. The serious or pathetic parts received full support from Henry, who played the Father, and from Mrs. Henry, who was the heroine. Wignell added to his reputation as a comic actor. The comedy was performed until the benefits commenced, in about three weeks after its appearance. The author made an attempt to soften the asperities which war had created, and to reconcile his countrymen to their British brethren. When the American Company ceased to be "one and indivisible"—when Wignell, who was the great favourite of the laughter-loving, seceded, the play was laid aside. Its merits have never entitled it to revival.

As "The Father of an Only Child" may claim some attention from the circumstance that it was the first drama which issued from the press after the revolution—the first American play printed that had been performed in a regular theatre—and the first performed of the many afterwards written by its author, we will give the cast of it, and take the opportunity of noticing the characters and their representatives.

Colonel Campbell, "the father of an only child," was played by Mr. Henry. The colonel, like several of our patriotic officers of 1775, is supposed to have been a physician previous to taking up the sword. When a student at Edinburgh he had clandestinely married, lost his wife, and when he returned home, left his only child with a friend, who had educated him and placed him in the British army under his own name. Campbell supposes he was killed at Bunker hill, and now arrives in New-York to visit two sisters, his wards. Racket, played by Mr. Hallam, had married one of these sisters, and is a dissipated, and of course unhappy man and bad husband. In his house the scene lies, and the unities are fully observed. Rusport, played by Mr. Biddle, is an impostor, pretending to be an officer in the English army, but really the fugitive servant of Haller, played by Mr. Harper, who proves to be the son of the colonel supposed to have fallen in battle. Tattle, played by Mr. Wignell, is the family physician and Marplot of the piece. Campley, played by Mr. Wools, is a companion of Haller's; Platoon, Mr. Ryan, is a kind of poor Corporal Trim to Colonel Campbell; Jacob, Mr. Lake, is a German soldier, left behind by the auxiliaries of England. Such are the males. Mrs. Racket, played by Mrs. Morris, encourages the addresses of Rusport in jest, and excites her husband's jealousy. Caroline, played by Mrs. Henry, had met

Haller in Halifax and been betrothed to him, and discovers to Campbell that his son was not killed at Bunker hill, but is only lost to him by subsequent events, as is suspected by her. Mrs. Grenade, played by Mrs. Harper, and Susannah, by Miss Tuke, thicken the plot and serve to unravel it. Haller detects his servant, discovers that he is somebody else and not himself, and is married to Caroline, and all the rest ends as a decent play ought to do. Such were the characters; of their representatives a few words.

Mr. John Henry was full six feet in height, and had been uncommonly handsome. He played Othello better, we believe, than any man had done before him in America; it is recorded that he wore "the uniform of a British general officer, his face black and hair woolly." This must not appear strange, however improper, for the writer saw John Kemble, in 1786–7, play the Moor (Mrs. Siddons the Desdemona) in a suit of modern military of scarlet and gold lace, coat, waist-coat, and breeches; he wore white silk stockings, his face was black, and his hair (not woolly, but long and black) was cued in the military fashion of the day. Bensley played Iago, and very well, in a modern uniform of blue and red. Thus Mr. Henry dressed in the manner of his contemporaries. He was at this time a victim to the gout. His Irishmen were very fine, and he had great merit in serious and pathetic fathers. Of the merits of Mr. Hallam we have repeatedly spoken. In person he was of middle stature or above, thin, straight, and well taught as a dancer and fencer. In learning the latter accomplishment, he had received a hurt in the corner of one of his eyes, which gave a slight cast, a scarcely perceptible but odd expression to it in some points of view; generally, his face was well adapted to his profession, particularly in comedy. Biddle was an actor merely decent. Harper, who was then considered handsome, was marked with the small-pox, had expressive eyes and fine teeth. Wools, formerly the singer of the company, was now old, and of little value as a player; he was a gentlemanly, modest, and honest man. Wignell was a man below the ordinary height, with a slight stoop of the shoulders; he was athletic, with handsomely formed lower extremities, the knees a little curved outwards, and feet remarkably small. His large blue eyes were rich in expression, and his comedy was luxuriant in humour, but always faithful to his author. He was a comic actor, not a buffoon. He was a clown who did not speak more than was set down in his part. The vice of impudently altering and adding to an author has always existed and is increasing in proportion to the increase of our theatres and the decline of the drama. In proportion as plays are worthless, players will foist in their own nonsense to amuse the auditors of worthless plays; but if the drama is to be supported or revived, the practice must meet the reprehension of managers and audience. Mr. Wignell's taste was too good to permit his falling into such an error. Ryan was passable, and Lake merely bearable. Ryan was the prompter, and occasionally played small parts. Another of the name (Dennis Ryan), had performed in New-York in 1781–2, with the officers of the British army.

Mrs. Morris, the fine lady of the company, was a tall and elegant woman. Her acting very spirited. Mrs. Henry was a very small, fair woman, with much talent both for speaking and singing, and though her figure gave her no aid, her spirit and judgment made her tragedy effective. Mrs. Harper was a woman of no personal beauty, but played the old women of comedy respectably. Miss Tuke was young, comely, and awkward. She afterwards, as Mrs. Hallam, became an actress of merit, and improved in beauty and elegance.

For the reasons above given we may be excused if we dwell a little longer on this comedy. The American Quarterly Review thus speaks of it. "The plot is sufficiently dramatic to carry an interest throughout; the characters are well drawn, and well employed, and the dialogue possesses what is indispensable to genuine comedy, a brief terseness and unstudied ease, which few of the productions of the present era afford."

As we have given a specimen of the first American comedy that was performed by professed actors, and it is selected as a fair specimen, likewise, by the editor of The New-England Magazine, we will give a short scene from the second, as selected by the American Quarterly Review.

> *Enter* TATTLE, *to* RACKET, MRS. RACKET, *and* RUSPORT.
>
> "*Tat.* Oh, Racket, my dear fellow, how d'ye do?
>
> *Rack.* So, another infernal coxcomb!
>
> *Tat.* What's the matter? You don't seem well. How d'ye do, ma'am? Your servant sir (*to Rusport*). Racket, you have not introduced me to this gentleman.
>
> *Rack.* Captain Rusport, this is my friend Doctor Tattle.
>
> *Tat.* Yes sir, Tattle. Terebrate Tattle, M.D.
>
> *Rack.* Doctor, this is Captain Rusport, just arrived in the last packet from Halifax.
>
> *Tat.* How d'ye do, sir? I'm very glad to see you, indeed. Very fine potatoes in Halifax. Racket! this way. Here, just come from abroad. You'll recommend me.
>
> *Rack.* If he wants a physician I certainly will (*half aside*), in the full hope that you will poison him.
>
> *Tat.* Thank you! thank you! Servant ma'am. Fine weather, ha? A little rainy, but that's good for the country. A fine season for coughs and colds, sir (*to Rusport*). O, Racket, my dear fellow, I had forgot that I heard of your accident. No great harm done, I perceive. What a tremendous fall you must have had—precipitated from the scaffolding of a three-story house, and your *os parietale* brought in contact with the pavement, while your heels were suspended in the air, entangled in a mason's ladder.
>
> *Rack.* Pooh! pooh! I broke my nose.

Tat. Is that all! Why I heard—so, so—only a contusion on the *pons nasi*. I was called up to a curious case last evening.

Rack. Then I'm off. (*While Tattle is speaking, Racket goes, and Rusport and Mrs. Racket retire laughing.*)

Tat. Very curious case indeed. I had just finished my studies for the evening, smoked out my last cigar, and got comfortably in bed. Pretty late. Very dark. Monstrous dark. Cursed cold. Monstrous cold for the season. Very often the case with us of the faculty; called up at all times and seasons. used to be so when I was a student in Paris. Called up one night to a dancing-master, who had his scull most elegantly fractured, his leg most beautifully broke, and the finest dislocation of the shoulder I ever witnessed. I soon put his shoulder in state to draw the bow again, and his leg to caper to the sounds it might draw from his kit, violin or fiddle; as for his head, a dancing-master's head, ma'am (*looking round*), head, head. Oh, there you are, are you? I beg your pardon, I thought you were by me. (*Follows them.*) So you see, ma'am, as I was saying, I was called up last night to witness the most curious case (*they avoid him, he follows*), curious case. The bone of the right thigh—(*Racket re-enters*).

Rack. So, the doctor is at it still.

Tat. Right thigh—I am glad you have come to hear it, Racket. The bone of the right thigh. (*Racket turns from him.*) The bone of the right thigh, ma'am. (*She turns away.*) Curious case; the bone of the right thigh, captain.

Rusp. You must have gained great credit by that cure, doctor.

Tat. Cure? Sir! What? O, you mean the dancing-master! I can assure you, I am sought for. I have a pretty practice, considering the partiality of the people of this country for old women's prescriptions——"

Notoriety being mentioned—

"*Mrs. Rack.* Notoriety, let me tell you, is often a sure passport to wealth.

Tat. Very true, ma'am; did I ever tell you—

Rack. A man becomes notorious by actions which bring him to the pillory or the gallows.

Tat. Very true, sir. You've heard me say, perhaps—

Mrs. Rack. In that case the stock of notoriety acquired can be of little service, as the subject of it is launched into eternity before he has an opportunity of trading upon his capital.

Tat. Very good, ma'am, capital! Did I ever—(*she retires with Rusport*). Racket, did I ever tell you of the child that—

Rack. That swallowed the pap-spoon? Yes, yes, you told me that.

Tat. Pap-spoon? Swallowed? Pap-spoon? I never heard of such a case,—and yet it might be,—and yet—no—no—I mean the case of the infant that broke—

Rack. Yes, yes, you told me that.

Tat. There is an East Indian nabob just arrived who has a cursed cachetic habit—

Rack. True, true,—he has—he has; but, doctor, how goes on your matrimonial negotiation?

Tat. My landlady—

Rack. Almost married,—ha? Miss Gingham has consented?

Tat. A clever old woman,—good old soul—

Rack. But you don't think of marrying her?

Tat. Ha, ha! Good, good! Poor old soul, she is very much affected with—

Rack. But Miss Gingham?

Tat. Pshaw,—what's Miss Gingham to a fine case of bilious fever?"

The doctor having left them, it is observed that he had travelled France, Italy, and Germany in pursuit of science.

"*Mrs. Rack.* But science travelled faster than he did, and cruelly eluded his pursuit. Poor doctor! The few ideas he has are always travelling post, his head is like New-York on May day, *all the furniture wandering.*"

When Wignell took his benefit this year, he requested something from the author of The Father of an Only Child, and the character of Darby in The Poor Soldier, in which he was as popular in America as Edwin was in England, suggested an Interlude, in which Darby, after various adventures in Europe and in the United States, returns to Ireland and recounts the sights he had seen. This trifle was called "Darby's Return," and was for years extremely popular, and several times published. The remembrance of this performance is rendered pleasing from the recollection of the pleasure evinced by the first president of the U. States, the immortal Washington, who attended its representation. The eyes of the audience were frequently bent on his countenance, and to watch the emotions produced by any particular passage upon him was the simultaneous employment of all. When Wignell, as Darby, recounts what had befallen him in America, in New-York, at the adoption of the Federal Constitution, and the inauguration of the president, the interest expressed by the audience in the looks and the changes of countenance of this great man became intense. He smiled at these lines alluding to the change in the government—

> "There too I saw some mighty pretty shows;
> A revolution, without blood or blows,
> For, as I understood, the cunning elves,
> The people, all revolted from themselves."

But at the lines

> "A man who fought to free the land from wo,
> *Like me,* had left his farm, a soldiering to go.
> But having gain'd his point, he had, *like me,*
> Return'd his own potato ground to see.

But there he could not rest. With one accord
He's call'd to be a kind of—not a lord—
I don't know what, he's not a *great man* sure,
For poor men love him just as he were poor.
They love like a father, or a brother,

DERMOT.

As we poor Irishmen love one another.

The president looked serious; and when Kathleen asked,

"How looked he, Darby? Was he short or tall?"

his countenance showed embarrassment, from the expectation of one of those eulogiums which he had been obliged to hear on many public occasions, and which must doubtless have been a severe trial to his feelings; but Darby's answer that he had *not seen him,* because he had mistaken a man "all lace and glitter, botherum and shine" for him until all the show had passed, relieved the hero from apprehension of further personality, and he indulged in that which was with him extremely rare, a hearty laugh.

The plays and farces above mentioned, the first efforts of our dramatists, were strictly local. Mr. Tyler, in The Contrast, and some later writers for the stage, seem to have thought that a Yankee character, a Jonathan, stamped the piece as American, forgetting that a clown is not the type of the nation he belongs to. It may here be a fit subject of inquiring how far we ought to wish for a national drama, distinct from that of our English forefathers, meaning the works of the dramatists before the restoration of Charles the Second. The plays of Shakespeare, and Jonson, and Ford, and Marlowe, of Beaumont and Fletcher, of Wycherly, and all the old poets of the drama are ours, as *much ours,* being the descendants of Englishmen, as if our fathers had never left the country in which they were written. We say the same of the philosophy of Milton, and Locke, and Newton. Old English literature, as well as that of remote antiquity, on which it is founded, is the basis on which we build, and is an integral part of our mental existence. Inasmuch as we may hereafter deviate from the models left us by our ancestors, it will only be, as we hope, in a more severe and manly character, induced by our republican institutions, and approaching the high tone of the Greek drama. A character created by our free government and the absence of debasing aristocratic grades in our society already marks our travellers in every European country they visit. Surely, if any people on earth can hope to rival the works of Sophocles and Euripides, it is that country which is destined to look back to the annals of long past ages for a record that ever a slave or a master polluted her soil. A people literally self-governed, and guided by the experience and accumulated science of

Asia, and Africa, and Europe, must appreciate liberty and feel patriotism as no other people ever did. But before our drama can approach the wished-for character, our theatres must be placed in other hands, or so controlled by the enlightened portion of the public that the accumulation of money shall not be the object of their directors.

Milton felt as a republican, and in his dramas wrote like a Greek. When the dramatists of France attempted to rear a stage on the model of Greece, the manners of a court and the effects of monarchy upon the people counteracted the effort, and with some exceptions, rendered the works of their poets feeble, unnatural, and consequently tedious. The translations and imitations of the French tragedy brought on the English stage are contemptible.

We find the following observations, from the pen of a popular American writer,* so much to the purpose, that we beg leave to insert them. He is speaking (see No. 2, American Quarterly Review) of a national drama. "By a national drama, we mean, not merely a class of dramatic productions written by Americans, but one appealing directly to the national feeling—founded upon domestic incidents—illustrating or satirizing domestic manners, and above all, displaying a generous chivalry in the maintenance and vindication of those great and illustrious peculiarities of situation and character by which we are distinguished from all other nations. We do not hesitate to say, that next to the interests of eternal truth, there is no object more worthy the exercise of the highest attributes of mind than that of administering to the just pride of national character, inspiring a feeling for national glory, and inculcating a love of country."

The first efforts at dramatic literature in this country were wild. The essays of youth, not sufficiently instructed in any thing, and deficient in literary education; and though received favourably by a people beginning to feel that they were called to a new state of existence, and wishing a literature identified with themselves, and distinct from that of Europe, both the dramatists and the people they addressed had not yet sufficiently matured their notions of the result of the great political changes which had taken place to know how far to assert independence in literature or government, or how far to imitate their European ancestors. In the procession on occasion of the adoption of the Federal Constitution, an association of young men, of which the writer was one, called the Philological Society, carried through the streets of New-York a book inscribed "Federal Language," as if any other than the English language, the language of our fathers, the contemporaries of Hampden and Milton, could be desirable for their sons and the inheritors of their spirit. When the whole character of our literature shall have received the impress of our republican government, when our writers,

---

* James K. Paulding, Esq.

wherever they may lay the scene or the plot of their works, shall warn mankind of the evils of governments usurped over the people, then our drama will be national and distinct from that of countries not blessed by liberty of thought.

It is our province to record facts showing the progress of the theatre, and noticing the attempts at improvement, both literary and histrionic, and it shall be attempted with that feeling which we hope may communicate to our labours a spirit conducive to the improvement of our fellow-men, and the correction of those defects which exist in the department of the fine arts of which we treat.

We have taken the opportunity afforded by the comedy of "The Father of an Only Child," to record the personal appearance and merits as comedians of the members of the company who represented it. They soon after went on their southern tour. The benefits, which began on the 21st of September, 1789, continued to the 9th of December, when the theatre closed. The new pieces brought out this season were, He would be a Soldier, Choleric Man, School for Soldiers, *The Father*, Who's the Dupe, Inkle and Yarico, Dead Alive, Duplicity, Miser, Toy, Barataria, Prisoner at Large, Critic, Cheats of Scapin, Half an Hour after Supper, Invasion, Air Balloon, *Darby's Return*. Some of these were *got up* for benefits, and in that hurried manner for want of time or money as to destroy them. "To revive a play," a wit has said, "is to murder it."

⇥ CHAPTER 8 ⇤

1790 — American Company go to Philadelphia — Widow of Malabar — Col. Humphreys — John Martin — Season of 1791-2 in New-York, the last in which the old Company remained the sole possessors of the United States — Ashton — Final separation of Wignell from Hallam and Henry — Henry and Wignell go to England — Henry brings out Mr. and Mrs. Hodgkinson, and others — Wignell returns with a great Company, and finds the Yellow Fever in Philadelphia, where the Chestnut-street Theatre had been built for him and Reinagle — Hodgkinson, Mrs. Hodgkinson, King, Prigmore, West.

The company, with the addition to the stock pieces mentioned in the last chapter, and of a female performer, Mrs. Hamilton, who afterwards played the old women of comedy, proceeded to Philadelphia, opened their theatre in January, 1790, and continued playing until spring, when they went to Baltimore, and again returned to Philadelphia, reopening the theatre in Southwark on the 27th of Nov., 1790.

During their second visit, the managers brought out a tragedy translated from the French by Col. David Humphreys, called The Widow of Malabar; it was ushered in by a prologue from an abler hand than that of the translator, Judge

Trumbull, the author of McFingall. This was not a national drama, according to the author above quoted, though given to us by an American. The prologue had a portion of the wit for which McFingall is deservedly celebrated. One line approaches to temerity, alluding to the Indian custom of sacrificing widows to the manes of their husbands,—

> "'Tis better, far, to marry than to burn."

Col. Humphreys and Judge Trumbull belonged to one of those bands of literary pioneers which, with pen instead of pickaxe, let light into the wilderness, and showed to Americans that all knowledge or wit did not reside on the eastern side of the Atlantic. President Dwight, Joel Barlow, Judge Trumbull, Doctor Hopkins, and Col. Humphreys were fellow-labourers in this work of utility.

David Humphreys was born at Derby, in the state of Connecticut, about the time the first company of players came to Virginia, 1752, and graduated at Yale College in 1767. President Dwight and Judge Trumbull preceded him in the labour of verse-making; and Barlow likewise owed his courage to the success of these gentlemen, and submitted his works to them. Humphreys entered the army of his country at an early period, and continued to serve honourably to the end of the contest for freedom. In 1778, he was aid to Gen. Putnam, whose life he afterwards published, and in 1780, he made one of Washington's aides-de-camp. He was intrusted by his illustrious friend with the standards taken under the capitulation of Cornwallis at Yorktown, and was presented by Congress with a sword. This memorable event, his presenting the standards, was painted by a Danish artist, when the poet and soldier was in Europe, between 1784 and 1786, as secretary of legation to Mr. Jefferson. On his return, he, with Judge Trumbull, Mr. Barlow, and Doctor Hopkins, published "The Anarchiad." He resided at Mount Vernon for some time previous to the adoption of the Federal Constitution, and then came with the first president to New-York. To Humphreys has been ascribed some of that anti-republican etiquette which attended the president's levees, and we know the colonel was attached to other pomp besides that of "glorious war." The president and Senate appointed him ambassador to Madrid, and he fulfilled his honourable duties in Europe until 1802. He resided in Boston some years, and endeavoured to persuade Bernard to bring out a comedy he had laboured on until he thought it worthy of the public—it was extremely unlike those comedies Bernard owed his fame to, and repaid by imparting the vivifying influence of his art—but the wary comedian heard the poet read, drank his Madeira, said "very well" now and then—but never brought out the play. Col. Humphreys owes his poetical fame principally to his "Address to the Armies," a poem of merit. We owe to him the introduction of the merino breed of sheep into this country. He resided for some years near New-Haven, and died honoured and regretted. About the year 1806, Malbone painted a miniature of him, in his best style, which is, to those who know his style, the highest praise; this is the only true portrait of this amiable man.

In the course of this winter, 1790–1, we find nothing further worth recording but the first appearance of *the first person of the male sex* born in America, who adopted the stage as a profession. Two females of the name of Tuke had been successively, the one after the death of the other, brought out by Mr. Hallam, but in the present instance a youth, induced by habits of idleness, and the applause bestowed upon his recitations by his idle companions, abandoned the profession chosen for him, and leaving his native place, New-York, made his debut as Young Norval, on the stage of Philadelphia. He was favourably received, and his destiny sealed. This was John Martin. His friends had intended him for the profession of the law, but what he thought a life of pleasure had allurements which caused their disappointment. He was of fair complexion, middle height, light figure, and played the youthful characters of many tragedies and comedies in a style called respectable, but mere respectability in any of the fine arts is ever associated with mediocrity. Mr. Martin will be hereafter mentioned, as he continued for some years a useful, though not a brilliant actor. He laboured hard, lived poor, and died young. Such is the lot of hundreds who see only pleasure in the profession of a player; a profession requiring splendid talents and assiduous application; and if adopted by one who cannot attain distinction, he is doomed to labour and privations, too often ending in low dissipation, disease, neglect, and early death. Labour and privation is the lot of the player who possesses distinguished talents and public favour, but the portion of the drudges of a theatre, the pawns of the chess-board, is little short of a sealed doom to a life of poverty, and if not redeemed by private virtues, of degradation.

Hallam and Henry opened their theatre in John-street, New-York, on the 10th of Oct., 1791. The company now consisted of Hallam, Henry, Wignell, Morris, and Wools, sharers; Harper, Martin, Hammond, Heard, Ryan, Robinson, Durang, Bissett, Biddle, and Macpherson, salaried actors. The females were Mrs. Henry, Mrs. Morris, sharers; Mrs. Hamilton, Mrs. Rankin, Mrs. Gray, Mrs. Harper, and Miss Tuke were salaried.

This was the last season that this sharing scheme, first projected in 1752, kept in operation. A person of the name of Ashton made his debut in Hotspur, without any powers except those of voice. He is remembered in the soliloquy when reading the letter, screaming out,

> "For the love ee bears hour ouse!
> Ee shows by this ee loves iz hone barn better
> Than ee loves hour ouse."

Of Hammond, Bissett, Macpherson, Mrs. Rankin, Mrs. Gray, and Mrs. Sewell nothing is remembered.

At the close of this theatrical season, Mr. Thomas Wignell seceded from the old American Company, carrying with him Mr. and Mrs. Morris. Wignell's talents and influence laid the foundation of that theatrical establishment in Philadelphia which flourished for many years more uniformly, and with actors of more general estimation as citizens and artists, than the rival institution in New-York, which continued for some time longer to be called the old American Company. Philadelphia and New-York became from this time territories of rival monarchs, who, after mutual invasions and hostile incursions for a short time, found it necessary to divide the United States between them, until other potentates raised independent standards, and every city, town, and village had its own stage, and its own "king of shreds and patches."

In the year 1792, this important division of the American Company took place. The writer knew, four years before, that discord and jealousy existed between Henry and Wignell. Hallam, who was Wignell's cousin, and had sent him out in 1775, sided with the latter in 1788. Thus the managers, Hallam and Henry, were at variance. Hallam through life professed to be guided by two maxims in the management of a theatre. They were, "keep down the expenses," and "divide and govern." The first may be right according to circumstances, as a general rule it is wrong. The second is always wrong. It is the base resource of the weak to govern by fraud and falsehood, when they find that they have not the ability to govern by truth and justice. It is the Machiavelian policy of tyrants. Hallam could divide, but could not govern, and the two more powerful minds took the reins of government into their own hands and divided the kingdom. The following statement of the immediate cause of the separation was communicated to the writer by Wignell, in 1802, and in the main agrees with Hallam's account of the transaction. The reader will see where they would necessarily differ, each stating his own case.

By recurring to the early account of the division of shares, it will be seen that the manager had a share as such, and another as performer. Two managers enjoyed the same source of emolument, each having his share as such, and Wignell, knowing himself to be at this time the favourite of the public, aspired to a share in the management and the advantages belonging thereto. Henry had given him repeated promises of taking him into *the firm;* Hallam appearing to wish for the same. In the winter of 1791–2, it had been considered necessary by the sharers to send an agent to England for the purpose of engaging performers. The sharers, it appears, were occasionally called together as a council to the joint kings, and they saw that the American public began to call for more than had satisfied the colonies of England, or the exhausted and jealous states immediately after their independence. In addition to more actors, scene painters, musicians, machinists, and a better wardrobe was wanted. Wignell requested that he might be the company's agent, and it had been promised to him. He had in consequence written to his friends, that after an absence of fifteen years he should see them again in London. In this stage of the business he had a more than usually violent quarrel with Henry, who threatened him that "his reign should not be long."

In 1792, while the company were playing in Philadelphia, the following paragraph appeared in one of the papers. "We have authority to say that John Henry, one of the managers of the old American Company, will soon embark for England, for the purpose of engaging performers for the company." On seeing this, Wignell called upon Hallam, and asked him if he knew of, or had sanctioned that paragraph. He replied, "No." "Who then authorized it?" The reply was, "Henry, I suppose, as it is in his usual way."

Wignell asserted his right to go home as agent, mentioned the promise given to him, and his desire to visit his friends. Henry persisted in his determination to take the business on himself, and as appeared by the sequel, had Hallam's assent to the plan. A meeting of the sharers was called to choose their agent for this important mission. When all were assembled, Hallam, we presume because the oldest manager and sharer, opened the business.

He expatiated on the condition of the company, the growth of the country, the demands of the public, the necessity of satisfying these demands that the company might prevent opposition, that for these reasons an agent must be sent to England to procure performers, as well as make purchases, and establish such a correspondence as would further their views, concluding with these words, "Mr. Henry is willing to go, and Mr. Wignell is anxious to go. If Mr. Henry goes, we can continue playing and maintain ourselves. If Mr. Wignell goes, we must shut up."

This shows the importance of Wignell to the company at that time, and the high estimation in which he stood with the public.

He proceeded thus. "This was the first idea I had of Hallam's duplicity, and I immediately saw my situation. I represented to the meeting the promise given to me, and the arrangements I had made in consequence of that promise. I repeated the threat of Mr. Henry to destroy me, and the mode in which I understood he intended to accomplish it, by bringing out an actor to supersede me in my business, which, by keeping me out of the management, he could effect, as by casting new plays, he could bring a new performer into public favour, and thereby ruin me in my profession. I therefore demanded either to be made a joint partner, purchasing at their own price, and without asking credit, or to be appointed the company's agent. Both demands were positively refused by the two managers, and the meeting of sharers broke up without electing their agent."

The next day another meeting was called, "which," said Wignell, "as I knew all had been previously determined, I declined to attend." Wignell resigned his situation in the company; Henry was appointed the agent, and soon after embarked.

The plan of a new theatre in Philadelphia, probably long contemplated by many, was now matured without loss of time. Mr. Reinagle, a professor of music, entered into partnership with Wignell. Their friends furnished such additional funds as were necessary. The site of the present theatre in Chestnut-street, not then as now in the centre of the city, was purchased before the opponents of theatrical establishments knew for what purpose it was to be used, and while an elegant theatre was building, Wignell followed Henry to England with power and inclination to engage such a company and such additional aids as would overwhelm his long-time enemy, Henry, and his ex-friend and cousin, Hallam.

A man by the name of Anderson was associated with Wignell and Reinagle in this scheme, and afterwards acted as their treasurer. He was the financier. He was, as were the managers, from Britain, and was a shrewd man of business. While preparations were making in Philadelphia for the reception of the new company, Wignell was successfully employed in securing all the adventurers of talent that could render his corps effective.

The rival managers were both men of insinuating manners, both experienced in theatrical affairs and theatrical manœuvrers, and equally animated by the desire of success and the desire of inflicting injury.

Wignell engaged and safely landed in America a company more complete and more replete with every species of talent for the establishment of a theatre than could have been contemplated by the most sanguine of his friends. Every thing was to be splendid, every thing was to be new, with the exception of himself and Mr. and Mrs. Morris, the only sharers who had seceded with him.

Fennell, Chalmers, Moreton, Marshall, Harwood, Whitlock, Green, Darley and son, Francis, Bates, Blissett, Warrell, Mrs. Whitlock, Mrs. Oldmixon, Mrs. Francis, Mrs. Marshall, Miss Broadhurst, Mrs. Warrell, Miss Willems (afterwards Mrs. Green), Miss Oldfield, and others of less note, joined to Wignell and Mr. and Mrs. Morris, composed a force that defied opposition. Besides, they had a splendid new theatre, larger and incomparably better than had been seen before in the New World, and every thing appeared to ensure the triumph of Wignell, notwithstanding that Henry had anticipated him by arriving with a strong reinforcement to the old American Company, and by taking the field in Philadelphia before him.

But another, an unexpected and more deadly enemy, had likewise taken the field. An enemy that mocked at their painted banners and gilded truncheons, and put to flight their quips and quirks and wreathed smiles. Death, in the loathsome form of yellow fever, had established himself in the beautiful city of Philadelphia, in the citadel which had been prepared for the reception of Mirth and her attendants. This plague had rendered that place a scene of mourning and desolation, in which the inhabitants had prepared to erect the standard of taste and pleasure.

All the usual occupations of life had ceased, and the streets were deserted. Bush hill and Potter's Field, the Hospital and the burying-ground were alone populous.

Although Bush hill is now the seat of business and pleasure, and Potter's Field metamorphosed into one of the most elegant squares of this elegant metropolis, there remain too many monuments of that season of pestilence to need an additional one here. Yellow fever is marked on every record of that day, and Charles Brockden Brown, like another De Foe, has painted the truth of these scenes in the pages of fiction.

Wignell and Reinagle distributed their forces in the states of Delaware and New-Jersey, quartering them as they could, in farm-houses or taverns, and anxiously awaiting the return of health to the afflicted city. But in the mean time opened the old theatre in Annapolis, which ancient metropolis of Maryland was destined not only to have the first temple to the Muses built within its precincts, the first to have plays acted within its walls by any professional histrionics, a part of the company of William Hallam, but the first to see the efforts and skill of the best and most powerful company that had ever been assembled in this country. Wignell then opened the Baltimore theatre with his very fine *corps,* and employed them in that place until the restored health of Philadelphia enabled him to take possession of his head-quarters.

We have said that Henry anticipated the arrival of Wignell on his return to America. He had been active in his recruiting service and prosperous in his voyages. He had visited the provincial theatres of England, engaged efficient performers, and returned to New-York long before Wignell's company arrived or his new theatre in Philadelphia was ready.

As early as September, 1792, Henry and his recruits arrived at New-York, and immediately proceeded to join Hallam in Philadelphia, who was prepared to open the old theatre in Southwark. Their first play was the West Indian, in which Henry's O'Flaherty could only be surpassed by the original, Moody, or his successor, Johnstone. Hodgkinson, so long the admiration of the frequenters of the theatre, made his first appearance before an American audience on this occasion in the character of Belcour.

After a very successful season in the old theatre, Philadelphia, Hallam and Henry opened the theatre, John-street, New-York, on the 28th of January, 1793, with Reynold's new comedy of The Dramatist, and the musical farce of The Padlock.

The reinforcement brought from England by Henry, consisted of Hodgkinson, King, West, Prigmore, West, jun., Robins, Mrs. Hodgkinson, and Miss Brett (afterwards Mrs. King). If we remember that the whole of the old company, except Wignell, Morris, and Mrs. Morris, were still united with Hallam and Henry and their wives (for Hallam had married Miss Tuke), it will be seen that the corps was numerous, and those who remember the principals, know that it was strong in professional art. But insubordination and discord, jealousy and rivalry were mixed in even an uncommon degree with the body thus brought together. Hallam, who had fatally for himself and Henry, joined the latter by deserting Wignell, now adhered to his old diabolical maxim of divide and govern, notwithstanding he had found it easier to do the first than the last. There was a cause of discord in the jealousy with which the old members of the company, now feeling as Americans, viewed the new-comers, who on their part considered the Americans as inferiors, a thing of course with all Europeans, the well-informed excepted; and these actors were very far from being well-informed except in affairs of the stage and green-room. The old members of the company, treated as inferiors by the recruits, stood on the defensive, but had no bond of union. Besides this general cause of discord there were the usual conflicting claims of the individuals, which were soon perceivable by those not behind the curtain.

Even on the first night of exhibition, Hallam had to come forward before the play began and beg permission for Mr. Henry to read the part of "Lord Scratch," as Mr. Prigmore, who was announced for it, positively refused to appear. Henry accordingly read the part, and Prigmore the next day published an insolent tirade in which he talked of men who,

> "Dress'd in a little brief authority,
> Play such fantastic tricks before high heaven
> As make the angels weep."

Considering the person and occasion, this beautiful passage was probably never more misapplied. The conduct of this weak and ignorant man can only be accounted for by supposing that he had assurance of support from the new corps.

As Henry's recruits came before the public both of Philadelphia and New-York in advance of Wignell's company, they must take precedence of them in this record. And first John Hodgkinson.

Hodgkinson arrived in America on the 6th of September, 1792, at the age of twenty-six, having already passed through more scenes in real life, and played more parts in the mimic life of the stage, than most men even in his profession of changing scenes and varying characters are cast into during a life of protracted existence.

Believing as we do that the stage might be made subservient to the moral improvement of man, and that its productions in very many instances have enlightened the mind and improved the heart, we shall not conceal the important truth that those persons who have made acting the business of their lives have been in an uncommon degree the slaves of their passions. The causes and the remedy we have mentioned and must mention again. In most works dedicated to the history of the stage, or the biographies of actors, there is a gloss attempted, a false and glittering view of the subject presented to the reader calculated to do much mischief. The life of an actor is in many instances represented as a life of pleasure, how falsely hundreds could testify. It is a profession of toil and trouble, exposed to mortifications on one hand and temptations in an uncommon degree on the other. Many rise superior to both; those who fall become the inflictors of misery, and are repaid in bitterness with a tenfold portion of wretchedness. This is not alone the portion of the actor; it belongs to human nature: but until the profession is honoured by its professors and by society, the actor is exposed to this lot more than most men.

In this work we shall have occasion to mention many of both sexes who have been ornaments to their profession, and would have conferred honour on any society; but we shall not varnish the faults or cast a veil over the follies of those who have from any cause degraded a profession in itself as useful as it is liberal. The stage professes to show vice and folly their deformities as in a mirror. The historian of the stage is bound to do the same, and is as responsible to mankind for the truth and impartiality of his statements as the historian of the state. Nor can the actor claim indulgence from the historian more than any other public man or artist. He that places himself conspicuously before the world becomes accountable to the world for his actions, and must abide the judgment of those whose gaze he has attracted. He is responsible to society, as he is to his Creator, in proportion to the talents intrusted to him. The greater those talents, the greater is his power for good or ill; the more beneficial or destructive his example. The faults of a man in private life may be veiled, but the man who thrusts himself forward, and when made an object for the world to admire, then defies the maxims of morality and the decencies of life, can only be made to atone to society by exposure to infamy, and by the detail of those miseries, those inevitable miseries which his conduct entails upon himself and others. All he can ask is, "Nothing extenuate nor set down aught in malice."

The real name of Mr. Hodgkinson was Meadowcraft. He received from the care of his parents, who kept a small ale-house in Manchester, more education or schooling than usually falls to the lot of the common or lower classes of people in England. He was taught reading, writing, and ciphering, and made his debut in the drama of life as a pot-boy. In this situation he contrived to obtain some knowledge of fiddling; his ear was good and his voice melodious. Fiddling and singing were additional attractions to the ale-house. But it appears that his parents had too just notions of their duty to continue John in this dangerous situation; they removed him, perhaps too late, to the house of a manufacturer, and bound him as an apprentice.

There are very few inhabitants of towns but may remember some childish association for performing plays. To such a one this boy owed his first knowledge of that branch of literature, and it may be said that it was the only branch of which he obtained any knowledge. To say that Hodgkinson was a member of a troop of urchins for acting, is, to those who knew him, to say that he was the leader. Idleness, neglect of his master's business, and the deceit consequent upon all clandestine practices, were unfortunately the fruits of his boyish attempts at acting, and of the superiority his fiddling and singing gave him over his companions. This, of course, could not last, and at the age of fourteen, or between fourteen and fifteen, he ran away from his indentures, his master, and his mother (his father was dead), changed his name from Meadowcraft to Hodgkinson, and commenced a life of adventure, a life which teaches a knowledge of the worst portion of our species, gives unrestrained play to the passions, and while it sharpens the intellect, obscures the natural sense of moral propriety.

Such was the commencement of this man's life. Let it not be supposed that we record it as a stigma. On the contrary, we consider it as an excuse for many aberrations; and his having attained a high standing in a very difficult profession, from such a beginning, is a proof of natural endowments and talents of no common kind.

Hodgkinson used to say, that his principal dependence for the success of his scheme of elopement rested upon his knowledge of tunes and songs, which encouraged the hope of being received by some company of players. He had a crown in his pocket, which had been given to him by a traveller, who was pleased with his singing, when on a visit at his mother's ale-house.

He took the road to Bristol, and contrived, by joining a wagoner on the way, to reach an inn in that city, and gain admittance, while yet in the possession of the greater part of his fortune. An opportunity soon presented, to one of his enterprising disposition, for offering himself as a candidate to Mr. Keasbury, the manager of the Bristol theatre, for the honours and emoluments of the stage. "What can you do, my boy?" "I can sing, sir, and play on the fiddle—and I can snuff the candles." Keasbury was pleased with the boy's appearance—and surprised, on trial, at his musical powers. He was retained; and gladly, for the sake of gaining admittance within a theatre, agreed to do any thing, until he could be made of service on the stage. Mr. Keasbury seems never to have thought of doing justice to the boy, his master, or his parent, by sending him back to the house he had eloped from.

The first attempt of Hodgkinson to speak in public was something like that we have recorded of Hallam. To use his own expression, he "did not know whether he stood on his head or his heels," and the message he was intrusted with was probably not heard, certainly not understood, by the audience. He soon became useful, and by speaking a few lines now and then, singing in choruses, marching in processions, and snuffing candles, laid the foundation of his future theatrical fortunes. He was not singular in this. Many very excellent actors have had similar beginnings. The material was in him. It is ever a proof of superior powers, or superior virtue, to conquer difficulties, and from the lower of viler stations appendant on a profession, to arrive at the higher grades of the profession itself.

Most players have had provincial theatres or strolling companies for their schools; but we think it will be found that only those who have had a good, or at least a tolerably good early education, have arrived at the first rank in their profession. Not to go further back in theatrical history, Garrick, Henderson, Kemble, Siddons, Cooke, Merry, Cooper, Harwood, and other eminent performers, male and female, may be brought in proof. The attainments of Hodgkinson all partook of the imperfections of the provincial school, and were all limited by the deficiency of education and habits acquired from the associates of early life. His unbounded ambition, great physical powers, and youthful spirits carried him through every theatrical achievement with eclat. He was ready to attempt any thing, was always above mediocrity, and sometimes attained to excellence, though never in the highest department of the drama. His low comedy was his true excellence. In that he had gained his highest reputation before leaving England; but he played every thing from Harlequin to clown, from the fine gentleman of Congreve, or the Vapid of Reynolds, to the boor, the tinker, the cobbler, or the shelty, from the king to the foot-boy—his ambition made him ready to swallow any thing that might keep him before an audience—like Bottom, in the Midsummer's Night, he wished to play Pyramus and Thisbe, Wall, Moonshine, and Lion.

It is not our wish to follow this extraordinary man through the provincial theatres of England, in which he gained that skill which we witnessed in America. His power to please increased yearly, while going the rounds of Bristol, Liverpool, Manchester, and other theatrical towns, and he became the favourite actor in comedies, operas, and farces. His eulogist, Carpenter, in "The Mirror of Taste," says, "Co-ordinate with the rise of his fame and fortune, was the growth of the evils which were fated to endanger the one, and make shipwreck of the other; and his professional success and his gallantries, running parallel to each other, like the two wheels of a gig, left their marks on every road he travelled."

We may continue his friend's figure, by saying, that while the traces of one wheel were erased as soon as made by the next theatrical gig that followed him, the other, like the wheel of the car which bears the Hindoo idol, crushed the hapless victims who were fascinated by the rider, and left its traces permanently marked by ruin, anguish, and death. While he, apparently as insensible as the triumphant Juggernaut, passed on to immolate another and another.

Munden, afterward so celebrated in London, was then joint manager with Whitlock, in what is called the circuit of the northern towns in England. In their company, Hodgkinson rose to provincial celebrity; but being engaged for the Bath theatre, which was esteemed the next in rank to the London, left Munden, of whose family he was an inmate, carrying with him the mother of his children, and his nominal wife. At Bath they were Mr. and Mrs. Hodgkinson. At Bath, Henry engaged Hodgkinson for America, and with him another Mrs. Hodgkinson, whom he found as Miss Brett of the Bath theatre.

In person, Hodgkinson was five feet ten inches in height, but even at the period we speak of, at the age of twenty-six, he was too fleshy to appear tall, and in a few years became corpulent. He was strongly and well formed in the neck, shoulders, chest, and arms, but clumsily in the lower limbs, with thick ankles, and knees slightly inclining inward. His face was round, his nose broad and not prominent, his eyes gray, and of unequal sizes, but with large pupils and dark eyelashes. By some accident in early youth, one eye had been injured, as we have had occasion to mention in respect to one of Hallam's, and was smaller than the other, but this was not perceptible on the stage when he played in serious parts, and in the comic, added archness to the expression of his face. His complexion was white and almost colourless, and his hair dark brown. On the stage, paint is a part of costume; and at the time of which we write, powder was indispensable as a covering for the hair, on or off the stage, for those who played modern gentlemen, and theatrical heroes of antiquity had the resource of Brutus wigs of any colour.

This physiognomy was capable of varied expression, and with the unbounded animal spirits of the possessor, and skill in the stage toilette, Hodgkinson passed for handsome, and undoubtedly had the power of expressing every thing but the delicate or the sublime. He had great physical strength, and a memory capable of receiving and retaining the words of an author to an extent that was truly astonishing. What is called, in the technical language of the theatre, "a length," is forty lines. A *part* in a play is calculated by the number of *lengths*, and twenty is a long part. Hodgkinson would read over a new part of twenty lengths, and lay it aside until the night before he was to play it, attending the rehearsals meantime, then sit up pretty late to *study* it, as it is called, and the next morning, at rehearsal, repeat every word and prompt others. His ambi-

tion for play-house applause was inordinate, and he was as rapacious for characters as Bonaparte has since been for kingdoms.

Not content to be an actor, he would, in despite of every thing, be a poet and
author. As may be inferred from his want of education and course of life, his
ignorance of all beyond theatrical limits was profound. He did not know who
was the author of High Life below Stairs at the time he played the principal
character in the piece. And at a time when he was the delight of the town, the
companion of most of our wits, and the soul of our musical societies, he, having made out a *bill* for *poetical recitations,* was sportively asked by Judge Cozine,
"Who is that *anon* you have got in the bill among the poets?" and to the judge's
astonishment, he answered in serious earnest and with an air of one showing
his reading, "Oh, sir, he is one of our first poets."

As an actor he deserved great praise, and was at that time the delight of the New-
York audiences. From Jaffier to Dionysius, from Vapid to Shelty, he was the favourite, and was received with unbounded applause. His ear for music was good. He
had cultivated the art. He sung both serious and comic songs. From the Haunted
Tower to the Highland Reel, no one pleased so much as Hodgkinson. He had
played in the secondary theatres of England with Cooke and Mrs. Siddons in tragedy, and in comedy with Lewis and Munden, Miss Farren and Mrs. Wells. Such
was the man and the actor brought from England by John Henry to supplant
Wignell in the favour of the public. But the poisoned chalice was destined for his
own lips, and those of Hallam. All those characters which had been long considered as the property of himself and partner were usurped by the new-comer, and
the two kings were not long left in possession of the throne they had refused to
share with Thomas Wignell. Such are the decrees of "even-handed justice."

Among the recruits, Mrs. Hodgkinson was only second to her husband in
consequence. She had been born to and educated for the stage. She was the
daughter of Brett, a singer at Covent Garden and the Haymarket. The first time
the writer saw her was in 1784, at the Haymarket theatre, London, as the page
in the opera of the Noble Peasant. Hodgkinson became acquainted with her at
Bath, and brought her to New-York, where they were married by Bishop Moore.
She was an amiable woman and a good wife. As an actress in girls and romps
she was truly excellent. In high comedy she was far above mediocrity, and even
in tragedy she possessed much merit. In Ophelia she was touching in a powerful degree, as her singing gave her advantages in this character which tragic actresses do not usually possess. Her forte was opera. From her father she had
derived instructions; and her husband's practice on the violin continued to
improve her in knowledge in this branch of her profession. Her voice, both in
speaking and singing, was powerful and sweet.

Mrs. Hodgkinson was very fair, with blue eyes, and yellow hair approaching to the flaxen. Her nose was prominent or Roman; her visage oval, and rather long for her stature, which was below the middling. Her general carriage on the stage was suited to the character she performed; and in romps, full of archness, playfulness, and girlish simplicity. As a general actress, she was as valuable in female as her husband was in male characters.

The person next in importance to the Hodgkinsons among the new-comers was King. He was uncommonly handsome, but had not the skill that might entitle him to the rank of an artist. He could do nothing but as instructed by Hodgkinson. Sometimes his tall manly person, and fine face, under tuition and drilling, had an effect that might be called imposing. But he was dissipated and negligent of every duty.

Prigmore was a buffoon. He became the comic old man of the company, and with grimace, antiquated wigs, painted wrinkles and nose, became a favourite for a time of the gods and the groundlings—of those whose praise is censure. We have mentioned his refusal to play the part of *Lord Scratch*, in Reynold's first comedy, on the night that the theatre opened. It will give some notion of theatrical life and theatrical management to show the standing of this man in his own country among actors before his emigration. Bernard, who we shall have occasion to mention hereafter, gives, in his reminiscences, this anecdote and character of Prigmore. He says he was

> "a man of some vanity and little merit, whose opinion of himself was in inverse proportion to that of the public. One of the peculiarities of this person was to suppose (though he was neither handsome nor insinuating), that every woman whom he saw, through a mysterious fatality, fell in love with him. There was a very benevolent widow living in Plymouth, in respectable circumstances, who frequently came to the theatre, and was kind enough to inquire into the private situation of various members of the company. Among others she asked about Prigmore, and was told that he had but a small salary, and made a very poor appearance. Hearing this, she remembered that she had a pair of her late husband's indispensables in the house, which she resolved to offer to him. A servant was accordingly despatched to the object of her charity, who, meeting one of the actors, and partly disclosing his business, he went in search of Prigmore, and finding him, exclaimed, 'Prigmore, my boy, here's your fortune made at last; here's a rich widow has fallen in love with you, and wants to see you.' Prigmore, not suspecting his roguery, was led to the servant in a state of bewildered rapture, and by the latter was informed that the widow would be glad to see him any morning it was convenient. He appointed the following, and went home to his lodgings to indulge in a day-dream of golden independence. His friend (theatrical friend) in the meantime whispered the truth through the green-room, where there were two or three wicked enough to join in the conspiracy by walking to

Prigmore's house to tender their congratulations: Prigmore, as may be supposed, passed a sleepless night, and spent an extra hour at his toilette next
morning in adorning himself with a clean shirt and neckcloth. He then sal-
lied forth, and on reaching the widow's, was shown into her parlour, where,
casting his eyes around on the substantial sufficiency of the furniture, he
began to felicitate himself on the aspect of his future home.

"The lady at length appeared; she was upon the verge of forty, a very fashionable age at that time, which, resting upon the shoulders of a very comely-
looking woman, seemed to be in character with her comfortable dwelling.
Prigmore's satisfaction and her benevolence operated equally in producing
some confusion: at length a conversation commenced. She acquainted him
that she had heard his situation was not as agreeable as he could wish—that
his income was a confined one; she was, therefore, desirous to do him all the
service that lay in her power. Prigmore, considering this as an express declaration of her affection, was about to throw himself at her feet, when she suddenly summoned her servant, and exclaimed, 'Rachel, bring the breeches!'

"These words astounded him. The widow, on receiving the habiliments,
folded them carefully, and remarking that they were 'as good as new,' begged
his acceptance of them.

"'And was it for this you wanted me, madam?' 'Yes, sir.' He put on his hat
and walked to the door with indignation. The good woman, as much astonished as himself, followed him with 'won't you take the breeches, sir?' He
replied, pausing at the door to make some bitter retort, 'wear them yourself.'"

Such a man would not be worthy of the space he here occupies except as his
character and insignificance at home comports finely with his assumed importance after he had crossed the Atlantic. No uncommon thing.

West, known as the leather breeches beau (dandy was then unknown), was
imported as the singer and "walking-gentleman" of the company.

Robins was to be scene painter, occasionally sing a song, and join in the choruses.

West, jun., was literally nothing, and Miss Brett (afterwards Mrs. King) was
his equal; but as Mrs. Hodgkinson's sister, she was thrust before the public by
Hodgkinson's influence; she afterwards married King, and he dying in consequence of excessive dissipation, she married a German doctor on Long Island,
and made a notable housewife. Happier than her more talented sisters.

Those who now see actors moving in society like other men, at least in appearance, dressed as others dress, having the same fashions, manners, and behaviour
as their fellow-citizens, and not to be distinguished from them by the outside,
can hardly conceive the difference which then existed between these recruits to
the American Company and the townsfolk in all these particulars. Long after
others wore their hair short and of nature's colour, Hodgkinson had powdered

curls at each side, and long braided hair twisted into a club or knot behind! Instead of pantaloons and boots, breeches and stockings and shoes. This costume, with his hat on one side, and an air and manner then known by the appellation of theatrical, marked him among thousands. King displayed his fine person in another, but equally marked manner. West usually appeared in boots and leather breeches, always new, and three gold laced button-holes on each side of the high, upright collar of a scarlet coat. While Robins, a very tall and large-framed young man, in addition to the gold laced collar, wore three gold hat-bands.

West soon involved himself in debt, and being arrested by the breeches-maker for six pair of leather breeches, sent to Mr. Gaine, who still printed the play-bills, though no longer at the Bible and Crown, but only at the Bible, to request bail, as the prisoner's name was in the bill for that night.

The old gentleman took off his spectacles and exclaimed, "Six pair of leather breeches! Why I never had one pair in my life! Six pair! Why how many *legs* has the fellow got?"

⇥ CHAPTER 9 ⇤

The Miser's Wedding — Discord — Arbitration — Mrs. Hatton — Mrs. Melmoth — Twenty-fifth of November, 1793 — Mrs. Long — Mr. Crosby — Tammany — Ciceri — Mrs. Pownall — Mrs. Wilson — Mr. and Mrs. Henry's last appearance — He sells out to Hodgkinson and dies — Mrs. Henry's death — Tragedy of Lord Leicester — Literary Clubs.

On the 27th of March, 1793, The Fashionable Lover and No Song No Supper were performed in the New-York theatre for the benefit of the widows and orphans of a number of persons who were lost in a violent storm.

During the benefits, and in the hottest weather, though early in June, a comedy called "The Miser's Wedding," written by the author of The Father of an Only Child, was played without study or rehearsal, and in opposition to Henry, by the influence of Hodgkinson, who brought it out for the benefit of his wife's sister, Miss Brett. The character intended for Henry was refused by him, very properly under the circumstances, and accepted in opposition by Hallam. The piece was murdered—(it deserved death)—and never heard of more.

Hallam and Henry, after closing their theatre in John-street, on the 14th of June, led their company, flushed with success, to Philadelphia, to reap a second harvest in that city, before the arrival of Wignell and his troop. But this campaign with the new forces was soon ended, and the generals retreated before that enemy which, as we have said, met Wignell at his return—yellow fever.

The theatre in John-street was again opened on November 11th, 1793, the proceeds of the evening being for the benefit of the sufferers from the pestilence in Philadelphia.

Discord was now raging among the leaders of the mimic world. Henry had found himself opposed and thwarted by Hodgkinson from the first, and as the *latter* gained popularity, the former found his situation becoming worse. Hallam, upon his old Machiavelian policy of divide and govern, blew the coals, and sided with Hodgkinson against Henry. The first ostensible cause of quarrel was Henry not fulfilling engagements made with Hodgkinson and wife, respecting *parts, benefits,* &c., and in addition, a charge of neglect and inhumanity when Hodgkinson was sick, after flying from the yellow fever of Philadelphia. Inhumanity was a favourite word with Hodgkinson. The affair was submitted to arbitrators, who met Hallam and Henry, and Hodgkinson. Hallam sided with Hodgkinson. Henry admitted without making defence, except by a general denial of the positive assertions of his opponent; but he appeared literally overwhelmed by the audacious and unqualified assertions of the accuser, and by the evident treachery of his partner. The parties supped together, and the arbitrators declared in writing, that the charge of inhumanity was unfounded, but as by agreement Hodgkinson was to have two benefits in Philadelphia, which the calamity of the city had prevented, Hallam and Henry should compensate him by paying the average profits of two nights of the present season to him, the expenses per night being estimated at two hundred dollars. The arbitrators recommended that such harmony might thereafter exist between the parties, as might "have a tendency to make a profession *in itself* most respectable, respectable in the eyes of mankind."

About this time one of the Kemble family arrived in New-York, a sister of Mrs. Siddons, John Kemble, Mrs. Whitlock, Charles Kemble, Stephen Kemble, and the other children of that highly talented family. This person was called Mrs. Hatton, and had a husband with her, a vulgar man. She introduced herself to the American world by writing a play called Tammany, which she presented to the Tammany Society, who patronised it, and recommended it to the theatre through Hodgkinson, whose favour the authoress had secured. The managers would not have dared to reject any thing from the Sons of St. Tammany, and gladly received this production of the sister of Mrs. Siddons, seasoned high with spices hot from Paris, and swelling with rhodomontade for the sonorous voice of Hodgkinson, who was to represent the Indian saint. He did afterward represent him, as we shall see, and very much resembled the sons of the saint, who received the Cherokee, Choctaw, and other chiefs, when they marched from the East river where they landed, up Wall-street to the old Federal Hall, to be presented to the president and Congress of the United States. How these sons of the forest must have despised the sorry imitators of barbarism, who followed in their train with painted cheeks, rings in their noses, and bladders smeared with red ochre drawn over their powdered locks. Hodgkinson's Tammany dress was not so barbarous, for the actor took care not to excite disgust or laughter.

Another person of more consequence in the theatrical world appeared in New-York at this time, and finding a cold reception from the managers, threw herself into the train and under the protection of Hodgkinson. This was Mrs. Melmoth. Henry considered his wife as the only representative of Melpomene needed in the New-York theatre, and received Mrs. Melmoth coldly. Mrs. Hodgkinson did not yet play tragedy, and Hodgkinson wished to *patronise* any one in opposition to Henry. Hallam looked on. The public were told of Mrs. Melmoth's merits, and it was easy to create a call for her. This was irresistible; she appeared, and Mrs. Henry as a tragedian disappeared.

Mrs. Melmoth had been carried off from a boarding-school, when young, by Pratt, known as an author under the name of Courtney Melmoth. They both went on the stage, and played in several companies both in England and Ireland. They at length separated, and she continued to bear his assumed name. In 1782 she was a member of the Cork company, said to be at the time the best out of London. Miss Younge, afterwards Mrs. Pope, one of the best actresses of the English stage in either tragedy or comedy, and Miss Phillips, afterwards Mrs. Crouch, one of the best singers, and at that time, perhaps, the most beautiful girl in England or Ireland, made part of the company. Mrs. Melmoth must have been a remarkably handsome woman at the above-mentioned period. Bernard says, in his amusing reminiscences, that she "went out to America, where she purchased a plantation." Mrs. Melmoth prudently saved enough to purchase a small house on Long Island, between Brooklyn and Fort Swift, with land enough to keep some cows, whose milk contributed to supply the New-York market. This *trade,* and a few scholars as boarders at the seminary she for some time kept at the same place, occupied her latter years profitably. She was Irish by birth, a Roman Catholic by religion, and died in the bosom of the mother church.

On the 20th of November, 1793, Mrs. Melmoth appeared for the first time on the American stage. The character she had chosen was Euphrasia, in Murphy's tragedy of The Grecian Daughter. She was the best tragic actress the inhabitants of New-York, then living, had ever seen; unless it were those who had travelled, and they were at that time few. Mrs. Melmoth had played in Dublin and in Edinburgh with distinguished success. She had played in London without being distinguished. She was now past her prime, her face still handsome, her figure commanding, but not a little too large. Her dimensions were far beyond the sphere of embonpoint, and when Euphrasia invites Dionysius to strike her instead of her emaciated father, crying, "Strike here, here's blood enough!" an involuntary laugh from the audience had nearly destroyed, not only all illusion, but the hopes of the actress. Her merit, however, carried her through with great applause, and she long remained a favourite. By degrees, she relinquished the youthful heroines, and in the matrons she was unexceptionable, unless that she had rather too much of the Mrs. Overdone, and from a natural deficiency of the organs of speech, could not give utterance to that letter which her country-men generally sound double—the letter "R." She often repeated the Grecian Daughter at this period, but never repeated "here's blood enough!"

Ten years had now passed since we had witnessed the embarkation of the no longer hostile British troops, and the slow and dispirited retreat of the fleets of England, reluctantly turning their prows from the beautiful harbour they had entered in triumph. It was the tenth twenty-fifth of November on which the inhabitants of New-York had celebrated the day of the departure of their invad-ers, and the return of their exiles. The day was devoted, as usual, to rejoicing. The guns from the batteries were echoed by the ships of war of the French re-public visiting the harbour; and Citizen Genet, the first ambassador from re-publican France, waiting on the governor, the same who had guided the state through the scenes of war, delivered an address, in which we remember this passage: "The same all powerful arm which delivered your country from tyr-anny is now manifesting itself as the protector of the French people." That same evening the Grecian Daughter was repeated. We had joined in the enthusiasm of the day, we had witnessed the scene at the governor's house in Pearl-street, we now witnessed the scenes at the theatre in John-street, the most impressive of which were *before* the curtain.

One of the side boxes was filled by French officers from the ships of war in the harbour. The opposite box was filled with American officers. All were in their uniforms as dressed for the rejoicing day. French officers and soldier-sailors (we find the expression in a note made at the time), and many of the New-York militia, artillery, infantry, and dragoons, mingled with the crowd in the pit. The house was early filled. As soon as the musicians appeared in the orchestra, there was a general call for "*ça ira.*" The band struck up. The French in the pit joined first, and then the whole audience. Next followed the Marseillois Hymn. The audience stood up. The French took off their hats and sung in a full and sol-emn chorus. The Americans applauded by gestures and clapping of hands. We can yet recall the figure and voice of one Frenchman, who, standing on a bench in the pit, sung this solemn patriotic song with a clear loud voice, while his fine manly frame seemed to swell with the enthusiasm of the moment. The hymn ended, shouts of "Vivent les Français," "Vivent les Americains," were reiterat-ed until the curtain drew up, and all was silent.

When the Grecian Daughter saves her father, and strikes the tyrant to the earth, the applause usually bestowed on this catastrophe was drowned by the enthusiastic shouts of the excited spectators. Before or since we have never witnessed or felt such enthusiasm. Surely the theatre is a powerful engine—for evil or for good.

In a preceding chapter of this work, will be found the name of Miss Cheer as a principal actress in the American Company before the revolution. She now made her appearance as Mrs. Long, in The Jealous Wife of the elder Colman. Time had deprived the lady of all that can attract the spectator's attention to the moving pictures of the stage, and unless that attraction exists, the imagination cannot be enlisted in the service of the actor or author. Mrs. Long was received in silence by the audience, and never heard of more. Miss Cheer made her first appearance on the first opening of the theatre in John-street, in 1767.

On the 28th of December, Sir Richard Crosby made his appearance in the character of Barbarossa. He was announced as Mr. Richards, but after some time resumed his name of Crosby, dropping the distinguishing mark of his nobility. He was by birth and education a gentleman, and *spoke his parts* with propriety, but his face was of that species called pudding, and his person literally gigantic, without any of those swelling contours which render the Hercules Farnese so admirable. The contours of Crosby were all misplaced, and might remind a spectator of Foote's description of a nobleman of his day—"he looks like a grayhound that has the dropsy."

Crosby was some inches in height over six feet, and like many men who are conscious of being too tall, he sunk instead of elevating his head, and the stride of the tyrant was reduced to a gait between a trot and a pace. That with all this against him he should remain on the stage, and be tolerated, is one of the proofs of the triumphs of mind over matter. He was not likely to rival either of the managers, or the managers' manager, and he was supported behind the curtain and in the journals of the day.

This gentleman was an Irishman; he dissipated a fortune among the claret drinkers of the land of hospitality, had built a balloon, ascended in it, and like the ambitious high-flying Greek, had fallen into the sea. Sir Richard Crosby had been picked up by some fishing boats in the Irish channel, and preserved to fall, alien to his *caste*, a poor actor on the stage of the old American Company.

At about this date (December, 1793), the author of the comedy of The Father of an Only Child finished a tragedy, which was read aloud by Hodgkinson to his companions, of whom at that time he had many from among our literary citizens. The tragedy was applauded, and destined for the reader's benefit. Hodgkinson as now at the height of his popularity. His salaries and his benefits for himself and wife gave him more money than he knew what to do with, and he, by advice of some of his friends, bought land in the interior—not long held. Popularity is intoxicating. The favourite actor was late in making his appearance one evening, and some one or two of the audience hissed. He demanded the cause with an air of authority. A writer in the Daily Advertiser of December 25th, 1793, in a letter to Hallam and Henry, says, "in a manner and in language which would have been highly resented in the country whence he came," Hodgkinson told a long story to the audience of the insolence of some drunkard in the street towards Mrs. Hodgkinson, and his beating the ruffian. All this the writer says was unnecessary: "we wanted not recounted the words and actions of the ruffian towards Mrs. H., nor a particular description of the lady's shrieks, &c. The path of an actor," continued he, "is extremely plain; let him study his author, and endeavour to attain the summit of his professional excellence, with a decorous respect to the taste and judgment of the public." The writer described the audience of New-York as forbearing, and "never much disposed to look severely into the private actions or characters of performers."

The writer above quoted proposed Hallam (without naming him) as a model for imitation. Hallam had now begun to feel the influence of Hodgkinson, cherished by him against Henry, as rather detrimental to himself.

On the 28th, a friend of Hodgkinson published a vindication of his conduct, and an appeal to the public, in which we will notice these words: "In private life his conduct has procured him a large and respectable circle of friends; his splendid talents, united with the politeness of his manners, renders him a welcome visiter in the first families of the city." His "refinement of mind" is likewise stated. Such are the records of the day. Politeness or refinement he had none. But at this time he had a large and respectable circle of friends, or rather admirers, attracted by his popularity on the stage and his convivial dinners and suppers. His visits were soon found unsuited to the families of citizens, and by degrees even the attraction of song and wine ceased to draw the respectable to his habitation.

On the 3d of March, the long-forthcoming opera of Tammany, from the pen of Mrs. Hatton, appeared. The Daily Advertiser called upon republicans to support this effort from a female, filled with "simple and virtuous sentiments." It is needless to say that the opera was "received with unbounded applause." The Daily Advertiser has a communication that places this drama among the highest efforts of genius. It was literally a melange of bombast. The following, extracted from the Daily Advertiser of the 7th of March, 1794, shows that all the visiters of the theatre were not blinded by the puffs of the time. "I am among the many who were diverted with the piece in your paper of yesterday, signed a citizen, particularly where it supposes that 'surprise' at the merits of the opera lately exhibited 'astonished' our literati into silence. Much credit is due to Messrs. Hallam and Henry for the pains they have taken in decorations, scenery, &c.; and I doubt not, 'a citizen' will, whenever Tammany is performed, hear the warm though juvenile exclamation, 'Oh what a beautiful sight.'" A more severe and well-written communication takes notice of the *ruse* made use of to collect an audience for the support of the piece by circulating a report that a party had been made up to hiss it; and goes on to describe the audience assembled as made up of "the poorer class of mechanics and clerks," and of bankrupts who ought to "be content with the mischief they had already done, and who might be much better employed than in disturbing a theatre."

The disturbance alluded to was an attack upon James Hewitt, the leader in the orchestra, for not being ready with a popular air when called upon.

Heretofore the scenic decorations of the American theatre had been lamentably poor. Henry had not brought out with his recruits any artist to paint his scenes. Those of the old stock were originally of the lowest grade, and had become black with age. At this time, Charles Ciceri painted the scenes for Tammany. They were gaudy and unnatural, but had a brilliancy of colouring, reds and yellows being abundant. Ciceri afterwards made himself a better painter, and proved himself an excellent machinist. He was a man of exemplary habits, active mind, quick discernment, fertile in resources, and firm in purpose. His temper was quick, and his imperfect knowledge of our language occasioned misunderstandings and jealousies in his career as a scene painter, in times we have not yet reached. His story, like that of many whose stories are never told, was a romance of real life. Born in Milan, he lost his father when he was seven years of age, and was sent to an uncle in Paris. The uncle was strict, and made him improve the opportunity of acquiring the rudiments of science. He was likewise taught a little landscape drawing. The boy, however, was headstrong, and the uncle probably severe. Ciceri several times eloped. On one occasion he ran away and took the road to Flanders. After many adventures, the boy found his life abroad was worse than at home, and begged his way back to Paris almost in a starving condition. As he approached the age of manhood, he became ungovernable, again left his uncle, and enlisted in a troop of horse. After serving three months, his friends purchased his discharge. At length, determined to get out of the reach of family control, he, when about 16 or 17 years of age, again eloped, enlisted in a regiment destined for St. Domingo, and as a soldier, passed some years at Cape François. Here he formed the determination of acquiring property for himself, and he obtained permission to work at such employment as could be obtained in the town. It was the usage for the soldiers to purchase permission to pursue civil avocations by paying a portion of their earnings to the officer. The manager of the theatre wanted a scene painter, and Ciceri made himself sufficiently master of the mode of managing colours in *size*, and with his little knowledge of landscape, and greater proficiency in mathematics, he became invaluable. At the end of six months, from commencing foot-soldier, he was in possession of money enough to procure his discharge, and freight a vessel for the United States, determined to make his fortune. In five years he had accumulated a little fortune. St. Domingo became unsafe, and he determined to revisit Europe. He went to Paris, and was employed as assistant scene painter. He visited Bordeaux, and found employment in the splendid theatre of that place. The reign of terror drove him to England, and he was engaged at the Opera-house in London. With increased property he embarked as a merchant for St. Domingo, taking Jamaica in his way from England, but finding it unsafe to visit his former place of residence at *the Cape,* he embarked with all his property for Philadelphia. He lost all but life, shipwrecked on the Bahamas, and after remaining 17 days on a desert island, he was carried to Providence by a fisherman. At Providence, he, being almost starving, was asked what he could do. He answered "paint." He was offered employment as a miniature painter, and as he had said he was a painter, and an Italian, no excuse would be taken. The scene painter procured a piece of ivory, and was paid for a portrait in miniature, though he never could draw a face that might not pass as well for an owl as a man. He made friends, found his way to Philadelphia, commenced scene painter again, in the new theatre then building in that city, under Milbourne, the company not having yet arrived. Hallam and Henry engaged him for the old play-house in Southwark, and when the yellow fever of 1793 broke out, he came in their service to New-York. The first knowledge the writer had of him was as the painter of the scenery of his play of Fontainville Abbey. His architectural scenery was always good. He was long a most valuable auxiliary to the *corps dramatique,* and a faithful friend to the writer, in whose service he acquired sufficient property to send a stock of merchandise, with a partner, to St. Domingo, where Ciceri lost the goods, and the partner his head. He persevered, and when his manager failed, commenced trader in French merchandise between New-York and Paris, finally retiring in competence to his native country, from whence he sent his friendly remembrances to one who had not provided so well for old age as he had done.

The visit of Henry for recruits, and of Wignell to organize and fill a regiment, seems to have conveyed the intelligence to the players of England that a continent existed over sea, called America, where some of the people were white, spoke English, and went to see plays. We have mentioned the visit of Mrs. Hatton, who kindly came to instruct us in the history of the country, the value of liberty, and the duties of the patriot, and that of Mrs. Melmoth, who, whatever were her motives, added to the rational pleasures of society by her skill as an actress; and about this time, an actress long celebrated in London in comedy and opera, as Mrs. Wrighten, made her appearance in New-York as Mrs. Pownall.

This actress was a formidable rival to Mrs. Hodgkinson. But the latter had youth on her side. The skill of the veteran will not always compensate for the charms which belong alone to the freshness of youth. Mrs. Pownall had not lost her powers of song or of acting, which were both very great. Had she been permitted by Hodgkinson to play Margaretta, in No Song no Supper, Mrs. Hodgkinson would not have played the part again. What is called chance was propitious to Mrs. Hodgkinson, for shortly after Mrs. Pownall made her debut, she broke her leg, and was for a long time incapable of exerting her talents. At length she appeared on crutches in a musical piece put together for the occasion, the plot of which there was none, furnished by Mrs. Hatton, and the dialogue (introducing an apology), and the songs, by Mrs. Pownall.

The farce of The Irish Widow was got up on the 12th of March, 1794, to introduce an actress of the name of Wilson, in the Widow Brady.

As marking the state of the public mind at this time, we notice a circumstance, otherwise insignificant: Hodgkinson, when he came on the stage for Captain Flash, in Miss in her Teens, dressed, as the part always is, in an English uniform, was hissed and called upon by the French party, who could not look at an English officer's coat without being in a rage, to "take it off." He came forward, and to the satisfaction of the French partisans, said, he represented a coward and a bully. Unfortunately, this was running on Charybdis to avoid Scylla, and the English partisans threatened vengeance on the actor. Always ready to speak or to write, Hodgkinson came out in the Daily Advertiser, and to satisfy all parties, professed to give the exact words of his "address" made on compulsion, as follows: "Sir—the character I am going to portray is a bully and a coward, and however you may choose to quarrel with a red-coat, you would probably be a great deal more offended had I improperly disgraced the uniform of this or any other country, by wearing it on the back of a poltroon." Here it is to be observed, he admits that to wear the uniform of any country on the back of such a character was to disgrace it, and *he had worn* an English uniform. He goes on to say, that he was placed before the audience to represent an English officer, and should have deserved reprobation if he had worn an American or French uniform. This statement, under the signature of Verax, only made matters worse with the actor's countrymen, and other adherents of Old England, and on the 13th of March, 1794, the following appeared in print. "The situation I was placed in on Saturday evening last, and the explanation I was compelled to enter into, having given an opportunity to some evil-minded person to grossly mistake my words, I beg, through the medium of your paper, to lay before that part of the public who have heard the fabrication, the true meaning of what I said—'However angry you may be at the sight of a red-coat, you would probably be more displeased, had I appeared in the uniform of this or any other country, usually worn on the stage, for a character that is a disgrace to his cloth, by being a bully and a poltroon.' This was my meaning, and so plain, that I thought to misrepresent it was

impossible; for I trust it will need no great argument to convince, that if I, who have constantly worn a British uniform for a British officer, had upon this occasion altered it, I might have expected that just resentment which pointed insult deserves. However, upon this, as every other occasion, I trust to the candour of my fellow-citizens at large, and leave the being, capable of an endeavour at injury, to the disappointment and malice of his own heart. I am, gentlemen, &c.
(Signed)   "JOHN HODGKINSON."

In the beginning of April, Henry, who had gained great credit in the character of Beverley, in The Gamester, made an effort to revive his popularity, and the play was performed, he and his wife playing the hero and heroine. But this was considered as injurious to the young tragedian, who would play all, and wished that Mrs. Melmoth should be the only tragic actress. The house was thin, and the public were told in the Daily Advertiser, that it was owing to the preoccupation of parts by incompetent persons, when others more capable were ready to fill them. This was Henry's last effort at resistance to the fate he had invited. He made overtures to Hodgkinson for a sale of his share in the theatrical partnership, which were eagerly met, and we find the next theatrical campaign opened under the firm of Hallam and Hodgkinson.

In a letter from John Hodgkinson to Lewis Hallam, dated Philadelphia, October 12th, 1803 (when Hodgkinson was endeavouring to obtain a commission of bankruptcy by the aid of Richard Morris of New-York, and Richard Potter of Philadelphia, and Hallam had made a claim of debt), a threat of exposing Hallam occurs, which throws light upon this transaction, and on the characters of both Hodgkinson and Hallam. It is in these words: "I wish to hold you again forward to the world, and without being *compelled* to show the world too much, or adverting to any cause that may have tended to produce a share of our present misery. Recollect, and *weigh this calmly,* that if I am obliged to give any further statement of our affairs, I *must* BEGIN them, and that beginning *must* run thus. In the year 1794, John Henry, weary of the trouble he met with from various sources in the management of the property at that time known and generally styled the old American Company, offered by his friend Hugh Smith, to sell to John Hodgkinson all his share of the said property, in all American theatres; and John Hodgkinson, wishing to purchase, *advised* with Lewis Hallam, who seemed anxious that said Hodgkinson *should* become a purchaser, but at the same time wished that *himself* might be a purchaser from Henry, and that Hodgkinson should *re*purchase from Hallam. This was done, and Hodkinson purchased from Hallam *such part as he conceived Hallam had purchased from Henry,* giving Hallam exactly the counterpart of the deeds Hallam had given Henry for the payment. It has since appeared, that Lewis Hallam, so far from selling John Hodgkinson the same proportion, only held at the period he purchased *two* shares out of *six,* or one-third of the property, and that John Henry sold Lewis Hallam three shares for $10,000—and this additional one share not only added to himself, but also saddled Hodgkinson with half of an annuity to Stephen Wools, which was paid by John Hodgkinson to said Wools to the hour of his death; and all this while John Hodgkinson had purchased under the idea that Hallam and Henry were equal holders and partners; nor was Hodgkinson made acquainted *till some years* after of the disadvantageous bargain he had made—though Hallam by this contract, supposing the shares to amount to $10,000 annually, would have received $5000 instead of $3333 33! Mark, dear sir, that I do not find fault with that *now,* or *arraign* it, but it is a solemn truth which I don't wish to be compelled to give to the assignees." This curious document is signed, "Yours sincerely, JOHN HODGKINSON."

From the stage of life, as well as the stage of the theatre, Henry and his family were at once swept. His daughter eloped, and soon after died. While on a voyage to Rhode Island, he died on board a small coasting vessel, and was buried without ceremony under the sand of an island in the sound. His wife, who was with him, it is supposed never recovered the shock, and died deprived of reason at Philadelphia, 25th April, 1795, after having had the dead body of her husband brought to her, from its first place of unceremonious interment.

We find a memorandum that the theatre was shut on the 12th of April, 1794, on account of Passion week, and reopened on the 21st for the benefits, which continued until the 28th of June, when the last season of the theatrical partnership of Hallam and Henry closed. During these benefits, the first American tragedy that was performed by professed players, was brought out for the benefit of Mr. Hodgkinson.

We have already mentioned that a tragedy by the author of "The Father of an Only Child," had been read to a literary company by Hodgkinson. It was first called "Leicester." It was now played, 24th of April, 1794, under the title of "The Fatal Deception, or the Progress of Guilt." It was afterward published under the title of "Lord Leicester."

The characters and cast stand thus:—

Henry Cecil,	Mr. Hodgkinson.
Dudley Cecil,	King.
Edred,	Richards.*
Leicester,	Hallam.
Howard,	Martin.
Elwina,	Mrs. Hodgkinson.
Matilda,	Melmoth.

* Sir Richard Crosby.

As the author had formerly written an interlude for Wignell when he was the favourite Darby, and called it "Darby's Return," so now he gave Hodgkinson, the delight of the public in Shelty, a piece called "Shelty's Travels." The house was overflowing—the applause was great—and the actor cleared above the expenses, which were $200, full $500. The play was forgotten after a few repetitions, but one line was often repeated by the author's friends, as a description of a youth driven from his parental home,

> "A barefoot pilgrim on a flinty world."

Nevertheless, as a tragedy, it is justly doomed to oblivion. Mrs. Hodgkinson on this occasion first played an important part in this branch of the drama, and evinced great powers. Hodgkinson, Mrs. Melmoth, and Mrs. Hodgkinson produced great effect in their respective characters: of the remainder of the performers, some were passable, while others were attended by all the imperfection of a first exhibition, united to the unavoidable hurry of a *benefit play.*—A few words on the subject of our literary men.

Of those giants in letters and politics who, from being dependent colonists of a country that despised them, raised an independent empire whose inhabitants to the latest ages will adore them, the Franklins, Jeffersons, Hopkinsons, Henrys, Adamses, Dickinsons, and their fellow-labourers, we shall not speak. They had created a vast republic, whose institutions were so dissimilar to those of Europe, that a new tone seemed necessary for that literature which was to form the education of the rising generations. To open the highways by which truth should approach all who desired her acquaintance, required the united labour of her friends. Bands of pioneers were formed, who aided each other in removing rubbish, and hewing down prejudices of stubborn texture from long growth, and mischievous from the veneration bestowed upon worthless old age.

The first pioneers in this patriotic path-making were, at the time we are now considering, many of them yet in existence. Others had arisen and were at work opening the way for the Coopers, Irvings, Pauldings, Bryants, Walshes, Hallocks, Channings, and the hundreds who are the pride or the hope of the present day. The dramatic author, whose tragedy has passed under our notice, was connected with the aspirants who resided in New-York. He was intimately associated with Elihu H. Smith, Charles Brockden Brown, James Kent, Edward Miller, Samuel L. Mitchill, Saml. Miller, Wm. Johnson, Wm. Coleman, John Wells, and others who have distinguished themselves in the regions of fancy and science. Filled with youthful ardour, and pleased with the applause of the public and the encouragement of his associates, he thought only of future triumphs; and tragedies and comedies, operas and farces, occupied his mind, his time, and his pen.

The young men above named, with Richard Alsop, Mason Cogswell, and The-odore Dwight, of Connecticut, formed a club—projected many literary works, and executed some. A magazine was supported for a short time—a review was published. Some of these gentlemen had previously been associated under the name of the Philological Society. Perhaps to this association, of which Noah Webster was a member, may be attributed those labours which have given to the world the most perfect English dictionary in existence. The youthful dra-matist owed much to such associates, and particularly to the brotherly bond which long subsisted between him, Elihu Hubbard Smith, and Charles Brock-den Brown—only broken by death. Let us return to the theatre.

Having brought our history down to the abdication of Henry and succession of Hodgkinson, we will commence another chapter with the opening of the new house in Philadelphia. For a list of the company at the time of its arrival, see Chapter VIII.

But before we drop the curtain on the dramatic reign of Kings Hallam and Henry, we must mention one act of sovereignty which we omitted in its chro-nological order. During the season of 1790–1, they produced a farce, in two acts, written by one of the company, Mr. J. Robinson, which was received with uni-versal applause by the public.

It was called "The Yorker's Stratagem." The scene is laid in the West Indies, and the principal character the Yorker, whose stratagem is to personate a Yan-kee trader for the purpose of obtaining a West Indian heiress, was performed by Mr. Harper.

There is much dramatic skill evinced in this trifle, and dialogue well suited to the characters. The author played in it as a mongrel creole—a kind of tawny Mungo.

↦ CHAPTER 10 ↤

Opening of the new Theatre in Philadelphia by Wignell and Reinagle — Mrs. Oldmixon — Sir John Oldmixon — Mr. Moreton — Mr. Fennell — Mr. and Mrs. Francis — Mr. Green — Mr. Harwood — Mr. Darley — Mr. John Darley — Mr. Blissett — Mr. and Mrs. Whitlock — Mr. Chalmers — Mr. and Mrs. Marshall — Mr. Bates — Miss Broadhurst.

After the long delay occasioned by the yellow fever, Wignell opened the splen-did theatre which had been prepared for him in 1792, on the 17th of Feb-ruary, 1794. He had brought from England Mr. Milbourne, an excellent scene painter, who decorated the house and furnished the necessary scenery, as far sur-

passing any stage decorations heretofore seen in the country, as the building surpassed former American theatres.

The plan of this building was furnished by Mr. Richards, who was Wignell's
brother-in-law, and secretary to the Royal Academy. The model was burnt when
the house was consumed. Mr. Richards likewise presented to the managers several very fine scenes, and the beautiful drop-curtain, which was destroyed likewise by the fire of 1820.

The part of the theatre before the curtain formed a semicircle, having two complete rows of boxes, and higher up, on a line with the gallery, side-boxes. The boxes
were supported by pillars formed of bunches of reeds, tied together with red fillets
and gilt. Festoons of curtains and numerous chandeliers gave a brilliant effect to
the whole. The first dramatic pieces presented to the public of Philadelphia by
the new company were the Castle of Andalusia, and Who's the Dupe?

The orchestra, under the direction of Reinagle, who sat at the harpsichord, was
equally superior in power and talent with the other departments of the drama.

Mr. Reinagle was the brother of the great animal painter, and father of our
worthy fellow-citizen Mr. Hugh Reinagle; he was a very genteel man and skilful musician. The first piece played was an opera, and we are informed that
notwithstanding the great dramatic strength of the company of 1793, Mr. Wignell
was led to rest his hopes on the operatic department. Mr. Wood says, he "has
often declared to me, that had he devoted *all* his care to the drama, instead of
music, he might have been rich instead of a bankrupt." (He opened in Annapolis, as in Philadelphia, with the Castle of Andalusia.) "The first year I visited
Philadelphia," says Mr. Wood, "I saw the opera of Robin Hood *greatly* played
and sung, to a house of forty dollars."

The same friendly correspondent has furnished us with a *cast* of "Every One
has his Fault," as performed by Wignell's company in 1794, which will give an
idea of the strength of the corps to all who remember the principal performers,
or who may turn back to this page after reading the notices we shall give of them.
"Lord Norland, Mr. Whitlock (his best part); Captain Irwin, Fennell; Placid,
Moreton; Sir Robert Ramble, Chalmers; Solus, Morris; Hammond, Green; Mrs.
Placid, Mrs. Shaw; Miss Spinster, Mrs. Bates; Lady Elinor, Mrs. Whitlock; Miss
Wooburn, Mrs. Morris; Edward (a matchless performance), Mrs. Marshall."

We proceed to give a sketch of the lives and dramatic education of some of
the most prominent performers in this very efficient company.

Mrs. Oldmixon was first seen by the writer in London as Miss George filling
the station of first comic singer, and the line of comic girls and chambermaids,
at the Haymarket theatre. She held the same station at Drury Lane in the winter. She was so distinguished a favourite at this time, 1785–6, that, in company
with John Palmer's, her portrait was exhibited at Somerset House, by Russell,

the best painter in *pastels* or crayons that we remember. The expression was very characteristic, full of archness, and might have passed for that of the Comic Muse. Mrs. Oldmixon retained for the many years she was on the stage great vivacity and force; in the later years of her stage history, she frequently played the old woman of comedy, and with peculiar effect.

She changed her name by marriage with Sir John Oldmixon, recorded by Bernard as the Bath beau. As Lady Oldmixon, a stage player, would appear incongruous, and unsanctioned by custom, the title does not appear in the playbills; neither was it assumed in private life. The lady was called universally Mrs. Oldmixon, except by old Philip, the door-keeper of the stage, who was a German by birth, and had been brought hither with other slaves of the Prince of Hesse. Philip could see no propriety in putting the Mrs. before the "old." "De fools! dey are always axing for Mrs. Oldmixon! Mrs. Oldmixon! ven I tell 'em dey mean old Mrs. Mixon, and yet de vont larn." Such was the complaint the porter made of the stupid Yankees to the lady herself; and none would enjoy the joke more.

Sir John, though not an actor or an author, is so intimately connected with the stage, that we must not omit him. Bernard, who will be entitled to a place in our narrative of stage events, and collection of theatrical characters, says he first met Sir John at Bath in 1784. "It was during one of my morning calls that I met Sir John Oldmixon at his lordship's:" one Lord Conyngham, who was the model of Bernard's Lord Ogilby. "And the flattering introduction I then received, improved our previously distant street acquaintance into a lasting intimacy. This gentleman, from the refinement of his dress and manners, bore the peculiar appellation of the 'Bath beau,' and upon all points of good breeding was looked up to as an oracle. This distinction in the metropolis of fashion he was not slightly proud of; it acknowledged him as the legitimate successor in the dynasty of Nash. Certainly, the mechanism of his dress was a profound study, and his science in manœuvring a snuff-box and a cane was, for many months, in my eyes, an impenetrable mystery. I have been told that Sir John was the original of Mrs. Cowley's Lord Sparkle; he certainly was of mine, accident having thrown him in my way on my first visit to Bath. Whatever success I obtained in the fops and fine gentlemen (which were the characters I played mostly in London), I am willing to acknowledge that I owe it all to the strong impressions I received from Sir John Oldmixon. But this gentleman enjoyed the additional celebrity of having founded an order of his own—the 'full curl' order, as it might have been called, grateful to the memories of the peruquiers of the last generation. Our first performance of 'Which is the Man' was so successful, that in the course of the ensuing week it was repeated. The next day Sir John met and stopped me in the street, saying, 'Bernard, I saw your Sparkle last night; they say you imitate me!' 'It is my object, Sir John,' I replied, 'to imitate the manners of an English nobleman!' 'Ah, ah, true; but your dress was incorrect.' 'In that respect,' said I, 'I must confess, Sir John, I did intend to imitate you.' 'Oh no, quite wrong; you had only twelve curls of a side; I never wear under sixteen!'"

Such is the picture an English writer gives of an English nobleman. Our motive for introducing this extract is to contrast the situation of this man, "the successor" of Nash, the oracle of fashion "in the metropolis of fashion," with that he held in society among the plebeians of the New World. The following appeared in the London papers of 1796. "Sir John Oldmixon, whose equipage was once the gaze of Bond-street, is now a gardener near Philadelphia. He drives his own cabbages to market in his own cart! His wife, formerly Miss George, sings at the theatre, and returns in the conveyance which brought vegetables for sale."

The fact is, Sir John did, with the earnings of his wife, purchase or hire a cottage at Germantown, and drove vegetables to market in a conveyance which would allow of his wife's going to town to attend her professional duties, and return when they were over for the time. Thus a family was maintained and educated by industry and economy, and Sir John only retained of the Bath beau the snuff-box, which he certainly *tapped, opened,* and presented with the air of a finished gentleman, and manners which indicated his familiarity with a state of society very dissimilar to that found in America. What broke up this Germantown establishment, and separated the family, is not for us to inquire into—most probably, something more congenial to the Bath beau than the American gardener. In 1816, Sir John was living obscurely at Sag Harbor, Long Island.

The principal gentleman comedian in this splendid company, at the time under review, was Mr. Moreton. He was, as remembered by the writer, the most elegant gentleman performer that our long acquaintance with the London and American theatres has made known to us. Tall, slender, straight-limbed, and perfectly at ease, his regular features, light complexion, and blue eyes, with the perfect air and manner of a finished gentleman, united to the talent, vivacity, and mind which must combine to make a real actor, gave to the spectator a combination rarely seen on any stage.

Mr. Wood, the worthy successor to this gentleman in the Philadelphia company, has furnished us, in answer to our inquiries, among other information important to our work, with the following notice of Mr. Moreton.

"Of Mr. Moreton, my splendid predecessor, this much I know from Mr. Wignell (*the best authority*). John Pollard, Moreton being an assumed name, was born in America, somewhere in the neighbourhood of Niagara Falls. He was early in life taken to England, and from thence sent to India, and became assistant cashier in the Calcutta Bank. His confidence was abused by a friend whom he suffered to overdraw the bank to a large amount, on the most sacred assurances that it should be replaced in time to prevent the irregularity being known. The overdraw was repaid, but not in time to prevent the knowledge of Pollard's imprudence—the friend failed to keep his word, and Pollard lost his situation, and the confidence necessary to success—he returned to England, and there met with Wignell, who engaged him as a member of his company in 1793. His first thirty or forty appearances, I have been assured by Mr. Wignell and others, were any thing but promising: but his early good breeding and close study soon made him the first of high comedians, either native or imported. I declare I think him in the easy (not spirited) comedy the best, except Lewis, I ever saw."

Mr. Wood saw Mr. Lewis after he had passed his meridian, when he played the characters which were written for him by Reynolds, Morton, and Colman; the writer saw him in earlier life the delight of London, in Ranger, Mercutio, the Copper Captain, Sir Charles Rackett, and that range of better comedy which preceded. He was more like Moreton than any other actor we have seen, and his superior as an artist. Moreton died before he could have attained the skill his talents would have certainly achieved.

Mr. Wood says, "Moreton was in very ill health a long time. The last part he played was Lothario, in The Fair Penitent. (I saw it.) He was obliged to lie long on the stage after falling; the night being severe, he was taken into the green-room in a very exhausted state. He never played again. He died of consumption. His case, like many we meet with in that disease, was a very flattering one. I spent an hour with him on Friday, when he talked confidently of playing soon. Calling on Monday, he was dead—passing away as in a gentle sleep—nor was his death noticed by his attendant." He died April 2d, 1798, at Philadelphia, and the theatre was closed three days as a tribute of respect to his memory.

Mr. James Fennell was born in London, received a good education, which was finished at the University of Cambridge. Rejecting the study of the law, he offered himself to the manager of the Edinburgh theatre in 1787, under the assumed name of Cambray, and was well received by the public in the characters of Jaffier and Othello. Othello continued long a favourite character with Fennell, and with another sooty-face (Zanga), placed him high among the heroes of tragedy. Returning to London, he offered himself to Mr. Harris, and, still under the name of Cambray, played with some success, though not enough to fix him on the boards of Covent Garden.

He returned to Edinburgh, and played with some eclat, but a dispute arising respecting parts with a favourite actor, the populace drove Mr. Fennell from the stage. A law-suit was the consequence, and after a time a return to London, where in 1789 he again had an engagement at Covent Garden, without rising in the profession.

Between this time and his engagement with Wignell for Philadelphia, he appeared in Paris as my Lord Anglais, and supported a hotel in great style, at the expense of all who trusted to his specious manners and fine appearance.

He was a remarkably handsome figure, although above the just height, being considerably over six feet. His complexion and hair light, with a blush ready for every occasion on which a blush could be graceful. His features were not handsome, his nose being round, thick, and too fleshy, and his eyes a very light gray, with yellowish lashes and brows. His appearance in the Moors, Othello, and Zanga, was noble; his face appeared better and more expressive, and his towering figure superb. His Glenalvon was a fine piece of acting, and generally, his villains appeared very natural. Deceit seemed to be at home in all his words and actions.

His style of living in Philadelphia was modelled on the plan he had tried in Paris, and with the same short-sighted system of dishonest extravagance, ended in the same disgraceful poverty, without the opportunity of flight. He was the idol of the literary youth of Philadelphia, and for a time revelled in the luxury of stylish living, and applause on and off the stage. We shall often have occasion to mention this singular man, who abused the gifts of his Creator, and the cares bestowed upon his education by his father; and after a series of acts which, if an honourable and liberal profession could be disgraced by an unworthy member, would have disgraced it,—and after all that obloquy and misery inseparable from a career of fraud,—after sporting with the credulity of the inhabitants on the seashore, from Chesapeake bay to Massachusetts, by pretended new modes of making salt, and with that of every city of note at that time in the Union by other pretences,—after passing from the palace to the prison again and again,—this unhappy man appeared for the last time on the stage of the Chestnut-street theatres, where he had been idolized in 1794, and exhibited the powerless remains of what God had made man, and vice had debased to a wretched driveller. He was allowed to attempt Lear in 1815, but even his memory was gone. And the scene of his former triumphs witnessed his last public exhibition of pitiable imbecility—the fruit of selfish indulgence, deviation from truth, and final intemperance. He died shortly after, in what, according to the course of nature, would have been the season of perfect manhood.

Of Mr. and Mrs. Francis, little is known previous to their coming to America. Mr. Francis had been a dancer, but for many years gout had possession of his legs and feet, a sore enemy to grace and activity. He played old men respectably. When Cooke arrived in Philadelphia, he met in Francis and his wife old companions of the provincial theatre, and hearty friends. Billy Francis and George Frederick clasped hands with the cordiality of two sailors who had navigated the same ship, shared the same toils, storms, and pleasures, and met again in a foreign country, after a separation of years.

Mrs. Francis, always respectable in her profession, was in private life a model of cheerful benevolence. This worthy pair, having no children, adopted and shared their professional earnings with those who had no parents. Joseph Harris, Miss Hunt, late Mrs. Bray of the Boston theatre, and another orphan, may attest their parental care and beneficence, and the inhabitants of Philadelphia generally their estimable qualities. Francis died worn out by frequent attacks of gout; Mrs. Francis lives at an advanced age, cheerful and happy, though rendered inactive by a partial paralysis. Sickness, decay, and death, is the lot of all; cheerfulness, resignation, and happiness, is the reward of those who love their God and their neighbour—the benevolent.

Mr. Green was not much of an actor when he enlisted with Wignell, but a young, tall, good-looking man. Of his previous history we know nothing. He married a pretty girl, Miss Willems, who came out from England at the same time, and was a member of the corps. Green became a good second actor in first parts, was the manager of several southern theatres, and had the misfortune to lose a daughter, one of the loveliest creatures as a girl that we remember, in that dreadful conflagration which destroyed the theatre of Richmond, and filled the town with mourning.

John E. Harwood was, from talents and education, one of the brightest ornaments of the Philadelphia company. A young man at the time of forming his engagement with Wignell, he was engaging in manners, and remarkably handsome in the form and expression of his countenance. He was inclined to indulgence, and became somewhat corpulent; but never lost the expression of humour, and the power of delighting an audience, although the exertion of that power was checked, and sometimes paralyzed by indolence. He had been intended for the law, and probably chose the stage to avoid labour, although only labour can ensure success on the stage.

Mr. Harwood married Miss Bache, a granddaughter of our great philosopher and politician Franklin, a man to whom we owe more than perhaps to any one man of the revolution, except Washington.

We shall come in contact with Harwood again in this work, and though we never think of him without regret, it is regret for one whose good qualities we admired and loved, whose faults we would willingly throw into the huge mass of nature's frailties, and cover them with the pall of oblivion. "Alas, poor Jack!"

Mr. Darley, the father of the well-known Mr. John Darley, long before the public as an actor and singer, and hereafter to be mentioned, was brought into public notice on the London stage by the uncommon powers and melody of his voice. In the winter of 1784–5, a farce called "The Positive Man" had a run at Covent Garden, its success being much owing to the pleasure received from a song by Mrs. Kennedy, in the character of a sailor. The song was "Sweet Poll of

Plymouth," not yet forgotten. The next winter the manager brought forward the farce, and attempted to deprive John Bull of the song; but John was *uproarious*, and doubtless delighted with the opportunity of managing the manager; hisses and groans, and stick-thumps, with catcalls, evinced his sense of harmony, and at length came apology to conciliate the "Gentlemen and Ladies." Apology stated that Mrs. Kennedy was not in the theatre, but if Mr. Darley would be accepted, he was ready to attempt the song. Accordingly, Darley came forward, dressed as a sailor, and never was the simple melody of Sweet Poll given with more effect, or received with greater pleasure. This is among the reminiscences of the writer, who enjoyed the *fun* and the song.

Mr. Darley was afterwards famous among English lovers of English opera for his Farmer Blackberry, which pleased as much at least as Incledon's Valentine in the same afterpiece of the Farmer. Mr. Darley was a stout, perhaps we might say, a fat man, and his appearance was not suited to any great variety of character. After his return to his native country, he enjoyed public favour, and esteem in private life; and died respected as the keeper of a porter-house in Oxford-street, London.

John Darley, the son of the above, came out to America when a boy with his father, and was occasionally introduced as a singer on the stage of Philadelphia, but left the service of the Muses for the United States' service as a lieutenant of marines; in which branch of our naval establishment, had he remained, he would now have been nearly at the head; but he returned to the stage in 1800, and married Miss E. Westray, forming a union of histrionic and musical ability which ensured competence, and has resulted in a numerous and talented domestic circle that will make the evening of their lives as tranquil as the morning and noon has been pleasant to the eyes and ears of their fellow-citizens.

Mr. and Mrs. Darley will again be met with in the pages of our theatrical record.

Blissett was unknown to the writer. He was the best of actors in a small part. He returned to England in 1821, and has played in Guernsey and Jersey. As a low comedian, he has been spoken of as possessing talent and humour of a high grade.

"He was very great in Jerry Sneak and Doctor Last," says Mr. Wood, "and incomparably the best Frenchman I ever saw; his Doctor Caius, Doctor Dablancour, and Monsieur le Medecin, were considered *perfect*,—his Sheepface, in The Village Lawyer, was excellent. He seldom succeeded in a very long part." We have heard that, having inherited property from his father, Mr. Blissett now resides in ease and retirement on the continent of Europe.

Mr. Whitlock was, at the time of coming to America, past the meridian of life, and in appearance and manner "every inch" a gentleman. He filled the parts of fathers, serious or tragic, and played some comic characters, but not with equal success. He had been long on the English provincial stage, and was a partner in management with the afterwards famous Munden. Munden's London celebrity, and Whitlock's emigration to America, may be traced to Hodgkinson, who had been received into the company and family of Munden, as has been mentioned. Whitlock was afterwards under Hodgkinson's management in this country; but returned home with his talented wife, and passed the evening of his life in quiet competency, more owing to the energy of her character than his own.

Mrs. Whitlock was one of the many children of Roger Kemble, and of course sister to Mrs. Siddons, John Kemble, Stephen Kemble, Charles Kemble, and all the rest of this celebrated and fortunate family; fortunate that in so numerous a circle there should be but one, the before-mentioned author of Tammany, who could call up a blush or a sigh at the mention of name or act: and that one was not on the stage.

Mrs. Whitlock had been the support and ornament of the company of Whitlock and Munden, and had played at Bath and in London before the engagement which brought her to Philadelphia in 1793. She was what may truly be called a fine-looking woman, with some of the Siddons and Kemble physiognomy, but fairer of complexion, and not so towering in stature. Her eye and voice were powerful, and reminded the spectator and hearer of her sister, sometimes raising expectations which were not fully realized, of seeing a second Siddons. She was of great value in her profession, and out of it an honour to her family. She still lives respected and beloved, enjoying the fruits of her exertions in that branch of the fine arts which owes so much to the family of her father.

Of Mr. Warrell we know nothing but that he was a respectable man.

Mrs. Warrell was a good singer, and added strength to this very fine company in its operatic department.

Master Warrell, the son of the above, was one of the *corps de ballet.*

Chalmers was brought out by Wignell as his first gentleman comedian, and occasional tragedian. He was soon superseded by Moreton in the first, and immediately by Fennell in the second branch of acting. He had talents and powers as an actor in comedy, but no application; and consummate vanity, with utter carelessness of any thing but self-gratification, ruined him. He sank into insignificance, returned to England about the year 1805–6, and died suddenly.

Mr. Marshall was engaged to fill the line of fops and Frenchmen, and that of first singer. His previous life is unknown to us, except that he played at Covent Garden, and was the very successful successor of Wewitzer, in Bagatelle. He returned to England in 1801, and is perhaps still living. "Some few years ago," says Mr. Wood, "I learned that he was totally blind, and living comfortably on the theatrical fund, a noble institution." The same gentleman remarks that every attempt to establish such a fund had failed in this country, as is much to be regretted. Mr. Marshall made his debut in America at the theatre of Annapolis, where Wignell carried his splendid troop to employ them, while Philadelphia was shut against them by pestilence. The house, then occupied by the company, is now, and has been for years, a public school. There is now another theatre in Annapolis.

Mrs. Marshall was a pretty little woman, and a most charming actress in the Pickles and romps of the drama. Her Edward, in Every One has his Fault, is spoken of to this day as perfection. She was afterwards, when less young, less beautiful, and less admired, Mrs. Wilmot.

Bates was Wignell's principal low comedian, after himself, without one-twentieth part of Harwood's talent, but the latter was then young and new to the stage, and "Billy Bates" was an old stager. He was a broad, short, strong-built man, with some comedy in his face, but it was all low, conceited, and cunning. Bates had been, like the celebrated Rich, both a Harlequin and a manager, and was found as an underling at Drury Lane by Wignell. Bernard, in his amusing book, thus mentions him as an acting manager. "Bates, as most acting managers are, was the commander of his company on the stage and in the closet. He played all the best parts, and thus laid claim to the character of the superior actor." As an actor he is thus mentioned, when under another management very dissimilar to his own. His manager was present in a first rate character at rehearsal, when Bates entered to deliver a message, which he did with all the flourish of a hero who had been preceded by the sound of a trumpet. "Mr. Bates," says the principal, "You surely don't intend to deliver that message in that manner to-night?" "Yes, sir, but I do." "you ar∫*too loud, sir." "Loud, sir! not at all, sir; I'm only energetic. I've got a benefit to make as well as you, sir." It used to be said in Philadelphia, that Bates had a standing, falling, practical joke, more profitable to the dealers in glass than to those with whom he dined. He would contrive to place a wine-glass, slyly, near the edge of the table, and then as by accident brush it off, exclaiming, "There, I have turned a wine-glass into a tumbler!"

Miss Broadhurst, a genteel and amiable young lady, was engaged in this great company as a second singer in serious opera, Mrs. Oldmixon being the first, and dividing the comic with Mrs. Marshall.

Miss Broadhurst had science, but not personal beauty, or skill as an actress to recommend her. She was attended by her mother in this visit to the New World, and left Wignell's company after the first season.

→→ CHAPTER 11 ←←

Boston — Law against Stage-plays by the General Court of Massachusetts, 1750 — Hallam and Henry petition and are refused — Perez Morton's petition, 1791 — Instructions given by the town of Boston to their Representatives — Committee appointed, who report against a Theatre — Mr. and Mrs. Morris and Harper go to Boston — A theatre built in Broad-alley — Charles Powell — Plays performed as Moral Lectures — Players arrested on the Stage — Governor Hancock's Speech — Law against Theatres repealed — Federalstreet Theatre built and opened — Prologue by Mr. T. Paine — Opposition Prologue.

M assachusetts, both as a colony of Great Britain and as an independent state, had been forbidden ground to all Thespians. As early as the year 1750, before any of that dangerous class of people had ventured over the Atlantic, the General Court of Massachusetts, that is, in the language of other parts of our country, the House of Assembly or Representatives, passed an act to prevent stage-plays and other theatrical entertainments. The historian of Massachusetts says, that the cause of "this moral regulation" was, that two young Englishmen, assisted by some townsmen, tried to represent Otway's tragedy of "The Orphan," and the inhabitants were so eager to see the entertainment, that some disturbances took place at the door of the coffee-house where they were amusing themselves. This so alarmed the lieutenant-governor, council, and House of Representatives, that, "For preventing and avoiding the many and great mischiefs which arise from public stage-plays, &c.—which not only occasion great and unnecessary expenses, and discourage industry and frugality, but likewise tend generally to increase immorality, impiety, and a contempt of religion," they enacted as follows: "that from and after the publication of this act, no person or persons whatsoever may, for his or their gain, or for any price or valuable consideration, let, or suffer to be used or improved, any house, room, or place whatsoever, for acting or carrying on any stage-plays, interludes, or other theatrical entertainments, on pain of forfeiting and paying for each and every day, or time, such house, room, or place, shall be let, used, or improved, contrary to this act, twenty pounds. And if, at any time or times whatsoever, from and after the publication of this act, any person or persons shall be present as an actor in, or spectator of any stage-play, &c. in any house, &c. where a greater number of persons than twenty shall be assembled together, every such person shall forfeit for each time five pounds. One-half to his majesty, and one-half to the informer."

Such were the feelings and opinions of the representatives of the people of Massachusetts in 1750; "but," says the author of Dramatic Reminiscences in The New-England Magazine, "as the Puritanic sentiments of the older inhabitants gave place to more liberal and extended views in religion and morals, much of the prejudice against theatrical amusements subsided."

After Wignell had separated from Hallam and Henry, they, foreseeing that he would occupy the south, petitioned the legislature of Massachusetts, on the 5th of June, 1790, "for leave to open a theatre in Boston, under proper regulations." The petition was not granted.

In 1791, a petition was presented to the select-men of Boston, drawn up by Perez Morton, Esq., and signed by him and thirty-eight other gentlemen of the town, setting forth "the advantages of well-regulated public amusements in large towns," and stating that, "being desirous of encouraging the interests of genius and literature, by encouraging such theatrical exhibitions as are calculated to promote the cause of morality and virtue, and conduce to polish the manners and habits of society," and for other reasons assigned, they respectfully solicit the board of select-men to take the opinion of the inhabitants "on the subject of admitting a theatre in the town of Boston," and of instructing their representatives "to obtain a repeal" of the prohibitory act of 1750, which law had been revived in 1784, to be in force 15 years.

On the 26th of October, this subject was debated in town meeting, and a committee appointed to prepare instructions to the representatives of the town in the legislature, and on the ninth of November following, the committee presented their report to the adjourned town-meeting, which was accepted.

The instructions state, that the inhabitants of Boston consider the prohibitory law of 1750 as an infringement of their privileges; and that a "theatre, where the actions of great and virtuous men are represented, will advance the interests of private and political virtue." They, for these and similar reasons, instruct the representatives to endeavour to effect the "repeal of the law alluded to, so far, at least, as respects the town of Boston." They farther instruct, that "the law of repeal may be so constructed that no dramatic composition shall be the subjects of theatrical representation" till sanctioned "by some authority appointed for the purpose;" that no "immoral expressions may ever disgrace the American stage;" but, on the contrary, all "subserve the great and beneficial purposes of public and private virtue."

In January, 1792, Mr. Tudor brought the subject before the House of Representatives, and moved for a committee to "consider the expediency of bringing in a bill to repeal the prohibitory law of 1750. After opposition, a committee was appointed, and "a remonstrance against the repeal" was referred to the same committee.

The committee reported on the 20th, that it was inexpedient to repeal the law. Notwithstanding the efforts of Mr. Gardiner and Dr. Jarvis against this report, it was accepted on the 25th. The names of Samuel Adams and Benjamin Austin are enrolled as opponents to a theatre. The latter wrote "a series of essays," says the author of Reminiscences, "to prove that Shakespeare had no genius." The principal advocates for stage exhibitions were William Tudor and Dr. Charles Jarvis.

We see from the above instructions, given by Boston to her representatives, that the opinions of the people of the capital of Massachusetts had undergone a change. We shall soon see, that notwithstanding present opposition to these opinions, they were triumphant, and the drama established in the cradle of the liberties of America.

The secession of Wignell from the old American Company, and his crossing the Atlantic in search of performers, caused the immediate voyage of John Henry, also for the same purpose. It has been stated that Mr. and Mrs. Morris, and Stephen Wools, were sharers in the *scheme* of the old company. Harper was not. Mr. and Mrs. Morris took their part with Wignell, and were, during his absence, to seek employment. Harper was not engaged with either party. Wools adhered to the property in which he was a sharer, but was left for the present unemployed.

Under these circumstances, the above-named four individuals united for the purpose of trying their fortunes in Boston, invited by the efforts for the establishment of a theatre which a portion of the inhabitants were making. Notwithstanding the denial of the legislature to repeal the law of 1750, a number of gentlemen formed an association for the purpose of introducing the drama. A committee was formed to carry their purpose into effect, and ground purchased on which to erect a building in Broad-alley, near Hawley-street. The committee were, according to Mr. Buckingham, "Joseph Russell, Esq., who also acted as treasurer to the association, Dr. Jarvis, Gen. Henry Jackson, Joseph Barrell, and Joseph Russell, jun." "A theatre in every thing but the name" was erected. A pit, one row of boxes, and a gallery, could contain about five hundred persons, and it was called the "New Exhibition Room." "The boxes formed three sides of a regular square, the stage making the fourth. The scenery was tolerably well executed." But before its completion, Charles Powell arrived from England, and advertised an entertainment, which he called "The Evening Brush for rubbing off the Rust of Care," to consist of songs and farcical recitations. This was on Monday, August 13th, 1792, and on the 16th, the New Exhibition Room was opened by Harper as manager, with feats on the tight rope by Mons. Placide, songs by Mr. Wools, feats on the slack rope and tumbling by Mons. Martine, hornpipes and minuets by Mons. and Madame Placide, and the gallery of portraits by Mr. Harper, the manager. "These entertainments," says The New-England Magazine, "continued with slight variations, for several weeks."

Thus we see a theatre was put in operation in open defiance of the law of the state, and as the good people of Boston were denied rational amusement, they accepted the efforts of the tumbler and rope dancer, and eagerly seized on the entertainments of Sadler's Wells, when prohibited by law from listening to the lines of the wit or the poet, as recited at Old Drury or Covent Garden.

But this could not last long; the company of performers increased in numbers; Mr. and Mrs. Morris, and Harper, were really actors; to these were added the names of Mr. and Mrs. Solomon, Messrs. Roberts, Adams, Watts, Jones, Redfield, Tucker, Murry, Mrs. Gray, Miss Smith, and Miss Chapman—names only mentioned as being the first professional actors who performed plays in Boston. Roberts was deformed, and almost an idiot; Watts a vulgar fellow with a wry neck; Miss Smith became soon after Mrs. Harper, the rest are only names. Charles Powell joined Harper.

Plays were now performed; but as the theatre was called an exhibition room, Douglas was represented as a Moral Lecture in five parts, "delivered by Messrs." so and so. And all the songs of The Poor Soldier were to be "delivered by Messrs. Watts, Murry, Redfield, Solomon, Jones, Mrs. Solomon, and Miss Chapman." The play-bill for this entertainment, Douglas and The Poor Soldier, thus disguised, was dated September 26th, 1792. Wools, who was attached to Hallam and Henry's company, had before this joined his leaders, they having opened the odd theatre in Philadelphia.

Thus were the laws defied, and the people and their magistrates insulted for several weeks. The municipal authorities criminally suffered this nuisance to exist until "about the end of October or beginning of November, when," as Mr. Buckingham says, "during the representation of The School for Scandal, while Morris and his wife were on the stage in the characters of Sir Peter and Lady Teazle, the sheriff of the county suddenly and very unexpectedly *made his first appearance on that stage,* and arrested them by virtue of a peace-warrant." Some of the audience leaped on the stage from the pit, "tore down the arms of the state, which decorated a tablet between one of the stage-boxes and the door, and trampled it under their feet. Several gentlemen immediately came forward and became bound for the appearance of the persons arrested." And shortly after, an association was formed for erecting a permanent theatre.

"It does not appear," says Mr. Buckingham, who writes on the spot, and has every source of information at command, "that those whose duty it was to see the laws executed, pursued the offenders with much rigour."

The legislature of Massachusetts at this time sat at Concord, and Governor

Hancock, in his speech, thus alludes to what he justly considered "an open insult upon the laws and government of the Commonwealth.

"Whether the apprehensions of the evils which might flow from theatrical exhibitions, so fully expressed in the preamble of that act" (the act of 1750, to be continued in force till 1799), "are well founded or not, may be a proper subject of legislative disquisition on a motion for the continuance or the repeal of the law; but the act is now a law of the Commonwealth; the principles on which it is predicated, have been recognised by and derive support from several legislatures, and surely it ought to claim the respect and obedience of all persons who live, or happen to be within the Commonwealth. Yet a number of aliens or foreigners have lately entered the state, and in the metropolis of the government, under advertisements insulting to the habits and education of the citizens, have been pleased to invite them to, and to exhibit before such as have attended, *stageplays, interludes,* and *theatrical* entertainments, under the style and appellation of moral lectures;" he proceeds to say, "no measures have been taken to punish a most open breach of the laws, and a most contemptuous insult upon the powers of government." He then calls upon the legislature to take measures to rectify the abuse, and punish the offenders.

The legislature in reply concur with the governor, and promise to endeavour to remedy any defect that may be found in the statute. The consequence was, that in December, a warrant was issued for the apprehension of the offenders, and the sheriff, in obedience to his precept, took the body of Mr. Harper, and as to the rest returned *non inventus.* The justices (Barrett and Greenleaf), with a view to accommodate the numerous spectators who waited with anxious expectation the result of this important inquiry, held their sitting at Faneuil Hall. Upon Mr. Harper's appearance before them, the attorney-general read a special order from the governor and council, directing him to prosecute and bring to condign punishment these contemners of the law; and then read his complaint filed with the aforesaid justices, upon which they had issued their warrant as above.

Messrs. Tudor and Otis, for the defendant, suggested the illegality of the complaint, it not being grounded upon an oath, as required by the 14th article of the declaration of rights. The objection prevailed, and Mr. Harper was released from his arrest amid the loud applauses of a "numerous and respectable audience."

On the 5th of December, a few evenings subsequent to the preceding measures, just after the first act of the play had been performed, the sheriff executed a second warrant on Mr. Harper, and put a stop to the performance. The audience finding themselves thus disappointed, became riotous, and it was at this time (according to this statement) that the painting of the state arms was pulled down and torn to pieces. Judge Tudor addressed the audience, and begged the company to withdraw, which has its effect, and great order was observed in retiring from the house.

The existence of a legislative enactment, which has become obsolete, or is contrary to the sense or will of the community, is at all times the source of evil. It is broken with impunity, or if the offender is punished, he is considered as a martyr, and praised and supported, while the laws, the only safeguard of society, are rendered of less effect in the eyes of the people, both of those they are intended to restrain, and those for whose protection they are enacted.

In 1793, the Legislature of Massachusetts repealed the law against theatrical amusements, and the Federal-street theatre was opened February 4th, 1794, with a prologue written by Thomas Paine, the son of the Honourable Robert Treat Paine, one of the signers of the Declaration of Independence. The poet petitioned the legislature afterwards to give him a *Christian name,* as he then had none. They granted the prayer, and gave him the one of his choice, that of his father. Charles Powell (who, as we have seen, had joined Harper and others in giving moral lectures on Jane Shore, Douglas, and The School for Scandal) spoke the prologue, which, as the beginning of the Boston regular and lawful theatrical history, we give.

A gold medal had been offered by the proprietors for the best, and the prize adjudged to this.

> When first o'er Athens learning's dawning ray
> Gleam'd the dim twilight of the Attic day;
> To charm, improve the hours of state repose,
> The deathless father of the drama rose.
> No gorgeous pageantry adorned the show;
> The plot was simple, and the scene was low.
> Without the wardrobe of the Graces, dress'd;
> Without the mimic blush of art, caress'd;
> Heroic virtue held her throne secure,
> For vice was *modest,* and ambition *poor.*
>
> But soon the muse, by nobler ardours fir'd,
> To loftier heights of scenic verse aspir'd.
> From useful life her comic fable rose,
> And curbless passions formed the tale of woes;
> For daring drama Heav'n itself explored,
> And gods descending trod the Grecian board.
> Each scene expanding through the temple swelled,
> Each bosom acted what each eye beheld:
> Warm to the heart, the *chymic fiction* stole,
> And purged, by *moral alchymy,* the soul.

Hence artists grac'd, and heroes nerved the age,
The sons or pupils of a patriot stage.
Hence in this forum of the virtues fir'd;
Hence in this school of eloquence inspir'd,
With bolder crest the dauntless warrior strode;
With nobler tongue the ardent statesman glow'd;—
And Athens reigned Minerva of the globe;
First in the helmet—fairest in the robe:
In arms she triumphed, as in letters shone,
Of taste the palace, and of war the throne.

But lo! where rising in majestic flight,
The Roman eagle sails th' expanse of light!
His wings, like Heaven's vast canopy, unfurl'd,
Spread their broad plumage o'er the subject world.
Behold! he soars where golden Phœbus rolls,
And perching on his car, o'erlooks the poles.
Far, as revolves the chariot's radiant way,
He wafts his empire o'er the tide of day;
From where it rolls on yon bright sea of suns,
To where in light's remotest ebb it runs.

The globe half ravaged by the storm of war,
The gates of Greece admit the victor's car;
Chain'd to his wheels is captive science led,
And taste transplanted, blooms at Tiber's head.
O'er the rude minds of empire's hardy race
The opening *pupil* beam'd of letter'd grace:
With charms so sweet, the houseless drama smil'd,
That Rome adopted Athens' orphan child.
Fledg'd by her hand, the Mantuan Swan aspir'd;
Aw'd by her power, e'en Pompey's self retir'd;
Sheath'd was the sword by which a world had bled;
And Janus blushing to his temple fled:
The globe's proud butcher grew humanely brave;
Earth stanch'd her wounds, and ocean hush'd his wave.

At length, like huge Enceladus depress'd,
Groaning with slavery's mountain on their breast,
The supine nations struggled from disgrace,
And Rome, like Etna, totter'd from her base.

Thus set the sun of intellectual light,
And wrapt in clouds, lower'd on the Gothic night.
Dark gloom'd the storm—the rushing torrent pour'd,

And wide the deep Cimmerian deluge showered;
E'en learning's loftiest hills were covered o'er,
And seas of *dulness* rolled without a shore.
Yet ere the surge Parnassus' top o'erflowed,
The banish'd muses fled their bless'd abode.
Frail was their ark, the heaven-topp'd seas to brave,
The wind their compass, and their helm the wave;
No port to cheer them, and no star to guide,
From clime to clime, they rov'd the billowy tide;
At length by storms and tempests wafted o'er,
They found an Ararat on Albion's shore.

 Yet long so steril prov'd the ravag'd age,
That scarcely seem'd to vegetate the stage;
Nature, in dotage, second childhood mourn'd,
And to her infant cradle had return'd.
But hark! her mighty rival sweeps the strings;—
Sweet Avon, flow not!—'tis thy Shakespeare sings!
With Blanchard's wing, in fancy's heaven he soars;
With Herschel's eye another world explores!
Taught by the tones of his melodious song,
The scenic muses tuned their barbarous tongue;
With subtle powers the crudest soul refined,
And warm'd the *Zembla* of the frozen mind.
The world's new queen, Augusta, own'd their charms,
And clasp'd the Grecian nymphs in British arms.
Then shone the drama with imperial art,
And made a province of the human heart.
What nerve of verse can sketch th' ecstatic view,
When she and Garrick sighed their last adieu!
Description but a shadow's shade appears,
When Siddons looks a nation into tears!

 But ah! while thus unrivall'd reigns the muse,
Her soul o'erflows, and grief her face bedews;
Sworn at the altar, proud oppression's foe,
She weeps indignant for her Britain's wo.
Long has she cast a fondly wishful eye
On the pure climate of this western sky;
And now while Europe bleeds at every vein,
And pinion'd forests shake the crimson'd main;
While Gallia wall'd by foes collected stands,
And hurls her thunders from a hundred hands:—
Lur'd by a clime, where,—hostile arms afar,—

Peace rolls luxurious in her dove-drawn car;
Where freedom first awoke the human mind,
And broke the enchantment which enslaved mankind;
Behold Apollo seeks this liberal plain,
And brings the Thespian goddess in his train.
Oh! happy realm, to whom are richly given
The noblest bounties of indulgent heaven;
For whom has earth her wealthiest mine bestow'd,
And commerce bridg'd old ocean's broadest flood!
To you, a stranger guest, the drama flies;
An angel wanderer in a pilgrim's guise!
To charm the fancy, and to feast the heart,
She spreads the banquet of the scenic art.
By you supported, shall her infant stage
Portray, adorn, and regulate the age.
When faction rages with intemperate sway,
And gray-hair'd vices shame the face of day,
Drawn from their covert to th' indignant pit,
Be such the *game* to stock the *park of wit;*
That *park,* where genius all his shafts may draw,
Nor dread the terrors of a *forest law.*
But not to scenes of pravity confined,
Here polish'd life an ample field shall find;
Reflected here, its fair *perspective,* view
The *stage,* the *camera*—the *landscape, you.*

Ye lovely fair, whose circling beauties shine
A radiant galaxy of charms divine:
Whose gentle hearts those tender scenes approve,
Where pity begs, or kneels adoring love:—
Ye sons of sentiment, whose bosom fire
The song of pathos and the epic lyre;
Whose glowing souls with tragic grandeur rise,
When bleeds a hero or a nation dies:—
And ye, who thron'd on high a synod sit,
And rule the lofty atmosphere of wit;
From whom a flash of comic lightning draws
A bursting thunder-clap of loud applause:
If here those eyes, whose tears, with peerless sway,
Have wept the vices of an age away;
If here those lips, whose smiles, with magic art,
Have laughed the foibles from the cheated heart:
On mirth's gay cheek can one gay dimple light;

In sorrow's breast one passion'd sigh excite:
With nobler streams the buskin's grief shall fall;
With pangs sublimer throb this breathing wall;
Thalia too, more blythe, shall trip the stage,
Of care the wrinkles smooth, and thaw the veins of age.

And now, thou dome, by Freedom's patrons rear'd,
With beauty blazon'd and by taste rever'd;
Apollo consecrates thy walls profane,—
Hence be thou sacred to the muses reign!
In thee, *three ages* shall in *one* conspire;—
A SOPHOCLES shall swell his chastened lyre;
A TERENCE rise in native charms serene;
A SHERIDAN display the perfect scene:—
And Athens, Rome, August blush to see
Their *virtues, beauty, grace,* all shine—combin'd in THEE.

Mr. Paine was then a very young man. Like many others, his connexion with a theatre was a source of evil to himself; of regret to his friends. Mr. Charles Powell, the speaker of this prize prologue (for which we are indebted to Carpenter's The Mirror of Taste, 1810), went to England while the theatre was being built, and the company he brought out now opened with Gustavus Vasa and Modern Antiques. Mr. and Mrs. Powell, Mr. Mrs. and Miss Barker, Mr. and Mrs. Collins, Mr. and Mrs. Jones, Messrs. Bartlett, Kenny, Nelson, and S. Powell (brother to Charles, and afterwards manager), Mrs. Abbot, and Miss Harrison, who will be noticed by us, with the respect due to her talents and virtues, as Mrs. S. Powell.

Mr. Buckingham says, that "none of the *rejected addresses* were ever published," but gives us a prologue by an adversary to the theatre, which we think superior in some respects to Mr. Paine's prize poem. The salutary "if," the great poet's great peace-maker, renders these lines as acceptable to the friend of the drama as to the enemy; and appropriate to the opening of any play-house whatever. The line in italics is a fair and palpable hit given to Mr. Paine and the directors.

PROLOGUE.

"Apollo consecrates thy walls profane."
Ye sons of liberty, with awe profound,
Survey these walls and tread this classic ground
And you, ye fair, whose footsteps here incline,
To pay your vespers at Apollo's shrine,
At this, his porch, in solemn stillness, hear
The friendly voice, which asks a list'ning ear.

If here the drama rapturous scenes disclose,
And all the heart with liveliest passion glows;
If in this dome, gay pleasure's luring smile
Enchant the soul, and midnight hours beguile;
If here, entranced, ye nobler views forego,
And cares domestic yield to *fancied* wo;
If at your home, the babe, or prattling boy,
ye, heedless left, for visionary joy;
If, borne from far, the wit of Albion's race,
As dissolute as gay, these walls disgrace;
If foreign brogues and foreign manners strive
Your speech to dictate, and the *ton* to give;
If alien vices, here unknown before,
Come, shameless, to pollute Columbia's shore;
If, here profan'd, Religion's sacred name,
Be dress'd in ridicule and mark'd with shame;
If yon bright temples which the good revere,
And rites most sacred, meet the pointing sneer;
If dipp'd in gall, the unhallow'd comic rod,
Touch, unprovoked, the ministers of God;
If here, regardless of the powers on high
The impious buskin dare his wrath defy;
Indignant rise! and fly these curs'd abodes,
To vice devoted and to heathen gods:
And save, while yet ye may, your spotless name,
Your own chaste virtue, and your country's fame.

But if this voice be doom'd in vain to call,
If, deaf to counsel, ye approach this hall;
If here, triumphant, vice her standard rear,
And ye, as votaries to her throne, repair;
If from this dome the dire contagion spread,
And blushing virtue hide her drooping head;
O, may the lightning rend these walls profane,
And desolation o'er the ruins reign.

A master of ceremonies was appointed by the trustees of the theatre, whose business it was to see that those who had taken seats should be accommodated according to contract—to direct the manner of taking up and putting down those who came to the door in coaches—and other matters of equal importance, besides suppressing "all kinds of disorder and indecorum." The trustees reserved to themselves the power of dismissing any performer from the stage or orchestra for misconduct—a power to be exercised in the form of a request to the manager.

The season ended with the fourth of July, before which time, Mr. Buckingham says, "Powell and Baker quarrelled; from what cause is not very material to be known. The dispute was brought before the public in the newspapers, and resulted in the secession of Baker, his wife, and daughter, from the company." We hope the Bakers made bread elsewhere, but we hear no more of them.

✣ CHAPTER 12 ✣

Hallam and Hodgkinson open the New-York Theatre, December 1794 — Mr. Benjamin Carr — Mr. and Mrs. Marriott — Mr. Munto — Mr. Nelson — Mrs. Solomons — Mons. and Madame Gardie — Mrs. Faugeres's Belisarius — Fontainville Abbey — Mr. Fawcet — First plan of the Park Theatre — Mrs. Hallam withdrawn from the Stage — Hartford — Providence Theatre — The Friendly Club.

The old American Company, under Hallam and Hodgkinson, visited Philadelphia in the summer of 1794, and opened the old theatre in Southwark, but with little success, as might have been anticipated. The citizens had been satiated with dramatic novelties and excellences. Such as were friends of the drama gave their countenance to the splendid establishment of Wignell and Reinagle, and frowned on those who took advantage of the closing of the new house for the summer, to intrude upon the territory now devoted to the men who had so eminently gratified taste by the introduction of a company that might defy all opposition.

Hallam and Hodgkinson opened the theatre in John-street, New-York, on the 15th of December, 1794. The opening pieces were Love in a Village, and The Liar.

In the opera, Mr. Benjamin Carr, well known afterwards, and much esteemed in Philadelphia as a teacher of music, made his first appearance in Young Meadows. His deportment was correct, but timid, and he never acquired or deserved reputation as an actor. His voice was mellow, and knowledge of music without the graces of action, made him more acceptable to the scientific than to the vulgar auditor. We shall have occasion to mention him again, although he did not continue long on the stage. An overture was performed, composed by him, and much approved: the orchestra had been enlarged, and the best band collected that ever had been heard in the New-York theatre.

Mr. Munto was brought forward in Eustace, but was merely tolerable. An actress of the name of Solomons appeared for the first time, but soon disappeared.

In the afterpiece, to any one who had not seen John Palmer's admirable Young Wilding, Hodgkinson would appear unrivalled.

Miss Chaucer was another debutant on this evening; but the strength of the company was in the performers heretofore mentioned. Foote's admirable comedy of The Liar is an alteration from Sir Richard Steele's "Lying Lover." Still The Liar is Foote's.

Before the opening, a series of numbers on the theatre were commenced in The New-York Magazine for November, 1794, called the Theatrical Register, which thus speaks: "The next month is the time fixed for commencing the first campaign under the new managers," Hallam and Hodgkinson. After announcing the projected new house, and the intended abandonment of the John-street theatre, the writer proceeds. "Under these circumstances, we have thought proper to begin this monthly publication, with a view to watch over the conduct of the managers and the company. A well-regulated stage tends to suppress those paltry exhibitions with which every city is infested which has not a regular theatre, or during those seasons that the theatre is closed. The very refuse of society associate to exercise a profession which requires the utmost powers of humanity. Their audiences are composed of people like themselves."

The author of The Father of an Only Child had now written a second tragedy, taking his plot from Mrs. Radcliff's Romance of the Forest. He called it "Fontainville Abbey." It was read to the author's associates, and communicated to Dr. Dwight. It was approved of by them, and accepted by the managers. The author's friend, Dr. E. H. Smith, finished at this time a drama called "Edwin and Angelina," which was likewise accepted for performance.

The theatre at Newport was at this time under the direction of Harper. He had now a second wife, who was the heroine of his company. He was of course the hero, and appeared indeed a hero among those who formed his troop. Huggins, afterwards so noted in New-York, was one of the actors.

Three days after the opening, a Mr. Marriot was announced as from the Edinburgh boards. He was received quietly by the audience, and condemned by the critics of the newspapers. His wife, Mrs. Marriott, a pretty young woman, was likewise added to the company, but made no addition to its strength. The same must be repeated respecting Mr. Nelson, who appeared in the character of Lubin, in the Quaker.

In the orchestra was a genteel man of the name of Gardie; he was from St. Domingo, and brought with him his wife, a beautiful woman, who now made her appearance as the heroine of a pantomime called "Sophia of Brabant." This was the first introduction of serious pantomime on our stage. The music was composed by M. Pelesier. The impression made by Madame Gardie was extremely great, and after a little time a second serious pantomime was got up, in which she was the principal attraction, called "Le Foret Noir." She is thus noticed in the Theatrical Register: "Her face, figure, and action were enchanting.

The appearance and manners of this lady are prepossessing, beyond any example on our stage."

Gardie, like most of the gentlemen composing the band, had seen better days. He appeared a melancholy man. The lady had all the fascinating vivacity of her nation. The termination of her triumphs over the people of America was a tragedy of real life, performed in the well-known house where a sublime drama of a very different character had been enacted; where Washington took leave of his companions in arms when he retired to his beloved Mount Vernon. The house is still in being at the corner of Pearl and Broad-streets. The story of the unfortunate Gardie and his fascinating wife will occupy another page.

In February, 1795, Mrs. Faugeres showed to several literary persons a tragedy called "Belisarius." It was not played. Although it possessed merit, the lady had not that knowledge of the stage which is necessary to produce an acting play. It was afterwards published.

On the 17th of February, 1795, the second tragedy by the author of The Father of an Only Child, was played and applauded. "Fontainville Abbey" was thus cast.

La Motte,	Mr. Hodgkinson.
Marquis,	King.
Peter,	Richards (alias Crosby).
Madame La Motte,	Mrs. Melmoth.
Adeline,	Hodgkinson.

The new tragedy was not announced as the production of an American, and we find in a publication of the day the following remark. "Can it be possible that the author thinks that such an avowal would operate against it?" There can be no doubt that he did think so, and no doubt but that such an avowal at that time would have been enough to condemn the piece. The writers of the day, however, whether from mistaking its origin or not, did praise it in good set terms.

This tragedy, after a few repetitions, was suffered to sleep with its predecessor. It was published by Longworth some years after, and is forgotten.

Among the inefficient performers brought out or added to the American Company, we are sorry to add the name of Hallam. Mr. Hallam, brought forward his son, Mirvan Hallam, and he made his appearance under his father's influence and instruction as Belcour, in the West Indian. But he was any thing rather than the elegant Belcour. He had neither talents nor education, and sunk into that insignificance which mediocrity in the fine arts must experience. Nay worse, discouraged by disappointed hopes, and without mental resources, that fate awaited him which sweeps into oblivion or worse so many who attempt this dangerous and alluring profession, and so many who have brighter prospects in other professions.

It was not to be expected that the inhabitants of New-York would be content with a paltry wooden theatre in John-street, when their neighbours and rivals, who outdid them at all times in fish and butter, had a new brick splendid building in Chestnut-street, the centre of Philadelphia fashion. Accordingly, a scheme for a new theatre, to surpass all new theatres, had now been some time in agitation. Eighty subscribers at 375 dollars each were obtained, making the sum of 30,000 dollars. This was to be sufficient. The number of subscribers was increased to 100; and more it was soon found were wanted. It was reported that Hodgkinson was to go to England for performers, and leave his partner to manage in America, but the partners were by this time, to use the common phrase, "at swords' points;" neither was the one fitted for the mission abroad, nor the other to manage at home.

Mr. Fawcet made his appearance in Mahomet, and added to the number, rather than to the strength of the company.

About this time Mrs. Melmoth, whose bulk had almost rendered her talents in tragedy unavailing, the towering Mrs. Melmoth, made herself ridiculous as the romping Roxalana, in the farce of The Sultan. So we remember Mrs. Abington playing Scrub, and Mrs. Webb, Falstaff.

A Mrs. Spencer appeared in Juliet, on the evening of the 2d of March, but made no impression, and deserved no support in so high a flight.

Mrs. Hallam, who has been mentioned as Miss Tuke, and who became the wife of the manager after the death of his first wife, long separated from him, and become a pleasing actress, and filled many of the first parts in comedy. About this time she was withdrawn from the stage, in consequence of an unfavourable impression made upon the audience by her appearance in the principal lady's character in Cumberland's comedy of The Jew. Mr. Hallam attributed the very strange exhibition to opium. The audience were shocked and disgusted. The actress was withdrawn from the public eye. Discontent ensued. Hodgkinson was charged in an anonymous letter with being the enemy of Mrs. Hallam, and the cause of her being withdrawn, and he attributed the charge to Hallam. Discord and ill-will raged, and partisans were enlisted on both sides. A meeting was brought about by the writer, and a seeming reconciliation effected.

Hodgkinson offered to sell out to a third party for 5,000 pounds, or 12,500 dollars.

Wignell, whose territory had been invaded by Hallam and Henry, and by Hallam and Hodgkinson, contemplated an invasion in return, and about this time commenced preparations for carrying the war into the enemy's country. A circus had been built in Greenwich-street, and occupied by a company of equestrians under a man of the name of Ricketts, and Wignell made proposals to him for his circus as a summer theatre, confident that not only novelty, but strength, ensured success. Ricketts declined the offer, and was charged in the Daily Advertiser of March 14th, 1795, with having refused "through fear of displeasing a small part of the public, or rather some gentlemen of the profession," and by that refusal having prevented the citizens of New-York seeing "some of the best actors on the continent." Four days after, the charge was answered from behind the curtain, saying the refusal was in consequence of the citizens being opposed to a second theatre, and denying that the best actors, "or near the best, are in Philadelphia;" thus denying what had not been asserted. The writer goes on to praise the New-York managers, and to show that the citizens were bound to support Mr. Hodgkinson, who had become a resident in New-York "in preference to any part of the continent." To keep the good-will of Ricketts, the managers put off a play on the 24th of March, rather than interfere with the performances of the circus. Sheridan and the School for Scandal gave way to Ricketts and clown.

Boston had before this established a theatre within her precincts, and now Hartford imitated most unwisely her example. Hartford was a mere village at that time. What may be a good in a large and populous city, may be an evil if not under the supervision of the government and other strict regulations where the population is sparse. But a theatre had been recently erected in Hartford, and Hodgkinson, with part of the old American Company, opened it in August, 1795.

Providence, Rhode Island, had likewise her play-house, and the remainder of the company were led by Hallam to that rising and flourishing town.

The two divisions united and proceeded to Boston, where they continued until the end of January, 1796. But before we follow them thither, we must bring up the history of the Boston stage to this time.

From July 4th, 1794, till December 15th, the theatre of Boston was closed. On the last named day theatrical representations recommenced with As You like It, and Rosina.

The company consisted of Mr. and Mrs. C. Powell, Mr. and Mrs. S. Powell, Mr. and Mrs. Jones, Mr. and Mrs. Collins, Mr. and Mrs. Hughes, Messrs. Bartlett, Taylor, Kenny, Heely, Hipworth, Villiers, Mrs. Heelyer (afterwards Mrs. Graupner), and Miss Harrison (afterwards Mrs. Dickinson).

Mr. Taylor gained great celebrity in Boston by his personation of Octavian; but it must be remembered that no other Octavian had been seen. We remember Mr. Taylor's Octavian. It was in our estimation at the time a failure. It was remarkable for what would be unnoticed in 1832, a growth of beard cherished for the purpose.

Mr. Hipworth was at the time thought highly of in the part of Sheva, then first played in Boston, and in Vapid. Hodgkinson had not yet been seen. But Mr. Hipworth is praised for something beyond good playing; "he was respected," says Mr. Buckingham, "for his good conduct, both before the public and in his private life." That he should have personated with success the varied characters of Sheva, Vapid, Cato, Shylock, Rover, Beverley, Petruchio, Jaffier, and Jaques, proves more than ordinary talent. This gentleman died in Charleston, South Carolina, in 1795.

Mr. Jones was the favourite low comedian of the place at that time, and a rebellious subject of King Powell's. It appears from a circumstance related by Mr. Buckingham, that the monarch could not decide the differences which arose among his subjects, in respect to parts, and that Mr. Jones could.

"Mrs. Jones and Mrs. Hughes both laid claim to the part of Cowslip, in *The Agreeable Surprise.* One evening when it was performed, they both prepared for the character, both came on the stage at the same instant, and each presented her bowl of cream to Lingo. Jones, who was playing the part of the pedagogue, received the offering from his wife, and the rival Cowslip was obliged to retire from the contest." He died in Charleston, S. Carolina, in 1797.

As the name of Jones might mislead, we will remark that the comedians Mr. and Mrs. Jones were not the same we have elsewhere mentioned. The Mrs. Jones, mother of Mrs. Simpson, who was the favourite of New-York in the winter of 1805–6, could have had no rival as Cowslip. Her husband died at Charleston in the year 1806.

A play was performed in Boston, written by a citizen of the United States, called "The Medium, or Happy Tea-party." It was not played a second time, and was not printed. It was attributed for a time to a clergyman, but denied by him as his offspring.

Mr. C. Powell became bankrupt; and at the end of the season, Col. John S. Tyler was appointed manager by the proprietors. Col. John S. Tyler was appointed manager by the proprietors. Col. Tyler made an arrangement with Messrs. Hallam and Hodgkinson to bring on the New-York company to Boston; and having engaged a part of the former Boston company, the whole formed a very effective and numerous corps; made more so by the addition of Mr. and Mrs. Johnson, Mr. and Mrs. Tyler, Mr. Jefferson, Mrs. Brett, and Miss Arabella Brett, all of whom arrived from England and joined the New-York company.

Mr. Buckingham mentions it as worthy of record that the tragedies of *Macbeth* and *Othello* were played for the first time this season, Hodgkinson playing the hero of each piece.

The company of Hallam and Hodgkinson closed their performance in Boston on the 20th of January, 1796, and opened in New-York on the 10th of February following.

In the course of the spring of 1796, the project of building a new play-house in Boston was started, a subscription opened and almost immediately filled up.

Such was the prevailing taste for theatrical performances, that men of capital were willing to invest their property to almost any amount in the erection of theatres; and mechanics did not hesitate to take shares in payment for their labour. Contracts were made, the building went on rapidly, and before the first of January, 1797, the Haymarket theatre, an immense wooden pile, proudly overtopping every other building in the metropolis, was completed. It is believed that the idea of raising a rival house was first suggested by C. Powell, or some of his friends, who thought him injured by the proprietors of the Federal-street theatre; but there was another and more potent principle exerted in producing the establishment than mere theatrical rivalry, and that was political feeling. Political excitement at that time, between the parties then denominated *Federal* and *Jacobin,* was high and furious. Every man joined himself to one or the other of those parties, and each was jealous of the ascendency of the other. It was suspected, and not without some reason, that party politics, which pervaded almost every private as well as public concern, had some influence in the management of the Federal-street house; and that the trustees who were all of the Federal school of politics, had upheld and justified the manager in the introduction of pieces tending to provoke the resentments and animosities of their political opponents. It was customary (and very naturally so), for the actors, who were all emigrants from the English stage, to interpolate jests and witticisms at the expense of the French, who were then at war with England; and these often gave great offence, excited disapprobation, and sometimes created great uproar in the house. The anti-Federal (or as it was then called, the Jacobin) party, were so exceedingly sensitive that they took great offence at the representation of *The Poor Soldier,* pretending that the character of Bagatelle was a libel on the character of the whole French nation. They were encouraged in this by the French consul, then residing in Boston. A pretty smart quarrel was excited between him and the editor of the Boston Gazette; and the controversy at last became so bitter, that a mob on one occasion attempted to stop the performance of this farce, and did considerable damage to the benches, doors, and windows of the offending house.

After a short recess, which commenced about the last of May, Williamson again drew up the curtain of the Federal-street stage. He retained many of the principal performers of the preceding season, and enriched the company by adding the talents of Chalmers, Bates, and Mrs. Whitlock. Chalmers was introduced on the first night of the season, as Vapid, in *The Dramatist.* Mrs. Whitlock came out as Isabella, in Southern's *Fatal Marriage,* and repeated the part several times within a short period. Bates was reserved till the season was near two months advanced, and then brought forward as Justice Woodcock, in Bickerstaff's delightful opera, *Love in a Village,* and Sharp, in *The Lying Valet.* Jones, who had returned from Charleston, to pass the summer in New-England, joined the company at the commencement of the season, and played for several weeks with a popularity equal to that which attended his first performances. Mr. and Mrs. Rowson, Mr. and Mrs. Hogg, and their daughter, Mr. and Mrs. Solomon, with two daughters, and Mr. Downie, were in the Federal-street company of this season.

In the month of December, the Haymarket theatre was completed. It was an immense building, constructed entirely of wood. It had three tiers of boxes and a gallery. The lobbies and staircases were spacious and convenient. On each side of the stage was a suite of dressing-rooms, constructed in wings, projecting from the second story to the main edifice, and nearly on a level with the stage. The entrance to the pit was up a flight of steps.

This theatre was first opened on Monday, the 26th day of December. C. Powell had made a voyage to England during the preceding summer, to complete his company by the enlistment of recruits, and returned with Mr. and Mrs. Barrett, Mr. and Mrs. Simpson, three Misses Westray (daughters of Mrs. Simpson by a former marriage), and a corps of ballet dancers and mimes. Among these were the celebrated French performers, Francisquy, Val, Legé, and their wives. The company was numerous, and embraced a great variety and excellence of talent. The opening play was *The Belle's Stratagem,* which was thus cast. Doricourt, S. Powell; Sir George Touchwood, Marriott (first appearance); Flutter, C. Powell; Saville, Dickson (first appearance on any stage); Courtall, Taylor; Villars, a young American; Hardy, Simpson (first appearance); Letitia Hardy, Mrs. S. Powell; Lady Frances, Miss Hughes; Miss Ogle, Miss Harrison (afterwards Mrs. Dickson); Mrs. Rackett, Mrs. Simpson (first appearance). The comedy was succeeded by a ballet, pantomime, &c. in which the whole corps displayed their powers to the utmost extent.

On the Wednesday following, Barrett made his first bow to the American audience in the character of Ranger. Mrs. Barrett's first appearance was in Mrs. Beverley, in Moore's popular tragedy of *The Gamester.*

The acting management of the Federal-street stage devolved on J. B. Williamson, whom we have mentioned elsewhere as the tragedian of the summer theatre in the Haymarket, London, where tragedies were very rare, and Mrs. Wells the heroine. We remember hearing Williamson, with all the swelling port of *My Lord Duke,* tell Hodgkinson that Tyler, the Yankee manager, had *run away,* and then thank Heaven that he was not a *regular bred manager.*

Williamson's wife, the Miss Fontenelle of the English stage, was a very fine actress in *Little Pickle* and romps. She was the original *Moggy M'Gilpin* of the Highland Reel. She was powerful, but her playfulness lacked delicacy.

From Mr. Buckingham we learn that "Mrs. Arnold, from Covent Garden, made her *debut* in Rosetta, in *Love in a Village*." She is mentioned with praise, and is supposed to have died many years after in Virginia.

We make use of the accurate information of Mr. Buckingham for the origin of the Boston Haymarket, and the opening of the Federal-street theatre under J. B. Williamson.

In December, Mr. William Charles White, who will be better known to the reader by our account of his attempts and failure in New-York, made his first appearance with great applause as a boy on the Boston stage.

While the house, first called the new theatre, and since the Park theatre, in New-York, was building, the following queries were suggested by one who had afterwards the direction of it, accompanied by care and misery, but at this time was happy in competence, ardent wishes for the happiness of his fellow-creatures, delightful society of enlightened friends, and in daily pursuit of knowledge. "Is not the present situation of the drama in New-York, while the power of regulating it seems to be in the subscribers to a new building, a good opportunity for effecting a reform? It is very much wanted. May I not address a letter to the subscribers through the medium of the press, and show the power which a theatrical establishment possesses of being eminently useful? May not errors be pointed out in former and existing establishments?

The use which governments have made of the stage shows the absurdity of allowing the erroneous opinions of Europe to be propagated in the most alluring form, in opposition to those which our superior form of government is calculated to generate. May I not offer a plan for a more perfect mode of conducting theatres in this country? Cannot the stage be made a vehicle for the furtherance of useful knowledge, second to none but the press?" Such were the thoughts and wishes of one who on trial found circumstances too strong for his desires of reform, and who, after a struggle of years (with ruined health and fortunes), gave up the contest, without giving up the wish or the hope.

Charles Brockden Brown had been destined for the bar, and received early education accordingly, but disappointed his friends by positively refusing to enter into the profession of the law. He became intimate with Elihu Hubbard Smith while the latter studied under the physicians of Philadelphia, and Smith having determined to practise in New-York, Brown visited that city and joined those who have been denominated pioneers, becoming a member of the Friendly Club. Already he had commenced novel writing, and the young physician, the future novelist, and the dramatist, soon became inseparables. A young lawyer, William Johnson, well known since as a reporter, being likewise a member of the club, commenced his career about the same time with Elihu H. Smith, and they established themselves in the house of Alderman Waddell, in Pine-street, near Nassau. This is the same Alderman Waddell who became a subject for the theatrical historian by selling play tickets in conjunction with David Matthews, mayor of New-York, in the year 1777. At that time the alderman was a member of a club of wits, very dissimilar to the Friendly Club both in habits and politics; but they were certainly wits, although as certainly bon-vivants. The names of William Franklin, the son of Benjamin, and of James Rivington, the printer of the Royal Gazette, are enough to justify the character here given of that club of 1777. Waddell lived now in the same house with Johnson and Smith, occupying upper apartments, and perhaps his tenants did not see him once a month, so regular were all parties, and so different their habits of regularity.

The apartments of Johnson and Smith were the resort of the members of their club, and the novelist was divided between them and the dramatist; sleeping at Bachelor's Hall, and otherwise domesticated in the family of the author of "The Father;" until a long and severe illness rendered it necessary to remove him altogether to the house of the latter. While thus situated, and surrounded by such friends, we shall see that the dramatist was induced to become a manager of the New-York theatre.

⇥ CHAPTER 13 ⇤

1796 — Mr. and Mrs. Johnson — Mr. and Mrs. Tyler — Mr. Jefferson — Mrs. and Miss Brett — Mr. and Mrs. Cleveland — Mons. and Madame Val — M. Francisquy — M. Dubois — Opera of the Archers — Mr. Hogg — A third Manager added to the partnership of Messrs. Hallam and Hodgkinson, whose violent quarrels had threatened destruction to the Company — Endeavours to mediate — Williamson of the Haymarket, London — Revived Quarrels — Mrs. Hallam withdrawn, and a new Agreement among the Directors — Company at Hartford — John D. Miller — Old American Company open in New-York, 1796 — Mysterious Monk — Arrival of Wignell with Mrs. Merry, Mr. Cooper, &c. — Godwin — Holcroft — Edwin and Angelina — Bourville Castle — John Blair Linn — Doctor Elihu Hubbard Smith — Tell Truth and Shame the Devil — The Comet — Mr. Miller — Vexations of Theatrical Management — Wignell opens the Philadelphia theatre, December 5, 1796 — Mrs. Merry — Mr. Cooper.

February 10th, 1796, was a remarkable era in the history of the theatre of New-York. We have seen that Hallam and Hodgkinson had successfully quartered their troop upon the good people of Boston, to the mutual satisfaction of the strangers and citizens. They now opened the house in John-street, New-York, with the good old comedy of the Provoked Husband, and by a very judicious cast of the play showed an accession of strength, as well as numbers, which warranted the success they met with this season. Mr. and Mrs. Johnson, Mr. and Mrs. Tyler, Mr. Jefferson, and Mrs. Brett, all made their debut at the same time. Mr. Johnson, and Mrs. Brett in Sir Francis and Lady Wronghead; Mr. and Mrs. Tyler as Manley and Lady Grace; Mr. Jefferson as Squire Richard, and Mrs. Johnson as Lady Townley.

We will speak of these in succession, according to our estimate of their value as players; and first,

Mrs. Johnson was a tall, elegant, beautiful young woman, whose taste in dress made her a model for the belles of the city, and whose manners were as fascinating off as on the stage. Her irreproachable character and demeanour rendered her playfulness harmless to herself or others, for the most licentious would see at a glance that he must not approach, in that character, within the circle of her influence. She was almost too tall, yet the spectator did not wish her shorter, and if any movement appeared like an approach to awkwardness, it was only to be attributed to modesty. She had not the self-possession of Miss Farren or Mrs. Merry, though more like the first than the last. She was more beautiful, but not so good an actress as either, and at the time we now speak of, America had not seen so perfect a fine lady in comedy.

This lady made her first appearance in Mr. Brunton's company, and Mrs. Merry has told the writer that she could not recognise in the elegant Mrs. Johnson the tall awkward girl of that period. She had prudently accepted the hand of Mr. Johnson, much her senior, but one who could protect and instruct her. She lived respected and esteemed, and after several visits to her native land, she died in America, in the arms of a beloved and most worthy daughter.

As an actor, Mr. Jefferson stands next. Perhaps, as an actor, he ought to have been placed first, but "place aux dames" where any doubt exists. He was then a youth, but even then an artist. Of a small and light figure, well formed, with a singular physiognomy, a nose perfectly Grecian, and blue eyes full of laughter, he had the faculty of exciting mirth to as great a degree by power of feature, although handsome, as any ugly featured low comedian ever seen. The Squire Richard of Mr. Jefferson made a strong impression on the writer; his Sadi, in the Mountaineers, a stronger; and, strange to say, his Verges, in Much Ado about Nothing, a yet stronger.

Joseph Jefferson was invited to this country by Mr. C. Powell, for Boston (he paying the passage money and agreeing to give seventeen dollars per week salary), and arrived in 1795. Powell having failed, Jefferson engaged with Hallam and Hodgkinson. He was the son of Mr. Jefferson, a contemporary and friend of Garrick. Mr. J. Jefferson had been under Bernard's management in England.

We shall often have occasion to mention this excellent comedian, who lived among us, admired as an actor, and esteemed as a man, for six-and-thirty years, paying the debt of nature while this work is passing through the press in 1832.

Joseph Tyler was, at the time of his debut in New-York, a manly figure; had had good provincial practice as an actor and singer, and was a most valuable acquisition to the American stage. In time, he became the representative of what, on the French theatre, is called the "*pere noble*," and long continued a favourite on the stage and an estimable man in private life. That his appearance and manner on the stage and elsewhere should have been so highly respectable is the more to be remarked, and is the more creditable to him, as he was originally a practitioner of a trade certainly not high in the scale among ordinary occupations. Mr. Tyler was in early life a barber; and consequently an uneducated man. It is the more to his honour that he could represent the *pere noble* on the stage, and play the part of the "noblest work of God," an honest man, in society. He does not stand alone among histrionics in the circumstance of having sprung from the barber's-shop to the stage. Mr. Thomas King, long at the head of his profession as a comic actor in London, was likewise a knight of the pole. Bernard says, King was extremely "sensitive of any allusions to his early occupation," and tells from Mrs. Clive, the celebrated actress, who had retired in honourable competency from the stage, the following anecdote:

"In playing a particular character one evening which required a stick, King mislaid his own, and seized another at the wings which was too large and clumsy. Garrick met him as he was going on, and observed it: 'Eh, eh, Tom, what's that?—That won't do;—cudgel, Irish shilalegh;—you're a man in high life,— ought to have a gold-headed cane.' King was conscious of the impropriety, and Garrick's observation nettled him; he therefore answered, rather testily, that 'he had lost his own, and must use that or go on without one.' 'Curse it Tom,' said the manager, 'the people will say you're going back to your old business, and have brought your *pole* with you.' King threw down the stick, and instantly ran to find another." It is but fair to add, that in theatrical biography, Mr. King is said to have been educated for a barrister. Mr. Tyler's early destination was communicated to the writer by his friend Johnson, who emigrated with him, and was afterwards his partner as a manager. Mr. Tyler died, January, 1823, aged 72 years and 4 days.

Mrs. Brett comes next in order. She was the wife of Brett of Covent Garden and the Haymarket, London, and mother of Mrs. Hodgkinson, Mrs. King, and Miss Arabella Brett, the latter of whom now arrived with her. She was a good actress, and filled the line of comedy old women better than had heretofore been seen.

Mrs. Tyler was no addition to the strength of the company.

It will be perceived from this account of the accessions made to the already powerful company of Hallam and Hodgkinson, that the comedy of the Provoked Husband must have given satisfaction to all, and delight to most of the audience. Mr. Hodgkinson spoke an opening address, written by Mr. Milns. It was commonplace in the serious, and silly in the attempted comic parts. But Hodgkinson could make any thing pass at that time, and with eclat.

On the 12th of February, Miss Broadhurst and Miss Brett made their first appearance in Yarico and Narcissa, in the opera of Inkle and Yarico, Mrs. Hodgkinson playing Wowski, her husband Trudge, and Tyler Inkle. Miss Broadhurst we have spoken of as one of Wignell's company. Miss Brett was a child in years, but a woman in appearance, with a powerful voice as a singer, but destitute of personal beauty. Mr. Tyler's first singing character established him in the favour of the audience.

Mr. and Mrs. Cleveland were brought out the succeeding night, he playing Zaphna and she Palmira, in Voltaire's tragedy of Mahomet. They were genteel and useful performers;—young and handsome, but in talent not above mediocrity.

In the beginning of March, some French performers were engaged. M. and Madame Val, M. Francisquy, and M. Dubois. Francisquy became useful and attractive in pantomime; these performers supported the beautiful and very fine actress, Madame Gardie, in serious or heroic exhibitions of that description.

The story of William Tell and the struggle for Helvetic liberty was at this time moulded into dramatic form by the author of The Father of an Only Child, and with songs, choruses, &c., was called an opera. The subject was suggested to the author by an English play, recently published, which was utterly unfit, and perhaps not intended for the stage. Mr. Carr, for whom the principal singing part was allotted, composed the music. Comic parts were introduced with some effect. Schiller's play on the same subject did not then exist. We have had, of late years, a popular English drama on the same subject, made more so by the talents of an American actor.

I find the following curious passage in Keyslar's Travels. "At the end of this hall," the arsenal at Bern, "is an excellent wooden image of the famous William Tell; he is aiming at the apple on the head of his little son, who stands opposite to him; the hands and eyes are admirably expressed. He appears to have been a tall, raw-boned man, with a very honest countenance; and according to the fashion of the times, one-half of his coat is red, and the other black and yellow stripes alternately, his breeches and stockings are of one single piece, and an arrow sticks in his coat behind his head; the boy is laughing, as apprehending no danger."

The writer of the American play gave it a very bad title, "The Archers."

On the 30th of March, 1796, Mr. John Hogg, long a favourite actor in New-York, made his first appearance on the American stage, perhaps on any stage, and so unpromising was it that he did not appear again this season. He had given his

name to an actress who is recorded in a previous chapter of our history as having come to this country in the year 1767, as Miss Ann Storer, being saved from
the burning ship at sea, and landed at Newport, Rhode Island. Mrs. Hogg was
many years the representative of comedy old women, and an excellent actress.

The character chosen for Mr. Hogg to appear in was that of Virolet, in the
Mountaineers. He was no otherwise qualified for the part than as he was a good-
looking young man. Always diffident and easily disconcerted, he never received
favour or deserved it from the audience until he fell into the line of comic old
men. Once possessed of popular favour, he played many comic parts well. Whenever it was his ill fate to be thrust into a tragedy, he invariably lost his recollection, and as the time for his appearance approached would be in perfect agony,
every moment losing his hold of the words of the part, and conscious that he
only went on the stage to stand mute or to utter nonsense. On such occasions
he would make a desperate effort, and generally shouted out in a voice louder
than necessary, and perfectly distinct, something either unintelligible or foreign
to the purpose. On one occasion, having to tell Cooper, who represented the hero,
that one of his generals could not be in the field for fifteen days, Hogg roared,
"he says he cannot bring his powers these fifteen years!" This was received with
bursts of laughter; the actor standing like a statue, and perfectly unconscious that
he had said any thing amiss.

He made his first very great impression on the audience in John Bull, when
he played Job Thornberry. We shall often have occasion to mention honest John
Hogg in the course of these annals.

About this time, Hodgkinson pressed upon the author of The Father of an
Only Child, whom we have called the dramatist, a purchase of his half in the
concerns of the theatre, with the tempting bait of having the sole control of the
pieces to be brought before the public. The proposition was made on the 19th
of March. The bait took. The enthusiastic dramatist seriously persuaded himself that it was his duty to take the direction of so powerful an engine as the stage;
his thoughts at the time lay open before me. "If the effects of the stage are as
great as its friends and enemies have concurred in representing it, surely I should
have the power to do much good." The power of the engine is certain; his powers to direct it he ought to have doubted.

The proposer was to obtain Hallam's concurrence. The price of the purchase
to be valued by the purchaser. Time of payment unlimited. Mr. Hodgkinson's
services as an actor and manager warranted. Tempting prospects of profit were
displayed. It was stated that the theatre had cleared, in the last six weeks, between
four and five thousand dollars. The power (not forgetting the power to bring out
his own plays) offered to the dramatist,—the control of the stage in a large portion of the continent,—and wealth unbounded,—were irresistible; we shall see

how the visions were realized. Hallam's concurrence was obtained by Hodgkinson in April, and every arrangement made for the dramatist to commence manager in May.

On the 18th of April, 1796, the opera of The Archers was performed for the first time, and received with great applause. The music by Carr was pleasing, and well got up. Hodgkinson and Mrs. Melmoth were forcible in Tell and wife. The comic parts told well with Hallam and Mrs. Hodgkinson, although Conrad ought to have been given to Jefferson. The piece was repeatedly played, and was printed immediately.

At a meeting of the two managers and the dramatist for the purpose of signing articles of agreement, Hallam began to raise difficulties. "There may be a difference among us, who is to decide? You two being a majority, am I to be bound by your acts?" It was replied, that as his property was equal to that of the two, his voice in every thing relative to property must be equal to both his colleagues. This appeared satisfactory, but he still declined signing the papers. The dramatist now found that he had to be mediator between two men who were jealous of each other, and at variance in the most violent degree, and on the 1st of May, Hallam laid open his grievances, complaining of Hodgkinson's encroachments, and usurpations of power and of parts; having deprived him of all those characters which gave him consequence with the public, either playing them, or contriving to keep the plays from being played. His wife, he said, was likewise aggrieved, misrepresented, and deprived of her consequence by the introduction of others. She had been restored to the stage after the exposure above mentioned. Mr. Hallam professed perfect confidence in the new manager, and appealed to him for justice. The dramatist promised to see Hodgkinson immediately, and did so. He ridiculed Hallam's wish to keep young parts from him, declared that they were his right, and he would have them or quit the stage. After repeated mediatorial visits, the characters in dispute were reduced to six, and then to four—Orestes, Hamlet, Ranger, and Benedict; these Hodgkinson swore he would have, or not play, although he had just bound himself to the new manager and purchaser. The dramatist, in all this disagreeable business, consulted and followed the advice of his friends. Hallam declared that he was "as much surprised at Hodgkinson's demand of the *parts* as if he had demanded his tables and chairs."

This shows the view actors took of this subject. A dispute for *parts* appears ridiculous to the public; but upon the *line of business* played depends the favour of the actor with the audience, and his emolument from salary and benefit.

The new manager by degrees quieted, if not reconciled his colleagues, and entered upon the business of directing a theatre with the approbation of his former friends and associates, and without immediate change in his mode of life. As the theatrical season was drawing to a close, benefits were the only con-cern of the actors, and the principal occupation of all connected with the the-atre. But the discord between Hallam and Hodgkinson was flaming out daily, and made the situation of their associate any thing but enviable. Hodgkinson threw out hints that he would leave the company—said he was subjected to insult from Hallam's family. "If he did stay with the company, he would have a higher salary for himself and wife than Hallam and his wife received, but would not be joint manager with Hallam." The latter being told this demand respect-ing salary, swore solemnly, that Hodgkinson should not, in *his* company, have a higher salary than himself. Such are the scenes in theatres, such in many other places; but actors seem to be jostled against each other more than most men. The new manager began to desire a retreat from the incessant quarrels of those with whom he had connected himself.

Williamson, remembered by us as the principal tragedian at the summer theatre in London in 1786, where tragedies were not the order of the day, and a kind of stiff, handsome "walking-gentleman" of comedy, was now a manager of one of the Boston theatres, and was at this time in New-York. He stimulated Hodgkinson to hostility against Hallam. Wignell, by offers of advantageous terms to Hodgkinson if he would come to Philadelphia, strengthened his op-position to his first partner; indeed he knew that he could command a great engagement anywhere.

With his friend Doctor E. H. Smith, the unfortunate dramatist repaired to Hodgkinson, on the last day of May, 1796, and demanded, "Will you, or will you not remain in the old American Company as a performer and assistant man-ager according to your agreement?" He hesitated, wished that his answer "should be deferred until the crisis between him and Hallam had passed." He was told that his answer must determine the conduct of the man he had invited into the business; and he answered, "If I stay, my salary must be raised, and that dam-nably," thus at once destroying the basis of the agreement. "I have received my answer," was the reply, and the friends departed.

As Mr. and Mrs. Johnson and Mr. and Mrs. Tyler had been engaged by let-ters to them from Hodgkinson, written in his own name, he considered them as bound to him, and threatened to withdraw them from the company. The ri-valry between Mrs. Johnson and Mrs. Hallam, the latter supported by her hus-band's influence, rendered this a probable event. Mr. Johnson anxiously asked the new director if Hallam and Hodgkinson were likely to be reconciled. He was answered that Hodgkinson said he would leave the company, but that all en-gagements should be fulfilled. He replied that he and his wife wished to remain in New-York, but feared the Hallams, and complained of Mrs. Hallam particu-larly, as an actress and woman.

After several letters from the new manager on the one part, submitted by him to his friend Smith, and intemperate answers to them from Hodgkinson, the latter made apologies and concessions, gave up the demand for exorbitant salaries, and expressed a wish for reconciliation with Hallam. The mediator represented all this to Hallam, who expressed his wish for accommodation, and made proposals to relinquish parts and make an equitable adjustment; but two days after he retracted, and said his friends advised him not to give up any thing. Hodgkinson now proposed to leave the company, vesting all his property in it and all his rights in the new manager, and settling his accounts with Mr. Hallam. He wrote to this purpose to Hallam, and it was agreed upon. Under this new arrangement, engagements were offered to the principal performers, but here difficulties arose; Mrs. Johnson, always of consequence, but rendered more so by the withdrawal of Mrs. Hodgkinson, could not be reconciled to sharing business with a woman like Mrs. Hallam, and putting herself under the direction of such a woman's husband. Hallam became furious on hearing these objections, and the dramatist, utterly disgusted, made known to him and to Hodgkinson his determination to relinquish the connexion.

The dramatist consulted Mr. Hugh Gaine, who agreed that Hallam could only be saved from ruin by withdrawing his wife from the stage, and undertook to deliver a letter to him stating that her continuance in the theatre would prevent the fulfilling of the recent engagement with the writer, who at the same time offered to give up accounts and money, and retire. Mr. Gaine delivered this letter, and advised Hallam to remove his wife from the stage, but said he did not believe he would do it. "You have done your duty," said this worthy man to the dramatist, "and so have I."

Hallam, by the advice of his oldest friends, among whom were Mr. Gaine and Mr. M'Cormick, concluded to remove Mrs. Hallam from the eye of the public; and the dramatist, supposing all settled to Hodgkinson's satisfaction, was surprised by his demand for more of the parts played by Hallam, and finally by his avowing that he had engaged himself to Wignell, having made the first overture, in consequence of which Wignell had been in New-York, and Anderson, his agent, was at this time on the spot to secure Hodgkinson. The letters were produced, and the person he had been employing as a mediator with the view of keeping him with Hallam and in New-York, now for the first time knew of the long-existing negotiation. Hodgkinson consulted his friends, and determined to break off with Wignell and remain in New-York. The consequence of this was that new articles of agreement were entered into between Hallam, Hodgkinson, and Dunlap, for two years, the latter having that power which he still hoped to use for good purposes; but the two first were in a state of bitter enmity, and so continued.

Let us for a moment pause and consider, merely as a curious speculation, what must have been the changes in theatrical history, if the mediation of the new manager had not prevented Hodgkinson's leaving the New-York for the Philadelphia theatre. The acquisition of Mr. and Mrs. Hodgkinson, Mrs. Brett and Miss Brett, with probably Mr. and Mrs. Johnson, would have prevented Wignell's voyage to England, now on the eve of taking place, and America might never have seen Mrs. Merry and Mr. Cooper,—and of course all those events hanging on their presence and actions must have given place to others; what, we know not. Thus it is that the actions of one man, either in the great or little world, change the whole course of future events to eternity. Thus the strife and bickerings in palaces and play-houses have their influence in circles so wide that the imagination cannot keep pace with them, or the human mind trace their consequences.

It appears necessary to give some brief statement of these difficulties and disagreements, and yet I fear the reader will say, "What do I care for the quarrels and jealousies of these men?" The subject has been stated as briefly as possible, and only because future transactions would be unintelligible without this information, and because truth requires it.

July the 4th, 1796, found the old American Company at Hartford, and their new manager with them. The day, as usual, was a day of rejoicing and festivity. The theatre of Hartford was opened on the 11th with the Provoked Husband and Purse, and it immediately appeared that the receipts could not support such a company of comedians.

About this time, John D. Miller made his first appearance on the stage as Clement, in The Deserted Daughter. He was a good-looking young man, but destitute of education or talent. He wisely retired in a few years, became rich, an alderman, and a 4th of July orator.

These civic honours entitle Mr. Miller to more space on our pages than any distinction he gained as a player. He was a native of New-York, and the son of Mr. Philip Miller, a German baker. John D. was born in 1771, and preferring the ever-changing temperature of the stage to the eternal heat of the oven, he determined to be a hero. After fighting against nature for a few years, he wisely became a partner with his brother, a grocer, and being a *tall man*, soon became an orator among the sachems of Tammany Hall, a common-council-man, and alderman.

Miller's debut is fresh in our recollection as connected with the admirable acting of Jefferson in the character of Item, the attorney, whose clerk Miller represented. Worked up to a phrensy of feigned passion, Jefferson, a small-sized man, seized Miller by the breast, and while uttering the language of rage, shook him violently. Miller, not aware that he was to be treated so roughly, was at first astonished; but as Jefferson continued shaking and the audience laughing, the young baker's blood boiled, and calling on his physical energies, he seized the comedian with an Herculean grasp, and threw him off violently. Certainly John D. Miller never played with so much spirit or nature on any subsequent occasion. This may remind the reader of John Kemble's regret at the death of Suett, the low comedian, who played Weazel to Kemble's Penruddock. The lament of the tragedian is characteristic, as told by Kelly. "My dear Mic., Penruddock has lost a powerful ally in Suett; sir, I have acted the part with many Weazels, and good ones too, but none of them could work up my passions to the pitch Suett did; he had a comical impertinent way of thrusting his head into my face, which called forth all my irritable sensations; the effect upon me was irresistible." Such was the effect of Jefferson's shaking upon Miller, and Jefferson found the Yankee's arm equally irresistible.

On the 19th of July, the new manager, after several delightful days passed with his friends Dwight, Alsop, and Cogswell, left Connecticut, leaving the business altogether with Hodgkinson. It was intended that the company should remove to Philadelphia, and open the old theatre in Southwark. Funds were already wanted, and the dramatist, instead of reaping a harvest, had advanced between four and five hundred dollars. His partners made no offers to assist in the expenses necessary to remove the company and repair the theatre, and the plan was given up.

Mr. William King, who has been mentioned as one of the recruits brought out by Henry at the same time with Hodgkinson, and who married Mrs. Hodgkinson's sister, died early in October, 1796, at Norfolk, in the flower of his youth, a victim to vice. He had left New-York and joined the Virginia company, now a distinct corps, and moving from one town to another in that state which had first received the Thespians in 1752.

About this time died Mrs. Pownall, once Mrs. Wrighten of Drury Lane theatre.

The summer had now passed. Hodgkinson had continued with the company; Hallam on Long Island, in retirement; and their partner at Perth Amboy, where Charles B. Brown was an inmate with him, and occasionally Elihu H. Smith. In September he was engaged in New-York, preparing for the opening of the campaign.

By the 19th of September, the company had assembled at New-York, and Hodgkinson demanded a rise in his wife's salary, or threatened she should not play. This was the commencement of violations of agreement, which, with other disgusting affairs relative to the theatre, made the additional manager heartily sick of his situation. The first demand was resisted, and the threat waived.

On the 26th, the theatre in John-street, New-York, was opened with The Wonder, and The Poor Soldier. The new theatre (or Park) was in progress. A tragedy, called "The Mysterious Monk," was preparing, written by the author of The Father of an Only Child. A serious drama, accepted from John B. Linn, called "Bourville Castle, or the Gallic Orphan;" and an opera, called "Edwin and Angelina, or the Bandit," by Doctor Elihu Hubbard Smith, were in rehearsal. A farce was likewise nearly ready, written by the author of the tragedy, called "Tell Truth and Shame the Devil." To these American productions must be added another play, by an English author, "The Comet," by Mr. Milns, an intimate of Mr. Hodgkinson's.

"The Mysterious Monk," the third tragedy written by the author of The Father of an Only Child, was performed with success on the last day of October.

The plot of this play turns on the revenge a vassal or *villain* takes for blows and injuries inflicted upon him by his *feudal lord,* whose princely soul, according to the creed of those days, had nothing in common with *mere men.* The degraded vassal contrives to destroy his lord's peace, makes him jealous of his wife, the murderer, as he supposes, of his friend, and of the mother of his only son. The friend, however, recovers from the wounds he had received, and in the disguise of a monk, saves the wife from her husband's jealousy, ultimately restoring all to peace and happiness. But while he is working for the salvation of his friend, the baron communicates the story of guilt to his son, and the vassal having secured, as he supposes, his own safety, writes a letter disclosing to the baron the innocence of his wife, and the means he had used for his revenge. The son follows the author of his parent's misery and kills him, but is condemned to die for the murder. All, however, is rectified by *The Mysterious Monk.* The play is not skilfully managed; but there are passages deserving preservation. The young lord speaks thus to the monk:

> "Remember that thou speakest to thy master:
> Be fair and open—leave thy wonted arts,
> Or thou may'st raise a storm to blast thee, monk!

> MANUEL.
> Irreverend boy! I was mistaken in thee.
> Rash and unthinking, dost thou mean by threats
> To win the confidence of one like me.
> I am a Christian, boy! and own no master,
> Save one alone.—Oh, how unlike to thee!

The son says, speaking of his father,

> ———Honour is his idol.

> MANUEL.
> What is this boasted honour?
> This prince's, soldier's, ruffian's, robber's honour?

Oft-times at honour's call, the haughty lord
Arms 'gainst his neighbour chief his vassal train,
And leads them on to massacre and carnage.
Then flames the peasant's cot. The midnight shrieks
Of infants slaughtered—virgin's violated—
Rise on the wo-fraught cloud to Heaven for vengeance!
And gratify the ear of princely honour!

Manuel, speaking to the baron,

The work was all thine own: accuse not Heaven.
Even now the self-same demons rend thy soul
Which led thee on to murder innocence:
Thy passions.

RIBBEMONT.

Doth it not seem that Heaven denies its grace
Where most it gifts vain man with worldly glory?

MANUEL.

The snow, which as a fleecy mantle falls,
Covering the tender plant, its seeds preserving,
Is spread alike on hill and lowly vale;
So falls the soul-preserving grace of God,
In equal portions on the rich and poor.
But as the wind drifteth the wholesome snow,
Uncovering the lofty hill's proud summit,
And doubly blanketing the lowly vale;
So do the furious blasts of lawless passion
Sweep from the haughty head Heaven's balmy grace,
And doubly gift the humble."

But a brick, as has been said, or even two or three bricks, give no idea of a house.

It may be remarked that the fable of this play can be traced in Tobins's posthumous drama of the Curfew, written many years after. The principal parts were correctly played by Hodgkinson, Martin, Tyler, and Mrs. Melmoth. The characters and incidents were not in sufficient number, and the piece is long since, though published under the title of Ribbemont, of the Feudal Baron, forgotten.

On the 19th of October, Mr. Wignell arrived at New-York from England with the very important reinforcement to his company of Mrs. Merry (late Miss Brunton), Mr. Cooper, then a youth of twenty, Mr. Warren, Mr. and Mrs. Byrne, and Mr. and Mrs. L'Estrange.

In the evening of the 20th, while Cumberland's comedy of First Love was performing, Wignell renewed his cordial acquaintance with the author of Darby's return, now one of the New-York managers, and told him that he had a message for him from Holcroft, the author of the Road to Ruin, and many other popular works, and an apology for not writing. A correspondence had previously commenced. Godwin being mentioned, Wignell said, "I have with me a young man, educated from infancy with Mr. Godwin, of the name of Cooper." The manager sought and found Mr. Cooper in the green-room, and seating himself beside him, told him that Wignell had said he was intimate with Mr. Godwin. "As much so as any man," he replied; "I have lived with him from infancy; I am his son, not in the course of nature, but much more than a common father is he to me; he has cherished and instructed me." He then mentioned several particulars respecting the amiable William Godwin and his friend Thomas Holcroft. Such was the first interview between Mr. Cooper and one who for years was connected with him in theatrical affairs and by reciprocal acts of friendship.

Hallam and Wignell at this time met, and were apparently reconciled.

On the 2d of November happened one of those riots which tend to throw obloquy on the theatre unjustly. Two sea captains, doubtless intoxicated, being in one of the stage-boxes, called during an overture for "Yankee Doodle." The audience hissed them, they threw missiles in the orchestra, and defied the audience, some of whom pressed on the stage and attacked the rioters in conjunction with the peace officers; one of the latter was injured by a blow from a club. The rioters were dragged from their box, one turned into the street, and the other carried into a dressing-room. These mad-men afterwards with a number of sailors, attacked the doors of the theatre, and were only secured by the city watch. The principal in this transaction, Hayley, afterwards ran away with a ship of Mr. Isaac Clason's, and carried her into a French port.

On the 19th of December, 1796, "Edwin and Angelina, or the Bandit," was performed for the first time. This only dramatic production from the pen of Doctor Elihu Hubbard Smith, was, like himself, pure and energetic. But it was not sufficiently dramatic, and the characters of Edwin and Angelina too familiar to all readers. He wrote many sonnets and essays, but published little except on subjects connected with his profession. The drama of Edwin and Angelina was printed, with a dedication to the author's parents, "Reuben and Abigail Smith."

This amiable and highly gifted man was born at Litchfield, in Connecticut, in the year 1771. He was fitted for entering Yale College at so early an age, and graduated while so young, that his father, Doctor Reuben Smith, of Litchfield, very judiciously placed him, although he had passed through College honourably, for further tuition under the care of Doctor Dwight, at Greenfield. He received his first medical education under his worthy father, and the accomplishment of it under the professors of Philadelphia. There he became the friend of Charles Brockden Brown, whom he introduced to the knowledge and friendship of the writer. Doctor E. H. Smith practised his profession in New-York, and there, with Doctors Edward Miller and Samuel Latham Mitchill, established the work entitled "The Medical Repository." These men, with the others above mentioned, formed the before-mentioned band of literary pioneers. Of these the three last named were all distinguished as writers and physicians; another, Noah Webster, as a philologist and lexicographer; James Kent and William Johnson as jurists; Richard Alsop as a poet; and Samuel Miller as a theologian. To such men were the dramas of the American manager read and submitted.

Doctor Elihu Hubbard Smith fell a victim to yellow fever in September, 1798. This was one of those returns of devastating pestilence which destroyed the hopes of fortune and usefulness which his friend the manager had entertained, and robbed that friend of one dearer to him than any earthly wealth. Elihu H. Smith feared no danger in the exercise of his professional duties, or of his duty as a man. He relied, likewise, upon his habitual temperance, perhaps carried to excess. He continued amidst the dead and dying, firmly and cheerfully exposing himself to infection. Finally, a young and amiable foreigner, an Italian, arrived from Philadelphia, where the plague likewise raged. He was seized with the symptoms before he reached New-York. Smith and his friend Johnson had him removed to their house before mentioned, in Pine-street, that he might have every aid humanity could render. He died. His nurse and physician sickened, and when he saw the last black symptoms of dissolution in his own case, calmly remarked, "decomposition," and expired.

Thus the young, the temperate, the virtuous, the benevolent, sank under the hoofs of the pale horse and pierced by his rider's darts—but they had enjoyed life and the happiness flowing from conscious rectitude, and they died doing their duty, and calmly bowing to the will of their God.

On the 9th of January, 1797, was first performed a piece in two acts, written by the American manager, called "Tell Truth and Shame the Devil." It was an alteration from a French one-act piece called "Jerome Pointu." So little of the French *proverbe* was retained, that it may be considered as original. It was played a few times and forgotten. It was printed by Longworth, and was (as altered to suit the place and people) played at Covent Garden on the 18th of May, 1799.

Seven days after "Tell Truth and Shame the Devil," "Bourville Castle" made its appearance, written by John Blair Linn. This young man was the son of Doctor Linn, of the Presbyterian Church, had graduated at Columbia College, New-York, and was at the time studying law with Alexander Hamilton. One of the most remarkable circumstances attending Bourville Castle is, that Charles Brockden Brown, and the American manager, whose guest he was, corrected the manuscript and wrote out the parts for the performers. Mr. Linn studied divinity, and was for some years pastor of a church in Philadelphia, much esteemed as a preacher, and beloved as a man. After his death, Brown published an elegant biographical eulogium on him.

On the 1st of February, "The Comet," a comedy by Mr. Milns, was performed. It was soon afterwards put down to a farce, which it had been originally, when it was acted in London for John Bannister's benefit.

It appears that although the American manager had been empowered to cast all plays, that is, to appropriate parts, this source of discord, even between Hallam and Hodgkinson, was not removed. Hallam gave up most that Hodgkinson wished, but he wished all. Hallam had played Goldfinch in the Road to Ruin, and Hodgkinson Harry Dornton. On occasion of preparing the play for performance, the latter told the manager that Hallam was unfit for Goldfinch, and he must have it, or he would not play in the piece. The manager made a proper stand, and told him he must play Harry Dornton, as it was the part he had played by choice, and his name should be put in the bill. The consequence was, that he went so far as to consult the illustrious Hamilton respecting the force of the articles he had signed, and swayed by his legal advice, submitted to play this very fine part rather than forfeit his bond. It had been agreed that no money should be expended, or salaries granted, without consent of the three concerned; Hallam, as being proprietor of half, to have a voice equal to the other two. The salaries of the three were fixed. But a proposal was soon made to obtain higher salaries for Hodgkinson and wife, accompanied by threats of leaving the company, or ceasing to play. The irritation between Hallam and Hodgkinson was incessant, and the determination of Hallam to bring his wife on the stage again, in which he found supporters, made the internal business of the theatre a constant source of vexations. Instead of the promised assistance in the management, every obstacle was increased, and every error exulted over, by both the contending parties.

The frequent applications of *would-be* authors and actors is a source of trouble to all managers. Sometimes the applications are vexatious, sometimes ludicrous.

"Are you the gentleman that takes in play-actors?" asked a youth of seventeen or eighteen, slender, awkward, neatly dressed in a short blue jacket, striped waistcoat, pantaloons of nankeen, and half-boots. The reply was, "I have the direction of the theatre."

"Do you want any actors?"

"Any person of extraordinary talents would find employment. Do you know of any one wanting to engage as an actor?"

"I want to go on the stage myself."

"You! Did you ever attempt to go on the stage?"

"Only at the Academy."

"You are an American?"

"Yes."

"Where were you educated?"

"At Goshen."

"What plays did you perform in at the Academy?"

"Why, we played the Catos, and Tamerlanes, and such."

"And what did you play?"

"I played Cato and Bajazet—and in the Bold Stroke for a Wife, I played the Colonel. I was the biggest boy, and so I played the biggest parts."

Sometimes a young Scotchman would present himself for Douglas, because "*Hairy Johnson* was successful in London;" or an Irishman, realizing Murphy's Othello in the Apprentice.

On the 5th of December, 1796, Wignell having returned to Philadelphia with his powerful reinforcement, opened his theatre with Romeo and Juliet; Juliet, Mrs. Merry, perhaps the best representative of Juliet that ever was seen or heard. On the 7th, the ballet dancers, Mr. and Mrs. Byrne, were brought out; and on the Friday following, the 9th, Mr. Cooper made his first appearance in America, playing Macbeth.

⇥ CHAPTER 14 ⇤

Letter from T. Holcroft — New Theatre, Park — Boston Theatres — John B. Williamson — Bunker Hill, a Tragedy — John Burk — The Hallam Riot — Hodgkinson hissed off the Stage — Hallam breaks into Jail — The author's visit to Philadelphia, May, 1797 — Convention from the Abolition Societies — Doctors Barton, Rush, Griffiths — Bartram the Botanist — Uriah Tracy — Oliver Wolcott — Joseph Bringhurst — Wm. Cobbett — "The Ancient Day" — Natural History — Man of Fortitude — Boston and Charleston Theatres — Names of Performers known at this time in the United States (1797) — Wignell and Reinagle, and the Philadelphia Company in Greenwich-street, New-York.

The writer having sent some manuscripts to Mr. Holcroft, with whom he had exchanged letters before, received the following from him; which, as it gives the opinions of a veteran dramatist on the play of The Archers, or William Tell, recently acted, and on other subjects connected with this work, we will insert.

"To Mr. Dunlap.

"DEAR SIR,

"I received your last letters dated May and October; as I had done others some months ago, in which you wished me to read your manuscripts. Your friend, Mr. Brewer, offered to put these manuscripts into my hands; this I declined, and I will state my motives.

"The reading of manuscripts I have found to be attended with danger. I once read two acts of a manuscript play, and was afterwards accused of having purloined one of the characters. The accusation had some semblance of truth: latent ideas floated in my mind, and there were two or three traits in the character drawn by me similar to the one I had read; though I was very unconscious of this when I wrote the character.

"A still more potent reason is the improbability of good that is to result from reading manuscripts. To read carefully, examine conscientiously, and detail with perspicuity the errors which the judgment of a critic might think deserving of amendment, is a laborious task: it devours time and fatigues the mind, and but seldom to any good purpose. Books of criticism abound, and may be consulted by an author who is anxious to improve. I grant that the critical remarks of a friend may be of great service. If a man have attained that elegance of diction, depth of penetration, and strength of feeling which constitute genius, to criticize his works before they are presented to the public, may be a useful and a dignified task. Men acquire these high qualities gradually, when compelled by that restless desire which is incessant in its endeavours after excellence; and for these gradations the books already written are, in my opinion, sufficient. Your friend gave me William Tell to read: it proves you have made some progress; but it likewise proves, as far as I am a judge, that much remains for you to accomplish. Common thoughts, common characters, and common sensations have little attraction: we must soar beyond them, or be contented to walk the earth and join the crowd. Far be it from me to discourage those efforts of mind in which I delight: but far be it from me to deceive. If you would attain the high gifts after which you so virtuously aspire, your perseverance must be energetic and unremitting. I consider America as unfavourable to genius: not from any qualities of air, earth, or water: but because the efforts of mind are neither so great, so numerous, or so urgent as in England or France.

"You wish for an independence. That man is independent whose mind is prepared to meet all fortunes, and be happy under the worst; who is conscious that industry in any country will supply the very few real wants of his species; and who, while he can enjoy the delicacies of taste as exquisitely as a glutton, can transfer that luxury by the activity of his mind and body to the simplest viands. Every other man is a slave, though he were more wealthy than Midas.

"I send you my narrative, but am surprised that there should be any difficulty in procuring it at New-York. To a bookseller, the conveyance of such things is familiar and easy; to an individual it has the inconvenience of calling his attention to trifles, and disturbing his ordinary progress. I am not certain that the man of literature is not benefited by these little jolts that awaken him, or rather endeavours to awaken: but I know from experience he is very unwilling to notice them, they therefore easily slip his memory. This is the reason that I did not send it before as you desired.

"With respect to the stage, it is a question which cannot be effectually discussed in a letter: but I have no doubt whatever of its high moral tendency. Neither, in my opinion, was Rousseau right relative to Geneva: for that, which is in itself essentially good, will, as I suppose, be good at all times and in all places.

"T. HOLCROFT.

"London, Newman-street, ⎫
    December 10th, 1796." ⎭

Here was no flattery to the young author, but much excellent advice. He probably flattered himself that if the stern critic had read the manuscript instead of the printed play, he might have found something more than "common thoughts, common characters, and common sensations;" and yet it would probably have been merely self-flattery. The remark respecting America as being "unfavourable to genius," was at that time perfectly true: but the efforts of mind are now, and must be henceforward, greater, more numerous, and more urgent than heretofore. The remark only applies to literature and the fine arts. It is applicable to a time past. The men of the present day have advantages which their predecessors had not.

At this time, January, 1797, the managers were negotiating with the proprietors of the new theatre, Park, for that building, and Hodgkinson was anxious to go to England to procure wardrobe and performers. This was discouraged by the American partner, who now knew the man and his motives too well. Hallam was decidedly opposed to the scheme. In February, every engine that Hallam could move was put in operation to force a consent to the return of Mrs. Hallam to the stage.

Mr. John B. Williamson, before mentioned as remembered when playing at the Haymarket theatre, London, in 1785–6, was now manager of the Federal-street theatre, Boston, and wished to take the Hartford theatre for one season. A portion of his letter to Hodgkinson is characteristic: "You wish to be informed 'how we go on;' I scarcely need to point out what your own judgment and experience here will suggest. *We* have the opinion hollow as to the merits of the company, and the patronage of the '*better sort.*' But the rage for *novelty* in Boston, and prevailing Jacobin spirit in the lower ranks, are our strongest opponents.

Two theatres cannot be supported—an additional public could not be created with an additional theatre. Could the *joint* receipts of *both houses* be fairly averaged, I will venture to assert they would not exceed *five hundred and fifty* dollars, while we are expending upwards of *twelve hundred* nightly, to take—'a plague upon both the houses'—the deficiency must fall *somewhere.* However we *pay* punctually—it is in proof that our opponents *do not.* They have brought out a new piece, called 'Bunker Hill,' a tragedy, the most execrable of the Grubstreet kind—but from its locality in title, the burning of Charlestown, and *peppering* the *British* (which are superadded to the tragedy in pantomime), to the utter disgrace of Boston theatricals, has brought them *full houses.*"

This deplorable Bunker Hill was offered to the New-York stage, by the author, for one hundred guineas. He published it, and we are sorry to say it was afterwards played in New-York. The author's letter accompanying the play is too great a curiosity to be suppressed.

Mr. Burk's History of Virginia proves that it was not want of talent or learning that occasioned this odd production.

"To J. Hodgkinson, Esq.

"DEAR SIR,

"From a wish that you should be possessed of my play as early as possible, I have preferred sending on the original copy rather than wait to have a fair one transcribed—where it was incomplete I have written and made it good, interspersing occasionally such remarks as, from seeing the effect in representation, appeared to me serviceable in getting it up. It was played seven nights successively, and on the last night was received with the same enthusiasm as on the first—it revived old scenes, and united all parts of the house. Mr. Powell intends it for a stock play, and it will be represented on all festivals—such as 4th July, 19th June, &c. It will be played here in a few nights again, immediately after Columbus. The lines marked by inverted commas are those spoken. The hill is raised gradually by boards extended from the stage to a bench. Three men should walk abreast on it, and the side where the English march up, should for the most part be turned towards the wings; on our hill there was room for eighteen or twenty men, and they were concealed by a board painted mud colour, and having two cannons painted on it—which board was three feet and a half high. The English marched in two divisions from one extremity of the stage, where they ranged, after coming from the wings, when they come to the foot of the hill. The Americans fire—the English fire—six or seven of your men should be taught to fall—the fire should be frequent for some minutes. The English retire to the front of the stage—second line of English advance from the wing near the hill—firing commences—they are again beaten back—windows on the stage should be open to let out the smoak. All the English make the attack and mount the hill. After a brisk fire, the Americans leave works and meet them. Here is room for effect, if the scuffle be nicely managed. Sometimes the English falling back, sometimes the Americans—two or three Englishmen rolling down the hill. A square piece about nine feet high and five wide, having some houses and a meeting-house painted on fire, with flame and smoak issuing from it, should be raised two feet distance from the horizon scene at the back of your stage, the windows and doors cut out for transparencies— in a word, it should have the appearance of a town on fire. We had painted smoak suspended—it is raised at the back wing, and is intended to represent Charlestown, and is on a line with the hill, and where it is lowest. The fire should be played skilfully" (this puts one in mind of Bottom playing Moon-shine) "behind this burning town, and the smoak to evaporate. When the curtain rises in the fifth, the appearance of the whole is good—Charlestown on fire, the breastwork of wood, the Americans appearing over the works and the muzzles of their guns, the English and the American music, the attack of the hill, the falling of the English troops, Warren's half descending the hill and animating the Americans, the smoak and confusion, all together produce an effect scarce credible. We had a scene of State-street— if you had one it would not be amiss—we used it instead of the scene of Boston Neck—it appears to me you need not be particular, but the hill and Charlestown on fire. We had English uniforms for men and officers. You can procure the coats of some company at New-York which dresses in red. Small cannon should be fired during the battle, which continued with us for twelve or fifteen minutes. I am thus prolix that you may find the less difficulty in getting it up—it is not expensive, and will always be a valuable stock piece. I should not wonder if every person in New-York, and some miles round it, should go to see it represented. There will no doubt be some who will call in question your prudence in getting up this piece, as being not in favour of England. Those are blockheads, and know not the public opinion in America. Boston is as much divided as New-York—party was forgotten in the representation of it. Others there are who will endeavour to prejudice you against its merit; of them I shall say nothing. You have the play and can judge for yourself—my reason for mentioning the latter description of men is, that a man from Boston, who pretends to criticise without knowing how to *spell,* has been industrious in depreciating the value of my piece in Boston, and I conceived it not improbable that he would act in the same manner in New-York. When he found it had succeeded, he ascribed its success alone to its locality. This man took a letter to you from Mr. Barrett. I send you the prologue and elegy.

"After consulting Mr. Barrett, who was delicate in advising, lest he should be thought partial to one interest or the other, I have concluded to charge you one hundred guineas for the copy, seventy of which I request you will send to Mr. Barrett immediately on receipt of the piece, the remaining thirty on the fourth night of representation. Mr. Barrett thinks it will run ten nights in succession at New-York. I think not of printing it for one year, when I do I shall dedicate it to the President. Mr. Bates has sent on to me for a copy. I am in treaty with Mr. Wignell. The terms shall not be lower than with you. I shall send you on from time to time such pantomimes and entertainments as I shall arrange, on reasonable terms. I have three at present, which I shall send on when you please, as cheap as you can get a pirated copy of a farce. My new tragedy, entitled Joan of Arc, or the Maid of Orleans, is ready for representation. Excuse this wretched scrawl, it has been written too hastily.

"JOHN BURK.

"We had our hill on the left side of the stage—the painting of Charlestown on fire should not be seen till the fifth act. If there is any thing you would wish to be informed on further, by directing a line to me, you shall receive the speediest answer. As I look on this only as the *basis* of a future negotiation, I shall not be averse to abate something of my demand, if you think it high, though I am tolerably certain you will clear four thousand dollars in its run only."

This is literal and faithful. He cleared by it $2000 in Boston. Hodgkinson sent the piece back immediately, but it was returned with a letter offering it on the usual terms given by him for new pieces.

The elegy mentioned in the letter begins,

"He died for his country—rain our tears."

And the first stanza concludes thus:—

"His sacred blood was shed for you,
Oh let us shed our tears in lieu."

The author styles himself, "late of Trinity College, Dublin." He says, "never less than 2500 persons attended, sometimes 3000; our pit and boxes were as good the last night as the first." Again, "this act kept the audience in one incessant roar of applause, from beginning to end," and "the fifth act was received with still greater enthusiasm than the fourth."

After some attempts to induce Mr. Hallam to sell out altogether, which failed, the American manager relinquished his salary to Hodgkinson, who agreed to become the acting manager. It was further agreed that the former articles should be made void after the present season, the one quitting theatrical management, the other leaving the old American Company and New-York. Happy would it have been if *so* it had been!

The re-engagement of Mrs. Hallam being refused, notwithstanding threats and hints of combinations to create riots and coerce the managers, her husband gave it out that she should play for his benefit. The following regulations were put up in the green-room.

> "*Regulations for the old American Company, at the ensuing Benefits.*
>
> March 24th, 1797.
>
> The nights on which benefit plays will be performed, to be thrown for in two classes, as on the last season.
>
> Any performer giving notice, after this date, to the acting manager for the time being, of his or her wish to get up any new piece, on his or her night, will obtain by such notice a prior right to such new piece.
>
> No piece shall be performed in any other manner than as cast by the acting manager for the time being, that cast to be obtained previous to advertising the piece.
>
> No bill to be published until submitted to the correction of the acting manager for the time being, and one of the other proprietors.
>
> No performer can be required to study more than four lengths, from play night to play night, and in the same proportion for a longer time."

The evening after this notice was put up, Hodgkinson, on playing Puff, in the Critic, mentioned himself as is usual, it being intended by the author that the actor shall do so; but on this occasion, there was a long and audible hiss among the plaudits; he then added "to be sure he was goosed, but that's of little consequence; it is not the first time this season that some envious scoundrel has insulted him," and then went on with the part apparently at ease.

On the 27th, Hallam informed Hodgkinson that he would not agree to the regulations which had been put up in the green-room, and had torn them down. James Kent and William Johnson, Esqrs. were consulted upon the articles of agreement, and gave their opinion that a suit might be commenced for their breach, but advised that no steps of the kind should be then taken, except that they would write to him.

On the evening of the 29th, the Hallams had concerted an appeal to the public from the stage, and had planned their measures with such secrecy that Hodgkinson, then the acting manager, had no intimation of them. He had been told that Mrs. Hallam was behind the scenes, but that was all. He was to play Colin M'Cleod, in the Fashionable Lover, and had come on the stage from the left side to begin the comedy, when he was saluted by hisses and the cry of "off! off!" He stood astounded, and the noise and hissing continued undiminished. Mrs. Hallam entered from the right, dressed in black silk, her hair parted on the top of her head, combed down on each side of her face, and powdered. She looked beauty in distress. She held a paper in her hands, and courtesied most profoundly. The plaudit which saluted her entrance caused Hodgkinson to look over his shoulder, and he then first perceived that she was not only in the house, but on the stage. There was a momentary silence, when a person in the pit cried out "Insolence," on which a man sprang up, likewise in the pit, and brandishing a cudgel, with which many appeared to be armed, cried, "Out with the rascal," which was repeated by others, until it was superseded by another cry of "Hear Mrs. Hallam." And now Hallam was seen, dressed in black, stalking down the centre of the stage, and advancing with many bows to the audience. A messenger was despatched to give notice to the magistrates that a riot had commenced at the theatre. Hallam addressed the audience and asked permission for Mrs. Hallam to read the paper she held in her hand. Mrs. Hallam then read a statement of injuries received in being deprived of the means of earning her bread, asserted that she never intentionally offended that audience, and expressed her eternal gratitude to those who now supported her. She then retired amid plaudits. Hallam and Hodgkinson remained on the stage, the one in stately black, the other in the Highland Colin's dress. They both addressed the audience, but Hodgkinson was constantly interrupted by hisses, he however succeeded in stating that the offer to withdraw Mrs. Hallam from the stage was the basis of the present copartnership, and had been made by Mr. Hallam. This Hallam denied. The other appealed to Mr. Philip Ten Eyck, as the person bringing the offer from Hallam. This was affirmed by Mr. Ten Eyck, who was present, and pledged himself to state the affair in the papers. Hodgkinson now obtained a hearing, and appealed to the audience eloquently. He represented the injustice of attacking a player when on the stage and defenceless, by a combination of numbers determined to prejudge and insult him. "If I have offended any one, I am known and to be found, but I know not the persons or the names of those who insult me." Some one cried out, "We are not ashamed of our names."

"Give me your name, sir;—you who last spoke."

But the champion drew back and sheltered himself in the crowd. Hodgkinson made use of the word riot. This called forth vehement marks of disapprobation.

John Cozine, Esq., afterwards Judge Cozine, got up in a side-box not far from the stage, and addressed the rioters. They hissed. He proceeded, "You are guilty of a riot, and liable to all the consequent damage that may ensue. You have no right to demand any thing or person at the theatre, or on the stage, not advertised expressly in the bill. If Mr. Hallam is aggrieved, he has his remedy in a court of justice. You are rioters; you will know to-morrow that the grand jury are sitting."

Another gentleman got up in a side-box and told Hodgkinson that he degraded his profession by speaking to men who had entered into a conspiracy to injure him, and would only hear his adversaries.

The tide was turning, and Hallam requested that the play might commence, saying he would withdraw Mrs. Hallam.

Some one said, "It is very hard that the public are not to be indulged with a

favourite actress." Hodgkinson promptly replied, "You are not the public, sir."
He was asked if he would not permit Mrs. Hallam to play. He answered, "Never,
while I have any thing to do with the theatre." He said he would appeal to the
public and the laws of the country. He was now generally applauded, and the
rioters put down. The mayor and other magistrates were by this time in the house.

There was a general call for the play. Hodgkinson said he could not proceed
after what had passed, but was soon persuaded; and commenced with the first
line of Colin M'Cleod. "Hoot awa," &c. amidst a shout of applause, and uninterrupted plaudits continued throughout the evening's entertainment.

On the 30th of March, Mr. Philip Ten Eyck made a statement of facts respecting Hallam's withdrawing Mrs. Hallam from the stage, which statement was
given for publication to the Daily Advertiser and Patriotic Register.

On the next play night Hodgkinson was hissed, until he finally took his leave,
went home, and the audience retired. He now declined appearing as actor or
manager, and with difficulty the performers' benefits were arranged, and in a
slovenly manner carried through.

It was necessary to commence suits against Hallam; but Hodgkinson, justly
fearful that an improper impression on the public might be made thereby, gave
instructions that Mr. Hallam's person should not be molested; such an opportunity, however, was not to be missed, and he would go to jail in spite of the
sheriff. Hodgkinson wrote to the deputy sheriff thus. "Sir, the impression has
gone forth among a number of citizens that Mr. Hallam is in confinement at
my instance. I will thank you to say in return what my request was to you respecting the suit for damages between Mr. Hallam and me, and how, after the
conversation that passed this morning he is surrendered at all, or whether he is
not permitted to leave custody if he pleases." The answer was:

April 18th, 1797.—"Sir: I waited upon Mr. Hallam yesterday before I had seen
you upon the business of the writ, and agreeable to the nature of the precept,
asked him to endorse his appearance. After a few minutes' consideration he
declined, and said he would go to jail. I remonstrated against his resolution,
and begged him not to let the impulse of the moment lead him to put it in
execution. He promised to wait upon me this morning at nine o'clock, and
conclusively determine what to do. He came and said he had made up his
mind to remain in custody. I begged him to think better of it—that I desired
no endorsement from him, and he was at liberty to go when he pleased. He
would content himself with nothing short of actual confinement, and though
I told him the turnkeys should have orders to let him out whenever he called
upon them, he was determined not to be liberated. I am sorry the contest
between you has taken so serious an aspect; I certainly have a high esteem for
Mr. Hallam, and would go great lengths to serve him, yet I must do you the

justice to declare when I waited upon you at your request this morning, you told me you was heartily willing he should be left at his word, and wished no difficulty to arise that might savour of coercion. But having supposed a breach of covenant had taken place on the part of Mr. Hallam, you found no other way left you but the step which you had taken, and trusted I would do every thing in my power to convince him he was free from constraint.

"Signed, Arondt Van Hook.

Thus Mr. Hallam broke into jail, and the jailer, after begging him not to do so, asked the lawyer who issued the writ for advice, who laughing, told him, "Turn him out of doors, unless you keep him as a companion." After playing this farce some hours, Hallam walked home again and then played sick, or was sick from disappointment and vexation.

During the benefits, Mrs. Hallam again appeared before the public as Lady Teazle, on the night appropriated to her husband's son. Hodgkinson had been driven from the stage. The writer had only continued in the direction to prevent total loss; and on the 2d of May, 1797, went to Philadelphia as a deputy to the Convention there meeting, from the Abolition Societies of the several states. The deputies from New-York, among others, were Doctor E. H. Smith, Doctor Samuel L. Mitchill, and Lawrence Embree, the same whose conscience refused 100 dollars for the poor, because it came from the manager of a play-house. Uriah Tracy, of Connecticut, represented the Abolition Society of Connecticut in Convention, as well as the good people of the state in Congress.

To relieve the monotony of a work on one subject, we will extract from a diary, kept at the time, some notices of men and events of that day which may not prove uninteresting. Charles Brockden Brown was now at home in his father's house in Philadelphia. E. H. Smith had preceded the writer. Extracts:

Went by appointment and drank tea with Charles. He showed me a letter from Joseph Bringhurst, in which he gives his reason for being a Christian; the letter is highly pleasing and lovely. We walk in the state-house yard, and thence into the library. Here I read with much pleasure a translation of *Leonora*. The bewildered dream of a heart-broken girl ending in death is finely imagined and executed. We leave the library to see the circus and exhibitions of a French equestrian (Lailson). Smith joins and goes with us. The *coup d'œil* of the house, lights, and company were pleasing, but a pleasure fleeting in the extreme. Compare the pleasures of yesterday (a day the writer had passed in the place of his nativity, Perth Amboy), rambling over meadows and clover fields, amid orchards whose blossoms filled the air with fragrance, while birds of every kind warbled or whistled their expressions of happiness. To-day encircled in a huge enclosure from which the light and air of Heaven is excluded, surrounded by beings like myself, pretending to rationality, yet sitting hour after hour to see men and women, in fool's coats, display the gambols of the monkey as the highest attainment of their persevering industry. We did not stay the show over. I found Tracy at home, and passed an agreeable hour with him.

May 3d. Smith and self call on Brown. Bringhurst came hither from Wilmington yesterday; we cannot yet find him. Go to the theatre, but do not find Wignell. We called on Mr. John Leib, who read us a dissection of Peter Porcupine, by his brother Doctor Leib. We call to see Leffert: Volney is not in town, so we are disappointed in our expected introduction to him. We went to Cobbett's bookstore. He is a stout, well-looking man, plain and manly, speaks well, but has an aspect of ill temper. Bought Adam's Defence, in 3 octavo vols., just published by Cobbett from the last London edition. We now find Bringhurst at Brown's, and pass a very pleasant hour with him. Evening, Bringhurst and Brown called on us and staid until the hour appointed for the meeting of the Convention. Doctor Rush I had met in the course of the day; we now met him again, and Doctor Griffith, Gen. Bloomfield, and others of my acquaintance. On returning home, Tracy, who had been at the theatre, gave us an account of a new drama, in three acts, called "The Ancient Day," by a citizen of Philadelphia, which he says is execrable.

May 4th. Go with Tracy and Smith to the "United States" frigate now nearly ready for launching. Met Wignell and Reinagle, who took me to the theatre. I saw Cooper, who apologized for not writing to me. He says he has not written to Holcroft. Wignell left me, and I soon left the theatre, which looks quite small after seeing Lailson's circus. Declined an invitation to dine with Wignell on Saturday. Dine at Brown's, with Smith and Bringhurst. Afternoon, met Oliver Wolcott, who walked with my hand locked in his nearly the length of a square; he reproached me with not calling on him, and took my address. He asked me for news. I told him I had just read a letter attributed to Mr. Jefferson, which was very surprising to me. He said it was not so to him, that it corresponded with his manner of talking. I promised to call on him, and went to my lodgings, where he came with the attorney-general, and invited Tracy, Smith, and self to dine with him.

May 6th. Attend to the laws respecting slavery, in consequence of a nomination as chairman of committee for that purpose. Tracy, Smith, Mitchill, and self, dined with Secretary Wolcott, and passed an agreeable afternoon. He gave us some wine sent by Joel Barlow to him from Algiers, made from grapes the growth of that soil, and manufactured by the hands of the poet and ambassador. Evening, theatre—"Way to get Married." Pleased with Morton's Tangent. It was easy and elegant, nothing overstrained. Cooper exceeded my expectations in Faulkner. Mrs. Merry was certainly every thing that an actress could be in Julia. Her voice charming; her person far exceeding my expectation from having seen her in a riding habit at New-York, but I am not quite satisfied with her countenance, and see or imagine some defect in her eyes.

May 7th. Smith, Mitchill, and self breakfast with Doctor Benjamin Smith Barton. Here I had a feast of physical science. He showed us a number of drawings in natural history, executed by himself, with eminent accuracy and taste, among which were two species of jerboa, lately discovered by himself. He has promised me a list of such plants of our country as have not been yet drawn, or have only imperfect drawings or engravings made of them. He showed us, in a small box, curiously preserved, a number of grasshoppers, each of which was transfixed with a thorn, and gave us the following history of them. "A gentleman, going into a young apple orchard, was surprised to see the trees hung with grasshoppers thus transfixed on the thorny branches. The farmer laughed at his surprise, and told him that the birds did it. For what purpose, or what birds, the farmer never inquired. This was late in the autumn. The gentleman's curiosity was strongly awakened; he collected specimens of the insect, and watched for the birds. The result of his observations in this and the succeeding year was, that the "great ash-coloured butcher-bird, or 'shrike,' a specimen of which Doctor Barton produced (taken in the act), is the bird that dresses out such curious shambles; not only to serve as provision after the insect tribes have run their little race of life, but as a bait whereby to catch the small birds who remain late in the autumn, or winter, among us. The bird-catcher having baited the thorns, sits ready until a bird is attracted by the bait, then pounces on and secures his victim."

May 8th. Dine with James Todd, who had other members of the Convention with him. Go to Convention at 3. Mr. Patterson asserted that what was morally right could not be politically wrong, applying it to the sudden and total abolition of slavery, as it respects the Southern states, and the acts of the French convention, which liberated all their West India slaves. Doctor Rush got up and approved this, repeating with admiration Condorcet's expression of "perish our West India islands rather than we should depart from the principles of justice." This he gave as sublime, and said he did homage to it. Do these gentlemen consider that justice is due to the inhabitants of those countries where there are unhappily slaves, and to slave-holders as well as slaves? ('Fiat Justitia' is in the mouths of many who do not consider that to liberate the slave does not restore him to his original condition, but probably devotes him and his holder to misery, and that many a slave-holder is innocently such—that, in short, justice is due to all God's creatures, as is every act of love; but this subject is better understood now, and Colonization Societies are superseding the Abolitionists, who are to be blessed for beginning the good work.)

May 9th. Rise about 5 o'clock, and join Charles Brockden Brown about 6, for the purpose of walking to Bartram's Botanic Garden. We breakfasted at Gray's Gardens, and then continued our walk. Arrived at the Botanist's Garden, we approached an old man who, with a rake in his hand, was breaking the clods of earth in a tulip bed. His hat was old and flapped over his face, his coarse shirt was seen near his neck, as he wore no cravat or kerchief; his waistcoat and breeches were both of leather, and his shoes were tied with leather strings. We approached and accosted him. He ceased his work, and entered into conversation with the ease and politeness of nature's noblemen. His countenance was expressive of benignity and happiness. This was the botanist, traveller, and philosopher we had come to see. He had pointed out many curious plants. He said there was in New-Jersey a third species of azalea, somewhat like the viscosa; that at Passaic falls, his father John Bartram and himself had found in a shady hollow, near the cascade, a species of geranium; and in the neighbourhood, the larch-tree. He had heard of, but had never seen Wangenheim's book. Dine with Smith and Mitchill at Doctor Rush's. He mentions several cases of hydrophobia cured by *copious bleeding.*

We will return to New-York, and the drama.

During the month of May, negotiations were in progress respecting the new theatre, which were not concluded until some time after, and the result shall be noticed in due time.

In the letter from T. Holcroft to W. Dunlap, we find the first-mentioned person noticing the accusation made against him of appropriating a portion of a manuscript left with him for reading to his own purposes in composition. Managers have been accused of such thefts time out of mind. But a most curious fact of that nature we will notice, as characteristic of the extraordinary individual who was one of the parties in the affair.

The person we have designated the American manager, had written a piece in one act for the stage, and called it the "Knight's Adventure." It was in blank verse. He left it with Mr. Hodgkinson, and it was almost forgotten, when Hodgkinson told him that he had written a play, and called it "The Man of Fortitude." This was the whole of the "Knight's Adventure," partly in prose, with the addition of a comic buffoon, and a lady. The author of the first piece remarked this to Hodgkinson, who did not deny it, only said he had "altered every thing," and truly every thing was altered. "And you see I have added so and so." The other laughed and asked for his one-act piece, but it was not forthcoming. The Man of Fortitude was read to companions at the dinner table, to the company in the greenroom, and on the 7th of June, 1797, played for a benefit. We scarcely believe the author was conscious of wrong in the transaction, as far as injury to another was concerned. The Knight's Adventure was afterwards recovered.

At a benefit given at the Boston theatre, in the early part of March, 1797, the sum of 887 dollars was raised for the prisoners recently released from Algiers. As we have no occurrence to record belonging to this period, we will close this chapter with an extract from the Minerva of July 29th, 1797, and some other "notes of preparation."

The citizens of Boston are assured, that for five years to come, their amusements will not be disturbed by an opposition between the two theatres. A formal agreement has taken place between Mr. Hodgkinson, manager of the N. York company, and the proprietor of the City theatre, Charleston, who have engaged the two theatres in town. The Haymarket will be reserved for summer exhibitions, the Federal-street for winter. The plan for the winter theatre is to have one company for Boston and one for Charleston, to be exchanged every season. The persons already fixed upon and partly engaged are,

In Boston, Mr. and Mrs. Barrett, Mr. and Mrs. Marshall, Mr. and Mrs. C. Powell, Mr. and Mrs. S. Powell, Mr. and Mrs. Harper, Mr. and Mrs. Graupner, M. and Madame Lege, M. and Madame Gardie, Messrs. Villiers, Kenny, Dickinson, and J. Jones. Mrs. Allen, and Miss Harrison.

For Charleston, Mr. and Mrs. Williamson, Mr. and Mrs. Whitlock, Mr. and Mrs. Jones, Mr. and Mrs. Cleveland, Mr. and Mrs. Hughes, Mr. and Mrs. Placide, Mr. and Mrs. Rowson, Messrs. Chalmers, Williamson (a singer), Downie, and M'Kenzie. Misses Broadhurst and Green.

When this catalogue of names is added to that which may be composed from the two companies at Philadelphia and New-York, we may form an estimate of the progress of the theatre, and in some measure of the country, since the year 1752.

In New-York were Mr. and Mrs. Hodgkinson, Mr. and Mrs. Hallam, Mr. and Mrs. Johnson, Mr. and Mrs. Tyler, Mr. and Mrs. Seymour, Mr. and Mrs. Munto, Messrs. Jefferson, Hallam, jun., Martin, Crosby, Fawcet, Prigmore, Miller, Lee, Wools, M'Grath, Durang, Mrs. Melmoth, Mrs. Brett, and Misses Brett and Hardinge.

And the Philadelphia company consisted of Messrs. Wignell, Fennell, Cooper, Moreton, Harwood, Marshall, Blissett, Francis, Hardinge, Fox, Warren, Warrell, Byrne, Green, and L'Estrange. Bernard joined after they opened in Greenwich-street, New-York. Mesdames Merry, Marshall, Oldmixon, Hardinge, Francis, Warrell, L'Estrange, and Misses Oldfield, Milbourne, &c. such were the successors, in 1797, to the company sent from Goodman's Fields to Virginia in 1752, and playing for the first time in New-York in 1753.

On the 17th of August, the following notice appeared in the New-York newspapers. "The public are respectfully informed, the entertainments of the theatre, Greenwich-street, will commence on Monday, the twenty-first instant. Wignell and Reinagle." And on the 18th appeared thus. "The public are informed, that several principal performers of the Boston and Charleston theatres, on their way to Philadelphia, will perform, on Friday evening, a comedy called The Wonder, with the farce of The Spoiled Child."

⇢ CHAPTER 15 ⇠

Solee and Company open in John-street, August 18th, 1797 — Mr. Whitlock — Wignell and Reinagle's Company in Greenwich-street — Mrs. Merry — Mr. Cooper — Mr. Bernard — Mr. and Mrs. L'Estrange — Mr. Fox — Mr. and Mrs. Hardinge — Mr. and Mrs. Byrne — Mr. John Joseph Holland.

The performers announced in the last chapter as of the Boston and Charleston theatres, played in the John-street theatre, the New-York company being elsewhere. Mr. Solee, a French gentleman, was the manager. He was imperfectly acquainted with the English language, and utterly unacquainted with English literature, especially dramatic. The performers directed the business, which was very bad in every sense, though some excellent actors were employed in it. Mrs. Whitlock appeared in Isabella, and was thus announced. "Mrs. Whitlock, the sister of Mrs. Siddons, and the Siddons of America, is arrived, and will perform at the theatre in John-street the short time the company remains in this city." But the Siddons of America, as we shall see, was playing at the other house, the circus in Greenwich-street, fitted up as an elegant summer theatre.

We shall dwell at some length upon such performers attached to the company of Wignell and Reinagle as have not already occupied our pages, and although the order in which we shall notice them is not intended to denote the rank which they hold in our estimation, yet we begin with the person who will long be entitled to the character of the most perfect actor America has seen—Mrs. Ann Merry.

This lady was born in the year 1770, and was the daughter of Mr. John Brunton. She made her debut at Bristol in the winter of 1785–6. Her father was manager of a provincial theatre, and a very respectable and truly worthy man. He was an actor, but though a man of excellent good sense, was not a star in his profession.

Mr. Brunton married Miss Friend, of Bristol, he being then a grocer in that place. He afterwards established himself as a tea-dealer in London; but fondness for the stage and an acquaintance with Mr. Younge, of Covent Garden, induced him to try his success at his friend's benefit, which led finally to leaving trade and becoming professionally an actor. He was successful in the Norwich, Bath, and Bristol companies, and becoming manager of the Norwich theatre, sustained an exemplary character, and reared a family of six children, three of whom have been distinguished for good acting off and on the stage, and have given celebrity to the name of Brunton.

Mr. Brunton commenced his theatrical career when his daughter Ann was five years of age, in the year 1774. Though her father was an actor and manager, Ann had seen very few plays. The family resided in an elegant cottage near Bath, and Mrs. Brunton was the instructer of her children. Nothing was further from the thoughts of Mr. Brunton than a future career of fame for his children in the profession he had chosen for himself.

He taught his daughter to read Shakespeare, without any view to her becoming an actress. "Coming home from rehearsal one day, he overheard her reciting Calista's speech upon the unfortunate condition of her sex," and on expressing his surprise at the talents she displayed, he found that she had studied and could recite the parts of Juliet, Belvidera, and Euphrasia. After consulting his friends, the determination was suddenly taken to bring the young lady on the stage. Mr. Palmer, the Bath and Bristol manager, having pronounced her "another Siddons." In less than a week from the discovery of her talent for acting, she was brought on the stage in the character of Euphrasia, and received with the most unqualified applause by the public of Bristol. Her first appearance was for her father's benefit, he playing Evander. The father and daughter played a father and daughter.

Mr. Brunton spoke a prologue, written by Meyler, as an introduction to the young heroine of sixteen. All this was judicious preparation; but still the audience only expected to see a girl, a novice, perhaps a mawkin, but they saw with astonishment a graceful and accomplished actress. The applause and commendation in and out of the theatre were proportionate to the surprise and admiration. The characters of Horatia, in The Roman Father, and Palmyra, in Mahomet, parts suited to her age and figure, succeeded, and increased her fame. Thus Siddons, the greatest tragedian we have ever seen, had to struggle through difficulties to reach that pinnacle on which she towered for almost half a century unrivalled, while Ann Brunton, a child in years, soared at once to almost an equal height. Mrs. Siddons had person, power, art, beyond all contemporaries— Mrs. Merry had voice and feeling, that went as direct to the heart of a feeling auditor as the ray of light to its destination.

Mr. Harris soon after engaged both her and her father for Covent Garden. In the season of 1785–6, the writer witnessed her first appearance on the London boards in the character of Horatia, in The Roman Father, Henderson playing Horatius. The streets adjacent to the theatre were crowded before the opening of the doors, and all the usual consequences of a rush ensued. Borne into the pit, we remained wedged in, where the crowd placed us, but we were amply repaid for the sufferings experienced in narrow passages while moved (although motionless from the shoulders downward) to the seat we were thrust into. The extraordinary self-possession of this young lady, not yet sixteen, when she appeared at Bristol the preceding year, has been recorded by a witness, and it apparently did not desert her on this occasion. Her voice, never exceeded in sweetness and clearness, did not falter, her action was perfect, she was the Horatia of the poet, and London confirmed Mr. Palmer's opinion that she was "another Siddons." Yet there was no similarity except in mind. Their persons and manners were indeed opposite, and, as we have said above, though Mrs. Merry made her way direct to the heart, the prize was won by gentleness. But Siddons seized upon it with a force that was irresistible. We speak of her such as she was at the time Miss Brunton appeared in London in the height of her power and popularity.

The town was prepared to see a wonder in Miss Brunton, and it was not disappointed. She was ushered in with those attentions which Mr. Harris thought due to merit. Murphy wrote a prologue to introduce her. Holman, then a young man, and new to the London audience, spoke the veteran's lines. Pope, likewise new in London, and Holman's rival, played the young hero of the piece. And Henderson, incomparably greater than either of them, played the father.

Holman, who had made his debut as the Romeo of Miss Younge the preceding winter, was now better mated in respect to age and personal appearance with the Juliet of Miss Brunton. And in the Orphan, her Monimia was supported by Holman, Pope, and Henderson in Chamont, Castalio, and Acasto. While Lear was in preparation for her Cordelia, and Henderson's aged king and father, he died—the greatest loss the English stage has sustained since Garrick. He was not so great a tragedian as Siddons, though greater than any other of his time; but he was as great a comedian as tragedian, and his Leon, Don John, and Falstaff were perhaps never equalled.

Miss Brunton attracted the admiration of Mr. Robert Merry soon after her engagement at Covent Garden, and his person, fashion, address, and amiable disposition, added to the eclat of the Della Crusca poetry, then estimated higher than since, won her heart and hand. She became Mrs. Merry, and retired from the stage as soon as her engagement was at an end. She was never known on the stage as Mrs. Merry in London.

In 1792, Miss Brunton was removed from the English dramatic world, and as Mrs. Merry, visited the continent of Europe with her husband. Returning, they lived in retirement until 1796, when Merry's reduced fortune and his wife's love of a profession in which she was so eminently qualified to shine, led to an engagement with Wignell for Philadelphia, the poet being willing that his wife should appear as such, on the stage, in a foreign land and among republicans, though averse to the same public exhibition of her talents before his former acquaintance of St. James's and Bond-street. We have mentioned their arrival at New-York on the 10th of October, 1796, and on the 5th of December, she was introduced to the public of Philadelphia as Juliet, Moreton being her Romeo.

Notwithstanding this great accession to the strength of the company, and Mrs. Merry playing all her great characters, the manager was a loser by the season; and, as we have seen, led his forces to New-York, and opened as a theatre what was then known as Rickett's circus in Greenwich-street.

Our most valuable correspondent, Mr. William B. Wood, of Philadelphia, whose opinions and recollections of acting and actors is in unison with our own, and who has furnished us many valuable facts for this work, says, "The delight of the New-York people was at its height when Mr. Wignell opened the Greenwich-street circus with Venice Preserved, Jaffier, Moreton; Pierre, Cooper; Belvidera, Mrs. Merry, and all the inferior parts well played." And well might they be delighted.

Of this highly gifted lady we shall have to speak, a pleasing task, again and again in the course of our work.

Her accomplished husband was born in London, April, 1755, and was educated at Harrow. He entered at Christ's Church College, Cambridge, but left the university without taking a degree. He was entered of Lincoln's Inn, but on the death of his father, bought into the Horse Guards, and served as adjutant and lieutenant. Quitting the service, he went abroad, and resided some years at Florence, where he was elected a member of the Della Crusca Academy. This name he used on his return to England in his poetical publications. His first performed play was "Lorenzo," and in *that,* the same lady played as Miss Brunton, who supported his last dramatic production by her talents as Mrs. Merry.

Mr. Merry wrote several dramas, but they do not live as acting plays. His Della Crusca and Mrs. Cowley's Anna Matilda occupied public attention for a time. He wrote for the London Journal under the signature of "Tom Thorne," and felt the vengeance of the ministerial prints for expressing his republican opinions. Gifford, in the Baviad and Mæviad, put an end to Della Crusca poetry.

All those who enjoyed the acquaintance of Mr. Merry have represented him as a well-informed, intelligent, amiable man of genius. A *bon-vivant* in early life. A good husband and steadfast friend, but indolent, and more addicted to ease and punning than disposed to the severe duties man in society is called upon to fulfil.

On the first night of The School for Scandal, Merry whispered to a companion, "I wish the *dramatis personæ* would leave off talking, and let the play begin." Being in company with one of the cabinet ministers, the noble duke remarked, that by supporting the constitution, his majesty had proved himself a good *upholder*. "True," said Merry, "but a bad *cabinet-maker*."

The only play he wrote (either the whole or in part) in America was called "The Abbey of St. Augustine." It was played in Philadelphia in 1797. His dramatic productions in England were "Ambitious Vengeance," tragic drama, 1790. "Lorenzo," tragic, 1791, in which Miss Brunton, afterwards Mrs. Merry, performed the heroine. "The Magician no Conjuror," comic opera, 1792, and "Fenelon," serious drama, 1795.

Mr. Merry died at Baltimore in the latter part of the year 1798. The day before Christmas he walked out into the garden, apparently well, and was found helpless on the ground soon after. Mr. Wood, in a letter before us, says, "Mr. Merry's is an interesting recollection to me. In my early theatrical efforts I felt myself indebted to him and his gifted wife for the best instructions I ever received. His death was to me a severe loss. He literally died in my arms, as some years after did his wife. No man possessed less guile. His latest words were most cheerful."

Mr. Thomas Abthorpe Cooper will command our attention next. We have spoken of his arrival in New-York at the same time that Mrs. Merry, accompanied by her accomplished and well-known husband, landed on the shores of America.

Mr. Cooper was born in 1776. His father was an Irish gentleman, a surgeon by profession, and long resided at *Harrow on the Hill*, but entered into the service of the East India Company, and died in India. His mother going to Holland when he was between eight and nine years of age, the celebrated William Godwin, a friend of the deceased father, prevailed upon her to leave the boy with him, and was to him a father. We have noticed that at the time of his arrival and first visit to the John-street theatre, he called himself, in conversation, the son of Godwin; "much more than a common father is he to me; he has cherished and instructed me." Mr. Godwin was his preceptor, his monitor, his friend. He instructed him, as he could receive the instruction, in French, Latin, Italian, and Greek. He regularly read to him every day after dinner. Among the books thus read and explained were Clarissa Harlowe, and all Shakespeare's plays. It was customary for Mr. Godwin to dine every Sunday with his friend Holcroft, and Tom always went with him. Thus he lived with one of the most pure and benevolent of men until he was sixteen years of age, when one morning, to the astonishment of the philosopher, Tom told him abruptly that he was tired of studying Latin and Greek, and thought it was time to go into the world, as he was able to take care of himself. Godwin, although surprised, asked him what he wished to do. Cooper replied, "Walk to Paris and join the republican army." Mr. Godwin only said, "We will talk further on the subject to-morrow morning."

By the persuasion of his friends, Godwin and Holcroft, the youth relinquished his military schemes, and as his great object was to be independent, he proposed, among other projects, that of becoming a chorus singer at one of the theatres. Whether in earnest, or only to gain time and turn his attention to something else, Holcroft made an appointment for Cooper to come to him that he might judge of his voice. On trial, Holcroft said it would not do.

Singing was given up, and acting was thought of. The young aspirant read Zaphna, and Holcroft declared it was hopeless; but on his speaking a speech of Richard, hope was revived. Holcroft had played on, as well as written for the stage, and was doubtless an admirable critic. He acted the part of Figaro when his translation of Beaumarchais's The Marriage of Figaro was performed at Covent Garden in 1785, under the title of The Follies of a Day. He was not then a player by profession, but for some reason performed the part on the first night, Bonner appearing in it on the second.

Cooper's friends finding his determination to be a hero of *some sort* invincible, preferred the stage to the army, and after preparatory drilling and much deliberation as to the scene of operation, he was furnished with money and letters, and sent by the stage-coach to Edinburgh, where Stephen Kemble, commonly called the great Kemble from his bulk, was manager.

Arrived at the Scottish capital, Tom, who had heretofore retained the dress of a boy, put on the apparel of manhood. His dangling locks were frizzed, powdered, and cued according to the fashion, or the folly of that day, and in all the awkwardness which novelty of dress and situation bestowed, with a figure neither that of man or boy, he waited upon that awe-inspiring personage, the manager. He was received politely, but when King Stephen opened his letter, and found him recommended for Young Norval, his smiles fled, and chagrin marked his countenance. Tom, though awkward from novelty of circumstances, was handsome, and nothing doubting his own talents or appearance. The manager took time to consider the business, and after another cool reception, a rehearsal was called, and Mr. Cooper was flattered with the idea of playing Young Norval, with Mrs. Siddons for the Lady Randolph. The lady, however, did not attend rehearsal, but her husband was present to judge of the young debutant. Tom ranted. Kemble walked up and down the stage in silence. The rehearsal was over, and Cooper, perfectly satisfied with himself, concluded that Kemble, if dumb, was only so in consequence of extreme admiration, and waited the opening of the great man's mouth to receive his meed of praise—but all that fell from it was a request that he would wait on the manager next day. Still full of confidence, he kept the appointment to a minute. No thought had yet entered his head that could damp the heroic ardour of Young Norval, or lower the tone in which he had shouted, "The blood of Douglas can support itself."

"This is a very difficult part you have chosen, Mr. Cooper."

"Very difficult sir," with a smile which said, "but not too difficult for me."

"You had better think of something else."

Here the veil was drawn aside; the reality appeared. Tom was rejected. The play of Douglas was performed. He saw another hero fill the space he expected to occupy, and receive the plaudits hope had promised to him and dreams had already given him.

He remained with the company unemployed until they removed to Newcastle-upon-Tyne; there he was occasionally "sent on," as the phrase is, remaining unnoticed, dependent, and in the very worst school a youth of seventeen could be in, until by some chance, or as the last resort of the manager, the part of Malcolm, in the tragedy of Macbeth, was assigned to him. In this humble part, in that play which appeared to receive new lustre from his representing the principal character at a day not far distant, did this great tragedian make his debut. And he was hissed before he got through this first effort. Till the last scene, he passed through either unnoticed or applauded; but when he came to the lines which conclude the play, called by players the *tag,* and the audience expected to hear the well-known lines,

> "So thanks to all at once, and to each one
> Whom we invite to see us crown'd at Scone,"

the heir of Duncan and successor of Macbeth stretched forth his hand and assumed the royal smile of condescension, he saw the people rising in the theatre to depart, he lost his presence of mind and all recollection of the gracious words he had been prepared to utter—confusion begat terror, and he stood silent and motionless, his royal hand held forth and lips unclosed—the prompter was heard, "So thanks to all"—Macduff whispered, "So thanks to all"—Macbeth, though long dead, echoed, "So thanks to all"—the audience spoke to him no thanks but hisses—Tom continued with outstretched hand and unmeaning smile, and so might have continued, had not Macbeth ordered the trumpet to sound, and the curtain to fall, amid the hootings of the audience.

The manager rose, and ordered young Malcolm to follow him. Then, and not till then, did Tom move or cease to play Orator Mum.

"Order the treasurer to pay Mr. Cooper five pounds. Mr. Cooper, I have no further service for you."

Thus terminated our hero's first campaign, and he was happy to find himself once more at the hospitable hearth of William Godwin, after having expended his last penny to pay his passage back to London in a collier.

His friends being convinced that he had the requisites for a tragedian, or, to use Sheridan's words of himself, "that he had it in him," advised him to try some of the country theatres, and he was sent to Portsmouth. He here first met Tyler, a short time before his engagement with Hodgkinson for America. Tyler has told the writer that he thought him a most unpromising boy, and was astonished when in New-York, to hear that this same good-for-naught stripling was playing Hamlet and Macbeth with success in London.

At Portsmouth he received a small salary, was not intrusted with any business that called forth his exertion or excited his ambition, and in idleness and dissipation he was forgetting the precious precepts implanted by his instructers. They recalled him to London, and finding him still determined to be a player, they set themselves anew to the task of qualifying him for success.

Cooper now no longer lived under Mr. Godwin's roof, but that friend and Holcroft directed his studies, avowedly for the stage, and he was well instructed in Hamlet and Macbeth before he again exposed himself to an audience. Hamlet was chosen for his trial part, and every account of that night's performance mentions it as one of the most successful ever remembered. Macklin, the Nestor of the stage, so pronounced it, and congratulated the triumphant youth accordingly. Macbeth followed with equal success. Thus, before he was nineteen years of age, the despised boy had triumphed in the two most difficult characters of the drama, and received the applauses of those who had witnessed the veteran skill of Garrick, Henderson, and Kemble.

Mr. Cooper was brought forward soon after in Lothario—"the gallant gay Lothario;" if Godwin and Holcroft advised this, it was lamentably misjudged. The qualifications for Hamlet or Macbeth may be possessed by an actor, and not one requisite for Lothario be in his possession. To add to his *stiffness,* Mr. Lewis put him in a suit of clothes too small—it was a failure. He was offered an inferior line of business by Mr. Harris, with an engagement for Covent Garden, but refused it. Fifty guineas was the payment for his services, and he retired into Wales to study. It appears, however, that in September, 1796, Mr. Cooper was performing at Cheltenham.

Wignell now arrived in London and heard of Cooper's fame. Holcroft was applied to, as was Godwin, in respect to an engagement for Philadelphia, and offers made to induce the young actor to leave England. The following letter will show their sentiments on the subject. The first part appears to be in reply to some complaints made by Cooper.

> "You do not like the word lamentation. You will less like the word I am going to use. But before I use it, I will most sincerely assure you I mean it kindly. I do not like rhodomontade heroics. They are discordant, grating, and degrading. They are the very reverse of what you imagine them to be. It was not from report, but from your letter itself, that I collected my idea of lamentation: and compared to your sufferings, I repeat, Jeremiah never lamented so loudly: at least, such is my opinion, and I hope you did not intend, by a hackneyed and coarse quotation, to deter me from saying that which I think

may awaken your attention. If you did, it was in a moment of forgetfulness; for you know that a man of principle ought not to be so deterred. I speak plainly from the very sincere wish, which I so long have cherished, of rousing you at once to the exertions of genius, and the sagacity of benevolence and urbanity. It is to exercise benevolence and urbanity myself, that I am thus intent in wiping from your mind all impressions of supposed rudeness or rigour in thus addressing you.

"And now to business: after just reminding you that, though you did not wish me to apply for a London engagement for you, it would have looked quite as friendly had you written to me without this personal motive.

"Mr. Wignell, the manager of the theatres of Philadelphia and Baltimore, in America, has applied to me, offering you four, five, and six guineas a week, forty weeks each year, for three succeeding years; and ensuring benefits to the amount of a hundred and fifty guineas. I have reflected on the subject, and have consulted your other true and tried friend, Mr. Godwin; and notwithstanding that this offer is so alluring, it is our decided opinion that, were it ten times as great, it ought to be rejected. As an actor, you would be extinct, and the very season of energy and improvement would be for ever passed. I speak of men as they are now constituted; and after the manner, as experience tells me, that their habits become fixed; eradicably fixed. Mr. Godwin indeed expresses himself with great force, mixed with some little dread, lest money should be a temptation that you could not withstand. However, we both knew it to be but right that the decision should be entirely your own; and I therefore send you this information. Be kind enough to return me your answer; and without regarding my, or any man's opinion, judge for yourself. It is right that Mr. Wignell should not be kept in suspense. Yours, kindly and sincerely,

"T. HOLCROFT.

"September 3d, 1796.

"The above is a transcript of a letter which was dated August the 26th, and directed to you at Swansea, where I suppose it is left. Let me request an immediate answer.

"A gentleman has just been with me on the part of Mr. Daly, who is to be in town in nine or ten days, and wishes to engage you for the winter season, but this I think as prejudicial, except that it is something nearer home, and not so durable an engagement as America. Ireland is certainly the school of idleness. However, all these matters must be left to yourself."

This was directed, "Mr. Cooper, Theatre, Cheltenham," by as true a friend as ever man had, but the views of youth are ever widely different from those of age. Cooper chose to embark upon the sea of adventure, and the Atlantic, and to try a new scene in a New World.

Mr. Cooper, before embarking for America, went to London to see and take leave of his two best friends, and both Godwin and Holcroft attended him to the coach when he left the metropolis to join the companions of his voyage.

Godwin and Holcroft are both important in literary history generally, and particularly entitled to notice as dramatists. Mr. Cooper remembered Godwin, when he first knew him, in his clerical dress. A black suit, large cocked hat, his hair frizzed at the sides and curled stiffly behind. He is a small, well-made man, with a thin face, large nose, blue eyes, and most placid countenance. He changed his dress to a blue coat, yellow cassimere breeches, very blue white silk stockings (the same in which he equipped Cooper for his Scotch expedition), his hair plaited behind, instead of the single clerical curl, and the large cocked hat was dismissed and replaced by a round one. At this time he put on spectacles. The last dress his pupil saw him in when he left home was a plain suit, with short unpowdered hair; and the dress of Holcroft was perfectly similar.

Mr. Godwin is principally known among the readers of the present day as the author of Caleb Williams, but will be known hereafter as the historian of the English Commonwealth, the vindicator of our forefathers, the glorious republicans to whose enlightened opposition, when the first Charles asserted the divine rights of monarchy, England and America may trace the origin of their liberty. That Godwin's History of the Commonwealth has not been reprinted among us, shows an apathy or an ignorance that ought to be amended. Mr. Godwin wrote one tragedy, called Anthonio. He is now between 70 and 80 years of age, and to use his own expression, "A destitute man of letters." We will add—a man of first-rate talents, poor and neglected, in the land he has loved and faithfully served. But he is a republican.

We have mentioned Mr. Cooper's arrival in New-York on the 18th of October, 1796, whence he proceeded with Wignell to Philadelphia, and made his first appearance in America in the character of Macbeth, on the 9th of December, 1796.

The first line in tragedy was preoccupied in Philadelphia by Fennell, who, having come out with the first company of Wignell and Reinagle, had preoccupied likewise the favour of the public, especially the literary men. Tall, handsome in person, specious in manner, well educated, and ever courteous, Fennell as a gentleman at this time stood high. He lived splendidly, and far beyond his income, courted the world, and was courted in return. Cooper's character and conduct was as opposite as possible. Frank, fearless, and too careless—he soon made friends, but they were the younger and less influential portion of the population. Such was the state of things at that time, and discontent was the consequence. He had refused an engagement to play inferior parts in London, and the great parts were preoccupied in Philadelphia.

When the time arrived for his first benefit, the seats were not taken. To be sure he was ensured by the manger to a certain amount. This did not satisfy Cooper, and he hired for sixty dollars an elephant that had just arrived, and advertised the new performer for Mr. Cooper's benefit. Those who had declined to take seats to see and support the best tragedian, although not yet so finished as afterwards, that had yet played in America, filled the house to overflowing to see the stage dishonoured by an elephant.

Early in May, 1797, the writer saw Mr. Cooper for the second time. It was on the stage at a rehearsal, in the Chestnut-street theatre. The first time we had an opportunity of seeing him play was not in a character suited to him—it was *The Serious Father,* in the comedy of The Way to get Married. Yet in this he exceeded expectation. Mrs. Merry was the Julia Falkner, and Moreton the finest Tangent we ever saw.

We shall next notice a great comedian.

Mr. John Bernard was the son of a lieutenant in the English navy, and born at Portsmouth in 1756. His first applause was gained at the academy where he had been educated, and where, like the Goshen youth already mentioned, he played the biggest parts because he was the biggest boy. John played Hamlet, he being then sixteen, and about leaving school. "All went on very smoothly," he says, "until the scene with the ghost, when a bungling rascal, whose part for the night was to sit above on a beam and pull up the three baize table-cloths tacked together into a curtain, and at the moment I pronounced the words, 'Alas, poor ghost!' the roller becoming disengaged, descended with a swift thwack upon the royal Dane's head, and prostrated him to the earth, amid an uproar of laughter!" Bernard's father being at sea, and the boy now idle, thought only of acting, and determined to try his hand with a strolling company that had put up their flag at the Black Bull in Farnham. As this may serve for a picture of such theatricals, we will extract the description of Manager Jackson's establishment.

"He had engaged the largest room at the said Black Bull, suspended a collection of tatters along its middle for a curtain, erected a pair of paper screens right hand and left for wings; arranged four candles in front of said wings, to divide the stage from the orchestra (the fiddlers' chairs being the legitimate division of the orchestra from the pit); and with all the spare benches of the inn to form boxes, and a hoop suspended from the ceiling (perforated with a dozen nails to receive as many tallow candles) to suggest the idea of a chandelier; he had constructed and embellished what he called a theatre. The scenery consisted of two drops,"—scenes which roll up,—"the inside of a house and the outside of a house." The first was a kitchen, with all its implements; "by the simple introduction of two chairs and a table, this was constituted a gentleman's parlour; and in the further presence of a crimson-cushioned yellow-legged elbow-chair, with a banner behind and a stool in front, was elevated into a royal hall of audience. The other drop (which I have termed outside of a house) presented on its surface two houses peeping in at the sides, a hill, a wood, a stream, a bridge, and a distant plain."

Thus, the spectator might imagine himself in a street, a wood, by a stream, &c. Some other boys joined Bernard in filling Manager Jackson's theatre; but their parents finding out what was going forward, their mothers agreed to go in a body to the spot and witness the scene; the consequence was, that Jaffier and Pierre, and all the rest of the conspirators, were made prisoners, and conducted home by the good ladies, amid the shouts of the clowns of the village.

Bernard's father being disappointed in getting him on board a ship of war, articled him to an attorney. The boy jumped out of the window and ran away. Being rejected at Bristol, he made his *debut* at the village of Chew Magna, in the character of Jaffier. Engaged, he was regularly inserted in the bills as Mr. Budd, a young gentleman only seventeen years of age. He received for his first payment a share of eight shillings and three tallow candles. After various strolling adventures and starvations, he met his mother at Weymouth, and returned home with her, promising amendment. But notwithstanding every inducement which duty to a good and indulgent mother could present, the worse than thoughtless boy again left his employment and his parent; and after wandering about in want, among those who disgrace a profession by assuming its title without possessing its requisites, he again returned to his sorrowing mother. With the consent of both his parents, the youth subsequently was devoted to the stage, a profession for which he had talents of a high order, and in which, having obtained the necessary skill, he became a distinguished artist.

Having married a prudent woman and good actress, and found in Griffiths, the Norwich manager, a judicious friend, Bernard renounced the faults and vices contracted during his low rambling life, and by degrees became what we in America have seen him, an excellent comic actor. In the winter of 1777–8, Mr. and Mrs. Bernard made their appearance on the Bath boards as Gratiano and Portia; Henderson, the best actor the writer of this work ever saw except Mrs. Siddons, played Shylock. Henderson was about this time engaged for Covent Garden, and remained the unrivalled actor of London until 1786–7, dying in the flower of life and fulness of fame, as a gentleman, a scholar, and an actor. He was preparing to play Lear to Miss Brunton's Cordelia when he died.

In 1782, Mr. and Mrs. Bernard made an engagement with "Daly, the Irish manager," and played at Cork and Dublin. At Cork he quarrelled with his manager; his wife fell sick; and his circumstances were in a very sorry condition, when John Kemble relieved him by a proffered loan in the most friendly and delicate manner. "This was a kindness I never forgot. John Kemble was a reserved man, a peculiar man, perhaps a proud man; but to the last hour of my life, I will maintain that he was an honourable man, a faithful man, and a man of as much tenderness as integrity."

Travelling from Cork to Limerick, and stopping for the night at a village called Mallow, he and his companions were invited to attend a theatrical exhibition which he thus describes. "The construction of the theatre did not importantly differ from that of many I had played in in my early days. It was the interior of a barn; the hayloft being naturally adapted for the gallery; the boxes formed by rough boards nailed to four uprights; the stage being divided from the pit by a board bored with holes as the sockets for so many candles or foot lights; the scenery was *secundem artem,* things of shreds and patches; and the green curtain a piece of gray antiquity that went up and down, in momentary danger of dissolution.

Our amusement commenced the moment we entered the house, in listening to a conversation that was going on between the gallery and the orchestra, the latter composed of a performer on the violin and one on the big drum. "Mr. Patrick Moriarty," shouted the combiner of horse-hair and catgut, "how are you, my jewel?" "Aisy and impudent, Teddy O'Hoone; how are you? How's your sow?" "Mischievous and tender like all her sex. What tune would it plase you to have, Mr. Patrick Moriarty?" Mr. Patrick was indifferent, and referred the matter to a committee of females. In the mean time, Teddy began to tune up, at which another of his "divine" companions above assailed him: "Arra! Teddy O'Hoone! Teddy, you divil,"—"What do you say, Larry Kennedy?"—"Tip us a tune on your fiddle-de-dee, and don't stand there making the cratcher squake like a hog in a holly-bush. Paddy Byrne" (to the drummer)—"What do you say, Mr. Kennedy?"—"Aint you a jewel now to be sitting there at your aise, when here's a whole cockloft full of jontlemen come to hear you thump your big bit of cowhide on the top of a butter tub."

This specimen of "wild Irish theatricals," with the former description of Manager Jackson's display, will suffice for our readers. The actors in both cases suited the scenery and the audience. A refined audience will only tolerate a refined moral exhibition, and such performers as are fitting to amuse and instruct them. It is the audience that gives the tone to every part of the theatre. Where there is the best audience, there will be the best actors, and the best plays, and the most attractive decorations, music, and scenery, and to such a place even the vulgar will come for his own pleasure; and being restrained, will be eventually amended.

Bernard, in 1784, performed with the Bath company. Here he first met with Mr. Blanchard, afterwards well known on the London stage, and recently [1832] arrived in this country.

No person meets so many adventures or becomes acquainted with so many characters as an actor whose talents give him eclat. Among the many recorded by Bernard are the late Sir Thomas Lawrence and his father, who had been an actor, and was in 1786 an innkeeper, at Devizes.* Fond of his original profession, he frequented the Bath theatre, and brought his son Tom with him, who was remarkable for good recitation as well as early cleverness with the pencil. In his sixteenth year, the future president of the Royal Academy was a candidate for the stage, and was with difficulty persuaded to give up a profession so alluring to a beautiful and talented youth. His father was opposed to his wishes, and filial duty was rewarded by a splendid life of honour, and an immortal name as the best of English portrait painters.

Mr. Bernard's first attempt as an author was in a farce called the "Whimsical Ladies," which produced profit to the theatre and the writer.

In the winter of 1787, Mr. Bernard attained the height of his wishes as an actor, by a successful appearance and engagement at Covent Garden theatre, his salary fixed at "ten, eleven, twelve, and thirteen pounds." His engagement was for the fops, fine gentlemen, and higher line of comedy; but owing to Edwin's frequent indisposition from a cause similar to that which destroyed Cooke, Bernard was thrust into low comedy, and became very excellent in that line of playing. Mrs. Bernard not being satisfied at Covent Garden, we find Bernard in 1791 at Plymouth, under the management of Mr. Jefferson, the father of that excellent comedian, Joseph Jefferson, late of the New-York and Philadelphia companies.

Bernard had the direction of several minor theatres, and among others, that of Guernsey. At this place he employed as a prompter a non-commissioned officer, quartered there, who is connected indirectly with the drama of America. Archibald McLaren was a native of the Highlands of Scotland, and had served as a private under Sir William Howe, in the American war of 1776. This soldier cultivated a taste for poetry during the hardships of war and the privations incident to his ineligible situation. He wrote, in America, a farce called "The Coup de Main," which, on his return to Scotland, was performed at Edinburgh in the year 1783.

After trying a round of provincial theatres, Mr. Bernard returned to Covent Garden, and opened in Lord Ogilby, which he played in a style that rivalled the original Lord Ogilby of King. He produced that season a second farce, called "The Poor Sailor."

In the summer of 1797, Mr. Bernard engaged with Mr. Wignell, after procur-

* This circumstance is not mentioned by D. E. Williams, Esq., in his Life of Lawrence; but we rely upon Bernard's testimony.

ing a release from Mr. Harris, and embarked for America the 4th of June, 1797, making his first appearance at the Greenwich-street theatre, New-York, as Goldfinch, in the Road to Ruin. We shall have occasion to mention this gentleman frequently in the course of this work, for although the claim he makes of being one of the founders of the American stage is totally *unfounded*, he was a support and an ornament to it, and his memory is cherished as an actor and a man. At this place we will briefly state, that on the company of Wignell and Reinagle removing to their winter-quarters in Philadelphia, Mr. Bernard was brought out in Ruttekin, the tinker in Robin Hood, and Young Wilding in The Liar. He remained in the Philadelphia company until 1803, when Mr. Powell engaged him for Boston, and brought him out in Humphrey Gubbins, in the Battle of Hexham.

In the winter of 1804, Mr. Bernard gained additional fame by his representation of Lovegold in The Miser, and in 1806, he became one of the managers of the Boston theatre, and in the summer of that year went to England for recruits.

Of Mr. William Warren we have ample materials for such brief notice as our limits will allow. He was born in the year 1767, in the city of Bath. His father, a respectable mechanic, gave him an education intended to fit him for following in his steps; but the boy, like many others we have noticed, preferred idleness and pleasure to application and labour, and having been applauded for boyish attempts at acting, was unfit for the occupation of a cabinet-maker, which was that of his father, and was intended for him.

At the age of seventeen, Warren made his appearance as a player in the character of Young Norval, with a company who were making tragedy comical, and lowering comedy to farce, in a village near Bath, called Chippenham. His reception encouraged him to proceed in the career he had chosen. In this strolling company, under the management of one Biggs, he played all the first parts in tragedy and comedy, and of course gained some professional knowledge though the school was bad. For this first line of playing the young hero received less than four shillings per week.

Leaving Manager Biggs, he joined the forces of another stroller called "Tag Davis," who had a company of a higher order; among them was Riley, known as the author of an amusing book called the Itinerant, and Bignel, afterwards in America, but only known to the South. At the end of the season, Warren, too poor to pay for a place in the stage, walked home to the house of his indulgent parents.

There appears to be no cure for the disease of strolling, or as De Foe has it in his Robinson Crusoe, "What is bred in the bone will never be out of the flesh." Warren had become attached to Davis, as well as to a rambling life, and again joined him. Poverty was as much attached to that company now as before, and Riley records their situation at Lyme, utterly penniless, and without food, which could only be procured by stratagem. On this occasion he mentions Warren as exclaiming in mock heroics, "Was it or this I left my father's shop," and then adding from Dogberry, "would he were here to write me down an ass!"

Biggs, his first manager, having a company in the neighbourhood of Davis's barn, Warren now did double duty, *starring* it in both companies, walking from Lyme to Bedminster, and back again, to serve his two masters, not having profit enough from his "double toil and trouble" to pay for any other "leathern convenience" than his shoes.

Warren's next engagement was with Manager Jefferson, the father of the excellent comedian we have mentioned as joining the old American Company at Boston, and coming with them to New-York in 1796. From Jefferson's company he was induced to return to his friend Biggs by the tempting offer of ten shillings per week, a little more than two dollars. This enabled the rising young hero to ride, on the top of the stage, to the place of destination. In Warren's rambles, he met two performers afterwards well known in New-York and Boston, Mrs. Hogg and Mr. Baker.

After several changes of place and manager, Biggs, having been deserted by most of his company, followed Warren and another stroller of the name of Woolley, and being unable to persuade them to return, arrested them both; and carrying them, guarded by a constable, before a magistrate, swore they were journeymen tailors who had deserted from him, and left clothes unfinished which they had engaged to complete. The magistrate discharged the young men, advising them to return to their homes and parents. This advice was not followed, and Tag Davis having a *new opposition* house built for him in Exeter, by a man who was rich enough to indulge his desire to overthrow the established dynasty, Tag invited Warren to join his company, which he accordingly accepted.

To give the American reader an idea of the contempt shown in England by people of every condition towards the members of strolling companies, we will relate two anecdotes of Warren. Biggs, who seems to have considered Warren essential to his well-being, again followed him, and endeavoured to prevail on him to rejoin his company; but not succeeding, changed his persuasive tone to abuse, which he carried so far as to provoke Warren to break his pipe over the manager's head. For this assault on majesty, Biggs again took him, with the aid of a constable, on charge of assault and battery, and the justice hearing the accuser state that the accused was a strolling player, was about committing him to jail; but Warren retorted the title of strolling manager on Biggs, and the magistrate dismissed both with contempt and injurious epithets from his august presence.

The second concerns the treatment of the whole of Mr. Jefferson's company. One Mr. Carey, a man of fortune, on occasion of some family festival, applied to Jefferson and engaged his company to come to Tor Abbey, his place of residence, and perform a play. Accordingly, they all proceeded thither, not in carts or on foot, as most of them travelled usually, but attended by their very respectable manager, in coaches, post-chaises, and gigs. When they arrived at Tor Abbey, they were shown into the servant's hall, where a table and dinner was prepared for them.

Jefferson sent a remonstrance to Carey, and the company prevailed on the manager to take a coach and turn his back on the aristocrat, while they performed a play for his emolument. They then refused food in the inhospitable mansion, and Mr. Carey finding the actors so stomachful, made his appearance and apologies, showed them into a more dignified part of his house, and prevailed on them to take food more nourishing than the air of offended pride which they had assumed and were endeavouring to digest for the occasion. They ate and drank, and played their play and farce for the amusement of the great man and his family, and returned home content.

That most actors receive an education in the school of folly, thoughtless dissipation, or positive vice, which the degrading scenes belonging to the life of a strolling player in England invariably furnish, must be apparent to every one who reads the books which have been published on the subject. That so many come out of the furnace, if not purified, yet so far uninjured as to assume the rank of respectable and honourable men, is truly wonderful. If we look back upon the lives of most of those performers who have come to America and have challenged admiration as actors and respect as men, we shall find that they have passed through, from early youth to manhood, a succession of scenes sufficient to destroy all sense of moral propriety. To have passed through such scenes with such debased and debasing associates, and yet stand erect in society, is proof of uncommon merit; that many sink never to rise is plain.

This evil does not exist in this country to any great extent, and may be prevented altogether. We see those who have submitted to the disgrace of a stroller's life in England, take a higher stand in this country, and maintain it. They feel that they are not degraded by the presence of a privileged order; and if the mere moneyed aristocrat assumes airs of superiority, they feel authorized to resist the assumption. Having thrown off the stigma which the laws of their own country had affixed to them, they feel bound to assume, with the more elevated character, a more elevated deportment and conduct.

The frequent recurrence of poverty, insult, and disgrace at length, as the novelty and enticements of licentious liberty began to lose their charms, brought Warren to reflect upon the folly of his conduct. "He had experienced," says Carpenter, "poverty in its most intolerable shape, hunger." He had found that innocence was not a protection to the player, if accused of a crime, for the magistrates considered him as a vagabond. "Indeed," he continues, "what could he hope, seeing as he did so much penury around him, and at the same time so much ignorance and incapacity in many of his associates." While thus ruminating on his sad condition, he received a letter from his father inviting him home. And hoping to qualify himself for, and obtain a higher post in the profession he had chosen, he returned to the paternal roof.

After a few weeks at home, through the influence of Incledon, Blanchard, and other London actors with whom he became acquainted, he got a situation in a respectable provincial theatre, and obtained the friendship of Mr. Dowton. He now strove to make himself truly an artist, and by industry and good conduct acquired and skill importance in his profession.

Warren was a member of the Salisbury theatrical corps in 1787, when a prosecution was instituted through malice against the proprietor, and he was cast on the old vagrant act. This caused the repeal of the statute, and a protecting act was passed, by which justices of peace were enjoined to license and protect any manager who chose to establish a theatre. From this time the now prudent actor increased in reputation and emoluments. In 1788, he was engaged by Tate Wilkinson, well known by all who have attended to the English theatre, and Mrs. Siddons being engaged to play at York, Mr. Warren had the advantage of playing several characters with that first of tragedians. His habits of industry and attention to the business of the scene gained him the approbation of this lady, who in her provincial tours was annoyed very generally by the absence of those virtues.

In this situation, a favoured performer in a respectable company, directed by a man of talents, Mr. Wignell, in 1796, found the subject of this notice, and made him offers which engaged him for America. Warren was then married, and as the highest salary in the company was a guinea and a half a week, the salaries given by American managers must have appeared tempting. Mr. Warren was engaged for Philadelphia, and repairing to London, embarked at Gravesend, from whence dropping down to the Downs, the vessel took in Mr. and Mrs. Merry, and Mr. Cooper, and reached New-York in 21 days. Mr. Warren's first characters in Philadelphia were Friar Lawrence in Romeo and Juliet, and Bundle in the Waterman.

Thus Mr. Warren, after passing through scenes in real life which, as we have seen, seem sufficient to destroy every good habit, if not principle in man, was landed on a shore where he was safe from such contact, for in the company of such performers as composed the company of Philadelphia for many years, the ill habits acquired in English strolling companies would be discouraged, and if possible, eradicated. In Mr. Warren's case we have reason to believe that what might have been wrong had been previously rectified, and we only remember him as a pleasant companion and an upright man. The characters he sustained with the highest reputation in the drama, were Falstaff, Sir Peter Teazle, Old Norval, Brabantio, Sir Anthony Absolute, and the like in tragedy and comedy.

It will be seen by referring to the list of names at the end of chapter XIV., that Mr. and Mrs. Whitlock, the Darleys, father and son, Chalmers, Miss Broadhurst, and Mr. Bates, are not on the list; having already parted from their companions of 1794. Their successors, already noticed, were Mr. Cooper, Mrs. Merry, Mr. Warren, Mr. Bernard, Mr. and Mrs. L'Estrange; to these are to be added Messrs. Fox, Hardinge, and Byrne, with Mesdames Hardinge and Byrne.

Mr. Fox, originally an engraver, was yet a youth, and added to talents as an actor a voice for, and some knowledge of music.

Mr. Hardinge was the Irishman of the company, and Mrs. Hardinge a second lady for comedy or tragedy.

Mr. and Mrs. Byrne were dancers; he a ballet-master, and both had been first in their line at Covent Garden theatre. We remember him as Master Byrne, 1786.

In addition to Milbourne, as his scene painter, Mr. Wignell engaged the services of Mr. John Joseph Holland, whom he found at the Opera-house, London, where he had been educated for his profession. Mr. Holland was still a young man, although married, and with his wife, arrived in 1796 at New-York. Holland has often laughed at his profound ignorance of the country to which he was emigrating, an ignorance which is perpetuated as far as possible to this day by the efforts of the government, or at least those writers who have the sanction of the government and the confidence of the people. This ignorance is fast passing away, but at the time Holland came to New-York, 1796, not having an opportunity to consult Wignell on the subject, he brought out his household and kitchen furniture with him, fully persuaded that such articles could not be procured (at least of equal good quality) in the savage country he was embarking for. The ship arrived in the evening, and was anchored in the East river, and Holland went on shore to reconnoitre—all was astonishment and enchantment—he was among white men who spoke English, not but that he had been told this before, but we never realize the objects we are to meet abroad from mere description or information, until travelling has given us a second education, and no Englishman ever expects to find any thing good out of his own blessed isle. The young painter walked up to Wall-street, by the light of lamps and on good flag-stone pavement; he saw tall brick houses; he saw pillars, pilasters, and porticoes; he arrived in Broadway, and was still more astonished; he got as far as St. Paul's, but when he saw the beautiful Roman Ionic columns of that chapel, he could go no further, but hastened back to congratulate his wife that they were in a civilized land, and to recount the wonders he had seen. Holland's feelings were such as a native of our seaboard cities feels when travelling into the country of the Iroquois he finds, instead of forests, the cities of Utica and Rochester.

This accomplished architect and artist had prepared the house, which had been previously occupied as a circus, for the reception of the best company of performers that have ever been seen in America. The Greenwich-street circus was fitted up and decorated as an elegant summer theatre. The John-street house, in its decay, was occupied as we have seen by Solee, and an ill-assorted, ill-directed company; many of them excellent actors. The Park theatre was now being prepared for the old American Company.

On the 18th of August, 1797, "the principal performers of the Boston and Charleston theatres" opened in John-street with The Wonder, and The Spoiled Child; and on the 21st, played The Mountaineers, and The Spoiled Child.

The same evening, the 21st, the Greenwich-street theatre opened with Venice Preserved, Mrs. Merry, Mr. Cooper, and Mr. Moreton playing the principal characters.

The two houses went on striving against each other, and each injuring the other, and neither company supported by the receipt of expenses. A brief notice of some of the plays for a short time will convey the best image of the mimic world at this period in New-York.

August 30th, John-street, Isabella, by Mrs. Whitlock. Greenwich-street, Child of Nature—Amanthis, Mrs. Merry; Critic—Puff, Mr. Bernard.

September 1st, John-street, The School for Scandal. Greenwich-street the same. John-street was sick and put off; and the next day announced, "that the *celebrated* tragedy of Bunker Hill was in preparation, and would soon be performed."

Accordingly, Bunker Hill was brought out, with all the smoke, noise, and nonsense belonging to Mr. John Burk's muse; and Greenwich-street had nothing to oppose but Shakespeare's and Mrs. Merry's Juliet. The Romeo by Moreton, the Mercutio by Bernard, and every part supported by the names we have above recorded. But what were these to "a scuffle nicely managed," the "English falling back," and "two or three Englishmen rolling down the hill, a meeting-house on fire, with flames and smoak issuing from it, the smoak and confusion producing an effect scarce credible," as described in the author's letter given above?

Wignell, finding that fire and smoke pleased the public, determined to give them a volcano. Morton's Columbus was got up with all the taste, splendour, and skill of such a manager, such a company, and such a scene painter as Holland, combined. Wignell spoke the prologue, Cooper played Columbus; Mrs. Merry, Cora; Mr. Moreton, Alonzo. And, notwithstanding that the John-street hill was turned into a volcano, and Columbus advertised for the same night, September 11, 1797, the combined corps of Boston and Charleston were obliged to retreat soon after, and not with flying colours.

Wignell closed his temporary establishment with loss, but credit; and drew off his forces to their winter-quarters.

⤜ CHAPTER 16 ⤛

Critics — Critiques — Plays, Players, and Playwrights — Remarks of John Wells, Esq. on altering the titles of English Plays and passing them for American — A Hint to English Dramatists on the same Subject.

In the year 1796, that memorable year in the theatrical history of the New World which gave to New-York a band of distinguished actors, at the head of whom stood Mr. and Mrs. Johnson and Mr. Jefferson; and to Philadelphia, Mrs. Merry, and Messrs. Cooper and Warren; a company of critics was organized, who may not unaptly be characterized as sharp-shooters.

These gentlemen were regular frequenters of the New-York theatre, enjoyed its productions as men of education and lovers of literature, and wished to correct the abuses existing in the costume, demeanour, and general conduct of the actors *on the stage.*

Messrs. John Wells, Elias Hicks, Samuel Jones, William Cutting, Peter Irving, and Charles Adams, formed themselves into a species of dramatic censorship, and by turns put down their remarks on the play of the evening, meeting *next* evening to criticise the critique, and give it passport to the press. The last named of these gentlemen was only distinguished as being the son and brother of presidents of the United States; others are known as distinguished by their own talents and attainments. They signed with the initials of their names, the last letter being the actual writer. Finding that these initials led to the detection of the offenders against the liberty of murdering plays at will, they inserted other letters to mislead, but still continued the *last* as the initial of the writer. The letter D is frequently inserted, although no person whose name begins with that letter belonged to, or wrote for the club; the rogues intended to throw some of the credit on the writer of this work. We will review these effusions of the *box* critics of that day—for the pit had even then ceased to be the centre from which public opinion was to be enlightened on subjects of theatrical taste.

Farquhar's "The Inconstant," injudiciously revived by Hodgkinson, they condemn; and do not approve Cumberland's "The Wheel of Fortune," a play which with Cooper's Penruddock, and other alterations of the cast, became a favourite. They speak respectfully of Mr. Hodgkinson's Penruddock, and of Mrs. Johnson's Emily Tempest—of Mr. Jefferson's *Daw* they say it had "confirmed the favourable impression he had made." Of Prigmore, who played Tempest, they say, "We have desisted from remarking on our old acquaintance, Prigmore, in the hope he might (at least by accident) afford us something to applaud. But

that same uniformity of acting, which has ever characterized him, still continues, and we can find in him no other difference than may be found in a 'cocked
up hat' and a 'hat cocked up.'" They speak of attempts behind the scenes *to get
up* applause, by beginning to knock or clap, "whenever the manager has delivered any thing extremely witty or sentimental. Whether it is by direction of him
'whose sole ambition is the lust of praise,' or proceeds from the officiousness
of some candidate for managerial favour, we shall not pretend to determine."

Mr. King and Mr. Cleveland, in Woodville and Harry, they censure altogether.

The farce of "The Flitch of Bacon," they condemn *in toto.* Of "The Agreeable
Surprise" they speak in terms of high praise, and especially Hodgkinson's *Lingo*—
but they justly censure him for casting the part of "Widow Cheshire" to a *man* of
the name of Lee—a heavy, stupid, vulgar fellow, with no requisite for the stage
but a bass voice and some knowledge of music. So was the Widow Cheshire personated on the 9th of March, 1796.

O'Keefe's "Young Quaker" calls forth the approbation of our sharp-shooters, and they praise Mr. Hallam's Clod, and Mrs. Hallam's pretty Dinah Prim-
rose. Of "No Song no Supper," the approbation is full, particularly of Hodgkinson's matchless Robin. Jefferson falls under the lash as *Endless,* but, for once,
Prigmore is praised, and he deserved it, in *Crop.* He played the part and sung
the songs in perfection. Miss Broadhurst, a little timid gentle creature, is always
a favourite with these Mohawks.

It appears by the remarks of this band of scalpers and tomahawkers on "The
School for Scandal," that they truly estimated its beauties and its immoralities,
and that they had seen the play played in times past. They remark: "Though Mrs.
Hallam in *Lady Teazle,* and Mr. *Hallam* in *Sir Peter,* equalled our expectations,
we could not forget that Mr. and Mrs. *Henry* formerly appeared in those characters: we could not but remember that such things were, and were most precious to us." They praise Dibdin's "The Quaker," but justly remark, that play-
house representations of Quakers are unnatural, and generally disgusting.

It appears by Critique No. 8, that the body of critics had been called "liar and
assassin," but they say "they are none"—and go on as usual. They talk of Hodgkinson's "*bawling,*" and of "Poor Vulcan," that it is "insipid, tasteless, and unenter-
taining"—praising the "modest diffidence" of Miss Broadhurst in all she does.

In remarking on the comedy of Know Your own Mind, and its performance,
they ask, "Why was not the part of *Miss Neville* given to Mrs. Johnson, or Mrs.
Hallam?" (It was played by Mrs. Cleveland.) "Where was Mr. Hallam when the
part of Captain Bygrove was *cast* upon Mr. *Munto,* who, whenever he appears
'in uniform,' perpetually reminds us of a servant in livery." Madame Gardie the
fascinating dancer and pantomime actress, whose story ended so fatally in tragedy, played in this comedy a *speaking part, Madame Larouge,* and was "perfect-

ly natural." They laugh at the manager's apology for the nonappearance of a performer, who he said could not appear, but "at the risk of her life and future health."

Cumberland's The Jew was performed, March 21st, 1796, and Hodgkinson played Sheva with that versatile excellence which rendered him so remarkable, and after it, his Walter in The Children in the Wood, showed even superior powers. Miss Harding and Master Stockwell were the children. The first, Mr. Hodgkinson's ward, a pretty, innocent, black-eyed girl, looking as if she might be destined to a life of purity and happiness. The comedy is deservedly praised by the critics as abounding in "the purest morality, and the most instructive lessons of disinterested virtue."

The principal thing to be noted in the *critique* on the excellent comedy of The Clandestine Marriage, is the just reprehension of the manager for putting a poor deformed idiot, of the name of *Roberts*, into the fine part of *Canton*. Those who remember Baddely and Wewitzer, in London, and Darley and Harwood, in New-York, will think of the murder of poor Canton in the hands of one thus described by the Mohawks, one "whose dress and figure reminds us of the *ponies* in the races at the *circus*." They lament that they could not express at the time their disapprobation of the manager, without hurting the feelings of the *actor*. Gentle savages!

In their notice of Jane Shore, the savages are *really gentle*. They are more—they are complimentary. The ladies, however, have the greater share in their praise, and we know they deserved it. Mrs. Melmoth's Alicia, and Mrs. Johnson's penitent Jane, were, the first full of fiery passion, the second of tender pathos. Mr. Hallam had the merit of being respectable in Hastings, at the same time that he was, as Mercutio, in *high*, and *Jabel, Mungo, Clod*, and many other *low* comedy parts, far above mediocrity.

The Belle's Stratagem, The Mountaineers, The Irish Widow, Florizel, and Pirdetta, Alexander the Great, Maid of the Mill, &c., pass under review, and are treated fairly; and the performers quite as gently as heretofore. Of The Archers, we have spoken elsewhere—we may observe here, that the critics treat it with as much favour as it deserves. They take the occasion to recommend a national drama, and an independence in literature, as well as politics. In a second critique on the piece, they express themselves more fully in its favour, both in the serious and comic parts.

As the benefits came on, the critiques became more complimentary and less discriminating. Charlotte and Werter, by Reynolds, was *got up*, but received very coldly; and the critics censured both the play and the performance of it.

On the 20th of May, the band of censors were called to an account for all their missayings and misdoings, by *Verax*—who tells them they are *ignorant*, for they have not travelled—they are young—they are malicious—and that they war upon the actors because they are emigrants. The critics made no answer to this attack on them—probably they thought it *unanswerable.* This curious performance was known to come from Mr. Hodgkinson.

As the young men took no notice of Verax, and continued to give good advice to the actors, particularly Mr. William King, he challenged them to mortal combat, severally and individually—but strange to say, they took no more notice of Mr. King than they had done of his friend and brother *Verax.*

There is something so very characteristic in Hodgkinson's advertisement, notifying his approaching benefit, that we will insert it.

"Mr. HODGKINSON—respectfully acquaints the public in general, that his benefit will be on MONDAY, May 30, when will be presented the comedy of MUCH ADO ABOUT NOTHING, written by Shakespeare."

The same Mr. Prigmore, so utterly worthless as a man and an actor, the hero of the tale of the widow and the breeches, furnishes us occasion to call from their obscure resting-place some just remarks in a style of elegance, which alone would entitle them to a place in this history of our dramatic literature; but when we know that they are from the pen of John Wells, they receive additional value.

Prigmore, being entitled to a benefit, and having certain claims upon a certain class of theatrical visiters, whose favour he secured, by what players call *mumming,* contrived to attract a full house composed of *patrons* who could see his merits. A full house on a benefit night is considered by an actor as a mark of the estimation he or she is held in by the public. There is nothing more fallacious. To produce this evidence of public favour, and the dollars attendant on it, every art is resorted to, and a benefit-bill is generally a gull-trap. We have recorded elsewhere the *Melocosmiotis* of Chalmers, who was no favourite, and its success, and might mention many other instances. On this occasion, May 16th, 1796, Prigmore produced what was called a new play, "The School for Citizens," and with "Jonathan's description of New-York," "Auld Robin Grey," "Slaves in Algiers," &c. &c. succeeded in obtaining his object.

The play is *our object,* particularly as it called into exertion the pen of a distinguished friend, a portion of whose remarks we extract. "The School for Citizens," says he, "is an altered comedy from an English one of a different name, and an attempt made to adapt the language and incidents to this country. The design, unhappy in its conception, is rendered still more so in the execution, and it robs the original piece of much of its consistency, and leaves us one marked with many irregularities, though not the irregularities of genius. The practice of borrowing an original work from another nation, and accommodating it to our own, is a species of plagiarism, which involves the reputation of a country in which it is permitted. Our infancy as a people, the equal though moderate distribution of property, and the consequent necessity for personal industry, have hitherto, with us, suppressed the exercise of talents to any extensive degree in the dramatic line. Early occupied with procuring the means of subsistence, and the cares of providing for a family, the mind, with us, is naturally directed to the cultivation of that knowledge which most effectually answers the common purposes of life: hence the learning of America is rather of the useful than splendid kind, rather calculated to form the massy Doric, than the Corinthian capitals of science. As our literary pursuits, therefore, are of the robust kind, and we are obliged to resort to the foreign source for the more delicate productions of genius, which serve to amuse our leisure hours, and soften for a time the cares of real life, we cannot too severely reprehend the mean and unmanly spirit which would supply by a pitiful alteration of names, to the people of America, those sentiments of national compliments which were originally devoted to the service of another: It is an appropriation too disgraceful ever to become an acceptable offering to a sensible people."

The American dramatist, who steals the whole or a part of an English play, cannot escape detection, and can only, like Mr. Prigmore, hope for a harvest from the benefit nights. English dramatists have for ages translated from the Continental languages, and given no credit to the original authors. At the time Kotzebue brought the German school into fashion, the playwrights employed to measure out dialogue and pantomime by the yard for the London theatres, were superseded by the honest, homely translators of German plays, the Thomsons and Plumtrees. They took the alarm, and all joined in crying down the German drama; the hired journalists followed in the hue and cry, and John Bull was convinced that nothing could be so absurd as the exhibitions he had been weeping over, or had received with shouts of applause, and peals of laughter. This done, the cunning manufacturers for the theatres had the poor Germans at their mercy; and for years whole scenes and whole plots were given to admiring audiences as English *every inch,* and filled with *true British* patriotism, although they were stolen from those very Dutchmen, the plagiarists had decried by sound of trumpet.

At an after period appeared some playful strictures upon plays, managers, actors, and audiences, under the names of Jonathan Oldstyle and Andrew Quoz, which we shall hereafter quote largely from. They are from the pen of Washington Irving, and first published in the Morning Chronicle, then edited by his brother Doctor Peter Irving, a gentleman of the first talents, and of feelings as purely honourable as ever resided in the breast of man.

⇥ CHAPTER 17 ⇤

Agreement between John Hodgkinson and William Dunlap, on the one part, and the Committee empowered by the Proprietors of the Park Theatre, on the other — Reappearance of Mrs. Hallam on the Stage, June, 1797 — Agreement with the Proprietors of the Haymarket Theatre, Boston — Hodgkinson and Company in Boston, July, 1797.

We will continue the history of the old American or New-York Company, to the conclusion of the season of 1796–7, and of the formation of a new company for the Park theatre.

On the 25th of May, 1797, after various tedious preliminary negotiations, which had ended in an expressed wish that William Dunlap and John Hodgkinson should become joint lessees of the new or Park theatre, and make such arrangement with Lewis Hallam as should be satisfactory, a meeting took place between William Henderson, the acting agent or the committee of proprietors, and Messrs. Dunlap and Hodgkinson, and the following terms were agreed upon for three years and a half, for four playing seasons, to commence the ensuing autumn as soon as the house could be made ready for exhibitions. The lessees agreed to pay on the gross receipts of the house nightly, thus: on any sum from 450 to 500 dollars, 5 per cent.; from 5 to 600 dollars, 10 per cent.; from 6 to 700 dollars, 12½ per cent.; from 7 to 800 dollars, 15 per cent.; from 8 to 1200 dollars, 17 per cent.; 1200 dollars and upwards, 20 per cent. On benefit nights the rent was to be 10 per cent. on the receipt. Thus for a receipt under 450 dollars, no house-rent was to be paid; but the night which gave a receipt of 1200 dollars, paid 240 dollars rent. The managers were to proceed to the organization of the company, and the proprietors to the finishing that part of the building necessary to the commencement of theatrical performances, and such scenery and machinery as might be sufficient to begin with.

By the agreement of the managers, they were jointly to direct the theatre. The actor was to receive, as such, 20 dollars a week, 5 dollars a week for his wardrobe, and 30 dollars a week for superintending the stage, rehearsals, &c., making 55 dollars per week. His partner was to have as treasurer and joint director, 24 dollars per week.

The managers offered to Lewis Hallam to become purchasers of his theatrical property, and, in addition, to give him one-fourth of any profits they might make during the time of their lease of the new theatre.

Early in June a formal meeting took place between the managers attended by Dr. E. H. Smith, and Mr. Hallam attended by Philip Brasher, Esq., in which Mr.

Hallam agreed to sell his share in wardrobe, &c., and to accept the offer of one-fourth of the profits of the new theatre, and the managers agreed to engage him and his wife as actors in the company at the first salaries.

Mrs. Hallam reappeared on the John-street stage playing Lady Teazle, and spoke the following prologue, written by Mr. Milne. It was printed in the papers of the day, and the words marked as here in italics.

> "These flattering plaudits cannot fail to raise
> A *wish* to merit such transcendent praise;
> It can but be a *wish,* for Ah!—my heart
> Knows *merit* could not claim a thousandth part:
> But like the lavish hand of Heaven, you
> Give largely e'en though nothing should be due.
> O'ercome with joy, my anxious throbbing heart,
> Disdaining all the little tricks of art,
> Conceals those feelings in a grateful breast
> Which *may* be *felt,* but *cannot* be *express'd.*
> Time has now swept ten rolling years away,
> Since flattering plaudits graced my first essay,*
> Young, giddy, rash, ambitious, and untaught,
> You still caress'd, excusing many a fault;
> With friendly hand safe led me through the way
> Where lurking error watches to betray:
> And shall I such advantages forego
> With my consent? I frankly answer, No:
> I may through inadvertency have stray'd,
> But who by folly *never* was betray'd?
> If e'er my judgment played the foolish part,
> I acted not in concert with my heart.
> I boldly can defy the world to say
> From my first entrée to the present day,
> Whate'er my errors, numerous or few,
> I never wanted gratitude to you.
> On your indulgence still I'll rest my cause;
> Will you support me with your kind applause?
> You verify the truth of Pope's fine line—
> 'To err is human; to forgive, divine.'"

Thus, literally, was this extraordinary performance spoken and published at the time.

---

* She made her first appearance in the afterpiece of The Guardian, Hallam playing the Guardian, she the ward.

J. B. Williamson, the manager of the Boston Federal-street theatre, about this time, June, 1797, broke up his company, and part of them joined Harper's company at Providence. Hodgkinson left New-York for Boston, to pass through Newport, and to employ a portion of the New-York company there, and make arrangements for opening the Haymarket.

Mr. Williamson went to Charleston, S.C. and was for a time the principal performer there, and his wife a great favourite in the romps and other lively characters of comedy. She died at Charleston on the 31st of October, 1799.

On the 18th of June, three of the proprietors of the Boston Haymarket theatre, viz. Messrs. Osborne, Gardner, and Blake, arrived in New-York. They wished to see Hodgkinson, to make an agreement with him for their property. "He might have it on his own terms." The next day Hodgkinson returned from Boston, having engaged the Haymarket for four years for himself and partner. This theatre was a large wooden building, which had been erected from a spirit of opposition, partly political, and was owned by the democrats or anti-federalists. It was opposite to the southern corner of the Mall or Common.

The articles of agreement were, that for the use of said house for four *seasons,* consisting of sixty playing nights, commencing in June or July, and terminating in October or November, and for the use of all scenery, wardrobe, &c. belonging to the theatre, the managers shall pay 10 per cent. on the gross receipts. The house not to be used as a theatre during this period, except by consent of said managers—and after the present year, if the managers choose, they may pay fifty dollars per night, in lieu of the ten per cent. This agreement was signed by John Winthrop, Caleb Stimson, Joseph Blake, jun., and George Blake. This was an additional step in the road to ruin.

On the 24th of June, the articles of agreement between the managers of the old American Company, and Carlisle Pollock, Jacob Morton, Edward Livingston, and William Henderson, on behalf of the proprietors of the new theatre, were formally agreed to on the plan above stated. The seasons to be from the first of October to the tenth of June, and at least one hundred nights of playing "unless some public calamity prevents it."

Hodgkinson went on with the company, and opened the theatre in Hartford on the 3d of July. Sixty-seven dollars in the house. Another step on the downhill road. After a few nights' playing the house was closed, and the deficiencies remitted from New-York. The proprietors of the Hartford theatre were discontented, and Hodgkinson, to satisfy them, promised to send on a company of comedians, when he arrived in Boston. In consequence of this promise, he entered into engagements with Solee, forwarding him to Hartford and afterwards to New-York, where he opened the John-street theatre in opposition to Wignell's Greenwich-street house.

On the 24th of July, 1797, Hodgkinson opened the Haymarket theatre, Boston, with The Grecian Daughter and Romp. His receipts were 220 dollars. He engaged Mr. and Mrs. C. Powell, at 32 dollars per week; Mr. and Mrs. S. Powell, and Miss Harrison, at 42 dollars; Mr. and Mrs. Simpson, and two Miss Westrays, at 50 dollars; and Mrs. Peck, at 12 dollars; in addition to his company, already too large for the time.

Collins and Crosby having quarrelled, were preparing for the settlement which honour required; but the magistracy interfered, and the heroes, after lying in jail some hours, were examined. Sir Richard was dismissed and Collins remanded to prison, but afterwards liberated, on condition of removing his honour out of the Commonwealth. This man's real name was Phipps.

Mr. and Mrs. S. Powell were afterwards at New-York, valuable members of the company, and will be hereafter mentioned. The Miss Westrays proved distinguished ornaments to the drama, in every point of view. The history of the American theatre would be deficient if many pages were not devoted to Mrs. Wood, (then Miss Westray), and Mrs. Darley (Miss E. Westray). Their mother, Mrs. Simpson, was long on the New-York theatre, playing the line of old women.

Mr. Hodgkinson had now increased his expenses in Boston to upwards of 1100 dollars per week, and played on his second night (Mrs. Johnson's first appearance that season) to 144 dollars, which at three nights the week, at that rate, amounted to 432 dollars for the week's receipts. To oppose Wignell he had engaged Solee to go to New-York and Philadelphia, with Mr. and Mrs. Barrett, Mr. and Mrs. Jones, Mr. and Mrs. Williamson, Mr. and Mrs. Cleveland, Mr. and Mrs. Bernard (who wisely joined Wignell), Mr. and Mrs. Hughes, and Mr. and Mrs. Whitlock. This company, many of them good performers, failed in John-street, New-York, as we have seen, and Hodgkinson's letters induced his partner to support Solee by his credit, ultimately to great loss.

Hodgkinson's next managerial step was to engage Chalmers at 25 dollars, and Williamson, a singer, at 18, and despatch them with Messrs. Cleveland, S. Powell, Dickinson, Kenny, Seymour, M'Knight, and Simpson—and Mesdames S. Powell, Cleveland, Simpson, Seymour, with Misses Westray, and E. Westray, to Hartford, paying all expenses and guarantying their salaries. Mr. Hodgkinson's partner sent on money and advice. The one was taken, the other rejected.

→→ CHAPTER 18 ←←

The Orchestra — The Swiss Catholic Priest — The Inquisition — The Victim's Tale — The ex-noble — Monsieur and Madame Gardie, their Story and Tragical Death.

We have noticed the improvements made by Mr. Hodgkinson in the orchestra at New-York, improvements rendered necessary by the excellence of this branch of theatrical arrangement in the rival company of Philadelphia. Instead of the "one Mr. Pelham," and his harpsichord, or the single fiddle of Mr. Hewlett, performers of great skill filled the bands of the two rival cities. In New-York the musicians were principally French. Most of them gentlemen who had seen better days, some driven from Paris by the revolution, some of them nobles, some officers in the army of the king, others who had sought refuge from the devastation of St. Domingo.

The stories of these men would fill volumes. We will select one. The subject of it was not French, and the cause of his taking refuge in America was not revolutionary. The singularity of his appearance and behaviour attracted the notice of the manager, and on inquiry he was stated to have been a priest, and to be versed in languages, ancient and modern. The manager was studying German, and busied in translating the popular plays of the day, and as the musician's native tongue was German, he being a native of a German canton of Switzerland, and being master of English as well as most other modern tongues, he became very acceptable as a companion, and was soon employed as a teacher in the manager's family.

He was a man of Herculean mould, past the meridian of life, heavy in his movements unless excited, and then both his person and face became suddenly animated from listlessness to wildness. His large blue eyes, generally mild, were often suffused with tears; but when certain subjects were touched upon, glared madly, while his teeth were set convulsively. The manager had a retreat at Perth Amboy, and when released from the cares of the theatre, retired thither with his family, of which the musician made an interesting and acceptable member. He spoke of his having been a priest. He talked of his having experienced the horrors of the Inquisition in Madrid.

There are few subjects which take so decided a hold on the imagination as tales of the Inquisition. The mystery involving its enormous power, the darkness surrounding its black officials, and the silence attendant upon their movements, the sufferings in the solitary cells, the tortures inflicted at its tribunals, the manifold miseries attendant upon its victims living, and the awful horrors of death at the *auto-da-fé*, all combine to form one hideous, indistinct, gigantic image at which the soul sickens. There are few but have had an insatiable desire to read any thing relative to this gloomy, and terrifying, and mysterious power. The triumphs of the *auto-da-fé* are plain, full, and apparent—but imagination retires from these midday horrors, where power, wealth, beauty, regal magnificence, and the emblems and ministers of the religion of mercy and love exult over, and feast upon the tortures of their fellow-creatures, to the blacker and more secret horrors of the dark dungeons, solitary cells, subterranean galleries, and midnight tribunals of the impenetrable prison-house—impenetrable to all but its fiendlike ministers, and the pre-doomed wretches who have fallen within their iron grasp.

Such were the feelings of the man who found himself the inmate and host of one who had been a tenant of those dungeons, and could unfold their mysteries; and who hinted that he had experienced the power of this infernal institution in sufferings worse than death. When he appeared lost and abstracted in thought, or sought solitude, or laughed bitterly,—or when at the relation of some instance of virtue in his presence, his eyes became suffused with tears, and he was unable to restrain his morbid sensibility—the image of that power which had broken down such a frame and such a mind immediately presented itself.

One day, as he accompanied his friend in a ramble over the fields of the neighbourhood, and conversed of European affairs and manners, the abuses which had crept into the church, as we Protestants believe, occupied their attention, and he descanted with eloquent bitterness on the vices and corruption of the popish clergy in Europe.

"Why, you have told me that you yourself are one of the priesthood."

"Yes," he replied, "accursed be the hour that enrolled me on the list of those who vow to renounce nature, and bid defiance to the first command of God! Accursed be the moment when the folly of my mother devoted me to hypocrisy, guilt, and misery! Yes, in my mother's womb I was devoted a sacrifice on the altar. Such is superstition! A mother, the tenderest of all characters, to make, as she thinks, her peace with Heaven, offers up her unborn child as a victim, to be trained from the cradle in ceremonies and observations, to be bound in manhood by vows to contravene the laws of nature, to be dragged, for his obedience to the commands of his Creator, from the air and light of Heaven to the dungeons and tortures of the hellish Inquisition." He could speak no more. His eyes, which had glared furiously while he spoke, became dim—his teeth grated, and then became fixed—his hands were clenched—his whole frame convulsed—an hysteric laugh relieved him—tears followed—he continued the walk for some time in silence. After becoming calm he thus told his story.

"I was told, before I was capable of comprehending the nature of any obligation, that I was vowed by my mother to the priesthood. All my education
tended to that point. As a child I could have no objection. It appeared desirable to become one of those whose appearance inspired awe, and whose dress
and occupation marked them as superiors. I had afterwards my doubts and
misgivings; but no circumstance occurred to break the chain by which I was
led to destruction. I went through the studies and the forms: I took the vows,
and became a servant of the Church of Rome. My mind acquiesced—I had
an unshaken reverence for the ministers of the church; for in my simple and
free country, virtue was an inmate of every dwelling, whatever the faith its
possessor professed, or whatever his condition of life. I was pure in intention, and virtuous in action. A regiment was raised in our canton for the
service of the King of Spain, and I was appointed its chaplain. To visit a foreign country, surrounded by hundreds of my countrymen, who looked up
to me as a father and instructer was a delightful prospect to a young man,
for the desire to travel is common to youth; and to be revered and beloved,
and return good offices for love, I felt to be common to man. The regiment
was marched to Spain, and quartered in Madrid.

"Oh what a contrast between the inhabitants of cities and those of the
country! The love of God and of my neighbour fills my breast in the fields
and in the woods, and on the hill-top—even now—even now—but in the
streets and crowds of the city my God is forgotten, and my neighbour appears unworthy of love. What a contrast was there between these Spaniards,
slaves to their king, their nobles, and their vices, and the freeborn rustic sons
of the mountains. The surrounding objects, the manners I saw, both in the
laity and clergy, had a powerful, deteriorating effect upon my young and
inexperienced mind. My passions, which had been restrained by awe, not
subdued by a rational sense of duty, were here aroused, and they aroused my
mind to an examination of those vows, in making which I had forsworn
nature and contravened the mandates of God.

"The passion which is given to be our greatest joy, the bond of social union,
the source of virtuous action, I had forsworn, and that sin against nature
ruined me. I saw and loved a Spanish lady. I appeared worthy in her eyes of
reciprocal affection. I was not then the wretched thing you see. I was full of
youth, and life, and health, and strength. I could have bounded from rock to
rock, like the chamois of my native hills—I could—pshaw! Fool!"

He wiped the drops from his forehead and proceeded.

"I saw in the clearest point of view the horrible state of bondage to which I
had been doomed before my birth, and I determined to free myself. At my
confessional I met the object of my love, a love pure and holy, and there and
only there—in a situation where apparently the possibility of being overheard

was provided against—our plans of flight, and marriage, and future life were arranged. First England was to receive us, and then America—the refuge of the oppressed! This blessed country was to be our asylum and our country. The day was fixed—it had nearly arrived, when I was seized, bound, and hurried to the dungeons of the Inquisition."

A long pause ensued, and struggles almost to convulsion took place before he could proceed. "No third person had been confided in. I felt confident that my secret was unknown—I had dreadful misgivings and forebodings—but hope assured me that I had been seized through error. I demanded the cause of my arrest; but these adamantine demons gave no answer; nor after the first scrutinizing stare did they deign to cast a glance on my visage. Then the truth rushed on me—even the confessional was subject to the espionage of the terrible power that had cast its net around me, and held me a helpless, hopeless victim. The key of my cell turned, the bolts grated, and was left to darkness and solitude. Do not expect me to describe the mental tortures I endured; if I could recall them, I should go mad—where, where was the dear one on whom my hope of earthly happiness had been fixed? What would be her torture when she found herself abandoned!

"Hours, days, weeks, months passed before these demons deigned to relieve this suspense, and give me the comparative felicity of despair. At length four mute ministers of the inhuman power visited me, and the light of a lamp for the second time showed me the walls of my dungeon. They decorated me with the insignia of guilt, and led me to the dread tribunal of those who condemn before trial, and torture their victims to force the confession of guilt for the justification of the judges. I was required to confess my crime without having any charge made against me. I remained silent. They threatened. I persisted in silence and was remanded to my dungeon. A second time I was brought before them, and the instruments of torture displayed. I preserved my silence, and I was sent back to darkness and solitude. The third time on which I was led to my condemners, I was charged with the crime of intending to abjure my vows, and throw off my allegiance to the church; and my whole plan was detailed to me with a faithfulness which a transcript from my soul could only have equalled. My heart died within me. A cloud came over my bewildered mind, my senses failed, and when I awoke I was alone in my horrible cell. In my horrible cell I remained, alone, two years. I have been able since to compute the time, not then. All was then a void of darkness; or when I could reflect and look back on past days, pangs which made the moments of madness desirable racked me, until I howled curses on the authors of my existence. When I looked back upon the manner in which I had been devoted to misery before my birth, then led on from infancy, an unsuspecting victim, in the way marked out for me before I saw the light, and my feet trained to the pit in which I now groaned—when I looked forward to the years in which I must endure my sufferings, before my strength would yield and death relieve me—I arraigned the justice of Heaven—my mind, loathing the error which had led to my destruction, rebelled against truth, and abandoned its Creator—I abandoned and was abandoned by my God! At the end of two years I was roused from sleep—for even such a wretch had the consolation of sleep—the ministers of cruelty entered, seized me—stretched me on the stone floor of my dungeon, bound my limbs with cords to the iron rings which were fixed for the purposes of torture, near the corner of the cell, and— see—my mutilated body testifies the truth of my tale—how long it was before I recovered the use of my senses I know not—let me end. When I was sufficiently recovered to be able to totter a few steps, I was led from my cell, a most loathsome object, and thrust from a private gate of the infernal region into the street, about the hour of midnight. The demon who turned me thus, powerless, shelterless, and without the means of procuring subsistence, upon a world which had been deprived of all its charms to me, opened his mouth and accosted me with the first words I had heard for years, except my own ravings. I remember them well. 'Go, be not seen near this building. Be not found in Spain ten days hence. You always will have, as you always have had, the eye of the holy Inquisition on you.'

"I crawled by the aid of the walls. I remembered a friend who might shelter me, and reached his dwelling before the dawn of the first daylight I had seen in three years. When with difficulty I could make myself known to my friend—he proved himself truly such—he did all that could be done to alleviate my misery, and I embarked for America in less than ten days from the time I saw the light which had no longer joy for my eyes or my heart." "The lady?" "She had disappeared about the time I was missing, and never was heard of more."

Such was one of the members of the orchestra. Most of his companions considered themselves as the victims of democracy. He knew himself to be the victim of an institution which could only exist in a monarchy or aristocracy. He was bitter in his expressions against those institutions which they loved. His hate of monarchies and hierarchies was deep; *they* adored the source of their former ease and splendour. He had no companions in the theatre. A brother arrived from Switzerland, and the ex-priest stripped himself of all the property he had accumulated to help his brother. He received offers from Havanna of a situation as a musician, went thither, and yellow fever soon ended his unfortunate life.

Among the musicians was a former captain of Bourbon horses, a fine fellow, who now eked out his income by making ice-creams. Another, a ci-devant noble is remembered, always mild, gentlemanly, and silent. There was one, who without circumlocution offered his services as a go-between in any affair of what is called gallantry, that might suit those who could pay or patronize him. He was a noble by the rotten institutions of Europe—the Swiss peasant was a noble from the hand of nature, persecuted and destroyed by those institutions.

Young, an Englishman, was the bassoon player of the orchestra. He had contracted debts and on the deputy sheriff or constable attempting to arrest him, he drew forth a pistol and shot him. The desperate man was immediately secured, shortly after tried, condemned, and executed. He committed the murder on the 29th of June, 1797. About the middle of August the governor requested, by letter, James Kent, Esq., then recorder of the city, to attend, with the other magistrates, upon the execution of this miserable man; the sheriff being apprehensive of a rescue, the governor ordered out a large detachment of the militia, with arms and ammunition to support the sheriff. The criminal was accordingly guarded thus to the place of expiation, but no tumult of any kind occurred.

Mons. Victor Pellesier must not be forgotten in a notice of the orchestra. He was a performer on the horn, and a composer. His music for an opera called "Sterne's Maria, or the Vintage," is remembered with pleasure. He was a short old gentleman, and so near-sighted as to be nearly blind. Always cheerful, and his thoughts as fully occupied by notes as any banker or broker in Wall-street.

We have slightly mentioned in a former chapter, the sad story and death of Monseiur and Madame Gardie. From Messrs. Ciceri and Pellesier the writer obtained a more detailed account of the catastrophe, and the story of the former part of the lives of these unhappy young people, than could be given by persons not acquainted personally with them, speaking their language and frequenting the house which was their place of abode, and where the desperate act of the deluded man was achieved.

Gardie was the son of a nobleman, the king's receiver-general at La Rochelle, and possessor of great wealth. The young man was idle and dissipated; the expectation of inheriting great riches operated to the destruction of that ambition which would have rendered him worthy of their possession. His father, wishing to remove him from the haunts of idleness, and to give that employment which would correct present unprofitable habits, sent him to St. Domingo, as his agent in some commercial business. There he saw and formed an intimacy with a beautiful and fascinating woman, the mother of a male infant, who, as an actress, for that was her profession, enchanted the public when on the stage, and in private life was the charmer of all who approached her. This woman had lived as a wife with a performer of the name of Maurison, who was the father of the infant, at this time her solace and care, for she had separated herself from Maurison, on finding him unworthy of her affections. He had gone to France, and being a man of abilities, and carrying with him property from the Cape, he was elected one of the municipality of Lyons after the revolution, and shared the fate of thousands, the fate of blood and death, during the reign of terror.

Gardie and the fascinating actress became united, and she accompanied him on his return to La Rochelle; she continued to exercise her professional abilities, and was not received into his father's family. The revolution, although it deprived the elder Gardie of his title, neither took from him his wealth nor his office; he was alive at the time of which we write, and receiver-general at La Rochelle.

One evening when the beautiful actress was on the stage, she was called upon to sing the Marseillois Hymn. She refused. The cause of her refusal is not stated. The audience were enraged—she was withdrawn from the stage, and at that time of universal excitement, found it necessary to fly the country. Gardie left country and family, and accompanied the mistress of his destiny. They returned to Cape Françoise. On the insurrection of the blacks, they took refuge in this country, where they lived as man and wife, he principally supported by her salary as a dancer and pantomime actress, for her skill as a comedian was nugatory, where her language could not be understood by the frequenters of the theatre. The boy knew him as a father and the husband of his mother; as a husband and a father he was exemplary. The ballet and pantomime establishment had been lopped off from the New-York theatre in consequence of scanty receipts. Gardie's principal resource for support was copying music. When Mr. Hodgkinson, in 1798, had determined to leave New-York for Boston, he employed Gardie to copy the orchestra music belonging to the theatre of the first place. He went away, and even that source failed. The young man was in debt, and as he himself thought without resource—he was helpless and friendless. His wife, for such she was in the eye of law and society here, solicited, importuned him to write to his father. He now resolved to return to him. He wished her to return with him, but she could not conquer her repugnance to the family which had rejected her, and the people who had chased her from the stage and the country. She refused to return. It appears that a separation had been agreed upon, whether final or temporary, is not known. He had engaged his passage for France, and she had been the evening before her death at Mr. Hallam's, consulting as to the means of enabling her return to St. Domingo.

On the fatal and horrible night, Gardie occupied a small bed in the third story, in the same chamber in which his wife and her boy, now about eight years of age, slept. The boy was waked in the night, and found himself in his supposed father's arms, who was in the act of removing him from his mother's bed, to place him in that which had witnessed his agonies while he watched until his victim should sleep. There was no light. On the boy inquiring why he removed him from his mother, he bade him be quiet and not wake his mamma; then laid him in the bed from which he had himself risen, and the boy again fell asleep; but soon starting at the sound of a groan, which he thought proceeded from his mother, the little lad in great terror called out, "What is the matter, papa? What is the matter with mamma?"—"Hush," was the reply, "your mamma is not well—but she sleeps—don't disturb her."

Again the child slept, unconscious that death in his most horrid forms of murder and suicide was at his side, and the murderer's task half achieved. A noise of falling, struggling, and groans a third time awoke the boy; his calls were unanswered—all was dark and silent—his terror increased when he found that he received no answer to his repeated calls on his father and mother—he left his bed, and groping his way, his little hands encountered the yet warm corpse of his father on the floor; and he felt the blood, as it yet oozed from the wounds, and unknowing what he did, he pressed his little fingers into the gaping gashes, whence life had scarcely escaped.

Wild with terror, the child reached the door of the chamber, and it not being fastened he fled, leaving the door open, and found his way to the mistress of the boarding-house, who was awakened by his cries. His tale was incoherent and unintelligible. His "papa, and his mamma—his papa, and his mamma," were the only words understood. His cries were not attended to, and he was sternly ordered to go to bed. Thus repulsed, and not daring to return to the dreadful chamber, he sought the bed of one of the negro servants, and crept trembling to his side.

About the break of day the dogs of the house found their way to the scene of blood, and with the most piteous cries gave vent to their feelings. Several times they ran howling up and down stairs before the family were alarmed.

On entering the room, they found the miserable murderer lying in the middle of the floor weltering in his blood; his right hand above his head still grasping the knife, his face and limbs horribly distorted—it appeared that he had been forced to inflict several wounds on himself before he fell. She had been killed by one blow, and lay as if asleep. He had probably thought to be merciful in murder.

Such misery and such crime are not to be charged to the theatre. They are found everywhere. They are the fruits of error and vicious indulgence.

⇥ CHAPTER 19 ⇤

Cause of the decline of the Drama, and Remedies proposed — A dull, short Chapter.

In a former chapter we have recommended the interference of the state in the regulation of the theatre. The more we reflect upon the subject the more we are convinced of the propriety, utility, and necessity of the measure. It is a great and powerful engine for good or ill; and though its general tendency may have been favourable to civilization and morals, evils have attended, and do attend it. In Germany, where it is altogether under the direction and control of the government, one of these evils is unknown; and where it is under the supervision and partial direction of the rulers, it is in its worst form avoided; as in France. The evil we mean, and shall protest against, is that which arises from the English and American regulation of theatres, which allots a distinct portion of the proscenium to those unfortunate females who have been the victims of seduction. In Germany, the theatre is the prince's; it is directed by a literary man in his service. The director and players are paid by the government, and being chosen for talents and moral conduct, are honoured by the prince and his court. Here the theatre is the people's, as all things are. And the representatives and guardians of the people ought to prevent the misuse and perversion of it in any way. The directors ought to be controlled to their own and the public good by the official servants of the public, and in the particular abuse above mentioned, the prohibition of the immoral display would remove a just stigma from the theatre, and would further the views of managers by increasing their receipts.

In France the theatres are under strict control, and some of them are supported by the government. The abominable regulation which causes this evil is there unknown, and the evil is unknown. It is not practicable to exclude the impure and the vicious from public resorts, neither is it to be wished. If the drama is such as a good government ought to permit, its influence cannot be ill on the immoral auditor, and may be good. But no separate place should be set apart, to present to the gaze of the matron and virgin the unabashed votaries of vice, and to tempt the yet unsullied youth by the example of the false face which depravity assumes for the purposes of enticing to guilt.

We see by a late debate in the French Chamber of Deputies, that one million three hundred thousand francs was the grant of the present year, 1832, for the support of the theatres. A member wished a reduction, but M. J. de Larochefaucauld considered that the national theatres would be ruined by any diminution of the assistance afforded to them, and therefore opposed the amendment.

The minister of commerce entered into a detailed history of the connexion between the government and the theatres, from the time of the Empire, when the police received the proceeds of the tax on the gaming-houses, and paid the subventions to the theatres. It appears by the same debate, that the Opera-house, the Theatre Françoise, and the opera Comique, had advocates for greater support by additional allowance of money.

We would not propose that our countrymen should take any European mode of government for a model; or that the theatres of America should be regulated according to the usages of Germany and France; but we do hope that what is good, will be adopted from the laws and customs of every country, as far as it can be adapted to our republican institutions. In France the audience see no display of the nature we have mentioned. It is only in England and America that the nuisance exists. If a regulation was enforced, that no female should come to a theatre unattended by a protector of the other sex, except such whose standing in society is a passport to every place, the evil would be effectually remedied. The moral would not be deterred from a rational amusement, and the public and the manager would both be benefited.

The improper, indecent, and scandalous practice of setting apart a portion of the boxes for this most disgusting display of shameless vice, has no connexion with the question of the utility of theatres. The prostitution of the pencil, the graver, or that mighty engine the press, to the purposes of vice, immorality, or irreligion, might with equal propriety be charged against those modes of ameliorating or instructing society.

It is to be lamented that when the people of Massachusetts introduced the theatre in their capital, having the experience of the world before them, they had not set an example to their fellow-citizens, by purifying the dramatic establishment and abolishing this evil. They appear to have noticed it, but instead of remedying, they, if possible, made it worse. The Federal-street theatre provided a separate entrance for those who came for the express purpose of alluring to vice. The boxes displayed the same row of miserable victims, decked in smiles and borrowed finery, and the entrance could only, by its separation from those appropriated to the residue of the audience, become a screen inviting to secret guilt. The new theatre of Philadelphia gave an opportunity for reform, as did that of New-York; but these opportunities were neglected, and those who wished to support, as a mode of improvement, the representation of good dramatic works, have been driven from the boxes by the spectacle presented, not on the stage, but on seats placed opposite to them, and attracting their attention *from* the stage.

Since writing the above, we have seen the English theatre charged by an English writer, with "disgraceful arrangements which would not be endured in the most dissolute capital of the continent, and which seem intended to justify the severe denunciations of those who entertain religious scruples about the stage." The same writer says: "We venture to hope, that one theatre will break the unholy association with open vice and immorality, by imitating the stricter police of the Continental theatres."

We will venture to hope that, not only one theatre, but all will break this unholy alliance. There is the more reason to hope, from the conviction that, as a mere money-making speculation, it would be found for the interest of all concerned. But if managers will not so regulate the police of the theatre, we hope that grand juries or legislative bodies will take the regulation into their hands.

Our forefathers, both in America and England, saw the noblest efforts of the mind of man, when presented by the stage, accompanied by meanness in theatres and decorations, and frequently by mediocrity in the performers who gave them utterance. We see splendid theatres, excellent performers, beautiful scenery, classical decorations, and appropriate dresses, but the plays brought out as meager, mean, and despicable as the barns and sail-lofts which formerly echoed with the inspirations of Shakespeare, or the laughter excited by the wit of Congreve. Have not the dimensions of theatres been one cause of the degradation of the drama? We can hardly conceive that the perfection of the painter and the player has caused the deterioration of the dramatist—unless, that dramatists have been induced to write plays to suit the ability or whim of the player, and relied on his support instead of their own resources—or, that managers have thought it cheaper or more profitable to display gilding and paint, accompanied by the inanity of a playwright hired by the week, than the effusions of a poet, whose words could not be heard from a stage removed beyond the sound of human voice. The huge house requires an exertion of the actor's voice which destroys its melody, and renders variety of intonation impossible. The expression of the actor's face cannot be seen by the spectator, and to endeavour to convey ideas by the countenance, exaggeration and grimace are resorted to. To see or to hear, the spectator and auditor must overstrain attention, and overstrained attention causes pain and weariness, instead of the delight we seek.

Another evil flowing from large theatres, is that desire to fill them, which as induced the shameful exhibitions of monsters and beasts, and other vulgar shows. This is one reason of their being left to such audiences as are fit for such exhibitions; and, until this evil, and the still greater which we have combatted in the commencement of this chapter, are removed, we cannot hope to see audiences of the learned, the wise, and the good, attending to the productions of the poet, the wit, and the moralist.

✦ CHAPTER 20 ✦

1797 — The two Theatres in New-York — Lailson's Circus — Two Theatres in Boston — Wignell returns to Philadelphia and Hodgkinson to New-York — Mr. Cooper joins the New-York Company — The New, or Park Theatre opened, January 29th, 1798 — Mr. Wignell closes the Philadelphia Theatre, and assigns as the causes, Mr. Moreton's ill-health, and the defection of Messrs. Fennell and Cooper — Mr. Cooper's Hamlet — Tragedy of André — Joan of Arc — Chalmers and Melocosmiotis — Mr. Hodgkinson determines to relinquish New-York, and engages both the Boston houses — The Park Theatre leased to Mr. Dunlap — Biography of William B. Wood, Esq.

The yellow fever having taken possession of Philadelphia, in August, 1797, Solee's intended opening in the old theatre in Southwark was prevented, and, as before noticed, he (or rather the company directed by their own whims) was playing at John-street, and Wignell's company, well directed and organized, in Greenwich-street. An extract from a letter will give a notion of the relative success. "Solee opened here last Friday, the 18th of August, to $374, and played again on Monday to $315. I hear much praise of Mrs. Williamson's Little Pickle. Last Wednesday, the 23d of August, Wignell opened with Venice Preserved, and Who's the Dupe? to upwards of $1000. The performance was highly approved, and Mrs. Merry left a lasting impression."

This splendid exhibition has been noticed. Harwood appeared in *Gradus,* which he played very finely. Another extract: "We went to John-street where, to a very thin audience ($130), was performed The Gamester and Romp. Mrs. Barrett's personation of Mrs. Beverley was very respectable, and her appearance majestic; there was not much else to praise, except Mrs. Williamson's Romp. Barrett is not equal to a first place in a company *now* and *here.* Wignell was present and most of his performers, who were tittering at the performance of the tragedy." On the other hand, "Williamson declares Cooper's Pierre 'execrable,' Moreton's Jaffier 'very so-so,' and Mrs. Merry's last night's performance 'below par.' Barrett says, 'he saw nothing to be frightened at.'"

Fennell made his first appearance in New-York, in the character of Zanga, early in September, adding still more to the reputation of the Greenwich-street company.

Another extract: "I last night (September 11th, 1797) saw Mrs. Merry's Juliet with much delight. There were a great many people present, the first and most respectable of our people, while at John-street, Bunker Hill was performing to a mere rabble, amounting to a house of $200, and even the rabble execrated it.

On Friday night Wignell played Columbus to something above $600. The John-street company put off until Saturday. On Saturday Wignell repeated Columbus to, I think, less than $200. The John-street company put off until further notice."

Thus Hodgkinson was playing in the Haymarket theatre, Boston, to houses below expenses, but paying the salaries of himself and family, and his partner borrowing money in the hope to keep together the company for the new house, and be repaid in the autumn by opening it. He advanced to Solee, as one engaged by Hodgkinson, to a large amount, which he had finally to lose.

The John-street theatre, under Solee, was closed October 3d, 1797, with Jane Shore and The Poor Soldier. Jane Shore, by an American lady; Alicia, by an English lady; both first appearances. The American had figure and voice, though in the main abominably bad. The English woman was Irish, and played several times in other places; it was an Irish first appearance, and reminds us of the gentleman who, coming to join a company after they had left the place, exclaims—"I'm *first, after all.*"

While Wignell was using Rickett's circus as a theatre, Lailson was building a new one, likewise in Greenwich-street. No vestige of either remains.

Cooper, dissatisfied with Wignell's preference of Fennell, and Wignell, perhaps, dissatisfied with Cooper's inattention to business, were not openly at variance, and it was prophesied that the young tragedian would not submit to the rule of one who treated him *en cavalier.* Indeed, it was already reported, that he was going to Charleston, S.C. with Solee. On the other hand, Wignell threatened to arrest him. This difference was made up, and Cooper continued to play in Greenwich-street, and occasionally had an opportunity of bursting forth with a force and fire, guided by genius and taste, that won the audience of New-York, and made him a decided favourite before the theatre closed. His Hastings, in Jane Shore, made a great impression. On some, more than his Pierre had done.

Solee, having made arrangements with Hodgkinson for occupying the Haymarket theatre, Boston, and having carried his company thither, and Hodgkinson having broke up for New-York, his partner in this losing business left home for Boston, thinking to meet him on the road, and deeming it necessary to be on the spot, to secure, if possible, the sums lent to Solee. They did not meet. And Solee had not yet opened the theatre at Boston. All parties appear to have been playing at cross-purposes, and every step was leading to ultimate bankruptcy.

The Haymarket theatre, Boston, was opened in December, the Federal-street theatre being open likewise, and both playing to loss. After in vain waiting, in the hope of obtaining something more than promises from Solee, the disappointed manager retraced his way to New-York, where Hodgkinson had opened the John-street theatre, the new house being yet unfinished. The first play and farce were, The School for Arrogance, and The Adopted Child. The company consisted of Messrs. Hallam, Hodgkinson, Tyler, Johnson, Fawcet, Jefferson, Hallam, jun., Martin, Prigmore, Seymour, Miller, Lee, Leonard, Chalmers, Williamson the singer, and Simpson the Irishman;—Mesdames Hallam, Hodgkinson, Melmoth, Johnson, Tyler, Brett, Seymour, Collins, and Simpson;—Misses Broadhurst, Westray, E. Westray, Brett, Harding, and Hogg.

As might be expected, the loss on such an establishment (kept up with the hope of opening the costly new theatre, so long in anticipation, and which was to have been ready in October) was as regular as the play-day or pay-day; but there was now no retreat, and the managers were urgent with the proprietors of the new building to complete the portion absolutely necessary, and let them take possession.

On the 27th of December, the two *stars*, Chalmers (who was a good comedian), and Williamson (a singer from Covent Garden), were produced, the first as Vapid, in Reynolds's first comedy, the second as Tom Tug in The Waterman. The receipts of the house $222. Chalmers failed after Hodgkinson's Vapid; but Williamson's singing was approved.

Even New-Year's day could not give profit to the loaded and sinking establishment. The holy-day play only produced $494.

On the 1st of January, 1798, Mr. Cooper arrived from Philadelphia. His discontents, perhaps the mutual discontents, in regard to his situation with Messrs. Wignell and Reinagle were increased. The public of New-York had preferred him to all tragic actors they had seen. He was now solicited by a number of gentlemen, with whom he had become intimate during the summer and autumn, to play one night while in New-York, for his amusement and their gratification, and he yielded to their requests, writing to Wignell and informing him of the circumstance. The character of Pierre in Venice Preserved, was selected, and on the 4th of January he rehearsed it with Hodgkinson's Jaffier.

Wignell, by letter, forbade Cooper's playing in New-York. There had been a money transaction, in which the managers had suffered a note given to Mr. Cooper to be protested. In this letter there was a proviso that the note should be paid, provided he was on the spot by a certain day. A previous day had been stipulated for. Mr. Cooper continued his determination to gratify his New-York friends, and wrote to Wignell that he would be in Philadelphia by the time appointed. "I might, perhaps, fail my friend," said he, "in an appointment; never my enemy."

Wignell wrote to Hodgkinson, and used an expression conveying the idea that Cooper had informed him (Wignell), that Hodgkinson had solicited him to play in New-York. This was denied by Mr. Cooper, in his letter to Wignell, with the assertion that he had told him the simple truth, and asked his permission.

On the 5th of January, Mr. Cooper played Pierre in the John-street theatre, but even this novelty only produced a receipt of $240, and to his Penruddock, next night, $160. Hodgkinson never played Jaffier so well as with Cooper's Pierre.

It appears that Messrs. Hodgkinson and Dunlap had been proceeding in this long course of exertion with continued loss, to support a company for the new building, without having obtained the signatures of the committee of proprietors to the agreement, which secured the possession of that theatre to them, which was expected to repay the money lost, and discharge the debts contracted. It was now necessary to stop the business at John-street, which added by every succeeding exhibition to the losses already incurred, and to open the new house in its unfinished state as a *dernier resource.*

In this state of the business Mr. William Henderson, who was the acting man of the committee, proposed to the managers that they should admit the proprietors with free tickets into the theatre. The number of proprietors was 130. Thus, in addition to the deduction to be made from the receipts as above stated on every occasion when the theatre had extraordinary attraction from extraordinary exertion, novelty, or expense, the managers might be deprived of 130 dollars by the admission of those free of expense, who were most likely to attend and pay for admission.

It appears that the committee had contracted debts for the building on their own responsibility, and now were about to call upon the proprietors to assume them. They therefore wished to present this additional view of advantage from their contract.

In a conversation between Mr. Henderson and one of the managers it was objected, that no such diminution of the receipts was contemplated when the agreement with the committee was made; that in consequence of that agreement great loss had been sustained. The free admittance was then talked of as a temporary thing, to cease after a short time. It was objected that if once granted it could not without offence be withdrawn.

Here was a lesson. The managers had proceeded upon an unsigned contract, and one of them jeoparded his mercantile property and credit upon an agreement which, if not fulfilled, would make ruin certain.

On the 13th of January, 1798, the writer went, as was usual with him, to see how the new building was progressing, and his friend Dr. E. H. Smith went with him. We had scarcely entered the lower boxes when Mr. Henderson accosted us from the third row on the opposite side, and we went to him. Mr. Carlisle Pollock was with him (one of the committee), and was reading a paper. "I have just given Mr. Pollock a piece to read which I have drawn up for publication." He took it from Pollock's hand and put it in the hand of the manager.

In this paper the committee informed the proprietors or subscribers, that the theatre would be opened; apologized for its not being furnished in the style contemplated, and told them that by a temporary agreement, or arrangement with the managers, the proprietors would be admitted free of expense with untransferable tickets. The manager returned the paper with his thumb upon the part respecting the admission tickets, and Pollock and Smith both attending, he pointedly observed that there had been "no such arrangement or agreement." This was admitted. The manager, in answer to suggestions that such an arrangement would be for the benefit of the lessees, said that on the profits from opening he had relied for relief from debt contracted in consequence of his agreement with the committee; that it was now many months since the agreement; that the idea of granting free tickets had not been suggested; that the terms were publicly known, and no dissatisfaction on the part of the proprietors expressed; that if the idea of free admission was suggested by the committee, the subscribers would not be satisfied if the managers did not comply with the demand. Mr. Henderson said that all the subscribers to whom he had mentioned it, expected free admission. As Pollock and Henderson both protested that they only wished to devise means for mutual benefit, the parties separated by agreement to meet at the house of Mr. Pollock. A meeting accordingly took place between the managers and the committee, the result of which was, that the proprietors should be admitted free, and a reduction made on the per centage before agreed upon. The first took place, but not the second. This was another step in the downhill road.

Mr. Cooper returned to Philadelphia, was arrested by the managers of the Chestnut-street theatre, gave bail, and returned to New-York, where his admirers had assured him of a welcome reception.

On the 22d of January, 1798, Mr. Wm. Henderson put into the hands of the New-York managers a memorandum of agreement to be substituted for that which had been acted upon. By this the free tickets to 113 subscribers were to be given. No free admissions were to be given except to performers for themselves, and those as few as possible. The managers were not to cause any scenery or machinery to be made without the consent of the proprietors, and such to be valued and paid for by the proprietors on the occupants' leaving the house. No alterations to be made to the scenery and machinery without the consent of the proprietors, and the managers to be answerable for all damage done to either, necessary use and fire excepted. The proprietors reserved to themselves all the rooms in front of the building, except one for a box-office. And finally, stipulated that the agreement should continue in force until such time as the proprietors shall decide "in what mode the debts for which the property is liable shall be paid."

Such is a faithful abstract of this most extraordinary proposal of an agreement as a substitute for that which had been made and acted upon, but had not been rendered legal by the forms required.

One of the partners wrote a plain statement of the objections to this proposed substitute. The reader will observe that the agreement by this proposal might be annulled at the pleasure of the proprietors; that the managers could not prepare for a new play or afterpiece without the consent of the committee; that authors of plays could not be made free of the house; that the friends of the lessees, or even their families, could not have free admission; and in short that the managers were to consent to annul the agreement on the faith of which they had contracted debts and sustained losses, and so bind themselves as to render the prospect of future success impossible.

Subsequently the committee professed not to intend their memorandum to convey the meaning understood by the managers, but said they could not lease the theatre for a definite time. They requested some memorandum before giving possession. One was drawn up, leaving the time for which the theatre was leased undefined, but stating that the first agreement with the committee was for three and a half years, and pledging the committee to use their influence with the proprietors so to continue the occupants. The most objectionable parts of the memorandum as proposed by Mr. Henderson were omitted.

At length on the 29th of January, 1798, the new theatre was opened in an unfinished state, and with a scanty supply of scenes. The scenery, machinery, and stage were under the direction of Mr. Charles Ciceri, heretofore mentioned. The landscapes were painted by Mr. Audin, his assistant. The play of the night was "As You like It," the farce was "The Purse." The house was opened with an address written by Dr. E. H. Smith, and spoken by Mr. Hodgkinson. A prelude was performed, written by Mr. Milne, and called "All in a Bustle." The house was overflowing, but such was the confusion from the press of the crowd, and the want of such precautions as experience would have suggested, that great numbers entered without paying at the doors or delivering tickets. Mr. Cooper seeing the confusion and the want of energy in one of the box door-keepers, took his place, and restored order at one of the entrances. The amount received on this first evening of performance was $1232. The next night, January 31st, sunk to $513, and the third, with Mr. Chalmers's first appearance in the new theatre, to $265. The succeeding week only averaged $333 each evening.

The theatre in John-street was soon after pulled down, and on the site three brick houses and their out-houses built, which are at this time (1832) Nos. 13, 15, and 17.

Mr. Cooper was now out of employment in his profession, as he felt it impossible to continue under the management of Mr. Wignell; and the managers of the New-York company had been formally threatened with legal prosecution if they suffered him to play on their stage. He consulted James Kent, Esq., whose opinion was that the managers would be liable to a suit and damages for every time Mr. Cooper played for them.

Early in February, 1798, the Federal-street theatre, Boston, was burnt. In consequence of this incident and of the apparent continuance of poor if not losing business in New-York, Mr. Hodgkinson, already formed a plan for himself of breaking off from the latter place and establishing himself in the Haymarket, now the only theatre in Boston. He even wished to go immediately, and communicated his scheme to others without giving any intimation to his partner. Barrett, who had been thrown out of employ by the burning of the Federal-street theatre, of which he had been manager, arrived in New-York with a letter from Mr. Blake, one of the proprietors of the Haymarket, recommending that Barrett should be put in possession of that theatre. It being necessary that this should be communicated by Hodgkinson to his partner, he for the first time, on the 15th of February, showed him two letters from Mr. Winthrop, advising him to come on immediately and establish himself there.

At this time Mr. Hodgkinson declared his wish to leave New-York, and proposed that a separation should take place, he forming a company for the ensuing winter and going to Boston. His partner raised no objections to his wishes. Mr. Hodgkinson even desired to leave New-York immediately, but that was objected to, and it was concluded to consent to the Boston company taking possession of the Haymarket theatre for a certain number of nights, they paying a rent to the proprietors to be credited to the lessees. Barrett and company were to play until the 23d of March, 1798, and pay 10 per cent. on the receipts. Two days after Hodgkinson received a letter signed by Stimson, Winthrop, and two other trustees, disapproving of the agreement.

The following address of the managers of the theatre in Philadelphia will convey an idea of the difficulties and embarrassments they had to encounter at this period. It appears that Fennell, who had been the cherished object of their attentions, and whose popularity, supported by them, had been one cause for that dissatisfaction which deprived them of Cooper, repaid their partiality by ingratitude.

"*New Theatre.*—The managers deem it their duty to inform the public that the entertainments of the theatre are unavoidably suspended till Monday next, in consequence of the unfortunate indisposition of Mr. Moreton, the injurious defection of Mr. Cooper, and the unprecedented, peremptory refusal of Mr. Fennell to perform the character twice announced for him. Of the first gentleman, the managers must ever speak in terms of acknowledgment, approbation, and friendship, for that uniform exertion in his profession, which has at once advanced the interests of the drama, and justly rendered him the favourite of its patrons.

"On Mr. Cooper's conduct they can make no remark at this time, as the violation of his contract is the subject of a suit now depending in the Supreme Court; and in relation to Mr. Fennell, they are content at present to observe, that independent of the good faith which his engagements ought to inspire, the liberality he has hitherto experienced from the managers, as well as from the public, had naturally raised an expectation that he would not ungratefully have taken advantage of the existing state of the theatre either to embarrass the former or to obstruct the amusements of the latter.

"The managers, having thus respectfully represented the real cause of the postponement of their entertainments (an event equally unexpected and prejudicial) cannot avoid adverting to the difficulty of executing with universal approbation so arduous a task as that which they have undertaken; but they solemnly declare that in every department of their duty towards the public, and in all their transactions with the performers, their incessant effort has been to give satisfaction; and under that declaration they anxiously hope that they shall experience favour and protection, a candid interpretation of their conduct, and a spirit of mutual accommodation.

"WIGNELL & REINAGLE.

"February 20, 1798."

In the meantime Mr. Cooper's friends in New-York made up the sum of £500 sterling, being the penalty of his bond, and he carried the money to Philadelphia, and formally tendered it to Wignell & Reinagle, who refused it. It was tendered to them jointly and severally in the presence of two witnesses, and refused, but the managers afterwards sent for Cooper, who refused to return, but offered Dallas, their attorney, $1200, which he refused, pressing him to pay the whole sum and accept a discharge. This Mr. Cooper refused, and returning to New-York, brought back the money.

On the 28th of February, 1798, the bill announced Mr. Cooper's engagement, and was headed, "To the public.—Mr. Cooper, by certain unfortunate circumstances, being prevented from the future exercise of his profession for nearly two years, unless he pays the penalty of his article to Messrs. Wignell & Reinagle, the managers of this theatre propose to appropriate the profits of this his first night's performance towards the discharge of the same."

The play was "Hamlet," and the farce "The Adopted Child;" and never, probably, was the Danish prince so well played in America, for the actor knew he was playing to those who justly appreciated his talent, and had no prejudices in favour of a rival tragedian. Until this night he had displayed this dramatic character to an audience whose first love had been won by Fennell, and whose prejudice in favour of that actor had been cherished by the directors of the theatre in which they were both engaged. The amount of the receipts was $895. The young actor was received with enthusiasm.

On the 21st of February, 1798, the proprietors of the new theatre met, and their committee reported that after expending the original money subscribed, a debt was incurred of £34,000, or $85,000. We have before stated that the first scheme consisted of 80 shares at 375 dollars, which makes an amount of $127,000. As there were at this time 113 subscribers who had paid, we may state the amount paid at 42,375 dollars, to which add the debt contracted, and we have a total of 127,375 dollars, and the building far from being completed. The waste, mistakes, and mismanagement in erecting this building are perhaps unexampled. The useless excavations under the stage and pit remain as testimonies, for though the house has been rebuilt and burnt, and rebuilt again, these yawning abysses still remain, and, though covered over, will long remain monuments of "alacrity at sinking."

Mr. Hodgkinson's partner in the management had now finished another tragedy called André,—a most unfortunate subject for the stage, at a period so near the time of the event dramatized. Mr. Burk, the author of Bunker Hill, had likewise a tragedy ready for the stage, which was left for perusal with the author of Andre.

A few days after, the two dramatists met, and the following is part of a dialogue which passed in the street.

"Well, sir, have you read my play?"

"Yes."

"And how do you like it?"

"It wants correction."

"What do you mean by correction? I am sure there are no grammatical errors."

"Unless I had the book before me, it is impossible for me to explain my meaning precisely, or point out the parts which I think would be better for your revisal. As far as I recollect, there are some false or confused metaphors, easily remedied when you look it over again, and I recommend it to your severe attention before it is put into the prompter's hands."

"Sir, I have bestowed the utmost attention on it. I am proud of it. It has received every attention, sir."

"But there are few literary productions that could not be made more perfect. There appears to be an incongruity in the character of the heroine. Joan of Arc is first brought forward as a person really inspired, as in Shakespeare's drama, or at least believing herself to be directly inspired from above; subsequently she represents herself as inspired only by her patriotism; and finally, she is a prophetess, again inspired by Heaven, and possessed of foreknowledge, which she communicates in a letter to her countrymen sent from the stake."

The author vehemently defended his heroine, and his play, but agreed to take it back and re-write it.

Early in March, it being generally known that Hodgkinson had determined on leaving New-York for Boston, there to commence manager of the Haymarket theatre on his sole account, Mr. Henderson offered the lease of the house to Mr. Dunlap, if the proprietors agreed, for the sum of five thousand dollars per year. Such an agreement was subsequently entered into.

The receipts in the new theatre were now uniformly below the expenses, except on the night Cooper played Romeo, March 9th, when the amount was $735. It became necessary either to stop or retrench. Chalmers was perfectly useless. He would only play first comedy or tragedy, and the public preferred, justly, Hodgkinson, in one or both, and Cooper in the last. He was perfectly at his ease—did nothing—received his salary—dined with Hodgkinson every day, and sat by his Madeira, as long as he and friend Williamson, the singer, found it convenient or agreeable. If the host said, "I must go to the theatre to dress," the friends were unmoved by the hint. If it was repeated, Chalmers would say, "Very well, Hodge, leave the big bottle with us, we will take care of it."

It was, however, hinted to the free and easy gentleman, that salaries must be reduced and more work done, and he chose to give up his situation, provided he might take his benefit. This was agreed to, and he was allowed to make his own bill. The entertainments were, the "Road to Ruin," and readings by Mr. Chalmers, with songs, &c. &c., under the unintelligible title of a "Melocosmiotis." The incomprehensible title, and the novelty of readings from the stage, succeeded to the comedian's wishes. The house was nearly full. The receipts $1177. After the comedy, in which he played Goldfinch, Melocosmiotis commenced. Chalmers, in full dress, was discovered seated on the stage. He read passages of prose and poetry. The pit hissed—the gallery called for Melocosmiotis! Chalmers knew the bait had taken, he saw the trap full; he laughed in his sleeve, and gravely rose, and bowed whenever he was saluted with a hiss.

The next night "Robin Hood," and "Next Door Neighbours" were played to $99. "Zorinski" was got up with care and expense, and produced $293 receipts.

The tragedy of "André" was performed for the first time on the 30th of March, 1798. The receipts were $817, a temporary relief. The play was received with warm applause, until Mr. Cooper, in the character of a young American officer, who had been treated as a brother by André, when a prisoner with the British, in his zeal and gratitude, having pleaded for the life of the spy in vain, tears the American cockade from his casque, and throws it from him. This was not, perhaps could not be, understood by a mixed assembly; they thought the country and its defenders insulted, and a hiss ensued—it was soon quieted, and the play ended with applause. But the feeling excited by the incident was propagated out of doors. Cooper's friends wished the play withdrawn, on his account, fearing for his popularity. However, the author made an alteration in the incident, and subsequently all went on to the end with applause. The applause of a theatre! The play was printed, and is forgotten. A portion of it was incorporated with a holy-day drama, which the author afterwards put together, and called "The Glory of Columbia, her Yeomanry," which was likewise published, and is occasionally murdered for the amusement of holy-day fools. The tragedy of André was thus cast:

The general, Mr. Hallam; André, Hodgkinson; Bland, Cooper; M'Donald, Tyler; Melville, Williamson; Seward, Martin; British Officer, Hogg; American Officer, Miller; Mrs. Bland, Mrs. Melmoth; Honora, Mrs. Johnson. Children, Miss Hogg, and Master Stockwell.

Our friend Cooper was at this time rather in the habit of neglecting such *parts* as were not *first,* or exactly to his mind. Young Bland was not the hero of the piece, and very little of the author's blank verse came *unamended* from the mouth of the tragedian. In what was intended as the most pathetic scene of the play, between Cooper and Hodgkinson, the first, as Bland, after repeating, "Oh, André—oh, André," as often as "Jemmy Thomson" wrote "Oh, Sophronisba," approached the unfortunate André, who in vain waited for *his* cue, and falling in a burst of sorrow on his neck, cried, loud enough to be heard at the side scene, "Oh, André—damn the prompter!—Oh, André! What's next, Hodgkinson?" and sunk in unutterable sorrow on the breast of his overwhelmed friend, upon whose more practised stage cleverness he relied for support in the trying scene— *trying* to the author as well as actor and audience.

The Nestor of histrionics, Colley Cibber, says, "to show respect to an audience is worth the best actor's labour; and his business considered, he must be a very impudent one that comes before them with a conscious negligence of what he is about."

As most of the part of Bland was never spoken, and as the printed book is long forgotten, we will insert a few lines, to be *skipped,* or read, at pleasure.

"The south teems with events, convulsing ones;
The Briton there plays at no mimic war,
With gallant face he moves and gallantly is met,
Brave spirits throng the camp. And not a clown
But from his youth is trained with steady aim
To speed the unerring bullet to the mark,
To climb the steep, to struggle with the stream,
To toil unshrinking under scorching skies—
This—and that trust in Heaven which animates
The patriot breast, shall far outweigh the lack
Of discipline————."

In a subsequent scene, we have these lines.

> "The men of other climes from this shall see
> How easy 'tis to shake oppression from them.
> How all-resistless is a unioned people.
> And hence from our success, which by my soul
> I feel as well secured as though our foes
> Were now within their floating prisons hous'd
> And their proud prows all pointing to the east,
> The nations of the earth, encouraged, rous'd,
> Shall break their chains—throw down their pageant idols—
> And reassume the dignity of man."

M'Donald, the son of Scotch parents, thanks them for making him,

> "Native of fair nature's world with room
> To grow and thrive in—."

He is censured for uncharitably speaking of Andre as playing the tempter's part; and reminded that fortune had "hurled him from her topmost height," but sturdily replies,

> "Fortune and chance! O, most convenient words!
> Man runs the wild career of blind ambition,
> Plunges in vice, takes falsehood for his buoy,
> And when he feels the waves encircling him,
> Curses, in good set terms, 'poor lady fortune.'"

It was now necessary to know Mr. Hodgkinson's intentions definitely, and Mr. Henderson, having requested an answer to the query, whether he intended to continue in New-York, it was given in the negative. He said that he had written to the proprietors of the Haymarket theatre, that unless he could have the Federal-street theatre for the winter, and the Haymarket for the summer, he would not take either. The Federal-street theatre was then being rebuilt, and the proprietors offered it to him. He said if he staid in New-York, it would be as an actor only: that he had a letter from the Federal-street proprietors, in which they expressed their satisfaction in his acceptance of their offer. "You wrote to them that you would come?" "Yes. But the terms are not yet settled. At any rate, I will never be a manager here." This passed with his partner, who was advised by him to make up a company immediately, and in consequence proceeded to Philadelphia, with a view to engaging Mr. Bernard as stage manager, and first comedian for the ensuing season, his engagements with Wignell and Reinagle being at an end in the month of August of this year. Mr. Bernard declined the offer. His note of

Thursday the 12th of April, 1798, concludes with offers of services with other performers in England, or elsewhere—wishes for success, &c. "I am sorry circumstances will not permit me to quit Philadelphia, but a promise has been extorted from me to continue, by those friends that I cannot disoblige, I once more return your sincere thanks for your polite offer, and friendly wishes."

Mr. Benjamin Carr was at this time a publisher and teacher of music at Philadelphia. The reader will perhaps recollect that he was the composer of the music for the manager's "William Tell," or "The Archers," and performed in it. At his house by appointment a negotiation was commenced with Mrs. Oldmixon. She stated that she had received offers from Mr. Whitlock, for Charleston, S.C.—Her previous engagement at Philadelphia had been seven guineas per week, and a benefit ensured. That she would engage for the best old women, in comedy, the comic singing characters, and occasionally a serious one, and the best chambermaids—and referred the manager to Sir John.

The manager had an interview also with Harwood. These eminent performers are introduced to the reader in chapter X. On the 13th of April, the New-York manager rode to Germantown, in the stage, and found waiting for him at the inn, a horse, sent by Sir John Oldmixon, for his accommodation, and servant with a horse and cart, the identical market cart before mentioned. The manager preferred a walk of a mile and a half to Sir John's cottage, where he passed the night, having in the evening engaged the lady at the salary above mentioned (she finding her own dresses for the stage). Her benefit was to be free from charges, and 38 weeks in the year to be paid for, unless the theatre was shut by some unavoidable calamity. The knight's signature is to the engagement, in very gentlemanly illegible letters.

On returning to New-York the following note was written to Mr. Hallam.—

"Sir, the committee of proprietors of the new theatre, not choosing, or not having the power to prolong the lease of it beyond the present season on the terms agreed to with Mr. Hodgkinson and myself, and Mr. Hodgkinson declining all further concern in the holding or improving said theatre, all engagements, agreements, or contracts depending upon our jointly holding and improving it must necessarily cease at the close of the season. The abovementioned committee have, however, in consideration of the loss sustained by me in the management, offered the house to me for the ensuing year for the sum of $5000, and it is my intention, immediately on the close of the present season, to proceed in decorating the house and preparing a full stock of scenery, and to open it early in September.

"Your situation and theatrical character entitle you to every consideration on a change of this kind, and I hereby offer to sell to you my lease for the sum which shall appear on closing the present season to have been lost by me, in consequence of my having hired the new theatre, provided I can obtain the consent of the proprietors so to do; in which case I will altogether withdraw; or I will for the half or fourth of my aforesaid loss sell the half or fourth of any profit I may gain the ensuing year, you joining with me in the business and leaving the direction to me; or, I offer for your assistance and the assistance of Mrs. Hallam as performers, 50 dollars weekly, you both finding your stage clothes; and, in addition, a weekly sum to be determined upon for the use of your theatrical property, to be agreed upon by us or left to indifferent persons."

To the last proposal he acceded.

On the 27th of April, 1798, articles of agreement were signed by Carlisle Pollock, Jacob Morton, and Wm. Henderson, on the one part, and Wm. Dunlap on the other, and witnessed by E. H. Smith and Wm. Johnson, by which the theatre and "the property belonging to it" were leased, and possession agreed to be given immediately on closing the present season, for the sum of $5000 for one year, to be paid at eight payments. Untransferable rights of free admission to be given to 113 persons, except on benefit nights. If from war, prevailing sickness, or other public calamity, the theatre should not be opened for eight months during the year, a deduction to be made of one hundred and forty seven dollars and five cents for each week it is so closed. Scenery made during the year to be valued fairly and paid for by the proprietors.

On the 13th of April Mr. Burk's tragedy of Joan of Arc was brought out. It was execrably performed by the male actors. The female performers were never deficient in their duty. The receipts were 238 dollars. The managers declined repeating it, unless the author gave security for the expenses. He said Brockholst Livingston, Esq. had consented to be his security, but on a note being addressed to that gentleman he returned for answer, that "Mr. Burk had *mistaken* him, and that he had advised him not to risk the repetition of his play."

Mr. Hodgkinson brought out a farce written by his friend Milne, called "A Flash in the Pan."—It proved so.

The benefits commenced on the 10th of April, and several new dramatic pieces were hastily got up, all of which were consigned to merited oblivion. Among them we must mention one called "The Federal Oath, or Americans strike Home," by the infamous Anthony Pasquin. This man was introduced to the writer by Mr. Hodgkinson. His appearance was not more prepossessing than his writings. He afterwards offered to hire himself for a low salary to puff the theatre. The offer was declined. His real name was Williams. He obtained a living in London for years, by writing libels on players and painters. A judge on the bench, we think Lord Mansfield, said, "his touch is pollution." Yet we see this man's opinions, in matters of art, gravely quoted in modern books.

Mr. Cooper, Mr. Jefferson, Mrs. Melmoth, Miss Westray, Miss E. Westray, and generally the most valued of the company, chose to re-engage with the New-York director. Mr. Martin was engaged as a deputy stage-manager. Mr. Johnson made a verbal engagement for himself and wife at $25 per week each, but shortly after informed the manager that he had determined to go to England in consequence of a letter, which he produced and read, from a friend, who informed him that both Harris and Wroughton wished for Mrs. Johnson's services, and a situation was open to her at either house. "Harris," he said, "offers her a salary which will entitle her to give orders" (this was explained as meaning a sum not under six guineas), "and in case of success as good a salary as any woman in the company." The offer of Mr. Harris was accepted.

The theatre closed on the 29th of June, 1798, and Mr. Hodgkinson, with a part of the company, went on to Boston and opened the Haymarket.

The company of Wignell and Reinagle were employed this summer at Annapolis and Baltimore. At the former place Mr. Wm. B. Wood made his first appearance on the stage, to which his talents have been an ornament, and his conduct through life an honour. Of the following biographical sketch of this gentleman he says, "it is positively true, though not flattering. It was drawn up by one of (now) the first men of the country, and at my request, for fear the violent zeal at that moment of '*Carpenter*' should make me ridiculous."

BIOGRAPHY OF MR. WOOD.
—(From The Mirror of Taste.)

"Individuals who are constantly before the world naturally excite its interests, and awake its curiosity. The public require further information with respect to them, than that which arises from the professional intercourse that subsists, and they have a right to be informed. In the subject of this sketch a double interest will be felt; both as it exhibits a gentleman who has for a considerable time engaged a large portion of public attention, and as it forms a striking illustration of the effects of industry and laudable ambition in triumphing over the opposition of nature, and establishing a reputation solid, brilliant, and beneficial.

Mr. Wood, the father of our present subject, was a respectable goldsmith of New-York. He left his native city when the British took possession of it in the revolution, and retired to Montreal. During his residence there, on the 26th of May, 1779, Mr. William B. Wood was born. At four years of age he was brought by his father to New-York, and during the first years of infancy was treated and educated as boys generally are. At the early age of eleven years he was placed in a counting-house, not long before the celebrated scrip speculation, which terminated in the failure of many respectable houses, and among others of that to which he was attached. Left to seek his fortune out of trade, young Wood was placed in the office of an attorney, where he remained twelve

months. Thus early bustled about from school to counting-house, and from
counting-house to office, it may be expected that our young gentleman was
somewhat manly for his years, as he had at least learnt a lesson that he must
take care of himself. Anxious, therefore, for something like an independence,
he entered again into a merchant's counting-house as clerk, at a small salary,
with little recommendation except integrity and the faculty or writing an
excellent hand. A prospect now opened for a voyage to the West Indies with
commercial views, which was gladly embraced, and in the year '97 Mr. Wood
embarked on this expedition. He remained abroad a twelvemonth, and returned extremely poor, somewhat profligate, and very proud. These qualities,
as might be expected, brought on difficulty after difficulty, and heaped embarrassment upon embarrassment, until his career was brought up (though
still some years short of manhood), by imprisonment for debt in the Philadelphia jail. While in confinement, and revolving the various means of struggling through life, he recollected that he had obtained some premiums and
praise for his elocution when at school, and he saw through the bars of his
prison an eminence of theatrical fame, which he fancied would readily be
obtained. As soon as an arrangement could be made with his few creditors,
he left this city for Annapolis, where Mr. Wignell was then performing with
the Philadelphia company, and presented himself to the manager, full of expectation, and throbbing with the certainty of success. This was in 1798.

This was the dawn of Mr. Wood's theatrical life; and never did a more
inauspicious sun arise. He was feeble in health, indolent, little habituated to
theatrical studies, indifferent as to voice, and extremely young. Mr. Wignell,
therefore, who was a friend to his father, strenuously advised him to relinquish his idea of a dramatic life, but all in vain—the young gentleman "had
heard of battles," and was resolved to be a tragedy hero.

It was somewhat strange that at this time, and for some years afterwards,
Mr. Wood never thought of genteel comedy, on which principally his present
fame is founded, as a road to reputation; and looked down with ineffable
contempt upon every thing but the dagger and the buskin.

After much persuasion, Mr. Wignell, with that goodness of heart which
always characterized him, determined to gratify the young man, and George
Barnwell was fixed upon as the proper *debut* of this tragic actor. Wood's
figure, albeit not corpulent at best, was reduced to a skeleton by a recent illness, and he appeared more like George Barnwell, a year after his execution,
than the blooming lover of Milwood. As the manager expected, the performance absolutely failed. Not a ray of merit shone form the character, and our
friend Wood, since declares, that it was the most execrable thing that ever
came before the public. He was, however, not disheartened: baffled in a great
attempt, he had at least the consolation of Phaeton—*magnis tamen excidit
ausis;* and he must perforce clip his wings, and content himself for a while,
with an humble flight. And much more lowly it was indeed, for during the

whole of that season, at Annapolis and Baltimore, he figured away in the next grade above message carriers, until his patience, and even his ambition were nearly exhausted. In Philadelphia he opened in the part of Plethora, in "Secrets Worth Knowing," and so miserably meagre was his frame, and so consumptive and sickly his hue, that the audience were at a loss whether to consider the player as performing a part, or exhibiting the unaffected symptoms of disease.

After performing some little time with no improvement, and of course with miserable prospects, Mr. Wood's father interposed, and insisted upon his quitting the stage. To this he consented, and embarked a second time for the West Indies, with the view of establishing himself permanently there. Prospects were now fair, and a fortune would, probably, have been acquired, but that the climate proved so hostile to his constitution, as to force our friend to return to this country. After an eight months' absence he returned home, and wrung from his father "a slow leave" to resume his occupations on the stage. During his absence, however, Mr. Cain had come forward with *eclat,* and had given promise of great excellence, so that the place which Wood's ambition had sometimes marked out for him, in her most extravagant moments, was already occupied, and Mr. Wignell received him with greater reluctance than before. He continued to play inferior, very inferior parts, principally in tragedy, until accident brought to light some sparks of merit in another line. When the play of the "Heir at Law," was first *got up,* the part of Dick Dowlas was allotted to Mr. Blissett. That gentleman, either thinking the character ill adapted to his style of acting, or perhaps really indisposed, gave it up, when of necessity the part fell upon Wood. He appeared after a few hours of hasty study, and gained considerable reputation in the piece, which was a favourite and often repeated. This was the first character that Mr. Wood played really well, and from this time forth he turned his attention towards genteel comedy, in which now he performs the whole range of first-rate parts. Wignell, in Dr. Pangloss, Warren, in Baron Duberly, and we may add Wood, in Dick Dowlas, rendered the "Heir at Law" an excellent play.

When "Speed the Plough" was brought forward, Wood took Bob Hardy, and did it extremely well. From this time forward he began to be tolerated, though still not admired. Mr. Wignell, although from the first he considered him a bad actor, always entertained for him the highest esteem as a man. He therefore, in the year, 1799, appointed him treasurer of the theatre, in which station he continued until 1803. When Mr. Cooper went to England, the necessity of filling up a stock play, threw Wood into the part of Rolla, which he performed frequently, and always with increasing reputation.

In the month of January, 1803, Mr. Wignell died: Mr. Warren undertook the management of the theatre, and Wood continued for some time, as his assistant or coadjutor in the task. In this capacity he went to England, in June, 1803, with a view to recruit the company, that had sustained some heavy losses. Here was a glorious opportunity for improvement. An opportunity which we believe was not neglected. His taste had been formed upon very imperfect models, and it was difficult for him to conceive an accurate idea of chaste performance from any thing he had seen in America. With an enthusiastic devotion to his business, it is not to be wondered at that he carried to an extravagant length his admiration of Mr. Kemble, Mr. Lewis, and Mrs. Siddons. He attended the theatre faithfully, during his continuance in England, and returned greatly improved in his knowledge of acting, bringing with him some additions to the Philadelphia corps.

Soon after his return from England, Mr. Wood married Miss Juliana Westray, who was then rising rapidly into distinction, and is now an excellent actress on our boards. He was thus rescued from all danger of falling again into his habits of dissipation, and henceforth devoted himself entirely to his profession and his family. From this period he has progressively advanced in merit, and of consequence in public estimation. The inattention, or ill-health of Cain, soon enabled our friend Wood to overtake and outstrip him in the course, and he assumed a station of the first respectability on the Philadelphia stage.

In the winter of 1808–9, the labours of the theatre falling upon him with peculiar weight, Mr. Wood's health sunk under the exertions. While performing the part of Charles de Moor, he broke a small blood-vessel, and was for some time confined extremely ill. Before a recovery could be entirely effected he renewed his labours, and induced by that means a relapse, which had nearly carried him to his grave. A sea voyage was recommended, as a last resort, and he took leave of his friends, and embarked for England. While absent report stated him to be dead, and many who knew his worth, lamented him as such. They were, however, equally surprised and delighted, by his resurrection *in propria persona,* and that too in perfect health and renewed strength.

The winter following, Mr. Wood reaped a whole harvest of laurels, and established his fame on the most solid basis. He played Perez, Iago, and a variety of other parts with great effect. At the close of the season, he purchased into the management with Mr. Warren, and renewed the lease of the theatre for five years: so that the Philadelphia audience are secured in the possession of this valuable actor, for at least a considerable length of time.

The manager of the New-York theatre invited Wood to go and play a few nights there. The invitation was accepted, and the impression made was such as to extend his reputation, and gratify his pride in the highest degree. While there, he performed De Valmont twice, Don Felix, in the Wonder, Penruddock, and Rolla. His Penruddock, particularly, we understand, though seen after that of Mr. Cooper, was universally applauded, and warmly admired.

Perhaps the best piece of acting exhibited by our friend is that of De Valmont, in The Foundling of the Forest; a part for which the author has done little, but left much for the genius of the actor. The feeling and gentlemanly deportment of Mr. Wood peculiarly calculated him for the character, and he has performed it frequently with augmented reputation and success.

Mr. Wood's forte is decidedly genteel comedy, but he succeeds admirably well in tragedy too. His striking excellence is a never-failing perfect knowledge of his author, both as to sentiment and language. If we were to designate the parts in which he particularly excels, we should say that his Belcour, Reuben Glenroy, Vapid, Tangent, Sir Charles Rackett, Michael Perez, Mercutio, and Benedick, in comedy; and in tragedy, his Brutus, Jaffier, Iago, Alonzo in The Revenge, Charles de Moor, and Penruddock, were all excellent performances.

We have before hinted that Mr. Wood's reputation was not so much the effect of natural endowments as the legitimate offspring of long and unwearied application, persevering ambition, and an enthusiastic love of the profession which he embraced almost from necessity. These qualities have enabled him successfully to combat, and finally to defeat the disadvantages of a delicate frame and an unmelodious voice, and they have gained a reputation scarcely surpassed on this side of the Atlantic. They are enforced, indeed, by the advantages of a person tall and genteel, a deportment easy and graceful, manners engaging and polite, and a most amiable character in private life. We have therefore always confidence that an actor so endowed must perpetually improve, since the mind cannot be affected by accident, nor its varieties rendered uninteresting by time."

One of the most disagreeable, perhaps humiliating circumstances attending the life of an actor *is,* that personal enmity, or partiality to a rival, or mere caprice in the most despicable portion of the community, may subject him to insult when on the stage. On the 19th of March, 1810, Mr. Wood was suddenly taken ill on a benefit night. The play was changed. The friends of the actor, who had assembled for his benefit, chose to be irritated against Wood, and threats were loudly uttered of hissing him on his next appearance. He however wisely addressed the audience, and by what was termed an apology, but which was only a plain statement of a fact, deprived the valiant heroes who in the safety of numbers and obscurity had purposed to insult him, of an apology even to themselves for the outrage.

Mr. Wood's most successful efforts have been in the Copper Captain, Prince of Wales, and generally the characters in which Mr. Lewis, of Covent Garden, shone unrivalled in his best days; yet in very many serious and tragic performances, in De Valmont, Reuben Glenroy, Jaffier, and many other characters of first-rate importance, he has gained reputation, and may be considered as an actor of uncommon versatility of talent.

→→ CHAPTER 21 ←←

Autobiography — Scenes before the American Revolution — Scenes during the War of the Revolution — First Visit to a Theatre — London and its Theatres — Pedestrian Tour to Oxford with Dr. S. L. Mitchill — Old Soldier of the 47th.

That the reader may decide how far the person who in 1798 assumed the direction of that powerful and complicated engine, the theatre of a great metropolis, was fitted for the delicate task and great responsibility, it is necessary that a brief retrospect of his past life should be taken. The opinion of the writer is (an opinion perhaps founded upon the result of the experiment) that he was not fitted for the arduous task. Had it been his lot to direct a theatre patronized by an enlightened government, having no care but that of selecting such dramas and such performers as would best promote the great end of human happiness, he might perhaps have been entitled to the grateful remembrance of his fellow-men; but he was now, after a trial of management in conjunction with another person, forced by previous circumstances to burthen himself with a hazardous speculation, which, as far as it had been proved, was unsuccessful; and the power he once possessed of meeting temporary losses and providing the means of success, had been lamentably diminished. Instead of having an unembarrassed mind whose entire powers could be directed to that which should be the object of such an institution, he was tempted to seek resources for the supply of the treasury and the fulfillment of his moneyed engagements. Instead of studying to gain the approbation of the wise, pressing necessities turned his thoughts to the common methods of attracting the vulgar.

The subject of the present chapter was born in the city of Perth Amboy on the 19th of February, 1766. The writer has endeavoured to avoid the much-dreaded pronoun "I" in the previous part of the work, but in what must be known as autobiography it would appear affectation; besides, a change of style even thus unimportant may be agreeable to the reader, and to leave the theatre for a time may render a return to it perhaps pleasant, certainly less tiresome.

My father was Samuel Dunlap, from the town of Londonderry, in the north of Ireland. My mother's maiden name was Sargeant, and her mother's Stone, both natives of New-Jersey, and of English descent, as were all the original families in that part of New-Jersey which lies adjacent to its then capital. The names of Sargeant, Stone, Barron, Bell, Bloodgood, Freeman, Parker, Heriot, and others, testify this as fully as those of Van Rensselaer, Knickerbocker, Schermerhorne, Ten Broek, and others, show the origin of the New-York or New-Netherland settlement in that great metropolis and its adjacent villages and islands of Bergen, Harlæm, Nassau, and Staaten.

My father "had been a soldier in his youth, and fought in famous battles;" and the name, originally Dunlop, is now well known in the world of literature by distinguished authors bearing it, and more generally as connected with Scott's Jenny Deans and the Dunlop cheeses.

Among my earliest recollections are those connected with sickness, and the relief derived from being carried in the arms of my father. I was an only child. When old enough, I listened to the story of his early life with intense interest. He told of crossing the deep with the army that came to wrest Canada from the French, for he was an officer in the forty-seventh, and carried the colours of *Wolfe's own*. He told of the difficulties they encountered in the great river St. Lawrence; of the attempts upon the fleet by the French fire-ships, and the gallant cheerings of the English tars as they towed off from their destination, and rendered harmless the blazing engines of destruction; of the landing and scaling the banks to gain the plains of Abraham; of his being wounded and carried off the field, and, as suspended in his sash and borne to the ships, the pioneers throwing down their tools, supposing they saw their young commander disabled and leaving them, for Wolfe and his regiment wore that day one and the same plain uniform of scarlet without facings. In short, before I knew the meaning of the tale, I had heard all the circumstances of that important day, which fixed the destiny of this great continent of North America—which decided that from Hudson bay to Mexico the descendants of Englishmen, or those deriving from them their civil and religious principles, should spread the language of Shakespeare and Milton, and plant the independent spirit of Hampden and Pym throughout a moiety of the globe.

Another portion of my early education was not so favourable. Slavery had been introduced into the colonies and fostered by the commercial spirit of the mother country. Every family was served by negro slaves, and every kitchen swarmed with them. To be petted, indulged, spoiled, and have their example before his eyes, was the lot of the only child of the master of the family.

But, on the other and brighter side again, it was my happiness to become the favourite of a being of a very different description, and to become attached, in early childhood, to an aged man who lived almost the life of a hermit, having neither wife nor child, in the midst of fruits and flowers *without* doors, and *within* surrounded by books.

Thomas Bartow was a small thin old man, with straight gray hair, pale face, plain dark-coloured clothes, and stockings to suit—his well-polished square-toed shoes were ornamented with little silver buckles, and his white cambric stock, neatly plaited, was fastened behind with a silver clasp. When he walked, a cane with an ivory head aided his steps, which halted through age and rheumatism. His house stood on a corner of the market-square—none other near it—and *the green* before it. It was surrounded on three sides by a garden with the best fruits our climate affords. His person, his house, his garden, were equally neat. I, and I alone, had the full command of the two last, and very nearly of the first.

By some arrangement with my indulgent parents, I was permitted to go every Sunday to this still more indulgent old gentleman. Invariably I found the venerable man alone, seated by a small table, his Bible or other book before him, and his spectacles on his nose—gladly lifted to welcome one who was yet untainted by the world he seemed to shun. The boy was his companion at home, and his only companion when he rode or walked abroad. In winter, he gambolled about the room while the old man read; or was sent into the garret to bring down dried grapes which hung on frames, preserved carefully after ripening on the vines in his garden; or took the key of his library and selected books, to place on the table before him, that he might explain the pictures, or tell the stories. In summer, the favoured boy had the range of the garden, and the choice of the fruit, with the same course of instruction from his books and his lips. Thus, before I could read, Pope's Iliad, Dryden's Virgil, and Milton's Paradise Lost were familiar to me, as to the fable and incident, and every plate was patiently explained, and the passages read or repeated. The good old man was repaid by the unsophisticated remarks of childhood, and the development of intellect in an infant mind. He laughed when the boy pronounced it false that Hector fled from Achilles, and remarked that the story was told by a Greek.

While every other house in the village, nominally a city, was encumbered by negroes, and every family degraded by the presence of slaves, his alone was free from the stain and the curse. Two domestics, both white and free, served, and were served by him. One respectable old female managed his household and culinary concerns, and was as neat, but not as free from frowns, as himself, and a rustic youth attended to the stable and old sorrel, the garden, the wood-pile, and the square-toed shoes. In these domestics I remember no change. The good master made good servants.

Among the evils of the war of the revolution, the greatest to me appeared the loss of my aged friend and companion. He retired from the scene of approaching conflict when the British fleet appeared off Sandy Hook, and I never saw him again, except in my dreams. Through a long life his image has visited my hours of sleep—always changed—generally sick—or insane—or confined to his chamber and forbidding my approach to him. At his death, I was mentioned in his will.

My limits, and the reader's patience, will not allow of details like these; but it is my wish to notice the circumstances which caused the future pursuits, and formed the character of the individual. Great Britain maintained an army in the colonies, and sometimes a regiment was quartered at the place of my nativity, sometimes distributed among the three towns of Brunswick, Elizabethtown, and Perth Amboy. My father's former profession drew to his house the officers, and they carried his son to the barracks. The 47th, in which he had served, were *thus* quartered, during the years 1773, 1774, and part of 1775, in the last year mentioned they were transported to New-York, and thence to Boston. Familiarity with military pomp and revelry, guns, drums, and all the allurements which such an artificial state presents, formed another part of my education.

Schools were as widely different then from what they now are, as every thing else has become. But reading was soon my delight, for my school was at Mr. Bartow's. I read every thing, *skipping* what I could not understand. The Fool of Quality made more impression on me than any other book, and the author's lesson respecting the good and evil propensities of our nature, the good and the naughty boy united in the same person, is often present in my mind to this day. In the year 1775 my father took me on a visit to New-York, and my recollections are vivid of what that city then was. I remember the preparations then making for the struggle which was to ensue.

War approached. The English troops had been withdrawn, the townsfolk of Perth Amboy were arming and forming themselves into a company of infantry. The boys imitated them. The militia from inland poured down to the coast, and filled the village—some *Continentals* (troops raised by order of Congress) passed through on their way to Canada. Their appearance and discipline were a contrast to the militia, and, in many respects, to the red-coated veterans I had been accustomed to. Some in rifle frocks of brown linen, with trousers of the same—but well equipped, though more like hunters than soldiers—others in blue and red uniforms and white trousers, a black cap on the head, the cartouch-box and bayonet slung in black belts, and a round canteen for water, with a bright musket, formed the equipment of these fine young men, now marching to the north to be placed under Montgomery. The militia were an almost unarmed rabble, of every age and description.

The British appeared on the shore of Staten Island, opposite Perth Amboy, and I was removed up the Raritan near to a small village called *Piscataway,* about two miles east of Brunswick. The summer of 1776 I rambled about the fields, caught perch in the brooks, or sunfish in the mill-ponds—was as happy as liberty from school and nearly all restraint could make me; but I read the whole of Shakespeare. I remember that the historical plays were my favourites. I read every book that fell in my way.

The English army marched in hostile array through New-Jersey, and my father walked to the high road passing through the village, to present himself to General Grant as an adherent to the cause of Britain. He took me with him, and

I saw the soldiers plundering the houses, the women of the village trembling and weeping, or flying with their children—the men had retired to await the time of retribution.

In many houses helpless old men, or widowed females anxiously awaited the soldiers of monarchy. A scene of promiscuous pillage was in full operation. Here a soldier was seen issuing from a house armed with a frying-pan and gridiron, and hastening to deposit them with the store over which his helpmate kept watch.

The women who had followed the army assisted their husbands in bringing the furniture from the houses, or stood as sentinels to guard the pile of kitchen utensils, or other articles already secured and claimed by right of war. Here was seen a woman bearing a looking-glass, and here a soldier with a feather-bed—but as this was rather an inconvenient article to carry on a march, the ticking was soon ripped open, and a shower of goose feathers were seen taking higher flight than their original owners ever soared to. This scene was a lesson.

The family returned to Perth Amboy, and remained during that winter surrounded by their English friends, and a medley of Highlanders, Hessians, and other German troops of every description. Wallenstein's camp, as described by Schiller, has since reminded me of the scenes of that winter.

Washington captured the Hessians at Trenton—drove in the 17th, 55th, and 40th regiments of English from Princeton. Amboy was thronged with troops, my father's house filled with officers, his kitchen and out-houses with their servants and soldiers. The grenadiers and light infantry of the army arrived in transport ships from Rhode Island, and lay off in the stream. They were landed on a fine clear winter's day, and with all the "pride, pomp, and circumstance of glorious war," I saw them march into the rebellious country adjacent, attended by a long train of wagons to procure forage. I walked out of the village to see the last of the brilliant show, and tried to keep up with a tall grenadier of the 42d, whose height and beauty particularly attracted my attention. I returned and placed myself by a garret window, which commanded a view of the roads leading on the left to Brunswick, on the right to Woodbridge, that I might catch another view of the long procession, which I saw passing over the hill, and vanishing as it moved on towards the nearest village. I have a confused recollection that my thoughts, that day, were occupied altogether by the proud display I had witnessed, and the events which might be passing in the interior; and the sound of distant musketry gave activity to these thoughts—my mind was on the stretch. I took my way up the road by which the army had passed, and I met a wounded man returning, assisted by a less injured comrade. A little further on, stragglers were met returning, more or less hurt, and evincing pain. I next met the gigantic grenadier of the 42d—his musket on his left shoulder, his right-hand bound up—he walked fast, but he no longer looked like the hero I had admired. I turned about and followed him. It was soon known that the militia had assembled, and were skirmishing with the *regulars*. In the evening it was known that this gallant military array were returning, their wagons loaded with wounded, instead of the booty they went in search of. By the fireside I heard the heavy rumbling of the wagons over the frozen earth, and the groans of those who were borne to the hospitals. I had now seen something of war.

In the spring of 1777, my father removed his family to New-York. I have spoken of New-York as it then was. After a year's interval I again went to school, and a worthy man, Thomas Steele, then a Quaker, once a soldier of artillery, and Englishman by birth, gave me all the instruction I ever received from such institutions. But I read Shakespeare again—and Pope's Homer for the first time, with recollections of my first instructer. I read every thing I could lay hands on, until, by the loss of my right eye from a wound inflicted by a missile, while playing with the boys after dinner, at Andrew Elliot's, my reading and education were for months interrupted. This memorable incident in my life, occurred behind the house for years known as the Sailors' Snug Harbour; then the residence of Mr. Elliot, and a beautiful country-seat, surrounded by pleasure grounds. The north side of the house is the only part now bearing the shape of the original mansion. By this incident my application to drawing, one of my sources of pleasure, was suspended. And I was prohibited from visiting the theatre, as the glare of light was painful and injurious. But the manager, the surgeon-general, Doctor Beaumont, was one of my friendly attendants during this season of pain and long confinement.

Iffland, the great German actor, and one of those dramatists who had raised the theatre of that country to a proud eminence, has, in his autobiography, given a most animated description of the effects produced upon a young mind, by the first enjoyment of the splendid illusions, and seductive excitement of a theatrical exhibition. The crowd of well-dressed people, tier above tier, added to the novelty of the building and its decorations; the lights, the music, the drop-curtain, the mysterious anticipations of the wonders behind it; its rising, and the anxious attention of the audience, on the signal for the long-expected *something*, to be developed; then the magic and moving pictures; the blooming personages of the drama, separated as by enchantment from those to whose view they are exposed, and only connected in joy or sorrow, with each—the creatures of another world, or of ages long gone by.

The feelings he describes were mine on that important evening, when I saw a play for the first time. It was Farquhar's The Beaux' Stratagem. The surgeon-general played Scrub, and colonels, majors, captains, and subalterns, personated the other characters. Thus, until deprived of this pleasure, by the accident above mentioned, I was occasionally indulged in going to the theatre in John-

street, and enjoyed the delight of reading over the plays after seeing them acted, and recalling actors to my mind's eye.

My health being restored, I passed my life until the age of seventeen, attending to my father's store, and in desultory reading, drawing with Indian ink from
such good prints as I could obtain, and finally attempting to paint portraits of
my friends with crayons or pastels. I likewise began two dramas; one on the story
of Abon Hassan, in the Arabian Nights, and the other a tragedy on some incidents in Persian history. At this period, 1783, the preliminaries of peace opened
the way for a return to my native place. I was permitted to visit New-Jersey and
Philadelphia.

For eight years of my life the name of Washington had been familiar to my
ear, though surrounded by his enemies. I had seen the Howes, the Clintons, and
the Carltons of the British army. And the renegades, Brooke Watson, and Benedict Arnold. My attempts at painting attracted the attention of the second named,
commander-in-chief of the English forces, who with other generals and a train
of aids, visited the young aspirant.

When Washington was first heard of, his name was coupled with sarcasms
or taunts, but with the occasional alleviation of "He was with Braddock, and
did good service, though a provincial," and sometimes the acknowledgment—
"He saved the remains of the army from destruction." After the Trenton and
Princeton affairs, Englishmen spoke of him with respect. His name grew with
my growth—it was by-and-by in every month—every transaction of moment
was connected with it. After the capture of Cornwallis, awe and admiration were
constantly connected with the character of Washington.

I was now to see this great man. Congress were in session at Princeton. The
commander-in-chief had his head-quarters at the house of Mr. Berrien, at Rocky
Hill, within two miles. In a solitary walk on the road, between Princeton and
Trenton, while ascending a hill, suddenly appeared from the opposite side a party
of military horsemen. They gained the height, and their figures were relieved
darkly by a light and brilliant sky. They were all dressed in the well-known old
staff uniform of the United States, blue and buff, with the black and white cockade, marking the union with France, in their cocked hats, which were worn, as
generally at that time in the American army, with the greatest breadth (to use a
sea phrase), fore and aft, so as to screen the eyes; they were gallantly equipped
and mounted; each had the glittering gold epaulet on either shoulder, and at
first view all appeared equal, and all above the ordinary height. But the centre
figure was tallest of the group, and I knew that I saw in him the man on whom
every thought centred. The eyes of the company were turned upon me as they
approached. The salutation of taking off my cocked hat was performed with a
feeling which probably my face expressed. Instantly the salute was returned in

the same manner by the chief, and every hat of the company was lowered with its waving plume to me. They passed, and I gazed after them. It was a precious moment. I had seen Washington.

At the hospitable mansion of Mr. John Van Horne, at Rocky Hill, where I passed some weeks amusing myself with my flute, my music books, and my crayons, I was established within a mile of head-quarters. The General and Mrs. Washington were frequently visiters. In his daily rides he usually stopped, and passed an hour with the family. Thus I became, as far as my youth and admiration permitted, an associate with the greatest man of the age. My attempts at painting, miserable as they were, attracted attention, and I was stimulated by words of encouragement. I was invited to head-quarters, and there met at breakfasts and dinners the eminent men who then legislated for, and guided the councils of the country.

I must not indulge in these reminiscences. The portraits I painted at Mr. Van Horne's, led to the painting of the General and Mrs. Washington, and head-quarters for a time was almost my home.

After a visit to Philadelphia, which I saw for the first time, having for my companion a young officer of Lee's legion, I returned to New-York in the month of November, 1783; and on the 4th of May, 1784, embarked for England, in the good ship Betsey, Thomas Watson, commander, with letters to Benjamin West, and for the purpose of studying the arts of design.

To Benjamin West, and the painters of that day, a more ample notice is due from my recollections, than comports with the intentions of this chapter, which is to give some idea of the facilities which I had for obtaining that species of knowledge, which might form a good director of a theatre. It is only as such, and as a dramatic writer, that I am entitled to notice in a history of the American stage.

During the summer of 1784, frequent visits to Colman's theatre, made me familiar with many of the comedians belonging to the winter theatres, and with the pieces then popular, as well as those being introduced as novelties, by the dramatists of the day. Colman the younger's first drama, "Two to One," was then brought out, and the first recollections I have of the elegant John Palmer, is as the speaker of the prologue to it, in which, in allusion to the son's treading in the steps of his father, is the line—

"And dunce the second follows dunce the first."

Mrs. Oldmixon, then Miss George, is vividly impressed on my memory, in the character of Tippet; the elder Bannister, in the man who derives his consequence from the amount of his debts, and Bannister, jun. in the hero of the piece, are before me. But the face and manner of Edwin in Dicky Ditto, who would rather be treated civilly by the debtor he comes to dun, than receive his money and be told to leave the presence of quality customers, is perhaps the most distinct of the whole.

O'Keefe produced farce after farce, some in two acts and some in five. The Agreeable Surprise with the Lingo of Edwin, and the Cowslip of Mrs. Wells, can never be forgotten. And even great Mrs. Webb, in Mrs. Cheshire, and that automaton Davies, are stamped on the tablet of my brain. The Young Quaker, with Palmer's Sadboy, and Edwin's Clod, might be dwelt upon with more delight to the writer than the reader.

Wilson, in Rory the blacksmith of Gretna Green, and Parsons, in every comic piece brought out, are among the strong recollections of the pleasures of that day.

A man's companions form, as well as mark his character. Samuel L. Mitchill, passed through London, to Edinburgh. He was my former intimate at home. Wright Post came to London, and remained about two years, studying and residing with Sheldon. Our intimacy was of the strictest kind. Young officers who had served in America, were too much my companions. Raphael West, the oldest of the great painter's sons, was another intimate associate. When my friend Mitchill returned an M.D. from Edinburgh, in 1786, we renewed our intimacy, and made a pedestrian tour, of which hereafter.

At the opening of the winter theatres, my first visit was to old Drury, Garrick's Drury Lane. I went in at half price, and Messrs. Smith and Bensley were on the stage, in the Lord Townley and Manly of the Provoked Husband. The first impression was very unfavourable. The discordant nasal utterance of Bensley, and the sharp tone of Smith, almost disgusted me. When Miss Farren as Lady Townley appeared, all was enchantment. Suett's Squire Richard, and Parson's Sir Francis, are remembered, and the remainder of the dramatis personæ fade from recollection. Except the Lady Townley, I have seen all better in America.

The first play I saw at Covent Garden was, "As You like It." Miss Younge was Rosalind herself. Lewis, no more than a common, or passable Orlando—Lewis, the best of all gentlemen comedians! Henderson was the Jaques, and he was in every thing the best performer on the stage at that time in all the higher branches of the drama, that we have assigned to, Lewis only excepted. Quick was the clown, and Mrs. Wilson the Audrey. Quick was a great comedian, but I feel confident that the Touchstone of Mr. Hilson is better than Quick's then was.

My first opportunity of seeing Mrs. Siddons was in Isabella. My opinion of this transcendent actress has been given. At this time she was in her prime, and her face and figure as perfect as her acting. Smith was the Biron; Palmer the Villeroy; the Carlos, Barrymore. Mrs. Siddons's Lady Macbeth was played with Smith's Macbeth, and Kemble's Macduff. Her majestic Constance with Kemble's King John, Bensley's Hubert, Smith's Bastard. Her Desdemona with Kemble's

Othello, dressed in a suit of coat, waistcoat, and breeches of scarlet, white silk stockings, and a long military cue. Bensley's Iago, in a blue uniform, and the rest of the characters conformably. John Bannister was the Cassio, and Dodd the Roderigo. Dodd, the *beau ideal* of fops of the old school! Mrs. Hopkins was the Emilia. Mrs. Melmoth played it better. Mrs. Siddons's Grecian Daughter is alone remembered when the performance of that tragedy is thought of. In Mrs. Beverley she was as true to nature in the amiable, as in the sublime and terrible of Lady Macbeth and Constance. Kemble was the Beverley, and Bensley the Lewson; but Palmer's Stukeley surpassed all the performances of the male part of the dramatis personæ.

Of Mr. Henderson, I will only remark that his Hamlet was then the best in London, though I doubt not that Mr. Kemble's surpassed it in after-years. Mr. Henderson's Leonatus Posthumus in "Cymbeline," Horatius in "The Roman Father," and Sir Giles Overreach in "A New Way to Pay Old Debts," are remembered as being perfection, and his Falstaff as the only Falstaff worth remembering; Cooke's being professedly a copy of it.

Of Mr. Lewis I have spoken. His Mercutio, Michael Perez, Ranger, and Sir Charles Rackett have had no equal.

The same must be said of Mr. Palmer's Young Wilding; and when I remember his Bobadil, I can doubt the tradition which says Woodward's was better. It is only that my experience of acting and actors may be known that I risk being wearisome to the general reader. To those who are versed in stage history, such recollections may be interesting. To all who remember (and who that has read can forget?) the comedy of "The Twelfth Night," I may hope to bring pleasing images of the past perfection of casting a play, by detailing the names of those performers who were combined in its representation when I saw it at Drury Lane. Olivia, Miss Farren; Viola, Mrs. Jordan; Sir Andrew, Mr. Dodd; Sir Toby, Mr. Palmer; Malvolio, Mr. Bensley; Fool, Mr. Suett; Sebastian, Mr. Bannister, jun.

The picture presented, when the two knights are discovered with their pipes and potations, as exhibited by Dodd and Palmer, is ineffaceable. The driveller, rendered more contemptible by the effect of liquor,—the actor's thin legs in scarlet stockings, his knees raised nearly to his chin, by placing his feet on the front cross-piece of the chair (the degraded drunkards being seated with a table, tankards, pipes, and candles between them), a candle in one hand and pipe in the other, endeavouring in vain to bring the two together; while in representing the swaggering Sir Toby, Palmer's gigantic limbs outstretched, seemed to indicate the enjoyment of that physical superiority which nature had given him, even while debasing it by the lowest of all vices.

The School for Scandal I saw played in the author's own theatre, and the Critic in the same, with the original cast.

Mrs. Jordan's *debut* and successive characters were all witnessed when she was as perfect in figure as in skill. Her singing was sweet, not powerful. In Wyncherly's Peggy, and in Bickerstaff's Priscilla Tomboy, and The Virgin Unmasked, she was the model on which others have since obtained favour and reputation by the greater or less perfection of their copies. Nothing could be more sweet than her Viola; but in the higher walks of the drama, though always good, she was not the highest. Mrs. Abington *had been*—was still, in point of skill and spirit; but time, the inexorable enemy of beauty, had rendered it impossible for the spectator to believe that the matronly embonpoint of the actress belonged to Rosalind or Portia, Lady Teazle or Violante. Mrs. Mattocks was old, and (to use a phrase of my friend C. B. Brown's) "very remote from beauty." She still sustained a spirited chambermaid's part where youth or comeliness were not required. Mrs. Wrighten was yet in her prime, and those powers which gave her an eminent place as an actress and singer at Drury Lane, were little diminished when as Mrs. Pownall she joined the American stage.

Miss Brunton's reception I have already mentioned, when speaking of her as Mrs. Merry. Pope and Holman were seen in their prime. The Heiress of Burgoyne was seen in its first cast—King, Parsons, Palmer, Miss Farren, and Miss Pope, giving a force to the elegant drama of the unfortunate general, which had not been imparted by the author. Miss Phillips (afterwards, or perhaps at that time, Mrs. Crouch), by her musical talents and most perfect beauty, supported the tender or serious portion of the play.

If I were to speak of the merits of King, Parsons, Mrs. Wrighten, Miss Pope, and many others, I might fill pages, but doubt if they would be read with the pleasure the recollection causes to the writer.

In the autumn of 1786, Samuel Latham Mitchill, having finished his studies in Edinburgh, and taken his degree of M.D., returned to London on his way home. He immediately sought me, and soon after his arrival, proposed a pedestrian tour to the University of Oxford. Wright Post had returned home, or probably he would have joined us. We packed up what we deemed sufficient clothing in one trunk, and despatched it to the Angel Inn, Oxford, with a direction purporting that it was to be delivered to the bearer of the key.

Having determined our line of march by the map, we left London on a rainy morning in the month of November, each equipped with an overcoat and boots, and became travellers in that dreary month, "when Englishmen hang and drown themselves." But there was no dreariness for us; the cold gray sky and black muddy roads were "coleur de rose;" and when night came, and the landlady of a very indifferent inn, with her arms "akimbo," would have sent us on further in wet and darkness, after examining and condemning our appearance, it only excited mirth, for we knew that we bore the *passe pour toute* to the kitchen fire, and that our key would open the best parlour and best bedroom for our accommodation. Some travellers, who were journeying in broad-wheeled wagons to London, and had gained possession of the kitchen hearth, made room for us, and while drying our clothes, and waiting for a fire to be kindled in the parlour, afforded us ample amusement. All was new—all was full of interest. We ate heartily and slept soundly. Hunger sauced our supper—fatigue ensured rest.

We trudged with light hearts through heavy roads, at the rate of thirty miles a day, taking refreshment when most wanted, or most easily obtained, and enjoying every incident which chance threw in our way. We gained a view of the beautiful city of Oxford about mid-day, and the key of our trunk, aided by the key to the landlord's heart, soon made us comfortable at the Angel Inn.

We had letters to professors and students. The curiosities and libraries were shown to us. We dined in the halls. We drank port wine in the chambers of the students—and after some days of enjoyment (for two Americans were two lions at that day, and were stared at and caressed accordingly), we took staff in hand and walked to Blenheim, to view the wonders of that palace, one of the rewards bestowed on Churchill, the Wellington of his day. Woodstock and Blenheim would afford pages of recollections; even the works of Rubens alone, if pictures were the subject of my book, might detain the reader until he tired of descriptions of that which cannot be described, the works of the painter. We walked in the dark back to Oxford.

Of the many who were our companions, or who showed us civilities, only one is distinctly remembered, and that one only as connected with the theatre. Mr. Bland, a brother of Mrs. Jordan, was then a student at Oxford. He is remembered as a modest retiring youth. Another brother of this charming actress, the mother of dukes, and intimate of royalty, it will be seen was thrown in my way, when my way was far removed from the paths of Milton and Addison. The brothers were very dissimilar, and I hope my Oxford acquaintance has passed through life under more favourable auspices than those which governed the fate of him whom I knew as a member of the New-York company of Thespians.

After learning as much of university life as a week's residence could teach us, we prepared to return to London by the same mode of travelling as that which had so pleasantly brought us to the seat of the Muses and loyalty.

Determined to see as much as possible in our journey, we planned another route for our return to the metropolis, one which should lead us through the royal residence of Windsor. This place, which, although frequently visited by me, being a summer abode of Mr. West, and possessing the charm of a royal collection of paintings, was new to my companion.

One incident of our pedestrian wayfaring I will record here: it made a strong impression on my companion, and a stronger on me, as connected with the scenes of my childhood.

As the sun was rising one morning, and cheering our walk with his beams—for it did not rain all the time—as we ascended a hill, and looked forward to descry the welcome Red Lion or Black Bull of some breakfasting place, we saw a fellow footpad come from a turnip-field, and slowly make his way up the road before us. We were soon alongside, and, as was ever our wont, accosted him. But first a description of the new actor in the scene:—He was a short, sturdy man, but bent by the weight of years: he wore what had been regimentals, but tattered and torn; and the defacings of time, and hard wear and tear, had removed the facings which might denote the corps he belonged to. His military covered his thin gray hair, which was no longer plaistered with tallow and covered with flour, in emulation of his captain's perfumes and powder. The worsted lace, which makes the poor soldier strut with all the air of a commander—this mockery of pomp and pride—was gone from his threadbare and patched habiliment. He bore on his back something between a pack and a knapsack; and with a jack-knife he was paring a turnip, "which ever and anon he gave his" mouth, who, not "therewith offended," received the present graciously.

"A cold breakfast, fellow-traveller."

"Yes, your honour, but a keen appetite. This is my first mouthful since yesterday morning,—a long fast for a long march."

"Such as is often a soldier's lot."

"A poor man's lot."

"A soldier is never poor: the paymaster is his banker, and he finds forage in the fields of the enemy when the quartermaster is not at hand."

"Bless you, young gentleman, you talk as if you had seen soldiers, if not service; *that* you are too young for: I have seen and done some; but I'm too old now—no longer a soldier—though I have borne the musket many a year."

"And does your king and country leave you now in this poor plight, and without wherewithal to buy a mouthful of bread?"

"No—God bless his majesty! he takes care of me, though I can no longer fight for him."

"Care of you! It does not appear."

"Better care than I have taken of myself—that's the truth of it. I received my certificate from the war-office, and money to bear me to quarters for life; but when I came to present my papers, behold I had lost them! I had spent my money; and now, without a sixpence, I am on my way to the war-office at Whitehall again, for a renewal of billeting orders."

We had seen instances enough of imposture to be wary; and though the old man spoke frankly, and with a soldier's honesty in appearance, we chose to question him further before relieving his wants, although fully disposed to share with him in the breakfast we were approaching. The question was asked,

"Where have you served?"

"In America." We now thought if he played false, we should soon detect him.

"In what part?"

"God bless you, everywhere! From the St. Lawrence to the Ohio; from north to south, and back again."

"What regiment did you belong to?"

"The forty-seventh—Wolfe's own." I now thought the old man was coming near my home—he must be soon known for false or true. I eagerly asked,

"Where did you serve with the forty-seventh?"

"At Quebec," said the veteran, who now stopped, looked erect, and "every inch" a soldier: "on the Plains of Abraham, with Wolfe; in the woods of Pennsylvania, with Braddock; at Bunker's Hill, with Howe; at Bennington and Saratoga, with Burgoyne." At all these places I knew the regiment had fought; and at the last been surrendered, with their comrades, to my undisciplined countrymen.

"And before you went to Boston, where did you quarter?"

"In New-Jersey: I was stationed in the barracks at Perth Amboy; Col. Nesbitt commanded us then."

"And your major—your captain—"

"Major Smelt; I was in Captain Craig's company of light infantry." The old man ran over the names of the officers, who had taken me on their knees in my father's house, without seeming to enter into my motives for inquiry.

"Do you remember an officer of the name of Dunlap?"

"Not then: in the French war he was my lieutenant; he was at Amboy, but not then in the army."

"What would you say if I told you that I am his son?" He now seemed to understand the motives of my queries, and to be convinced that my assertion was a fact from the questions I had put; for he instantly clasped my hand, gazed in my face, and after "No" and "Yes," seemed to be overcome by recollections, made more vivid by the train previously excited; and he wiped his eyes with the back of his hand, while I added,

"Come—my father's old comrade shall not want a breakfast." and we proceeded together on our search for an inn. It was his turn now to inquire, and mine to answer.

This has so much the air of romance that I could scarcely expect credit, if my companion, now no more, had not often related the occurrence to the many of his numerous friends who survive him. That in the land of my fathers, three thousand miles from that of my birth, I should thus stumble upon one who had been familiar with the scenes of my infancy—had been my father's companion in arms and in triumph, and shared the defeats of those I so well remembered in my childhood, when they had been opposed to the same provincials who assisted them in their Canadian wars and victories, was certainly very singular; but it is an old remark, that the romance of real life outstrips the invention of poets; and if this rough and war-worn veteran could have told all he had witnessed, from Braddock's defeat to the surrender at Saratoga, the tale might have vied in incident, perhaps in interest, with the best which have been invented of battles lost and won.

It is needless to say, that this encounter rendered the soldier's journey to the war-office easy. We proceeded to Windsor.

Next day, after breakfast, we repaired to the chapel, and saw the king and royal family; and then gayly, with limbs inured to pedestrian travel, passed by the two-and-twenty milestones between Oxford and Hyde Park Corner.

Of the circumstances which after my return to my native country led to my connexion with the drama, the reader has already been informed; and now return we to the theatre, plays, players, and management. Between three and four years I had been principally a resident in the metropolis of Great Britain, at the most critical time of a man's life,—between the ages of 18 and 22. I was not fitted for the best society of this great nation: I sought companions like myself; and either young Americans, or those connected with America, were my associates. Of arts and artists,—paints, pictures, and painters,—I may on some other occasion speak. I returned home happily with dispositions favourable to mental improvement, and fell among young men who had, like myself, ambition, and the desire to cultivate the field of knowledge. The Friendly Club and the Philological Society counteracted the effects of the Bucks' Lodges of London, and the Friars' Society of New-York; and with the example and friendly intercourse of the men heretofore mentioned, another colour was added to the many-coloured, changeable habit which conceals or unvails the character of man.

With little knowledge of the world, and none of theatres and actors except as seen from before the curtain, I was little fitted for the task I had undertaken. Of plays, and the merits of their performers, I had some knowledge—more than most men of my age. I had read all the dramatic authors of England, and seen their best works represented by the best English players. Of music and operas I was profoundly ignorant—as ignorant as all but professors of music are. I could play *a first* or *second* on a flute, and had heard all the singers and performers who were before the English public from 1784 to 1788; and *Mic. Kelly* is my authority for saying they were among the best of Europe. I had witnessed Signor O'Kelly's *debut* as Lionel at Drury Lane, after he had figured in Italy and Germany, and imitated the Abbé Dá Ponte in his own opera; but my ear for music was such, that I preferred his friend Jack Johnstone (Irish Johnstone), who was first-singer at Covent Garden, to Signor O'Kelly. Perhaps I was influenced by Johnstone's acting, which was better than Kelly's, or by his tall and handsome person. Then, again, my taste was for simple melody, and I received more pleasure from the airs in Rosina than from all the bravuras of the Italian opera. I preferred Mrs. Crouch to Madame Mara or Mrs. Billington, and don't recollect any delight from an Italian singer until I heard Madame Malibran. My object in saying this is to prove my ignorance and want of taste, and I doubt not I shall be readily credited on that score. I was not quite so low as the manager of a provincial company, who threatened the horns in his orchestra that he would discharge them because they did not sound as long as the fiddlers.

Nothing can be further from simplicity than the combinations of Handel; and yet the delight, the thrilling pleasure experienced on hearing the complicated mass of voice and instrument at Westminster Abbey was such as is never to be forgotten. I doubt whether the scientific European ear was more enraptured by the sublime "Hallelujah" of the Messiah than my uninstructed Yankee organ; and yet I ought not to doubt it, for knowledge has in all things the advantage over ignorance.

My knowledge of music gave me no advantages as the manager of a theatre; neither had I sufficient skill or science as a painter to be of much service in directing the scenic department. I end as I began, with the avowal that I was not fitted for the task I had undertaken.

⤖ CHAPTER 22 ⤚

Salaries and Expenses — Miss Westray and Miss E. Westray — Holcroft — Mr. and Mrs. Barrett — Yellow Fever of 1798 — The Theatre of New-York not opened until the 3d of December, 1798 — Saved by bringing out The Stranger — Biographical Notice of Kotzebue.

The theatre of New-York had now but one director or manager,—a circumstance which had not occurred in the United States before. An estimate of the expenses of the theatre at this time, 1798–9, will perhaps be acceptable to the general reader, and useful to those concerned in similar establishments. The salaries to actors and actresses, as follows, amount to 480 dollars weekly, viz: Mr. and Mrs. Hallam, 50; Mr. and Mrs. Johnson, 45—the first 20, the second 25; Mrs. Oldmixon, 37; Mr. Cooper, 25; Mrs. Melmoth, 20; Mr. Tyler, 20; Mr. Jefferson, 23; Mr. Martin, 18 (and for superintending the stage and making properties, 7

more); Mr. Hallam, jun., 16; Mrs. Hogg, 14; Mr. Hogg, 13; Miss Westray, 13; Miss
E. Westray, 12; Mr. Lee, 12, as performer and property-man; two message-carriers
(each 8), 16; Mrs. Seymour, 16; Mr. Seymour, 9; Mr. Miller, 12; Miss Hogg, 4;
estimate for three others, 54; Mrs. Collins, 12; with supernumeraries, 32. To this
was added a wretched prompter of the name of Hughes, at 10, and an intelligent box-office-keeper, Mr. Joseph Falconer, at 14. Dressers, 20; orchestra, 140
(consisting of Mr. James Hewitt, as leader; Messrs. Everdel, Nicolai, Samo, Henri,
Ulshoeffer, Librecheki, Pellessier, Dupuy, Gilfert, Nicolai, jun., Adet, Hoffman,
and Dangle). Other expenses were estimated thus:—lights, 109; labourers, 24;
doors and constables, 50; cleaning, 5; printing, 68; properties, 6; wardrobe, 15;
fires, 15; Mr. Ciceri and his department (the scenery and painting, not including materials), 60; rent, 145; amounting to $1161, without including any remu-
neration for the personal services of the manager.

As Mr. Hodgkinson had repeatedly said that if he staid in New-York, it would
be as an actor only, the manager offered him by letter, the 2d of June, 1798, a salary
of 50 dollars for himself, and the same amount for his wife; and the salary of 14
as heretofore given to Mrs. Brett. This would have made the amount of expenses
$1271; and in the same offer it was stated that the expenses of the benefits of Mr.
and Mrs. Hodgkinson were to be estimated at $385, which, as the theatre opened
only three times a week, would have been $3375 under the actual expense of the
night,—probably much more, as never estimate yet came up to the real cost in
such cases. The offer was treated as an insult.

Miss Westray and Miss E. Westray, with a younger sister, afterwards a distinguished actress as Mrs. Twaits (as the two first were and are as Mrs. Wood and
Mrs. Darley) were at this time under the protection of their mother and their
father-in-law, Mr. and Mrs. Simpson, who were added to the company.

The first display of the histrionic talents of Miss Westray and Miss E. Westray,
that we recollect, was on the 14th of June, 1798, when Holcroft's comedy, then
very popular, of the "The Deserted Daughter" was played for their mutual benefit,
the elder sister representing the character of Sarsenet, and the younger Joanna.
The receipts were $559.

Holcroft, the author of this and many other successful comedies and novels,
is well known to the reading public. He was one of those energetic characters
that rise in despite of and superior to circumstances. By birth thrown in the
lowest class of European society, a beggar and a stable boy, he escaped the vices
and burst the bonds of ignorance by mental effort. He educated himself, and
although a sturdy oppositionist to every abuse, social or political, no power, even
that of the mighty aristocracy of Britain, could put him down. As a politician
and reformer, he was accused of treason. He surrendered himself and was ac-
quitted. As a dramatist, he combated abuses manfully; but the managers of the

Royal theatres at length dared not bring forward his plays as such. As a novelist, he gained the attention of the public and served the cause of truth. He attacked the vices of players in one of his novels (he had himself been one of the fraternity); the characters were acknowledged, and the cap made to fit by several performers, in consequence of which the actors of Covent Garden had a meeting, and agreed to show their displeasure to the author by withholding their society from him,—ordaining that he among them who should be guilty of speaking to the author of the offensive novel (the author of the Road to Ruin, and other comedies by which they subsisted,—for what is the actor without the author?) should be "sent to Coventry;" but the sturdy reformer pursued his way undaunted, triumphing over the combination of cabinet ministers and green-room dignitaries.

While the heart sickens at the contemplation of the perverted talents of men who are born to fortune, and receive every aid from education,—while we view with loathing the vices of a George the Fourth, or the cruelties of a Don Miguel,—while we turn with disgust from the cant and hypocrisy of the thousands who, though blessed with every good springing from the social system, devote every effort to the advancement of self,—we are relieved and refreshed by studying the lives of such men as have seen the beauty of virtue while apparently doomed to crime, and from the regions of poverty and darkness have by their unassisted efforts soared to that light and power which has enabled them to overthrow the giants of the earth, and relieve their fellow men from ignorance and thraldom. When we trace the progress of Franklin from the hour he entered the city of Philadelphia, unnoticed and unknown, and made his first meal without table or house in the streets of the metropolis which has erected statues to his memory, to the day he dictated terms to the ministry of Great Britain; or when we accompany Holcroft as a beggar-boy soliciting alms for his parents—as a menial in the stables of Newmarket, rejoicing that he could obtain food and clothing—and then rising to the useful occupation of shoemaking, and thereby obtaining the scanty means of educating himself; seeing through all these states of gloom the star which promised him the power he aspired to, the power to benefit mankind;—when we see such examples,—and they are to be found both in ancient and modern times,—we feel revived hope and renewed strength, as the assurance is given that man will not ever remain the thing he is. But we must descend from our hopes for the future, to the plain statement of the past, retaining and cherishing those feelings which such views and hopes inspire.

Mr. and Mrs. Johnson having, as before stated, left the country, the manager entered into a negotiation with Mr. G. L. Barrett for himself and Mrs. Barrett, which was followed by an engagement for the ensuing season. A few passages from the letters which effected the engagement may not be thought irrelevant.

Mr. Barrett writes from Boston, dated June 16th, 1798, "With regard to business I cannot suppose you *mean* any but the *first* in each *department*."—"Should we meet, I hope you will have no objection to my regulating the stage business of Mrs. B. and my own." To this the manager answered, "The company will be much lessened from what it has been, though I hope no less efficient. But the diminution of numbers, without which I have no hope of keeping the charges within those bounds which can alone give hope of success, renders it necessary that the members of the company should adjust themselves to its exigencies, and occasionally do such parts as in an over-abounding corps would fall into other hands. This has been agreed to by Mr. Cooper and others."—"I shall keep the direction of the business, the choice of plays, their cast, &c., entirely in my own hands. I expect usefulness to the best of your ability, and I trust that you may expect justice."—"In regulating stage business, I shall pay just deference to your opinion, and I think it not improbable that your knowledge may be rendered serviceable to me, and if so, by mutual agreement, beneficial to you (though I by no means at present propose such an agreement)."—"I would wish it clearly to be understood, that while I direct the stage, my opinion must be paramount to any other."

Mr. Barrett was at this time past the meridian of life. Tall, well formed, and skilful in fencing and other exercises. Though his figure was good for the stage, his face was far from it; round in its general form, and without one prominent feature. Nose short, eyes blue, and complexion fair by nature. He had been manager of Norwich theatre, England, and sustained the first line of business in some of the other provincial theatres. In Boston he had been a favourite until Hodgkinson superseded him. In the comparison he could not stand for a moment. He is thus mentioned by Bernard:—After giving an account of a suit at law, which he had at Plymouth (England), with a Mr. Wolfe, he adds, "One of his accomplices in this affair was Mr. G. L. Barrett, who, when called upon for his defence, raised some laughter in the court by saying that 'he had the pleasure of being an old friend and acquaintance of mine for many years.' About fifteen years after this, he rode up to my door in Boston (America) in a coach, and asked me if I would do him a last favour. I said, 'yes.' 'Well, then,' he added, 'John, I am dying; when I am dead, put me under the turf, and I will never trouble you again.' He kept his word and I mine."

Mrs. Barrett was a tall and commanding figure, and though neither young nor beautiful, possessed a countenance denoting mind, and her acting fulfilled the promise of her personal appearance.

Upon these performers the manager of the New-York theatre had to rely for a portion of Mr. Hodgkinson's and Mrs. Johnson's business. Mr. Cooper was his support in tragedy, and in low comedy he justly relied upon Mr. Jefferson;

Mr. Hogg was yet little known. Mr. Bates was engaged to fill an important portion of comedy business, for which he was found inadequate.

It is well known that September is the month when New-York is filled with visiters. And from that time until the commencement of winter is the harvest-time for those who have exhibitions of any kind, and especially for managers of theatres. It was intended that the New-York theatre should open early in September; but in this the manager was disappointed, and lost in this first year of his direction the whole of that month, with October and November. He did not commence until the 3d of December, after the city had been desolated by pestilence, and its remaining citizens had become little disposed to seek amusement or incur expense.

The yellow fever of this year commenced in Philadelphia earlier than in New-York. Wignell, after the Baltimore season, carried his company to Annapolis.

On the 5th of September, 1798, the manager of the New-York theatre received a letter, written by his three friends E. H. Smith, C. B. Brown, and William Johnson, who were then in New-York, and residing together in Pine-street; from which we make the following extracts. The first is Brown's:—

> "Your letter was very acceptable and seasonable: it cheered us poor solitary beings, with the plaguy fever at our doors, in our cupboards, and in our beds.
>
> "Johnson and I are pretty well; but E. H. S., by midnight sallyings forth, sudden changes of temperature, fatigue, and exposure to a noonday sun, is made sick: perhaps it would not have been so if this demon had not lurked in the air. To-morrow it is hoped that he will be able to answer your questions, as to the prevalence and comparative malignity of this disease, himself.
>
> "This afternoon I revised the last sheet of Wieland. It will form a handsome volume of 300 pages. Some ten or twelve have been added since you last saw it.
>
> "I have written something of the history of Carwin, which I will send. I have desisted for the present from the prosecution of this plan, and betook myself to another, which I mean to extend to the size of Wieland, and to finish by the end of this month, provided no yellow fever disconcert my schemes.
>
> "Your letter bespeaks you to be happy. Why is it so? I just now asked W. J. He says you are constitutionally cheerful; and having gotten rid of a certain pestering coadjutor, your constitution in that respect is at liberty to show itself."

This second extract is Johnson's:—

> "W. J. is, as you conjecture, doing nothing; not absolutely nothing, but nothing interesting to a "philosopher:" yet he rejoices in the works and fame of his friends. Charles feels all the joy and parental exultation of an author,

having this day been delivered, by the aid of H. Caritat and T. & J. Swords, of a handsome duodecimo, the offspring of that fertile brain which has already engendered two more volumes. This borders upon the *prodigious*—300 pages in a month! yet he is neither in a delirium or a fever. What an admirable antidote is philosophy! As to fever, it is a being of such unaccountable origin, such amazing attributes, and such inexplicable operations, that I deliver it over to the doctor, to be treated *secundum artem*—that is to say, according to his trade.

"I rejoice that you are happy at Amboy; I leave the philosopher Charles to search for the causes."

The next is from Smith:—

"These gay friends of mine have so covered the paper with their gambols, that nothing but coldness and conclusion, dullness and death-heads are left for me.

"Had you seen me extended on my bed yesterday, rejecting (alas, the while!) half a dozen applications from the sick, and confined to pills and potions, you would have trembled for the safety of your poor philosopher. To-day, however, I have sitten up till this hour; and, if the day be fair, to-morrow shall resume my customary functions."

After some account of the prevailing pestilence, he signs the letter,

"By order of the Com.,

                            "E. H. SMITH (this day 27).

"Tuesday noon, Sept. 4th, 1798."

The plague continued to prevail. The work-men employed under the direction of Mr. Ciceri in preparing the theatre, left the place through fear. On the 18th the manager received a letter from C. B. Brown and William Johnson, saying that they have in the house a young Italian, Signor Scandella, a physician, dangerously ill of the fever, and under the care of Elihu. In answer, they are pressed to come to Amboy. The next news was that Smith was ill. On the 20th the two surviving friends wrote that Elihu H. Smith was no more; C. B. Brown sick, but recovering; and both determined as soon as possible to leave the "hateful city." They joined their friend on the 24th.

Early in November the manager returned to New-York, and proceeded to prepare the theatre for use, Ciceri having finished the dome, which was at the last season in a sad, unsightly state.

Money was wanted to bring on the members of the company, and by great exertion obtained and forwarded. On Monday, December the 3d, the theatre was opened with the School for Scandal and High Life Below Stairs. In the house, $730.

Nothing could be more unpropitious than such an opening. The city was a city of mourning, and the winter already begun. But the step was taken that made it necessary to proceed.

On the 5th, Mr. Bates and Mrs. Oldmixon were *brought out* in the opera of Inkle and Yarico, and the receipts were $267. The third night of the week, Mrs. Oldmixon was taken ill when dressing for Ophelia: there was no performance, and the week's receipts only amounted to $997.

Happily, the manager had not been idle as an author. The fame of the Stranger, then playing in London, had reached New-York; and after his return to the city, having got possession of a wretched publication in which the plot and part of the dialogue of Kotzebue's play were given, in language neither German nor English, he wrote a play founded on these materials; and producing his manuscript without telling any one but Mr. Cooper his secret, the parts were distributed, the play studied, rehearsed, and brought before the public on the Monday of the second week of the season. The success of this piece alone enabled the author to keep open the theatre. It was thus cast:—The Stranger, Mr. Cooper; Francis, Mr. Martin; Baron Steinfort, Mr. Barrett; Solomon, Mr. Bates; Peter, Mr. Jefferson; Mrs. Haller, Mrs. Barrett; Chambermaid, Mrs. Seymour; Baroness Steinfort, Mrs. Hallam. Mr. Cooper was well studied in the principal character, and produced great effect; Mrs. Barrett was powerful and touching; Martin was correct; and Bates and Jefferson gave every opportunity for the lovers of farce (for such the comic portion of the play literally was) to enjoy themselves.

The author had adopted the names from the English play-bills, as well as the name by which Kotzebue's play was performed in London, and the public were at liberty to suppose that *that* which delighted them had been sanctioned by a London audience. The bills only announced "The Stranger." The success of this piece, undoubtedly owing to the merits of Kotzebue, determined the manager to study German, which he so far mastered in a very short time as to translate other plays from the same popular author.

The same effect was produced in England by the success of Thompson's translation of Kotzebue's Menschenhatz and Reue, or Misanthropy and Repentance, under the title of "The Stranger." Its success, as Iffland says in his memoirs of himself, was overwhelming in Germany, and rendered the author the idol of the public. German plays were the rage in England until the English playwrights found it necessary to write them down, and at the same time found it convenient to steal from them as unconscionably as they berated them unmercifully.

Although Kotzebue is far beneath many of the German dramatists, the great popularity his plays enjoyed at home and abroad render him worthy of a place in any work on the drama of the period in which he lived.

Mr. John A. Dunlap has assisted us by contributing to our work the follow-

ing biographical notice of this extraordinary, extravagant, successful, and unfortunate author:—

AUGUSTUS VON KOTZEBUE was born at Weimar on the third of May, 1761. His
mother, being early left a widow, devoted herself to the education of her children. Kotzebue was at first place under successive private tutors, was then a
scholar in the gymnasium of Weimar, and about the age of sixteen became a
student of the University of Jena. At a very early age he became enamoured of
theatrical exhibitions; his first literary efforts were usually of a dramatic character, and his darling amusement was the getting-up of private theatres, and with
his companions performing plays, which were frequently of his own composition. Of these boyish efforts we are not aware that any were ever published, nor
is it probable that any were worth publication.

He had, while still very young, frequent opportunities of admission to the
theatre of Weimar; and when he could not gain an entrance by fair means, he
would contrive to get in clandestinely. He observes,

> "My passion for the stage increased every day. As the theatre was entirely sup-
> ported by the court, there was no paying for admission, but a limited num-
> ber of tickets were regularly given out. Thus, on festival days, when a new
> piece or some grand pantomime-ballet was to be performed, and the con-
> course of company who wished to be present was unusually great, it often
> happened that so insignificant a person as myself could not procure a tick-
> et. But as my curiosity was on such occasions more strongly excited than ever,
> I was obliged to have recourse to stratagem for its gratification. Every ave-
> nue leading to the theatre, every corner of the house was as well known to
> me as the inside of my coat-pocket; even the passages under the stage were
> as familiar to me as to the man that lighted the lamps. When I was hard
> pressed for admittance, therefore, I used to stand at the entrance allotted to
> the performers, and slip in dexterously behind the guards. Then, to escape
> pursuit, I crept instantly under the stage, whence a little door led into the
> orchestra: through this I got behind the great drum, which being somewhat
> elevated, completely concealed my little person, and here I could see the
> performance very commodiously."

In his nineteenth year he closed his academical career at Jena, and soon after
returned to Weimar, where he studied the pandects with extreme diligence, was
examined by the principals in the law, and admitted as an advocate. "Here," he
says, "while I was waiting for clients, I continued to be myself a zealous client
of the muses."

In the autumn of 1781 Kotzebue went to St. Petersburg, where he obtained,
through the influence of a German officer of high rank in the employ of the
Empress Catherine, some office, of the nature of which we are not informed,

and where he married a Russian lady of rank. At Petersburg he wrote a tragedy, called *Demetrius, Tzar of Moscow,* which, after some difficulties of a political nature interposed by the police, was allowed to be performed at the German theatre at Petersburg, and was received with an applause which the author considers he could only have pretended to from the forbearance generally practised towards youth.

From the capital he removed to Revel, holding a higher appointment under the Russian government. "During the first summer of my residence there," he says, "I spent the greatest part of every day in the delicious, shady walks belonging to the Castle of Catharenenthall, and read more than I wrote. In the autumn I visited for the first time the dismal and dreary environs of Kiekel, abounding with forests and morasses."—"The two first dramas I ever wrote, which I consider as possessing some degree of real merit, *The Hermit of Formentera* and *Adelaide of Wulfingen,* were written at Kiekel. The former we played among ourselves; and this private performance revived my passion for the stage with even increased violence. To that passion Revel was indebted for the institution of an excellent private theatre, which produced both actors and actresses of no common talents. It was opened with a comedy of mine, called *Every Fool has his Cap.*"

In the autumn of 1787 he was seized with a severe and long-protracted illness, during the height of which he wrote *Misanthropy and Repentance* (anglicized by the name of *The Stranger*), and *The Indians in England.* In 1789 he wrote *The Virgin of the Sun, The Natural Son* (known in English under the title of *Lover's Vows*), and *Brother Maurice.* The story of the last, though worse than extravagant, is so characteristic, perhaps, of the author and his times, that we may be excused in transcribing a sketch of it from Taylor's *Historic Survey of German Poetry.*

> "Brother Maurice was a poor nobleman, obliged to leave his aunt and sisters in narrow circumstances, and to embark for the Indies in quest of a maintenance. After having rapidly acquired the fortune of a nabob, he attempted to return through Arabia, where he was plundered of that portion of his property which was intrusted to the caravan, and was himself made slave to a Bedouin sheik. Omar, the son of the Arab chieftain, attaches himself to Maurice, learns of him a European language, obtains his liberty, and accompanies him to Europe: he has saved the life and he enjoys the friendship of Maurice. The piece opens soon after the arrival of the two friends in the seaport at which the female relatives of Maurice reside in industrious obscurity. They have just been removed to better lodgings, and are engaged in hiring an additional maidservant. Maurice is represented as endowed with an excellent head and heart, but as having got rid of every prejudice which the freaks of modern philosophy have attacked. He proposes to each of his sis-

ters that she should marry him; but finding them otherwise inclined, he gives the one to a painter and the other to his friend Omar. He next applies to the maidservant, who, after various hesitations, thinks it her duty to tell him that she has already an illegitimate child five or six years of age, by a person who is lately dead. Maurice likes both the child and the mother, and is determined to marry her. He is willing to let his property become a common stock, and his friends are willing that he should: they agree to lay it out in what is necessary for colonization; and, being rather unfit for Europe, to set off together for the Pelew Islands."

Such is the plot of Brother Maurice, one of the most extravagant of Kotzebue's dramas.

In 1790, while on a visit to his mother at Weimar, together with his wife, she died. To assuage his grief he went to Paris, where he remained half a year, and from thence transferred his abode to Maynz. "Here I arranged for the press a detail of the heavy calamity I had experienced, and of my consequent wanderings, which was soon after published under the title of *My Flight to Paris.*"

On his return from Paris he married another Russian lady. He afterwards resided in Germany, principally at Vienna, for three years, where he produced *Count Benyowsky,* and other pieces, which made their first appearance in the theatre in Vienna. From Vienna he returned to Russia, and on the frontier was arrested and sent to Siberia, for what cause is not explained. He has, however, published an account of his exile, under the title of *The most Remarkable Year in the Life of Augustus Von Kotzebue.*

Recalled from banishment, he was restored to the imperial favour, which he continued to enjoy during the lifetime of Paul, and under his successor. He afterward went, with his wife, on a tour of pleasure to Italy, an account of which journey was published at Berlin in 1805. He then finally settled at Mannheim, where he conducted a periodical miscellany, which, though more than liberal as to religion, was devoted to the politics of the holy alliance. By this he drew upon himself the execration of the friends of freedom throughout Germany, and his own sacrifice was the result.

On the 11th of March, 1819, a young man of the name of Sandt, of whose previous character nothing amiss has transpired, and who was destined for the ecclesiastical profession, called upon Kotzebue at Mannheim, under some pretext, and stabbed him to the heart. Sandt did not attempt to escape: he stabbed himself, though not mortally; was arrested, disarmed, confined, cured, tried, condemned, and beheaded.

Such was the end of Kotzebue. Some talent he undoubtedly did possess; but it was not uniformly exerted in strengthening those moral restraints which are the safeguards of society and the foundation of human happiness: his pen was in early life devoted to wild and pernicious views of morals and manners, and afterwards to the defence of a system which can only be supported upon the debasement of the human race. Servility was one principal ingredient of Kotzebue's moral temperament: he was ready to lick the dust before a Paul or an Alexander. He received his reward in the patronage of tyrants, and from the dagger of an enthusiast.

Of his dramatic works, not already mentioned, we will notice the following:— *Hyperborean Ass, Female Jacobin Club, Blind Love, Der Wildfang* (a term hardly translatable), *The Reconciliation,* and *False Shame*—comedies. *The Count of Burgundy* and *Joanna of Montfaucon. Octavia,* a tragedy, founded on the history of Anthony and Cleopatra, and *Bayard; Hugo Grotius* and *Gustavus Vasa*—tragedies. *The Negro Slaves* is another of his productions—a piece of exaggerated, nauseous, overstrained sentimentality. *Self-immolation* is another monstrosity. His best plays are *The Death of Rolla (Pizarro), False Shame, Lover's Vows,* and *The Force of Calumny.*

Kotzebue revelled in revolting subjects. *Adelaide of Wolfingen,* already mentioned, is founded on an incestuous marriage, and the heroine, like Medea, slaughters her children. "Such plots," says Taylor, whom we have already cited, "may be borne in the closet, but good taste has ceased to patronize the exhibition of Œdipus, or of The Mysterious Mother. Prejudice may have led to excessive remorse; but not therefore would a civilized audience conspire to abolish it."

Kotzebue, according to Taylor, whom we have just cited, was "the greatest dramatic genius that Europe has evolved since Shakespeare." Leaving that point to be settled by others, we will conclude this notice of Kotzebue by extracting from the same writer a sketch of his *La Perouse,* the catastrophe of which is worthy of the author of *Brother Maurice.*

> "A play on the subject of the misfortunes of *La Perouse,* who is here supposed to have been shipwrecked in the South Seas. Malvina, a female savage, has saved him from the waves, and has conveyed him to an unoccupied island, where he lives with her, and has a son. In secret, he vents his sorrow for those whom he left behind in Europe: he observes a sail; he makes signals; the vessel approaches. A female and a boy are landed from a boat: they are the wife and son of *La Perouse.* The two women gradually discover each other's relation to *La Perouse:* their equal claims, their jealousy, their warm affection for him, and their children, supply interesting moments. The brother of Madame *La Perouse* now intervenes. He descants on the revolution of France and the insecurity of happiness in Europe; he proposes to the party to establish themselves in the South Seas, and to despatch him with the vessel for other companions. The plan is determined, and the two women consent to live *in sisterly union* with *La Perouse.*"

Kotzebue's great talent was facility of invention: his incidents are admirable; his delineation of character is often fine; but many of his characters partake of the age in which he lived, and of his own false philosophy and false estimate of the foundation on which society ought to rest.

➤➤ CHAPTER 23 ◄◄

Boston Theatre, autumn of 1798 — Names of Performers there engaged — Mrs. S. Powell — Mr. Villiers — New-York Theatre — Sterne's Maria, or the Vintage — The Natural Daughter — Great Success of the Stranger — Lover's Vows — Count Benyowski — Schiller's Don Carlos — Biography of Schiller.

In the meantime, Boston being free from pestilence, Mr. Hodgkinson had the good fortune to find profitable employment for himself, his family, and the company he had engaged. It appears that he gave dissatisfaction as a manager by raising the price of admission to the pit, from 50 to 75 cents. As an apology, he stated that in 1797, *he had lost* 5000 dollars by his theatrical business in Boston. On the 13th of November, he advertises the pit admission by 50 cents again.

The company consisted of Mr. and Mrs. Hodgkinson; Mr. and Mrs. Whitlock; Mr. and Mrs. S. Powell; Mrs. Brett; Miss Brett; Mr. and Mrs. Harper; Mr. Williamson (the singer); Mr. Chalmers; Mr. Turnbull; Mr. Simpson (Irish Simpson); Mr. Munto; Mr. Helmbold; Mr. Kedy; Mr. Price; Mr. Homer; Mr. Villiers; Mr. Kenny; Mr. Lathy; Miss Solomon; Miss S. Solomon; Miss Harding; and Mrs. King.

Of the most important personages in this list we have already spoken, except Mrs. S. Powell. This lady's early history is unknown to us. She came to this country as Miss Harrison in the first company that played in the Federal-street theatre, Boston. She was an elegant woman, and a good actress. She was exemplary in her social duties, and if now living enjoys competency and all the fruits of prudence and virtue. She filled respectably the highest lines of tragedy and comedy, and will long live in the memories of the public of Boston, as well as in the affections of those who knew her private worth.

Mr. Villiers was the low comedian of the company, and an actor of force and merit. He of course could only expect to play such characters as the manager thought unworthy of his attention, as must have been the case in respect to every portion of the drama, where Hodgkinson was the director, and in the greater part of every branch he had no competitor in this country at that time. Moreton was dead. Cooper, far his superior in tragedy, was yet negligent, and his great excellence confined to a few "characters. Fennell's walk was very confined, and his pursuits irregular.

On the 14th of January, 1799, the manager of the New-York theatre brought out an opera written by himself, founded on the story of Maria, and called "Sterne's Maria, or the Vintage." The music was composed by Victor Pellesier, and the piece pleased and was pleasing, but not sufficiently attractive or popular to keep the stage after the original performers in it were removed by those fluctuations common in theatrical establishments. Sterne's Maria was thus cast. Sir Harry Metland, Mr. Hallam, jun.; Yorick, Mr. Cooper; Pierre (an old man, father of Maria), Mr. Hogg; Henry (Maria's lover), Mr. Tyler; La Fleur, Mr. Jefferson; Landlords, Peasants, &c.—Maria, Miss E. Westray; Nannette, Mrs. Oldmixon; Lilla, Mrs. Seymour. It is not necessary to observe to those acquainted with any part of American theatrical history, that the music of the piece was confined to Messrs. Tyler and Jefferson among the males. The females were all singers; Mrs. Oldmixon the superior. After the opening chorus in the vineyard at sunset, and preparations for the peasants' dance, we will give a few lines to characterize the dialogue.

> "———Why should I wish a change?"
> *Pierre.* "But the change will come unwished, and to be happy we must be prepared for it. Yes, pretty Nannette, when the time of sport is past, and the roses have fled from your cheeks—your companions all married or dead—the young men will shun you, the young women jeer you."
> *Nannette.* "Then shall innocence sing the song of content to the bosom of humble Nannette!"

Sterne's words were kept for Yorick, with little variation, and the story of Maria told in his language. La Fleur is the lover of Nannette, and gives this account of taking leave of his drum and his military life.

"I loved my companions, did my duty, and was always as tight as my own drum-head when braced, and as trim and neat as the sticks. But one of my comrades was sentenced to the halberts, and I was ordered to inflict the sentence of the court on him. I could have cut my own throat as soon. 'No, no,' said I, 'I can't; I will beat on dried sheep's-skin as long as you please, but not on the quivering flesh of my fellow-creature.' I was sentenced to receive double the number of lashes for my refusal—but the soldiers winked at my escape.—I left glory and my drum behind me—let the court-martial determine which is the most noisy and empty of the two."

The principal performers of the New-York company this season were Messrs. Cooper, Hallam, Jefferson, Tyler, Barrett, Bates, Martin, and Hogg—Mesdames Barrett, Oldmixon, Hogg, Seymour, Hallam, Misses Westray, and e. Westray.

During the month of January, Mr. Cooper's Macbeth attracted attention. (Barrett refused to play Macduff.) The Stranger was the support of the theatre, and in February, Mr. Henderson, from the proprietors, proposed that Mr. Dunlap should purchase the theatre for 85,000 dollars, the amount of the debt due by the proprietors, after exhausting the money subscribed and paid, viz: 40,000. The property to be mortgaged with a right in the purchaser to redeem, and in case of destruction by fire, the land and ruins to revert to the original proprietors, and the purchaser to be exonerated.

On the 8th of February, 1799, the manager produced a comedy called "The Natural Daughter," which was in itself complicated and ineffective, and was most wretchedly played in a cold winter's storm, to empty benches, and never repeated. But the apparently indefatigable author and manager had already finished another comedy, "The Italian Father," and translated Kotzebue's Natural Son (under the name given it in England of "Lover's Vows"), and "Count Benyowski." The last piece was at this time in rehearsal, the scenery having been got ready under the direction of Ciceri, and the music from the pen of Pellesier. A piece called the "Temple of Independence," was likewise written and produced on Washington's birth-day, the 22d of February, 1799, with Romeo and Juliet, and the Romp. The receipts of the night in a storm 610 dollars, and the new occasional piece, which principally depended on Mrs. Barrett, was received with enthusiasm. The Stranger was played for the 10th time on the 8th of March, to 624 dollars.

On the 11th of March, the manager's version of Lover's Vows was played with full success, the receipts 622 dollars. In this play Mr. Cooper again gave great delight in the character of The Natural Son, and Mr. Tyler supported the Baron with great success; but the eminent popularity of the piece was as much to be attributed to the happy combination of youth, beauty, judgment, and naiveté of manner which Miss E. Westray displayed in the daughter of the Baron, and sister of Frederick. Neither The Stranger, nor Lover's Vows, as written for the American theatre, are published; and the versions from London have been preferred by London players. But we will remark here, that when Mrs. Merry read the American Stranger, she declined playing Mrs. Haller in New-York, as studied from the London copy.

In a letter about this time to Mr. Cooper, it appears that an engagement was proposed by him for another year, he being secured a salary of 30 dollars for 42 weeks. All the characters he named (the first and best), were given to him, but a proposal that he should withhold his services from new pieces if the principal part did not please him, was objected to.

On the first of April, the play of Count Benyowski was brought out with great expense and care. Receipts first night 800 dollars. The audience were much gratified, and expectation, though on tip-toe, fully satisfied. The costume of Russia and Siberia were strictly conformed to, and the snow and ice scenes of Kamschatka would have been invaluable in the dog-days. The play was thus cast. The Governor of Bolcheretsk, Mr. Hallam; Hettman of the Cossacks, Mr. Bates; Benyowski, Mr. Cooper; Crustiew, Mr. Tyler; Stepenoff, Mr. Barrett; Kudrin, Mr. Jefferson; Gurcinin, Mr. Martin; Exiles, Conspirators, &c.—Athanasia, Mrs. Barrett; Feodora, Mrs. Oldmixon.

The play was well performed for a first representation. It is necessary to say that the literal translations of Count Benyowski can give no idea of the drama as prepared for the New-York stage. Mr. Barrett's Stepenoff was good, and Mrs. Barrett, though not youthful enough for the heroine, played it with truth and force. Mr. Jefferson and Mrs. Oldmixon supported the comedy of the piece, and Bates, as usual, said any thing but what was put down for him.

The next play of note, as a novelty, was performed on the 6th of May, 1799, Schiller's "Don Carlos." Those who have read this voluminous poem in the original, or in translation, will know that only a meager curtailment of it could be performed within the ordinary time allowed to an English play. The manager curtailed it, and it was more curtailed in the performance. The receipts were 676 dollars. It was not repeated. It was unmercifully shorn of its beams.

As this is the first time that Schiller, the greatest dramatist of his age, has become a legitimate subject of notice, as connected with the history of the American theatre, we seize the opportunity of closing this chapter with a biographical sketch from the same pen which furnished us with that of Augustus Von Kotzebue, John A. Dunlap, Esq.

FREDERICK SCHILLER was born at Marback, a small town of Wirtemburg, on the 10th of November, 1759. His father had been a surgeon in the Bavarian army, and was afterwards taken into the service of the Duke of Wirtemburg. Frederick's original destination was the church, and his early studies were adapted to that object; but circumstances rendered a change advisable; law was adopted, and with this view he was placed in the Ducal Seminary at Stuttgart, where he continued six years, with increasing dislike for the pursuit, until he was allowed to abandon it for the study of medicine, in the same seminary. Having completed his medical studies, he, in 1780, obtained the post of surgeon in the Wirtemburg army, but in a year or two afterwards he relinquished his profession, never to resume it.

Schiller never pursued professional studies with alacrity. Poetry and dramatic literature had peculiar charms for him; while a student he produced several poetical effusions, and a tragedy, "Cosmo de Medicis," some fragments of which he retained and inserted in his The Robbers. It is by "The Robbers" that Schiller is best known in this country. He commenced it in his nineteenth year, and, after his emancipation from school, printed it at his own expense, not being able to find a bookseller who would undertake it. Notwithstanding its great faults, of which Schiller himself, in maturer life, became perfectly sensible, its popularity was immense; it was soon translated into most of the European languages, and was performed, for the first time, at Manheim, in 1781. A story has been extensively circulated, that a young German nobleman, allured by the character of Moor, the hero of the tragedy, had abandoned the fairest gifts and prospects, betaken himself to the forests, and begun a course of active operations, which, like Moor's, was terminated by a shameful death. "The German nobleman of the fairest gifts and prospects," observes the anonymous English biographer of Schiller (London, 1825), from whom this notice of his life is principally derived, "turns out on investigation to have been a German blackguard, whom debauchery and riotous extravagance had reduced to want; who took to the highway, when he could take to nothing else,—not allured by an ebullient enthusiasm, or any heroical and misdirected appetite for sublime actions, but driven by the more palpable stimulus of importunate duns, an empty purse, and five craving senses. Perhaps in his later days, this philosopher *may* have referred to Schiller's tragedy for the source from which he drew his theory of life; but if so, we believe he was mistaken. For characters like him, the great attraction was the charms of revelry, and the great restraint, the gallows,—before the period of Karl von Moor, just as they have been since, and will be to the end of time."

But whatever effect *The Robbers* may have had on the morals of the youth of Germany, its publication materially influenced the future destinies of Schiller, by drawing down upon him the displeasure of his master, the Duke of Wirtemburg, which, exhibited at first in petty vexations, at length reached so great a height, that Schiller, apprehensive of worse consequences, was obliged to elope clandestinely from Stuttgart. Concealing himself in Franconia, he produced within a year his tragedies of *Conspiracy of Fiesco,* and *Cabal and Love,* which were published together in 1783, and the former was soon after brought upon the Mannheim theatre with universal applause. In the same year he removed to that city, where, under a new sovereign, the Elector Palatine, he was secure from the malice of his former prince, and as poet to the theatre, held a post of respectability and moderate income.

From Mannheim, Schiller went to Leipzig, and from Leipzig to Dresden, but with what definite object we do not understand. It was at Dresden he completed his *Don Carlos* (published in 1786), which he had commenced at Mannheim. His former tragedies were written in prose: this was composed in blank verse, as were all its successors. During his residence at Dresden, he applied himself to the study of history, and produced the first volume of the *History of the Revolt of the United Netherlands,* published in 1788. The work, thought never completed, had its effect in procuring for Schiller the appointment of professor of history in the University of Jena, in the Duchy of Weimar, whither he removed in 1789, where he married, and where, and in Weimar the capital, he passed the residue of his days, and notwithstanding a pulmonary attack, which had at first almost terminated his existence, and which clung to him until he was finally brought to the grave, he still continued his studies with unintermitting exertion, supported principally by a pension from the Duke of Weimar, which was from time to time increased, enjoying the friendship and munificence of that liberal prince, under whom it was now his good fortune to be placed, and with Wieland and Goethe, his friends and associates, forming one of the great literary triumvirates which has made Weimar the Athens of Germany.

A long interval had intervened, until Schiller, in 1799, brought forward his *Wallenstein,* which had for seven years been before him in irregular and often suspended progress. This is not one single drama, but a series of three plays, under different titles, all of which—not like the historical plays of Shakespeare, having no other connexion than mere chronological sequence—tend to the grand catastrophe, the tragical and mysterious death of the hero.

In 1800 appeared his *Mary Stuart;* the next year the *Maid of Orleans;* and in 1803 the *Bride of Messina,* which, as being little known out of its native language, we will introduce, from Taylor's *Historic Sketch of German Poetry,* an account of its fable, first premising that choruses, though not precisely in the style of the Greek drama, form a part of its *dramatis personæ.*

"A duke of Messina is recently dead, who leaves two sons, both of age, but separated from each other by factious rivalry. Isabella, their widowed mother, endeavours to produce a reconciliation, and succeeds in bringing them together. They have both fallen in love with Beatrice, a beautiful woman of unknown parentage, resident in a convent near Mount Etna. In her presence they unexpectedly meet, and Don Cæsar, the younger brother, in a fit of jealousy, kills Don Manuel, the elder brother, who was preferred by Beatrice. Meanwhile it appears that Isabella had once a younger daughter, of whom it was prophesied that she should occasion the extinction of the whole house, and whom the father had therefore ordered to be drowned; but the mother had secretly preserved the girl, and caused her to be reared in a convent of nuns on Mount Etna. This is the Beatrice for whom both the brothers have formed a passion. The successive discoveries of the relationships between the parties, give occasion to terrible situations; at length Don Cæsar, to atone for the murder of his brother, and to terminate a remediless disappointment of love, closes the play with a deliberate suicide." This tragedy was not successful, although it is highly praised as a specimen of poetry.

In 1804 he produced *William Tell.* This was his last effort; and *this* and *Wal-*

lenstein are regarded not only as his greatest efforts, but as among the greatest which have appeared for ages. The same year brought back a return of disease, which had never wholly left him since its first access, and which was doubtless increased by his habits of nocturnal study, and keeping up his strength and spirits by artificial stimulus. In May, 1805, it reached its crisis, and on the 9th of that month he expired, aged forty-five years and some months, leaving a widow, two sons, and two daughters.

Thus removed, by a hopeless disease, from a circle who idolized him, and from a world he had laboured to serve, while still in the vigour of manhood, his sufferings were alleviated by the best of children, and by a wife who merited the attachment he ever evinced for her. Some hours before his death he was asked how he found himself. "More and more at ease each moment," he replied. "Had he not reason," says Madame de Stael, from whom we translate the passage,— "Had he not reason to confide in that God whose servant he had faithfully been?" "He had a motive of action through life," says the same eloquent writer, "even above the love of glory—*the love of truth.* He was the best of friends, of fathers, and of husbands—respect for women, enthusiasm for the fine arts, and adoration of the Divinity, animated the genius of Schiller."

He was interred in the ducal chapel of Weimar, alongside of the place which the then reigning duke intended for himself, designing to be supported in the grave, on one side by Schiller, and on the other by the other literary luminary of his court, Schiller's warm and constant friend, the celebrated Göethe. Göethe, on the 22d of March, 1832, departed to take the place assigned him, at the age of nearly ninety years.

Schiller, besides his tragedies, the unfinished romance of the *Ghost Seer,* and his *History of the Thirty Years' War,* conducted, or contributed to, for some years, several periodical journals, principally devoted to poetry, and dramatic literature, and criticisms on the stage—wrote a number of ballads and lyrical poems, many of which are much admired—several essays, philosophical and miscellaneous—and translated, among other works, Shakespeare's *Macbeth,* and the *Iphigenia in Tauris* of Euripides.

Schiller's plays are well known to the literary world, but, except the Robbers, are not familiar to the frequenters of the English or American theatres. And The Robbers is so mutilated and mangled as to give no adequate idea of the great German poet.

→→ CHAPTER 24 ←←

1799 — "The Italian Father" — Philadelphia Company — New Agreement for the New-York Theatre — Wignell and Reinagle's failure in Philadelphia — Proposals to Mrs. Merry — Her Letter in answer — Mr. Hodgkinson offers himself and family for the New-York Theatre, and is engaged — Death of Stephen Wools — Fennell opens a Theatre in New-York and shuts it again — Yellow Fever of 1799 — Letter from Kotzebue — New-York Theatre opens 18th of November — False Shame — The Force of Calumny — Wild-goose Chase — The Robbers — Death of Washington — Mr. Cooper leaves New-York — Virgin of the Sun — Pizarro.

On the 15th of April, 1799, the comedy of "The Italian Father" was played at the New-York theatre, and as it was supposed to be one of Kotzebue's, though nothing was said to mislead the public or the performers, it was received with great applause, and extolled by many as the best of the great German dramatist's productions.

Nothing can be more unlike the style of the German plays than the style of this play. The manager-author had adopted the German mode of concluding the last act, and this tended to confirm the pre-conceived opinion that it was a continuation of his labours in the German mine. The play was announced without mentioning any author or any birthplace; otherwise it is probable, such was the prejudice of the *then* public, that few would have attended the first representation of a piece imperfectly and negligently committed to memory by actors prejudiced against it, and that those few would have gone away dissatisfied or coldly approving. As it was, the actors studied assiduously, played spiritedly, and the play was received with enthusiasm. Decker furnished many of the finest passages of this drama.

This comedy was published in 1810, with a note by the author prefixed, acknowledging that he had "enriched his work" from the obsolete sources afforded by the old English dramatists, but "without forfeiting his claim to originality in the composition." As this play is considered by the author as the best of the many he has written, we may be allowed to give the cast as first performed, and a few extracts. It was thus cast:—Michael Brazzo (the father), Mr. Tyler, who played it correctly, but was altogether inadequate to the deep, concentrated, and varied feelings of the character; Beraldo, Mr. Cooper, who ought, as he afterwards acknowledged, to have played Brazzo; Hippolito, Martin; Lodovico, Bates; Fool, finely played by Mr. Jefferson; Beatrice, Miss E. Westray; Astrabel (the discarded daughter of Brazzo, and married to Beraldo), well performed by Mrs. Barrett; Leonora, written for, and perfectly played by Mrs. Oldmixon.

As a specimen of the quaint style the author adopted in this comedy, to conform to the old English plays, we give a few lines from the opening scene, in which Lodovico tells some one on the stage, by way of telling the audience, that Hippolito was that day married to Beatrice, the Duke of Milan's daughter; and that Beraldo, who had seduced Astrabel, the daughter of Brazzo, and had been compelled to marry her, was a disgraced and desperate man, and then in prison. Lodovico is the old-time fop or coxcomb.

"Hippolito was, before his marriage with my Lady Beatrice, as simple a gentleman as I who now confront you, and much the same for merit, except not so abundant in wit; and for personal beauty, I think I ever had the advantage. Ah, there was music in the trios which Hippolito, Beraldo, and Lodovico performed! But so it turns with the wheel of dame Fortune—up goes Hippolito for a prince— down goes Beraldo for a beggar—while I stick to the hub of the wheel, and, though constantly turning round, remain in the middle still." A few lines of the next scene.

> "——Lodovico is a wit.
> *Leonora.*—Not a dry one—for he is ever drenched in wine after dinner.
> *Beatrice.*—Yet if not dry, why is he ever drinking?
> *Leonora.*—He has a thirsty wit, I grant you, lady. And here comes your father's fool. Let us bless Heaven, lady, that we had not the wit and the fool both on our hands at one time." *Hilario,* the fool, enters.
> "*Beatrice.*—How now, Hilario?
> *Fool.*—Well, now, madonna—but not well then—yet, pretty well—now and then.
> *Leonora.*—Still say I, Heaven be praised, wit fled as folly approached."

Astrabel seeks Hippolito, once her husband's companion, now the prince's heir, and petitions for the release of Beraldo, her husband, from prison. It is promised, and Hippolito questions her of her father, Brazzo. She says,

> "Michael Brazzo remembers not he had a daughter."
> "What does he for you?"
> "All he should. When children start from duty, parents may swerve from love. He nothing does, for nothing I deserve. You may restore my husband from the jaws of death—but to restore me to a father's love—Impossible! Impossible!"
> "It shall be put to trial." Brazzo being informed of the extreme poverty of his daughter, exclaims, when alone, "Alas, my girl! Art thou so poor? Poverty dwells next door to despair—there is but a thin and broken wall between them."

One more extract. Hippolito, to further the reconcilation of Brazzo to his daughter, visits the house of Beraldo.

> "*Hippolito.*—I must chide thee, Beraldo, for thy long estrangement from me. How has it happened that, being neighbours here in Milan, we have been thus distant?
> *Beraldo.*—O, my lord, though the hovel of the beggar should touch the palace of the prince, still is the distance between them measureless.
> *Hippolito.*—But thou didst know me, Beraldo.
> *Beraldo.*—As Hippolito I knew you, not as the heir of Milan.
> *Hippolito.*—And didst thou think that fortune so had changed me that I was not still Hippolito?
> *Beraldo.*—Pardon me, my lord, I have been a fool—I am still a fool. When fortune smiled upon me, I was praised for a certain bluntness which, in a laced coat, was called honesty: of late days it hath gone by the different names of sullenness and impertinence. I will try what you will call it. I felt that if I had been Beraldo in the palace, I should not have waited until Hippolito had crept from the hovel to find me."

There are some wholesome lessons against becoming a debtor. O, never let the smooth-tongued, smiling, sycophantic dealer, wheedle you into purchasing wares for which you cannot immediately pay. Every one who contracts a debt promises to pay, and if the time of payment arrives and he is unable, he may be charged with breach of promise. The same wheedling trader, no longer with fascinating smiles, will tell you that you have been living upon his property—you cannot deny it—he will then insolently add, that when you contracted the debt you did not mean to pay it—and, though conscious of honest purpose you may look in his coward eye till it quails and seeks the earth, the same loquacious shopboy tongue will continue its false assertions, which you will not repel—for, though indignant at the foul charges, you know that you are—a debtor to the wretch who insults you.

There is an upper and under plot. One to reconcile the father to his disobedient, but long-suffering, virtuous, and repentant daughter, and one to punish the coxcomb Lodovico, to unite the fool and the lady's attendant, and to cure the young bride of jealousy produced by her husband's agency in the first plot. Perhaps too much of this. We will resume our history.

The Philadelphia theatre, in the season of 1799–1800, was tenanted by the following very strong company:—Messrs. Warren, Wood, Cooper, Bernard, Marshall, Cain, Blissett, Darley, sen., L'Estrange, Warrell, Francis, Wignell, Doctor, Morris, Robbins, Cromwell, Warrell, jun., Mitchell, Hopkins, and Master Harris; Messrs. Holland, Milbourne, and Robins, artists in the scene department;

Mesdames Merry, Marshall, Morris, Warrell, Francis, Doctor, Gillingham, Salmon, Bernard; Misses L'Estrange, Arnold, Solomon, and Broadhurst.

As the theatrical season drew to a close in New-York, it had become necessary that the manager should have a renewed lease of the house, or become, as was proposed, the purchaser. A company was to be formed, and arrangements made for the next campaign. His reputation as a director and author had not declined. He had, certainly, not been idle this season. Besides the general direction of the great machine, he had superintended the stage, acted as treasurer, and produced six plays, original and translated, and some occasional interludes.

On the 26th of March he addressed a note to the proprietors, from which the following is an extract:—"My expectations of profit from the business have proved fallacious; I have laboured to the extent of my strength through this winter, and have gained nothing. My hopes are now reduced to the profit which may arise from the month of April, which I shall be happy to realize at the amount of the debt incurred before the opening." The purchase is mentioned, and he declines taking the house on the present terms. Mr. Henderson informed him that he was confident the purchase could be effected, but wished proposals for leasing it another year, such proposals to be void if the purchase was made. The result was, taking the theatre at $4000.

Mr. Robert Merry died in December, 1798, and Mrs. Merry's engagement with Mr. Wignell having closed a letter, of which the following is part, was addressed to her. "Rumour says that your intention is to return to your native land this spring: to arrest the execution of that purpose, and prevail upon you to exert your talents upon the stage of the theatre under my direction at New-York, is the intent of this letter. Is there any emolument that an American theatre can yield to a performer, sufficient to induce you to reside a year longer in the country?" It is then stated that for 34 or 40 weeks, 60 dollars salary, and 600 dollars profit on a benefit shall be ensured. The following answer was received:—

"Philadelphia, April 29th, 1799.
"SIR—In answer to your polite letter, I have to inform you that it is not my intention at present to return to Europe. I am every day in expectation of receiving letters from my connexions in England, and before I know what their wishes are, it will be improper for me to enter into any new engagement.

"Mr. Wignell has invariably behaved to me like a man of honour and a sincere friend; my article with him has in every point been fulfilled to this moment. What the situation of this theatre may be next winter is past conjecture; but I think it *more than probable* that the present holders will still retain the management.

"In the course of the month I think I shall know to a certainty how to proceed in my arrangements for the next season, and will take the earliest opportunity of informing you if any change in this theatre should induce me to leave Philadelphia.

"Permit me to say, there is no situation on the continent I should accept with greater pleasure than the one offered me in your establishment.

"I remain, &c. &c.

"ANN MERRY."

As early as the 16th of April, an agent of Mr. Hodgkinson's called on the manager of the New-York theatre, and read to him part of a letter, in which Mr. Hodgkinson says he is coming to New-York, and that he is willing to engage as a performer. About the same time it was known that he was overwhelmed with debt, from the management at Boston, and at variance with the proprietors of the Federal-street theatre.

On the 27th of April, a letter was received from Mr. Hodgkinson, offering himself and family for New-York. He says, "my pecuniary embarrassments will not allow me to leave the company until June." He offers himself as a partner to the manager, "or if not, what *allowance of salary and list of characters* would you undertake to give myself and Mrs. Hodgkinson in a *private capacity?* Mrs. and Miss Brett, and Miss Harding, with Mrs. King, being *after considerations.*" The words marked by italics are underscored, as was the custom of their writer. The letter concludes with what is intended as a threat of "a *compelled* statement to the public of New-York of the "circumstances" he "labours under."

In the answer to this are these lines: "It appears to contain" (his letter) "an appeal, an offer, and a threat. Of the latter I shall take no notice. It seems to be a matter in dispute which is the debtor of the other." "Now as two parties holding diametrically opposite opinions, seldom succeed in convincing each other, it is generally necessary to call in the aid of a third. In our case let that third by mutual agreement be a jury of our fellow-citizens. If you can make it conformable to your views of interest to come hither and exert your talents under my direction, for a certain pre-determined emolument, let us agree to abide by such a decision." On the subject of salary (the idea of renewed partnership was passed over), the offer was 50 dollars a week for himself, and 30 for Mrs. Hodgkinson, they finding their own wardrobes, servants, and dresses. Benefit charges to be 380 dollars. The complicated business of characters to be performed or not to be performed, made an important part of this negotiation, but could not be rendered interesting to a reader. It was the wish of the actor to play every thing: it was the wish of the manager to reserve some power of directing his business in his own hands, and, that two such excellent performers as Mr. and Mrs. Hodgkinson should stand in their proper places before the public. As to the family of "after considerations," the manager plainly said that he did not wish to have any thing to do with them; but if the principals were only to be had by taking the accessories, it must be determined what the cost would be.

Before sending his answer, the manager called on Mr. Henderson, as agent for the proprietors of the theatre, and *he* read a letter he had just received from Hodgkinson, offering himself "a candidate" for the management of the New-York theatre. It being Mr. Henderson's wish that Hodgkinson should be engaged, the letter in answer to the above proposals was sent.

Mr. Hodgkinson's reply is dated, Boston, May 2d, 1799. In speaking of the contract formerly entered into with the proprietors of the Haymarket theatre, Boston, he says, "It is the opinion of the first lawyer in Massachusetts, 'that as the law prohibiting every species of theatrical performance has never been repealed, no contract can be a legal one which the law does not sanction.'" He offers to engage for himself and wife, for 100 dollars per week, and adds, "Mr. Hodgkinson *shall not* have the *power* of objecting to any character appointed by the manager, provided such character be in tragedy the *first* character, *also in genteel comedy;* and if Mr. Hodgkinson *should* object, he shall pay for every such objection a forfeit of five pounds sterling." The stipulation for Mrs. Hodgkinson is much the same, with the same forfeit or penalty. The terms of engagement for Mrs. and Miss Brett, Mrs. King, and Miss Harding, are left to the manager's "generosity." A list of one hundred and forty-six characters was inclosed, which Mr. H. wished to play, and nearly as many for his wife. He asks the list to be returned with a mark on such characters as the manager does not wish him to play, and requests the loan of the plays of Count Benyowski, and The Italian Father. The manuscripts were sent to him. After some further stipulations for characters, and after Mr. Cooper had given up some he held by agreement, the business was concluded, and the family engaged.

On the 6th of May, a notice was attached to the bill of the play, saying, "Last night of the season, for the benefit of the lessee of the theatre; after which, the individual in whose name the bill of the night will be made out, takes every risk and is alone responsible to the public for the pieces exhibited." This was ill judged, to say no more of it.

This regulation made the actor master of the house for his benefit. We will mention an incident resulting from it. There was a standing law which prohibited performers during the time of exhibition from encumbering the wings, and impeding the carpenters. John D. Miller, before mentioned, not being yet an alderman, was in the habit of breaking the law by gliding from his dressing-room and placing himself in the carpenter's gallery. Mr. George Concklin, long the head carpenter, found it necessary to exert his legal authority, and expel the embryo alderman from the premises. Miller submitted. But, when he on his benefit night became master of the house, and lord of the ascendant, he thought that he had an opportunity for retaliation. Concklin had a key which admitted him from the carpenter's gallery into the upper boxes; by this means he could in a moment pass from the scene of labour to that of enjoyment, and could see the effect produced by the machinery he superintended. Miller had observed this, and on his night, seeing Concklin pass into the boxes, without having locked the door after him, the alderman followed and ordered him triumphantly, by virtue of the regulation which made the house his, to retire from his seat of ease and light, to the region of labour and darkness. Concklin obeyed the law, and passed the door to his own domain; but as the actor, in all the paint and embroidery of his assumed character for the stage, was following, the carpenter suddenly closed the door in his face, and the key being inside, locked him in that portion of the house he had claimed as his own. This passed in the upper region, and the alderman had no resource but to descend through his congregated friends, as they were crowding to the boxes, then by the front door to the street, and through the admiring boys and coachmen, until he could gain an asylum behind the scenes again, by means of the dark and dirty passage of Theatre Alley.

"It's a mad world, my masters," and a mutable. We have seen John D. Miller, the baker's boy, sitting on the judge's bench, dispensing life or death, liberty or imprisonment, labour and chains. We see and hope long to see George Concklin, who slapped the door in his face, the owner of squares, and the chairman of ward committees. It has passed or is passing—let us pass on to another subject, still marking the mutation in the shifting scenes of the world, and its epitome the stage.

Mr. Stephen Wools, so long in presence of the public as a singer and performer, before and after the war of our revolution, died on the 14th of June, 1799, aged 70, and was buried in the cemetery of the Roman chapel, in Barclay-street. A benefit night was given for the widow and daughter of Mr. Wools, on the 15th. The amount of the benefit evinced the esteem entertained for the man.

Fennell, notwithstanding his salt-making, and catching gulls "all along shore," from Chesapeake bay to Sandy Hook, had found means to get possession of the last built circus in Greenwich-street, on the west side, nearly opposite that in which Wignell's company played in 1797, and which was now removed. Although he had been incarcerated again and again in almost every place at which he had resided, Fennell now prepared to open this circus, and engaged performers for a summer theatre in New-York. But, after commencing about the 20th of June, with such actors as were not re-engaged for the Park house, he finally gave up the plan. He had advertised "The Roman Father," with Barrett's Horatius, his own Publius, and Mrs. Barrett's Horatia; nobody came to see them, and he shut up the house. He then began to collect subscribers for a salt manufactory, to be put in operation in the circus, the back part of which rested on the water, and he commenced altering the building accordingly, buying up lumber from any North river dealer in the article who could be persuaded to receive promises in payment. He used at this time to dress his lofty and handsome person in a black suit, with silk stockings and gilt shoe-buckles, and his cocked hat was ornamented with a gold button and loop. The result was a residence in the debtor's prison of New-York.

The manager of the Park house having produced his seventh new play for this season, an alteration from "The Deserter" of the French, called "The School for Soldiers," and it having been played on the 4th of July, 1799, with his piece called the "Temple of Independence," he closed the house for the summer.

In August, 1799, the yellow fever again appeared in New-York. The manager of the theatre resided at Perth Amboy, his native place, and was employed in translating Kotzebue's comedy of "False Shame," and turning the farce of "Der Wildfang" into an opera, which he called the "Wild-goose Chase." A title which some wiseacres thought was intended as a translation of the German appellation.

The Boston theatre was opened under the direction of Mr. Barrett, who by agreement was to get up "Count Benyowski," "The Italian Father," and the other plays written or translated by W. Dunlap, and share the profits arising from them.

Mr. Hodgkinson had a company at Hartford. This was the last season of playing there, the legislature passing a law of prohibition soon after.

A letter was received on the 11th of October, directed "Herren Wm. Dunlap, Director des Theatres in New-York," from "August Von Kotzebue," in which he expresses his pleasure that the favourable reception of his muse in America should be owing to his correspondent. "I will, with great satisfaction, forward my new pieces to you. Those already printed are to be had of the bookseller, Kummer, in Leipzig. The new, unpublished pieces are six, namely, "The Epigram," in four acts; "The Reward of Truth," in five acts; "Joanna of Montfaucon," five acts; "The Writing Desk," in four acts; "The Two Klingsbergs," in four acts; "The Wise Woman in the Wood," in five acts. These will not be printed in 18 months or two years. I am accustomed for such a period to sell my manuscripts to the best theatres in Germany, and also to the London theatre of Covent Garden. The price to be regulated by the power of the theatre; leaving to the justice and delicacy of the director to remunerate me according to his power and the profit derived from the pieces. Covent Garden has given for each piece one hundred pounds sterling. According to the foregoing, you may regulate the sum you can give, and if you wish the six pieces, to save time, as the distance between us is great, whatever sum you can, and are willing to give, may be transmitted to Mr. Casper Voght, at Hamburgh, who will send you the manuscripts. You will have the same right as that given to Covent Garden, to sell again to any stage in America, guarantying to me that they shall not be printed. With thanks, &c. Your friend and servant, August Von Kotzebue."

The New-York plays were successful in Boston, and yielded some profit to their author, who commenced his business as manager for this winter, on the 18th of November, 1799; thus again losing the best portion of the theatrical season,— the autumn.

The opening pieces were the Heir at Law, and The Old Maid. The receipts 636 dollars. On the second evening, The Carmelite, and The Poor Soldier, were played, and introduced Mr. Fox as Montgomery and Bagatelle. This young man was a singer, and possessed merit as an actor. He was the only novelty of the company, which stood thus, and thus salaried—Mr. and Mrs. Hodgkinson, 100 dollars; Mr. and Mrs. Hallam, 50; Mr. Cooper, 32; Mr. Jefferson, 25; Mr. Martin, 25; Mr. Tyler, 25; Mr. Fox, 18; Mr. and Mrs. and Miss Hogg, 32; Lee, 12; Stockwell, 4; Mrs. Melmoth, 25; Mr. and Mrs. Seymour, 25; Miss E. Westray, 18; Mrs. Brett, 14; Miss Brett, 14; Miss Harding, 10; Mrs. King, 6; Mr. Hallam, jun., 18; Mr. Perkins, 12; Mrs. Perkins, 20.

A letter was received from Mr. Whitlock, saying, "that from Mr. Barrett's conduct, it was unlikely that himself and wife should remain in Boston." He adds, "when we part it shall be with honour to myself. It is now three years since I have been under the direction of a manager deserving the name of gentleman. If you and I, sir, can meet on terms of reciprocal advantage, I shall be happy."

The manager was at this time under the necessity of declining this offer. Mr. Powell now offered the services of himself and wife, and Barrett offered his wife. None could be accepted, as the company was full.

The comedy of "False Shame," as translated and adapted to the American theatre, by the translator of the previously played German plays, was performed with the utmost success on the 11th of December, 1799. This play, without scenery or decoration, by plain dialogue and natural character, supported the theatre this, the second season of the author's direction. As in the case of "The Stranger," it ran through the whole winter. "The Force of Calumny," "Fraternal Discord" (from the same pen), and other pieces, did their part; but "False Shame" was the pillar on which all rested. The cast of this play stood thus—The Baron, Mr. Tyler; Captain Erlach, Mr. Hodgkinson; Wieland, Mr. Cooper; John, Mr. Jefferson; Frelon, Mr. Fox; Maillac, Mr. Martin; Baroness, Mrs. Hodgkinson; Adelaide, Mrs. Hallam; Emmy, Miss E. Westray; Madame Moreau, Mrs. Melmoth. Never was part better suited to Mr. Hodgkinson than that of Erlach, and never was part better played. Emmy was for Miss E. Westray a second Amelia, as portrayed in Lover's Vows. Her youth and beauty contrasted finely with Hodgkinson's figure and manner, which were so well suited to the veteran German officer who had borne her when an infant from the flames of Charleston,—

the exquisitely natural playing of both—made an impression never to be forgotten, and rendered the comedy useless to the theatre of New-York when they ceased to perform the parts. All the piece was well played; and never were the critics of the green-room more disappointed than the performers in this piece were, when they found that audience after audience were delighted by this unadorned comedy.

On the 20th of December, 1799, it was known in New-York that Washington died on the 14th. The theatre was shut until the 30th, when it was opened with mourning emblems and a covering of black. Mr. Cooper spoke a monody, written by the director's friend, C. B. Brown: a new play was performed for the first time,—a piece translated from the French by the manager, and called "The Robbery." It was most imperfectly played: it was repeated but once. This mourning appearance and black dress was kept on the house until after the 22d of February, which, as Washington's birthday, was consecrated to the memory of his loss, and the theatre shut.

In the mean time, Mr. Cooper went to Philadelphia to settle the long-protracted business of his breach of articles with Wignell and Reinagle; and having received some insult from their attorney, demanded satisfaction, and delayed his return to New-York. He had been announced in the bills, and the play changed and apologies made, two nights in succession, which on his return he considered injurious to him, and gave notice to the manager that he would not continue with him.

"Der Wildfang," as translated and metamorphosed into an opera, called the "Wild-goose Chase," was first performed on the 24th of January, and continued a favourite as long as Hodgkinson continued to play the young baron.

"The Force of Calumny" had likewise been successful; but the secession of Mr. Cooper in March was a severe blow to the theatre and its receipts. However, Kotzebue, with the manager's industry, kept up the business. "The Virgin of the Sun" was brought out at great expense, with splendid scenery and dresses, and was attractive through the season. "Pizarro" was performed on the 26th, composed from the original and Sheridan's alterations: the concluding scene by Sheridan was omitted, and the sublime last lines of the author preferred. These two pieces, with all their faults, have great merit, and merited the thanks of the "manager in distress."

That amusing egotist, Michael Kelly, who tells us many pleasant stories, though he "pushes the duke" rather too hard, and certainly must have had a father who "drew a long bow at the battle of Hastings,"—Kelly says Sheridan wrote the last part of the play of Pizarro "up-stairs in the prompter's room," "while the earlier parts of the play were acting" to an overflowing house. And further, "that at the time the house was overflowing, on the first night's performance, all that was written of the play was actually rehearsing," and that "until the end of the fourth act, neither Mrs. Siddons, nor Charles Kemble, nor Barrymore, had all their speeches for the fifth." Now, we all know that Pizarro was *written* by Kotzebue; and it is most probable a translation was put into Sheridan's hands, he knowing nothing of German, and making little alteration but for the worse (instance the change at the end), except here and there a line or a song, and the anti-Gallican speech put into the mouth of Rolla to serve the time,—and yet, to take Mic.'s story, as it reads, we must believe that the *author-manager* had announced this great play of his, had paid severe attention to the splendid scenery and decorations, and yet had not written it when his actors were playing it.

That Mr. Cooper had become discontented with his situation in New-York before the unfortunate failure in keeping his appointment, and its consequences, no one can doubt. Hodgkinson's eternal appearance before the public, and eminent success in the German plays of the present season, threw the tragedian in the shade. The necessity for producing these attractive novelties rendered Hamlet and Macbeth, and all the glories of the drama, for the time a dead letter. In proportion as his consequence decreased, the carelessness for performing his duty increased, and every new character Mr. Cooper *went on for* (to use the stage phrase), was almost invariably marred by an ignorance even of the words of the author. It was perhaps well for his future fame and excellence that circumstances removed him from the stage of New-York at a time so inauspicious to his improvement as an actor.

The exertions of the manager had been so far successful that the engine he guided was kept in motion, and to the public eye appeared gay and prosperous. But all within was discord and discontent: even those plays which attracted the public, and gave bread to some and the means of destructive indulgence to others, were stigmatized by the actors as *Dutch stuff,* and by other epithets equally characteristic. But why dwell on evils of this disgusting kind? Can they be removed?

When a theatre is supported by a power, whether in a government or an association, which will not look for profit from it, but rather if any deficiency of money from the receipts occurs, is ready to make it good, as in France— when it is so cherished and supervised, and is directed by a man who has taste and knowledge, and whose faculties may be devoted to the true purposes of the institution,—then such a theatre will be truly a school of morality, of patriotism, and every virtue; the glory of the fine arts, and the delight of the wise and the good: such a theatre would be what the theatre of Weimar was when Göethe was its manager, or that of Berlin under the direction of Iffland,—the one directed by the first poet of the age, the other by the first actor of Germany, and both supported by government.

But while actors squabble for parts and intrigue for benefits, and managers are looking to the means of raising money, the theatre must be—what it now is.

Benefit-nights allowed to performers have ever been one source of mischief, one cause of degradation. This has been amended, but must be abolished before the theatre can be what, by its constituent parts and powers, it ought to be, or even what it has been.

It was the practice in the early days of the American drama for the performers of the company to *throw* for the nights of their respective benefits. As the benefits usually commenced in the spring and continued into summer, the earliest nights, or those of spring, were the prizes of the dice-box. We have seen that once the performer literally went from door to door to beg patronage. Since, other means, perhaps as degrading, and more injurious to the individual, were resorted to. The nights being determined, every thought of the performer is turned to promote his own particular interest; not more than the thoughts of men in other pursuits, but more promotive of jealousy and discord, from the nature of the institution, which is only fitted to be guided by one head and for one purpose. Plays are got up merely to make show-bills, the public are deceived, and the pieces that are performed are sacrificed. Dryden, in a couplet, which I cannot recollect or turn to, says that the actors murdered plays, and called it reviving them. Such is the fate of all revivals for benefit-nights.

This abuse has been, by the energy of managers subsequent to the time of which we write, in some degree remedied; but it should be abolished altogether. The actor ought to be liberally rewarded, according to his talents and his exertion of them, by a fixed income, and not left to look for an uncertain receipt from a benefit, which, like the prize in the lottery, is to pay his creditors, while he lives at an expense far beyond his income. We do not say that this is or has been generally the case; that it has been in some instances we know, and the temptation ought to be removed.

While a tier of boxes is appropriated as a gallery to display the allurements of vice,—while the actor looks for his reward from the popularity he can establish with the million, and the manager must please the vulgar or shut his theatre,—the stage is not a school of morality; it is a mockery to call it so. By its nature, and the powers it possesses, it is fitted to be one of the most effective.

✦✦ CHAPTER 25 ✦✦

1800 — Theatre at Mount Vernon Gardens — Mr. Corré — Effects of the Departure of Mr. Cooper — Theatre opens Oct. 20th, 1800 — Names of Performers — Mrs. Powell — Mr. Fennell — Fraternal Discord, or Bruder's Twist — Mr. Harper — Mrs. Jefferson's first appearance — Mr. White — Mr. Winstanley — Joanna of Montfaucon — Abælino — Zsokke — De Montfort — Joanna Bailey.

On the 9th of July, 1800, a summer theatre was opened in New-York at a place called by the proprietor "Mount Vernon Gardens," and which is now the north-west corner of Leonard-street and Broadway. This spot, as is mentioned in our fourth chapter, was in *good old times* far out of town, and here stood the "White Conduit House," which, with its gardens, were the summer resort of our citizens for many years; as Brennon's (afterwards Tyler's, and again Hogg's, and now the S. W. corner of Spring and Hudson-streets) was in after-times.

We will insert the first bill issued by the manager of this theatre:

> "Mount Vernon Gardens. Theatre.—JOSEPH CORRÉ presents his respects to the public: ever anxious to merit their patronage and contribute to their amusement, he has at a considerable expense engaged several of the principal performers belonging to the theatre, and proposes to exhibit theatrical entertainments on Mondays, Wednesdays, and Fridays, which he flatters himself will give additional satisfaction to those who have on former occasions honoured him with their company.
>
> "On Wednesday evening, July 9th, 1800, will be presented a much-admired farce, in two acts, called Miss in her Teens, or the Medley of Lovers. Capt. Flash, Mr. Jefferson; Capt. Loveit, Mr. Hallam, jun.; Puff, Mr. Hogg; Jasper, Mr. Fox; Fribble, Mr. Martin; Tag (with a song), Mrs. Seymour; Miss Biddy Bellair (with a song), Miss Brett. Tickets of admittance 4s. Performance to begin at 9 o'clock precisely."

Here we have a new manager. We have said, in our twentieth chapter, that we do not think the man who assumed the direction of "that powerful and complicated engine, the theatre of a great metropolis" (meaning the New-York theatre in 1798), "was fitted for the arduous task." Let us examine the qualifications which his previous situations in life's drama had, as far as we can judge by the retrospect, bestowed on Mr. Joseph Corré.

Mr. Corré will be long remembered by the elder citizens of New-York as an honest, industrious, and prosperous man. He was a Frenchman, and is first remembered as a cook in the service of Major Carew, of the 17th light dragoons, the servant of his Britannic majesty. The first time the writer saw

Corré he stood with knife in hand, and in the full costume of his trade, looking as important as the mysteries of his craft entitle every cook to look; "with fair round belly, with good capon lined," covered with a fair white apron, and his powdered locks compressed by an equally white cap. His rotundity of face and rotundity of person—for he was not related to Hogarth's cook at the gates of Calais—with this professional costume, made his figure, though by no means of gigantic height, appear awfully grand, as well as outré, and was stamped upon the young mind of his admirer in lights and shadows never to be erased. When we say the costume of his trade, we mean such as we see it in pictures, and as travellers see it; the writer had at that time never seen other than a female cook, and such always black as Erebus. This was in the winter of 1776–7, before the New-Jersey militia and the great chief of our citizen-soldiers had driven the English to the protection of their ships and the safety of water-girt islands. It was at Perth Amboy that Corré stood lord of the kitchen, which his lord, the major of dragoons, had wrested from the black cook of the writer's father, and held by the same title which made the Corsican lord of the continent of Europe,—*military force.* The gallant major occupied *and improved,* the upper part of the house, and Manager Corré ruled below.

Mr. Corré afterwards kept the City Tavern, in New-York, with reputation and success, and established those public gardens in State-street still existing, on the site of a part of what was Fort George when he first saw America. He was a thriving and worthy man, and his descendants have reason to respect his memory, although these situations in life might little qualify him to direct public taste, except in the way of his original employment. Mr. Corré and the writer were now, in 1800, both theatrical managers, and Mr. Corré proved the most successful manager of the two. In regard to literary qualifications, Mr. Corré was probably not far behind many other managers who have since ruled the fates of actors and destinies of authors.

It certainly appears to have been bad *management* to lose Mr. Cooper from a company in which he was so prominent a member. To the director of the theatre he was not only valuable as a performer, but as a check to another performer who had shown a disposition at all times to grasp and encroach. By the removal of the representative of Hamlet and Othello, Macbeth and Richard, Hodgkinson would be all-in-all with the playgoing public, and control his employer accordingly. It appears that by a very unmanagerlike love of truth, Mr. Cooper was lost for a time to the stage of New-York. He had asked permission to absent himself from Tuesday to Friday, on urgent business in Philadelphia,—on the latter day to be back to perform in the play of the evening. His punctuality was usually very great, even to an hour. On the afternoon of the day, he having been announced for the play as usual, a letter was received, explaining the cause of Mr. Cooper's detention in Philadelphia, prohibiting the making the cause known, and promising that nothing should prevent his "being ready for Monday night." In consequence of this, another play was substituted, and the audience were told that the change was in consequence of Mr. Cooper's having failed to return at the time engaged for. Monday came, and another disappointment: he had been again announced, and did not appear; and another apology was made, and the business for succeeding nights arranged without him. He went on the 18th of December, and returned the 27th; and, as appears at this distance of time, under the influence of irritation, determined to withdraw himself, as the manager had not used words which "might have been thrown together exculpatory of" himself, "without seriously inculpating" Mr. Cooper. A proposal was made by him that he should take a benefit, allowing half the profit to the manager, who, on an agreement that such an apparent permission to withdraw from his station should not be construed into an assent on the part of the director, made the arrangement.

Mr. Hodgkinson had previous to this, in conjunction with Mr. Hallam, two mortal enemies to each other, applied to one of the committee of proprietors for the lease of the theatre, and obtained a promise that they should have information before the theatre might be let to any other person. Now, by the removal of Mr. Cooper, the Hodgkinson family were the principal efficient force of the company, as will be seen by these names:—Mr. and Mrs. Hodgkinson, Mr. and Mrs. Hallam, Mr. and Mrs. Hogg, Mr. and Mrs. Powell, Mr. and Mrs. Harper, Mr. Tyler, Mr. Jefferson, Mr. Fox, Mr. Martin, Mr. Hallam, jun., Mr. Crosby, Mrs. Melmoth, Mrs. and Miss Brett, Misses Harding and Hogg. Mr. Jefferson's excellence was great, but not to be put in competition with Hodgkinson's, even in low comedy. Mrs. Powell might have balanced Mrs. Hodgkinson in high comedy and in tragedy, but her success was literally prevented by the influence of Mr. Hodgkinson, who wished that his wife should be the first tragedian, as well as the first opera-singer, first comedy lady, first romp, and first chambermaid; and if her figure had been equal to her talents, she would have seconded his views by her industry, and aptness for what is theatrically called study.

This summer, Mr. Wignell opened the first theatre in the capital of the United States, and called it "The United States' Theatre." His company for the winter of 1800 was considerably changed. Mrs. Morris went to England. Mr. and Mrs. Marshall, Mr. and Mrs. L'Estrange, two Mr. Warrells, Mr. Darley, sen., Mr. Doctor, Mr. Cromwell, Master Harris, Mr. Mitchell, Mrs. Warrell, Mrs. Gillingham, Mrs. Salmon, and the Misses Broadhurst and L'Estrange, are all off the list of the season; and instead, we have Mr. Darley, jun., Mr. Prigmore, Mr. Durang, Mr. Bailey, Mr. Usher, and Mr. Hammond; Mesdames Shaw, Snowden, and Stuart, and Misses Westray and E. Westray.

The theatre of New-York was not opened until the 20th of Oct., 1800. The fears of yellow fever, now considered as an annual scourge, kept the inhabitants from their winter homes, and traders from their periodical visits. The first play was Lover's Vows, Hodgkinson now playing Frederick, but very inferior to Cooper, and Mrs. Hodgkinson as much inferior to Miss E. Westray in the character of Amelia.

Mr. Fennell, oppressed by poverty and debt, and in the possession of those who would not receive promises as current coin, applied to the manager for a benefit, and promised his aid as a performer. He might now have been of real service. He published a card, announcing that, by permission of Mr. Dunlap, his benefit would take place, and "respectfully solicits the patronage of the public:" "flatters himself that by the ready and favourable attention of his friends to the object of his benefit, he may be enabled to offer his contributory efforts for their amusement on this and future occasions." Mr. Fennell's benefit, on which occasion he played Zanga, took place on the 10th of November, and was productive.

Mr. and Mrs. Powell made their first appearance on the 31st of October, 1800, as Muley and Angela, in the Castle Spectre. Mrs. Powell has been mentioned before. She was brought to Boston from England in the year 1794 by Mr. C. Powell, she being then Miss Harrison, and Mr. S. Powell, her present husband, being one of the company. Her beauty and talents soon placed her at the head of her profession in the theatres of New-England.

The first play the manager produced this season was perhaps the most meritorious of the many translations and alterations which came from his pen. "Fraternal Discord," altered and adapted from Kotzebue's "Bruder's Twist," was made more English, particularly in the *prominent characters* of Captain Bertram and his old brother-sailor and boatswain, than any of the previous pieces from the same source. The two parts were most admirably played, and nothing ever was finer of the kind than Jefferson's sailor, except the gouty captain of Hodgkinson. The merits of this piece have been so far acknowledged by English managers and actors, and even by American audiences, as to obtain a preference over the foreign version from the same source.

On the 28th of November, Mr. Harper, who abandoned the old American Company at the time Wignell separated his interests from those of Hallam and Henry, in the year 1792, now reappeared in Charles Surface. He was the first actor who had played it in America: he had been the favourite of the New-York public; but the words "had been" are generally ominous. Mr. Harper was very little changed by eight years; but he had not improved; and those who remembered him as Charles Surface had seen Cooper, and Hodgkinson, and Moreton represent the fascinating libertine, and wondered that they could ever have endured Mr. Harper. It was Mr. Harper's choice to play Charles; had he reappeared in a new piece, his reception would have been different: it was now cold. Mrs. Harper, his second wife, was, as a performer, his pupil, and not entitled to further notice.

Mr. Jefferson had married in New-York, and Mrs. Jefferson became a member of the company about this time. She made her first appearance in the character of Louisa Dudley. As a wife and mother, she has played well her part in life's drama, and continues to merit applause in the characters.

On the 5th of December, an opera, the music put together by James Hewit, and the dialogue by the manager, was performed, not approved of, repeated once, and forgotten. It was called the "Knight of the Guadalquiver." The usual receipts of the theatre appear to have been for weeks below the expenses.

On the 19th of January, 1801, Mr. White, a young man from Worcester, Massachusetts, was brought out with some promise of success in Young Norval. Curiosity was excited, and a house of $614 obtained. He had performed in Boston, when quite a boy, with that applause so freely, and often so injudiciously bestowed on such efforts—had since studied law, and was at this time a tall, handsome youth; but not destined by nature to shine. He was afterwards the author of three plays, which were performed in Boston,—The Clergyman's Daughter, The Poor Lodger, and Alonzo.

A play from Kotzebue, called the "Happy Family," was played (an English version) unsuccessfully.

We have mentioned the benevolent attempts that had been made to enlighten the country by those luminaries from the land of our fathers, Milne, Mrs. Hatton, and Williams (Anthony Pasquin). Another English genius now appeared among us, and wished his oracles delivered from the stage.

Mr. Winstanley called on the manager, and informed him that he had a comedy ready for representation, which would "draw twenty full houses in succession." "That is very desirable, sir." "Well, sir, what terms do you offer to successful authors?" "Half the profits of the third night's representation." "O, that's nothing, sir, for a piece that will overflow your treasury; nothing, sir, nothing!" "It is the established custom of my theatre." "Well, sir, when will it be played?" "I must first read it, and if I think it will do—" "Oh, sir, there's no doubt of that; it has been approved of by the first men in the country; it will *draw* during all your season." "I must judge of its merits for myself; and if I think it fit for representation—" "Fit!" "If I think it fit for representation, it shall be put in train." "And how long before it will be performed?" "Under favourable circumstances, three or four weeks." "Too long, sir; I wish to offer it to Wignell and Reinagle: after its run here, I intend to sell it to all the theatres on the continent. You will have it played in three weeks?" "The first step must be my approbation of it; I make you no promise." "Well, sir, I will read it to you." "Excuse me, I must read it myself, and at my own time." "But you can't read it; it—it—I must explain. If you will come to my lodgings I will read it to you: you will be delighted with it!"

Whether to get rid of importunity, or from a hope that the empty treasury might be filled, the manager consented to hear the author read his comedy the next evening. It was beyond measure long, and as tedious as it was long. Every defect that was pointed out was in the author's eyes a beauty. The weary manager took the manuscript home, and promised an answer. It was as follows:—"Being an author myself, I feel my situation peculiarly delicate when a new play is offered to me as a manager of the theatre: at the same time, I consider it my duty to give a prompt opinion and decision. It is my duty (and my interest) to present to the public those plays which I shall think most worthy of attention: therefore a piece, to be entitled to the time, labour, and expense of *getting up* (to use a technical phrase), ought to have a decided superiority over all the other new pieces which are in my possession, all having an equal claim on the ground of novelty. I frankly confess, that in my opinion your play, whatever its merits as a composition, does not possess this necessary superiority. As this opinion, if known, might injure your interests with Messrs. Wignell and Reinagle, to whom you first mentioned the piece, I shall be silent on the subject, and advise your carrying into effect your purposed offer of it to those gentlemen."

If he took the last piece of advice is not known; but the play was printed, and the manager's letter: the first (though not intended so to do) justified the opinion expressed in the last. But an inveterate enemy was made to the manager, whose inveterate foes at this time, and long after, were a few of the friends of Mr. Winstanley,—men of influence in matters connected with public amusement, associated as members of the Anacreontic Society, Rifle Company, and other clubs, whose chief business was singing and drinking. Mr. Winstanley's comedy was called "The Hypocrites Unmasked."

Mr. Gilbert Stewart, the celebrated portrait painter, used to tell, in his inimitable manner, an anecdote of Winstanley, which we will endeavour to relate: "When I lived at Germantown, a little, pert young man called on me, and addressed me thus,—'You are Mr. Stewart, sir, the great painter?' 'My name is Stewart, sir.'" Those who remember Mr. Stewart's athletic figure, quiet manner, sarcastic humour, and uncommon face, can alone imagine the picture he would have made as Winstanley proceeded:—"'My name is Winstanley, sir; you must have heard of me.' 'Not that I recollect, sir.' 'No! Well, Mr. Stewart, I have been copying your full-length of Washington; I have made a number of copies; I have now six that I have brought on to Philadelphia; I have got a room in the State-house, and I have put them up; but before I show them to the public, and offer them for sale, I have a proposal to make to you.' 'Go on, sir.' 'It would enhance their value, you know, if I could say that you had given them the last touch. Now, sir, all you have to do is to ride to town, and give each of them a tap, you know, with your riding-switch—just thus, you know.'"

Stewart, who had been feeding his capacious nostrils with Scotch snuff, shut the box, and deliberately placed it on the table. Winstanley proceeded, "'And we will share the amount of the sale.' 'Did you ever hear that I was a swindler?' 'Sir!—Oh, you mistake. You know—' The painter rose to his full height. 'You will please to walk down stairs, sir, very quickly, or I shall throw you out at the window.'" The genius would have added another "you know;" but seeing that the action was likely to be suited to the word, he took the hint, and preferred the stairs.

Kotzebue's "Joanna of Montfaucon" was brought out, but without success, compared to former plays by this author. Mrs. Powell's Joanna was a good performance; but it had been desired that Mrs. Hodgkinson should appear as the heroine, and every opportunity was taken to prejudice the public against a lady who was the only rival in tragedy.

Fennell had been a short time one of the company, but did not interfere with the predominant interests. On the 5th of February he withdrew his services, that he might receive the benefit of the bankrupt law.

We have endeavoured to avoid the particulars of those continual conflicts which were taking place between the interests of the theatre and the interests of individual performers. To be faithful, instances perhaps ought to be given; but they are painful in the recollection, and might be disagreeable to the reader in the recital. It has been seen that Mr. Hodgkinson retired from the partnership in the New-York business when it was unsuccessful, and went to Boston; that he there was disappointed; and that, finding the theatre he had left *looking up,* he proposed returning, as a partner or an actor. As the last he was accepted, at $100 per week for himself and wife. His next step was a demand of $20, in addition, to be called an allowance for his wardrobe: this was granted—there was no refusing. Mr. Cooper having withdrawn himself, the next demand was an equal share in the profits for his services, and $50 for Mrs. Hodgkinson: this was granted—but it was not enough. The next demand was that he should have an equal voice in the direction of the theatre. It was time to stop: it was refused. He was told that himself or agent might at any time inspect the books, and see that the division of profit was equitable. The result was—bitter hostility.

The manager had, in the midst of annoyance from sources as adverse to literary exertion as can well be imagined, translated and adapted to the American stage the play of "Abælino, the Great Bandit." Mr. Hodgkinson was of course to play the hero, and Mrs. Hodgkinson the heroine. The author had marked the business of the play, as author and manager, and as such he superintended the rehearsal. On an appeal from an inferior performer, who was reciting correctly, but was interrupted by Mr. Hodgkinson, the manager directed the performer to "go on." This caused offence where causes of offence were looked for. The rehearsal proceeded; and literally, before the end of it, the author was threatened with personal violence. The unmoved manner in which the threat was received was attributed to his carrying pistols concealed about his person, and it was so reported. The success of the piece was great, both in New-York and elsewhere. It was performed for the first time in the English language the 11th of February, 1801.

At the time it was brought out in its new dress, the name of the German author was unknown to the translator, and remained so for some years. His name is Zsokke. He was born in Magdeburg, and left, an orphan, to the care of distant relations, "a very unhappy, unloved, and therefore unloving boy." In crossing the Alps, when a young man, in order to visit Italy, he was persuaded to relinquish his travels and take charge of a school. Having brought this seminary from a deplorable state, in which he found it, to a flourishing condition, he was rewarded with the honours of citizenship. His peaceful and useful life was interrupted by the French invasion. He found means to make himself beloved by his adopted fellow-citizens, and they employed him in administrative offices in several of the Swiss cantons; but finally withdrawing from public life, he married, and commenced author and editor of a newspaper. "Abælino," the play which has made him known to the American public, and entitles him to notice in a history of the American theatre, was written upwards of forty years ago, probably about the same time that his translator commenced dramatist by writing "The Father of an Only Child." His principal works are novels, which have been very popular.

His Abælino has been translated into most of the languages of Europe, and brought forward on most of the European stages under various disguises. It was first played, in a language foreign to its author, in New-York, and only played in America by its original title. Never was a play more successful, or a successful play less productive to its author or translator. It was overwhelmed by snow.

On the 13th of April, "De Montfort," one of those grand and truly poetical, as well as philosophical dramas, written by Joanna Bailey, to portray the progress of the passions, was performed, but failed. If Mr. Cooper, instead of Mr. Hodgkinson, had represented the character of De Montfort, it might not have been so. The last-mentioned performer, with all his versatility and excellence, had nothing of the sublime or philosophic in his composition. He was incapable of understanding De Montfort. But let us remember that all the apparent sublimity and real black letter of John Kemble, and the greatly superior powers of his great sister, could not render De Montfort popular in London. It would not perhaps have been so in the time of Addison.

To dilate on the merits of Joanna Bailey, and to insert a notice of her literary life, would give us pleasure; but we are admonished that our limits are too circumscribed for even the facts immediately belonging to our history.

Charles Jared Ingersoll produced a tragedy at the Philadelphia theatre, called "Edwy and Elgiva." Mr. Cooper and Mrs. Merry played the principal characters, and the piece met with success. This gentleman has written a tragedy, called "Julian the Apostate," of much merit as far as we can remember from reading the manuscript many years since. It has neither been played nor printed.

⇥ CHAPTER 26 ⇤

Mr. Hodgkinson prefers being a salaried Performer to sharing Profits — Mr. White's Romeo — The Abbé de l'Epee — Philadelphia Company — Engagement of Mrs. Merry and Mr. Cooper for New-York — Starring — Miss E. A. Westray — Mr. Placide — Hodgkinson's Falstaff — Opening of the Theatre in October, 1802 — Mr. and Mrs. Whitlock — Mr. and Mrs. Johnson arrive from England — Mr. Prigmore — Mr. Wilson — Blue Beard — The Wheel of Truth — The Voice of Nature — Mr. Cooper departs for Drury Lane — Consequences of The Wheel of Truth — Jonathan Oldstyle and Andrew Quoz.

It now appearing that the profit upon the theatrical business when divided would not yield Mr. Hodgkinson as much as his salary by the agreement made at Boston, and the addition made afterward, he asked to be released from the sharing engagement, and be placed on the salary list again; but demanded for himself and wife $130 per week. The return to the salary list was finally agreed to, but the increase refused.

Mr. White attempted Romeo, and gave hopes of improvement; but much improvement was wanted to constitute him an artist.

The friends of Mr. Cooper, and among them the manager, wishing his return to the New-York theatre, mutual explanations took place; and the latter finding no difficulty in writing to invite him back, or in saying, "As far as my behaviour was influenced by anger in the unfortunate business which separated us, it was unwarrantable,—it is likewise highly probable that I though too much of myself and allowed too little for you, and consequently was erroneous," an engagement was concluded.

The next new play the manager produced was from the French, and called the "Abbé de l'Epee." In this piece Mrs. Powell exceeded all expectation as the deaf and dumb boy. The public voice did her justice at last. But Mr. White failed altogether in the part allotted to him, and it was given to Mr. Martin.

As an instance of sensitiveness, or jealousy, or morbid feeling of some kind, this anecdote is worth recording. Hodgkinson had refused the part of greatest importance, as it respects the display of passion or of skill, in the Abbé de l'Epee, and the manager yielded and gave it to Mr. Harper, very much to the injury of the piece. A short time after, while the piece was still in rehearsal, and after it was known that Mr. Cooper was re-engaged, Mr. Hodgkinson's attorney, Richardson, called on the manager and read a paper addressed to him, complaining of a plot formed for the purpose of calling Hodgkinson to account for not playing the above-mentioned part in the new play; and stating, "that on a certain day some one of 'the conspirators' is to call upon the manager for the reason Mr. Hodgkinson is not in the play, who is to answer that he refused; and then he is to be *cut up* for his slight of the public." He goes on to say that he hopes and believes that "the manager is not in the plot, but as *he* had read the play in a *certain lawyer's office, he* must know who the persons are, and have it in his power to prevent it; and that if it is not prevented, every thing must be at an end between the manager and Mr. Hodgkinson." As the accused and suspected manager had never read his play in a *"lawyer's office,"* and knew nothing of any conspiracy, he dismissed the agent satisfied by the assurance. But not so his principal—he wrote to the author of the play in these words: "I am satisfied that *you* are no way concerned in the business which hurt me so much; but my authority on the intended plan I think unquestionable:" and went on to say, that, as but a few had read the play, the author may "stop the attempt." He then proposes *friendship,* and pledges himself "not to be a candidate for the theatre, but to support the present lessee in it;" and concludes by asking for a copy of Abælino, *"as a matter of justice,* if *not of friendship."*

Mr. White consented to being withdrawn from the character of St. Alme, in the new piece, and announced it to the public as his wish, he finding the character too arduous; Martin prepared for the part, and Hodgkinson took Martin's place. The play was eminently successful.

Mr. Darley having thrown up his commission as an officer in the Marine Corps of the United States, had returned to the stage of Philadelphia, and Miss E. Westray had become Mrs. Darley. With this accession, and that of Mr. Cooper, and with the very great improvement of Mr. Wood, who now stood equal to any actor in the first line of genteel comedy, Mr. Wignell's company this season ranked higher than that of New-York.

On the 12th of March, 1801, the New-York manager made a visit to Philadelphia to make arrangements for future business. The consequence was that Mrs. Merry and Mr. Cooper were engaged for a short *summer season,* to commence in July, and the latter concluded his engagement for the ensuing winter. Mrs. Merry was engaged at $100 per week and a clear benefit, and Mr. Cooper for $30 per week for the summer (as long as the theatre could be kept open profitably), and for the ensuing winter at $50 for 34 weeks.

Dining one day with Wignell, the author of "The Father of an Only Child" found himself in company with two of the original performers of the company of 1789—Messrs. Morris and Wignell.

Mr. Whitlock had been the manager of the Boston theatre for the last season, and now intending to relinquish the business, Mrs. Whitlock applied for a situation in New-York. Her words were, "I have great obligations to the town of Boston; yet when Mr. Whitlock gives up the management, I fear it will fall into the power of those whose pleasure heretofore consisted in making me unhappy." Mr. and Mrs. Whitlock were engaged for the ensuing season.

That Mrs. Merry should be brought to New-York as the sun of the drama, around which the great and little planets and their satellites were to revolve, was a sore mortification to one who could allow of no merit out of the precincts of his own family. It must have been humiliating to consent to receive half salaries after the close of the regular season, knowing that the principal attraction was in another, and that *that* other was to receive the greater share of the profit from the business. But then a refusal would not stop the scheme, and Cooper would stand alone as the hero if Hodgkinson refused. After much struggling and many a hard epithet bestowed even on the very superior woman who for the first time in America was brought forward as (what is now called) a star, Mr. Hodgkinson submitted.

What is called "*starring*" is one cause of the degradation of the drama. The regular company of a theatre may be of an inferior order provided a succession of *stars* keep up attraction and fill the treasury. The manager has another advantage; by bringing in a *star,* he can lessen the influence of a performer over the public, and free himself from an oppressive tyranny. But if a theatre is ever established on the plan we have suggested, to be supported by an enlightened government, there would be no starring.

The delicate health of Mrs. Merry had nearly broken up the scheme for re-opening the New-York theatre. On the 10th of June, the following letter was received from Baltimore.

"TO WM. DUNLAP, ESQ.,

"Sir,—To the last moment have I delayed writing, expecting that every hour would bring me a return of health; but heavy is this short task of telling you the opinion of my physicians, that my recovery is far distant; the complaint is in my breast, and is severe indeed; it has prevented my performing for many nights past, and I have given up the idea of being able to appear again this season. I enclose a letter from Doctor Crawford, as my own feelings tell me his judgment is not erroneous: rash indeed would be the attempt of fulfilling my engagement with you this summer. Sincerely regretting the disappointment to myself and the inconvenience it may be to you, I remain &c. &c.

A. MERRY."

This was accompanied by a note from her physician, fully corroborating this statement: he says, "It has been obvious to all who have witnessed your sufferings, that on every occasion of considerable exertion since the commencement of the warm weather, you have been exhausted to an alarming degree."

In reply to Mrs. Merry's letter, it was said—"I confide in the generosity of your interpretation when I proceed to state that I have not only made numerous engagements, but have even issued notes, payable the first week in July, for which I have no other resource but the profits expected from your appearance. All this, or any pecuniary distress which I may experience, is nothing when weighed in the balance against the health of any individual—when your health is in question, it is less than nothing. But would the journey injure you? might it not be serviceable if made at leisure, and by short stages?" It was then suggested that her coming on and performing twice for the director, and once for herself, if not found injurious, might prove beneficial to her health. This was answered thus, "I will be in New-York by the 29th (June), after that all must depend upon circumstances. I again repeat that every exertion I can make you may depend upon."

On the 8th of June, 1801, Miss E. A. Westray made her first appearance in New-York as Angela, in the Castle Spectre, playing for the benefit of her stepfather, Mr. Simpson. This lady was afterward a performer of some note and consequence as Mrs. Villiers and Mrs. Twaits.

To support the treasury, the stage was degraded by the exhibitions of a man who could whirl round on his head with crackers and other fireworks attached to his heels.

On the 1st of July, 1801, the theatre was reopened, having been prepared for summer weather, with Venice Preserved; Belvidera, Pierre, and Jaffier, by Mrs. Merry, Messrs. Cooper and Hodgkinson. Receipts, $646.

On the 3d, Romeo and Juliet was played. On the 5th, Mrs. Merry played Calista, in The Fair Penitent. The unexpected excellence of Mr. Cooper's Lothario is more vivid in our remembrance than any other portion of this very perfect exhibition.

The warmth of the weather and the exertion brought on a renewal of the great actress's indisposition, and she announced that the next evening's play must be the last but one. On the 8th, she played Beatrice, in Much Ado about Nothing, and The Orphan was given out for her benefit and last appearance.

Cooper and Hodgkinson both solicited her to play for their respective benefits, but she answered that if she could play, it would be for the manager. The receipts on her night were $884.

Mr. Placide, manager of the Charleston theatre, the father of the excellent comedian now (in 1832) on the stage of the Park theatre, was, in 1801, with Mrs. Placide, in New-York, and had engaged as a rope dancer and pantomime performer, to join Hodgkinson and others in a summer theatre at Corré's gardens, at the corner of what is now (1832) Leonard-street and Broadway. Placide was dexterous and powerful on the rope; his wife, whom he married at Charleston after the loss of the excellent dancer and pantomime actress who accompanied him to America, was Miss Wrighten, the daughter of the celebrated actress of that name, who is better known as Mrs. Pownall in this country. Mr. Placide was likewise a great pantomime clown. He had exhibited in various parts of Europe, and was first seen by the writer in 1785 at Sadler's Wells, London, where he went by the name, from his feats as a tumbler, of "The great Devil." Placide's recital of the effects of a panic upon him when exhibiting before Louis XVI. and Marie Antoinette made so strong an impression upon us, that we are induced to think it may interest our readers. It was common for him at that time to perform the enormous feat of throwing himself at a leap, on the stage, over ten, twelve, or more files of soldiers, ranged two and two from the back to the front of the stage, and standing with their muskets perpendicularly erect, and the bayonets bristling above them. On this occasion, he had announced his leap over sixteen files of the grenadiers, so arranged. When the moment approached, he, for the first time, felt the sickening sensation of misgiving—then fear—then panic—a full conviction that he should fail and fall on the points of the bayonets glittering before him. He could not think of flinching from the trial, and his king and queen present. The honour of a tumbler forbade the thought—the drops of sweat oozed from his forehead—the prediction of his fear fulfilled itself—he dashed forward—threw himself into the air—and before he had passed the bayonets, found himself falling on their points. A cry from the audience perhaps saved him by shaking the steady ranks of the grenadiers—he fell—was wounded slightly in body, but in reputation most grievously. The last wound was only cured by adding another file of grenadiers to the line, and springing desperately over the whole.

Mrs. Merry's benefit took place on Friday, and Monday was fixed for the benefit of Mr. and Mrs. Hodgkinson (both having had benefits a few weeks before). Hodgkinson had engaged Placide to get up a pantomime, and perform in it, and likewise to exhibit on the rope, for his night.

On Friday the 10th, during the rehearsal previous to Mrs. Merry's benefit, Mr. Hodgkinson addressed the manager, saying, that the pantomime getting up for him could not be ready by Monday night, and he could not take the night. Astonishment was expressed at his proposing to throw up a night fixed for a benefit, and he was reminded that all the machinists had been employed from Tuesday last, and were employed then for him. This he acknowledged, "but how could he take Monday—he had not determined his play—besides, the house would be crowded to-night, it was very hot, the people would not come again on Monday—the house might be closed for one night—he would take Wednesday—the company would give up one night." He was told that such a sacrifice should not be asked of them. "Would not Robinson take it?" "I shall not ask him. If you, from Tuesday to Monday, could not get ready (the time he had for preparation), how is he to prepare in two days?" The conversation was broken off, and renewed in presence of Mr. Cooper. The manager offered to take the night provided Mr. Hodgkinson would give up Mr. Placide's first appearance to him, and take the second. "What shall I get by that?" was the answer. Cooper proposed to take the night, provided he could prevail on Mrs. Merry to play for him, with consent of the manager. The consent was given, and she agreed, provided Mr. Cooper was permitted to come to Philadelphia and play for her benefit; and, as she had said she would only stay, if she staid at all, for the manager's benefit, she insisted that half the profits of the night should be his. On these terms she stopped her preparations for departure, and her trunks were relanded from the packet, she having only retained the dress necessary for her benefit play. Previous to obtaining this arrangement, Mr. Hodgkinson, in presence of Mr. Cooper, was told that the night should be given to the last named, and Wednesday to him. Mr. Cooper asked him to play Horatius in the Roman Father—"Yes—but who is to play Horatia?" "Mrs. Melmoth," laughing, "or perhaps Mrs. Merry, if I can prevail on her."

On learning that Mrs. Merry had consented to stay and play for his rival, the rage of the jealous and disappointed man was extreme. He threatened not to play for her benefit, which was to take place that night—to leave New-York: he said, "a plot was formed to ruin him—she never intended to go on Monday." He concluded, however, that it was best to go to the theatre, play the character he was announced for (Castalio), and try his persuasive powers again with the lady. But they were not of the kind suited to her. She persisted in refusal—he offered money—she turned from him.

The next day, want of iteration not being his vice, he requested the manager to ask Mrs. Merry to stay and play for his night. The answer was, "I will ask her, as she has swerved from her first resolution, to continue the week; play for you on Wednesday, and me on Friday." On this being proposed, she politely declined; intimating that if importuned, she would consider herself bound to serve the manager. He dropped the subject.

In the afternoon, Mr. Hodgkinson called to know Mrs. Merry's answer, and said he had in the mean time written to her and received a polite but positive refusal, adding, "It seems to me she wants to be offered money." It was replied, "Depend upon it, no. Your offer of that nature last evening gave her great offence." In truth, she had expressed her disgust at his indelicacy.

It is due to Mrs. Merry to state that on the whole receipts of her benefit being presented to her, she would not receive the money, as her health had not permitted her to fulfil her original engagement; and with great difficulty she could be prevailed upon, in addition to her salary, to accept $750 of the $884 received.

On the evening of Mr. Cooper's benefit, Monday, the 13th of July, 1801, the printer's boy put the proof of the next night's bill into the hand of the manager for approbation, and he found it headed by an assertion that he had assured to Mr. and Mrs. Hodgkinson "the services of Mrs. Merry at their benefit, but that she had absolutely declined playing for them." He wrote the words, "in case it had been in her power to fulfil her *first* engagement," and carried them to Mr. Hodgkinson for his consent to their insertion. He refused. "Then an account of the whole transaction shall be published." He then assented. Notwithstanding this, the bills, as first printed, with the falsehood at the top, were attempted to be circulated, and in part succeeded; and the same was published in one of the morning papers—with difficulty prevented in the others.

We have been particular in stating this transaction, as it relates to a most distinguished actress and uncommonly fine woman; and as on the files of the newspapers of the day may be found a formal statement, signed "John Hodgkinson," saying, that the services of Mrs. Merry had been secured to him—that he had been induced to engage on the assurance that she should perform for his benefit, and other misrepresentations; and as the life of a gentleman who had been privy to the affair, and was so far interested for the lady as to come forward to vindicate her from what he thought and called a rude attack, was jeoparded on the occasion.

William Coleman, Esq., long editor of the Evening Post of New-York, under the signature of "Amicus," reprobated the attempt to injure Mrs. Merry with the public. The consequence was the long misstatement of July 15th, and rejoinders, which were near producing an appeal to the pistol. We have no reason to believe that Hodgkinson would have thought of such an argument, but he belonged to the English Rifle Company of the time, and they considered the honour of the corps concerned.

In the bills and advertisements of the theatre for July 20th, the manager took the opportunity of paying a just tribute to the merits and conduct of Mrs. Merry, and of stating "that Mr. Hodgkinson disclaimed any intention of charging the director of the theatre with any breach or violation of contract." By the aid of the peace-maker "if," bloodshed was prevented. We conclude this portion of theatrical history, with a part of a letter from the lady, whose favours were so violently sought.

> "SIR,—I own to you that I have been severely mortified to see my name so frequently before the public, in the New-York prints, and that attached to the name of a man whose conduct I despised, even before he had the opportunity of insulting me.
>
> "This is the second public attack of Mr. Hodgkinson within a short space of time—the subjects females. Surely the people of your city must think of

him as he deserves, and feel that all his assertions are indelicate, inhuman, and unmanly.

"On my return from the theatre, the last evening of my performance, I told Mr. Coleman that if he should observe any further insult from Mr. H. in the bills or papers, I must feel it as an obligation, as he was acquainted with all the circumstances, if he would answer for me, and not suffer Mr. H. to make an impression on the public mind entirely in his own favour. I do feel myself greatly obliged by Mr. Coleman, and only regret the *early* insertion of the first number of Amicus—all I wished was to stand on the defensive. I own myself a coward when armed against such a man, so unprincipled as Mr. H."

This is dated from Philadelphia, July 24th, 1801.

The summer theatre, at what was called Mount Vernon Gardens, was opened on the 10th of August, 1801. Company—Mr. and Mrs. Hodgkinson, Mr. and Mrs. Hallam, Mr. and Mrs. Hogg, Mrs. and Miss Brett, Mr. and Mrs. Jefferson, Mr. Martin, Mr. Darley, jun., Mr. and Mrs. Placide, Mr. Shapter, Mr. Story, Mr. and Mrs. Simpson, and Miss E. A. Westray. Miss Broadhurst appeared for a benefit.

The elder Mr. Darley, before mentioned as one of Wignell's company in 1793, and long a singer at Covent Garden, played Hawthorn, in Love in a Village, on the 29th of August. Mr. Hodgkinson, among his many parts in opera, as in every other department of the drama, was a very good Young Meadows.

Mr. and Mrs. Jones came to this country this summer. Mr. Wignell converted the building, now (in 1832) the post-office in the city of Washington, into a theatre. The opening play was Venice Preserved: Pierre, Mr. Cooper; Belvidera, Mrs. Merry. His winter establishment was deprived of Mr. Cooper, but enriched by the accession of Mr. and Mrs. Jones, and Mr. and Mrs. Whitlock, from the Boston company. Mr. Green also, who had been absent from Philadelphia some years, rejoined the company.

Again yellow fever prevented the opening of the New-York theatre at that time which is most propitious to the interest of the proprietor. On the 16th of November, 1801, the play of Lover's Vows (Cooper playing Frederick), and the farce of Fortune's Frolic, were performed. The company consisted of Mr. and Mrs. Hodgkinson, Mrs. Melmoth, Mr. Cooper, Mr. Fennell, Mr. and Mrs. Hallam, Mrs. Simpson, and her youngest daughter, Miss E. A. Westray, Mr. and Mrs. Hogg, Mr. Tyler, Mr. and Mrs. Jefferson, Mr. Martin, Mrs. and Miss Brett, Mrs. King, Misses Hogg and Harding, and Mr. Fox.

On the 4th of December, 1801, a farce, called "Where is He?" by the manager from the German, was played with success. "The Force of Calumny" was successful this season, but in the commencement the business was a losing one. Mr. Cooper's performances now assumed a higher tone, and he became the acknowledged hero of tragedy. This caused another uneasiness to the rival, besides the jealousy at seeing the tragedian's success. As every *good part* in afterpieces had been eagerly sought for, it now happened that when Mr. Cooper was the Richard, Mr. Hodgkinson might be called on for a character in a farce. This was represented as degrading.

On the 29th of January, 1802, Mr. Bland, a brother of Mrs. Jordan, from the theatres Royal, Drury Lane, and Haymarket, made his first appearance in America under the name of Welson. He played Frank Oatland, in the comedy of A Cure for the Heart Ache. He proved to be a man of indifferent character, but possessed talents for the stage. He afterwards was very serviceable in getting up the opera of Blue Beard, and played Shakabac with effect. This play, being got up with great care and expense, was successful, and yielded a support to the theatre for a time.

On the 26th of March, Schiller's Fiesco, curtailed, was performed (Cooper playing Fiesco); it was coldly received.

On the 28th of March, 1802, Mr. John Brown Williamson, one of the managers of the Charleston theatre, previously a manager of the Boston theatre, and in 1786 an actor on the boards of the Haymarket theatre, London, died in the city of Charleston, South Carolina.

Again the time had arrived for arranging a company for the ensuing winter. Offers were made to Mr. Hodgkinson for himself and wife, and the negotiation broken off upon his demanding that neither of them should be required to aid or assist in any theatrical piece, "except as principal performers in principal characters," and that in any new or revived piece, "they shall be secured, and have a right to demand an equal number of principal characters with any other principal performer or performers, as well in tragedy as in comedy"—all this formally drawn up by his lawyer. The answer was brief: "the demand cannot be complied with, without depriving me of that power which I consider as the basis of my future prosperity." Measures were taken to coerce a settlement of accounts, and Mr. Hodgkinson notified thereof. He then employed friends of the manager to interfere, and finally engaged himself and family for next season on the former terms, with unessential variation. Mr. Whitlock engaged for himself and wife.

It was probably during the season of 1801–2, that Doctor Stock, an English or Welsh gentleman, produced a comedy, which was played with success in Philadelphia, called "A Wedding in Wales."

The doctor had made himself obnoxious to the government of his country by his efforts in the cause of reform, and took refuge in America. He, however, returned home, and perhaps is living, and, we hope, still a reformer. In 1804, our friend William B. Wood, saw him in Liverpool. The doctor altered for the stage some of the translations from Kotzebue, by Miss Plumptree. "A Wedding in Wales" is said to have been a tame, genteel production, but not calculated to last.

Mrs. Merry, having arranged characters for two weeks, came on to New-York, and played Juliet, on the 19th of April, 1802, to $1000; Calista, on the 22d, to $676; Belvidera, on the 24th, to $624; Isabella, the 26th, to $760; Lady Teazle, the 28th, to $750; Jane Shore, the 30th, to $800; and Monimia, the 3d of May, to $900.

Mr. Johnson, in a letter from Hull, concluded an engagement for himself and wife.

Mr. Hodgkinson played Falstaff, for the first time, on the 5th of June, 1802. It was overcharged and hard. It was not like his general comedy playing, which, though sometimes too broad, was the reverse of hard in the sense here meant.

Mr. Cooper having informed the manager that he had received an offer of a purse, to be made up in Philadelphia, if he could come on and play the next winter, by which 3000 dollars would be added to his income, he was told that no obstacle should be raised to his good fortune. The scheme, however, did not take effect.

On the 5th of July, Sunday being the 4th, the rain driving the merrimakers of the day from the public gardens in the evening, the house overflowed to that vile trash, the play of Bunker Hill, and a piece by the manager called "The Retrospect." The receipts were the greatest ever known at that time, $1245.

On the 11th of October, 1802, the theatre of New-York was opened for the season with Adelmorn and The Quaker. The company consisted of Mr. Cooper, Mr. Fennell, Mr. and Mrs. Hodgkinson, Mr. and Mrs. Hallam, Mr. and Mrs. Whitlock, Mr. Tyler, Mr. and Mrs. Jefferson, Mr. and Mrs. Hogg, Mrs. and Miss Brett, Miss Hogg, Mr. Martin, Mr. Hallam, jun., Messrs. McDonald, Shapter, and Robinson, and Mr. Wilson (alias Bland).

Mrs. Melmoth withdrew for a time from before the public, and Miss Harding had been removed from Mr. Hodgkinson's house. Mrs. King, who had been always what is called a dead weight, had become the wife of some one on Long Island, and lived, as we hope, a useful member of society to a good old age. Her sister, Miss Brett, was still on the salary list, and a member of Mr. Hodgkinson's family, but unable to be of any service to the company. Mr. and Mrs. Johnson had not yet arrived from England.

Mr. Whitlock made his first appearance as Major O'Flaherty, and Mrs. Whitlock, on the 6th of November, played Lady Randolph, Cooper playing Young Norval, Hodgkinson Old Norval, Tyler Lord Randolph, and Fennell Glenalvon. Certainly the play had been seldom better performed. The Glenalvon of Mr. Fennell was the best character he ever played, and appeared to the writer better than even John Palmer's. Mrs. Whitlock, though a fine actress, was not Mrs. Siddons, but she imitated her; and in parts of this character was extremely like her great sister. Mr. Hodgkinson's Old Norval was not equal to Henderson's, but when Henderson played the part at Covent Garden, neither the Young Norval nor the Lady Randolph were equal to those of Cooper and Mrs. Whitlock; and Mr. Hodgkinson's representation was replete with excellence.

The manager had translated from the German and brought out, on the 15th of November, a play called "Peter the Great." Mr. Cooper, Mr. Hodgkinson, and Mrs. Whitlock were the principal performers, but the piece did not live.

At this time Mr. and Mrs. Johnson arrived, and the company was of course uncommonly strong. She made her first appearance in Lady Bell Bloomer, in "Which is the Man?" with great eclat, and her second in Lady Teazle, with her husband's Sir Peter. Her Lady Teazle was deemed even superior to Mrs. Merry's by the editor of the Evening Post, Mr. Coleman; and Mr. Irving, in the Morning Chronicle, gave due praise to the improved acting of a lady always justly a favourite. The arrival of this accomplished and elegant actress, and her success, was the cause of bitter animosity from the Hallam family, and of threats and abuse not to be recorded.

Mr. Prigmore, the hero of the tale of the widow and breeches, in a former chapter, had applied for an engagement, and been received on a salary of $14 per week, to do any thing; but feeling important again, or a desire to become so, wrote a letter saying that he had been *forfeited* for not attending in a certain piece, when directed so to do, complaining of injustice, concluding: "I may without boast say that I am held in as much estimation as any actor in the company, in my line of business." In answer, he was referred to the letter which engaged him, in consequence of a very humble application, "only adding, in consequence of yours now before me, I shall not again forfeit you, but if you neglect the business assigned by me, consider you as declining your engagement."

On the 3d of December, 1802, Mr. Wilson, or Bland, the brother of Mrs. Jordan, was carried to jail for debt. And the next day, poor Fennell was again incarcerated. His hope of relief, if not release, was placed on a farce he had written, and which the manager determined to bring out immediately, and to which, in the *bringing out,* the author and principal actor made such additions as called it into more notice than its merits would have done, as we shall see in the sequel.

Mr. John Kemble having retired from the stage at this time, and gone on a tour to the continent, Mr. Cooper had an invitation to try Drury Lane theatre, and wishing so to do, the manager immediately gave his assent, though aware of the difficulties he must encounter when deprived of his talents. He likewise agreed to Mr. Cooper's proposal of playing a week in Philadelphia, the profits to be shared equally.

On the 17th of December, 1802, "Le Judgment de Salomon" was placed by a friend in the hands of the manager, and on the 22d he had finished a translation of it, adapted to his theatre. On the 26th, he began to write a play called "The Blind Boy," altered from Kotzebue's "Epigram."

On the 1st of January, 1803, Blue Beard was played to $1090. Thus far the business of the theatre had been prosperous this season, and Mr. Cooper having in Philadelphia played Hamlet, Richard, Pierre, and Macbeth, to houses averaging $1100 each, the division of profit to the New-York establishment was $475. On the 10th, he sailed in the Chesterfield packet for England.

On the 14th of January, Fennell's farce of "The Wheel of Truth" was brought out, with Mrs. Johnson's Lady Townley preceding it, and the receipt was $215. The farce was played on its second night for the author's benefit, and the receipts were $600. Mr. Hodgkinson played a speaking Harlequin, and his figure in the motley dress gave occasion to some squibs, which annoyed him sadly. Washington Irving wrote for the Morning Chronicle under the signature of Jonathan Oldstyle, and though always playful, the irritation caused was excessive. In a supposed letter from *Quoz* to Jonathan, the actor's rights are thus defended, and Jonathan reprimanded for noticing certain peculiarities in a great performer's playing and dress. "Odsbud, hath not an actor eyes, and shall he not wink?—hath not an actor teeth, and shall he not grin?—feet, and shall he not stamp?—lungs, and shall he not roar?—breast, and shall he not slap it?—hair, and shall he not *club* it?" the immediate cause of this was a parody, put in Harlequin's mouth, of Shylock's "Hath not a Jew," &c. &c. *Harlequin-Shylock,* as one of the journals called him, says, "Hath not an actor eyes—feeling, &c.—if you wrong us, shall we not retort?" &c.

The play of "Liberal Opinions" was brought out—Old Liberal, Mr. Hogg; Young Liberal, Mr. Hodgkinson; but brought neither honour nor profit, and was laid aside. Mr. Hogg had by this time acquired confidence, when he played in old men or humourists, and had become a favourite with the audience.

On the 31st of January, a young man of the name of Cox made a first appearance in Theodore, in the manager's play of "The Mysterious Monk, or Ribbemont." The house was thin. The applause little. The papers next day damned the debutant with faint praise, and the play by the advice to return it to the shelf.

The manager's new play from "The Judgment of Solomon" of the French, was received with great applause, which, and its subsequent success, was without doubt owing to the author's adopting the same title for the piece as that by which it was played in London ("The Voice of Nature"), and calling the characters by the same names. It was supposed to be foreign, and it was admired accordingly. Such were the prejudices which the pioneers of American literature had to encounter. When The Italian Father, which was highly extolled when supposed to be a German play, was revived and known to be American, it was coldly received; and we shall have to record a similar instance in respect to Mr. Barker's play of Marmion—for the same spirit prevailed then in Philadelphia.

The receipts were now so inadequate to support the theatre, that on the 5th of February it was closed, and a part of the company went on to Philadelphia, and played with Wignell's company, now no longer directed by him.

Early in January, 1803, Mr. Wignell was married to Mrs. Merry, who appeared for the first time as Mrs. Wignell on the 12th of that month, in the character of Rosamunda, in the writer's play, from Zsokke, of Abælino. This was the first time *that piece* was performed in Philadelphia. Before the end of the month Mr. Wignell died, in consequence of injury received from a spring-lancet in blood-letting. Mrs. Wignell and Mr. Reinagle directed the business for some time, and Mr. Wood went to England to engage performers.

In the month of February, before the temporary closing of the theatre, Mr. Hodgkinson and Mr. Coleman had a second serious difference, arising from some severe remarks made by Mr. Coleman upon a portion of The Wheel of Truth, known to be written by Mr. Hodgkinson, and introduced as additions to the part he played.

Thus The Wheel of Truth, which was the slightest imaginable piece of patch-work, the only plot being to put the pretenders to a young lady into a wheel, and reward him with the fair who came out unchanged; and whose only aim was to relieve Fennell, by giving him a benefit, and gratify Hodgkinson by put-ting a critic (such as the actors would paint a critic on *their* performances, and who had censured them,) into the wheel, and turning him out "a goose"—thus, this most flimsy farce was made of consequence—first by Irving's pleasantries, and then by Coleman's severe animad-versions on the merits, as players, of Fennell and Hodgkinson.

Coleman said that instead of the silly questions put to the Critic by Harlequin, and more silly answers returned, as the actors had it all in their own hands *now*, being both authors and players, they should have made the Critic utter such ab-surdities as these: "Hodgkinson has merit, &c.; but his tragedy we pronounce rant, his comedy frequently degenerates into vulgar farce, from a want of chaste-ness of demeanour—his broad farce is the most successful; in Ruttikin and Shelty he is at home—buffoons are his forte. As Hodgkinson offends by his assurance, we are sometimes embarrassed by Fennell's diffidence," which he attributes to not having studied his author, and being afraid of "coming to a stand-still."

This produced an attack upon Coleman, which was signed "Justice," and which was pronounced by Hodgkinson, in a piece the next day, to be "correct generally in the charges against Coleman, but in part erroneous."

On Hodgkinson's disavowing the additions to the farce, and stating that "he had no agency whatever in the production of that piece," John Wells, Esq., who managed the matter as Coleman's friend, one of the Rifle Company appearing on the part of the actor, advised (although the evidence to the contrary was before them) that Mr. Coleman should say, "*that* being the case, he is sorry he was so severe upon him; for, considered only as the actor, he should certainly have stopped short of making him the subject of his mirth." Coleman then notices what he calls a "very rude attack" upon him in the Citizen of February 3d, 1803, signed "Justice," which in the paper of next day Hodgkinson in his own name had declared to be "the greater part *correct*, a few assertions *erroneous*," and Hodgkinson is called upon to "point out the parts to which he refers as correct, and those he considers as erroneous." Hodgkinson acknowledged that, in respect to this publication, he had written *with too much haste;* says he "does not know the author,"—that in respect to all the charges or assertions in that piece, nothing is true but that *he* became acquainted with Mr. Coleman in the year 1799—that *he* gave him orders for admission into the theatre, which were amply returned by Mr. C.'s services as a lawyer. That in respect to the compromise in the affair of Mrs. Merry, it was settled on fair and equal principles, and "not at all as a measure into which either of us was driven from any threatened or apprehended consequences." See Evening Post, No. 381, Monday, February 7th, 1803.

The pleasant effusions of an author, who, since the time of which we are writing, has become an object of attention and admiration in both hemispheres, will be better understood and appreciated in connexion with our work than in an isolated situation; or even when read in the journal where first published. We speak of Mr. Washington Irving's communications to his brother's paper, the Morning Chronicle, under the names of Jonathan Oldstyle and Andrew Quoz.

Under this impression we insert two or three of these communications, and a portion of one or two others, as intimately connected with the subjects of this chapter. It is perhaps unnecessary to remark that the *portly gentleman* and the Merry Andrew are the same actor, Mr. Hodgkinson; and the elegant lady who is censured for "mimickry" is Mrs. Johnson. The *white lion* is Prigmore, the hero of the breeches. The "Tripolitan Prize" was one of those vile alterations of an English piece, so justly censured by Mr. Wells in the critique published in an earlier chapter of this work.

> "I was much taken with a play-bill of last week, announcing, in large capitals, THE BATTLE OF HEXHAM; *or, Days of old.* Here, said I to myself, will be something grand—*days of old!*—my fancy fired at the words. I pictured to myself all the gallantry of chivalry; here, thought I, will be a display of court manners and true politeness; the play will no doubt be garnished with tilts and tournaments; and as to those *banditti,* whose names make such a formidable appearance on the bills, they will be hung up, every mother's son, for the edification of the gallery.
>
> "With such impressions, I took my seat in the pit, and was so impatient that I could hardly attend to the music, though I found it very good.

"The curtain rose. Out walked the queen with great majesty; she answered my idea, she was dressed well, she looked well, and she acted well. The queen was followed by a pretty gentleman, who, from his winking and grinning, I took to be the court fool. I soon found out my mistake. He was a courtier "*high in trust*," and either general, colonel, or something of *martial* dignity.

"They talked for some time, though I could not understand the drift of their discourse, so I amused myself with eating peanuts.

"In one of the scenes I was diverted with the stupidity of a corporal and his men, who sung a dull song and talked a great deal about nothing, though I found by their laughing there was a great deal of fun in the corporal's remarks. What this scene had to do with the rest of the piece, I could not comprehend: I suspect it was a part of some other play thrust in here by accident.

"I was introduced to a cavern where there were several hard-looking fellows sitting round a table carousing. They told the audience they were banditti. They then sung a *gallery song,* of which I could understand nothing but two lines:

> "'The Welchman had like to've been chok'd by a mouse,
> But he pull'd him out by the tail!'

"Just as they had ended this elegant song, their banquet was disturbed by the *melodious sound* of a horn, and in marched a *portly gentleman,* who I found was their captain. After this worthy gentleman had fumed his hour out: after he had slapped his breast and drawn his sword half-a-dozen times, the act ended.

"In the course of the play I learned that there had been, or was, or would be a battle; but how, or when, or where, I could not understand. The banditti once more made their appearance, and frightened the wife of the portly gentleman, who was dressed in man's clothes, and was seeking her husband. I could not enough admire the dignity of her deportment and the unaffected gracefulness of her action; but who the captain really was, or why he ran away from his spouse, I could not understand. However, they seemed very glad to find one another again; and so at last the play ended by the falling of the curtain.

"I wish the manager would use a drop scene at the close of the acts: we might then always ascertain the termination of the piece by the *green* curtain. On this occasion I was indebted to the polite bows of the actors for this pleasing information. I cannot say that I was entirely satisfied with the play, but I promised myself ample entertainment in the afterpiece, which was called the "*Tripolitan Prize.*" Now, thought I, we shall have some *sport* for our money; we will no doubt see a few of these Tripolitan scoundrels spitted like turkeys for our amusement. Well, sir, the curtain rose—the trees waved in front of the stage, and the sea rolled in the rear. All things looked very pleasant and smiling. Presently I heard a bustling behind the scenes—here, thought I, comes a fierce band of Tripolitans, with whiskers as long as my arm. No such thing— they were only a party of village masters and misses taking a walk for exercise, and very pretty behaved young gentlefolks they were, I assure you; but it was cruel in the manager to dress them in *buckram,* as it deprived them entirely of the use of their limbs. They arranged themselves very orderly on each side of the stage, and sang something, doubtless very affecting, for they all looked pitiful enough. By-and-by came up a most tremendous storm: the lightning flashed, the thunder roared, the rain descended in torrents: however, our pretty rustics stood gaping quietly at one another till they must have been wet to the skin. I was surprised at their torpidity, till I found they were each one afraid to move first, through fear of being laughed at for their awkwardness. How they got off I do not recollect, but I advise the manager, in a similar case, to furnish every one with a *trap-door,* through which to make his exit. Yet this would deprive the audience of much amusement, for nothing can be more laughable than to see a body of guards with their spears, or courtiers with their long robes, *get* across the stage at our theatre.

"Scene passed after scene. In vain I strained my eyes to catch a glimpse of a Mahometan phiz. I once heard a great bellowing behind the scenes, and expected to see a strapping Mussulman come bouncing in; but was miserably disappointed, on distinguishing his voice, to find out by his *swearing* that he was only a *Christian.* In he came—an American navy officer—worsted stockings—olive velvet small-clothes—scarlet vest—pea-jacket, and *gold-laced hat*—dressed quite *in character.* I soon found out by his talk that he was an American prize-master: that returning through the *Mediterranean* with his Tripolitan prize, he was driven by a storm on the *coast of England!*

"The honest gentleman seemed from his actions to be rather intoxicated; which I could account for in no other way than his having drank a great deal of salt water as he swam ashore.

"Several following scenes were taken up with hallooing and huzzaing between the captain, his crew, and the gallery; with several amusing tricks of the captain and his son, a very funny, mischievous little fellow. Then came the cream of the joke: the captain wanted to put to sea, and the young fellow, who had fallen desperately in love, to stay ashore. Here was a contest between love and honour—such piping of eyes, such blowing of noses, such slapping of pocket-holes! But *Old Junk* was inflexible! What! an American tar desert his duty! (three cheers from the gallery) impossible! American tars for ever!! true blue will never stain!! &c. &c. (a continual thundering among the gods).

"Here was a scene of distress—here was pathos. The author seemed as much puzzled how to dispose of the young tar as Old Junk was. It would not do to leave an American seaman on foreign ground; nor would it do to separate him from his mistress.

"Scene the last opened—it seems that another Tripolitan cruiser had borne down on the prize as she lay about a mile off shore. How a Barbary corsair had got in this part of the world—whether she had been driven there by the same storm, or whether she was cruising about to pick up a few English first-rates, I could not learn. However, here she was—again were we conducted to the seashore, where we found all the village gentry, in their buckram suits, ready assembled to be entertained with the rare show of an American and Tripolitan engaged yard-arm and yard-arm. The battle was conducted with proper decency and decorum, and the Tripolitan very politely gave in—as it would be indecent to conquer in the face of an American audience.

"After the engagement, the crew came ashore, joined with the captain and gallery in a few more huzzas, and the curtain fell. How Old Junk, his son, and his son's sweetheart settled it, I could not discover.

"I was somewhat puzzled to understand the meaning and necessity of this engagement between the ships, till an honest old countryman at my elbow said he supposed *this* was the *Battle of Hexham*, as he recollected no fighting in the first piece. With this explanation I was perfectly satisfied.

"My remarks upon the audience I shall postpone to another opportunity.
"JONATHAN OLDSTYLE."

We give part of the next communication.

"I observed that every part of the house has its different department. The good folks of the gallery have all the trouble of ordering the music (their directions, however, are not more frequently followed than they deserve). The mode by which they issue their mandates is stamping, hissing, roaring, whistling, and when the musicians are refractory, groaning in cadence. They also have the privilege of demanding a *bow* from *John* (by which name they designate every servant at the theatre who enters to move a table or snuff a candle); and of detecting those cunning dogs who peep from behind the curtain.

"'My friend,' said I, (to the countryman, who complained of candle-grease falling on his coat), 'we must put up with a few trifling inconveniences when in the pursuit of pleasure.' 'True,' said he:—'but I think I pay pretty dear for it:—first to give six shillings at the door, and then to have my head battered with rotten apples, and my coat spoiled by candle-grease: by-and-by I shall have my other clothes dirtied by sitting down, as I perceive every body mounted on the benches. I wonder if they could not see as well if they were all to stand upon the floor.'

"Here I could no longer defend our customs, for I could scarcely breathe while thus surrounded by a host of strapping fellows standing with their dirty boots on the seats of the benches. The little Frenchman who thus found a temporary shelter from the missive compliments of his gallery friends, was the only person benefited. At last the bell again rung, and the cry of 'down, down—hats off,' was the signal for the commencement of the play.

"If, Mr. Editor, the garrulity of an old fellow is not tiresome, and you choose to give this *view of a New-York theatre* a place in your paper, you may, perhaps, hear further from your friend,

"JONATHAN OLDSTYLE."

In his next, he says,—

"I had chosen a seat in the pit, as least subject to annoyance from a habit of talking loud that has lately crept into our theatres, and which particularly prevails in the boxes. In old times, people went to the theatre for the sake of the play and acting; but I now find it begins to answer the purpose of a coffee-house, or fashionable lounge, where many indulge in loud conversation, without any regard to the pain it inflicts on their more attentive neighbours. As this conversation is generally of the most trifling kind, it seldom repays the latter for the inconvenience they suffer, of not hearing one-half of the play.

"I found, however, that I had not much bettered my situation; but that every part of the house has its share of evils. Besides those I had already suffered, I was yet to undergo a new kind of torment. I had got in the neighbourhood of a very obliging personage, who had seen the play before, and was kindly anticipating every scene, and informing those about him what was to take place; to prevent, I suppose, any *disagreeable* surprise to which they would otherwise have been liable. Had there been any thing of a plot to the play, this might have been a serious inconvenience; but as the piece was entirely *innocent* of every thing of the kind, it was not of so much importance. As I generally contrive to extract amusement from every incident that happens, I now entertained myself with remarks on the self-important air with which he delivered his information, and the distressed and impatient looks of his unwilling auditors.

"My country neighbour was exceedingly delighted with the performance, though he did not half the time understand what was going forward. He sat staring with open mouth at the portly gentleman, as he strode across the stage, and in a furious rage drew his sword on the *white lion.* 'By George, but that's a brave fellow,' said he, when the act was over; 'that's what you call first-rate acting, I suppose.'

"'Yes,' said I, 'it is what the critics of the present day admire, but it is not altogether what I like; you should have seen an actor of the *old school* do this part; he would have given it to some purpose; you'd have had such ranting and roaring, and stamping and storming; to be sure this honest man gives us a *bounce* now and then in the true old style, but in the main he seems to prefer walking on plain ground to strutting on the *stilts* used by the tragic heroes of my day.'

"This is the chief of what passed between me and my companion during the play and entertainment, except an observation of his, that it would be well if the manager were to *drill* his nobility and gentry now and then, to enable them to go through their evolutions with more grace and spirit.

"'But what is your opinion of the house?' said I: 'don't you think it a very substantial, *solid-looking* building, both inside and out? Observe what a fine effect the dark colouring of the wall has upon the white faces of the audience, which glare like the stars in a dark night. And then what can be more pretty than the stars in a dark night. And then what can be more pretty than the paintings on the front of the boxes; those little masters and misses sucking their thumbs and making mouths at the audience.'

"'Very fine, upon my word—and what, pray, is the use of that chandelier, as you call it, that is hung among the clouds, and has showered down its favours on my coat?'

"'Oh, that is to illumine the heavens, and to set off to advantage the little periwigg'd cupids, tumbling head-over-heels, with which the painter has decorated the *dome*. You see we have no need of the chandelier below, as here the house is *perfectly well* illuminated; but I think it would have been a great saving of candle-light if the manager had ordered the painter, among his other pretty designs, to paint a moon up there, or if he was to hang up that sun with whose *intense light* our eyes were greatly annoyed in the beginning of the afterpiece.'

"'But don't you think, after all, there is rather a—sort of a—kind of *heavyishness* about the house? don't you think it has a little of an *under-groundish* appearance?'

"To this I could make no answer. I must confess I have thought myself the house had a *dungeonlike* look; so I proposed to him to make our exit, as the candles were putting out, and we should be left in the dark. Accordingly, groping our way through the dismal *subterraneous* passage that leads from the pit, and passing through the ragged bridewell-looking antichamber, we once more emerged into the purer air of the Park, when bidding my honest countryman good-night, I repaired home, considerably pleased with the entertainments of the evening.

"Thus, Mr. Editor, have I given you an account of the chief incidents that occurred in my visit to the theatre. I have shown you a few of its accommodations and its imperfections. Those who visit it more frequently may be able to give you a better statement.

"I shall conclude with a few words of advice for the benefit of every department of it.

"I would recommend,

"To the actors—less etiquette—less fustian—less buckram.

"To the orchestra—new music, and more of it.

"To the pit—patience—clean benches, and umbrellas.

"To the boxes—less affectation—less noise—less coxcombs.

"To the gallery—less grog, and better constables;—and

"To the whole house—inside and out—a total reformation.—And so much for the theatre.

"JONATHAN OLDSTYLE."

"TO JONATHAN OLDSTYLE, *Gent.*

"MY DEAR FRIEND—I perceive, by the late papers you have been entertaining the town with remarks on the theatre. As you do not seem from your writings to be much of an adept in the Thespian arcana, permit me to give you a few hints for your information.

"The theatre, you observe, begins to answer all the purposes of a coffeehouse. Here you are right: it is the polite lounge, where the idle and curious resort to pick up the news of the fashionable world; to meet their acquaintances, and to show themselves off to advantage. As to the dull souls who go for the sake of the play, why if their attention is interrupted by the conversation of their neighbours, they must bear it with patience—it is a custom authorized by fashion. Persons who go for the purpose of chatting with their friends are not to be deprived of their amusement: *they have paid their dollar,* and have a right to entertain themselves as well as they can. As to those who are annoyed by their talking, why they need not listen to it—*let them mind their own business.*

"I think you complain of the deficiency of the music, and say that we want a greater variety and more of it. But you must know that though this might have been a grievance in old times, when people attended to the musicians, it is a thing of but little moment at present. Our orchestra is kept principally for form sake. There is such a continual noise and bustle between the acts that it is difficult to hear a note; and if the musicians were to get up a new piece of the finest melody, so nicely tuned are the ears of their auditors, that I doubt whether nine hearers out of ten would not complain, on leaving the house, that they had been *bored* with the same old pieces they have heard these two or three years back. Indeed, many who go to the theatre carry their own music with them; and we are so often delighted with the crying of children by way of glee, and such coughing and sneezing from various parts of the house, by way of chorus—not to mention the regale of a sweet symphony from a sweep or two in the gallery—and occasionally a full piece, in which nasal, vocal, *whistling,* and *thumping* powers are admirably exerted and blended, that what want we of an orchestra?

"In your remarks on the actors, my dear friend, let me beg of you to be cautious. I would not for the world that you should *degenerate* into a critic. The critics, my dear Jonathan, are the very pests of society: they rob the actor of his reputation; the public of their amusement: they open the eyes of their readers to a full perception of the faults of our performers; they reduce our feelings to a state of miserable refinement, and destroy entirely all the enjoyments in which our coarser sensations delighted. I can remember the time when I could hardly keep my seat through laughing at the wretched buffoonery, the Merry Andrew tricks, and the unnatural grimaces played off by one of our theatric Jack Puddings; when I was struck with awful admiration at the roaring and ranting of a buskined hero; and hung with rapture on every word, while he was 'tearing a passion to tatters—to very rags!' I remember the time when he who could make the queerest mouth, roll his eyes, and twist his body with the most hideous distortions, was surest to please. Alas! how changed the times, or rather how changed the tastes! I can now sit with the gravest countenance, and look without a smile on all such *mimicry,*—their skipping, their squinting, their shrugging, their snuffling, delight not me; and as to their ranting and roaring,

> 'I'd rather hear a brazen candlestick turned,
> Or a dry wheel grate on the axletree,'

than any such fustian efforts to obtain a shallow gallery applause.

"Now, though I confess these critics have reformed the manners of the actors, as well as the tastes of the audience, so that these absurdities are almost banished from the New-York stage, yet I think they have employed a most unwarrantable liberty.

"A critic, my dear sir, has no more right to expose the faults of an actor than he has to detect the deceptions of a juggler, or the impositions of a quack. All trades must live; and as long as the public are satisfied to admire the tricks of the juggler, to swallow the drugs of the quack, or to applaud the fustian of the actor, whoever attempts to undeceive them, does but curtail the pleasures of the latter, and deprive the former of their bread.

"Odsbud! hath not an actor eyes, and shall he not *wink?* hath not an actor teeth, and shall he not grin? feet, and shall he not stamp? lungs, and shall he not roar? breast, and shall he not slap it? hair, and shall he not *club* it? Is he not fed with plaudits from the gods? delighted with thumpings from the groundlings? annoyed by hisses from the boxes?

"If you censure his follies, does he not complain? if you take away his bread, will he not starve? if you starve him, will he not die? and if you kill him, will not his wife and seven small infants, six at her back and one at her breast, rise up and cry vengeance against you? Ponder these things seriously, my friend Oldstyle, and you will agree with me that, as the actor is the most meritorious and faultless, so is the critic the most cruel and sanguinary character in the world, as I will show you more fully in my next.

"Your loving friend,   ANDREW QUOZ."

We will conclude with Mr. Oldstyle's account of the Wheel of Truth, which is the most cruel cut of all upon his favourite, the portly gentleman, who performed Harlequin, or the Merry Andrew.

"We found the play already commenced. I was particularly delighted with the appearance and manners of one of the female performers. What ease, what grace, what elegance of deportment! This is not acting, Cousin Jack, said I; this is reality.

"After the play, this lady again came forward, and delivered a ludicrous epilogue. I was extremely sorry to find her step so far out of that graceful line of character in which she is calculated to shine, and I perceived by the countenances around me that the sentiment was universal.

"Ah, said I, how much she forgets what is due to her dignity! That charming countenance was never made to be so unworthily distorted, nor that graceful person and carriage to represent the awkward movements of hobbling decrepitude. Take this word of advice, fair lady, from an old man and a *friend:*—Never, if you wish to retain that character for elegance you so deservedly possess,—never degrade yourself by assuming the part of a mimic.

"The curtain rose for the afterpiece. Out skipped a *jolly Merry Andrew.* Aha! said I, here is the *Jack Pudding.* I see he has forgot his broomstick and gridiron; he'll compensate for these wants, I suppose, by his wit and humour. But where is his master, the quack? He'll be here presently, said Jack Stylish; he's a queer old codger; his name's Puffaway; here's to be a rare roasting-match, and this quizzical-looking fellow turns the spit. The Merry Andrew now began to deal out his speeches with great rapidity; but, on a sudden, pulling off a black hood that covered his face, who should I recognise but my old acquaintance, the *portly gentleman!*

"I started back with astonishment. *Sic transit gloria mundi!* exclaimed I, with a melancholy shake of the head. Here's a *dreary* but true picture of the vicissitudes of life: one night paraded in regal robes, surrounded with a *splendid train* of nobility, the next degraded to a poor *Jack Pudding,* and without even a gridiron to help himself! What think you of this, my friend *Quoz?* said I; think you an actor has any right to sport with the *feelings* of his audience, by presenting them with such *distressing* contrasts? Quoz, who is of the melting mood, shook his head ruefully, and said nothing. I, however, saw the tear of *sympathy* tremble in his eye, and honoured him for his *sensibility.*

"The *Merry Andrew* went on with his part, and my pity increased as he progressed; when, all of a sudden, he exclaimed, 'And as to *Oldstyle,* I wish him to Old Nick!' My blood mounted into my cheeks at this insolent mention of my name. And what think you of *this,* friend Quoz? exclaimed I, vehemently; I presume this is one of your 'rights of actors!' I suppose we are now to have the stage a vehicle for lampoons and slanders; on which our fellow-citizens are to be caricatured by the clumsy hand of every dauber who can hold a brush!

"Let me tell you, Mr. Andrew Quoz, I have known the time when such insolence would have been hooted from the stage.

"After some persuasion, I resumed my seat, and attempted to listen patiently to the rest of the afterpiece; but I was so disgusted with the Merry Andrew, that in spite of all his skipping and jumping, and turning on his heel, I could not yield him a smile.

"Among the other *original* characters of the dramatis personæ, we were presented with an ancient maiden; and entertained with jests and remarks from the buffoon and his associates, containing equal *wit* and *novelty*. But jesting apart, I think these attempts to injure female happiness at once cruel and unmanly. I have ever been an enthusiast in my attachment to the fair sex; I have ever thought them possessed of the strongest claims on our admiration, our tenderness, and our protection. But when to these are added still stronger claims,—when we see them aged and infirm, solitary and neglected, without a partner to support them down the descent of life,—cold indeed must be that heart, and unmanly that spirit, that can point the shafts of ridicule at their defenceless bosoms,—that can poison the few drops of comfort Heaven has poured into their cup.

"The form of my sister Dorothy presented itself to my imagination; her hair silvered by time, but her face unwrinkled by sorrow or care.

"She 'hath borne her faculties so meekly' that age has marked no traces on her forehead. Amiable sister of my heart! cried I, who has jogged with me through so many years of existence, is this to be the recompense of all thy virtues! are thou who never, in thought or deed, injured the feelings of another, to have thy own massacred by the jeering insults of those to whom thou shouldst look for honour and protection?

"Away with such despicable trumpery,—such shallow, worn out attempts to obtain applause from the unfeeling! I'll no more of it. Come along, friend Quoz; if we stay much longer, I suppose we shall find our courts of justice insulted, and attempts to ridicule the characters of private persons. Jack Stylish entreated me to stay, and see the addition the manager had made to his live-stock, of an ass, a goose, and a monkey. Not I, said I; I'll see no more. I accordingly hobbled off with my friend Mr. Andrew Quoz, Jack declaring he would stay behind and see the end of the joke. On our way home, I asked friend Quoz how he could justify such clumsy attempts at personal satire. He seemed, however, rather reserved in his answers, and informed me he would write his sentiments on the subject.

"The next morning Jack Stylish related to me the conclusion of the piece: how several actors went into a wheel, one after another, and, after a little grinding, were converted into asses, geese, and monkeys, except the *Merry Andrew,* who was found such a *tough jockey* that the wheel could not digest him, so he came out as much a Jack Pudding as ever.

"JONATHAN OLDSTYLE."

A letter received by the manager about this time is of a character so different from the general tenor of this chapter, that we will reserve it for another, in which threats, and quarrels, and ill-will shall have no part.

✦ CHAPTER 27 ✦

Letter from John Murray, jun., to Wm. Dunlap, and the answer.

"2d mo. 15th, 1803.

"Impressed with sentiments of friendship, and influenced, I trust, from motives which are the offspring of a desire to promote the welfare of individuals, and the good of the community at large, I am induced to address thee on a subject in which I conceive thy happiness is not a little interested, as well as that of many others who may be more or less affected by thy conduct and example. Since I waited on thee in the case of the young man who had imprudently exposed himself, I have frequently been led to take a view of the pernicious effects resulting from theatrical exhibitions, and to lament that a person of thy understanding and sensibility should ever have been prevailed upon to become an active agent in promoting any kind of amusements which are calculated to weaken the moral principle and alienate the mind from the precepts and practices of the Christian religion. I wish not to enlarge much on the subject, but apprehending it was my religious duty to impart a few thoughts to thee relative thereto, I have therefore taken the liberty to do it in this way; with a request that thou would accept a book, entitled, The Power of Religion on the Mind, as also a pamphlet containing the sentiments of some pious characters touching the evil tendency of stageplays, &c. These I submit to thy perusal and serious consideration, and with an unfeigned solicitude for thy present and future welfare,

I subscribe myself thy sincere friend,

JNO. MURRAY, Jun."

Mr. Murray, the brother of Lindley Murray, was not at this time a young man, the jun. was adopted to distinguish him from the father of Mr. John R. Murray.

ANSWER.

February the 17th, 1803.

DEAR SIR,

Your kind and benevolent letter, and the books accompanying it, were put into my hands yesterday. You have given me a pleasure which does not often fall to my lot. In the first place I am flattered not only by your selecting me as an object worthy of the exertion of your benevolence, but that you should so liberally appreciate my understanding as to believe me capable of listening with profit to the voice which cries, 'Your ways are the ways of wickedness, and lead to destruction.' Secondly, I am pleased to see in you a proof that there are men among us who from purely disinterested motives take part in that which concerns their neighbour's welfare, and generously expose themselves to the risk of his displeasure from a wish to confer on him a benefit.

Although I am thus gratified by your attention to me, you must not conclude that I am insensible to the mortifying consideration that my conduct meets with the entire disapprobation of an enlightened and honest man. No thinking man ought to (nay, I may say no thinking man can) be so fortified in his opinions of the truth of those deductions which are the result of his own reasoning on an important subject, but that he is rejoiced to find his conclusions sanctioned and supported by others; and must always pause with a sensation of pain when a wise or good man differs from him in opinion.

I accept with pleasure the books, and shall keep them as a memorial of your friendship. I read the pamphlet yesterday, and looked over the other compilation. Collier, Rousseau, and Witherspoon have written against the stage with more force than any other authors whom I have read, and have brought forward all the arguments that are to be found in Mr. Lindley Murray's pamphlet, with others not there noticed. I would wish you to do me the justice to believe that subjects so momentous as those you recommend have not been passed over lightly in my previous studies; and that I did not become an author of plays and a director of their exhibition, before I had with my best ability examined the subject, and heard or read all the arguments against the drama which were within my reach. My decision, notwithstanding, was, and still is, in favour of theatrical establishments *in all great cities;* from a full conviction that with all the ills which may be imputed to them, the balance of good must be carried to their credit.

Far be it from me to suppose myself above error, or that my reason is so powerful as to be in no danger from the seductions of passion and selfishness, or the biases of early education and prejudices; and whenever I shall be convinced that I am acting upon erroneous principles, I will undoubtedly change my conduct. The path I am now in is not the path of pleasure; and *but* from the consciousness of its being my duty to continue in it, I should certainly seek another. You must suppose me in an error; and as the truth is always desirable, and in this instance concerns the welfare of many, I should be glad to submit to you the process of my reasoning on this subject, and by so doing give you an opportunity of detecting the mistakes I may have committed. With your permission, I will some time hence address you again on this subject. At present permit me to assure you of the grateful sense I entertain of the propriety of your conduct towards me, and to subscribe myself your sincere friend."

It is probable that at the present time the writer of the last letter would not have treated the subject exactly as above. A theatre well conducted, and under the charge of the government, is good in any place.

To avoid a repetition of ideas, and to be as brief as possible, instead of the subsequent letters to Mr. Murray, we will give a few extracts. As he made no reply the subject was dropped. In the second letter are these remarks on Mr. Lindley Murray's pamphlet, which accompanied his brother's letter.

"Mr. Lindley Murray introduces his theme with the language of a gentleman and a philosopher; and, unlike those dogmatical sectaries who, presuming upon the infallibility of their own opinions, stigmatize with the epithets trifling, dangerous, hurtful, vicious, criminal, intolerable, and profane, those opinions which differ from their own, he, with due respect to his fellow-men, invites to free inquiry; advances his opinion against dramatic exhibitions, and gives as a support to that opinion the words of certain well-known characters, whose names are supposed to add weight to his assertions.

"To oppose to the names Mr. Murray brings forward in formidable array, an equal number—I forbear to say a greater—of the most enlightened men and the most exemplary might be mentioned, who have assisted at stage representations. The first objection I make to Mr. Murray's pamphlet is the phrase on his titlepage—*Dramatic entertainments and other* VAIN *amusements*. As Mr. Murray invites to 'free inquiry,' and 'candid opinions *decently* advanced,' it appears to me to be improper to brand the subject with a degrading epithet before an attempt is made to discuss it.

"On page eight I find these words supported by the name of the Prince of Conti:—'It is a jest to fancy that a man need to pass three hours in filling his mind with follies at a play.' This is the first mention made of plays after the introduction. The wise Prince of Conti tells us that one has no need of filling the mind with follies—that it is a jest to think it needful. Is it only a jest? Indeed I think that it is lamentable that any human being should fill his mind with follies at any time or in any place. But we are not, on the authority of his royal highness, to take it for granted that by attention to a play the mind is filled with follies. By attention to a fable or parable, whether delivered from the stage or the press, whether in narrative or dialogue, by one person or many, the mind may imbibe the most useful and important truths.

"From the same author Mr. Murray quotes the following words, 'Now, among the pleasures of the world which extinguish the love of God, it may be said that plays and romances hold the first rank, because there is nothing more opposed to truth.'

"No play or romance that was ever written contains a greater falsehood than the above. Do the soul-debasing pleasures which engross the minds of the sensual extinguish the love of God less than reading or hearing the fables of the poet? The Prince of Conti has said so, and Lindley Murray has sanctioned the assertion.

"That 'there is nothing more opposed to truth' than plays and romances, is an assertion utterly void of just foundation. Plays, poems, and romances derive their value and popularity from the true delineation of nature, added to the just sentiments introduced, and the moral inculcated by the fable. It surely cannot be meant that they are opposed to truth because they are fictions, fables, or parables. Mr. Murray knows full well that by such fictions, fables, or parables, men are induced to listen to the voice of the teacher, and remembers with delight and reverence Jotham's beautiful fable of the trees, Nathan's fable of the poor man and the lamb, the parable of Dives and Lazarus, the sower, the ten virgins, the prodigal son, and many others, which are so instructively interspersed through the prophetical and other scriptures. Now, a poem, a play, a novel, or a romance, is a fable or parable of more or less length—the play written in a form to be recited by one or more persons,—otherwise in nothing differing.

"The general assertions of ignorant or misinformed writers or declaimers against stage-plays, as 'that nothing is represented in them but gallantries, or extraordinary adventures and discourses far distant from serious life,'—'that plays are full of wicked maxims,'—'that they notoriously minister to vice and immorality,'—'that by their lewdness they teach vice,' are so *notoriously* untrue, and such gross libels upon the thousands of good men who have attended to their representation, and encouraged their authors and those who have studied to give them force and effect by recitation and action, that they are unworthy of notice at this time and in this state of society.

"That many plays and other books may be found immoral in their tendency, and disgusting from their vulgar or obscene expressions, is too true. That some of the very many plays represented on the stage are objectionable, is likewise true; but that entertainments such as are described by Archbishop Tillotson and others are the favourites of the present time, is utterly untrue, and the assertion an indecent outrage upon those to whom it is addressed.

"The stage, as well as the press, brings before the public a great variety of literary effusions of unequal merits. But the stage can never produce works so vile as issue from the press; for men will endure to read that which, if spoken from the stage, no audience would tolerate for a moment. Shall we therefore abolish the press?

"There are many who cannot, and still more who will not, read, but will receive the lessons of wisdom, when impressed by the exertions of others. Evil maxims in plays are hurtful, but good maxims must be beneficial; and none will deny that there are plays whose whole and sole tendency is to good. The time may come when all shall be such."

With these extracts we will conclude this chapter, and proceed to chronicle events in our eventful history.

⇥ CHAPTER 28 ⇤

Boston Theatre and Mr. Powell — Miss F. Hodgkinson — Alphonso — Mrs. Gannett — Mrs. Wignell — Mrs. Hodgkinson — Miss Brett — Messrs. Claude and Clarke — Mr. Hodgkinson's Bankruptcy as a Merchant, &c. in Philadelphia — Death of Mrs. Hodgkinson, and Miss Brett, in 1803.

M r. S. Powell was this winter (1802–3) the manager of the Boston theatre, and Mrs. Powell the principal ornament of it. Mr. Powell had the use of the plays written by the New-York manager at this time, always remunerating him honourably.

When "The Voice of Nature" was brought out, Miss F. Hodgkinson was introduced to the public. She was the oldest child then living of Mr. and Mrs. Hodgkinson, and a beautiful girl. She has since proved an amiable and worthy woman.

One of the first effects of Mr. Cooper's departure was, that Mr. Fennell, who had been relieved and released by the aid of the manager, increased his demands, and threatened to go to Philadelphia. He however remained through the season.

Lewis's tragedy of "Alphonso" was brought out and applauded; but no attention was paid to the theatre at this time, the receipts not being generally more than half the expenses.

Col. Wm. Smith recommended Deborah Gannett, and wished that she should have an opportunity of delivering an oration from the stage, she having served three years as a soldier in the war of the revolution. It was an ill-judged exhibition, and failed accordingly.

On the 16th of March, 1803, Holcroft's melo-drama of the "Tale of Mystery" was performed in America. This was the first play of the kind seen in the New World; indeed, this kind of mixed drama was a novelty even in Europe. It was received with pleasure amounting to delight. The characters were thus played:— Bonamo, Tyler; Romaldi, Hodgkinson; Francisco, Fennell; Stephano, Martin; Montano, Johnson; Michelli, Jefferson; Piero, Hogg; First Gardener, Prigmore. Selina, Mrs. Johnson; Fiamella, Mrs. Hogg. Miss Hodgkinson danced "a *shantruse.*"

On the 30th of March, the manager's play of "The Blind Boy," with a dialogue epilogue, was performed to a thin audience,—parts much applauded. Its second night was better attended. It was never popular.

At this time Mr. Cooper was playing Hamlet, Macbeth, and Richard successfully in London.

Holcroft's comedy of "Hear both Sides" was received from James Brown, the friend of the manager of the New-York theatre, and brother of his friend C. B. Brown.

A play called "The Tournament" was brought out with expensive scenery and decorations, but without salutary effect upon the treasury.

In May, 1803, Mrs. Wignell gave notice, that as principal, she had engaged the theatre of Philadelphia, and that the business would be as usual carried on by Wignell and Reinagle. A letter had been addressed to her on hearing a report that she intended leaving America, to which the following is the answer:

"Baltimore, May 30, 1803.

"W. DUNLAP, ESQ.

"Dear Sir,—Before this time you must have seen by the papers that I have bound myself a slave for four years. Doubts and fears for the consequences of such an arduous undertaking prevented my answering your kind and friendly letter before. As I did not make up my mind to the task until the last moment, and as circumstances would have obliged me to remain in this country at least to the end of the next winter, it is more than probable I should have accepted your proposal, and be assured this is the only reason for my apparent neglect. Believe me, with all respect,

"Your obedient and obliged friend,

"ANNE WIGNELL."

Mrs. Hodgkinson had been for some time in declining health, and was in June, 1803, evidently too ill to exert herself in her profession. On Wednesday the 15th she appeared so unwell when playing "Letitia Hardy," that the manager spoke to her husband on the subject, hoping he would withdraw her. He said she could play "any speaking part;" that "those who took benefits must not put her in the bills for too much;" that "she could not sing, but could do any speaking part." In consequence she was announced for Mrs. Haller, in The Stranger, for Monday the 26th. She performed the part looking so as to make the writer's heart ache. Near the conclusion of the play she spoke to Mr. Ciceri, desiring him to give notice that "she could play no more." She spoke so as to give him the idea that she thought she had been compelled to play; and he assured her that to his knowledge the manager had long been averse to her coming before the public, and grieved to see the pain she suffered. She told him that "her physician had that evening told her, that if she performed any longer she could not live, but might recover by ease, care, and rest;" that "she had asked his opinion respecting Miss Brett's situation, and he told her that she could not live." They both died in a very short time after; the one in the prime of life, the other in age still a girl.

Mrs. Hodgkinson was written to thus:

"Madam:—Mr. Ciceri delivered your message to me yesterday. As I have long
seen the danger you incurred and the injury you sustained from playing, and
have sincerely wished that you would retire to that repose which you so evidently require, I was gratified to hear your determination, and hope that you
will soon experience the salutary effects of it. I remain, madam,
            "With respect and esteem, —— ——."

Upon the rumour that Mrs. Wignell was going to England it was supposed
that Mr. Hodgkinson would obtain the Philadelphia theatre, and Mr. Wood
prepared to shift his quarters to New-York. On the arrangement already mentioned, Mr. Jefferson engaged himself for Philadelphia, where he and his wife
remained in that permanent and highly respectable manner which seems to have
been peculiarly the lot of the performers of that company. Mr. Wood went to
England as Mrs. Wignell's agent. Mr. Harwood was subsequently engaged for
New-York to supply the place of Mr. Jefferson.

As the names of Messrs. Claude and Clarke are well known in theatrical story, their first appearance, not on the stage, but in a manager's office, shall be related. On the 23d of June, 1803, two young men, well dressed, called and expressed
a wish to go on the stage. They were told that the theatre would be closed in a
few days, and no opportunity offered. They expressed their disappointment, and
the youngest seemed chagrined at the idea of returning home. They said they
had come from Maryland, and begged to be heard recite. They were gratified,
and their defects pointed out, and advice very freely given not to think of going
on the stage, but to return home. In short, every thing was said to discourage them
from their pursuit. In the evening, a black man brought the following:

"Sir,—Having hitherto moved in a sphere of life respectable and independent, the idea of soliciting a favour from a gentleman to whom I am a perfect stranger, fills my bosom with the most exquisite pain. But there is no
alternative. Necessity commands it, and my heart, however reluctant, must
obey its dictates. When, sir, I left my native residence, it was under the firmest conviction that I should obtain a situation in the theatre, which would at
least furnish me with the means of returning to Maryland, should I become
dissatisfied. Disappointed in my expectations, my situation has become truly
distressing. A perfect stranger in New-York, without a shilling in my pocket,
more than will pay my bill in the house I live, and for a seat in the stage to
Philadelphia. To you, sir, under these circumstances, I have taken the liberty
to apply for assistance. I flattered myself with an idea that by the disposal of
a watch I have I might have got to Baltimore, where I am known; but in this
I have also been disappointed, not being able to find a purchaser. Should you

think proper to take this for whatever you may advance, I will with pleasure send it to you; or if you can place confidence in the honour of a distressed stranger, I will remit to you upon my return to Maryland. I am, with every sentiment of respect,

"Your obedient servant,
"JOHN CLAUDE."

The black was asked where the gentleman was who sent that letter. "Here, at the corner of the street,"—the corner of Nassau and Beekman. "Ask him if he will please to step here." It proved to be the tallest and handsomest of the two. He was taken by the hand, and being led into the office, burst into tears. On a chair being presented, he seated himself and sobbed aloud. On being assured that he should have the assistance he needed, he could not reply intelligibly. "Is your companion in the same destitute situation?" "I believe he is." "Is it the determination of both to return home?" "Yes." "Will twenty dollars carry you to your friends?" "I believe it will be quite sufficient." It was given with assurances of perfect confidence. "I do not wish to pry into your affairs; as soon as I saw you I feared what I now find true, that this expedition is the fruit of some sudden and unadvised impulse." "Madness, madness." "I cannot be sorry for your distress, if its effect will be to restore you to your friends, and turn your thoughts from any pursuits not sanctioned by them." "I have friends, sir—I have read law,—I—" He could not proceed. "If you find to-morrow the sum I have given you is not sufficient for you and your companion, call on me for more." He could not speak,—pressed my hand and departed. He did not call again.

Both of these young men are dead. I am sorry to say that it is probable this first step was never retrieved. They both became performers without distinguished excellence. Claude married Miss Hogg, and left her a young widow. Clarke, after Hodgkinson's death, married Miss Harding, who at the time went under the name of Mrs. Marshall.

This transaction will serve to give an idea of many similar adventures of youth and folly. Some doubtless terminating even worse.

The time had now arrived for forming the company for the succeeding winter, and it was necessary to know the determination of the most efficient actor in the country. The state of Mrs. Hodgkinson's health was a source of embarrassment. Messrs. P. Irving, John Wells, and William Coleman, concurred in advising and dictating the words of the following letter to Mr. Hodgkinson.

"Sir,—Our engagements having expired some time back, you may perhaps be at a loss to account for my silence in respect to a renewal of them. Give me leave to assure you, sir, that it has not proceeded from a want of a due sense of the importance of your support to the New-York theatre; yet I could not but hesitate in making you proposals, under the peculiar circumstances in which the theatre is unfortunately placed.

"You know as well as myself that the receipts have not been adequate to the payment of the engagements, and that, instead of accumulating property, I am accumulating debt. Thus situated, I have deferred making any offers for future engagements, and to the applications which have been made to me, have only given provisional answers.

"Knowing how justly you appreciate your talents, I have felt great reluctance to offer you less advantageous terms for the ensuing season than those you have enjoyed heretofore, especially as my circumstances, as well as those of the theatre generally, put it out of my power to hire your theatrical property as I have for some years done. If it should still be agreeable to you to enter into a negotiation on such terms as I am enabled to offer, I shall be happy in any arrangement which may secure to me your continuance in the New-York theatre."

The last paragraph was written by P. Irving.

Upon a supposition that in answer to the above, a definite offer would be called for, it was agreed that 45 dollars should be named as his salary, he finding his own dresses. That it should be stated in consideration of Mrs. Hodgkinson's delicate health, and the impropriety of calling upon her for professional exertions, when it was evident that her restoration depended upon long continued repose, another lady should be engaged for her business; but 20 dollars paid weekly during the engagement, she not being called upon more than once a week, and not even that, if her health should continue inadequate to such exertion.

But the offer was not called for—the following answer concluded the affair. "Sir,—The terms of renewing mine and Mrs. Hodgkinson's engagement with you for another season, are the establishment in point of property, business, and salary, as our former one: with the addition of certainty in its extension to ———— weeks. Your letter is so far from meeting ideas of this nature, that I have only to wish you every success and happiness in other negotiations and with other people."

In consequence of this, the engagement of Mr. Harwood was completed, he being to act as stage-manager, and receiving $35 as performer and $15 as manager.

The manager's play of "The Glory of Columbia, her Yeomanry," written for the 4th of July, was played (1803), and the receipts $1287. The theatre was kept open the next night, and the receipts $444, which was still more extraordinary. The money necessary to discharging accounts and salaries, and making necessary advances, was raised by mortgage on landed property in New-Jersey.

This summer was again a season of pestilence, both in New-York and Philadelphia. Mr. Hodgkinson's account had been sent to him, making him debtor $5395. He returned—*defiance!* and early in September he was declared bankrupt in Philadelphia, as "John Hodgkinson, merchant, dealer, and chapman, Philadelphia (late of New-York), to surrender on the 14th of September, 11th and 21st of October, 1803."

In September, Miss Arabella Brett died. Early in October, a letter was received from William Coleman, dated 27th of September, 1803, "Tyler's Gardens, Tuesday, 7 o'clock," from which we must make some extracts, or we should not be faithful to the task we have undertaken. "After considerable knocking, Mrs. Brett partly opened the door, in that kind of manner as if to say no one's at home. Seeing who it was, she beckoned me in with her hand, and pointed to the parlour. I desired her, in a whisper, not to awaken Mrs. Hodgkinson. She went softly up the stairs, and presently he came down; he called me 'Billy,' and took my hand, to be sure, with much softness and affection, and sighed very deeply! I asked him if Mrs. H. was worse. He said no, he did not think she was, but he would awake her. I desired him not; but he persisted, and went to her room, saying, '*You won't know her.*' She came rather dragging than walking; but when she inclined her head as she entered the door, though prepared for the sight of a melancholy object, I started. Her face had no sign of muscle about it; her lips skinning to a degree that showed all her front teeth as she breathed; her eyes glassy, and wandering apparently without the power of distinguishing objects; her whole countenance ghastly to a shocking degree: yet she seemed not alarmed at her situation, but talked of getting rid, some how, of her cough, and she said she should soon get well." "Mrs. Tyler was there the day after, and she consulted her about the fashion of a new bonnet she wanted, and even spoke of playing again." "About an hour since, Tyler told me *she was no more!* 'Tis a melancholy subject to dwell upon." After mentioning the death of Miss Brett, he continues, "Poor Bell!—her nearly last words were, I wish Mr. Hodgkinson might see me *after I am dead.*"

✦ CHAPTER 29 ✦

1803 — Albany — New-York Company — John E. Harwood — Parallel be-
tween Harwood and Hodgkinson — John Bull — Harwood's Dennis Brul-
gruddery — Mr. Hogg's Job Thornberry — Bonaparte in England — Mr.
Searson — The Theatre of New-York sold at Auction — Conceit can Kill,
Conceit can Cure — Lewis of Monte Blanco, or the Transplanted Irishman
— Harwood's Military Irishman — Mr. and Mrs. Darley — Mr. Hunting-
ton — Mr. Thomas A. Cooper returns from England — Bankruptcy of the
Manager of the New-York Theatre.

During this summer the performers of the New-York theatre played at
Mount Vernon Gardens a short time, and afterwards at Albany, with some
success.

A letter was addressed to William Henderson, Esq., wishing a weekly sum fixed
for rent of the theatre, until the chancery suit in which the property was involved
should be settled. It is stated that Mrs. Wignell and Mr. Reinagle pay for the
Philadelphia theatre and property $2500 per year. Mr. Henderson, in answer,
says, "The chancellor, as yet, has made no decree," and advises to open the house
on or before the middle of November.

The Philadelphia company for the winter of 1803–4 consisted of Messrs. War-
ren, Downie, Jefferson, Twaits, Blissett, Francis, Wood, Cain, Morris, Warrell,
Durang, Mestayer, Melbourne, Fox, Hardinge, L'Estrange, and Usher; Mesdames
Wignell, Oldmixon, Shaw, Francis, Wood (late Miss Westray), Solomon, Snowden,
Durang, Downie, Morris, and Miss Hunt. This was the first season in which Mr.
Jefferson was enrolled as a member of the Philadelphia *corps dramatique,* and he
continued a useful and extremely valuable member of that body unto the day of
his death, in August, 1832. He died at Harrisburg, Pennsylvania, aged 58.

The theatre of New-York was opened on the 14th of November, 1803, with
the comedy of "She Would and She Would Not," and the farce of "Ways and
Means,"—Trapanti and Sir David Dunder, Mr. John E. Harwood. The company now was Messrs. Fennell, Hallam, Harwood, Tyler, Johnson, Harper, Martin, Hallam, jun., Hogg, Prigmore, Saunderson, M'Donald, and Shapter; Mesdames Johnson, Melmoth, Hallam, Hogg, and Miss Hogg.

Mr. Harwood was received with well-merited applause, and soon became a
favourite, although the remembrance of Mr. Hodgkinson in many parts made
it impossible for any performer to follow him with perfect success. John E. Harwood has been mentioned in the catalogue of the splendid company brought out
to this country in 1793 for Philadelphia. He was a man endowed by nature with

brilliant talents, and had received in every respect the education of a gentleman. His Trapanti, Sir David Dunder, Lenitive, Dennis Brulgruddery, Canton, Gradus, Capt. Ironsides, and a long list of characters, were superior to any man's, in our opinion, yet seen in this country: he was more like John Bannister than any other actor of the English stage. His Falstaff was the best in this country until Cooke played it, except,—and it is a most formidable exception,—that it was not sufficiently studied. In truth, self-indulgence was the ruin of Harwood, as of thousands off and on the stage. After his marriage, he had retired from the stage, and kept a bookstore and circulating library: this retirement from a profession in which he was qualified to shine was probably not his own choice. He read his books, and neglected his business. Booksellers should never read; if they do, they are lost. There are brilliant exceptions; but then they wrote also: they did not read merely for the gratification of reading, or to *kill time*, but to gain knowledge, and they exerted themselves to impart it. The venerable Matthew Carey is an instance in point. Harwood was a poet, and had in early life published a volume of verses. He was a man of wit, and the favourite of every company; never obtrusive, and always willing to take a joke or to give one. He was lazy, and became corpulent; the first disqualified him for all business, and rendered many of his new characters, after he returned to the stage, less perfect than they would have been; the second spoiled his appearance and action for high or genteel comedy, for a corpulent *Michael Perez* (and he played it well) should not be placed by the side of *Cacofogo*. John E. Harwood, off the stage, would have shone as a man of fortune, and he had a wife equally fitted to be a man of fortune's wife; but as unfit for a poor man's wife as he was for a poor man. The consequence was the return to the stage, which brings him again before the reader.

Amusing parallels might be run, showing the similarity and dissimilarity between Messrs. Hodgkinson and Harwood, both highly talented, and with great physical powers; both addicted to indulgence; yet one lazy, and the other not only active, but restless; one refined, and the other coarse; one retiring, the other forward; but enough has been said to enable the reader to form his own opinion of both. They were two very excellent actors, the versatility and industry of one far surpassing the other.

On the 25th of November, "The Glory of Columbia, her Yeomanry" produced again a great receipt: it had been played three times, at an average of near $900. The author, no doubt, was flattered; yet perhaps Burk's "Bunker Hill" had been more attractive and applauded. The applause of the enlightened is gratifying, and ought to be so: Mr. Bulwer has made his "Eugene Aram" express the stirring of his ambition when he heard the plaudits bestowed on a play; but when the same audience greeted a tumbler with still louder testimonies of their approbation, the ambition was quickly smothered.

Colman the younger's excellent comedy of "John Bull" was brought out, and was a temporary support to the theatre. Mr. Harper was certainly a very inadequate representative of Tom Shuffleton; but the part was new, and the audience were satisfied, because they had not seen a better. No fault could have been found with Mrs. Johnson's Mary Thornberry, unless that she was too tall and too elegant for the brazier's daughter,—faults easily passed over,—and the pathos of the part was perfect. Mrs. Hallam had the same advantage which attended Mr. Harper, with the semblance of youth and the remains of beauty to aid her. Mr. Hallam's Dan was the production of an artist, but without any prominent excellence. Mr. Johnson's Sir Simon Rochdale was truly characteristic, and played with great effect. Mr. John Hogg had now reached to that point in his profession which ensured him favour generally; and in some parts, where a certain dry humour was required, he was "just the thing." Before he played Job Thornberry, he was unequal to the part: he could not have conceived or executed it: but by having it read to him, and by instruction at the rehearsals, he acquired a just possession of the character, and the representation of the brazier stamped him an actor. Mr. Hogg had been gradually acquiring a deserved popularity, first in the line of old men of a secondary character, and then in that of humourists. Besides his Job Thornberry, we remember with peculiar pleasure his *John Lump, Humphrey Dobbins,* and other comic characters. He was an uneducated man, with good sense and praiseworthy modesty; he was a warm-hearted man, and delicately grateful for favours received. He died on the 14th of February, 1813, at the age of 43; he having been born on the 16th of September, 1770, in the parish of Saint Ann, Soho, London. Mrs. Hogg was more than equal to *Mistress* Brulgruddery: she was in all her old women a most able actress, though she has been excelled far by a much younger woman, the truly admirable Mrs. Wheatley. But Dennis was, in Harwood's hands, one of the richest pieces of comic acting that we have ever witnessed. Nothing overcharged, nothing vulgar; but ripe, and having all the flavour of perfect ripeness in the mellow fruit of an author's genius. Mr. Tyler played Peregrine, a character which, by the intrigue of management, was assigned to George Frederick Cooke at Covent Garden. Mr. Tyler was always perfect in the words of his author, and respectable in the delineation of his characters.

On the 18th of December, Mr. Henderson left a paper with the manager, containing a scheme by which he was to purchase the theatre for $85,000. The sum was objected to, and a day or two after the sum of $40,000 substituted by him— these words accompanying the same—"These proposals I make, sir, not because my experience justifies me in offering such terms, for I have long laboured through distress and difficulty, and have yet received no reward, but because I am already so engaged in the business, that I must sacrifice much if I turn back;

yet that sacrifice I will make rather than add to the above offer." At this time the theatre was advertised for sale at auction.

December the 19th, was brought out a farce written by the manager, called "Bonaparte in England," which brought more applause and less money the third than the first night. Harwood played a German Jew broker, who being shipwrecked on the coast of England, is taken up as Jerome Bonaparte, for whom the English government were keeping watch, and the honours paid to Shadrach, by an Irish officer, who confounds Jerome with Napoleon, and insists upon treating the broker as First Consul or Emperor, constitute the *fun* of the farce.

Mr. Searson was tried in two or three characters, and failed. Mr. Claude, the young man before mentioned, having persisted in going on the stage, and having made his debut at Baltimore, now tried George Barnwell with some success, on the 3d of January, 1804.

On the 26th of January, The Tournament and Wags of Windsor produced 218 dollars, and such was now the *run of the business.* A splendid show called "The Chains of the Heart," was got up and played on the 1st of February, 1804, to 597 dollars. In this piece Miss Dellinger made her first appearance. Its second night yielded $525; third night $265; fourth, $197.

On the 10th of February, the theatre was purchased at auction, by a company of gentlemen, principally, or altogether the original subscribers, for 43,000 dollars. The original plan was a subscription of 100 shares, at $375, making an amount of $37,500. Twenty more shares were added, and this also being consumed, money was borrowed to complete it—it never was completed. The cost is stated at $130,500, which with interest to the 1st of May, 1803, is stated as amounting to $193,792 90/100. The new proprietors appointed a committee to manage the property, with full powers to lease. The committee was composed of William Henderson, John C. Shaw, Daniel McCormick, John McVickar, and Joshua Waddington.

On the 21st of February, 1804, the manager brought out a new comedy called, "Conceit can Cure, Conceit can Kill." It was attended on its first representation, it being known as American, by a very thin audience. It was coldly received, until the two last acts, which, with the epilogue, were warmly applauded. This is the notice of one of the journals. "The plot contains considerable novelty of incident. It exhibits a picture of mountebank quackery, common in Europe, though little known in this country. The quack, with his attendant apparatus of stage and Jack Pudding, is introduced. The plot turns on the manœuvres of a couple of gentlemen who assume the above disguises; the object of one being to regain a wife; the other to obtain the hand of a mistress."

Those who saw the play had never seen the stage of a mountebank, but the author had witnessed the whole when a boy. Since the revolution, nothing of the kind has been attempted in this country.

The second night of the new comedy it was received with still greater applause.

During two weeks of severe cold and snow, the theatre was shut, and opened with another new comedy by the manager, called "Lewis of Monte Blanco, or the Transplanted Irishman." This from its coming so soon after "Conceit can Cure, Conceit can Kill," was not supposed to be the manager's, and was attended by the audience yielding him 523 dollars (double any receipts for some time back), and received with great applause. It was repeatedly played to increasing applause. In this play the author had written the principal character expressly for Harwood, in consequence of his success in Dennis Brulgruddery, and made an effort to produce an Irishman worthy of the representative of Colman's Dennis. It was, however, a military Irishman, and of course distinct in every respect, as well in manner as incident, from the preceding. The effort was in a great degree successful, as far as memory serves, for the author, by lending the manuscript copies (of which several were made), finally lost all traces of the play. Harwood's representation of this character was even satisfactory to its author.

On the 14th of March, the very popular farce of "Raising the Wind" was played for the first time. Diddler, Harwood; Sam, Hogg. June 8th, Fennell announced his last appearance on the stage.

After a variety of plans for selling or leasing the theatre, it was, on the 18th of June, again leased to the same director, at 100 dollars the week, with taxes, and ground-rent for the building then occupied as a scene-house in Theatre Alley.

After another *great house* to The Glory of Columbia, her Yeomanry, the theatre closed. During the latter part of the season, Signor Bologna was employed to bring out pantomimes and play clown.

Meanwhile the theatre in Philadelphia had been prosperously conducted by Messrs. Warren and Reinagle, to whom Mrs. Wignell transferred the direction, the management being in fact with Mr. Wood. The principal performers were Messrs. Wood, Warren, Francis, Jefferson, Twaits, Mrs. Wignell, and Mrs. Oldmixon. Mr. Twaits and Mr. Jefferson, so different and both so excellent, gave great strength to comedy and farce. Old Mr. Morris still continued to perform.

The Boston theatre was conducted prosperously by Mr. Powell. Mr. Chalmers was the principal male performer.

Mr. Green directed the theatres in Virginia.

Mr. Placide was the proprietor of the theatrical business of Charleston, S.C. Mr. Hodgkinson being the manager, and as actor, the support of it.

Early in August, the lessee of the New-York theatre met Mr. Hodgkinson, and agreed to a settlement of accounts, according to which Hodgkinson was to pay $282 22/100 in cash, and give bills payable at Charleston, in November, for $400. This was at least an acknowledgment that former assertions were false, and that a debt was due, but the creditor never received a cent of the promised sum. Mr.

Hodgkinson borrowed copies of manuscript plays for Charleston. He said he did not think of Charleston as a permanent situation, and hinted his desire to return to New-York as an actor.

On the 22d of September, P. Irving, Esq. wrote thus to the director of the New-York theatre. "Dear sir—I have just received a letter from Mr. Cooper, in which he apologizes for not having written to you, and in some degree accounts for the omission. He proposes a short visit in the course of the ensuing season. Enclosed is an abstract from his letter relative to that business."

Mr. Cooper made several distinct proposals, the first, as being that agreed to, is inserted. "To sail for New-York about the 10th of February, 1805, and to engage to play in New-York for 12 nights in four weeks. The terms—to divide the profits with the manager, after deducting from the receipts of each night the expenses of the house." "To receive a clear benefit on the 13th night. His expenses to America, and his return, to be borne by himself."

On the 22d of October, 1804, the theatre of New-York was opened with The Clandestine Marriage, and The Village Lawyer,—the theatre having been materially improved. The company consisted of Mr. and Mrs. Hallam, Mr. Harwood, Mr. and Mrs. Johnson, Mr. Tyler, Mr. and Mrs. Hogg, Mr. Martin, Mr. and Mrs. Claude (Miss Hogg that was), Mr. and Mrs. Harper, Mr. and Mrs. Darley, Mr. Darby, Mrs. Melmoth, and Messrs. Hallam, jun., Shapter, Robinson, M'Donald, &c.

Mr. Harwood had by this time shown that he was not sufficiently a man of business, and the stage direction was neglected. Mr. Martin was an assistant.

Mr. Darley gave great pleasure as a singer, and in many characters in comedy. His Frenchmen were approved, and his fine manly figure and face gave him a superiority to most who represented the second gentlemen of the drama. In opera he was the first and best the New-York theatre had known.

Mrs. Darley, so long a favourite as Miss E. Westray, resumed her station with undiminished charms in that line which she had first filled and shone in beyond any compeer, and was much improved in opera, and the loftier branches of her profession.

On the 29th of October, Mr. Huntington tried Macbeth. He had made the attempt in London, and failed. He had studied the part well, the stage business and situations were familiar to him, and were regulated at rehearsal according to his wishes. But his failure was complete. He was the first debutant that the writer knows of who was treated harshly by an audience in America, and he was far from deserving it, though far from being equal to the part of Macbeth.

We have mentioned the laugh which had nearly destroyed Mrs. Melmoth's Euphrasia, when she, in 1793, cried "strike here! here's blood enough," and drew the attention of the audience from the author of The Grecian Daughter to the actress's over bulk—she got over the laugh—but when as Lady Macbeth, she said of her husband's behaviour, as represented by Huntington, "the king grows worse and worse," a killing shout was the response of the audience, and little more of the play was heard.

On the 2d of November, a letter was received from Mr. Cooper apologizing for not having written during his long absence. He states that he had often wished to leave England, but that his mother and other friends were extremely averse to his again coming to America. He had now obtained leave of absence for a short period. He concludes thus, "I shall endeavour to get a new play or two for you, but I cannot promise any thing. As to actors I have not seen one in England that should arrive in America with the sanction of my recommendation, except only a comedian called Emery."

ANSWER—"I was at Perth Amboy when Irving communicated your propositions, and immediately wrote to him my agreement to the first, in full confidence of your wish to do justice towards me. I have opened my theatre without a man in tragedy superior to Martin; Fennell being engaged in Connecticut making salt."

Mr. Fennell's *nets* for catching salt will long be remembered by some of the inhabitants of New-London.

The manager brought out a translation from the French by himself, called, "The Wife of Two Husbands," and the English comedies of "The Will (in which Mrs. Darley gave great delight) and "Guilty or Not," but all to no purpose as it respected profit.

On the 14th of November, 1804, Mr. Thomas A. Cooper arrived, and his playing for 12 nights was immediately arranged. After which he was to go to Philadelphia, or Boston, or both, and then return to finish the season on salary. An attempt was made to induce Fennell to play with Cooper, but he refused.

As a record, we state the plays and the receipts during this engagement of Mr. Cooper's—Macbeth, $950; Jane Shore, 690; Hamlet, 1080; The Wheel of Fortune, 676; Richard the Third, 925; Lover's Vows, 532; The Merchant of Venice, 643 50/100; Hamlet (2d time), 681; First part of Henry the Fourth (supported by a new pantomime called Black Beard), 819; Macbeth (2d time), 487; Pizarro, 770; Henry the Fifth (the tragedian's benefit), 883. Two additional performances were agreed to, and yielded, the first, Romeo and Juliet, 440, and the second, Othello, 558.

La Bottier, a dancer, was engaged to get up ballets—but from the departure of Mr. Cooper, the theatre sunk, irretrievably. The apparent success during his short engagement, and real receipts, made creditors pressing and impatient. After a struggle of years against the effects of the yellow fever, and all those curses belonging to the interior of an establishment, badly organized when he found it, the manager's health yielded to disappointment and incessant exertion, and his struggles became proportionably fainter.

On the first of January, 1805, he writes, "Oppressed with disease and debt, I commence another year of my life with sentiments of gloom and self-disapprobation. After the present week I must close the theatre for two weeks, to wait the return of Mr. Cooper, who is now playing in Philadelphia."

On the 4th of January, the theatre was closed, and re-opened on the 1st of February. Mr. Cooper played a few nights, but the attraction of novelty was gone, and on the 22d of February, the theatre was finally closed, and the management of the man who had sacrificed his health and property in the pursuit of that which eluded his grasp, ceased. He gave up his property of every kind. He had found the theatre unfinished outside and in—he left the interior finished and beautified—it was almost void of scenery, and totally so of wardrobe, and all other property—he left it amply furnished; and the performers under the direction of Messrs. Johnson and Tyler, opened it in the following March, with the use of his property, and all the manuscripts of the retreating author.

Fortunately, the late manager had the house of his mother in the place of his nativity to shelter him and his family; and though utterly destitute of property, he had the friendship of all those who had, previous to this voyage and wreck, been his associates. Being no longer connected with the theatre, he is no longer a subject for this work for the present.

⤜ CHAPTER 30 ⤛

1805 — Mr. Twaits — Twaits and Cooper — Captain Smith — Boston Theatre — Boston — Death of Mr. Hodgkinson — Philadelphia Company — Mr. Cain — Lessons on Intemperance — New-York Theatre under Johnson and Tyler — Miss Ross — Mrs. Wheatley — Mrs. Jones — Mr. and Mrs. Young — Mr. Fennell a star — Play of The Wanderer — Tars from Tripoli — Manhattan Stage — New-York Theatre leased to Mr. Cooper — Mr. Robinson — Mr. Jones — Mr. and Mrs. Johnson's return to Europe.

The theatre of New-York was now under the direction of Messrs. Johnson and Tyler, who demanded for their services as managers 50 dollars per week, in addition to their salaries as players. The republic of actors, for such it now was, agreed to give them 10. Mr. Ciceri was in fact their principal man of business.

Mr. Cooper went on to Boston, and was opposed by the company then about to take benefits. The citizens wished his performances, there was considerable discontent in the theatre, but he played his usual round of characters.

At Baltimore, a tragedy was printed this year called "Blow for Blow."

On the 21st of June, Mr. Cooper having arrived in New-York, and Mr. Twaits, of the Philadelphia theatre, being in the city, the late manager took a benefit-night, they playing for him, the first Zanga, the second Caleb Quotem. Nothing but Mr. Cooper's offer of performing on the occasion, which he made by letter from Boston, could have justified trying a night after the benefits of the actors, and in the heat of summer; the receipt was 600 dollars. Mrs. Villiers, late Miss E. A. Westray, played on this occasion Leonora, in The Revenge.

As this was the first appearance of Mr. Twaits on the stage of New-York, we will briefly notice his person, his peculiarities, and the characters in which he excelled, among which Caleb Quotem stood very prominent.

Mr. William Twaits was born on the 25th of April, 1781. His father died when he was very young, and he obtained admittance behind the scenes of Drury Lane, through the influence of a play-mate, the son of Phillemore, one of the performers. Having determined to be an actor, he stuck to the point, as Coleman says, "like a rusty weather-cock," and we suppose, like most of our heroes, ran away. He commenced acting at a place called Waltham Abbey.

We have mentioned that he was brought out to this country by Mr. Wood, for the company of Philadelphia. That gentleman found him at Birmingham in "old Macready's company," where, and at Sheffield he was a favourite, "particularly," says Mr. Wood, "being considered one of the best burletta singers in England. He came out on a salary of four guineas a week for three years, but soon after his arrival it was advanced to six. He was an admirable *opposite* to Jefferson, their styles being so very different." The same may be said of him and Harwood afterwards. Indeed, neither his style of playing, nor his face or person was like any other individual on or off the stage. Short and thin, yet appearing broad; muscular, yet meagre; a large head, with stiff, stubborn, carroty hair; long colourless face, prominent hooked nose, projecting large hazel eyes, thin lips, and large mouth, which could be twisted into a variety of expression, and which, combining with his other features, eminently served the purposes of the comic muse. Such was the physiognomy of William Twaits. Yet Twaits seriously thought that his features were fitted for tragedy, and that he only wanted height to be like John Kemble. Did Mr. Twaits want common sense? Far, far from it. He had good natural mental powers, which he cultivated occasionally by reading, but he was quite young, and his early education, none. His passions were strong, and had never been disciplined or controlled. He had probably been *his own master* and adviser from childhood, and was at this time a very young man. Besides, he was encouraged in thinking himself a tragedian, as he had been the Richard and Romeo of many a barn, when he had the promise of the highest salary in the company, nine shillings per week, and was obliged to be content with two-and-sixpence; when he feasted upon a hog's heart and vegetables (cost ninepence, baking a penny) for a week; when he was the best-dressed man in the theatre, owing to his making one clean shirt serve for two nights' playing. He had played every thing, but he was only fitted for comedy—and for that he was eminently fitted.

His voice was powerful, yet he was asthmatic; and his great powers of song, and *queer* humour, made him as great a favourite with convivialists as with the lovers of comedy. This, with the frequent exertions of his lungs in public and private, ultimately changed asthma into consumption, and he died at the age of twenty-six or under, wasted to a skeleton, a melancholy instance of youth misguided by passion and devoid of a counsellor.

Cooper being at Philadelphia when Twaits's engagement ended, and having become attached to the amusing comedian, induced him to go on to Boston, where the tragedian had an engagement. A greater contrast cannot well be conceived than that between these two, either in person or manners. The tragedian felt that he was by birth, education, and profession, a gentleman; and always in society asserted his claims in the strongest and firmest manner. Twaits had smaller pretensions, at least from education. When the companions, after a successful campaign at the Boston theatre, returned to New-York, Twaits used to tell *these,* and other anecdotes, for the purpose of playfully annoying Cooper.

"As we were returning from Boston, our style of travelling made the folks stare. Our carriage, and servant, and trunks, seemed particularly to excite the curiosity of the landlord at an inn where we stopped to breakfast; and he saw that Tom was a great man at once. I was only the great man's companion, and he took an opportunity to inquire who this might be. 'It's the great Mr. Cooper,' said I, 'going on from Boston to New-York.' 'What, a congress-man?' 'No, you must have heard of him—the play-actor.' 'Play-actor!—oh, oh! Tumbling—rope dancing—oh, ho!'

"All the landlord's awe of the traveller was gone, but his curiosity yet more fully alive, and he walked into the room which Cooper had taken possession of to await breakfast, and seated himself to gaze his fill. I followed, and soon after in ran a rough little urchin, and placed himself between his father's knees, who patting his white head and looking at Cooper, says, 'Sonny, that's Mr. Cooper, my dear—won't you go to New-York with Mr. Cooper?' 'For what, daddy?' 'Why he'll make an actor of you.' 'What's that, daddy?' 'Oh, he'll learn you to dance the rope, turn over head and heels, and play all kinds of tricks.'"

"Another time," said Twaits, "we had been dining with Andrew Allen, and he took us out to see a new house he was then erecting. Allen entered the unfinished building by a single plank, and invited us to follow. Tom hesitated. 'Come on, Cooper,' cries Allen. 'What,' says Cooper, 'do you bring us here to make us walk the plank?' One of the carpenters who looked on and was standing near Tom, says to him, 'That's a good one, Mr. Cooper, you can't walk that plank? Haven't I seen you walk the rope many a time in the play-house at New-York?'"

These stories Cooper took in good part; but, an opportunity offering for retaliation on "Billy," it was seized, and a piece of mischief commenced by Cooper and his companions, introduced by an accidental circumstance, and continued beyond any calculation of the contrivers, took all the comedian's sportiveness away for the time.

Shortly after Twaits's marriage, he one evening was standing in the gallery, looking at Mrs. Twaits's performance of a character in tragedy, when he heard two men near him make some vulgar remarks upon the actress. The husband felt indignant, and addressing the principal speaker, told him that the lady was his wife, and that he would chastise any scoundrel who used such language in respect to her. The fellow was a vulgar blackguard, probably drunk, and with his companion sneaked away. All this might have been very well, but during his excitement the comedian came into the green-room, and before Cooper and others, related the affair with some degree of swagger. The opportunity was not to be lost for retaliation, and next day Mr. Twaits received a letter requiring apology for the harsh language made use of on the preceding evening, and notifying him that the writer would expect to see him at a certain hour at the Albany coffee-house. This was signed John Smith. As was expected by the conspirators, Twaits carried this letter to Cooper, who being *au fait* in all the punctilios of the duello, told him that he must meet Mr. Smith. "But I will not apologize to the rascal." "Certainly not, he must apologize to you, or give you satisfaction." "Damn the fellow—I don't want to have any thing more to do with him." "You called him a ———." "I called him a scoundrel." "You must see him." "You will go with me, Tom?" "Certainly, if you put the affair into my hands." "I don't want to have any thing to do with the blackguard." "You see by this letter that it is a gentleman, and you must go through with it."

To the great delight of the conspirators, the comedian was tortured until the time appointed came, and with dauntless resolution, attended by his friend, he stalked to the Albany coffee-house, and inquired for Mr. Smith. There was no Mr. Smith there. They waited a due time. No John Smith appeared, and the comedian, breathing more freely, was escorted home by the witness of his courage.

The bar-keeper had said, in answer to queries respecting Mr. Smith, that one Captain Smith sometimes came there. This was a cue for further mischief. Poor Twaits had his dinner marred by receiving a letter with the Philadelphia postmark, apologizing for John Smith's not meeting him at the Albany coffee-house, he being under the necessity of going to Philadelphia to prepare his ship for a voyage to Europe, but would return to New-York, and require of Mr. Twaits an ample apology. Cooper was to decide on this, and an answer of polite defiance was dictated by him, and written by Twaits, and delivered to the incendiary. In due time the reply of Mr. Smith arrived from Philadelphia—he would be in New-York on such a day. Mr. Simkins, or Jenkins, his friend, would see Mr. Twaits's friend to arrange a meeting. "Damn the fellow, I don't want to have any thing to do with him—ha, Tom?" "You have put the affair in my hands." "Oh—yes—" "Very well, I will see Mr. Jenkins." "Do you know him?" "Yes—he's a gentleman—there will be no difficulty in arranging a meeting—have you pistols, Billy?" "No—pistols—no." "Mine are at your service."

The conspirators now found a person to represent Mr. Jenkins, and Twaits was a witness to a formal and very courteous interchange of civilities between his friend Tom and the friend of the imaginary Captain Smith, in Broadway, and was told that the result was an appointment next morning at Hoboken.

Thus was this young man tortured day after day. It was like the fable of the boys and frogs. No excuse can be offered for such a hoax—certainly the contrivers did not at first intend to inflict the misery which was the inevitable effect of their unjustifiable prosecution of their joke.

Instead of the meeting, however, another letter came informing the parties that Captain Smith had been obliged to sail with his ship to the Mediterranean. Captain Smith was pronounced a poltroon, and even *his friend* Mr. Jenkins gave him up.

The conspirators had been so much amused by this plot, and the odd effects produced upon their companion, that they renewed it at a period when Captain Smith might be supposed to have returned from Europe. He was made to write from Philadelphia, lamenting his former want of punctuality, and again calling upon Twaits for the meeting. It was, however, determined that his previous conduct had put him out of the pale of honour; though neither killed nor wounded, he was "*hors de combat,*" and the meeting denied. He was now brought to New-York by the same process which had brought him into existence, and made to threaten personal chastisement. The comedian was obliged by his tormentors to buy pocket pistols, and go armed against this phantom raised to haunt him.

It is supposed that Twaits never had this hoax explained to him. It had been carried to so great a length that the contrivers did not dare to undeceive him. He probably had a misgiving—but inquiry was both mortifying and dangerous—and Captain Smith and his antagonist were soon, both equally creatures of mere memory.

Mrs. Wignell and Mr. Cooper played together in the latter part of June and beginning of July at the Park theatre, New-York. She performing Calista, Monimia, Juliet, Ophelia, Elvira, and Roxana—he Lothario, Chamont, Romeo, Hamlet, Rolla, and Alexander. He afterwards played Octavian for Twaits's benefit. The theatre was closed on the 10th of July with Speed the Plough, and The Children in the Wood.

Mr. Hodgkinson applied for, and obtained the promise of the theatre. He had, as has been mentioned, played at Charleston, S.C. under Mr. Placide. He opened there in Osmond, and played all his best characters, except Captain Erlach, which, as False Shame had not been published, he could not do. Captain Bertram, in Fraternal Discord, he played—but his friend Carpenter calls the play an English comedy from the German. Mrs. Whitlock was the heroine of the Charleston company at that time.

In the autumn of 1805, the Boston theatre was successfully directed by Mr. S. Powell and Mr. Dickson. The principal performers were Mr. Cooper, Mr. Twaits, Mr. and Mrs. Powell, Mr. and Mrs. Dickson, Mr. and Mrs. Darley, Mr. Usher, Mrs. Shaw, Mr. and Mrs. Young, and Mr. Bernard.

The writer passed the months of September and October of the year 1805 in Boston, and witnessed the performances of the Federal-street theatre, frequently. He remembers with pleasure Bernard's old-school Doricourt, and Mrs. Darley's pleasing Letitia Hardy. Mr. Dickson was the Hardy; Twaits the Flutter. Of "Douglas" and "The Turnpike Gate," he remembers Mrs. Shaw's Lady Randolph as respectable, and Mr. Young's Glenalvon as very poor. Mr. Usher more than respectable in Old Norval, and Cooper uncommonly fine in Douglas. Twaits's *Crack* was excellent. Of "John Bull," he remembers the inferiority of Bernard's Dennis, when compared to Harwood's, and the excellence of Twaits's *Dan*. He remembers Young being substituted for Cooper (who was unwell), in Octavian, and received with applause, most undeserved. He remembers the pleasant comedy of the "Heir at Law," and "Inkle and Yarico" played to empty benches. Little more of Boston theatricals can be recorded as appertaining to this time, from frail and imperfect memory.

Col. David Humphreys then resided in Boston, and to his polite attentions the writer owed many pleasant hours. He communicated the manuscript of a comedy for his opinion. The piece was not calculated to add to Col. Humphreys's literary reputation.

The writer's first visit to Boston was in 1791, and again in 1796; this of 1805 was the third. In 1813 he passed some weeks there, and again in 1822. His note on the town of Boston in 1805 may be interesting to those who now see it a splendid city in 1832.

"On my first visit to this town, I received many civilities from Rev. Jedediah Morse, Dr. Lloyd, Mr. Blagg, Sheriff Allen, and Judge Lowell. Mr. Samuel Cooper was particularly attentive to me. All is changed. With the last-mentioned gentleman I remember a ride to a bowling-green, where I first saw John Quincy Adams, and was introduced to him. A very dissimilar person was among the *bowlers.* "That," said Cooper, "is ————, a fellow half knave, half idiot, who has made a fortune by speculations which have thrown money into his pocket as fools are sometimes enriched by a lottery ticket." The man was seated, and looking at the *players* with lack-lustre eye, but rising, displayed a thin meager figure dressed in vulgar finery, his round unmeaning face rendered more so by a flaxen tie-wig—when he spoke, his voice would suddenly break from something like manly bass to "childish treble," and *piped* and *whistled* most ludicrously. "I lost my voice," he said or attempted to say, "by eating too many oysters—Oh, how sick I was!"—I was introduced to him as from New-York. "Maybe the gentleman deals in paper—I just sold ten thousand dollars—strange how I manage it—ha! Don't know a figure—do it here (pointing to his head), reckon all here— I always thought I should be rich—there's the house at ————, and the farm at ————, and the house at ————, and ten thousand pounds in the bank—not to mention any thing of the lands in Ohio." "But," said Samuel Cooper, "when you bought your house from Chester, didn't he offer you his commission?" "Yes, his justice's commission for last year—s'pose he thought I would think it like a British officer's commission—thought I was a fool—great many people think so—I'll tell you how I served him. Says I, Mr. Chester, says I—I never make two words to a bargain—what I offered you for your house, says I, that I gave you— but I must have time to consider of it." So he went away. By-and-by he comes again. "Well," says he, "what will you give for my commission?" "Says I, Mr. Chester, says I—I never make many words to a bargain—what I say I'll give, I'll give, and no more. Now here's what I think its worth, says I,—and I put my hand in my pocket so—no—this pocket—no—why where?—I've lost—no! Here it is. Here, says I, is the worth of it—and I twisted off a quid of tobacco—so—that's the worth of the commission! He told afterward ————'s no fool, says he; never found a tighter fellow to make a bargain."

The town of Boston is built upon a peninsula, which projects from the main land and points north. It is connected with Roxbury by an isthmus. It is situated at the bottom of Massachusetts Bay, which to the west of the town is called Charles river. The deep indentations in its margin make the shape of the peninsula very irregular, and the streets, owing to this shape and the hilly surface, are equally so. The north part of the town, called "North End," and the parts adjacent, form the original town of Boston. There took place those important transactions on which the fate of America hung. The more recent town extends southward and westward, and will be in a short time joined to the village of Roxbury. Part of the new town is on high ground, surrounding a superb new state-house, which is on the loftiest eminence, only overtopped by its immediate neighbour, the apex of Beacon hill. Here the houses are spacious and elegant. In 1790, the population was estimated at 18,000, now (1805), 36,000. The greatest length of the town is two miles, its greatest width one mile and 417 feet. It is generally pretty well paved, and there is a sufficient number of lamps which are without oil six months in the year. In the winter they are permitted to give light to the night wanderer—in summer he must find his way without. The increase of population which follows successful commerce will occasion encroachments on the bay—already the ground is prepared for a new street to be called Broad-street, on the east of the town; and the hill called Mount Vernon is rapidly descending into the waters on the west. The harbour of Boston is very beautiful, and is studded with islands—though I think there is not point from which it can be viewed, that gives a view equal to that we have of the harbour of New-York from the Battery. From the bridge to Dorchester, yet unfinished, the view of Boston is very fine. The eye takes in the Neck, part of the harbour and shipping, the south part of the town, and the west town towering over it; the whole crowned by the statehouse, which from its situation is seen with its foundations apparently resting upon the tops of the houses, and looks like the dome of an immense building, whose body is hid by the surrounding trees and edifices.

So Boston appeared to the stranger in 1791, who was equally delighted by the surrounding country and villages. He has seen it since in its progressive improvement up to 1822. Ten years have doubtless added to its magnitude and splendour.

The yellow fever appeared again in New-York early in the autumn of 1805, and Mr. Hodgkinson having made an engagement for the city of Washington, left the first-named place without having made arrangements for the ensuing season, or even taking possession of the theatre—he went on to Philadelphia, as his friend Carpenter, in The Mirror of Taste, states, and staid four days with one of "his most zealous friends, Mr. Richard Potter, the merchant, elate with the good fortune that awaited him, and delighting his friends with his conversation, his anecdote, and song." He proceeded, after this four days' residence at Philadelphia, to Baltimore, and one of his companions told the writer that he passed the day at the Point, opposite the city, on a party of pleasure, crossing at midnight in an open boat much heated. The weather was warm, and he threw off his coat and crossed the water without it. Between Baltimore and Washington, Carpenter states that he stopped at a place called ——— Ferry, and went out shooting—"returned overheated, and wet with profuse perspiration," borrowed clothes of the landlord and "sat down to table," and "spent the time in jollity and song till night came on." Then put on his shirt which had been hanging in the open air till the heavy dew of the evening "saturated it"—fever followed, and being unable to go on with the stage, he stopped on the evening of Sunday, the 8th (of September, 1805), at an inn within 12 miles of Washington. On the arrival of the stage at Washington without him, Greene the manager and Harwood, "set off to meet him, and on Monday morning they arrived" at Stelle's tavern, where he died on the succeeding Thursday (the 12th of September), between 12 and 1 o'clock in the morning. This is Carpenter's account, and this is called dying of yellow fever taken at New-York.

The news of yellow fever being in New-York had reached Washington. Hodgkinson had come from New-York,—and Harwood told the writer that Greene and himself hearing from the stage driver (they being on the look-out for Hodgkinson), that a man answering to his description was left behind sick, took a carriage and went on to him. The next morning he was better, and returned with them to Washington, where at the hotel, they put him under the care of a physician, and left him. They did not see him again until the keeper sent word that he was worse. They went to the hotel, and were told that he was dying of yellow fever. Previous to entering his room, they "peeped in and saw him in agonies with his head hanging over the bed-side, and by him a negro girl." They entered, and remained in the room until he died. "He was in continual agitation, from pain and excessive terror of death, and presented the most horrid spectacle that the mind can imagine; he was, as soon as dead, wrapped in a blanket, and carried to the burying field by some negroes." There the body lay until Greene and Harwood had it put in a coffin and interred. Such is the account given to the writer by John E. Harwood, at Philadelphia, on the 22d of December, 1805, not three months after the event, and then minuted.

"His remains were wrapped up in a blanket by negroes," says Carpenter, "who were induced by a considerable reward to perform the office, and conveyed to an obscure burying-ground, on the Baltimore road, where they were left entirely unattended till a shell of a coffin was made, and a grave hastily dug into which he was thrown."

At this time, September, 1805, the Boston theatre was under the management of Mr. S. Powell. The company consisted of Mr. Cooper, Mr. Twaits, Mr. Bernard, Mr. and Mrs. Darley, Mrs. Powell, Mrs. Darby, and Messrs. Usher, Kenny, Fox, and Mr. Young. The writer had an opportunity of seeing Bernard's Dennis Brulgruddery, and Twaits's Dan together. The last by far the best. Mrs. Darley was Mary Thornberry herself.

In the winter of 1805–6, the theatre at Philadelphia was well conducted. The prominent performers were Warren, Wood, Jefferson, Francis, Morris, Harwood, Cain, Woodham; Mesdames Wignell, Jefferson, Wood, Woodham, Francis, Morris, Melmoth. Of these only three are new to this work. Mr. Woodham was a singer of merit. Mrs. Woodham played comedy and romps. She was a pretty woman, but not as an actress to be placed in the first rank.

In December, Harwood played for the first time in six years in that city.

Mr. Cain, for some time considered the rival of Mr. Wood in Philadelphia, was born at Deptford, near London, but was educated in the neighbourhood of Burlington, New-Jersey, and generally considered an American candidate for fame; while Wood, an American, was thought a foreigner. Mr. Cain was young, handsome, with "health, a remarkably juvenile appearance, fine voice, and ability; advantages," says Mr. Wood, "which nothing but the actor's *bane*, brandy, could have deprived him of." He was idle—the last is the inevitable consequence of the first.

To publish a list of the victims to brandy or intemperance who have fallen under the writer's view, and were among the professors of the histrionic art, would at first glance appear as a libel on the theatre. But if examined in connexion with the list the same writer could present, of those who had fewer seductive inducements, and stronger incitements to virtuous conduct, and yet have fallen, the melancholy truth would appear that, throughout society in England and America, the indulgence in drunkenness—let the vile thing have its vile name—has been frightful. May the blessings of mankind and the reward of well-doing rest on those who have rendered the vice as infamous as it is loathsome and destructive.

Has the theatre done its part, as a school of morality, to check this evil? No. It has been represented in plays as a venial vice—the drunkard has been a theme for laughter, but not an object of detestation. The consequence of drunkenness has only been (as we now remember) shown in its true light by one dramatist— and that the greatest—yet his lessons have not been strong enough for the subject. In the American play of "The Italian Father," it is true we have moral lessons on sobriety and temperance; but the scenes of riot at which the thoughtless laugh, remain indelible, while the strains of wisdom, even from Shakespeare's mouth, are forgotten. How few remember,

> —"He that doth the ravens feed,
> Yea, providently caters for the sparrow,
> Be comfort to my age!"—"Let me be your servant;
> Though I look old, yet I am strong and lusty:
> For in my youth I never did apply
> Hot and rebellious liquors in my blood;
> Nor did with unbashful forehead woo
> The means of weakness and debility;
> Therefore my age is as a lusty winter,
> Frosty, but kindly:"

or,—

> "What, are you hurt, lieutenant?"
> "*Cassio.* Ay, past all surgery."—"Reputation, reputation, reputation! I have
> lost my reputation. I have lost the immortal part, sir, of myself, and what re-

mains is bestial."—"Drunk? and speak parrot? and squabble? swagger? swear? and discourse fustian with one's shadow? O thou invisible spirit of wine, if thou hast no name to be known by, let us call thee—devil!"—"O that men should put an enemy in their mouths to steal away their brains! That we should with joy, revel, pleasure, and applause, transform ourselves into beasts."—"To be now a sensible man, by-and-by a fool, and presently a beast! O, strange!— every inordinate cup is unblessed, and the ingredient is a devil."

What can be finer, what more true than this?—but the million, we fear, are more apt to remember Iago's words than Cassio's. Locke tells us the story of the two parrots—one had learned to bully and blaspheme, and the other to repeat the words of wisdom. They were placed together in the hope of reforming the noisy blackguard—but noise prevailed, and both became bullies. May not some dramatist show the misery resulting from the beastly vice of drunkenness, not only to the wretched individual himself, but to parents and relatives, to the wife and the child? Or would the fastidious turn from the scene? or the jovial fellow hiss it? We believe, if made the theme of true genius, the lesson would be received from the stage, and aid the efforts which the friends of humanity are making to banish from society the most debasing and irrational of all the many sources of human misery.

The company of Messrs. Johnson and Tyler consisted of Mr. and Mrs. Johnson, Mr. Tyler, Mr. and Mrs. Barrett, Mr. and Mrs. Hallam, Mr. Martin, Mr. Hogg, Messrs. Hallam, jun., Saubere, Shapter, Sanderson, and Allen; Mesdames Jones, Simpson, Villiers, G. Marshall; and Misses White, Dellinger, Ross, and Graham.

The house was opened on the 18th of November, 1805, with Abælino and the Adopted Child, to a receipt of $800. Mr. Barrett playing Abælino, in which he had been eminently successful in Boston.

Miss Ross, so well known since and so justly admired as Mrs. Wheatley, made her first appearance as Kitty Sprightly, and evinced a dawning of talent. Mrs. Wheatley has long been one of the best performers on the American stage. She was born at St. Johns, Nova Scotia, in the year 1790. Her parents were Scotch. Her father was Lieutenant Ross, of the 42d regiment. He died when Miss Ross was two years of age, and her mother returned to New-York, the place of her marriage, and of course the infant with her. From that time it was the place of her residence. Miss Ross made her debut on the 12th of November, 1805. Mrs. Johnson saw her *promise*, and gave her instruction. She married Mr. Wheatley in 1806, and withdrew from the stage, until her husband failing in business, she returned to it again for the support of her family. Success has crowned her industry and talents, and she has long been one of the ornaments of the New-York theatre. She first exerted herself in this arduous profession for the support of her mother, and afterwards for the maintenance and education of her children. Her reward is an approving conscience, competency, and the esteem of all who know her. For several seasons her talents were not appreciated, perhaps not discovered.

Mrs. Jones was the great attraction of this season. She was announced as from the Theatre Royal, Haymarket, London, and late of the Boston theatre, where she had been a very great favourite. Her first appearance in New-York was on the 27th of November, as Albina, in The Will, and Leonora, in The Padlock. This lady's acting and singing were much approved. Her figure was petite, and face pleasing. She died on the 11th of November, 1806. She was the sister of those distinguished actors, the Messrs. Wallacks, and has left to the society of America a valuable member in the wife of Mr. Simpson, the manager (1832) of the Park theatre.

On the 9th of December, "The Voice of Nature" and "The Children in the Wood" were performed for the benefit of the orphan children of Mr. Hodgkinson. Fennell played Rinaldo in the first, and the little girls the children in the afterpiece.

On the 23d of December, Mr. and Mrs. Young, from Norwich, England, and from the Boston theatre, appeared in Octavian and Agnes, in The Mountaineers. Mrs. Young was young and beautiful, and her Agnes pleasing.

In January, 1806, Mr. Fennell became a star, and played Hamlet, Penruddock, Lord Hastings, Othello, Jaffier, Macbeth, and Richard. The last at his benefit.

Several candidates for stage honours appeared and disappeared, and one attempt was made by "a young gentleman of New-York" as a dramatist, probably thinking the way cleared by the removal of the monopolizing manager-author. "The Wanderer" was performed, condemned, and being, before condemnation, announced for repetition, another play was substituted.

"Tars from Tripoli," an alteration from Dibdin's "Naval Pillar," was played several times. Mr. Turnbull took a benefit as the author. For the sentiments of a distinguished man on such productions, we refer to our sixteenth chapter.

On the 3d of March, Mr. Cooper commenced playing in New-York on an engagement for five nights. Hamlet, Richard, Lord Hastings, Macbeth, and Leon, in Rule a Wife and Have a Wife. In this character he has been very successful. He played Beverly for his benefit, and repeated it for the benefit of the managers. On the 17th of March, Mr. Jefferson came from Philadelphia to play on the stage of his former fame, and performed Jacob Gawky, Diddler, Bobby Pendragon, Doctor Lenitive, Toby Allspice, and Ralph in Lock and Key. On the 9th of April, Mr. Harwood returned to New-York for the remainder of the season, opening in Dennis Brulgruddery.

In April, Williams, alias Anthony Pasquin, produced a piece, called "The Manhattan Stage," which was damned. Huggins, the hair-dresser, published a formal notification that he was not the author.

As this wretched man, by bringing forward his wretched play in New-York, is entitled to our notice, we will quote a few lines from Bernard's Reminiscences respecting him. "He wore his conscience in his pocket, and wore them both out together. Money was his only principle; and he fitted praise to the backs of ministers or actors as he would have done a coat, agreeably to price and order. Passing over this unpleasant ground of notoriety (which made its object walk continually between the two fires of horsewhip and pillory), in his person he presented a greater. Daniel Dancer himself was a clean and decent individual compared to Anthony Pasquin. He seemed to have a passion for dirt" (his ideas were as dirty as his clothes); "he always looked as if he had just been expelled from a poor-house or a prison."

We have before had occasion to notice the offer made by this individual to officiate as the manager's salaried *puff.* Yet this man's writings—a man who was characterized from the bench of one of the high courts of justice in his own country as *one* "whose praise was infamy, and touch pollution"—are gravely quoted as authority by an author of the same name, who has recently published two elegantly printed and valuable volumes, giving "The Life of sir Thomas Lawrence." The accuracy of this work in most respects cannot be doubted; in that which concerns America, however, it may be judged of by the following extract.

After stating that the American Academy of Fine Arts sent Lawrence a diploma certifying that he had been chosen an honorary member, he goes on to say: "In appreciation of this honour, Sir Thomas Lawrence immediately painted for the Academy a full-length likeness of Mr. West, the president of the English Academy, and, as it is well known, a native of America."

Now as we know that this is a fable, without wishing to deprive the eminent painter of any credit justly his due, we state that he did not make any present whatever in return for "this honour." On the contrary, he being applied to in the way of business to paint the portrait of Mr. West for New-York, and West consenting to sit, Lawrence fixed his price at two thousand dollars, which sum was raised by the subscription of lawyers, painters, physicians, and merchants, at one hundred dollars each, and remitted to the painter. The portrait was deposited with the Academy, and is one of the finest specimens of the art from the pencil of this eminent man. But it was ordered and paid for. As we constituted a part of the directory of the American Academy, we speak, not fearing contradiction. To Sir Thomas Lawrence, the artists of America owe pleasure and instruction; his works are their delight and their study; they admire him as a painter and as a man; but the Academy of the country received no particular favours from him.

To revert to the drama. About the time to which we have brought down our annals, Mr. John K. Beekman made an arrangement with Mr. Thomas A. Cooper, by which Beekman was to become proprietor, and Cooper lessee of the New-York theatre. Fifteen thousand dollars were to be appropriated to altering the building, and more if required. Mr. J. J. Holland was employed as the architect. The writer was engaged, at a liberal yearly income, to take a general superintendence of the business.

After making these arrangements, Mr. Cooper went on to Charleston, S.C., to repeat his list of characters, and Mr. Twaits made his appearance in Richard the Third!

In May, Mr. Barrett, the present very excellent performer in genteel comedy, played as Master Barrett for the benefit of his parents. He enacted Young Norval twice, on the 5th and on the 23d of May. In more advanced years, he very judiciously bade adieu to Melpomene.

The conduct of the Hallams, which has been a sore annoyance under the former management, now became so insupportable, that Messrs. Johnson and Tyler were obliged to dismiss Mr. Hallam, jun., for a brutal attempt to assault Mr. Tyler, made in presence of the elder Hallam, and only prevented by the interference of several performers, the outrage being attempted at the time the performance of a play was going forward. For this act of self-defence, the dismissal of Hallam, jun., Johnson and Tyler were arraigned in one of the public prints; and in their defence, they stated the conduct of father and son, and that "the eldest Mr. Hallam receives $60 weekly for such services as he can render in his infirmities."

Mr. Hopkins Robinson, who has the merit of having raised himself from the tailor's shopboard to the stage of the theatre, at this time filled respectably many parts of the drama.

In January, 1806, Master John Howard Payne, afterwards to be noticed as a performer and dramatist, commenced a publication, entitled "The Thespian Mirror," which was discontinued on the 18th of March. He was then under 14 years of age.

Mr. Jones died at Charleston, S.C., on the 7th of August, 1806. Mr. Jones possessed a good person, and talents for serious speaking of more than common magnitude. It will be remembered that a low comedian of the same name died at the same place many years before; i.e. in 1797.

Mr. and Mrs. Johnson did not engage with Mr. Cooper, but returned once more to England.

Mr. Holland being engaged at Philadelphia, and Mr. Ciceri not agreeing to Mr. Cooper's proposals, and going to France, the theatre was for a time without an architect or scene painter.

⤖ CHAPTER 31 ⤔

Philadelphia Company in 1806 — Mr. Cooper opens the New-York Theatre — Company — Mr. Morse — Mr. Cooper's second Season of Management — Theatre remodelled — Boston Theatre — New-York Theatre under Cooper and Price — Mr. Twaits's Prince of Wales — Death of Mr. Hallam — Theatre in Lexington, Kentucky — Death of Mrs. Warren — Master Payne's first Appearance — Comedy of "Man and Wife" — "The Duke of Buckingham" — Mr. and Mrs. Duff.

In the year 1806, the Philadelphia company was composed of Messrs. Wood, M'Kenzie, Warren, Mills, Webster, Woodham, Cone, Cross, Cain, Francis, Robins, Sanderson, Blissett, Bailey, Jefferson, Taylor, Durang, Bray, and Seymour; Mesdames Melmoth, Woodham, Wood, Warren (late Wignell), Francis, Seymour, Morris, Jefferson, Cunningham, Mills, and Miss Hunt.

On the 6th of October, 1806, the theatre of New-York was opened under the direction of Thomas A. Cooper, Esq. The company engaged were Messrs. Tyler, Harwood, Twaits, Hogg, Darley, Martin, Hallam, jun., Saubere, Fennell, Shapter, and Rutherford; Mesdames Villiers, Darley, Simpson, Oldmixon, and Miss Dellinger.

Mrs. Placide, the second wife of the Charleston (S.C.) manager, and daughter to Mrs. Pownall (once Wrighten), played two or three times successfully.

On the 28th of November, Mr. Morse made his first appearance on the stage in Pierre,—Cooper, his instructer, playing Jaffier. He succeeded so far that the play was repeated, and Mr. Morse continued in the company. This gentleman, the son of a Massachusetts yeoman, had been destined by his father for the law, and educated accordingly; but he travelled out of the record, and preferred a life of dissipation and adventure to the dull routine of duty, or the study of Coke upon Lyttleton: and a life of adventure he had. After playing under Cooper in various theatrical establishments, he was for a time the hero of the Boston company. He possessed a towering figure, more than six feet in height, a face rather round for a hero, limbs muscular and well formed, particularly the legs, which were a beautiful compound of the Hercules and Apollo; his voice was good, and his judgment of his author tolerable. His early associates had not been of the most polished kind, and consequently he lacked the ease of a gentleman at the time of his debut. With such talents and such a person, he determined to try London, and did so with some success; but in that vast metropolis the handsome Yankee's head was turned, and he was all but lost in unbridled dissipation. He returned to Boston little more than a skeleton, and with entire loss of the sight of an eye. He so far regained his health, that on the breaking out of the second war with England, he entered the army, and served in Macomb's regiment. At the close of the war, he was destitute; but he told a good story, and that recommended him for what a chaplain *then was* on board one of our famous frigates. He went one or more cruises in this capacity, and had leisure to reflect on his follies and his consequent sufferings: his health had been fully re-established; and he, with a grateful heart, determined to devote himself to the service of God and the instruction of his fellow-men, as a minister of the Episcopal Church. During his preparatory studies, he became a real chaplain to the frigate in which he had taken this salutary resolution from reflection and conviction.

In the year 1819, a gentleman who had known Mr. Morse in 1806, and subsequently while he was on the stage, and again when he was in the army, being at Norfolk, was struck by the elegant appearance of a gentleman in black, who had just landed from the Portsmouth ferryboat. This was on a Sunday morning, as the stranger stood at the door of his hotel, waiting the hour of attending the Episcopal Church, where, he was told, the Reverend Mr. Low, who had once been a player, was that day to take leave of his congregation, in consequence of ill-health. Mr. Low reserved his strength for his sermon, and the tall elegant gentleman, now in canonicals, read the service. The uncommon propriety of his reading, and the musical cadence of his powerful voice, arrested the stranger's attention, and some of the tones sounded familiar to his ear. He was at the greatest distance from the pulpit of which a very long church admitted, and in the gallery. He could not resist the desire to use an opera-glass, and immediately perceived that it was his old acquaintance the tragedian. Thus in the same pulpit, at one time, were two men who had both been players. Mr. Low was the son of the author mentioned in an early portion of this work, whose play was rejected by Hallam and Henry. The son was a man of talents and virtue; his talents were not fitted for the stage, but eminently so for the pulpit.

Mr. Morse was at this time still attached to the United States' frigate, but soon after received deacon's orders from Bishop Moore, of Virginia, and settled at Williamsburg, where the old American Company first played in 1752. In this ancient metropolis of Virginia he died, after a short, eventful life, passed as a lawyer, actor, soldier, sailor, and clergyman.

Mr. Rutherford, from the Philadelphia theatre, appeared for the first time in New-York, as George Barnwell, on the 2d of January, 1807; and on the 19th, Mr. Bernard commenced playing for six nights. His characters were Lord Ogilby, Sheva, Ruttekin (very like Edwin's), Lovegold, Touchstone, Farmer Ashfield, Sir Robert Ramble, Dennis Brulgruddery, and Sharp.

In February, the late Mrs. Wignell, now Mrs. Warren, played her usual characters in New-York; and in March, Mr. Cooper returned the compliment by playing in Philadelphia. In April, 1807, Mr. and Mrs. Darley, and Mr. Morse went to Charleston, S.C., and Mr. John E. Martin died of what is improperly called consumption.

In the July following, a theatre was opened at Vauxhall Gardens, in the Bowery, by a part of the Philadelphia company; and the two principal comedians of the New-York company, Twaits and Harwood, made an excursion to Ballston Springs, where they engaged a large room, and commenced a medley of entertainments, consisting of readings, recitations, and singing. They found for an assistant the celebrated Mr. Huggins (the same who formally denied being the author of Anthony Pasquin's or Williams's comedy of "The Manhattan Stage"). Huggins hailed them as brother-actors, for he had been one of Harper's company in Newport, and volunteered his services, officiating in the double capacity of hair-dresser and door-keeper.

1807. The second season of Mr. Cooper's management commenced on the 9th of September; the company consisted of the same performers as the last, with the addition of Mr. and Mrs. Claude, Messrs. Spear, Comer, and Green.

Mr. Green had now become an actor of considerable merit, and made his *debut* in Sir William Dorillon. Previous to this opening, the theatre had been taken to pieces, except the walls and the stage, and rebuilt under the direction of Mr. J. J. Holland. It was to appearance (within) a new house, and the whole proscenium was in fact new. We copy the following:—

> "NEW-YORK THEATRE.—This theatre has lately undergone considerable alterations, which have materially added to the comfort and convenience of the spectators. The audience part, which is entirely rebuilt, now consists of four rows of boxes; in the lower lobby, there is a handsome colonnade, with mirrors, and fireplaces at each end, the whole lighted by glass lamps between the columns. In every part of the theatre, the spectator may both hear and see the performance. The box-fronts, instead of being, as usual, perpendicular, fall in at top, and thus give room to the knees, which is considered an improvement upon the plan of all former theatres. There are several coffee-rooms, one of which is fitted in an elegant style for the accommodation of the ladies, where they may be supplied with every kind of fruit, confections, tea, coffee, &c. &c. This room is spacious, the furniture in the newest fashion, and is lighted by three elegant chandeliers suspended from the ceiling. In case of fire, there are three communications from the boxes with the street, and two from the pit. The boxes will accommodate upwards of 1600 persons, and the pit and gallery about 1100. The ceiling painted as a dome, with panels of a light purple, and gold mouldings; the centre a balustrade and sky. The box-fronts (except the fourth row) are divided into panels, blue ground, with white and gold ornaments; a crimson festoon drapery over each box. The lower boxes are lighted by ten glass chandeliers, projecting from the front,

and suspended from gilt iron brackets, and the whole house is extremely well lighted. There are four private boxes, with rooms to retire to on the stage. A beautiful effect is produced by a large oval mirror at the end of the stage-boxes, which reflects the whole of the audience on the first row.

"The whole of the alterations and improvements were completed under the superintendence of Mr. Holland, in the short space of three months, and the whole amount of expenditure (a circumstance which rarely happens) is less than the estimate, by five thousand dollars."

As the Park theatre was originally constructed, and as it remained until the proscenium was remodelled by Mr. Holland, there were no pillars as props to the upper boxes: they were supported by timbers projecting from the walls, and appeared, with their tenons, self-balanced. Of course, there were no obstructions in front of the boxes, as is commonly the case; and however ornamental pillars so placed may be, that they impede the view of the spectator, and prevent his seeing more or less of the stage, is undeniable.

Another peculiarity belonged to the boxes of this theatre, as first erected. There was a large box occupying the front of the second tier, and directly in front of the stage, capable of containing between two and three hundred persons, which was called "The Shakespeare," and was the resort of the critics, as the pit of the English theatres had been in former times.

The remodelled building had none of the above peculiarities. It was a more splendid and more commodious theatre than that which it superseded.

We have, in a preceding chapter, mentioned the engagement of Mr. Holland by Mr. Wignell, at the Italian Opera-house, London, and his arrival in this country. We have repeated from himself the story of his first landing in New-York, and his astonishment at finding himself in a great city, instead of a wilderness or a prairie.

Mr. Holland was very young, although a married man, at the time he arrived: many older persons form equally erroneous ideas of our country. It is but lately that it has been made a subject of contemplation or thought for Europeans. Some have crossed the Atlantic expecting a wilderness, and some, even of what are called the well informed, have looked for a Utopia,—the *best informed* forgetting that we have to contend not only against the vices of our own state of society, but all the complicated crimes engendered by the governments of Europe, and brought to us by those who fly from justice or oppression.

John Joseph Holland was a man of warm affections and amiable disposition. He was one of the few European artists of merit who have chosen this country as their own: he loved it, and learned to appreciate its manners and institutions.

He had been neglected by his father, but Marinelli, of the Opera-house, was pleased with the boy, and took him as a pupil at the age of nine. He made him an architect and a scene painter; and he made himself a good landscape painter in water-colours, by application in his hours of leisure from business. He was a favourite with his manager, Wignell, and the friend of Merry and his accomplished wife.

This excellent artist and truly good-hearted man died still in the prime of life. Of his pupils, we have with us two who, by their talent as artists and conduct as citizens, deserve the high esteem in which they are held. Mr. Hugh Reinagle, son of the professor of music, and former manager of the Chestnut-street theatre, Philadelphia, and Mr. John Evers, are the distinguished pupils of Mr. John Joseph Holland to whom we refer.

The theatre, as rebuilt by Mr. Holland, was destroyed by fire in 1820, shortly after the death of the architect, and the present Park house was erected on the same foundation and walls.

In January, 1808, the Boston theatre was at a very low ebb, and Bernard, the manager, playing in Philadelphia. Messrs. Cooper, Twaits, and Harwood went on to Boston, and the theatre, which had been closed, was re-opened, and revived by their exertions. Bernard, having finished his Philadelphia engagement, came on to New-York, and the theatre of that place was re-opened on the 17th of February, 1808. He played his usual round of characters, but without success; and Messrs. Cooper, Twaits, and Harwood returning on the 4th of March, "The Curfew" was brought out with some success: but "Cinderella," a pantomime, *got up* by Mr. Holland with great splendour and taste, eclipsed all other dramatic efforts, and silenced all dramatists who only spoke to the ear. Mr. Twaits directed the stage business of this splendid show. In rehearsing the piece, the duty required of the band was so great that they rebelled, but all difficulties yielded to the determination of the manager.

The New-York theatre was opened on the 9th of September, 1808, under the management of Messrs. Cooper and Price, the latter having purchased into the business. "The School of Reform" and "The Padlock" were the opening pieces. The company was the same as last year, except that Mr. Green and Mr. and Mrs. Claude were not with it, and Mrs. Hogg, Mrs. Lipman, and Messrs. Huntingdon, Doyle, and Lindsley were added. Mrs. Villiers was now Mrs. Twaits.

On the 7th of November, Mr. Twaits played the Prince of Wales, and the ridicule he drew upon himself was justly merited: his excellence within his proper sphere was great beyond praise; but for the hero or the gentleman, his figure, face, and manner all disqualified him. The irony of the following is cutting, but wholesome:—

"THEATRE.—On Monday evening, the admirers of the histrionic art were regaled with an exquisite repast, in the exhibition of Shakespeare's tragedy of Henry the Fourth, Part First.

"The waggeries of the merry old knight were never given with more richness, taste, and effect on our boards than by Mr. Harwood: we pronounce Falstaff the finest among all his characters.

"The fiery Hotspur found an able representative in Mr. Cooper, who undoubtedly is, in our opinion, an actor of great and sterling abilities.

"Mr. Twaits personated the Prince of Wales, and Mr. Shapter personified the king,—a most worthy father for such a worthy son.

"Hitherto our taste has been shocked with the constant repetition of heroes of the true Patagonian breed; but the judgment of the manager, justly offended at such huge representatives of true greatness, induced him to gratify us with one of natural and historical dimensions: besides, 'tis evident that Shakespeare intended the prince to be a little man, for his colleague Falstaff styles him "eel-skin, dried neat's tongue, tailor's yard," &c. Moreover, Alexander the Great was but five feet six inches in stature; Bonaparte within two inches of him; and Mr. Twaits but three inches under the smallest of them.

"From his able performance of Caleb Quotem, Lingo, Dr. Pangloss, Launcelot Gobbo, &c. &c. we were always of opinion that he was peculiarly adapted to the weightier parts of the drama, and our presages were amply realized in his personification of the prince. He looked the character to a tittle, and his manly face displayed the very seat and front of royalty: his action was totally disencumbered of those measured attitudes so contrary to simple elegance, but was easy and familiar: and above all, the deep sepulchral tones of his voice were modulated to the most touching pathos!

"Seldom have we witnessed such a scene as that in the third act, where the prince first meets his royal parent, and swears to expiate all his former follies. Mr. Shapter really outdid himself in the utterance of the speech beginning,

> 'Had I so lavish of my presence been,
> So common hackneyed in the eyes of men,
> So stale and cheap to vulgar company;
> *Opinion,* that did help me to the crown,
> Had left me in reputeless banishment,
> A fellow of no mark or likelihood:
> But being seldom seen, I could not stir
> But like a comet I was wondered at,
> That men shall tell their children, *there he is.*'

"Mr. Twaits's answer was given with equal force and eloquence, beginning,

> 'I shall hereafter, thrice gracious lord,
> *Be more myself,*' &c.

"The final scene was marked with the same glow of feeling and effect; where the prince tells Hotspur,

> 'And all the budding honours of thy crest
> I'll crop, to make a garland for my head!'

"We recommend to Mr. T. a larger stick than the one he wore.

"Mr. Tyler, though occasionally incorrect in the character of Worcester, is nevertheless an improving actor, and of considerable promise.

"Before we conclude this merited eulogium on dramatic merit, we must not omit the performance of young Mr. Oliff, in the character of Gadshill. This gentleman's figure is rather against him; but his voice is sonorous and musical; we recommend him to correct his gestures, which, though expressive, and like that excellent actor Mr. Twaits, *easy,*—nevertheless, they want the *grace* of that gentleman.

PHILO-DRAMA."

Mr. Lewis Hallam, whose uncle, William Hallam, had deserved the appellation of the father of the American stage, and whose father, Lewis Hallam, had actually planted the drama in America, died at Philadelphia on the 1st of November, 1808,—aged (according to the statement made by himself to the writer, that he was twelve years of age when he came from England with his father and mother in 1752), 68,—but according to the account of his death published at the time, 73. On Mr. Cooper's taking the New-York theatre, he declined engaging Mr. and Mrs. Hallam, for reasons which may be gathered from the preceding pages. A benefit was given to him on the 14th of January, 1807.

M. G. Lewis's tragedy of "Adelgitha" was played for the first time in America on the 14th of November, and was successful.

A farce of Charles Kemble's was brought out on the 18th, and condemned.

Mr. Cooper's practice at this time was to perform in New-York on Monday and Wednesday, and in Philadelphia on Friday and Saturday, which kept him on the road no small portion of his time.

1808. Dec. 12, Mr. Cooper's benefit, $810—Adelgitha, and Blind Boy. On the Wednesday following (14th), he closed his engagement with Octavian, and set off the next day for Philadelphia; where, having played for three nights, he took his benefit on the 21st, and proceeded on to Charleston. There was about $1000 in the Philadelphia house; and in Charleston his receipts were uncommonly great at this time.

Dec. 19. Mrs. Stanley, announced as from the London, Boston, and Philadelphia theatres, and engaged for four nights, made her *debut* in Lady Townley and Roxalana. This lady was the wife of the Hon. and Rev. Mr. Twistleton, brother to Lord Saye and Sele; but, seized with a theatrical mania, in despite of the rank and profession of her husband, resolved upon going on the stage: a separation, *a mensa et thoro,* was the consequence. She came out to America in 1807, engaged by Mr. Bernard for the Boston theatre. She played her round of characters at Philadelphia, concluding with Violante, on the 12th of December. At New-York she attracted but little attention; and on no one of the five nights that she performed did the manager make the expenses of the house. The characters she played were Widow Cheerly, Mrs. Sullen, and Portia, in "The Merchant of Venice," for her benefit: there were not more than $300 in the house. Mrs. Twistleton, or Stanley, died at Burlington, Vermont, suddenly, on her way from the United States to the provinces of Canada. She was not admired or successful in America.

Dec. 21. "Fraternal Discord," and "The Purse," were performed for the benefit of distressed seamen, and towards raising a fund "for the purpose of relieving the distresses of shipmasters, mates, and seamen who are out of employ, and have families to support." The managers, in unison with the wishes of the committee appointed for the above purpose, selected the comedy of "Fraternal Discord." Harwood and Twaits played the gouty captain and his trusty fellow-tar—almost as well as Hodgkinson and Jefferson, their first representatives. The weather was extremely bad; notwithstanding which there was $1177 in the house, $777 of which were acknowledged by the committee to have been received from the manager.

In October, 1808, Mr. Usher, whose name has occurred as a member of the Boston company, opened a theatre in Lexington, Kentucky, with "The Sailor's Daughter," and "Ways and Means," the characters performed by "the Thespian Society." The theatre is mentioned as superior to former accommodations of the kind: and it is said in the western journals, "The plan and decorations do credit to the judgment of the proprietor, Mr. Usher, as does the scenery, which competent judges pronounce equal to what is seen to the eastward." The "lovers of the drama" are congratulated, and the friends of morality, upon this first attempt which has been made to introduce a theatre in the western country.

With the exception of the above, and the French theatre of New-Orleans, established in 1809, all the western theatres have sprung up since the period to which this volume is limited. Mr. James H. Caldwell, who is known as an actor of talent and skill, has raised theatres for the English drama in most of the western states.

The year 1808 was rendered remarkable in theatrical history wherever the English language is spoken by the death of Mrs. Anne Warren, in the thirty-eighth year of her age, and in the full possession of all those eminent qualifications which rendered her, as a tragedian, only second to Mrs. Siddons.

She died at Alexandria on the 28th of June, 1808, having, contrary to the advice of her physicians, accompanied her husband on the southern tour required by his duties as actor and manager. As Mrs. Merry, she had been left in a foreign country a widow, and remained such four years, experiencing the friendship of the manager who engaged her to come to this country, Mr. Wignell; and then became his wife: seven weeks after their marriage, Mr. Wignell died. She was a second time a widow; and became in due time the mother of a beautiful girl, who could know no natural father. Mr. Warren became the friend and protector of the widow and the orphan. He had been the companion of herself and her first and second husband in the voyage from England. Between three and four years from the time Mr. Wignell died, she became Mrs. Warren, being married on the 15th of August, 1806, two years before her much-lamented death.

On the 2d of January, 1809, the play of The Glory of Columbia, her Yeomanry, cut and mangled, was played. And after an attempt at a Harlequin pantomime, in which the Harlequin, Columbine, and Pantaloon were like any thing but the beings intended, the theatre was closed until the 22d of February, and on the 26th, Master Payne made his first appearance in character on any stage. This young gentleman was now 16 years of age, and small for that age, looking still younger. His face was remarkably handsome, his countenance full of intelligence, and his manners fascinating. He appeared on the stage with the consent of his father, who was behind the scenes during the performance, as was Mr. John E. Seaman, who had previously placed this young gentleman at the academy of Dr. Nott, at Schenectady. The friendship of Mr. Seaman, and the instructions of Dr. Nott, aided in developing those talents which have made of this gentleman one of the successful dramatists of the English and American stage. He performed Young Norval with credit, and his succeeding characters with an increased display of talent. The applause bestowed on his Norval was very great—boy actors were then a novelty, and we have seen none since that equalled Master Payne. A child playing in the same scene with men and women, is in itself an absurdity, and the popularity of such exhibitions is a proof of vicious taste, or rather an absence of taste. It is the same feeling which carries the crowd to see monsters of every description. A little boy or a little girl playing Richard, or Shylock, where the other characters are supported by men and women, is to a person of taste an object of pity, or of ridicule. There was judgment in the choice of characters for Master Payne, which rendered his performances pleasing—Norval, Achmet, or even Romeo might be tolerated in a boy of 16, and the beauty and talent of the young performer made these youthful characters extremely pleasing as exhibited by him. Master Payne made his debut in Boston on the 3d of April, in Norval.

The Forty Thieves was brought out with great success on the 20th of March, and on the 10th of April, Mr. Cooper returned and was announced for ten nights, previous to his departure for Europe.

He played, 1st, Beverley (The Gamester), 2d, Guiscard (Adelgitha), 3d, Othello, 4th, Duke Aranza (The Honey-moon), 5th, Macbeth, 6th, Leon, 7th, 8th, and 9th, Charles (in Man and Wife), 10th, Petruchio, and 11th (his benefit), Rolla.

On the 5th of May, 1809, the comedy of "Man and Wife" was first performed in America.

"The School for Authors," by the late John Tobin, author of The Honey-moon, was performed, but without success.

On the 17th of May, 1809, Master Payne commenced a second engagement at

New-York, for six nights, with Norval. He played in succession Hastings, Octavian, Frederick Fribourg, Rolla, Edgar, and Hamlet for his benefit. The receipts averaged 500 dollars a night, exclusive of his benefit, which produced 755 dollars. Mr. Twaits played Lear on the 29th, with Master Payne's Edgar, and disappointed public expectation by playing it with great judgment. Few as his inches were, he did not look "every inch a king," still his personal appearance did not disqualify him for the feeble old man, and the heroic Edgar was as deficient in inches as the king.

In a publication dated 1815, printed for John Miller, London, Mr. Payne is styled "the American Roscius." With us, in imitation of those who bestowed the title of "Young Roscius" on Master Betty, and every other theatrical imp who became the wonder of the day, Master Payne was entitled the "Young American Roscius," not dreaming thereby to place him at the head of American actors. When we first knew John Howard Payne, he was a fascinating youth, and richly deserved, as a boy, the applause he met with in public, and the admiration his talents elicited in private. He was born in the city of New-York, the 9th of June, 1792, and his father removed with his family to Boston while John was yet an infant, and there, under the parental roof, he received the rudiments of education. On some public occasion, as we are informed, he delivered an address from the stage, which probably planted in the boy his love for the drama. At the age of thirteen he was sent to New-York, and placed in the counting-house of Messrs. Grant and Bennet Forbes. His propensity for literature and the drama led him astray from journal and ledger, and he commenced a weekly paper, entitled the "Thespian Mirror," which, as the production of a boy, justly excited admiration. William Coleman, the editor of the Evening Post, relates in his paper of January 24th, 1806, the manner in which he became acquainted with Master Payne, as the editor of the "Thespian Mirror," and his surprise at finding in a boy of thirteen such strength and maturity of intellect. "I conversed with him for an hour; inquired into his history—the time since he came to reside in this city—and his object in setting on foot the publication in question. His answers were such as to dispel all doubts as to any imposition, and I found that it required an effort, on my part, to keep up the conversation in as choice a style as his own." In short, Coleman pronounced the boy "a prodigy."

While at Schenectady with Dr. Nott, Master Payne published a second weekly paper, called "The Pastime." As we have said, on the 26th of February, 1809, he made his first appearance on any stage, except the occasional address at Boston as a child.

During our second war against the then insolent and overbearing pretensions of Great Britain, young Mr. Payne left his country, and took up his abode in England.

On the 4th of June, 1813, he made a successful debut at Drury Lane theatre, being then twenty-one years of age, and was offered a permanent situation; but the charms of starring were preferred, and finally literary pursuits, particularly those connected with the drama, withdrew him altogether from the profession of an actor. He played at the English provincial theatres, and in Ireland, with success, and everywhere received those tokens of esteem and admiration which his talents and manners entitled him to. We here insert a letter from a friend in London, recording a compliment paid by our old master, Benjamin West, to his young countryman.

"London, June 18th, 1813.

* * * "John Howard Payne, the young American Roscius, has played Douglas twice at Drury Lane, with unbounded applause. The house, however, was neither time crowded, but that may be attributed to his having kept his intention of playing as secret as possible, till the day of his appearance; so that the English part of the audience, of course nearly the whole, had no idea who he really was. Some said he was from the provincial theatres, and others that he came from Ireland. They were taken by surprise, and delighted with him.

"On the second night I had the honour of conducting Mr. West to see him. This was a great compliment to Payne, the old gentleman not having been at the theatre since the time of Garrick. He felt much interest for Payne, and was instrumental in procuring him his engagement. After the play, he said that our young Roscius had far exceeded his expectations. He thought his action extremely graceful, and his voice very fine; his dress picturesque and correct, and perfectly adapted to his figure.

"The next night he played Romeo, with Elliston's Mercutio."

During a part of the years 1826–7, Mr. Payne edited with great credit, in London, a periodical work, called "The Opera Glass," devoted to the drama. To this work, and the work on the French theatre, presented to Mr. Payne by Talma, and communicated to us, we are indebted for the laws, regulations, and police of the French theatre, which we give as a model for all countries that wish to abolish the abuses, and profit by the inherent powers of that great engine which can bring back with more vividness and force than any other—even the pencil or the press—the mighty events of the past, and those heroic exertions of virtue that are the most effective lessons to the present and the future.

Mr. Payne has recently returned from Europe. He has visited its continent, and contributed to the English and American stage several successful translations from French dramas. He has likewise produced a tragedy, which has been, and continues popular, Brutus. This is a combination from the plays which had preceded it on the same subject. How far his dramas of Adeline, Charles the Second, Clari, Therese, and Love in Humble Life, &c. &c., are translations or original, we do not know. We shall endeavour to give, in our catalogue of plays by Americans, or written in America, the titles of all his dramatic works. Many of them have been, and continue very popular in England and America.

June 5th, the benefits commenced, but under auspices so discouraging, that seven only, including Mr. Holland the architect, ventured to put up their names. The result verified the anticipation. Twaits exceeded the expenses $100. Harwood merely defrayed them; and Holland was short $70. Tyler, Hogg, and Mrs. Lipman, a performer of some merit, who was before the public but a short time, by dint of the exertion of their friends, made out somewhat better; and Mrs. Oldmixon, through the same, though not equally direct means, cleared about $80.

On the 21st, a new play, called "The Duke of Buckingham," written by an English lady of the name of Ellis, was brought out. The house was very thin, and its reception by no means flattering. Its fate was most deserved.

June 28th, ticket night. On such nights the minor performers, door-keepers, &c., are allowed to dispose of as many tickets as they please, they paying the manager half the price of them.

July 4th, the theatre closed at New-York.

Many of our very excellent actors made their first appearance in America on the Boston theatre. This was the case with Mr. and Mrs. Duff. Mr. Duff was an actor in the Dublin theatre at a time when Mrs. Jordan, and Mr. Dwyer, then in his prime, had a serious dispute, which ended in his leaving the theatre, and giving Duff an opportunity to show talents before kept from view. He soon after came to Boston, bringing with him a very beautiful lady, his wife, the sister of the first wife of the poet, Anacreon Moore. The sisters were dancers in Dublin, and their name Dyke. Mr. Duff appeared on the Philadelphia stage in 1811, playing the first night Macbeth, and Diddler. This is an instance of versatility of powers seldom met with, for in both he was eminently successful. The manager of that theatre at the time, tells us, "he succeeded beyond any instance I ever met with; for many months he attracted great houses in the Three and the Deuce, which I had performed as a first piece, Richard, Macbeth, Lear, &c.; and I am safe in saying that Mr. Duff brought more *positive profit* to the house, in two years, than any *star* that visited us." It must be remembered that the *stars* took care to share the profit with the managers, except the greatest of all stars, George Frederick Cooke, and the profits of his performances were secured by those to whom he had bound himself. The Philadelphia manager, Mr. Wood, proceeds: "there was no one demanding all, or the largest share of the profits from us,—Mr. Duff had six guineas a week, and often played (on his sole attraction) to 7, 8, and $900. His second benefit here was $1574, which greatly exceeds any of Cooke's, Kean's, or Mathews's. Mrs. Duff, at this time, was very pretty, but so tame and indolent as to give no hope of the improvement we afterwards witnessed. Connected with

Duff, I will mention an odd circumstance. James N. Barker, who had written several pieces before, and which had no fault *but* being American productions, at my request, dramatised *Marmion.* I well knew the *then* prejudice against any native play, and concerted with Cooper a very innocent fraud upon the public—we insinuated that the piece was a London one—had it sent from New-York, exactly packed up *like the pieces we were in the habit of receiving, and made it arrive in the middle of rehearsal, when it was opened with great gravity, and announced without any author* alluded to. None of the company were in the secret—(I well knew 'these actors cannot keep counsel')—not even the prompter. Well, sir, it was played with great success for six or seven nights, when I (believing it safe) announced the author, and from that moment it *ceased to attract.* This is not a very creditable story, but a true, and forms a strong contrast to the warmth with which Metamora and the Gladiator were received. Cooper also played Marmion in New-York, without a hint of its father."

Of Metamora or the Gladiator, the writer cannot speak, but it is probable that the talents of the principal actor in these pieces have aided their authors, as is always the case, when one character is the sole object in a play. They have been eminently successful.

⤞ CHAPTER 32 ⤝

1809 — Mr. and Mrs. Poe — Mr. and Mrs. Young — To Marry or Not to Marry — Grieving's a Folly — Mrs. Mason — Her Widow Cheerly — Mr. Simpson — His Debut — His Early History — Engaged by Dr. Irving for New-York — Mr. Cooper's De Montfort — The Foundling of the Forest — Venoni — Mr. Oliff, and other Prompters at New-York — Mr. Dwyer — His Debut and Early History — Mr. Cooper goes to England, 1810 — Mr. Bray — Mr. Wood at New-York — Mr. and Mrs. Stanley — Arrival of Mr. Cooke.

On the 6th of September, 1809, the theatre of New-York was opened for the winter campaign with Lewis's Castle Spectre, and Bickerstaff's Romp. Mrs. Poe was the Angela and Priscilla Tomboy. Mr. Young Osmond, and Mr. Poe Hassan. Mr. and Mrs. Poe, Mr. Anderson, Miss Delamater, Miss Martin (a daughter of John E. Martin, deceased), and Miss White, were the additions to the company—a feeble company of recruits—to replace Harwood, Mr. and Mrs. Darley, and Mr. Hogg. It appears to have been the intention to open the theatre on the 30th of August—"the favourable season, and unprecedented good health" of the city, say the managers, are their inducements—but then the great improvements could not be ready in time.

Mrs. Young was brought forward as Cowslip, on the third night of performance—but as Cowslip, she had only beauty to recommend her.

Mr. Cooper now went through his usual characters. Mrs. Twaits was the heroine of tragedy. Mr. Robinson played Cassio, and many other important parts, far beyond his abilities. Mr. Twaits played Michael Perez, and Mr. Young played Iago. The company was weak, but a reinforcement was crossing the seas, and soon arrived.

Mr. Foster, a brother of Mrs. Young, made his first appearance as Ganem, in The Forty Thieves, on the 15th of September.

As the year 1808 was rendered memorable in the history of the American theatre, by the death of the accomplished lady and talented actress, Mrs. Anne Warren, so 1809 is little less entitled to the same distinction from the loss the stage sustained in the death of Mr. John E. Harwood, one of the best comedians the American theatre has possessed. On the 21st of September, in the 39th year of his age, this accomplished man and excellent actor expired at Germantown.

On the 18th of November, in the same year, 1809, Mr. Giles Leonard Barrett died, at the age of 65. Mr. Barrett had been more successful in Boston, where he made his first appearance on coming to America, than in any other metropolis, and he breathed his last in that city. He had considerable versatility. His figure must have been fine in early life, his face never. At a later period, Mr. Barrett would not have been a prominent actor on the American boards. His son, Mr. George Barrett, is justly estimated as equal to any performer in the higher line of genteel comedy now among us.

In the same month of November, at Philadelphia, died Mr. Owen Morris, aged 90. He played the old men of comedy for many years in the old American Company, and afterwards in Wignell's Philadelphia Company. He had the appearance of a very old man in 1787, twenty-two years before his death. It is an error to suppose players are short-lived.

Actors, we mean good actors, and respectable men, are a long-lived race. A friend has remarked that he could recollect thirty actors, generally of high eminence, who died with the space of 40 years, at or beyond the age of 70; and adds, "it would be difficult to show as large a number out of the same proportion of merchants or traders." Macklin died more than 100 years of age; we saw him act, with power and spirit, his Shylock, and Sir Pertinax, at the age of 94; Mrs. Bracegirdle died at 85; Mr. Yates, 97; Mr. Blissett, the elder, 84; Colley Cibber, 86, and a very long list of names might be added of those who lived beyond the "threescore and ten" allotted to men in general who live to old age. There are now, or lately were living, in competency or affluence, many more who could be mentioned as proofs of longevity among actors. The improvidence of actors is another vulgar error. When we speak of actors, we do not mean message-carriers, or the candle-snuffers and dram-drinkers of the stage. Of the hundreds who have retired from the stage in affluence, or with competency, or now live and act with the same advantage, we will only mention the names of Quin, Yates, Garrick, Smith, Cibber, Farren, Siddons, Mathews, Darley, Jefferson, Wood, Hull, Mattocks, Melmoth, Barry, Clive, Pritchard, Johnson, O'Neil, Bartley, Pope, Quick, Dodd, Bannister—we could fill our page with names who are honoured for their talents, and enjoy in private life the more estimable reward of esteem for their virtues. It is the lot of the stage's historian to record vice and folly, and that record is remembered longer than the page which speaks of virtue—so the pages of the historian are filled with war and crime, and the years of peace passed over. Men's good deeds are written in sand—their evil ones on brass.

On the 9th of October, Mrs. Inchbald's comedy of "To Marry or Not to Marry" was performed. Lord Danbury by Mr. Twaits; Sir Osborn Moreland, Mr. Cooper; Willowear, Mr. Young; Lavensworth, Mr. Robinson; Amos, Mr. Poe; Lady Susan Courtley, Mrs. Oldmixon; Mrs. Sarah Moreland, Mrs. Hogg; Hester, Mrs. Young. This comedy was played several nights in succession—that is, on play-nights.

On the 18th of October, the comedy of "Grieving's a Folly" was played with little success; and on the 21st, the arrival of Mrs. Mason and Mr. Simpson was announced—a strong and very seasonable accession to the company. That evening the lady made her appearance in Mrs. Beverley. The choice was bad. Comedy was Mrs. Mason's forte, and a most charming comedian she was. But we have ever remarked the predilection of those who have great talents in comedy for exhibiting themselves on stilts, and luxuriating in tears and sighs. The best of all gentlemen comedians, Lewis, began with tragedy—Bannister, the first of rich, not low, comedy players, made his attempt as a votary of Melpomene—these were men of ordinary height; but if the comedian is low in stature, the more violent is the propensity to seize the sceptre and the truncheon. Mrs. Mason did not want size, but she had no other requisite for tragedy, except good sense, which did not appear in the choice of Mrs. Beverley. Her second character was the Widow Cheerly, in Cherry's pleasant comedy of The Soldier's Daughter, and we never expect to see the part so well played again. She was from that time established as a first-rate comedy actress.

Mr. Simpson made his debut as Harry Dornton, in the fine comedy of the Road to Ruin. Mr. Cooper had played the part, and played it well, but Mr. Simpson's Harry Dornton was fully successful. On Mrs. Mason's second appearance, Mr. Simpson played Frank Heartall, and lost no favour with his audience.

Of Mr. Simpson's early history, all we know is from himself, in a very obliging answer to our inquiries; and we know no better mode of conveying the knowledge so obtained than by using his own words:—

"DEAR SIR: I know not of any intelligence I can give you respecting the American stage which you are not already acquainted with. I came here from Dublin in October, 1809, with Mrs. Mason in company, likewise engaged. I opened in Harry Dornton, &c. &c., all of which you know. My early life has not been eventful, and therefore not to your purpose. I was born in 1784, educated for a mercantile life, but 'had a soul above buttons;' so I ran away, and took to the stage: opened first at a little village called Towcester, in May, 1806, in the Baron in The Stranger, and Fainwould in Raising the Wind. The theatre was a decent barn: salary twenty shillings a week. My first interview with the manager was when he was mounted on a ladder, cleaning his lamp at the barn door. I stopped a very short time with him, and went to Buckingham, where we had the pleasure of playing in a larger stable,—I used to put my clothes in the manger while dressing. Now, having just started from home, and having a new blue coat and white breeches, I played all the walking-gentlemen. I captivated the heart of a milliner in the town, who kept a very decent shop, and who offered to make me a sleeping partner; but it would not do. I then went to Dover, Margate, Brighton, and from thence to Dublin; from whence I arrived here, being engaged by Dr. Irving for Messrs. Price and Cooper. This is all that is material; I have had the usual difficulties of all country actors; but, unlike most of my brethren, I never wronged a man of a shilling, though I walked forty miles in one lamentable day without a shilling in my pocket. I shall never forget the smell of some pork and cabbage at a cottage door by the way-side: I've loved pork and greens ever since.

"Yours, truly,   E. SIMPSON."

"I must not forget to tell you that my first *penchant* for the stage was encouraged by my revered friend Thomas Hilson, who introduced me behind the scenes of a private theatre."

It is to be lamented that a true and faithful account of this same revered friend does not fall within the limits of this our present History of the American Theatre.

Mr. Simpson's life, as an American, has not been one of the eventful kind; and although he has doubtless experienced the miseries of management, no man has borne the weight with better grace, or stood the wear and tear with less injury to health and equanimity. He has invariably yielded his rank to give an opportunity for the display of new talent; and played second-fiddle ofttimes when he was entitled to play first. He cannot be charged with the besetting sin of actor-managers, the seeking to thrust himself into every character that gave a chance of gaining applause or enhancing consequence. Happily for him, he has not had a Mrs. Simpson for whose caprice or ambition he would, perhaps, like other managers whose wives are heroines, been obliged to sacrifice justice and propriety; but, still happier for him, he has had good sense to direct him as a manager, an actor, and a man; and his reward is self-approbation and the esteem of his fellow-citizens.

Mr. Cooper, about this time, played De Montfort: it did not succeed. Hodgkinson had failed in it. Cooper was better fitted for it, but it did not meet public expectation. Mrs. Twaits was not equal to Jane de Montfort. Mr. Young was as far from Rezenvelt as south from north—all failed. May we not yet see Forrest in De Montfort, Wood in Rezenvelt—but where is Jane? Mrs. Duff is remembered as being nearest to the great Jane de Montfort.

On the 27th of November, "The Foundling of the Forest," by Dimond, was first played, and had a great run. Mrs. Mason had her share in its success.

"Venoni" was played twice. Mr. Morrell, "a gentleman of this city," played twice.

January 2d, 1810, "The Africans" had a run. O'Keefe's "Fontainbleau" several times played with success. We remember a circumstance connected with this play, when first performed in London, which shows how "they manage these things" t'other side the Atlantic. Taking up a paper the day after we had witnessed Edwin's performance of The Yorkshire Jockey, we read a eulogium on the same actor's performance on that night, and in that of a Welshman. The author had made the alteration, and had not given notice to the editor.

On the 22d of January, 1810, Mr. Trazetta *brought forth* in the "great room of the City Hotel" a musical farce, written and set to music by himself. He was manager, author, composer, and performer. It is to be presumed that it made some noise at the time.

The theatre having been closed for the benefit of the managers, was re-opened on the 22d of February, with "Gustavus Vasa," a play thought appropriate for the birthday of Washington, and frequently, as such, brought forward. The hero was played by Mr. Robinson.

Miss Jones, now Mrs. Simpson, performed the interesting child in the popular play of "The Soldier's Daughter," made popular by the acting of the gentleman now her husband, and of Mrs. Mason, in addition to its own merits.

In March, Master Payne played four or five nights, beginning very injudiciously with Rolla. A child in Rolla, let his mind be ever so Herculean, must be far below the mark. It is something like a little girl playing Shylock, with some horsehair tied to her chin.

That well-known character, Mr. Oliff, appears frequently in the bills this season; he had before been seen on the stage—never heard—at least, never understood. He held the prompt-book at the P.S. entrance, and rung the bells for up and down curtain—up and down lamps—thunder, lightning, and fiddlers— gave the signals for the carpenters to storm with the crackling of tin sheets or rolling of iron cannon-balls—and served for performers to storm at when they had neglected to be perfect in their parts: but for the purpose which gives name to the office, viz. prompting,—Mr. Oliff being prompter—for *giving the word*, the pillar behind which he was ensconced was just as efficient as Mr. Oliff. Mr. Cooper's maxim, in respect to a prompter (*after he became a manager*), was, that the more unintelligible he was in prompting, the less the actors would rely on him, and the more on their own industry. Messrs. Hughes, Oliff, and M'Enery were perfect on Mr. Cooper's system: they succeeded each other in the office: Hughes couldn't see the word, and the two Hibernians couldn't speak it. But let us go on to a greater Hibernian.

Mr. Dwyer made his appearance on the stage of America, in New-York, the 14th day of March, 1810. He played, judiciously, his best character, Belcour, in "The West Indian," and was much admired: it was repeated. He then played in succession, Gossamer, Charles Surface, Goldfinch, Ranger, Archer, Octavian (a vile failure), Sir Charles Rackett, Captain Absolute, Rover, Vapid, Tangent, and Mercutio.

Most of these he was well studied in, and had played them at Drury Lane; for Mr. Dwyer had been kept up at Drury Lane for three winters, as the successor of John Palmer.

Mr. Dwyer is an actor of too much notoriety to be passed over slightly. His biographer, in "The Mirror of Taste," tells us that he is descended from the O'Dwyers of Tipperary, and that his father was the best fencer of the age; that our hero ran away, as most of our heroes do, to avoid study or work, and at seventeen commenced player in Dublin; that "with a degree of success never contemplated by himself, Mr. Dwyer played in many of the principal provincial theatres of England until the year 1802; when, on the first of May, in that year, he appeared in the character of Belcour (West Indian) at Drury Lane."

Of his success, for a time, we have spoken. He was a very handsome fellow, and his success was never marred by his diffidence. Mr. Dwyer was above all the vulgar prejudices of mankind, and much better suited to the aristocracy of Europe than the plebeian society of America.

After leaving Drury Lane "in disgust," and playing a few nights, as we find it recorded, "at great prices, in most of the cities and towns of Great Britain," Mr. Dwyer "determined on a trip across the Atlantic." He played at Boston and Philadelphia, and for a time with success wherever he came.

The Emerald Isle is so rich in talent, and can boast of such a long line of splendid statesmen, soldiers, orators, and artists, that she will not feel that we have diminished her glories by denying a crown to the head of the descendant of the O'Dwyers of Tipperary. We take this opportunity to remark, that the success of Irishmen, as dramatists and actors, has been surprisingly great. Writing from recollection, and at random, we put down the names of Sheridan, Macklin, Wilkes, Moody, Johnstone, Kelly, Pope, Murphy, Farquhar, Dogget, Henry, Ry-der, Quin, Bickerstaff, O'Neil, Barry, Rock: we need not look into our books for more: the eloquence of Ireland is proverbial, and her sons have exhibited a due portion of it on the stage. Let it not be inferred, from what we have said, that Mr. Dwyer was destitute of talent; far from it: but it was not of the first order, nor had it received the best cultivation.

Mr. Cooper returned in April from blazing abroad as a star, and "is engaged" (according to the advertisement) after the manner of any other performer, for a certain number of nights. Two of these nights the two stars shone together: Cooper, Horatio; Dwyer, Lothario—Cooper, Leon; Dwyer, Michael Perez. Mr. Dwyer then proceeded to Philadelphia to make the luminaries of that company "hide their diminished heads."

The theatre of New-York was shut from the 18th to the 27th of April, when it was re-opened with the play of the Exiles. On the 16th of May, the new comedy of "Riches" was performed; and on the 21st, it was announced, that "Mr. Cooper being about to sail for England, his engagement will terminate in eight nights." He then played Richard, Hamlet, Coriolanus, Lear, Alexander, Orsino, Othello, and Duke Aranza, in "The Honey-moon."

Mr. Cooper having departed, the benefits commenced the 15th of June, and the theatre closed immediately after the 4th of July.

On the 10th of September, 1810, the theatre of New-York re-opened, Mr. Cooper being then in England. Mr. and Mrs. Claude and Mr. Bray were added to the company. Mr. Bray was a man of good sense, good manners, and a valuable comedian. The opening play was "She Stoops to Conquer." Mr. Wood, the manager of the Philadelphia theatre, "shot," we will not say "wildly, from his sphere," and became the centre of light in the rival house. He was announced for four nights, and played five (as usual), the last for his benefit. He was received, as he merited, with welcome and applause: first in Count de Valmont (The Foundling of the Forest), a part he had at home gained great reputation in; second night, Don Felix, in "The Wonder;" third, Penruddock; fourth, Rolla; and for his benefit, "The Foundling" was repeated. Mr. Wood's engagement commenced on the 12th of September, and on the 28th, two recruits, enlisted by Mr. Cooper, who was now playing "Sergeant Kite," arrived to keep up the attention of the public. Mr. and Mrs. Stanley were announced in due form, and she made her *debut* in Adelgitha. On the 30th, they both played,—he Sir Anthony Absolute in Sheridan's "The Rivals,"—she, Julia. Mr. Stanley was deaf, and Mrs. Stanley did not prove an equal to her predecessors or contemporaries. To be dear, is only a misfortune in the man, but it is a fault in the player. It is in vain that he has a just conception of character, and is fraught with the spirit as well as words of his author: he must hear the *cue* and the prompter. He knows that the person he is making love to, or quarrelling with, ought to say certain words to which he is to answer; but players are not infallible, though popes are, and it may happen that a game of cross-purposes and silly answers may ensue.

Fennell was called in as an auxiliary for six nights; but he was soon sick—not before the public sickened. The theatre was in a decline; when lo! George Frederick Cooke arrived, and all was well again.

⤖ CHAPTER 33 ⤏

A short Chapter of additional Autobiography.

In my memoirs of George Frederick Cooke, it will be seen that I was connected with the theatre of New-York during the year 1810 and part of 1811.

In 1812 I resumed the pencil, many years neglected; and was again, in 1813, called from the palette and easel, by an unsolicited and very unexpected appointment as assistant paymaster-general to the militia of the state of New-York, then in the service of the United States. This appointment was made by Daniel D. Tompkins, governor of the state, and commander-in-chief of the third military district; and was conferred upon me in a manner which beyond measure enhanced the value of the office.

Happily the war terminated triumphantly, but my services were required until 1816.

During an absence from the city of New-York, on duty, in the western part of the state, in 1815, I was informed that my name was joined with that of my friend John Joseph Holland, as the intended managers of the New-York theatre; and soon after received a request from John K. Beekman, Esq. (who had called at my house repeatedly to see me), that I would immediately on my return call on John Jacob Astor, Esq. (if Mr. Beekman should be absent).

On my return to New-York, I accordingly called on Mr. Astor, and told him that I did so in compliance with Mr. Beekman's wishes. He took me into a private cabinet, and mentioned certain negotiations then pending for a renewed lease of the theatre. I repeated that my only motive for calling was the expressed desire of his partner in the property. He again mentioned that Messrs. Price and Simpson were in treaty with him, and asked if I had any proposal to make. I answered, "No," and took my leave. As I was retiring, he asked me to call again. I replied, "If you have any communication to make to me, you know my place of residence;" and without any further explanation I departed. As I left his counting-house, I saw Mr. Simpson go to his dwelling-house, and heard shortly after that the gentlemen holding the lease had renewed it.

I have been assured that my name was not used to further or hasten the agreement. I only know that I had no further connexion or agency in the business than above stated, although as free to bid for the lease as any other person; but I was without thought or desire of the kind.

Again: Being in Norfolk in the year 1821, engaged professionally, and enjoying the friendship of many in that region of hospitality, particularly that of Thomas Williamson, Esq., who had erected a building for my painting and pictures, I received a letter from Mr. Beekman, suggesting an engagement to conduct the New-York theatre on the account and risk of the proprietors, and an immediate voyage to England on the business. I notified my willingness to enter into a negotiation for such purpose. This was on the 27th of April. I received an answer, dated May 5th, saying that Mr. Simpson had that day concluded his agreement for the theatre.

How far, without my knowledge or intention, I have been made to influence the contracts of others, I know not. The facts above stated appear to belong to my theatrical history, and as such I record them.

It will be seen by the catalogue of American plays, that I wrote and translated some pieces for the Bowery theatre. This was at the request of the managers, and in the plain way of trade, receiving meager compensation for poor commodities. "Thirty Years, or the Life of a Gamester," was faithfully translated from the French, and was generally well played. Mr. George Barrett represented the hero skilfully, and Mrs. Gilfert (above mentioned as Miss Holman) played the heroine with great pathos. Mrs. G. Barrett added her talents and beauty, both of a high order, to the strength which gave success to the piece.

The last piece I wrote for the stage was a farce, called "A Trip to Niagara," the main intention of which was to display scenery.

⤞ CHAPTER 34 ⤝

Present State of the English Stage — Plan of and Wish for Reform.

We have spoken of the state of the English drama in the year 1752, when William Hallam sent off a colony, led by his brother, to settle in the North American wilderness; when Garrick directed the stage of the metropolis, and Johnson and Goldsmith, and their associates, wrote for it; when the pit was the centre of wit and learning, and the boxes of taste and elegance.

We have noticed slightly the London theatre of 1787,—when Sheridan was the manager of Drury Lane, Harris of Covent Garden, and Colman of the Haymarket,—when Henderson and Lewis, Mrs. Billington, Mrs. Martyr, Mrs. Mattocks, Mrs. Abbingdon, Miss Brunton, with Farren, Irish Johnstone, Pope, Holman, Macklin, Edwin, Quick, Wilson, and their inferiors, enlivened the stage of one house; and Smith, Bensley, Kemble, two Bannisters, Mrs. Siddons, Miss Farren, Mrs. Jordan, Mrs. Crouch, Palmer, Dodd, parsons, Suett, and King, with their followers, shone on the boards of the other,—when the *élite* of both houses joined at the minor theatre to sport the wit of Foote, and his successors, in warm weather, making the little theatre in the Haymarket the seat of the Comic Muse,—when Sheridan, Burgoyne, and Colman wrote comedies, and O'Keefe farces,—when wit yet lingered in the pit, and beauty and taste in the boxes;—and we now will take a glance at the drama of Great Britain in 1832.

A flippant and (though scurrilous) amusing writer in Frazer's Magazine, under the head of "Sock and Buskin," will serve our turn for a text-book, and our commentaries shall be brief.

"It is long," he says, "since we have said a word about these 'poor rogues;' like the rest of the world nowadays, we think very little of them: we seldom see them at the theatres, and never meet with them elsewhere: it was once otherwise: we adored the princesses, and affected the company of Doricourt and Hamlet. In fact, we knew them in every walk and every degree, from the haughty star, that to vulgar eyes shone afar off in the distant heavens a glory and a mystery, to the no less haughty farthing-candle that twinkled, an idol and an oracle to the Zoroasters of the pot-house."

He goes on to say, that they are "bad acquaintance,"—"worse, by Jupiter! than marching officers." "No player (not even Garrick) ever was a gentleman." "Take a player from the first—the *debut*—how is it that any creature who has ever known a decent hearth, the care of parents, the respect of men, can stand with a painted face and antic dress to mimic human passions and human actions,— exposed to the gaze of a thousand eyes, the curling of a thousand lips, the scorn of every purse-proud, idle blockhead, the mercy of every ruffian who chooses to pay sixpence for the privilege to hiss? And, above all, how is it that a woman can do this?"

The writer's definition of the word gentleman appears to be, one whose "demeanour" evinces good breeding by "unconsciousness of restraint, and that perfect ease which must be its result." Now, we have known English actors who, according to this idea of a gentleman, were fitted for the society of the writer of the "Sock and Buskin." But, according to his definition, we Yankees have no gentlemen among us; and Heaven grant that we never may! Our citizens are ever under restraint,—the restraint of law, of religion, of morality—of the ties and cares imposed by their political and social duties, and by those connected with the avocations of business,—for we are a busy people,—and having no hered-itary gentlemen, no laws of primogeniture, are likely to continue so. It is true, an actor is under restraint; and, to be a good actor, must attend sedulously to his avocations; and so must be the priest and the lawyer, the judge and the bishop, the painter and the sculptor, the merchant and the banker, and the many who think themselves gentlemen in our republican society.

Actors and actresses paint their faces, and put on mimic dresses and actions. The princess, dukes, and lords of Europe, with their ladies; and the gentlemen who are proud to be called their grooms, and pages, and chamberlains, do the same (without aiming at the same, or an equally moral purpose), in their mid-night orgies, where, indeed, the end is vicious dissipation, licentious intrigue, or ostentatious display of arrogance and vanity. The actor, as an artist, puts on the appearance of a picture, which the poet had already painted in words, to the intellectual eye; but which the player happily illustrates by action, emphasis, and semblance of passion. The purpose of both poet and player is to present a pic-ture fraught with instruction: there is no moral degradation in the act or the purpose. The European gentleman and lady, duke and duchess, prince and princ-es (and with grief we add their servile imitators in this country), cover their faces with painted pasteboard, and deck themselves in robes, to mimic historic or poetic characters, with purposes in view which, if not evil, cannot be good.

We are not the advocates of abuse of any description. It is our aim and pur-pose to point out that which needs correction. It is only by the abuse of the theatre that the actor is "exposed to the curling of a thousand lips, the scorn of every purse-proud idle blockhead, the mercy of every ruffian who chooses to pay sixpence for the privilege to hiss."

Were the theatre under the protection of the state, as in France, or of a pow-erful association of men, not seeking emolument from it,—under the direction of a learned and good man, of refinement, taste, and experience in the fine arts, who should have no pecuniary interest therein, further than the liberal income furnished by the state or the association; were the actors chosen for talents, in union with moral excellence, and made independent of popular favour for other reward than that of public esteem, they would not be doomed

"to rehearse,
Day after day, poor scraps of prose and verse,"

for then a Göethe, or a Johnson (men who could write the most sublime plays, or in the triumphant strains of true poetry, sing,

"When *learning's* triumph o'er her *barbarous foes,*
First rear'd the stage, immortal Shakespeare rose;"

such men), would select the "prose and verse;" and the most skilful *histrionics* would guide the rehearsal of it. "The purse-proud idle blockhead," and the "ruffian" would not dare insult the director, or the poet, or the artist who gave life, motion, and reality to the effusions of the poet, or to annoy those who listened to them; and even the gentleman (according to "Sock and Buskin's" notion of a gentleman)—the man who is without restraint in the company of other free and easy persons of the same description, would be awed into decorous attention. Is this an imaginary picture? It has been a reality—we presume is still so—in Germany—and it is by such a theatre, so supported, so directed, and so conducted, that *Weimar* has acquired the title of the *Athens of Modern Europe*.

It was the triumph of learning "o'er her barbarous foes" that "reared the stage." If those "barbarous foes" succeed in their attempts to overthrow the fabric, it will be in consequence of weakness in the tenants of the structure, and not from any inherent defect in the building itself. The strongest tower which the wit of man can devise to resist barbarism and ignorance, even the omnipotent press itself, may be overthrown, if the efforts of those who assault are seconded by the introduction of abuses, the traitors who undermine the walls, or open the gates to the enemy.

Let us return to the present state of the English theatres, so intimately connected with the welfare of the American.

"The large theatres," says this lively writer, "are proceeding to perdition as fast as any saint in England can desire." "At Drury Lane there have been the wild beasts and Mrs. Wood. It was a silly thing to turn the theatre into a *menagerie*." He represents Mrs. Wood and others, on the great theatres, as poor or indifferent, but pleasing the kind of people who attend them. The smaller theatres are represented as in every respect the best and most prosperous. "Jack Reeves," Madame Vestris, and Liston are praised, and the Haymarket and Adelphi said to be prosperous. "Victorine," a piece from the French, is eulogized, with Mrs. Yates the principal player in it. Then we are told that "all the pantomimes have failed," and that "the solicitros of the patentees have issued a notice to all the managers and performers of the minor theatres, declaring their intention to prosecute everybody 'who shall either act in, or cause to be acted, any interlude, tragedy, comedy, opera, play, farce, or other entertainment of the stage, or any part or parts therein, without the authority or license mentioned in the act of 10 Geo. 2d, c. 28.' The men of the minors seeing that their very existence was aimed at by this act, held a meeting on Christmas-eve, for the purpose of considering how they could best defend themselves against these dramatic Burkers." During this meeting we find it asserted that "Covent Garden seemed sunk so low, that he," the speaker, "did not deem it worthy of mention; but at Drury

Lane the poetry of the drama was reduced to Hyder Ali, the energy to an emaciated lion, and the force to a half-starved tigress."

The writer next notices an evil long existing, the employing for the manufacture of plays "dramatic *littérateurs*. We speak not of authors; for none, under the present system of theatrical management, could exist."

These notices and extracts may give the reader an idea of the present state of
the theatre in Great Britain. A plan of reform has been announced. Reform is
the fashion of the day, reform is needed, and we wish success to reformers, both
of the stage and the state.

Having given this portrait of the English drama in its present state, by an English writer, let us see how the original appears in the eyes of a European foreigner; one used to the stage representation, and theatrical etiquette of France
and Germany. "The most striking thing to a foreigner in English theatres," says
a German prince, "is the unheard-of coarseness and brutality of the audiences."
"It is not uncommon, in the midst of the most affecting part of a tragedy, or
the most charming 'cadenza' of a singer, to hear some coarse expression shouted from the galleries in stentor voice. This is followed, according to the state of
the bystanders, either by loud laughter and approbation, or by castigation and
expulsion of the offender," and in either case you lose what is passing on the
stage. He proceeds, "it is also no rarity for some one to throw the fragments of
his *goute*, which does not always consist of orange peel alone, without the smallest ceremony, on the heads of the people in the pit, or to shale them, with singular dexterity, into the boxes; while others hang their coats and waistcoats over
the railing of the gallery, and sit in their shirt-sleeves." "Another cause for the
absence of respectable families is the resort of hundreds of those unhappy wom-
en with whom London swarms. Between the acts, they fill the large and handsome *foyers*, and exhibit their boundless effrontery in the most revolting manner." "The evil goes to such an extent, that in the theatres it is often difficult to
keep off these repulsive beings, especially when they are drunk, which is not
seldom the case. They beg in the most shameless manner, and a pretty, elegantly dressed girl does not disdain to take a shilling or a sixpence, which she instantly spends in a glass of rum, like the meanest beggar. And these are the scenes,
I repeat, which are exhibited in the national theatre of England." "Is not this—
to say nothing of the immorality—in the highest degree low and undignified?
It is wholly *inconsistent with any real love of art, or conception of its office and
dignity.*" This portrait is undoubtedly true, and it is more than time that a rad-
ical remedy should be found, otherwise a line must be drawn between the friends
of the drama and the friends of the play-house. It must not be suffered that while
the theatre is giving the lessons of morality from its stage, the play-house saloons and upper boxes and lobbies are such as above described.

How different is all this from the appearance which presents itself to the eye in the theatres of France and Germany—of every part of the world, where the influence of English refinement and taste in amusement is not imitated.

It appears, however, that in France, as well as England, the minor theatres take the lead in popularity and fashion. The most prolific and successful dramatists of Paris have devoted their time and talents to the *vaudeville* or *petite comedie*, and other productions, distinct from the legitimate tragedy and comedy of good old times—legitimacy is out of fashion, even at the theatre. Another innovation has taken place in this age of innovation. Instead of a poet being employed in deep research and study, for months or years, to produce a poem of profound thought, and solid as well as bright materials, two, three, or more men of the present day will form a copartnership, such as formerly subsisted between Beaumont and Fletcher in England, but driving an infinitely brisker trade, and they will manufacture dramatic pieces on any subject which circumstance, or the manager may demand, with the rapidity that attends all sublunary transactions in these degenerate days.

But what is most extraordinary, these French manufacturers produce wares of a very superior quality, at least in comparison with their English neighbours, and supply not only the Parisian, but the London and American market. These plays or farces generally pass through the London theatres before they are presented to us. "Trente Ans, ou la vie d'un Joueur," one of these company-wrought productions was done into English by the writer, at the request of the managers of the Bowery theatre, who were justly dissatisfied with the garbled English play, called "The Gambler's Fate," from the same original. This play, and a subsequent piece called "Avant, Pendant, et Aprés," exhibit the same dramatic characters at different and distant periods of time, and by that means produce that variety and rapidity which seems to be the taste of the day.

Mons. Eugene Scribe and his *Collaborateurs* pour out comedy, opera, farce, or pieces uniting the three, and a spice of tragedy in the bargain, and all full of interest, wit, incident—in short, delightful performances. He has published eight vols. octavo, entitled *Theatre* d'Eugene Scribe, and dedicated them to his *Collaborateurs*, Messrs. Deletre, Desnoyers, Delavigne, &c. &c. The English dramas of "The White Phantom," "The Happiest Day of my Life," and many others, are from the workshop of Scribe and Co.

In our projects for a reformed theatre, we have spoken of the plans adopted in Germany. We have instanced Weimar, where Göethe was the director. We have noticed Berlin, where Iffland, one of the best dramatists as well as actors, was the manager. At Hamburgh, Schrœder long directed the stage, and was its ornament both as a player and writer. Schrœder wrote several original pieces, but was so much attached to the older English plays, that he devoted much time to their translation, and delighted to act the characters Shakespeare, Congreve, Farquhar, and Sheridan had portrayed. At Vienna, where the theatre is, as it ought to be, supported by the government, the direction was, and probably, is, in a committee of five performers, selected for their talents and literature. These directors were accountable to the government for the pieces represented. One of the five directors attended during the performance of every evening, in full dress, and announced the succeeding night's entertainments, it being his duty to address the audience when any occasion called for it. We give in our appendix the laws by which the Theatre Françoise is governed, where similar customs prevail.

The expenses of a theatre, governed by the state, or by an enlightened and patriotic association, would be defrayed by the visiters—but profit should not be the object—loss should not be feared. Men of learning, and belles-lettres scholars would be the directors and writers—they would be made independent. Actors who are artists, and scholars, would be the performers—equally made independent. Every abuse would vanish. The theatre would be the temple of the muses, the graces, and the virtues.

In Germany, the theatre being under the direction of despots, or of their privileged aristocratic minions, may be used as an engine to support the abuses of the state which protects and guides it. Not so here. It would only be used, if used as a political engine, for purposes congenial to our republican institutions.

With the rulers of Germany, the opera ranks as high as the drama. We, however, only write of the theatre as the home of Melpomene and Thalia, and view the sister, Euterpe, as a favoured guest in the household where they preside. Let music have a temple of her own; but when in unison with the drama, music and painting are only to be considered as accessories.

⇢ CHAPTER 35 ⇠

Charleston Theatre — Solee — Williamson — Placide — Copartnership of Placide, Greene, and Twaits — Destruction of the Richmond Theatre, and the dissolution of the Charleston management of that period — Mr. Caldwell, and the Theatres of Western States.

It will be remembered that David Douglass, the second manager of the old American Company, built a theatre in Charleston, in the year 1773.

Near the conclusion of our fifth chapter we have mentioned, as an event in chronological order, that a merchant of Charleston, and Mr. Goodwin, a comedian, erected a building called Harmony Hall, in that city, for theatrical and other amusements, in 1786. We have reason to believe that this is the same building now used as a theatre, and standing in Church-street, near Broad-street. This is the second theatre in that city; the first being that which was built by David Douglass in 1773, as above mentioned.

We will devote this chapter principally to such facts as we can collect and recollect, connected with the drama of South Carolina.

The place first called Harmony Hall came afterwards to be known as *Solee's Long Room*. We have had occasion to mention Mr. Solee as a manager at Boston and New-York. He was probably better fitted for his earliest management, as the entertainments first directed by him were in the French language, and he may have known something of French literature.

The company which Mr. Solee carried to Charleston in 1797 was very strong, and probably far superior to any that had exhibited in the Long Room theatre before. Mr. and Mrs. Williamson, were leaders, the first in tragedy and second-rate comedy, the second in romps; Mr. and Mrs. Whitlock were equally leaders, the first in fathers, and the second as the representative of the tragic muse; Chalmers was first gentleman comedian, and Mr. Hughes the low comedian; Mr. and Mrs. Jones added strength to the corps; Miss Broadhurst was the opera lady; the singing man was Chalmers's *inseparable*, Williamson the second; Mr. and Mrs. Cleveland were the walking gentleman and lady, and *both* young, handsome, and equal to their lines; Mr. and Mrs. Placide were powerful, the first in dance and pantomime, the second as an actress and singer; Mr. M'Kenzie was an improving second actor in tragedy or comedy: of Mr. Downie, Mrs. Hughes, and Mr. and Mrs. Rowson, who filled the list, we cannot speak from knowledge.

Mr. Williamson, who stands at the head of this list, succeeded Solee in management, and died in 1802. After the death of Mr. and Mrs. Williamson, the Charleston theatre was taken by Mr. Placide. His children, the oldest, Miss Caroline Placide, afterwards Mrs. Waring, was born in April, 1798, and Henry, the present excellent comedian, was born in September, 1799. These, and the younger boys and girls, as they could be made useful in dances and pantomimes, were trained to the stage, and have been its ornaments and support.

After a time, Mr. William Greene, mentioned as one of the great Chestnut-street company, joined Mr. Placide in the management at Charleston, and played the first line of business. Robinson, familiarly called Hop. Robinson, who had descended from the shopboard of the Park theatre to the stage, and exchanged the thimble and needle for the sword and truncheon, was Greene's second in the buskin. His success, though not great, proved that he had merit. Mat. Sully was the principal low comedian for years. Mr. and Mrs. Claude, Mr. and Mrs. Young, Mr. and Mrs. Clarke, with Messrs, Caulfield, Burke, Anderson, Sandford,

Huntingdon, and Mesdames Green, Placide, Poe, and others, occasionally changing, made the Charleston theatre rich in efficient performers.

When Mr. Placide, in 1803, engaged Mr. Hodgkinson for the Charleston theatre, he absorbed all the attention which had previously been diffused among
many. Mr. and Mrs. Whitlock had again returned to Charleston, and to her
Angela, Mr. Hodgkinson played Osmond as his opening part. When this was
succeeded by Shelty, and a long list of characters not only dissimilar, but opposite, which he performed with such uncommon powers, he gained that favour
and admiration which was justly his due on the stage. He, in the winter of 1803–
4, played in Charleston upwards of 80 different characters. Seven of these were
from the pen of the writer of this work, who will remark, *en passant,* that when
he played Captain Bertram, the play was advertised by the title of "Fraternal
Discord in *England,*" to make it appear as an English production, although the
whole dialogue indicates Germany as the scene of the action.

In the winter of 1804–5, Mr. Hodgkinson was again the great attraction of the
Charleston theatre, which he left in the summer of 1805, and died in the autumn
of the same, at Washington, as above recorded.

When Twaits, after his unfortunate quarrel with Captain Smith, and the subsequent disagreement with the managers of the Park theatre, joined himself to
the Southern company, he was justly, for a time, the favourite actor. The management was now in the hands of three directors—Messrs. Placide, Greene, and
Twaits. They occasionally divided their company, and occupied, with the Charleston theatre, the theatres of Norfolk and Richmond.

This company was broken up in consequence of an astounding calamity
which seemed to shake the American theatre for a time to its foundation. This
was the destruction by fire of the Richmond house, during the time of performance, and the loss of upwards of seventy persons, burned, or crushed to death,
in the course of a few minutes.

It is a curious circumstance that Cooke, who never played either at Charleston or Richmond, was the remote cause of this conflagration, and the ruin of
the Charleston company.

The divisions of the corps of Messrs. Placide, Greene, and Twaits had been
united at Richmond, in the autumn of 1811, preparatory to embarking for their
winter-quarters in Charleston. But it was known that if they could carry the great
George Frederick Cooke with them, even in his shattered condition, their season must be uncommonly productive. The calculation was good. Cooke, removed to a new theatre of action, so dissimilar from either England or the northern states, would have thrown off his damning vice for a time, exerted a renewed
energy, and enjoyed renewed health. He would have been idolized by the hospi-

table south, and he would have refrained, for the poor object of attaining applause as a player, from that which the great object of health, self-approbation, and universal esteem could not cause him to eschew—he would have made—that was the object of the managers—an overflowing treasury.

Mr. Placide had negotiated an engagement with the veteran, and had left a carriage in waiting for him at New-York to transport him to Richmond: there to play a few nights previous to embarking. But Mr. Cooke was sick—or did not choose to move. This caused the delay of the company at Richmond, and the keeping open the theatre until the night of the fatal 26th of December, 1811.

A new play and pantomime had been advertised for the benefit of Mr. Placide. The house was fuller than on any night of the season. The play was over, and the first act of the pantomime had passed. The second and last had begun. All was yet gayety, all so far had been pleasure, curiosity was yet alive, and further gratification anticipated—the orchestra sent forth its sounds of harmony and joy—when the audience perceived some confusion on the stage, and presently a shower of sparks falling from above. Some were startled, others thought it was a part of the scenic exhibition. A performer on the stage received a portion of the burning materials from on high, and it was perceived that others were tearing down the scenery. Some one cried out from the stage that there was no danger. Immediately after, Hopkins Robinson ran forward and cried out "the house is on fire!" pointing to the ceiling, where the flames were progressing like wildfire. In a moment, all was appalling horror and distress. Robinson handed several persons from the boxes to the stage, as a ready way for their escape. The cry of "Fire, fire!" ran through the house, mingled with the wailings of females and children. The general rush was to gain the lobbies. It appears from the following description of the house, and the scene that ensued, that this was the cause of the great loss of life.

The general entrance to the pit and boxes was through a door not more than large enough to admit three persons abreast. This outer entrance was within a trifling distance of the pit door, and gave an easy escape to those in that part of the house. But to attain the boxes from the street it was necessary to descend into a long passage, and ascend again by an angular staircase. The gallery had a distinct entrance, and its occupants escaped. The suffering and death fell on the occupants of the boxes, who, panic-struck, did not see that the pit was immediately left vacant, but pressed on to gain the crowded and tortuous way by which they had entered. The pit door was so near the general entrance, that those who occupied that portion of the house gained the street with ease. A gentleman who escaped from the pit among the last, saw it empty, and when in the street, looked back again upon the general entrance to the pit and boxes, and the door had not yet been reached by those from the lobbies. A gentleman and lady were saved by being thrown accidentally into the pit, and most of those who perished would have escaped if they had leaped from the boxes and sought that avenue to the street. But all darted to the lobbies. The stairways were blocked up. All was enveloped in hot scorching smoke and flame. The lights were extinguished by the black and smothering vapour, and the shrieks of despair were appalling. Happy for a moment were those who gained a window and inhaled the air of Heaven. Those who had issued to the street cried to the sufferers at the windows to leap down, and stretched out their arms to save them. Some were seen struggling to gain the apertures to inhale the fresh air. Men, women, and children precipitated themselves from the first and second stories. Some escaped unhurt—others were killed or mangled by the fall. Some with their clothes on fire, shrieking, leaped from the windows to gain a short reprieve and die in agonies.

"Who can picture," says a correspondent of the Mirror, "the distress of those who, unable to gain the windows or afraid to leap from them, were pent up in the long narrow passages." The cries of those who reached the upper windows are described as being heart-sickening. Many who found their way to the street were so scorched or burnt as to die in consequence, and some were crushed to death under foot after reaching the outer door.

Add to this mass of suffering, the feelings of those who knew that they had relatives or friends who had gone to the house that night. Such rushed half frantic to the spot with the crowds of citizens from all quarters—while the tolling bells sounded the knell of death to the heart of the father or mother whose child had been permitted to visit the theatre on that night of horror.

"As my father was leading me home," said Mr. Henry Placide, "we saw Mr. Greene, exhausted by previous exertion, leaning on a fence, and looking at the scene of ruin. For all was now one black mass of smoking destruction. "Thank God!" ejaculated Greene, "Thank God! I prohibited Nancy from coming to the house to-night! She is safe!"

Nancy was his only daughter, just springing into womanhood, still at the boarding-school of Mrs. Gibson; and as beautiful and lovely a girl as imagination can picture.

Mrs. Gibson and the boarders had made up a party for the theatre that evening, and Nancy Greene asked her father's permission to accompany them. He refused—but unfortunately added his reason—"the house will be crowded, and you will occupy a seat that would otherwise be paid for." On these words hung the fate of youth, innocence, and beauty. "I will pay for your ticket, said the kind instructress, we will not leave you behind." The teacher and the pupil were buried in the ruins on which the father gazed, and over which he returned thanks for the safety of his child. He went home and learned the truth.

An instance of the escape of a family is given. The husband, with three children, were in the second boxes; his wife, with a female friend, in another part of the house. The wife gained a window—leaped out and escaped unhurt. Her friend followed and was killed. The father clasped two helpless girls to his breast, and left a boy of twelve years of age to follow—the boy was forced from the father, and to a window—sprang out and was safe. The parent, with his precious charge, followed the stairway, pressed upon by those behind him, and those who mounted on the heads and shoulders of the crowd before them—he became unconscious, but was still borne along—he was taken up, carried to his bed, and opened his eyes to see all his family safe.

On the contrary, Lieut. Gibbon, of the navy, as exemplary in private life as heroic in the service of his country, and on the brink of a union with Miss Conyers, the pride of Richmond for every accomplishment and virtue—was swept into eternity while exerting himself to do all that man should do in such trying circumstances. He was with his mother at the theatre, and carried her to a place of safety—then rushed back to save her in whose fate his own was bound up— he caught her in his arms—had borne her partly down the staircase, when the steps gave way, and a body of flame swept them to eternity.

Friday, the 27th of December, 1811, was a day of mourning to Richmond. The banks and stores were closed. A law was passed prohibiting amusements of every kind for four months. A day was set apart for humiliation and prayer. A monument was resolved on—to be erected to the memory of the dead and the event.

George Frederick Cooke did not come on to Richmond, and the Thespians embarked for Charleston. They were shipwrecked: lost most of the property by water that the fire had spared. And in short, the company was broken up by the blow received at Richmond. Placide, Greene, and Twaits passed away in a few short months, or years, after the dreadful night of the 26th of December.

Of the theatres in Broadway and Anthony-streets, under the direction of Messrs. Holland and Twaits, or of the theatrical commonwealth, it is not within our province to speak in this work.

In his last illness, Mr. Twaits was attended by Dr. McLean, who requested Drs. Mott and H. U. Onderdonk to assist in an examination of the corpse, the day after death. Mr. Twaits had laboured under a very severe asthmatic affection. We insert an extract from the publication of these gentlemen, as it seems to prove that powerful and effective exertions of the voice, both in speaking and singing, can be made, when the organs which we suppose necessary to both are nearly obliterated. Those who remember Mr. Twaits will recollect the very powerful and distinct manner of both speaking and singing which he exhibited in his profession. The surgeons, after noticing the stomach, &c., say—"The lungs were adherent to the pleura costalis universally, and when cut into, exhibited a compact texture; one very small vomica was noticed; the heart natural; cartilages of the ribs considerably ossified; the œsophagus had a small contraction near its upper part, which, however, gave way to a finger introduced; the cartilages of the larynx were partly ossified, and both they and the soft parts somewhat thickened; the lining membrane rough, as if from chronic inflammation; sacculus laryngis of the right side entirely obliterated, that of the left side not so completely effaced; the trachea was very large, and the muscles of the voice very strong. Were not these morbid appearances of the larynx produced by frequent and powerful efforts of the voice in his public exercises?"

From our knowledge of this extraordinary young man, who died at the early age of 26 or 27, we should answer "NO"—but from the abuse of these great natural powers in the frequent and powerful efforts of the voice in his "private" exercises.

After the death of Mr. Placide, Mrs. Placide attempted the management of the Charleston theatre, but failed in it, or was discouraged, and relinquished the scheme.

Mr. Holman conducted the Southern theatre for one season, and went to England for recruits at the end of it. But though successful in his errand, his plans were frustrated by his sudden death.

The recent purchase of Louisiana, and settlement of the great valley of the Mississippi, will make the theatre of this vast and populous region a subject for a subsequent work; we will only briefly and rapidly notice the progress of the drama of the west.

The French theatre was planted in New-Orleans as early as 1809; but it did not flourish until a new house was built by John Davis, Esq., in 1818, and a regular company imported from France.

The gentleman who introduced the English drama into these regions, is entitled to our notice on many accounts. In a future work we shall speak more fully of him.

James H. Caldwell commenced his managerial career in 1817, in the District of Columbia, and built, by subscription, in 1818, a new theatre in Petersburg, Virginia. In the same year he performed the first play that had been witnessed in Richmond after the calamitous fire which we have recorded above. Having been invited to make an establishment at New-Orleans, he embarked with a company of great force at City Point, James river, and on the 7th of January, 1820, represented at New-Orleans the first English drama ever performed in that city by a regular *corps dramatique*. The Honey-moon, and Three and Deuce, were the pieces of the evening. After a season of four months, Mr. Caldwell returned to Petersburg, Va. He has continued annually to visit New-Orleans from that time, and has introduced most of the actors of merit, known to the continent, either as residents or visiters.

On the 29th of May, 1822, the corner stone of the first American theatre in New-Orleans was laid. This house is nearly on the model of the Chestnut-street theatre, Philadelphia. It has been recently enlarged and improved. It will contain 2000 people.

On the 9th of May, 1823, this house was first opened, with the Honey-moon, and Three and Deuce. It was not then finished, but in 1824, on the 1st of January, it was opened in a state of complete preparation, with an appropriate address.

The gradual decline of the drama in Virginia induced Mr. Caldwell to try Nashville, the capital of the state of Tennessee. Accordingly he built a handsome theatre, to contain 700 auditors, which was opened on the 9th of October, 1826. "The Honey-moon" was again the opening play, to which was added the farce of "Of Age To-morrow."

Several attempts had been made to establish the drama at Natchez, in the state of Mississippi. A temporary building for that purpose had been erected in 1818, and had been occupied by amateurs, and occasionally a corps of Thespians. In 1822, this building was destroyed by fire. On the 30th of April, 1828, Mr. Caldwell opened a very neat and commodious brick theatre, capable of containing 700 persons. The same enterprising manager established himself at St. Louis—and opened a new theatre at Huntsville, Alabama, in 1826.

Thus we see an intelligent and enterprising gentleman establishing himself and the drama in this great and rapidly increasing portion of the United States, and growing with its growth, which is beyond parallel in the history of the world.

→→ CHAPTER 36 ←←

Two Letters from two Dramatists.

In answer to queries made by us we have received two letters from two distinguished dramatists, written with such frankness, and in a style so congenial to the feelings intended to be expressed in this work, that we know no mode of communicating the information they contain that will be so acceptable to the reader as by giving them in the words of the writers.

The plays of these gentlemen are an honour to the dramatic literature of the country, and we feel that the brief and pleasant sketch given by the authors will induce those who have not before met with such as are published, to lose no time in becoming acquainted with them by perusal.

Both these dramatists are honourably employed in the civil service of their country, and we hope will be protected in their evening of life from those ills which some of their brethren have to encounter, who have not taken the tide of fortune at its flood, or, perhaps, merited public confidence.

"*To William Dunlap, Esq.,*
"Philadelphia, 10th June, 1832.

"DEAR SIR,

"My friend Wood informed me, a few days since, that you desired a list of my dramatic productions for your History of the American Stage. I had almost resolved, in these utilitarian times, to forget that I had ever indulged in such fantasies; but in drawing the poor neglected things from their obscure retreats, just to see what they were made of, I could not but feel something like a return of fatherly affection for them; sufficient, at least, to induce me, if not to sketch their lives and characters, to record their names, that posterity may know, through your immortal pages, that such things were. As I write on Sunday, the work-day world cannot find fault, however I may deserve the censure of *holy*-day folks.

"Very early in life I began a play of three acts, with a marquis and a banditti in it. Cervantes furnished the plot, and it was to be called the SPANISH ROVER. This was in the year 1804. The fate of the one act, which was completed, will be seen hereafter.

"In the next year, 1805, I wrote a mask, entitled AMERICA: a brief, one-act piece, consisting of poetic dialogue, and sung by the genius of America, Science, Liberty, and attendant spirits, after the manner of the mask in the Tempest. It was to close a drama I had projected on the adventures of Smith in Virginia, in the olden time. The drama, however, when completed, was found sufficiently long without it, and the mask was laid aside. It was never represented nor printed.

"ATTILA, a tragedy, suggested by Gibbon, of course, was commenced about this period, and nearly two acts were written. Should I ever be tempted to do any thing more in the dramatic way, it will be to finish Attila. He is certainly an excellent stage personage. I was, a year or two ago, on the point of bringing him forward for Forrest, when I was informed that Stone had an Attila almost ready for the stage: he since tells me that he has laid it up in lavender. When I commenced, I had not an idea that this hero had ever been, or could ever be thought of by dramatic mortal man, and behold ye, Corneille and Schiller have each written an Attila, Stone had almost done another, and just as I had determined to go at it, forth comes an Attila in London; which, however, is said to be a dull poem. But have you never yourself been the victim of these odd coincidences, and just as you had fixed upon a subject or a title, found yourself superseded—a thing next in atrocity to the ancients' stealing all one's fine thoughts. My comedy of *Tears and Smiles* was to be called *Name it Yourself,* when out comes a *Name it Yourself* in England, and out comes too a *Smiles and Tears,* with a widow, an Irishman, and almost all my dramat. pers. I write the *Indian Princess,* and an *Indian Princess* appears in England. Looking over the old English dramatists, I am struck with the *Damon and Pythias* of Edwards as a subject, but am scarcely set down to it, when lo, the modern play in London; and what is worse, with the fine part of Pythias absolutely transformed into a snivelling fellow, who bellows like a calf at the prospect of dying for his friend. *Wallace* was purloined from me in like manner, and several other heroes: at length I fix upon *Epaminondas,* as a 'learned Theban' of so philosophical a cast of character, that even the French had not thought of him for the boards. I form my plot, and begin, *con amore,* when I am told that Dr. Bird has written a *Pelopidas* and an *Epaminondas,* comprehending the whole life of the latter. There is something curious in this, is there not? But the coincidences are not restricted to dramatic subjects; half a dozen literary projects of mine have met a similar fate. I will mention one. Being botanically inclined, and fond of rural description, I had the material prepared for a book of poetico-prose botany, to be beautifully christened the *Circle of the Seasons*—when, by heavens, there is published in England not only a *Book of the Seasons,* but an identical *Circle of the Seasons!* This was too bad, and so, with Billy Black, 'I give it up.' Excuse me for this rambling: I return to my list.

"TEARS AND SMILES, a comedy, in five acts, was written between the 1st of May and the 12th of June, 1806. The idea of writing was suggested at a dinner of the fishing company, at their ancient castle on the Schuylkill, on which august occasion you yourself were a guest. The topic happened to be Breck's *Fox Chase,* which had been first acted on the preceding night. Manager Warren, who was present, asked me to enter the lists as a dramatist, and Jefferson put in for a Yankee character. By-the-way, such a Yankee as I drew! I wonder what Hackett would say to it. The truth is, I had never even seen a Yankee at the time. You may have forgotten all this; and also that in walking home, I having ventured to hint to you that I had already written a dramatic piece, you very frankly advised me to throw it into the fire, remarking that the first attempts of young dramatists were never fit to be seen, and always made their authors ashamed. When I got home, determined to obey the injunction of the oracle, I took up the mask 'with zeal to destroy.' But no: I could not immolate liberty, science, peace, plenty—nay, my country, *America*—and so I saved my conscience by bringing the *Spanish Rover,* robbers and all, to the stake, a fate which I dare say they richly deserved. 'Tears and Smiles' was cast with the whole strength of the company: Warren, Wood, Cain, Jefferson, Blissett, Mills, M'Kenzie, Bray; and Mesdames Melmoth, Wood, Woodham, Francis, Jefferson. It was first acted March 4th, 1807, to a brilliant audience, and with complete success. Notwithstanding, I must confess that one of the deities of the gallery, where I had ensconced me, did fall fast asleep (O all ye gods!)

in the second act. Nay, others appeared likely to follow his example, during the sentimental dialogue, and were perhaps only kept awake by the expectation of seeing 'that funny fellow, Jeff., again.' Never did I hail a 'funny fellow' with so much glee as on that eventful night. The prologue was kindly undertaken by Wood, who began in his most lofty manner,

"'With swelling port, imperious, and vain,'

and there he stopped, at a dead fault. After in vain endeavouring to recall what was to follow, he addressed the audience:—'Upon my soul, ladies and gentlemen, I am so unaccustomed to this kind of speaking, that I must beg, &c. &c.,' in his peculiar, janty way, and with his usual happy effect. The piece was announced for repetition on the next night, the author was 'trotted out,' and ambled through the lobbies and boxes, and the booksellers made proposals— what a triumph for a tyro! I gave the copyright to Blake, who transferred it to Longworth. On the second night, being in the green-room, several of the ladies complained, on coming off, that they were put out in their parts by the loud and impertinent remarks from one of the stage boxes. My course was instantly adopted. I went around to the box, and calling out one of the gentlemen, made such an expostulation as had the desired effect. The conduct of those persons had been so flagrantly indecent as to draw upon them sounds of disapprobation from several parts of the house. They were certain witlings about town—Samuel Ewing, a lawyer, was one—who, induced by the reputation the piece had gained on the first night, to lay aside their habitual apathy towards American productions, were now aroused only to malignant feeling, as I was neither politically nor socially of their set.

"THE EMBARGO; or, What News? liberally borrowed from Murphy's Upholsterer, was prepared for Blissett's benefit, on the 16th of March, 1808. The subject of an embargo, then existing, was rather ticklish, and some of the patriotic sentiments were somewhat coldly received by a portion of the audience; but the majority were of the right feeling, and bore me triumphantly through. Very much to their credit, several of our merchants were distinguished for the applause they bestowed. I know not what became of the manuscript: Blissett took the piece to Baltimore, where it was performed, and whence it was sent, at the request of Bernard, to Boston. It was never printed.

"THE INDIAN PRINCESS, in three acts, founded on the story of Captain Smith and Pocahontas, began some time before, was taken up in 1808, at the request of Bray, and worked up into an opera, the music to which he composed. It was first performed for his benefit on the 6th of April, 1808, to a crowded house: but Webster, particularly obnoxious, at that period, to a large party, having a part in it, a tremendous tumult took place, and it was scarcely heard. I was on the stage, and directed the curtain to be dropped. It has since been frequently acted in, I believe, all the theatres of the United States. A few years since, I observed, in an English magazine, a critique on a drama called *Pocahontas; or, the Indian Princess*, produced at Drury Lane. From the sketch given, this piece differs essentially from mine in the plan and arrangement; and yet, according to the critic, they were indebted for this very stupid production 'to America, where it is a great favourite, and is to be found in all the printed collections of stock plays.' The copyright of the 'Indian Princess' was also given to Blake, and transferred to Longworth. It was printed in 1808 or 1809. George Washington Custis, of Arlington, has, I am told, written a drama on the same subject.

"In 1809, at the request of the managers, I altered, that is, *Americanized* Cherry's *Travellers;* making it, I am afraid, little less absurd than I found it.

"MARMION, from Scott's poem, was finished early in 1812, at the special request of Wood. The Chronicles of Hollinshead supplied me with several characters, and particularly with a good speech for King James, in which a close parallel is run between the conduct of England to Scotland, and, (by allusion) to this country. As it was intended by Wood and Cooper that 'Marmion' should come out as an English play, I was fearful this 'one speech' might 'unkennel' the 'occult' design, but they declared it must remain as a powerful 'touch at the times;' and remain it did, and was always effective. A London critic, in *The Opera Glass,* quotes it, with the remark that it must have had a powerful effect when uttered on our stage at the period when hostilities were about commencing; and it is also quoted with applause by a critic in the American Quarterly Review. 'Marmion' was first acted in New-York, in April, 1812. Cooper announced it as a play by Thomas Morton, Esq., author of Columbus, &c. &c.; this was audacious enough in all conscience, but the finesse was successful, and a play most probably otherwise destined to neglect, ran like wild-fire through all our theatres. I never felt very proud of the circumstance. The war intervening, I had no leisure to attend to the publishing of 'Marmion' until when it was printed by Palmer, Philadelphia, I think, for I have not a copy of the first edition by me. It was again published, very much curtailed, in the 'Acting American Theatre.'

"Talking of coincidences, on the very day I sent Marmion to New-York, I received a note from a Mrs. Ellis, who had furnished the Olympic theatre with several pieces, 'Cinderella,' 'Otranto,' &c., begging me to furnish in the newspapers a puff or two for a new drama, 'Marmion,' that she was about producing.

"THE ARMOURER'S ESCAPE; or, *Three Years at Nootka Sound,* a melo-dramatic sketch, in two acts, founded on the adventures of John Jewitt, armourer of the ship Boston, was first acted at Philadelphia, 24th of March, 1817. Jewitt performed the hero himself. The only copy of the piece was taken by Jewitt.

"HOW TO TRY A LOVER, a comedy, in three acts, suggested by some passages in a whimsical novel of Le Brun's, and introducing the novelty, as I then thought it, of the 'Court of Love' to the stage. The play was written in 1817. It was cast, studied, rehearsed, and announced; and why it was not acted, I am unable to say, as it is the only drama I have written with which I was satisfied. It was printed, ready to be published after representation.

"SUPERSTITION, a serious dramatic tale, in five acts, was first performed 12th of March, 1824; it is published in the *Acting American Theatre*. The London 'Opera Glass' and the American Quarterly Review speak favourably, if not flatteringly, of it.

"I have written nothing since.

"In haste,

"Yours very truly,

"J. N. BARKER."

Mr. Noah's answer to our inquiries bears the same character with that received from Mr. Barker, and we insert it without alteration, for the reason assigned in respect to the letter of his brother dramatist.

"*To William Dunlap, Esq.*

"New-York July 11th, 1832.

"DEAR SIR,

"I am happy to hear that your work on the American drama is in press, and trust that you may realize from it that harvest of fame and money to which your untiring industry and diversified labours give you an eminent claim. You desire me to furnish you a list of my dramatic productions; it will, by dear sir, constitute a sorry link in the chain of American writers—my plays have all been *ad captandum:* a kind of *amateur* performance, with no claim to the character of a settled, regular, or domiciliated writer for the green-room—a sort of volunteer supernumerary—a dramatic writer by 'particular desire, and for this night only,' as they say in the bills of the play; my 'line,' as you well know, has been in the more rugged paths of politics, a line in which there is more fact than poetry, more feeling than fiction; in which, to be sure, there are 'exits and entrances'—where the 'prompter's whistle' is constantly heard in the voice of the people; but which, in our popular government, almost disqualifies us for the more soft and agreeable translation to the lofty conceptions of tragedy, the pure diction of genteel comedy, or the wit, gayety, and humour of broad farce.

"I had an early hankering for the national drama, a kind of juvenile patriotism, which burst forth, for the first time, in a few sorry doggerels in the form of a prologue to a play, with a Thespian company, of which I was a member, produced in the South-street theatre—the old American theatre in Philadelphia. The idea was probably suggested by the sign of the Federal Convention at the tavern opposite the theatre. You, no doubt, remember the picture and the motto: an excellent piece of painting of the kind, representing a group of venerable personages engaged in public discussions, with the following distich:

"'These thirty-eight great men have signed a powerful deed,
That better times, to us, shall very soon succeed.'

"The sign must have been painted soon after the adoption of the Federal
Constitution, and I remember to have stood 'many a time and oft,' gazing,
when a boy, at the assembled patriots, particularly the venerable head and
spectacles of Dr. Franklin, always in conspicuous relief. In our Thespian corps,
the honour of cutting the plays, substituting new passages, casting parts, and
writing couplets at the exits, was divided between myself and a fellow of infinite wit and humour, by the name of Helmbold; who subsequently became
the editor of a scandalous little paper, called the *Tickler:* he was a rare rascal,
perpetrated all kind of calumnies, was constantly mulcted in fines, sometimes
imprisoned, was full of faults, which were forgotten in his conversational
qualities and dry sallies of genuine wit, particularly his Dutch stories. After
years of singular vicissitudes, Helmbold joined the army as a common soldier, fought bravely during the late war, obtained a commission, and died.
Our little company soon dwindled away; the expenses were too heavy for our
pockets; our writings and performances were sufficiently wretched, but as
the audience was admitted without cost, they were too polite to express any
disapprobation. We recorded all our doings in a little weekly paper, published,
I believe, by Jemmy Riddle, at the corner of Chestnut and Third-streets,
opposite the tavern kept by that sturdy old democrat, Israel Israel.

"From a boy, I was a regular attendant of the Chestnut-street theatre,
during the management of Wignell and Reinagle, and made great efforts to
compass the purchase of a season ticket, which I obtained generally of the
treasurer, George Davis, for $18. Our habits through life are frequently gov-
erned and directed by our early steps. I seldom missed a night; and always
retired to bed, after witnessing a good play, gratified and improved: and thus,
probably, escaped the haunts of taverns, and the pursuits of depraved pleasures, which too frequently allure and destroy our young men; hence I was
always the firm friend of the drama, and had an undoubted right to oppose
my example through life to the horror and hostility expressed by sectarians
to plays and play-houses generally. Independent of several of your plays which
had obtained possession of the stage, and were duly incorporated in the legitimate drama, the first call to support the productions of a fellow towns-
man, was, I think, Barker's opera of the "Indian Princess." Charles Ingersoll
had previously written a tragedy, a very able production for a very young
man, which was supported by all the 'good society;' but Barker, who was 'one
of us,' an amiable and intelligent young fellow, who owed nothing to hered-
itary rank, though his father was a whig, and a soldier of the revolution, was
in reality a fine spirited poet, a patriotic ode writer, and finally a gallant soldier of the late war. The managers gave Barker an excellent chance with all
his plays, and he had merit and popularity to give them in return full houses.

"About this time, I ventured to attempt a little melo-drama, under the title of the *Fortress of Sorrento,* which, not having money enough to pay for printing, nor sufficient influence to have acted, I thrust the manuscript in my pocket, and having occasion to visit New-York, I called in at David Longworth's Dramatic Repository one day, spoke of the little piece, and struck a bargain with him, by giving him the manuscript in return for a copy of every play he had published, which at once furnished me with a tolerably large dramatic collection. I believe the play never was performed, and I was almost ashamed to own it; but it was my first regular attempt at dramatic composition.

"In the year 1812, while in Charleston, S.C., Mr. Young requested me to write a piece for his wife's benefit. You remember her, no doubt; remarkable as she was for her personal beauty and amiable deportment, it would have been very ungallant to have refused, particularly as he requested that it should be a '*breeches part,*' to use a green-room term, though she was equally attractive in every character. Poor Mrs. Young! she died last year in Philadelphia. When she first arrived in New-York, from London, it was difficult to conceive a more perfect beauty; her complexion was of dazzling whiteness, her golden hair and ruddy complexion, figure somewhat *embonpoint,* and graceful carriage, made her a great favourite. I soon produced the little piece, which was called *Paul and Alexis, or the Orphans of the Rhine.* I was, at that period, a very active politician, and my political opponents did me the honour to go to the theatre the night it was performed, for the purpose of hissing it, which was not attempted until the curtain fell, and the piece was successful. After three years' absence in Europe and Africa, I saw the same piece performed at the Park, under the title of the *Wandering Boys,* which even now holds possession of the stage. It seems Mr. Young sent the manuscript to London, where the title was changed, and the bantling cut up, altered, and considerably improved.

"About this time, John Miller, the American bookseller in London, paid us a visit. Among the passengers in the same ship was a fine English girl of great talent and promise, Miss Leesugg, afterwards Mrs. Hackett. She was engaged at the Park as a singer, and Phillips, who was here about the same period fulfilling a most successful engagement, was decided and unqualified in his admiration of her talent. Every one took an interest in her success: she was gay, kind-hearted, and popular, always in excellent spirits, and always perfect. Anxious for her success, I ventured to write a play for her benefit, and in three days finished the patriotic piece of *She would be a Soldier, or the Battle of Chippewa,* which, I was happy to find, produced her an excellent house. Mrs. Hackett retired from the stage after her marriage, and lost six or seven years of profitable and unrivalled engagement.

"After this play, I became in a manner domiciliated in the green-room. My friends, Price and Simpson, who had always been exceedingly kind and liberal, allowed me to stray about the premises like one of the family, and always anxious for their success, I ventured upon another attempt for a holy-day occasion, and produced *Marion, or the Hero of Lake George.* It was played on the 25th of November—Evacuation day, and I bustled about among my military friends, to raise a party in support of a military play, and what with generals, staff officers, rank and file, the Park theatre was so crammed, that not a word of the play was heard, which was a very fortunate affair for the author. The managers presented me with a pair of handsome silver pitchers, which I still retain as a memento of their good will and friendly consideration. You must bear in mind that while I was thus employed in occasional attempts at play-writing, I was engaged in editing a daily journal, and in all the fierce contests of political strife; I had, therefore, but little time to devote to all that study and reflection so essential to the success of dramatic composition.

"My next piece, I believe, was written for the benefit of a relative and friend, who wanted something to bring a house; and as the struggle for liberty in Greece was at that period the prevailing excitement, I finished the melo-drama of the *Grecian Captive,* which was brought out with all the advantages of good scenery and music. As a 'good house' was of more consequence to the actor than fame to the author, it was resolved that the hero of the piece should make his appearance on an elephant, and the heroine on a camel, which were procured from a neighbouring *menagerie,* and the *tout ensemble* was sufficiently imposing, only it happened that the huge elephant, in shaking his skin, so rocked the castle on his back, that the Grecian general nearly lost his balance, and was in imminent danger of coming down from his 'high estate,' to the infinite merriment of the audience. On this occasion, to use another significant phrase, a 'gag' was hit upon of a new character altogether. The play was printed, and each auditor was presented with a copy gratis, as he entered the house. Figure to yourself a thousand people in a theatre, each with a book of the play in hand—imagine the turning over a thousand leaves simultaneously, the buzz and fluttering it produced, and you will readily believe that the actors entirely forgot their parts, and even the equanimity of the elephant and camel was essentially disturbed.

"My last appearance as a dramatic writer was in another national piece, called the *Siege of Tripoli,* which the managers persuaded me to bring out for my own benefit, being my first attempt to derive any profit from dramatic efforts. The piece was elegantly got up—the house crowded with beauty and fashion—every thing went off in the happiest manner; when a short time after the audience had retired, the Park theatre was discovered to be on fire, and in a short time was a heap of ruins. This conflagration burnt out all my dramatic fire and energy, since which I have been, as you well know, peaceably employed in settling the affairs of the nation, and mildly engaged in the political differences and disagreements which are so fruitful in our great state.

"I still, however, retain a warm interest for the success of the drama, and all who are entitled to success engaged in sustaining it, and to none greater than to yourself, who has done more, in actual labour and successful efforts, than any man in America. That you may realize all you have promised yourself, and all that you are richly entitled to, is the sincere wish of

"Dear sir,

"Your friend and servant,

"M. M. NOAH.

"Wm. Dunlap, Esq."

⇥ CHAPTER 37 ⇤

Scraps — Mr. Cooke's Father — Miss Rock — Cooke and Mathews — Kean — Cooke's Monument — Mr. and Miss Holman — Doctor Wilson's Letter to Doctor Hosack — Doctor Hosack's Introductory Letter borne by Mr. Holman to a friend in Philadelphia — Letter to Doctor Hosack on the Death of Mr. Holman.

We have fulfilled our engagement, by bringing up the history of the American theatre to the arrival of George Frederick Cooke, the greatest Richard, Sir Giles Overreach, Falstaff, Iago, Sir Pertinax, and Sir Archy that the western world has seen. We have even gone a little beyond our limits; and as there is nothing so dear to man as liberty, we will, in this additional chapter, indulge ourselves in speaking of *any* thing, or *any* body, in *any* way connected with our subject, which, or who, may be presented to the imagination of an author delighted at seeing that he has reached the goal proposed at starting in his race,— the last chapter.

And first, Cooke. We have represented him in our two volumes, published by Longworth in New-York and Miller in London, as the son of a captain in the 4th dragoons; but have no doubt that the captain must be reduced to a sergeant, as we have had more accurate information on that subject from the widow of Mr. Rock, the tragedian's old and tried friend. In this we have misled Mr. Galt, who, in his Lives of Players, has trusted us as we trusted Cooke. The mother of the tragedian was a lady by birth and education; and his father dying when the boy was very young, he received his earliest impressions from, and under the eyes of, his widowed and probably too indulgent parent.

Mrs. Rock was in this country with her niece Miss Rock, a very accomplished young lady, carefully educated for the profession she ornamented, and one of the best actresses we have seen on our boards in a certain line of playing. But

Miss Rock, though pleasing, was deficient in the rare charms of superior personal beauty: she wanted height. She danced elegantly—not as a dancer, but as a lady; she was a musician, and sung well. With the figure and face of some we could name, her Letitia Hardy would have been the best in the world.

We have a little more to say of George Frederick Cooke, and it is connected with two of the most extraordinary characters of the drama that have dazzled the eyes of the good people of the western hemisphere,—Kean and Mathews.

And first, the mimic and comedian. What I have to say of him shall be told in my autobiographical style, and is another correction of my aforesaid memoirs of George Frederick.

It was in the month of April, in the year 1823, that I embarked with two hundred and fifty others, in the steamboat Chancellor Livingston, for Albany. After the bustle of leave-taking, and the various ceremonies and multifarious acts of hurried business which daily take place on the departure of one of these self-moving hotels from the city of New-York, I had leisure to look around me, with the intention of finding some acquaintance as a companion, or at least to satisfy my curiosity as to who were on board.

I had seen many faces known to me when I first entered the boat, but they had vanished: all appeared, at first, strange. I soon, however, observed James Fennimore Cooper, the justly celebrated novelist, in conversation with Dr. Francis. The last-mentioned gentleman I had long known, but with the first my acquaintance was of recent date. We had occasionally met at the bookstore of Wiley, his publisher; but it was not until after the circumstances I am now recording that an intimacy took place which has been to me a source of very great pleasure.

I soon after noted a man of extraordinary appearance, who moved rapidly about the deck, and occasionally joined the gentlemen above named. His age might be forty; his figure tall, thin, and muscular; one leg was shorter than the other, which, although it occasioned a halt in his gait, did not impede his activity; his features were extremely irregular, yet his physiognomy was intelligent, and his eyes remarkably searching and expressive. I had never seen Mathews, either in private or public, nor do I recollect that I had at that time ever seen any representation of him, or heard his person described; but I instantly concluded that this was no other than the celebrated mimic and player. Doubtless his dress and manner, which were evidently English, and that peculiarity which still marks some of the votaries of the histrionic art, helped me to this conclusion. I say, "still marks;" for I remember the time when the distinction was so gross that a child would say, "There goes a play-actor."

The afternoon was uncommonly fine for our climate in the cold month of April. The passengers generally kept the deck. We had not gone far on our voy-

age before the author of The Spy (for he was then chiefly known by that fascinating work) accosted me nearly thus:—"I understand from Mathews that you
and he have never met. He is on board, and has expressed a wish to be introduced to you. Have you seen him off the stage?"

"No—nor on."

"Is it possible! There he stands with Francis."

"I have been noticing that figure, and had come to a conclusion that it was
Mathews."

"His figure is odd enough, to be sure. I suppose you know that his lameness
and the deficiency in the regular symmetry of his face are owing to his being
thrown from a gig, and very much injured by the fall; but these defects are not
seen on the stage, or are turned to good account by his skill in his profession."

Part of this passed as we approached the subject of the dialogue, and I soon
made acquaintance with Charles Mathews. He introduced the subject of George
Frederick Cooke and his Memoirs, complimented the author of them, and of
course made himself agreeable. Fennimore was very attentive to me, and appeared to wish my gratification by a display of the talents of Mathews, who, as
the novelist afterwards told me, was at his suggestion making a voyage to Albany, that he might see something more of America and American manners than
are to be found in a seaport town.

The figure and manner of the actor were sufficiently uncommon to attract
the attention of a throng of men usually employed in active business, but here
placed in a situation which, of all others, calls for something to while away time;
but when some who traced the likeness between the actor on the deck of the
steamboat and the actor on the stage of the theatre, buzzed it about that this
was the mirth-inspiring Mathews, curiosity showed itself in as many modes as
there were varieties of character in the motley crowd around him.

This very natural and powerful propensity, which every person who exposes
himself, or herself, upon a public stage, to the gaze of the mixed multitude,
wishes ardently to excite, was, under the present peculiar circumstances of time,
place, and leisure, expressed in a manner rather annoying to the hero of the sock,
who would now willingly have appeared in the character of a private gentleman.

There are individuals who can generally overcome this difficulty by dint of
character, talent, or personal appearance; but in the case before us there was
nothing sufficiently dignified to repress the clownish propensities of such among
the crowd as were clowns, and they were not a few.

The passengers in the Chancellor Livingston finding themselves on the same
boards with the celebrated Mathews, and at liberty to gaze without paying for
it, at the man who had delighted them on the stage, gratified their curiosity
without much ceremony; and whenever Mathews was perceived to be station-

ary, and with his usual animation amusing his immediate companions, the watchful loungers closed around by degrees, and according to character, feeling, or education, became distant or nearer auditors and admirers of the wondrous man.

One clown, in particular, followed the object of his very sincere admiration with a pertinacity which deserved a better return than it met. He was to Mathews a perfect Monsieur Tonson, and his appearance seemed to excite the same feelings. The novelist and physician pointed out to me the impertinent curiosity of this admirer of the actor, and we all took some portion of mischievous delight in observing the irritability of Mathews. It increased to a ludicrous degree when Mathews found that no effort or change of place could exclude his tormentor from his sight; and when, after having made an effort to avoid him, he, on turning his head, saw Monsieur Tonson fixed as a statue, again listening in motionless admiration to his honeyed words; the actor would suddenly change from the animated relation of story or anecdote, with which he had been entertaining his companions, to the outpouring of a rhapsody of incoherent nonsense, uttered with incredible volubility; without altering his former manner, he would rattle off something like, "Sardanapalus Heliogabalus Faustina and Kitty Fisher with their fourteen children Cecrops Moses Ariadne Robinson Crusoe Nimrod Captain Cooke Bonaparte and Jack the Giant-killer had a long confab with Nebuchadonozer Sir Walter Raleigh and the pope on the best mode of making caraway comfits." But he found that this only made his admirer listen more intently, and open his eyes and mouth more widely and earnestly. As happens with many other orators, the more unintelligible his nonsense, the greater was the admiration of the auditor.

We had but one regular meal on the passage, a very plentiful supper, at about seven o'clock, with tea and coffee. We had embarked at 5 P.M., and arrived at Albany by sunrise. The meal was not suited to the habits of Mr. Mathews, and he was offended by both the matter and manner of it; but when the preparations for sleeping took place, and he found that the whole company, females excepted, must seek rest in the same cabin, some in berths and others accommodated with mattresses on the floor, his feelings revolted, and he protested against taking rest on such terms.

To this feeling I am indebted for a night of much amusement; I should be unjust if I did not add, and some instruction. I had secured a mattress on the floor of one of the cabins, and should have dully slept away at least part of the night, but that Fennimore Cooper gave me intimation of Mathews's wish to sit up, and of his (Cooper's) success in obtaining the captain's cabin on the deck of the vessel, where Mathews, Francis, and himself had determined to enjoy a supper, whiskey-punch, and such convivial pleasure as could be extracted from such circumstances, and such a meeting. I was invited to make one, and readily accepted the invitation.

Seated in the captain's cabin, and freed from all annoyance, Mathews became, as usual, the fiddle of the company; and story, anecdote, imitation, and song poured from him with the rapidity and brilliancy of the stars which burst from a rocket on a rejoicing night. To make himself still more agreeable to the senior, he introduced the memoirs of George Frederick, with that flattery which is delicious to all men, and peculiarly so to an author. "The story of Cooke and Mrs. Burns," he added, "you have told remarkably well, and when I have introduced it in my "*Youthful Days,*" I have always taken your words; but Tom. Cooper from whom, as I understand, you had it, forgot the termination of the story,—the real *denouement,*—which makes it infinitely more dramatic." All joined in the request that Mathews would tell the story in his own way, and he, nothing loath, began:—

"I was a raw recruit in the Thespian corps, and it was my first campaign in Dublin. Chance made me a fellow-lodger with Cooke, at the house of Mistress Burns. I had looked at the great actor with an awful reverence, but had not yet been honoured by any notice from him.

"In getting up Macklin's *Love a la Mode,* I had been cast for Beau Mordecai, and assuredly a more unfit representative of the *little Jew* can scarcely be imagined. As tall as I now am, I had then all the rawboned awkwardness of a *hobbletehoy,* and no knowledge of the world or of the stage. But Mr. Cooke must be shown to the Dublin public in Sir Archy, and there was no other Mordecai to be had. I was, however, perfect in the words; and if I murdered the Jew, I did it impartially; I murdered him 'every inch.'

"After the farce, I *tarried,* as you Yankees say, *a considerable time* at the theatre, rather choosing to linger among the almost expiring dipped candles of the dressing-rooms than to seek, through mist and mud, my lofty but comfortless abode in Mrs. Burns's garret; but the property-man gave me my cue to depart, by putting out the lights; and I was slowly mounting to my bed, when, as I passed the room of the great man, I saw him (the door being open) sitting with a jug before him, indulging after the labours of the evening. I was stealing by, and had already one foot on the flight of stairs which led to my exalted apartment, when I was arrested by a loud, high-pitched voice, crying, 'Come hither, young man.' I could scarcely believe my senses: I hesitated. 'Come in,' was repeated. I advanced. 'Shut the door, and sit down.' I obeyed. He assumed an air of courtesy, and calling upon Mistress Burns for another tumbler, filled for himself and me. 'You will be so kind, my good Mistress Burns, as to bring another pitcher of whiskey-punch in honour of our young friend.' 'To be sure and I will, Mr. Cooke.' The punch was brought, and a hot supper, an unusual luxury then to me.

After supper, the veteran, quite refreshed and at ease, chatted incessantly of plays and players,—lashing some, commending others,—while I, delighted to be thus honoured, listened and laughed; thus playing naturally and sincerely the part of a most agreeable companion. After the third jug of punch, I was sufficiently inspired to ask a few questions, and even to praise the acting of the veteran.

"To use your own words, as I have often before done," said Mathews, addressing himself to the biographer, "'one jug of whiskey-punch followed the other;' and Cooke began to advise his young companion how to conduct himself on the real and on the mimic scene of life. 'You are young, and want a friend to guide you. Talent you have; but talent without prudence is worthless, and may be pernicious. Take my word for it, there is nothing can place a man at the head of his profession but industry and sobriety. Mistress Burns!—Shun ebriety as you would shun destruction. Mistress Burns! another jug of whiskey-punch, Mistress Burns.'

"'Oh, Mister Cooke—'

"'You make it so good, Mistress Burns; another jug.'

"'Yes, Mister Cooke.'

"'In our profession, my young friend, dissipation is the bane of hundreds; 'villanous company'—low company leads to drinking; and the precious time is lost which should have been employed in gaining that knowledge which alone can make men respectable. Ah! thank you, Mistress Burns: this has the true Hibernian smack!'

"'You may say that, Mister Cooke.'"

It is needless to remind the reader, that with the aid of Mathews's powers of imitation, sometimes called ventriloquism in this hum-bugging world, all this and much more would be extremely pleasant, and the more especially as the company had repeated supplies of the same inspiring beverage from the steward, and almost as good, certainly as strong, as that of Mistress Burns's.

Mathews went on to describe the progress of Cooke's intoxication, during which his protests against drunkenness became stronger with each glass. He then undertook to instruct the tyro in the histrionic art, and especially in the manner of exhibiting the passions. Here it would be vain to endeavour to follow Mathews: Cooke's grimaces and voice,—while his physical powers, under the government of whiskey, rebelled at every effort against the intention of the lecturer,—were depicted by the mimic in a manner beyond the conception of even those who have seen the public exhibition of his talents: here all was unrestrained gig and fun, and the painting truly *con amore,* and glowing from heart and glass.

"It must be remembered," continued Mr. Mathews, "that I was but a boy, and Cooke in the full vigour of manhood, with strength of limb and voice Herculean. I had the highest reverence for his talents, and literally stood in awe of him; so that when he made his horrible faces, and called upon me to name the passion he had depicted, I was truly frightened,—overwhelmed with the dread of offending him, and utterly at a loss to distinguish one grimace from another, except as one was *more* and another *most* savage and disgusting.

"'Now, sir—observe—what's that?'

"'Revenge—'

"'Revenge, you booby! Pity! pity!'

"Then, after making another hideous contortion of countenance, he cries,

"'What is that, sir?'

"'Very fine, sir; very fine, indeed.'

"'But *what* is it, sir?'

"Forced to answer, and utterly unable to guess the meaning of the distorted face which he then again thrust before me, I stammered out,

"'Anger, sir.'

"'Anger!'

"'Yes, sir; anger, to be sure.'

"'To be sure you are a blockhead! Look again, sir, look again! It's fear, sir—fear. You play! you a player!'"

Mathews then exhibited the face of Cooke, as he distorted it to express the tender passion,—a composition of Satanic malignity and the brutal leering of a drunken satyr,—and imitating Cooke's most discordant voice, cried,

"'There, sir; that's love.'

"This," continued Mathews, "was more than I could bear: even my fears could not restrain my laughter: I roared. He stared at first; but immediately assuming a most furious aspect, he cried,

"'What do you laugh at, sir! Is George Frederick Cooke to be made a laughing-stock for a booby! What, sir!'

"Luckily, at that moment Mrs. Burns stood with the door partly opened, and another jug in her hands. 'You must pardon me, sir,' I said, with a quickness which must have been the inspiration of whiskey, 'but you happened to turn your soft and languishing look towards the door just as Mrs. Burns opened it, and I could not but think of the dangerous effect of such a look upon her sex's softness.'

"He laughed; and embracing the jug as the good woman put it down, he looked at Mrs. Burns, and with some humour endeavoured to sing, *How happy could I be with either, were t'other dear charmer away,* but with a voice which defies art and nature for a comparison.

"Mrs. Burns now protested against any more punch; but after some time agreed, upon Cooke's solemn promise to be satisfied with one more jug, to bring it.

"'But remember your honour, Mister Cooke; and *that* is the jewel of a jontleman; and sure you have pledged it to me, you have.'

"'I have, my good Mistress Burns; and it is 'the immediate jewel of the soul,' as you say.'

"'I said no such thing; but I'll be as good as my word; and one more jug you shall have, and the divil a bit more, jewel or no jewel!'

"I was heartily tired by this time, and placed my hope on Mrs. Burns's resolution. The last jug came, and was finished; and I wished him good night.'

"'Not yet, my dear boy.'

"'It's very late, sir.'

"'Early, early: one jug more.'

"'Mrs. Burns will not let us have it, sir.'

"'She will not! I'll show you that presently!'"

Then followed a fine specimen of imitation; Mathews, as Cooke, calling upon Mrs. Burns (who was in the room below, and in bed), and then giving her answers, as coming up through the floor, in the manner called ventriloquism.

"Mistress Burns! Do you hear, Mistress Burns?"

"Indeed *and I do,* Mister Cooke."

"Bring me another jug of whiskey-punch, Mistress Burns!"

"Indeed *and I won't,* Mister Cooke!"

"You won't?"

"Indeed and indeed *so I won't.*"

"Do you hear that, Mistress Burns?" (smashing the jug on the floor).

"Indeed *and I do,* and you'll be sorry for it to-morrow."

He then regularly took the chairs, one by one, and broke them on the floor immediately over Mrs. Burns's head, after every crash crying, "Do you hear that, Mistress Burns?" and she as regularly answering, "Indeed *and I do,* Mister Cooke." He next opened the window, and threw the looking-glass into the street.

"I stood," continued Mathews, "in a state of stupid amazement during this scene; but now attempted to make my escape, edging towards the door, and making a long stride to gain the garret stairs.

"'Come back, sir! Where are you going?'

"'To bed, sir.'

"'To bed, sir! What, sir! desert me! I command you to remain, on your allegiance! Desert me in time of war! Traitor!'

"I now determined to make resistance; and feeling pot-valiant, looked big, and boldly answered,

"'I will *not* be commanded! I *will* go to bed!'

"'Aha!' cried the madman, in his highest key, 'Aha! do you rebel? Caitiff! wretch! murderer!'

"He advanced upon me, and I shrank to nothing before his flashing eye. 'Murderer!' and he seized me by the collar with Herculean grip, 'You will go! I will send you to the place you are fittest for! Murderer, I'll drag you to your doom! I'll give you up to Fate! Come along, caitiff!' and he dragged me to the open window, vociferating, 'Watch! watch! murder! murder!' in his highest and loudest key.

"Immediately the rattles were heard approaching in all directions, and a crowd instantly collected. He continued vociferating, 'Watch! watch! murder!' until the rattles and exclamations of the watchmen almost drowned his stentorian voice.

"'What's the matter? who's kilt? who's murdered? Where's the murderer?'

"'Silence!' screamed Cooke; 'hear me!' All became hushed. Then holding me up to the window, the raving tragedian audibly addressed the crowd:— 'In the name of Charles Macklin, I charge this culprit, Charles Mathews, with the most foul, cruel, deliberate, and unnatural murder of the unfortunate Jew, Beau Mordecai, in the farce of Love a la Mode.' Then pulling down the window, he cried, 'Now go to bed, you booby! go to bed! go to bed! go to bed!'"

The steamboat party remained together until near morning, and then retired to rest. Let it not be supposed that they imitated the folly of the hero of the above tale because whiskey-punch has been mentioned. The evening, or night, was one of real interchange of mind, heightened by the peculiar powers and habits of the very extraordinary histrionic artist who gave this instance of Cooke's eccentric and pernicious propensities.

I shall only now add to what has been said of Cooke a notice of the respect paid to his talents by his successor, Kean. It is known that Doctors M'Lean, Francis, and Hosack were the physicians who endeavoured to save Cooke from the effects of his own folly. These gentleman I am proud to call my friends, and from them I have received the knowledge of facts connected with the last scene in the actor's life, and the attention paid to his mortal remains after death.

The present dramatic record terminates, by agreement, with the arrival of Cooke in this country. The reader who is solicitous for further details of the drama, and dramatic literature, will probably turn to my Memoirs of George Frederick Cooke, which gives a general view of the subject to the time of his death. As a further continuation of the American theatre may not be called for, I have thought it not uninteresting to give in this place some account of the respect paid to his memory by a most distinguished successor in his line of professional life.

Shortly after the arrival of the celebrated Edmund Kean in New-York, which was in November, 1820, he paid a visit to the place of the interment of Mr. Cooke; and then determined, prior to his departure for Europe, to erect a suitable monument to the memory of him whose extraordinary powers, though he himself had never witnessed them, had been so highly lauded by every admirer of Shakespeare and lover of nature.

Accordingly, in June, 1821, the body of Mr. Cooke was removed from the strangers' vault, in St. Paul's church-yard to a most eligible spot in the centre of that extensive burial-ground. Mr. Cooke died in September, 1812, and the monument over his remains was erected on the 4th of June, 1821. It is a well-executed work, by the Frazees, in marble, consisting of a square pedestal on two steps, surmounted by an urn, from the top of which a flame issues towards the Park theatre, the scene of Mr. Cooke's greatest efforts in this country. The inscription on the tomb, which was furnished by Dr. Francis, who had superintended the removal of his remains, is as follows:—

> "Erected to the memory of George Frederick Cooke, by Edmund Kean, of the Theatre Royal, Drury Lane, 1821.
>
> > "Three kingdoms claim his birth,
> > Both hemispheres pronounce his worth."

There have been published several engraved representations of this monument, in which the figures of Mr. Kean and Dr. Francis, and a medallion with a portrait of Mr. Cooke are introduced. As a specimen of this species of work, the monument is worthy of the subject of it, and equally so of the liberality of Mr. Kean. If what old Fuller says be correct, that the shortest, plainest, and truest epitaphs are the best, no fault can be found with the inscription of Cooke's tomb. The place of his nativity is yet disputed: each portion of the United Kingdom claims him as its own, though there is no doubt that he was born in Westminster, as he told us, and we have recorded. He long enjoyed an unrivalled reputation, both in the Old and in the New World; and although it may hereafter be found that his surgeon possesses his skull, and his successor, Kean, the bones of the forefinger of his right-hand,—that dictatorial finger,—still the monument covers the *remains* of George Frederick Cooke.

Having gone beyond our limits, we will mention another actor and actress who followed Cooke to this country:—Mr. Holman and his accomplished daughter.

The histrionic career of Mr. Holman was checkered in America no less perhaps than in Great Britain; nevertheless, through all vicissitudes, he sustained the character of the scholar, the man of honour, and the gentleman. He who shall at some future day continue the History of the American Theatre, will fail in doing justice to an excellent man and a distinguished actor, if he does not enrich his materials with interesting incidents connected with the industry, talents, and strenuous efforts of Mr. Holman to elevate the standard of the profession he had chosen. In the city of New-York, Mr. Holman might be considered as having secured a fair and honourable distinction by the public display of his talents; all that European criticism has awarded to him for his Lord Townley, was realized by a New-York audience. His projects and measures to enlarge the dramatic taste in Albany, were marred and circumscribed by his want of sagacity in his pecuniary arrangements. In the south he unquestionably might have reaped a fair harvest of profit and fame, had not circumstances beyond his control blighted his harvest.

The notice which was taken abroad of his life and death, seems to have been intended to operate as an *in terrorem* to future dramatic adventure in this country. He was subjected, neither more nor less than other individuals, to the influence of pestilence, or the stroke of lightnings; and though his English biographer deems his demise as arising from the too great prevalence of these mighty agents in America, which, he says, carried him off in common with many others, it deserves to be here stated, that he died after an illness short indeed, but of a common cause of death, apoplexy (as we are informed by his attending physician, Dr. Francis), at Rockaway, Long Island, on the morning of Sunday, the 24th of August, 1817, and in the 53d year of his age.

We live in America about as well and as long as in any country on earth; and foreigners who leave their prejudices and their vices at home, will enjoy the blessings we are willing to share with them and be thankful. We believe Mr. Holman did so. But death will meet us, go where we will; and the man born in Europe will surely die in America, if he comes here and stays long enough.

The following notice of Mr. Holman was published shortly after his decease.

> "Mr. Holman was a native of England, and a descendant of Sir John Holman, Bart., of Warkeworth Castle, Banbury. He received the early part of his education at the academy Soho Square, London, with the view on the part of his friends to the church. In 1780, he entered Queen's College, Oxford, and such was the estimation in which he was held, that he received the honours of the university after he became attached to the theatrical corps. While at school he distinguished himself by his scenic exhibitions, and Garrick, who there witnessed his representation of Hamlet, pronounced most favourably of his performance.
>
> His first appearance on a public stage was in the character of Romeo, at Covent Garden theatre, in 1784; his reception is said by many to have been in the highest degree flattering, and fully justified the expectations of his friends. He arrived in this country in the fall of 1812, since which time he uninterruptedly persued his histrionic career.
>
> The abilities of Mr. Holman, as an actor, are sufficiently declared by his maintaining a powerful rivalship with Kemble; and his Lord Townley will long be remembered by the lovers of the drama in both hemispheres. He was distinguished as a gentleman and a scholar; and by the urbanity of his manners, and the force of his talents, greatly contributed to enhance the character of his profession. The virtues of his heart are known to all with whom he was in habits of intercourse."

We copy the above, but deny that Mr. Holman was ever the powerful rival of John Kemble.

The principal of Mr. Holman's writings for the stage were—"Abroad and at

Home!" "The Red Cross Knights," "The Votary of Wealth," "What a Blunder!" "Love gives the Alarm," and "The Gazette Extraordinary."

As early as 1811, it was known that Mr. Holman, probably induced by the accounts of Cooke's great reception, intended to visit America. "I came away, sir, without preparation," said Cooke: "without my stage-clothes, without my books—as if I was running away by stealth from my creditors—like a criminal flying from the laws of his country. Now Holman will come out after making every preparation; after making a bargain by which he will put that money into his own pocket which I am putting into the pockets of men who treat me as if I was an idiot."

Accordingly, in 1812, Mr. Holman and his amiable and accomplished daughter arrived. Between the landing-place and his hotel, looking up at the corner, as all persons of his profession are apt to do, he saw his own play of "Abroad and at Home" announced as the play of the evening. It was a curious coincidence, and hailed by him as a lucky omen.

We witnessed Mr. Holman's first appearance before a London audience in the autumn of 1784. He played Romeo to the Juliet of Miss Younge. He was apparently twenty-one years of age, and remarkably handsome. The Juliet was only young in name, and not by any means a beauty; but she was so fine an actress that the discrepancy was not observed—or only for the moment. The next winter his Romeo had a Juliet better suited in youth and beauty, and even greater than the first in all the requisites for the impassioned maid—Miss Brunton, known to Americans as Mrs. Merry. And in the mean time, Pope, Mr. Holman's rival in the young heroes of tragedy, had taken his first Juliet to the altar.

We saw Mr. Holman in many characters at that period, from 1784 to 1787, and particularly remember his excellent personification of Chamont, in the Orphan.

Mr. Holman's reasons for leaving London for Dublin are recorded in English dramatic history. When he arrived on our shores he brought letters to many gentlemen of distinction, among which was the following to Dr. Hosack, who has kindly permitted us to insert it.

> "London, Great Windmill-street, July 1st, 1812.
>
> "MY DEAR SIR,
>
> "Presuming upon our having been fellow-students in the Anatomical school in Great Windmill-street, to which I succeeded on the retirement of Dr. Baillie and death of Mr. Cruikshank, that I am not unknown to you, I take the liberty of introducing a very particular friend of mine to your acquaintance, and am sure, as a stranger in America, he will receive from you all those attentions which your countrymen are so well known to pay to dramatic merit and to respectable and honourable men. Mr. Holman, who will deliver to you this letter, was, when you were in London, the first actor in Covent Garden theatre; with his

professional character you must therefore be well acquainted. He has been offered such terms to visit your country that induces him to take with him his daughter, and they mean to exercise their professional talents for some time. I beg to say that you will find him a most honorable and well-educated man; he is a fellow of Queen's College, Oxford, and is connected with some of the first families in this kingdom. He is quite a stranger in your city, and I shall feel most particularly obliged by every attention you may have it in your power to show him, and shall be most happy to return them to any of your friends visiting this country. Dr. Baillie, Mr. Home, and most of your old friends are well; but to Mr. Holman I refer you for any news this part of the world produces. I have this summer made an arrangement for receiving Mr. Charles Bell as a partner in teaching anatomy, as my business now prevents me taking the whole concern on myself. I am, my dear sir,

"With great respect,

"Your very obedient servant,

"JAMES WILSON."

Of this gentleman Reynolds gives the following anecdote, connected with a club of which he was a member. In this literary club they had a rule that every member, on publishing a literary composition, should give a dozen of claret to the club. Topham, Merry, Morton, Rogers, Reynolds, Andrews regularly paid the fine; but the "choice spirits of the club" asserted that Wilson should pay the penalty for an advertisement announcing the commencement of his course of lectures, and, by a majority of votes, it was decided that the advertisement was a literary composition, and the unwilling author was compelled to pay the fine.

In connexion with this slight notice of Mr. Holman and his daughter, we must not omit to notice again the ephemeral existence of what was entitled the Theatrical Commonwealth.

An association under this title, at the head of which was Mr. Twaits, commenced their performances in New-York on the 3d of November, 1813 at a theatre fitted up for the purpose, which had been built as a circus, and stood at the corner of White-street and Broadway, on the east sides of the latter street.

The members of the Commonwealth were Mr. and Mrs. Twaits, Mr. and Mrs. Burke, Mr. and Mrs. Clarke, Mr. and Mrs. Fisher, Messrs. Robinson, Waring, Fennell, jun., Caulfield, Anderson, Jacobs, Ringwood, and Mrs. Goldson.

Mr. and Miss Holman commenced playing at the opening of this new theatre, and were to have a share of the profits and a benefit for each. The managers of the Park theatre, in order to distress the Commonwealth, and aware of the consequences of withdrawing Miss Holman from the association, or obliging the concern to increase her compensation, offered her an engagement for seven nights, at $200 a night. Twaits immediately engaged her on the same terms, and Mr. Holman generously volunteered his own services, and to prolong the period of the performances until the terms of the engagement could be fulfilled.

Bernard and Dwyer both played a few nights. The house continued open until the 9th of January, 1814, when the Commonwealth removed to Philadelphia and opened the old Southwark play-house as we have elsewhere mentioned.

Mr. Holman's *Lord Townley,* and the *Lady Townley* of Miss Holman, have been considered among the perfections of the art histrionic. In 1813, this gentleman and lady played with success at the Chestnut-street theatre, Philadelphia, on which occasion Doctor Hosack thus writes to his friend in that city.

> *An Introductory Letter from Dr. Hosack to his friend in Philadelphia.*

"DEAR SIR,

"I beg leave to introduce to your acquaintance my friend, Mr. Holman, who, with his daughter, proceeds to Philadelphia to pass a few weeks—fame has gone before them—it is therefore unnecessary for me to say any thing that can add to the favorable opinion you must already entertain of them. Both Mr. and Miss Holman have been very cordially received in this city; we part with them with great reluctance, and shall gladly welcome their return.

"Mr. Holman unites with his high professional character the advantages of education and the accomplishments of a gentleman. Mr. H. is a fellow of Queen's College, Oxford, and is connected with some of the first families of Great Britain, and has ever enjoyed the best society. Miss Holman you will also find a very interesting woman, and in her professional character is universally esteemed. She possesses more of the accomplishments and manner of Miss Farren than I have met with. Miss H.'s Lady Townley is one of the finest pieces of acting I have ever witnessed, with the exception of her great prototype just mentioned.

"Your attentions will greatly oblige,
"Dear sir,
"Your friend,
"DAVID HOSACK."

Unfortunately, Mr. Holman embarked in an opposition theatre in Philadelphia, in Walnut-street, and did not succeed. He afterward went to Charleston, South Carolina, and after conducting that theatre one season very much to the satisfaction of the public, went to England for additional performers. He brought out a lady of great talent as a singer, and of distinguished beauty and merit, whom he shortly afterward married; and, while at Rockaway, on Long Island, died suddenly. His death gave occasion to the following letter, which is one among many testimonies of the high estimation in which this accomplished gentleman was held.

"*To Doctor David Hosack.*
"Charleston, September 6th, 1817.

"MY DEAR SIR,

"The melancholy and afflicting intelligence of the death of my revered friend, the late Joseph George Holman, Esq., reached me a few days since. No event of my life has ever excited so deep and unaffected a sensation of grief. Connected to him by the warmest ties of friendship, and happy in the certainty of an affection on his part as disinterested as it was noble and ingenuous, his premature and unexpected dissolution has overwhelmed me with the bitterest sorrow. My acquaintance with him commenced a few weeks after his arrival in this city, in the fall of the year 1815. Though short, it was crowded with the improvement of years, and with recollections that can never fade from my heart. The superiority of his mind, the suavity of his manners, the goodness of his heart, added to the high and chivalric honour of his feelings, secured at once my admiration and esteem. Upon a closer intimacy, I loved him with the most permanent affection. I regarded him as a parent, and I feel persuaded from the interest he exhibited upon every occasion touching my advancement in life, that he felt for me all the solicitude of so tender a relation. Believe me, sir, I do not use these terms as the commonplace expressions of ordinary grief. My heart bleeds when I recall the many endearing hours we have passed together. It feels as if a link were stricken from the chain that binds it to existence *now that he is no more.* Judge then with what agony of feeling I have heard the death of a friend around whose melancholy and untimely tomb so many recollections hover. God protect and comfort those who stand in a more intimate relation than even that of friendship.

"Although personally a stranger to you, sir, I claim the privilege of this introduction, which I pray you to pardon, as well from the circumstance of your having professionally attended him in his last illness, as from the long-established reputation you enjoy—we look to such men with veneration, though unknown, and humanity has a kind of prescriptive right to approach them with the same freedom that strangers are permitted to enter our habitations, to derive the information they require, and share our hospitality and kindness: there is something in my heart that whispers to me you will not refuse me the favour of an answer.

"You must be aware, my dear sir, that every circumstance, even the most minute, respecting the cause, approach, progress, and final determination of his distressing malady, will afford me some consolation at least. It is painful indeed beyond expression, to know how so dear, so very dear a friend died, under the pressure of so fatal and so melancholy an affection; yet there is some comfort even in its dismal relation. It is like extracting a bullet: we writhe under the operation, but feel somewhat more composed after its removal, though the wound may be equally as painful.

"I am truly sorry, my dear sir, even for a moment to interrupt your useful and important avocations with the recital and petition of my personal sorrows: I pray you to pardon me, and attribute this liberty to the excitement of a feeling too stubborn to be subdued. It will be a proud moment to me, if that moment shall ever arrive, when I can personally declare to Dr. Hosack my respect and veneration for both his mind and heart. It will be a feeble tribute, truly, but I am sure of one thing, it will not want sincerity. God preserve you, sir, many years, to extend the circle of your usefulness. I am, very respectfully and sincerely,

"Your most obedient servant,

"EDWIN C. HOLLAND."

⤞ CONCLUSION ⤝

A continuation of American theatrical history would be rich in biographical subjects. Cooke, Kean, McCready, Forrest, Wallack, Conway, Hamblin, Barnes, Bartley, Gilfert, Rock, Kelly, Fisher, Hilson, Kemble, Mathews, Caldwell, Maywood, Barry, Placide, Hackett, Sharpe, Malibran, Austin—but why go on with the catalogue? The field is perhaps too wide; and although the writer of this volume alone possessed much of the information it contains, there are many who are more fully in possession of recent events and facts—more intimately acquainted with the characters of those who now possess or have recently passed over the American stage, than one whose pursuits have for years diverted his attention in part from the drama and its adherents.

As we have gone beyond the bounds prescribed by mentioning some of those actors who flourished in America after the arrival of Cooke, we may be excused for paying our respects to two distinguished men of the histrionic profession, on the ground of their being natives of the soil. The one has taken his stand as a leader of the high, and the other of the low drama. We allude to Messrs. Forrest and Hackett.

Ample biographical notices of both these gentlemen belong to a continuation of the history of the drama in this country, and will be interesting to the reader and honourable to the subjects. At this time, and in this place, we merely mention them to pay our respects *en passant.*

The very great success and distinguished talents of Mr. Forrest entitle him to an ample portion of the time and attention of the future historians of the American stage.

Of Mr. Hackett's talents in public and worth in private life, we have more intimate and personal knowledge. We have been the witness of his talent for imitation, and pleased by his accurate delineation of the manners and peculiarities of American low life, which, though full of absurdities, is free from the disgusting characteristics of the European. There are three distinct species of clown in our country, the descendants of English, Low Dutch, and German emigrants.

In all these Mr. Hackett is *true* and *original*. In that compound monster which is found on our western frontiers we are told he has been as successful in the representation as Mr. Paulding has been in the sketching. Mr. Hackett's success has been proportionate to the enterprise and observation he has evinced. He has been from his *debut* a star. Without regular training, or the toil of *working up* in a company of comedians, he has seized the crown at a leap, and may say with Richard, "I am myself alone."

It is to two American actors, Messrs. Forrest and Hackett, that we are indebted for (what we hope may become a custom) the encouraging of American dramatists by offering liberal remunerations for works of talent. The managers of our theatres, while they are such as they have been, looking only to the treasury, calculate to procure their new plays at eighteen-pence a piece. They are not even obliged, as the London directors are, to employ translators or playwrights, hired by the month, to produce dramas to order. The London translator suits the French piece to the market, fits it to the taste of a royal theatre and loyal audience, or the caprice of an English manager; and it must be given to us in America in the same shape, however mutilated or deformed, because it is cheap. To employ an American to suit the foreign piece to the feelings of republicans, or to give it as originally suited to the atmosphere of Paris, would cost more than the price of the English pamphlet, or the manuscript purloined by the prompter. We owe to Messrs. Forrest and Hackett an example, and we believe a successful one, which may induce even managers to call forth the latent talent of the country, and raise up a patriotic drama.

To return to Mr. Hackett—and not to be too serious when speaking of a comedian, we will consider another debt which his country owes him. He has identified himself with the American stage, therefore we go out of our way to notice him, and overleap a chronological line which we had drawn as our limits, within which he does not fall by many years. We hope we shall be excused, and that those who may justly feel that they are entitled as actors to as much or more attention, will remember that as an American, the writer of this history has obligations to Mr. Hackett outweighing all ordinary considerations. We have noticed his claim upon us for exhibiting the peculiarities of the clowns of the New World; but we are indebted to him for more than plays or encouragement of playwrights in the way of amusement and improvement. An actor was introduced to the western world by Mr. Hackett, who is also, like himself, "himself alone," and in himself a host. We mean that most entertaining and instructing performer and philosopher—*Punch*. Punch, an ingenious French author has said—nay demonstrated—is at least as old as the globe we inhabit. The memory of man does not go back to the time when Punch *was not;* and the earliest records prove the past existence of Punch. But although Asia, Europe, and Africa were at all times blessed by his presence, his ubiquity was not perfect. America did not know Punch. The patriotism of Mr. Hackett remedied the defect. The representative of the American clown went to Europe, and Punch followed in his train on his return. Punch is not only the most popular of all actors, but in himself a play—and not only a play, but, as the shell and the shellfish are one, a play-house—stage, scenes, and curtain, author, player, prompter, orchestra, and singer—a *star* dimming the lustre of all other stars—the only theatrical star who is independent of managers and theatres, being in himself actor, manager, and theatre. But Americans had not refinement enough to relish Punch, and disgusted with democracy, he returned, like other mistaken Whig travellers, to the hereditary orders of Europe and to European refinement.

Mrs. Trollope, another European traveller, finds America deficient in many things. She laments that there is no established church, and no Punch. The natural consequences following from their absence are revivals and camp-meetings, inordinate eating and drinking, melancholy contentment in the women, and in the men ignorance, dollar-hunting, and spitting. A king, lords, established church, and Punch, would remedy all this. We admire Mrs. Trollope's book, and recommend it to our readers as entertaining and instructive, full of truth, and replete with novelties to the inhabitant of America. We say Mrs. Trollope, although it is evident that Captain Basil Hall wrote both the book and the review of it in the English Quarterly. If any one doubts, let him call to mind the extreme sensitiveness of the lady and the captain—their tender fears lest the American generals, colonels, and majors should cut their mouths;—the dread of edgetools identifies the lady and the captain-reviewer. Be that as it may, we like the book, whether Mrs. Trollope is a captain in his Britannic majesty's navy or an old woman. But we have not yet done with Punch.

We doubt not but those patriots who introduced the Italian opera into America will be immortalized in the history of the march of mind, yet their title to the gratitude of posterity is much less than his who introduced Punch. It is strange, but true, that neither the one nor the other appeared suited to our state of society. It is only when men have attained to a refinement of the highest character that those exhibitions can be relished which are above making appeal to the understanding. Another attempt is being made to establish the Italian opera, and if it succeeds, Punch will return

In the mean time let us listen to Shakespeare in his own language, and if possible, be patient under the matrimonial lessons of Sir Charles and Lady Rackett, Sir Peter and Lady Teazle, or Lord and Lady Townley, until Punch and his wife Joan make a second appearance.

We resume the grave style which becomes us on making our bow to the courteous reader who has accompanied us through some hundred pages, and doubtless parts from us with regret.

Let us not be supposed inimical to the opera. Though ignorant of music, we delight in it. The opera-house combines all the magic of sweet sound, as the picture-gallery exhibits the magic of the pencil. Music and painting, when combined with the theatre of a country, are subordinates—poetry is the mistress. But in the opera-house and the picture-gallery, music and painting are the "leading gods," and poetry is an accessory.

We have promised ourselves and our readers some remarks on the causes of the deterioration of the drama. It has been suggested that the perfection to which acting has been carried, with its accompaniments of costume, music, and scenery, has been injurious to the drama, by withdrawing attention from the poet to the player, painter, and the machinist. Can it be supposed that the perfection to which players have attained in representing the author's images should cause the skilful writer to turn his efforts from the drama to compositions for the closet? It is the necessities and cupidity of managers, and the absence of wholesome regulations in theatres, that cause the lover of literature rather to depend upon the closet than the stage. In France the theatre is protected and supported by the government. Mr. Harris, the proprietor of Covent Garden theatre, tells us, that "the performers are not 'his majesty's servants,' but they may be said to be the servants of the constituted authorities." One theatre alone, he says, costs the government more than "thirty thousand pounds sterling per annum." We will not repeat what we have said on this subject, but we are confident that this control may be exercised at little expense (probably none), and the cause of literature, which is the cause of humanity, essentially served. If the expenses of the national theatre should exceed the receipts, let it be supplied by increased taxes on taverns and tippling houses. We refer to our appendix for the regulations of the Theatre Françoise.

It may be, that as men have advanced in civilization, refinement, and knowledge, the theatre, necessary to their progress at an early period, ceases to be so. This may be true as it respects those who are of the highest, the most refined grade—the capital of the Corinthian column of society. But the mass of mankind yet want every aid in rising to the level which republican governments make necessary for those who are henceforward to be self-guided and self-ruled—the people.

When we speak of the theatre of America, we mean the drama of the country. A theatre is used synonymously with a play-house. But the theatre of a country may be its loftiest and most efficient literature, when its play-houses may be, as in England, unhappily at present, and in a less degree in America (though soon we hope in no respect whatever), the open marts of vice and portals to destruction. We should as soon think of confounding the church of a country with the tabernacles where folly, madness, and blasphemy preside, as its theatre with the saloons and bar-rooms of a play-house.

If, as we believe, the world is to be in the future a democratic world, and the people thereof hereafter to be governed by those who form and compose the nation; by those whose interest it is that peace and good-will among men should exist, and not by those who have considered men as their property to be used or abused for their pleasure,—in short, if mankind are to govern themselves, as we know they ought to do, and as we believe they will—it is expedient that every source of knowledge should be opened to the governors, *the people*— every obstacle to their improvement removed, and every inducement held forth to qualify them for the high office they are destined to fill. If, in the progress to that high state of moral perfection enjoyed by the favoured few who prefer the lessons of wisdom taught in the closet to those received in public assemblies, another state less refined must be passed through—a state in which the attractions of oratory or even scenic decorations are useful—let us give to theatres that purity, as well as power, which shall produce the high moral purpose here aimed at.

To conclude our conclusion. We have endeavoured to trace the growth of the drama in our country from the time the shoot was planted in the soil to the maturity of the tree. We have seen it flourish in vigour, and put forth branches in every direction. It may be feared, worms in the bark, not the root, may cause decay.

We have compared the theatre to a mighty engine. It is such. We have shown how that engine was introduced among us. We have endeavoured to state facts that may guide others in their efforts to make this mode of diffusing knowledge a blessing to society. We have spoken of men connected with the stage as we have found them, always remembering that there is no "palace whereinto sometimes foul things intrude not." We have noticed individuals and circumstances unworthy of record only as links in the chain of historical events. We have interspersed reflections as they were suggested by the subject matter, and ventured to propose a project for the improvement of the drama. The drama *will* exist in good or evil repute, to guide or mislead, whether legislators will it or not. The people will have it so. The choice of the legislator is only to render that beneficial which may be made otherwise.

We might have been more particular in describing the manner of certain great actors in delivering well-known passages from the works of the established dramatists, or delineating certain characters in well-known plays; and if this work is received favourably, and a History of the American Theatre to the present time required, we may yet do so.

A review of the dramatic works which have been produced to this day, in our country, would be useful; and a due reprobation of much vile trash which has disgraced the stage and the press.

A comparison between the actors of the time past, by one who knew their merits and faults, with those who have succeeded them, and a candid criticism on many excellent performers now before the public, in our widely extended and extending republic, would serve the cause of literature and the arts.

We have seen the rise and the fall of many, in every pursuit and profession. The great cause that renders vain the ability of the individual in one, is the same in all—vicious indulgence. Either the indulgence of sensuality and idleness, or of inordinate vanity and cupidity. We say "renders vain the ability of the individual"—many fail from utter inability in every pursuit.

One great theatre in each great city of the Union, supported and guided by the state, would remedy every evil attendant on our present play-house system.

We should have no managers seeking *only* to fill the treasury, or pay hungry creditors—no stars rendering all attraction but that of novelty unprofitable—no benefit-plays tempting actors to exceed their stated and certain income, and to descend to practices, for the purpose of gaining *patrons,* which tend to disgrace their profession, and sometimes end in destroying themselves—no display of impudent vice before the stage, or of immoral precept upon it. A theatre, so supported and conducted, must exhibit plays no less attractive for the purpose of mere amusement, and no less popular, but like the novels of Walter Scott, and James Fennimore Cooper, incomparably more fascinating as well as instructive, than much of the trash of the stage or the circulating library in former days. Actors, however witty, would not be indulged in extempory effusions or expletives, but speak "that which is set down for them."

When we speak of a theatre supported by the state, or by a powerful association, we do not mean that the state should prohibit others, or discourage others, any further than such a theatre must have a preference over any that cannot rival it by the exhibition of talent in plays and performers. When plays are not submitted to the decision of the ignorant or the interested, they may be written by the first in the land, and the best in the land will attend their representation. When the director is paid by the state, he will not be a manager who has debts to liquidate or coffers to fill, and actors may be well remunerated. The stage-manager should always be an actor, relieved from the duties of acting, and the prompter should be an intelligent gentleman. This would be a kind of theatrical millennium—we hope the scheme is not altogether Utopian. What has been done, may be done; and again we refer to France and Germany.

The enemies of the drama have misrepresented it; they have stigmatized the theatre, and cast every term of reproach upon it, through successive ages; and if good name is taken from man he may become reckless of his conduct when "the immediate jewel of his soul is filched from him." If the profession was considered honourable, as in justice it ought to be, persons would be educated for it as for other honourable professions, and as they are for the French theatre. Of course the evil of youth abandoning their homes and their parents would cease—or, if theatres were conducted as we have suggested, no youth would be permitted to tread the stage without the parents' sanction.

By those who have considered the actor's calling a good and reputable one, children have been trained to it, and are among the best and worthiest, as artists and members of society.

If the theatre is represented as the scene of licentiousness, the licentious will seek it. And if, as now in most theatres, they see a display of the votaries and victims of vice in one part of the house, and the allurements to inebriation in another, they may have just grounds to believe that they are indeed in the palace of Circe, instead of the temple of the Muses. The frail or the vicious must be admitted to every temple, but not when they are openly marked and arrayed as such. If not known, their power of evil is abridged, and the disposition to it may be changed. We advocate no abuse, but earnestly wish reform:—that *that,* which is in itself good, may be the means of good. It was the triumph of learning over her barbarous foes that reared the stage; let us not aid those barbarous foes in their attempts to destroy it.

⤜ APPENDIX ⤛

Catalogue of American Plays and Their Authors *

Anonymous.—The Americans Roused, or a Cure for the Spleen; printed 1775. Guilt; translated from the German. The Ancient Day. He was a Soldier at the Battle of North Point. The Irish Patriot. Is it a lie? The Jubilee, or Triumph of Freedom. Julia, or the Wanderer. Life in New-York, or Firemen on Duty. Love in a Cloud. Lucinda. The Green Mountain Boys. Greece and Liberty. Miontonomon. New-York and London. The Poor Student. The Return from the Camp. Road to Honour. Rokeby. Ruffian Boy. Shakespeare in Love; acted in Boston. Sylla; acted in New-York. A tale of the Crusade; a tragedy, acted in New-York. Blow for Blow; tragedy printed in Baltimore. The Medium, or Happy Tea-party; acted in Boston 1795. The Pilot, and others from James F. Cooper's novels.

Barker, James N.—America, a mask. Attila, tragedy. The Embargo, or What News? acted 1808. Indian Princess. Tears and Smiles; comedy, 5 acts. How to try a Lover. Marmion. Travellers. The Armourer's Escape. Superstition. All acted with great success.

Barnard—The Wilderness.

Barton, Andrew—The Disappointment.

Bayley—The Sultan.

Beach, L.—Jonathan Postfree.

Biddle, Barnaby—The Mercenary Match; tragedy, acted at Yale College.

Booth, Lucius Junius—Ugolino; tragedy.

Bray, John—The Toothache, farce.

Breck, Charles—The Trust. The Fox Chase.

Brown, John Paul—Sertorius; tragedy.

Brown, Mrs.—The Pirate.

Burgoyne, Gen.—The Blockade of Boston; acted in Boston, during the blockade, by British officers.

Burk, John—Bunker Hill. Joan of Arc. Death of Montgomery. Fortunes of Nigel. Inn-

---

* To J. F. Foote, Esq. I am indebted for access to a collection of materials made by him for a new and improved Biographia Dramatica, the publication of which I hope will repay his labours.

keeper of Abbeville. Bethlehem Gabor. Female Patriotism. Which do you like best, the Poor Man or the Lord?

Carr, Mrs.—The Fair Americans.

Chapman, Samuel—Doctor Foster. Gasperoni.

Clinch, Charles P.—The Spy; from James Fennimore Cooper's novel. The Avenger's Vow. The Expelled Collegian. The First of May in New-York. All acted with distinguished success.

Cooper and Grey, Doctors—The Renegade.

Crafts—The Sea Serpent.

Cromwell—The Ocean Spectre.

Custis, George Washington—Pocahontas.

Da Ponti—The Italian Husband; tragedy. The Roman Wife; tragedy.

Darling, David—Beaux without Belles; farce, acted in Petersburg, Va.

Dearing, Mrs.—Carabasset, tragedy; acted in Portland, 1831.

Dumont, J. B.—The Invisible Witness; acted 1824.

Dunlap, Wm.—The Modest Soldier; comedy. The Father of an Only Child; acted in New-York in 1788. The Miser's Wedding. Darby's Return; interlude. Lord Leicester; tragedy. William Tell, or the Archers; opera. Fontainville Abbey; tragedy. Ribbemont, or the Feudal Baron; tragedy. André; tragedy. Tell Truth and Shame the Devil; farce. The Natural Daughter; comedy. The Stranger; comedy. Lovers' Vows; comedy. Sterne's Maria, or the Vintage; opera. Count Benyowsky; tragi-comedy. The Italian Father; comedy. False Shame; comedy. Force of Calumny; comedy. Wild-goose Chase; opera. The Robbery; drama. Fraternal Discord; comedy. Abælino. Where is He? farce. The Voice of Nature; drama. The Glory of Columbia, her Yeomanry; play in five acts. Bonaparte in England; farce. The Proverb, or Conceit can kill, Conceit can cure; comedy. Lewis of Monte Blanco; play in five acts. The Wife of two Husbands. Peter the Great. The Blind Boy. Yankee Chronology; interlude. The Soldier of '76. La Perouse. The Stranger's Birth Day. The Good Neighbour. Indians in England. The Merry Gardener; opera. Battle of New-Orleans. Forty and Twenty; comedy. School for Soldiers. Rinaldo Rinaldini. The Flying Dutchman. Thirty Years, or the Life of a Gambler. A Trip to Niagara. The Knight of the Guadalquiver; opera. Nina. The Knight's Adventure. Robespierre. The Africans; and other pieces unpublished. Most of these acted successfully.

Ellis, Mrs.—The Duke of Buckingham; acted unsuccessfully in N.Y.

Ellison, James—The American Captives, or the Siege of Tripoli; acted in Boston in 1812.

Ewing, Robert W.—Le Solitaire. Sponge Again. The Frontier Maid. The Highland Seer. The Election. Imperial Victim. La Fayette. Quentin Durward. Exit in a Hurry. Bride of Death.

Faugeres, Margaret V.—Belisarius; tragedy, printed 1795.

Fennell, James—The Wheel of Truth.

Field—France and Liberty. Rhyme without Reason; farce.

Finn, Henry J.—Montgomery, or the Falls of Montmorency.

Foote, J. F.—The Little Thief, or the Night Walker.

Foster—The Inheritance.

Fowler, Manly B.—The Prophecy. Orlando. Female Revenge.

Godfrey, Thomas (son of the inventor of the quadrant)—The Prince of Parthia; tragedy, printed Philadelphia, 1765, in 4to. (written at the age of twenty-two).

Grice, C. E.—The Battle of New-Orleans.

Hall, Everard—Nolens Volens, or the Biter Bit.

Hamilton, Col.—The Enterprise; opera, acted in Baltimore, 1823.

Harby, Isaac—Alberti; tragedy, in five acts, acted in Charleston, 1818. The Gordian Knot; tragedy. The author of this tragedy died in New-York much regretted.

Hatton, Mrs.—Tammany.

Hawkins, M.—The Saw-mill.

Henry, John—The School for Soldiers.

Hillhouse, James A.—Percy's Mask. Hadad.

Hodgkinson, John—The Man of Fortitude.

Holland, Edwin C.—The Corsair.

Humphreys, David—The Widow of Malabar; tragedy, and a comedy, name not known (never published).

Hutton, Joseph—Cuffee and Duffee. The School for Prodigals. Modern Honour. The Wounded Hussar. The Orphan of Prague. Fashionable Follies.

Hyer, Wm. G.—Rosa; melo-drama, printed 1822.

Ingersoll, Charles Jared—Edwy and Elgiva; tragedy, acted in Philadelphia, 1801. Julian the Apostate; tragedy.

Ingham, John—The Times. The Usurper; tragedy, acted in Phila.

Joor, Wm.—Battle of Eutaw Springs; played in Charleston, 1817.

Judah, Samuel B.—A Tale of Lexington; acted in New-York. The Mountain Torrent; acted in New-York. The Rose of Arragon. Odofriede.

Lawson, J.—Giordano; tragedy, acted in New-York.

Leacock, John—Disappointed; printed 1796, Philadelphia.

Lillibridge, Gardner R.—Tancred, or the Rightful Heir of Rochdale Castle; printed in Rhode Island, 1824.

Lindsley, A. B.—Love and Friendship, or Yankee Notions.

Linn, John Blair—Bourville Castle; acted in New-York.

Low, Samuel—The Politician Outwitted; printed in New-York, 1790.

Maddocks—The Bohemian Mother; translated from the French; acted at Boston, 1829.

Markoe, Peter—The Patriot Chief; printed 1784. Reconciliation.

McHenry, James—Genius; comedy, in five acts, acted in Phila., 1829.

McLaren, Archibald—The Coup de Main.

Merry, Robert—The Abbey of St. Augustine; tragedy, acted at the Chestnut-street theatre, Philadelphia.

Milne—The Comet. All in a Bustle; prel. A Flash in the Pan; farce.

Morris, George P.—Brier Cliff; performed at Chatham-street theatre, New-York, 1825; often repeated, and very successful.

Murdoch, J.—The Triumph of Love.

Noah, M. M.—The Fortress of Sorrento. The Grecian Captive. The Grand Canal. Marion, or the Hero of Lake George. Oh Yes, or the New Constitution. She Would be a Soldier. The Siege of Yorktown. Paul and Alexis. Yesef Caramatti. All acted with great success.

Paulding, James. K.—The Lion of the West; comedy, acted in New-York with great success, and often repeated.

Payne, John Howard—The Lancers, Brutus; tragedy. Oswali of Athens. Peter Smink, or Which is the Miller. Proclamation. Richelieu. Therese. 'Twas I. Two Galley Slaves. Accusation. Adeline. Ali Pacha, or the Signet Ring. King Charles the Second, or the Merry Monarch. Clari.

Phillips, J. D.—The Female Spy; acted in New-York, 1828. Paul Clifford. Beauty and Booty.

Potter, Reuben—Phelles, King of Tyre; tragedy. Don Alonzo; tragedy.

Rittenhouse, David—Lucy Sampson; translated from Lessing, printed in 1789.

Robinson, J.—The Yorker's Stratagem.

Rowson, Mrs.—The Female Patriot; acted in Philadelphia in 1795. Slaves in Algiers.

Sawyer, Lemuel—Black Beard. The Wreck of Honour.

Smith, Elihu Hubbard—Edwin and Angelina, or the Bandit; opera, played at New-York in 1796.

Smith, Richard Penn—William Penn; acted in Philadelphia. The Divorce. The Avengers. The Disowned. The Deformed. Eighth of January. A Wife at a Venture. Quite Correct. The Sentinels. The Pelican. The Recluse.

Smith, Charles—Several bad translations from Kotzebue.

Smith, W. R.—The Happy Return; a monologue.

Stock, Thomas—A Wedding in Wales; acted in Philadelphia.

Stone, John Augustus—Fauntleroy; tragedy, acted in Charleston. Metamora; tragedy, acted in New-York with great success. Edwin Forrest, the tragedian, paid the author $500 for this play. La Roque the Regicide; acted in Charleston. The Demoniac. Tancred. Touretoun. The Restoration, or the Diamond Cross. All pieces of distinguished merit.

Strong—The Fall of Iturbide; tragedy.

Talbot, Charles—Paddy's Trip to America.

Taylor—The Water-Witch.

Troubat, Francis—The Phrenologist; farce.

Turnbull, J. D.—Love and War. Cottage of the Forest. Rudolph; acted in Boston. Victor. Maid of Hungary.

Tyler, Royall—The Contrast; comedy, acted in New-York, 1787. May Day; farce, 1787.

Warren, Mrs.—The Sack of Rome; Boston, 1790.

Warren, M.—The Ladies of Castile; tragedy, Boston, 1790.

Wetmore, Alphonso—The Pedlar; farce in three acts.

White, Wm. Charles—The Clergyman's Daughter; tragedy. The Poor Lodger. Alonzo.

White, M. M.—Liberty in Louisiana; acted in Petersburg, Va.

Williamson, J. B.—Preservation, 1800.

Wilson, Jane—Percy.

Winstanley—The Hypocrites Unmasked; comedy, printed in N.Y.

Wood, Mrs.—The North American; in five acts.

Woodworth, Samuel—The Deed of Gift, acted in Boston. La Fayette, or the Castle of Olmutz; acted in New-York. The Widow's Son; acted in New-York. The Forest Rose; acted in New-York. This author's plays have been very successful.

Wright, Frances—Altorf; tragedy, played in New-York, 1819.

Regulations of the Theatre Françoise: Established by the Government

One hundred thousand francs per year is allowed by the government for the support of the *Theatre Françoise*. A franc is about 18³/₄ cents.

SUPERINTENDENT.—An officer of government has the direction of the theatre, and his orders are transmitted to the actors by another officer, called a commissioner, who is to superintend the administration, and the financial concerns. This commissioner must personally give all orders, and is personally responsible for the carrying into effect the same. In case of violation of the rules, it is the duty of the commissioner to report to the superintendent. His other duties will be mentioned below.

ASSOCIATES.—The ACTORS are united in a society. The associates employ salaried actors.

SHARES.—The receipts of all exhibitions, after deducting expenses, are divided into 24 shares: one share for contingencies; but if not called for (or any surplus remaining), it is divided at the end of the year among the associates.

A half-share is appropriated to augment the pension-fund; and another half-share is appropriated to repairs, scenery, wardrobe, and properties.

The 22 remaining shares are divided among the associate actors, from the eighth of a share to a whole share.

Every associate contracts an engagement to perform 20 years; and after 20 years of uninterrupted service, is at liberty to retire, unless the superintendent thinks it advisable that he or she should be retained. The associate so retiring has a right—first, to a pension for life of 2000 francs, from the appropriation of 100,000 francs made by government; and secondly, to a like sum from the funds of the society, which are supplied by the half-share mentioned above, and other sources. Thus, the actor retires upon a pension for life of 4000 francs per year. Here permanency and respectability are secured.

If the superintendent prolongs the service of an associate beyond the 20 years, there is added, whenever he or she retires, 100 francs more for each year of added service from each of the above funds; that is, 200 francs is added to the pension of 4000, on retiring, for each year of service beyond the 20 originally contracted for.

If an associate should be compelled by any accident arising immediately from the service of the theatre, to retire before the end of the 20 years, he or she shall receive the full pension of 4000 francs. (About 750 dollars.)

In case of incapacity to serve, resulting from any other cause, the associate may retire upon a pension of 200 francs for each year he or she may have served, if amounting to 10 years, provided such associate held a whole share; or 150 if only three-fourths of a share, and so on in proportion to the share held by the associate in the profits of the society. [I do not find in what manner the shares and parts of shares are divided among the associates: we must conjecture that it is according to the talents of the individual.]

If the associate has served less than ten years, the superintendent shall propose to the government such pension as he may deem just.

For the payment of these pensions, the government, as above said, provides 100,000 francs per year, and 50,000 francs per year are drawn by monthly drafts from the receipts, and placed in safe keeping at interest. No associate can transfer or mortgage his or her contribution to the funds of this income. On the retirement or the death of an associate, the reimbursement of the capital of this reservation is made to such associate, or his or her heirs, proportionably to the amount of his or her contribution. Thus, the actor retires not only on the pension above mentioned, but on an immediate payment of the money he or she has loaned to the fund.

Any associate who shall quit the theatre without permission from the superintendent, forfeits all claims upon the fund, either for pension or repayment of money contributed.

Should there be any balance remaining after the annual payment of the pensions, it is disposed of for the benefit of the society, under the sanction of the superintendent.

SALARIED ACTORS.—Besides the associates, the theatre may have salaried actors; and in case such salaried actor shall serve 20 years, or only 10 years if accident in service prevents further service, a pension may be given by the government's superintendent, from the above fund, not exceeding half the income the actor may have received during the three last years of his or her service. The same rule extends to the commissioner on his retiring, only that his pension must be solely taken from the fund supplied by the government.

COMMITTEE OF ADMINISTRATION.—We have said the commissioner is to superintend the administration of the society. It is provided that a committee of six male associates, presided over by the commissioner, and having a secretary, shall be the administrators. They shall be appointed by the commissioner yearly: three of this six are charged with the execution of the resolutions of the committee.

The duties of this committee are, to make out each year an estimate of the presumed expenses; to give orders for purchases and drafts for payments; to inspect every department of the establishment, as well the audience part of the house as the work-rooms, and the treasury, with the payment of pensions, shares, salaries, and every branch of the financial concerns.

TREASURER.—There must be a treasurer employed, who must give ample security. The receipt and expenditure is adjusted monthly, and approved by the commissioner. In making payments, this is the order: First, the claims of authors; next, salaries of actors and wages of work-men; then the sum named for the pension fund; lastly, all bills. The residue of the receipts to be divided as above. The treasurer will receive quarterly the money appropriated by government, to be applied as above stated. The treasurer's accounts are to be submitted to the associates, and must, before accepted, be approved by the superintendent.

Upon the share held in reserve for contingencies, the superintendent may grant to actors or actresses assistance in respect to dresses which may fall too heavy on them, according to circumstances.

GENERAL ASSEMBLY.—The committee must call a general assembly of the associates once a year, to decide on the expenses of the coming year, and once to examine the accounts of the preceding year; and likewise every time there are funds to put out, lawsuits to be sustained, or any extraordinary occurrence needing it. The superintendent may convoke the associates at his pleasure for business of the society.

The committee are charged with every thing relative to management, making a list of stock pieces, regulating *debuts* and reception of new pieces, under the control of the commissioner and superintendent.

LINES OF ACTING.—The superintendent determines the lines of acting. He draws up an estimate of pieces to be studied, names the actors and actresses who are to play as principals, doubles, or thirds, assigning the parts according the respective line and seniority. No performer can hold as principal two different lines, without permission of the superintendent—rarely granted. A performer in possession of a line as principal, wishing to act in another line, such actor or actress can only do so as second, even though senior to the person first in possession.

STOCK PLAYS.—When the committee form the stock-list, they must have added to them two of the associate actresses. This list must be so arranged that each part may have a second or double specified, to perform it in case of the absence of the principal.

Two associates, in rotation, are added to the committee each week, to assist in the direction.

If a double should fall sick, the principal, if in health, must take his character on notice from one of the committee. No principal may refuse a part in his line, or resign one altogether to his double. The principals must yield all or any of their parts to their doubles occasionally, or at least three or four times a month, that the doubles (who are actors on probation) may have an opportunity for improvement, and give an opportunity to judge of their progress. If deprived of this opportunity, the double may appeal to the superintendent; and those who have injured him may be fined 300 francs for such opposition to his right, and the commissioner is held responsible for any injustice done to the double by his negligence.

The association are bound to bring out a full piece every month, and two lesser pieces, either new or revived. Among these must be the works of living authors.

ALL THE ACTORS must be assembled once a week to receive notice of performances, and a programme of the week's business is delivered to each. If any performer makes objection to the intended business, their reasons for such objection must be addressed to the commissioner, to be determined on by the superintendent. The arrangement for the succeeding performances once determined, each performer will be expected to act the part placed opposite his or her name, under a penalty of 150 francs, unless sufficient cause is shown to the superintendent. If any performer has caused a performance to be changed on a plea of illness, and shall be seen out of his or her house, the fine is 300 francs.

DEBUTS.—The superintendent alone can give permission for a *debut*. The permission is presented to the committee, who register it, and place in the next week's performance the three pieces required by the person so permitted. The performers having parts in these pieces will not be permitted to refuse acting, under a penalty of 150 francs. A general rehearsal of each new piece, in which a *debutant* is to play, is insisted on, the forfeit for absence 25 francs. The committee will afterwards propose, and the superintendent elect other parts for the *debutant*. He will then have several private rehearsals, and one general rehearsal for each part. A successful *debutant* is received upon probation for not less than one year, and then the superintendent has power to receive him or her as an associate.

NEW PIECES are to be read before a committee of nine, selected from the associates of longest standing by the superintendent. A majority of votes decides the reception. If part of the vote is for sending back the piece for correction, the question is taken by yeas and nays: if there are but four votes for sending it back, it is accepted.

THE SHARE OF AN AUTHOR from the receipts, one-third being first deducted for expenses, is one-eighth for a piece of five or four acts; one-twelfth for a piece in three; and one-sixteenth for a piece of one or two. Nevertheless, the actors and authors make other arrangements to suit circumstances. The author enjoys his free admission to the house from the moment the piece is put in rehearsal: and for three years after the first representation of a piece of five or four acts; two years for one of three; and one year for a piece in one or two. The author of two pieces of five or four acts, or three pieces of three acts, or four pieces in one or two acts, remaining on the stage, is entitled to his free admission for life.

THE PENALTIES that may be imposed on an actor are for causing a piece to be changed, or refusing to perform a part in his line, or if not at his post at the hour appointed; and are, according to the gravity of the case, fines, exclusion from the assemblies of associates and committee of administration, temporary or final expulsion from the theatre, forfeiture of pension, and *imprisonment.* These penalties are imposed by the committee in the mildest degree, and by the superintendent in the harshest, with the concurrence of the committee. No performer can be absent without permission from the superintendent, and never more than two at a time, nor for more than two months.

RETIRING FROM THE STAGE.—If an associate, after 10 years' service, applies more than once in one year for permission to retire, and declares his intention never more to perform, he is permitted to retire; but he will have no right to any pension, nor to withdraw his share from the fund of 50,000 francs.

If the company does not perform every evening, unless excused by the superintendent, they pay for each time of omission 500 francs to the poor.

BENEFITS.—Any associate who has served 30 years may have a benefit on his retiring. Any actor who retires from the Theatre Françoise is not permitted to play any where else without permission of the superintendent.

The internal regulation of the theatre depends on the superintendent.

STUDENTS are by law attached to the theatre,—nine of each sex, not under 15 years of age.

TEACHERS are appointed in music, declamation, grammar, history, mythology, and the dramatic art.

If a student gives no promise, he or she is withdrawn, and another substituted. These students may be permitted to try their strength at inferior or minor theatres, sanctioned by the superintendent of the T.F. When deemed capable, they are permitted to make a *debut* as above at the T.F. The expenses of these students and salaries of their teachers are paid by the government.

In addition to these laws for the government of the theatre, we give an abridged translation of the superintendent's *Regulations for the internal administration of the Theatre Françoise.*

THE COMMITTEE must meet every Wednesday at one o'clock. Extra meetings are called by the commissioner. All letters intended for the committee are addressed to the commissioner, who is the presiding-officer, and he takes the votes of the committee on all questions discussed. When the votes are equal, the opinion of the commissioner decides. If a question interests a member of the committee, he must withdraw. This rule applies likewise to questions before the general meetings. The resolutions of the committee must be signed by every member, however he may have voted.

THE GENERAL MEETINGS of the associates take place at ten o'clock, and none but members can be present. No subjects can be discussed but those for which the meeting is called. Decisions by vote, as in the committee. All decisions are registered, and signed by all present.

STOCK-LIST.—The committee which makes out the stock-list, or list of acting plays, must assemble every Saturday at noon. This is the ordinary committee, with the addition of two associates, as *semanieres,* or weekly directors. If an actor wishes a day for particular business, he must write to the committee or the directors before the time of meeting. The list of plays to be acted shall be formed in such manner that tragedy and comedy shall be alternated. When the committee shall have made out the list of plays for the succeeding week, they next distribute the parts according to the laws of the theatre. All shall then be placed with the directors to communicate to the general assembly. Revived pieces must be distributed to the principals and their doubles, so that if the principal is not ready at the time fixed, the double may perform the part. Every actor who performs as a double or third in a piece when first played, has a right to perform that part twice in succession.

THE GENERAL ASSEMBLY of the actors for receiving the list of pieces for the next week must convene at one o'clock every Saturday. Every associate who shall be on the spot when the green-room clock strikes one, and shall remain until the sitting is over, shall receive a token of six francs. This makes it necessary that the roll shall be called over at one o'clock and at the conclusion of business.

When the list of plays shall have been made known, and sanctioned according to the rules prescribed, the weekly directors shall make no change, except authorized by the committee, under a penalty of 150 francs. If an actor, on any pretext whatever, shall, after the above meeting, refuse to perform the part assigned to him, he must pay 150 francs.

OF CHANGING A PLAY.—If, from any legitimate cause, the weekly directors shall be obliged to change any arrangement of the list, without having time to refer the subject to the committee, they must make a written report to the commissioner, under penalty of 50 francs; and this report must be instantly sent to the superintendent for his decision. Any actor who, without legitimate cause, shall occasion the closing of the theatre, shall be punished by a fine equal to the probable receipt of the intended representation, and even by severer penalty in case of repeating the offence, or of aggravating circumstances.

WEEKLY DIRECTORS.—No male associate (the senior excepted) can be excused from performing the duties of weekly director, under penalty of 50 francs; but it, from particular circumstances, unable to fulfil the duties, he may, by permission of the commissioner, be aided by another associate, who shall have the same authority. The weekly directors are bound so to consult each other, that in case of the absence of one, the other shall be present to fulfil the joint duties of the two. One of them must be at the theatre at six o'clock to see that every thing is ready, and all the actors who are to play are present. He is to see that the performance begins at the appointed time, and mark those who are not ready: the penalty for not being ready is 10 francs if 10 minutes after the time, and 20 if the actor causes a delay of 15 minutes; for a longer delay, the superintendent has power to increase the penalty at discretion, and also if the fault is repeated. Every actor is forbidden, under any pretext whatever, to make alterations or additions to his parts. Should any circumstance require an address to the public during performance, it must be made by one of the weekly directors, or if they are absent, by the senior actor present, who shall use such terms as he may communicate to the commissioner, or to the committee, or to the oldest actors who shall happen to be in the theatre. Any circumstance which may occur that can be interesting to the government, must be communicated by the weekly directors in a written report to the commissioner, under a penalty of 100 francs.

FUEL.—Every actor is allowed two francs for each day of performance for fuel.

The regulations respecting bills and advertisements provide that the directors make them out during the time of performing,—the names of the actors being inserted for every piece according to their rank of seniority; and it is the duty of the director to see that these notifications are sent to the printer and to the journalists. No actor can be announced separately on the bill, unless he has been absent at least two months from the theatre from some legitimate cause, and in that case only for the first three times of performance. If, from any cause whatever, an actor shall be substituted for one announced, the weekly directors must notify the change upon bills at the doors and in the hall of the theatre; and when the play announced is changed, it must be announced by the bills in like manner (the French says, by putting *bandeaux* on the bills; we presume a well-known signal). If a sudden close of the house takes place, the notice must express the cause; and the directors are bound, under penalty of 100 francs each, to notify the police and the commander of the armed force (precautions happily not needed with us). On all such occasions, the directors, under penalty of 50 francs each, must notify the superintendent by immediate report. When it is necessary to change the play, no actor can refuse to play in another piece, under a fine of 100 francs; and if he was to have played in the piece so put off or changed, the above fine is increased to 300 francs.

REHEARSALS are to be notified when the list of plays for the ensuing week is made known, on each Saturday, as above. The hours must not be the same as those of the meetings of the committee or general assembly. Rehearsals so notified cannot be changed, except the cause is approved by the committee, under penalty of 10 francs, to be paid by the person causing the change. Every actor absent from rehearsal at the moment of the scene in which he is to play, is fined 3 francs. The fine is 10 if absent the whole rehearsal. If absent from the next rehearsal of the same piece, 20 francs. For further offence, the superintendent may punish at will. The prompter is bound, under penalty of 3 francs, to return the absentees to the directors, they present it to the committee, whose duty it is to inflict the fines. The directors may admit strangers to rehearsals of old pieces, or stock-plays, but the permission of the *author of a new piece* must be obtained for that purpose, and then the actors must be notified thereof. An auditor disturbing a rehearsal, shall be immediately turned out.

The SALARIED ACTORS must be present when the list of plays for each succeeding week is made known,—*i.e.* at the general assembly each Saturday; and at the end of three months' admission or attendance, they will have a right to the token of three francs on the terms specified.

Every actor who is on trial, or on salary, must play any part cast for him or her, unless received upon other terms. Any salaried actor not re-engaged three months before the 1st of April, is at that time no longer a member of the company.

THE ORCHESTRA is placed under a leader, through whom the administration will transmit its orders. When a situation is vacant, the leader must report to the committee, who will appoint a successor. The leader must appoint those wanted for rehearsals, and they must attend, under penalty of 10 francs each. The musicians must be at the house at six o'clock every evening, and in their apartment, ready to obey the signal for action. Any one missing an overture, must pay $2^1/_2$ francs—a whole performance, 5 francs. When the performance is once commenced, no musician can leave the orchestra, except from indisposition. No substitute can be received for a musician, except for reasons approved by the leader, and a notice of a day. Never more than two substitutes at a time can be allowed. Any musician failing in the respect due to the public during a representation, or to the actors on the stage, must pay 10 francs; and for a repetition, be discharged. Every evening the leader shall report to the prompter, or to the weekly directors, any failure of duty, under penalty of being himself accountable for the fines incurred.

TICKETS AND DOORS.—Every thing relative to the offices for receipt and door-keepers is under charge of an inspector-general. Officers called comptrollers are under him, the principal of whom takes his place in his absence. The tickets are entrusted to him. He must see that the offices are open one hour before the rising of the curtain, and that all the door keepers are at their posts. He must frequently, during the performance, go the rounds, to see that every one is in his place, and the number of tickets received.

SEASON BOXES.—An officer is employed to let out the boxes, which are to be taken for a year or shorter period, not under six months. He keeps a register and account of receipts, with the names of the lessees, periods for which they are let, &c., and this register must be exhibited to the inspector-general once a month. This register and account must be examined by a member of the committee. A register is likewise kept of boxes let for one evening. The tickets are given to the office-keepers under inspection of the inspector-general. There are many strict regulations to preserve order and prevent imposition. It appears that the openers of the boxes are females. Those boxes hired are marked as such by the openers, who are liable to fine if they mark as hired a box which is not taken. These openers have a list of boxes taken given to them, by whom taken, &c. A comptroller, in the presence of the inspector, counts the tickets that are to be delivered to the office-keepers. When delivered, an account signed by the comptroller is delivered with them, and he is bound at the commencement of the second piece to examine and take account of the number of tickets sold.

No actor or actress can take tickets at the offices (*caisse*) even on paying for them, under a penalty of 300 francs for a first offence, and a punishment according to the superintendent's pleasure for a second. No comptroller, overseer, or office-keeper shall deliver to any person a ticket before the opening of the ticket-offices.

ORDERS.—Each associate is entitled to give or sell orders for two (upon the office only) for places in the first and second boxes, the orchestra, and the balconies, or the first gallery, except at representations of new pieces, or on evenings when new performers make *debuts,* or on any other occasion when the administration think proper to prohibit orders.

TICKETS.—More tickets shall never be given out than there are seats. On days of *debut,* the debutant is entitled to 12 places in front, i.e., four in the pit, four in the orchestra or first boxes, and four in the second gallery, or third boxes.

The treasurer must attend every evening in his office. The ticket-office-keepers must present to him their accounts, verified and signed by the inspector-general, and the amount of sales. The overseer of leased boxes must likewise account with and pay to him. All must give receipts, and their accounts must be settled every evening.

RIGHTS OF ACTORS.—Every associate, besides his two orders for free admission, is entitled to three seats for his relatives. An actor on trial, or a salaried actor, is only entitled to one seat or order for admission.

The two orders for free admission belonging to the associates may be sold by them, but not for less nor more than one year. The persons having free admission must have a written order from two of the committee or the commissioner.

Admissions to relatives are suspended during the three first performances of new or revived pieces, if the administration think fit. No admission of this kind can be sold, and only persons known as relatives can be entered on the list of admission as such. This list is prepared by the committee, and authorized by the commissioner, and no change made without his authority. The list of free admissions, whether of retired actors of the Theatre Françoise, or of authors, or of any persons having this privilege, is made out once a year, sanctioned by the superintendent, and unalterable but by his approbation.

Fines and penalties of expulsion are enforced against any comptroller, door-keeper, overseer, &c. who contravenes these rules.

The door communicating from the front to the interior is locked during the whole of the exhibition, and guarded by a sentinel and a servant of the theatre. This door shall not be opened until eight o'clock, and only for actors, their relatives (having free admission), and authors. A sentinel and a servant of the theatre are likewise posted at the door for entrance of actors, and only the same description of persons permitted to pass, and the necessary attendants.

THE POLICE OF THE INTERIOR, and of the wings, is entrusted to a particular officer appointed by the superintendent, called the inspector, who shall be bound to see the above rules enforced. He shall have a list of all who are entitled to entrance, and if he finds any intruder, he must turn him out instantly. Any person attached to the theatre contravening these rules, shall be fined 10 francs for the first offence, 20 for the second, and lose his or her place for the third.

No orders for admission are allowed: if one is given it must be carried by the door-keeper to the cashier, and by him charged to the person signing it at the rate of 6 francs, 60–100 for each seat.

RIGHTS OF AUTHORS AND RULES FOR READINGS.—To prevent all confusion respecting the rights of authors for priority of readings, reception, or representation, a register shall be kept of all authors who have works to read; of all works received, and the names of their authors; of all works returned for correction, and of all works rejected, with the names of their authors. This register shall be under charge of the commissioner. A request for a reading must be made in writing to the committee by the author, or an associate for the author. No new piece can be read whose author has not already one or more works accepted, unless an associate certifies in writing that he has read it, and that it has merit entitling it to be heard. Every new author must send his work to the committee, who will have it examined; if the examiner thinks it ought not to be admitted to a reading, he explains his reasons; if the contrary, it is entered on the register for reading. There shall never be more than one reading in a week, except specially ordered by the superintendent. If, however, the piece is of two or three acts, another short piece may be read at the same time. Three pieces of one act may be read at one sitting. Friday is the day for readings, at 1 o'clock. No member of the reading committee can be excused except for legitimate reasons made known to the directors the day before. Authors or their representatives are alone admitted to the readings. Every work shall be read according to the register, except by special order of the superintendent. An author must be apprised of the time of reading his work eight days before, and if he is not ready the next on the list is substituted, and his work carried down to the bottom of the list. An author not wishing to read his work, can have it read by any actor he chooses. After the reading, every member of the committee gives in his judgment in writing, always concluding with "I accept," "I accept for correction," or "I cannot accept." These opinions must be couched in decorous and cautious terms. The author has his choice, to hear these opinions read or to have the result sent to him, drawn up by the secretary. If an author agrees to make corrections, he is entitled to a second reading, on which occasion it must be accepted or rejected. This reading must take place as soon as the author is ready. Every piece accepted is registered with the name of the author or his representative. Every new piece shall be put in study in its turn of acceptance. The distribution of parts and the choice of doubles belongs to the author, but no actor can be compelled to go out of his line. If an actor shall, without consent of the superintendent, refuse a part in his line, cast by the author, he shall forfeit 300 francs, and further punishment at the discretion of the superintendent if he repeats the offence. No double is permitted in a new piece unless the principal has played it at least six times. An actor may, at the request of the author, play a new part out of his line, but when he ceases to play it, the part returns to its line, as adjudged by the committee.

During the six first nights of a piece of five or four acts, the author shall be allowed 30 seats, viz: 20 in the pit and 10 in the first boxes. For pieces of three acts, 12 in the pit and 8 in the first boxes. For pieces of one or two acts, 10 in the pit and 5 in the first boxes. After the six first nights, the seats are reduced to 6 for a piece of 5 or 4 acts; 4 for a piece of three acts; and 2 for a piece of one or two.

Let all persons interested in the drama study these laws and regulations. Any manager or association who shall conduct a theatre on a similar plan, varying it according to circumstances, will avoid the abuses which have lowered the drama in the estimation of the world, and may raise it again to its proper level among the institutions which benefit the human race. It may then be truly deserving of the epithet bestowed upon it in the last of the following lines.

> "Time rushes o'er us; thick as evening clouds
> Ages roll back; what calls them from their shrouds?
> What in full vision brings their good and great,—
> The men whose virtues make the nation's fate;
> The far, forgotten stars of human kind?
> The STAGE—the MIGHTY TELESCOPE OF MIND!"

THE END.

➤➤ INDEX ◄◄

WILLIAM DUNLAP (1766–1839) was a
playwright, adapter, and producer. He was a partner
in William Hallam's American Company—
the first theatrical company in the United States—
and a founder of the National Academy of Design.

TICE L. MILLER is a professor of theatre arts at
the University of Nebraska-Lincoln. He is the
author of *Bohemians and Critics* and coeditor of
the *Cambridge Guide to American Theatre.*

The University of Illinois Press
is a founding member of the
Association of American University Presses.

Composed in 10.3/13 Adobe Minion
with Bulmer display
by Celia Shapland
for the University of Illinois Press
Designed by Copenhaver Cumpston
Manufactured by Maple-Vail Book Manufacturing Group

UNIVERSITY OF ILLINOIS PRESS
1325 South Oak Street Champaign, IL 61820-6903
www.press.uillinois.edu